RANDOM HOUSE WEBSTER'S

STUDENT
notebook
THESAURUS
3rd Ed.

A

abandon, *v.* **1.** go away from, depart from, leave, forsake, jilt, walk out on, desert. **2.** resign, retire, quit, withdraw. **3.** drop, discontinue, abstain from, abdicate, renounce, repudiate.
—Ant. keep, maintain; pursue.

abandoned, *adj.* **1.** forsaken, left, left alone, forsaken, neglected, deserted, dropped, discarded, cast aside, cast out, dropped, rejected. **2.** unrestrained, uninhibited, loose, wanton, wild, reckless, intemperate.

abase, *v.* lower, reduce, humble, degrade, downgrade, demote; disgrace, dishonor, debase, take down a peg, humiliate, mortify, shame.
—Ant. elevate, exalt, honor.

abash, *v.* shame, embarrass, mortify, disconcert, discompose, confound, confuse; cow, humble, humiliate, discountenance, affront.

abate, *v.* lessen, diminish, reduce, decrease, lower, slow, subside, decline, sink, wane, ebb, slack off, slacken, fade, fade out, fade away.
—Ant. increase, intensify.

abatement, *n.* **1.** alleviation, mitigation, lessening, diminution, decrease, slackening, let-up. **2.** suppression, termination, ending, end, cessation. **3.** subsidence, decline, sinking, ebb, slack, fade-out, fading.
—Ant. intensification, increase.

abbreviate, *v.* shorten, abridge, reduce, curtail, cut, contract, compress; crop, dock, pare down, trim, prune, truncate; condense, digest, epitomize, summarize, abstract.
—Ant. lengthen, expand.
—Syn. Study. See SHORTEN.

abbreviation, *n.* shortening, abridgment, reduction, curtailment, cut, contraction, compression; truncation; condensation, digest, epitome, brief, essence, heart, core, soul.
—Ant. lengthening, expansion.

ABC's, *n.* essentials, rudiments, basics, fundamentals, principles, grammar, elements.

abdicate, *v.* renounce, disclaim, disavow, disown, repudiate; resign, retire, quit, relinquish, abandon, surrender, cede, give up, yield, waive.
—Ant. retain.

abdication, *n.* renunciation, disclaimer, disavowal, repudiation, resignation, retirement, quittance; abandonment, surrender, cession, waiver.
—Ant. commitment.

abdomen, *n.* stomach, belly, visceral cavity, viscera; paunch, pot, guts, gut, potbelly, tummy, bay window, breadbasket, spare tire, beer belly.

abduct, *v.* kidnap, carry off, bear off, capture, carry away, ravish, steal away, run away *or* off with, seize, snatch, grab.

abduction, *n.* kidnapping, capture, ravishment, seizure.

aberrant, *adj.* **1.** straying, stray, deviating, deviate, wandering, errant, erring, devious, erratic, rambling, diverging, divergent. **2.** abnormal, irregular, unusual, odd, eccentric, peculiar, exceptional, weird, queer, curious, singular, strange; unconforming, nonconforming, anomalous.
—Ant. direct; normal.

aberration, *n.* **1.** wandering, straying, deviation, rambling, divergence, departure. **2.** strangeness, abnormality, abnormity, oddness, anomaly, irregularity, eccentricity;

peculiarity, curiosity, oddity. **3.** unsoundness, illusion, hallucination, delusion.

abet, *v.* aid, assist, help, support, back, succor, sustain; countenance, sanction, uphold, second, condone, approve, favor; encourage, incite, instigate, urge, provoke, egg on, prod, goad, promote, conduce, advocate, advance, further, subsidize.
—Ant. hinder.

abeyance, *n.* suspension, suspense, inactivity, hiatus, recess, deferral, intermission, interregnum, dormancy, quiescence, adjournment, postponement.
—Ant. operation, action.

abhor, *v.* hate, detest, loathe, abominate, despise, regard with repugnance *or* loathing *or* disgust, execrate, view with horror, shrink from, shudder at, bear malice *or* spleen, recoil from, be aghast at.
—Ant. love.
—Syn. Study. See HATE.

abhorrent, *adj.* **1.** hating, loathing, loathsome, execrating, execratory, antipathetic, detesting, detestable. **2.** horrible, horrifying, shocking, disgusting, revolting, sickening, nauseating, obnoxious, repellant, offensive, repugnant, repulsive, odious; hateful, detestable, abominable, invidious, contemptible, loathsome, horrid, heinous, execrable. **3.** remote, far, distant, removed.
—Ant. amiable, lovable.

abide, *v.* **1.** remain, stay, wait, wait for, tarry, continue, linger, rest, sojourn. **2.** dwell, reside, live, inhabit, tenant, stay. **3.** remain, continue, endure, last, persist, persevere, remain steadfast *or* faithful *or* constant, go on, keep on. **4.** stand by, support, second; await *or* accept the consequences of. **5.** await, attend, wait for. **6.** stand one's ground against, await *or* sustain defiantly. **7.** put up with, stand, suffer, brook, allow, tolerate, bear, endure, submit to, accept.

ability, *n.* **1.** power, proficiency, expertness, dexterity, capacity, ableness, adeptness, know-how, mastery, capability, knack, facility, competency, competence, enablement; puissance, prepotency. **2.** faculty, talent, aptitude, skill, skillfulness, aptness, ingenuity, facility, knack, cleverness, wit, gift, genius.
—Ant. inability.
—Syn. Study. ABILITY, FACULTY, TALENT denote power or capacity to do something. ABILITY is the general word for a natural or acquired capacity to do things; it usually implies doing them well: *a leader of great ability; ability in mathematics.* FACULTY denotes a natural or acquired ability for a particular kind of action: *a faculty for putting people at ease.* TALENT usually denotes an exceptional natural ability or aptitude in a particular field: *a talent for music.*

abject, *adj.* **1.** humiliating, disheartening, debasing, degrading. **2.** contemptible, despicable, scurvy, hateful; base, mean, low, vile, groveling, corrupt; faithless, treacherous, perfidious, dishonorable, inglorious, dishonest, false, fraudulent; disgraceful, ignominious, discreditable.
—Ant. exalted.

able, *adj.* **1.** qualified, fit, fitted, competent, capable, apt. **2.** talented, accomplished, gifted, endowed, superior; skilled, clever, adroit, expert, ingenious, skillful, masterful, masterly, adept, proficient, versed.
—Ant. unable, incompetent, inept.

able-bodied, *adj.* well-knit, brawny, burly, sturdy, strapping, strong, powerful, vigorous, red-blooded, robust, vital, lusty.

abnormal, *adj.* nonconforming, unconventional, irregular, unusual, unnatural, strange, singular, idiosyncratic, freakish, bizarre, deviant, deviating, (*slang*) off-beat, kinky.
—Ant. normal, regular.

abolish, *v.* end, annul, invalidate, nullify, cancel, revoke, expunge, extirpate, erase, extinguish, eliminate, terminate.
—Ant. establish.

abominable, *adj.* detestable, hateful, loathsome, abhorrent, odious, contemptible, despicable, vile, horrid, deplorable, horrible.
—Ant. likable, admirable, delightful.

abominate, *v.* abhor, detest, hate, loathe, despise.
—Ant. like, love, enjoy.

abomination, *n.* **1.** hatred, loathing, abhorrence, detestation, revulsion, aversion. **2.** vice, sin, impurity, corruption, wickedness, evil, depravity, immorality, filth.

abound, *v.* prevail, teem, swarm, be very prevalent, thrive, flourish, proliferate, throng, flow, overflow with, be filled with, be rich in.
—Ant. lack, be scarce.

about, *prep.* **1.** of, concerning, regarding, in the matter of, apropos, in regard to, respecting, with regard *or* respect *or* reference to, relating *or* relative to. **2.** near, around, round, not far from, close to. **3.** near, close to, approximately, almost. **4.** around, circling, encircling, inclosing, enclosing, on every side, surrounding. **5.** on the point of, ready, prepared. **6.** here and there, in, on, hither and yon, to and fro, back and forth, hither and thither. —*adv.* **7.** near, approximately, nearly, almost, well-nigh. **8.** nearby, close, not far, around. **9.** on every side, in every direction, all around, everywhere, every place, all over. **10.** half round, reversed, backwards, opposite direction. **11.** to and fro, back and forth, hither and thither, hither and yon, here and there. **12.** in succession, alternately, in rotation.

about-face, *n.* 180° turn, reversal, turnabout, reverse, changeabout, reversion, volte-face.

above, *adv.* **1.** overhead, aloft, on high, atop, on top of. **2.** higher, beyond, over, superior, surpassing. **3.** (*in writing*) before, prior, earlier, sooner, previous, first. **4.** in heaven, on high, *in excelsis.* —*prep.* **5.** over, in a higher place than, higher than, superior to. **6.** more, greater than, more than, exceeding. **7.** better than, superior to, beyond, surpassing. —*adj.* **8.** supra, said, written, mentioned previously, foregoing, preceding.

aboveboard, *adv.* **1.** in open sight, without tricks, without disguise, openly, overtly, candidly, honestly, frankly, sincerely, guilelessly, unequivocally. —*adj.* **2.** open, candid, overt, honest, frank, sincere, guileless, unequivocal.
—Ant. underhand, treacherous, seditious.

abrade, *v.* wear off, wear down, scrape off; erode, wear away, rub off.

abrasion, *n.* **1.** sore, scrape, cut, scratch. **2.** friction, abrading, rubbing, erosion, wearing down, rubbing off.

abreast, *adv., adj.* side by side, alongside, equal, aligned.

abridge, *v.* **1.** shorten, condense, digest, scale down, reduce, abstract. **2.** curtail, reduce, lessen, diminish, contract. **3.** deprive, cut off, dispossess, divest.
—Ant. expand, extend.
—Syn. Study. See SHORTEN.

abridgment, *n.* **1.** condensation, shortening, digest, curtailment, reduction, abbreviation, contraction, compendium, synopsis, abstract, summary, brief, outline, précis. **2.** dispossession, limitation.
—Ant. expansion, extension, enlargement.

abroad, *adv.* **1.** overseas, beyond the sea, away. **2.** out-of-doors, outside. **3.** astir, in circulation. **4.** broadly, widely, expansively, at large, everywhere, ubiquitously, in all directions.
—Ant. here, domestically.

abrogate, *v.* abolish, cancel, annul, repeal, disannul, revoke, rescind, nullify, void, invalidate.
—Ant. ratify, establish.

abrupt, *adj.* sudden, short, precipitous, hasty, blunt, curt, brusque, uncomplaisant; rude, rough, discourteous, inconsiderate, boorish.
—Ant. gradual, slow, deliberate.

abscond, *v.* depart suddenly *or* secretly, steal away, sneak off *or* out.
—Ant. remain.

absence, *n.* **1.** want, lack, need. **2.** nonappearance.
—Ant. presence.

absent, *adj.* **1.** away, out, not present, off. **2.** lacking, missing, away.
—Ant. present.

absent-minded, *adj.* forgetful, preoccupied, abstracted, inattentive, daydreaming.
—Ant. attentive.

absolute, *adj.* **1.** complete, whole, entire. **2.** pure, unmixed, unadulterated. **3.** unqualified, utter, total, entire, unconditional, unrestricted, unlimited, unbound, unbounded. **4.** positive, affirmative, unquestionable, certain, sure, unequivocal, firm, definite.
—Ant. mixed; relative.

absolutely, *adv.* **1.** completely, wholly, entirely, unqualifiedly, definitely, unconditionally. **2.** positively, affirmatively, unquestionably, definitely, unequivocally, really, without doubt.

absolve, *v.* **1.** acquit, exonerate, free from blame, exculpate, excuse, forgive, pardon, clear, release. **2.** set free, loose, release, liberate, exempt. **3.** pardon, excuse, forgive.
—Ant. blame, censure.
—Syn. Study. ABSOLVE, ACQUIT, EXONERATE all mean to free from blame. ABSOLVE is a general word for this idea. To ACQUIT is to release from a specific and usu. formal accusation: *The court must acquit the accused if there is insufficient evidence of guilt.* To EXONERATE is to consider a person clear of blame or consequences for an act (even when the act is admitted), or to justify the person for having done it: *to be exonerated for a crime committed in self-defense.*

absorb, *v.* **1.** consume, assimilate, amalgamate, engulf. **2.** engross, occupy.

abstinence, *n.* **1.** abstemiousness, sobriety, soberness, teetotalism, moderation, temperance. **2.** self-restraint, avoidance, self-denial.
—Ant. indulgence.

abstract, *adj.* **1.** apart, special, unrelated, separate, isolated. **2.** theoretical, unpractical. **3.** abstruse, difficult, deep, complex, complicated. **4.** (*art*) nonrepresentational, unrealistic, unphotographic. —*n.* **5.** (*in writing*) summary, digest, abridgment, synopsis, compendium, condensation, brief. **6.** essence, distillation, condensation, substance; core, heart, idea. —*v.* **7.** draw away, take away, remove, distill; separate, fractionate. **8.** divert, disengage. **9.** steal, purloin, rob, pilfer, shoplift, hijack. **10.** separate, consider apart, isolate, ociate; disjoin, disunite. **11.** mmarize, epitomize, distill, abridge, abbreviate, outline, condense, edit, digest.

—**Ant.** concrete; interpolate.

absurd, *adj.* ridiculous, preposterous, silly, nonsensical, senseless, outlandish, farcical, childish, laughable, ludicrous, asinine, stupid, irrational, illogical, unsound.

—**Ant.** sensible, rational.

—**Syn. Study.** ABSURD, RIDICULOUS, PREPOSTEROUS all mean inconsistent with reason or common sense. ABSURD means utterly opposed to truth or reason: *an absurd claim.* RIDICULOUS implies that something is fit only to be laughed at, perhaps contemptuously: *a ridiculous suggestion.* PREPOSTEROUS implies an extreme of foolishness: *a preposterous proposal.*

abundant, *adj.* abounding, teeming, thick, plentiful, copious, profuse, rich, replete, ample, bountiful, bounteous, abounding in, rich in, luxuriant, lavish.

—**Ant.** sparse, scarce, poor.

—**Syn. Study.** See PLENTIFUL.

abuse, *v.* **1.** misuse, misapply, misemploy, misappropriate. **2.** maltreat, ill-use, injure, harm, hurt, wrong, mistreat, manhandle, ill-treat, damage. **3.** revile, malign, vilify, berate, rate, scold, carp at, censure, assail, lambaste, rebuke, bawl out, inveigh against, reproach; traduce, slander, defame, denounce, criticize, insult, curse, libel, calumniate, disparage. —*n.* **4.** mistreatment, misappropriation; desecration, profanation, deception, betrayal, seduction, subversion. **5.** adverse criticism, blame, condemnation, denunciation, vilification, tongue-lashing, scolding, insult, slander, defamation, aspersion, curse, disparagement; scorn, reproach, opprobrium.

—**Ant.** esteem; praise, acclaim.

—**Syn. Study.** ABUSE, CENSURE, INVECTIVE all mean strongly expressed disapproval. ABUSE implies an outburst of harsh and scathing words, often against one who is defenseless: *abuse directed against an opponent.* CENSURE implies blame, adverse criticism, or condemnation: *severe censure of her bad judgment.* INVECTIVE applies to strong but formal denunciation in speech or print, often in the public interest: *invective against graft.*

abyss, *n.* chasm, gulf, bottomless pit, pit, crater, crevasse, shaft, well, hollow, cavity, void, deep.

academic, *adj.* **1.** scholarly, scholastic, lettered, literary, humanistic, erudite, learned, cultured, scientific, pedagogical, pedagogic, educational, professorial, donnish, collegiate. **2.** theoretical, hypothetical, speculative, conjectural, abstract, *Informal* ivory-tower. **3.** conventional, formal, dry, standard, traditional, unoriginal, orthodox, commonplace, formulaic, pro forma, trite, conformist, prosaic, stale, uninspired, boring, tiresome.

—**Ant.** illiterate, informal.

accept, *v.* **1.** receive, take, allow, permit. **2.** admit, agree to, accede to, acquiesce in, assent to, approve, allow, concede, acknowledge. **3.** resign oneself to, reconcile oneself to, stomach, bear, endure, brook, take, tolerate, accommodate oneself to.

—**Ant.** reject.

access, *n.* **1.** entry, entrance, doorway, ingress, entrée, passage, admittance, way, way in, route, approach. —*v.* **2.** reach, approach, contact, enter.

accident, *n.* **1.** blunder, mistake, mischance, misfortune. **2.** disaster, calamity, catastrophe, casualty, mishap. **3.** fortuity, chance, fortune, luck, fluke, serendipity.

—**Ant.** design, premeditation.

accidental, *adj.* **1.** casual, fortuitous, chance, lucky, unlucky, unfortunate, serendipitous, unintentional, unwitting, inadvertent, unexpected, unanticipated, random, unforeseen, unplanned. **2.** nonessential, incidental, expendable, adventitious.

—**Ant.** planned, designed, essential.

acclaimed, *adj.* notable, distinguished, great, major, famous, honored, famed, renowned, celebrated, prominent, world-renowned, world-famous, stellar, world-class, outstanding, preeminent, premier.

accommodate, *v.* **1.** oblige, serve; aid, assist, help, abet. **2.** make suitable, suit, fit, adapt, adjust. **3.** bring into harmony, adjust, reconcile, compose, harmonize. **4.** contain, hold. **5.** conform, agree, concur, assent.

—**Ant.** inconvenience, incommode.

—**Syn. Study.** See OBLIGE. See also CONTAIN.

accompany, *v.* **1.** attend, join, convoy, escort, chaperone, squire, usher, come with. **2.** coexist with, belong with, associate with.

—**Ant.** desert, abandon, forsake.

—**Syn. Study.** ACCOMPANY, ATTEND, CONVOY, ESCORT mean to go along with. To ACCOMPANY is to go as an associate or companion, usu. on equal terms: *My daughter accompanied me on the trip.* ATTEND usu. implies going along as a subordinate, as to render service: *to attend the queen.* To CONVOY is to accompany ships or other vehicles with an armed guard: *to convoy a fleet of merchant vessels.* To ESCORT is to accompany in order to protect, honor, or show courtesy: *to escort a visiting dignitary.*

accomplice, *n.* associate, partner, confederate, accessory, ally, colleague, collaborator, coconspirator, partner in crime, abettor.

accomplish, *v.* **1.** fulfill, complete, achieve, execute, do, carry out, perform, finish, attain. **2.** succeed in, be successful with *or* in, triumph over, win over.

—**Ant.** fail.

accomplishment, *n.* **1.** fulfillment, completion, conclusion, culmination, execution. **2.** achievement, success, consummation, triumph, coup, feat. **3.** attainment, proficiency. **4.** talent, skill, ability, gift, aptitude, faculty, capability, forte.

—**Ant.** failure.

accord, *v.* **1.** agree, assent, concur, correspond, coincide, conform. **2.** adapt, accommodate, reconcile, suit, fit. **3.** grant, concede, yield.

—**Ant.** conflict, disagree.

accordingly, *adv.* in due course, consequently, hence, therefore, thus, so, wherefore.

account, *n.* **1.** narrative, narration, recital, report, history, chronicle, journal, anecdote, description, story, exposé, tale. **2.** explication, clearing up, exposition. **3.** reason, consideration, motive, excuse, purpose. **4.** consequence, importance, value, consideration, worth, distinction, repute, reputation. **5.** estimation, judgment, consideration, regard. **6.** profit, advantage, benefit. **7.** record, ledger; balance. —*v.* **8.** count, reckon, estimate, consider, regard, judge, deem, rate, assess, hold, see, view, look upon. **9.** account for, give an explanation for, explain, elucidate, make excuses for, give reasons for, answer, reply.

accurate, *adj.* **1.** correct, exact, precise, true, unerring, error-free, on target, (*slang*) on the money, verified, valid, real, factual, scientific. **2.** (*of a person*) meticulous, scrupulous, careful, conscientious.

—**Ant.** inaccurate.

—**Syn. Study.** See CORRECT.

accuse, *v.* **1.** arraign, indict, charge, impeach. **2.** blame, charge, censure, hold responsible, denounce, cite.

—**Ant.** exonerate.

acerbic, *adj.* **1.** sour, tart, acid, acidy. **2.** sarcastic, sardonic, ironic, wry, caustic, biting, scathing.

—**Ant.** sweet, dulcet, generous, upbeat, Pollyannaish, goody-goody.

ache, *v.* **1.** suffer, hurt, suffer pain, throb, smart, sting. **2.** long, yearn, hunger, hanker. —*n.* **3.** pain, continued *or* dull pain, agony, pang, soreness, smarting, throbbing.

achieve, *v.* **1.** accomplish, complete, effect, execute, do, perform, realize. **2.** gain, obtain, acquire, realize, win.

—**Ant.** fail.

achievement, *n.* **1.** exploit, feat, victory, triumph. **2.** accomplishment, realization, attainment, completion.

—**Ant.** failure.

acid, *adj.* **1.** (*of a taste*) acerbic, sour, tart, vinegary. **2.** (*of a person or words*) acerbic, caustic, scathing, biting, sarcastic, wry.

—**Ant.** sweet, mild.

acknowledge, *v.* **1.** admit, confess, concede. **2.** appreciate, be grateful for. **3.** reply to, answer, react to, respond to.

—**Syn. Study.** ACKNOWLEDGE, ADMIT, CONFESS agree in the idea of declaring something to be true. ACKNOWLEDGE implies making a statement reluctantly, often about something previously doubted or denied: *to acknowledge one's mistakes.* ADMIT esp. implies acknowledging under pressure: *to admit a charge.* CONFESS usu. means stating somewhat formally an admission of wrongdoing or shortcoming: *to confess guilt; to confess an inability to understand.*

acquaintance, *n.* **1.** associate, companion, friend. **2.** personal knowledge, familiarity, understanding, awareness; experience.

—**Syn. Study.** ACQUAINTANCE, ASSOCIATE, COMPANION, FRIEND refer to a person with whom one is in contact. An ACQUAINTANCE is a person one knows, though not intimately: *a casual acquaintance at school.* An ASSOCIATE is a person who is often in one's company, usu. because of some work or pursuit in common: *a business associate.* A COMPANION is a person who shares one's activities or fortunes; the term usu. suggests a familiar relationship: *a traveling companion; a companion in despair.* A FRIEND is a person with whom one is on intimate terms and for whom one feels a warm affection: *a trusted friend.*

acquiesce, *v.* assent, accede, comply, agree, concur, consent, yield.

—**Ant.** protest, object.

acquire, *n.* get, appropriate, gain, win, earn, attain; take possession of, obtain, get.

—**Ant.** forfeit, lose.

—**Syn. Study.** See GET.

acquit, *v.* **1.** absolve, exonerate, exculpate, pardon, excuse, forgive. **2.** release *or* discharge, liberate, set free. **3.** settle, pay, fulfill. **4.** behave, conduct oneself.

—**Ant.** convict, condemn.

—**Syn. Study.** See ABSOLVE.

acrimonious, *adj.* angry, harsh, bitter, biting, sharp, rancorous, contentious, antagonistic, hostile, vitriolic.

—**Ant.** peaceful, pacific, irenic, tactful, diplomatic.

act, *n.* **1.** feat, exploit, achievement, accomplishment, performance. **2.** deed. **3.** decree, edict, law, statute. **4.** record, deed, enactment, ordinance. **5.** turn, routine, performance, stint. —*v.* **6.** operate, function, perform, do, work. **7.** behave, perform, conduct *or* deport *or* comport oneself. **8.** pretend, dissemble, feign, fake. **9.** play parts. **10.** represent, impersonate, imitate, play the part of.

action, *n.* **1.** movement, work, performance, operation. **2.** deed, act. **3.** (*plural*) conduct. **4.** energetic activity. **5.** exertion, energy, effort. **6.** gesture. **7.** engagement, conflict, combat, fight, battle, clash, sortie.

—**Ant.** lethargy, inactivity.

active, *adj.* **1.** acting, moving, working, operative, functioning. **2.** busy, dynamic, lively, brisk, bustling, energetic, strenuous, vigorous, animated. **3.** nimble, sprightly, agile, alert, smart, quick, animated, spry, spirited, lively. **4.** practical, working.

—**Ant.** inactive, lazy.

actual, *adj.* **1.** true, genuine, real, veritable, factual, verifiable, authentic, verified, manifest, realistic, tangible, certain. **2.** current, existent, physical, now existing, present, here and now.

—**Ant.** unreal, untrue, fake.

acute, *adj.* **1.** pointed, sharp, sharpened. **2.** intense, poignant, touching. **3.** severe, distressing, crucial, critical, dangerous, grave, serious. **4.** sharp, penetrating, perceptive, keen, astute, incisive, insightful, sensitive, discriminating, discerning, intelligent, perspicacious, sharp-witted, shrewd, clever.

—**Ant.** blunt.

adapt, *v.* **1.** adjust, modify, alter, change, remodel, customize, tailor, reshape, shape, fashion, fit, reconcile, accommodate **2.** acclimate, habituate, get used to.

—**Syn. Study.** See ADJUST.

add, *v.* **1.** unite, annex, connect, affix, join; append, attach, supplement, increase, make an addition, augment, adjoin, tack on. **2.** total, sum up, combine, count up, tote up, reckon, sum, aggregate.

—**Ant.** subtract, deduct.

addiction, *n.* dependency, compulsive need, obsession, fixation, habit, craving, appetite, itch, lust, passion, monkey on one's back, jones, substance abuse.

addition, *n.* **1.** uniting, adding, joining. **2.** summing up, totaling, summation, counting up, reckoning. **3.** increase, increment, enlargement, aggrandizement, augmentation, extension, accession. **4.** accessory, adjunct, attachment, supplement, appendix, addendum, appendage.

—**Ant.** deduction, subtraction.

—**Syn. Study.** ADDITION, ACCESSORY, ADJUNCT, ATTACHMENT refer to something joined to or used with something else. ADDITION is the general word for anything joined to something previously existing; it carries no implication of size, importance, or kind: *to build an addition to the town library.* An ACCESSORY is a nonessential part or object that makes something more complete, convenient, or attractive: *clothing accessories; camera accessories.* An ADJUNCT is a subordinate addition that aids or assists but is usu. separate: *a second machine as an adjunct to the first.* An ATTACHMENT is a supplementary part that may be easily connected and removed: *a sewing machine attachment for pleating.*

address, *n.* **1.** discourse, lecture, speech, oration, talk, sermon. **2.** residence, domicile, abode, dwelling, home quarters, house. —*v.* **3.** talk to, deliver *or* give a speech to, lecture, direct (speech *or* writing to), speak to. **4.** greet, hail, approach,

accost.
—**Syn. Study.** See SPEECH.

adequate, *adj.* suitable, suited, fit for, competent, good enough, satisfactory; sufficient, enough, ample, plenty; acceptable, passable, average, fair, tolerable, all right, O.K., okay, not bad, so-so.
—**Ant.** inadequate, insufficient.

adhere, *v.* **1.** stick fast, cleave, cling, stick, hold, cohere. **2.** be a follower. **3.** hold closely *or* firmly to.
—**Ant.** separate.
—**Syn. Study.** See STICK.

adherent, *n.* **1.** supporter, follower, partisan, disciple; devotee, enthusiast, groupie, fan, aficionado. —*adj.* **2.** clinging, adhering, sticking, cleaving.
—**Ant.** recreant, deserter.
—**Syn. Study.** See FOLLOWER.

adjacent, *adj.* near, close, contiguous, adjoining, juxtaposed, abutting, neighboring, nearby, touching.
—**Ant.** distant.
—**Syn. Study.** See ADJOINING.

adjoining, *adj.* adjacent, bordering, neighboring, abutting, contiguous, near *or* close *or* next to, touching.
—**Syn. Study.** ADJOINING, ADJACENT both mean near or close to something. ADJOINING implies touching at a common point or line: *adjoining rooms.* ADJACENT implies being nearby or next to something else, with nothing of the same sort intervening: *a motel adjacent to the highway; the adjacent houses.*

adjourn, *v.* suspend, postpone, interrupt, put off, defer, delay.
—**Ant.** convene, begin.

adjunct, *n.* **1.** addition, appendix, supplement, attachment. **2.** aide, attaché, subordinate, accessory.
—**Syn. Study.** See ADDITION.

adjust, *v.* **1.** adapt, alter, fit, accommodate, suit. **2.** regulate, set, repair, fix; change, modify, alter, tweak. **3.** rectify, put to rights, correct, patch up. **4.** adapt oneself, make oneself suitable *or* suited for, acclimate, accustom.
—**Syn. Study.** ADJUST, ADAPT, ALTER imply making necessary or desirable changes, as in position, shape, or the like. To ADJUST is to make a minor change, as to move into proper position for use: *to adjust the eyepiece of a telescope.* To ADAPT is to make a change in character, or to make something useful in a new way: *to adapt a method to a new task.* To ALTER is to change the appearance but not the use: *to alter a suit.*

ad-lib, *v.* **1.** improvise, extemporize, make up, invent, throw away, (*slang*) wing it. —*n.* **2.** improvisation, extemporization. —*adj.* **3.** improvised, extemporized, extemporaneous, impromptu, unrehearsed, spur of the moment, ad hoc.

administer, *v.* **1.** manage, conduct, control, execute; rule, govern; direct, superintend, oversee, supervise. **2.** give, dispense, apply, dose, deal out, dole out.

admirable, *adj.* estimable, praiseworthy, fine, rare, excellent, wonderful, awe-inspiring, splendid, marvelous, superior, great, brilliant, first-rate, world-class.
—**Ant.** abhorrent.

admiration, *n.* esteem, appreciation, reverence, veneration.
—**Ant.** abhorrence, disgust, hatred.

admire, *v.* esteem; revere, respect, regard highly, look up to, idolize, venerate.
—**Ant.** detest, hate.

admission, *n.* **1.** entrance, introduction, access, admittance, entry, entrée, ticket, pass. **2.** confession, acknowledgment.
—**Ant.** rejection; denial.

admit, *v.* **1.** allow to enter, let in, receive. **2.** acknowledge, own, avow, confess.
—**Ant.** reject; deny.
—**Syn. Study.** See ACKNOWLEDGE.

admonish, *v.* **1.** caution, advise, warn, counsel. **2.** rebuke, censure, reprove.
—**Syn. Study.** See WARN.

ado, *n.* fuss, stir, flurry, dither, commotion, disturbance, turmoil.
—**Ant.** calm, serenity, tranquillity.

adolescent, *adj.* **1.** immature, puerile, juvenile; pubescent, teenaged, youthful, young. —*n.* **2.** youth, teenager, teen, juvenile, minor.
—**Ant.** adult.

adore, *v.* **1.** idolize, worship, love, dote on. **2.** respect, honor, esteem, revere, venerate, idolize, admire, exalt.
—**Ant.** abhor, detest, abominate, hate.

adorn, *v.* **1.** embellish, add luster to. **2.** decorate, enhance, beautify, deck, bedeck, ornament, trim, array.
—**Ant.** disfigure, deface.

adroit, *adj.* expert, ingenious, skillful, dexterous, clever, resourceful, ready, quick, apt, adept, agile, nimble, astute, shrewd, knowing.
—**Ant.** clumsy, maladroit.
—**Syn. Study.** See DEXTEROUS.

adult, *adj.* **1.** mature, grown up, full-grown, of age. —*n.* **2.** grown-up, man, woman.
—**Ant.** immature, adolescent.

advance, *v.* **1.** move *or* set *or* push *or* bring forward, further, forward. **2.** propose, bring to view *or* notice, propound, offer. **3.** improve, further, forward, strengthen. **4.** promote, elevate. **5.** increase, raise the price of, augment. **6.** update, accelerate, quicken, hasten, speed up, bring forward. **7.** furnish *or* supply on credit, lend, loan. **8.** move *or* go forward, proceed, move on. **9.** improve, progress, make progress. **10.** rise, increase, appreciate. —*n.* **11.** moving forward, progress, procedure, way; march, procession. **12.** advancement, promotion, improvement, advance, rise. **13.** overture, proposal, proposition, tender, offer, proffer, offering. —*adj.* **14.** going before, preceding, precedent. **15.** beyond, ahead, before.
—**Ant.** retreat.

advantage, *n.* **1.** favorable opportunity *or* state *or* circumstance *or* means *or* situation, vantage point. **2.** benefit, interest, gain, profit. **3.** superiority, ascendancy, preeminence, dominance, edge, head start, (*informal*) upper hand, win-win situation. **4.** behalf, vantage; privilege, prerogative, convenience, accommodation.
—**Ant.** disadvantage.
—**Syn. Study.** ADVANTAGE, BENEFIT, PROFIT all mean something that is of use or value. ADVANTAGE is anything that places a person in a favorable or superior position, esp. in coping with competition or difficulties: *It is to your advantage to have traveled widely.* BENEFIT is anything that promotes the welfare or improves the state of a person or group: *The new factory will be a great benefit to our town.* PROFIT is any valuable or useful gain, usually financial, moral, or educational: *profit from trade; profit from experience.*

adventurous, *adj.* daring, bold, intrepid, brave, heroic, fearless, audacious, courageous, dashing, risk-taking, reckless, devil-may-care, risky, dangerous, perilous.
—**Ant.** timid, tame, docile, cautious, unadventurous.

adversary, *n.* antagonist, opponent, enemy, foe, competitor, rival.
—**Ant.** ally, compatriot, friend.
—**Syn. Study.** ADVERSARY, ANTAGONIST refer to a person, group, or personified force contending against another. ADVERSARY suggests an enemy who fights determinedly, continuously, and relentlessly: *a formidable adversary.* ANTAGONIST suggests one who, in hostile spirit, opposes another, often in a particular contest or struggle: *a duel with an antagonist.*

adverse, *adj.* **1.** antagonistic, contrary, opposite, conflicting, opposed, hostile, against. **2.** unfavorable, calamitous, disastrous, catastrophic.
—**Ant.** favorable, beneficial.

adversity, *n.* calamity, catastrophe, disaster; bad luck, misfortune.
—**Ant.** happiness, wealth.

advice, *n.* **1.** counsel, recommendation, guidance, suggestion, admonition, warning, caution. **2.** communication, information, news, report, intelligence,.
—**Syn. Study.** ADVICE, COUNSEL refer to opinions offered as worthy bases for thought, conduct, or action. ADVICE is a practical recommendation, generally from a person with relevant knowledge or experience: *Get a lawyer's advice about the purchase.* COUNSEL is weighty and serious advice, given after careful deliberation and consultation: *to seek counsel during a personal crisis.*

advisable, *adj.* expedient, advantageous, politic, proper, fit, suitable, desirable, correct, prudent, practical, sound, wise (*informal*) win-win.

advise, *v.* **1.** give counsel to, counsel, caution, warn, recommend to, suggest, guide. **2.** tell, announce, make known, inform, notify, apprise.

advocate, *v.* **1.** plead in favor of, support, urge, argue for, speak for, recommend, champion, back, endorse, uphold, stand behind, second, favor. —*n.* **2.** lawyer, attorney, counselor, counselor-at-law, counsel. **3.** defender, vindicator, upholder, supporter, champion, backer, exponent, proponent, apologist.
—**Ant.** oppose; opponent.

aesthete, *n.* art lover, dilettante, connoisseur, virtuoso, expert, collector, tastemaker, maven.

affable, *adj.* approachable, polite, friendly, cordial, pleasant, amiable, obliging, gracious; benign, mild, easy, casual, social.
—**Ant.** boorish, reserved.

affect, *v.* **1.** exert influence on, bring about, influence, sway, act on; modify, alter, transform, change. **2.** move, strike, impress, touch, stir, overcome. **3.** pretend, feign, fake, assume, adopt.
—**Syn. Study.** See PRETEND.

affectation, *n.* pretension, pretentiousness, posturing, pomposity, airs, mannerisms, artificiality, affectedness, unnaturalness, insincerity.
—**Ant.** sincerity.

affected, *adj.* **1.** unnatural, artificial, contrived, stilted, studied, stiff, mannered, awkward. **2.** assumed, pretended, feigned, simulated, hollow, false, fake, insincere, counterfeit, bogus, sham, phony. **3.** pretentious, pompous. **4.** afflicted, attacked, seized, moved, stirred, touched.
—**Ant.** sincere, genuine.

affecting, *adj.* touching, moving, impressive.

affection, *n.* attachment, liking, friendliness, fondness, devotion, tenderness, regard.
—**Ant.** abhorrence.

affectionate, *adj.* tender, loving, fond, attentive, attached, devoted.
—**Ant.** apathetic.

affectless, *adj.* unemotional, unfeeling, remote, numb, dead, distant, passionless, dispassionate, detached, disinterested, indifferent.
—**Ant.** emotional, animated, passionate, excitable.

affirm, *v.* **1.** state, assert, aver, maintain, declare, depose, testify, say, pronounce. **2.** establish, confirm, ratify, approve, endorse.
—**Ant.** deny.
—**Syn. Study.** See DECLARE.

affliction, *n.* **1.** pain, distress, grief, adversity, misfortune, hardship, ordeal, torment, trial, mishap, trouble, tribulation, calamity, catastrophe, disaster. **2.** sickness, suffering, curse, disease, plague, scourge, epidemic.
—**Ant.** relief.

affront, *n.* **1.** offense, slight, disrespect, insult, impertinence, scorn. **2.** shame, disgrace, degradation. —*v.* **3.** offend, insult, slight, abuse, outrage. **4.** shame, disgrace, discountenance, confuse, confound, disconcert, abash.
—**Ant.** compliment.
—**Syn. Study.** See INSULT.

afraid, *adj.* scared, fearful, alarmed, frightened, agitated, intimidated, panic-stricken, weak-kneed, fainthearted, tremulous, traumatized, terrified, apprehensive, timid, cowardly, timorous.
—**Ant.** bold, sanguine, confident.

age, *n.* **1.** lifetime, lifespan, stage, period, life, duration. **2.** maturity, adulthood. **3.** old age, decline, twilight of life, dotage. **4.** epoch, era, period, time, date. —*v.* **5.** grow old, mature, ripen.
—**Ant.** youth.
—**Syn.** AGE, EPOCH, ERA, PERIOD all refer to an extent of time. AGE usu. implies a considerable extent of time, esp. one associated with a dominant personality, influence, characteristic, or institution: *the age of chivalry.* EPOCH and ERA are often used interchangeably to refer to an extent of time characterized by changed conditions and new undertakings: *an era* (*or epoch*) *of invention.* EPOCH sometimes refers esp. to the beginning of an era: *The steam engine marked a new epoch in technology.* A PERIOD usu. has a marked condition or feature: *a period of industrial expansion; the Victorian period.*

aged, *adj.* **1.** old, ancient, elderly, superannuated, gray, venerable, long-lived, full of years. **2.** decrepit, past one's prime, run-down, worn-out. **3.** ripe, mature, ready.
—**Ant.** young.

aggravate, *v.* **1.** worsen, make severe, intensify, heighten, increase, make serious *or* grave, exacerbate, magnify, inflame. **2.** (*sometimes criticized*) annoy, irritate, exasperate, vex, bother.
—**Ant.** assuage, improve, better.

aggregate, *adj.* **1.** added, combined, total, complete. —*n.* **2.** sum, mass, assemblage, total, gross, body, amount. —*v.* **3.** bring together, assemble, collect, amass, accumulate, gather. **4.** amount to, add up to. **5.** combine into a mass, form a collection.
—**Ant.** particular.

aggressive, *adj.* **1.** belligerent, hostile, unfriendly, quarrelsome, combative, warlike, take-no-prisoners, martial, bellicose, disputatious. **2.** energetic, vigorous, pushing, enterprising, assertive, determined, forward, forceful, bold, pushy.
—**Ant.** retiring, bashful, shy.

aghast, *adj.* dismayed, horrified, appalled, horror-struck, undone, stricken, stunned, shocked, agape, dumbfounded, thunderstruck, overwhelmed, jolted, jarred, shaken up, shook up.

agile, *adj.* **1.** (*of the body*) quick,

light, nimble, sprightly, active, lively, brisk, swift, lithe, limber, supple, flexible, animated. **2.** (*of the mind*) ready, smart, alert, keen, sharp, dextrous, resourceful, acute, adroit.
—Ant. awkward, clumsy, maladroit.
agitate, *v.* **1.** shake *or* move briskly, disturb, toss, jar. **2.** disturb, ruffle, perturb, excite, fluster, disquiet, rattle, disconcert, unsettle, upset, unnerve, rock, shake up. **3.** discuss, debate, dispute, promote, protest. **4.** ferment, disturb, rouse.
—Ant. tranquilize.
agitation, *n.* **1.** agitating, shaking, jarring. **2.** turbulence, commotion, ferment, stimulation, disturbance, excitement, turmoil, tumult. **3.** urging, persistence; debate, discussion, dispute, argument, campaign.
—Ant. serenity, calm, tranquility.
agony, *n.* pain, distress, anguish, grief, angst, trouble, misery, woe, wretchedness, affliction, suffering, torment, torture.
—Ant. comfort.
agree, *v.* **1.** assent, yield, consent, accede, settle, concede, acquiesce, allow, comply. **2.** harmonize, concur, unite. **3.** come to an agreement *or* arrangement *or* understanding, compromise, arrive at a settlement, see eye to eye. **4.** accord, correspond, compare favorably, coincide, conform, tally, match, stand up, suit. **5.** be applicable *or* appropriate *or* similar, resemble. **6.** make *or* write a contract *or* bargain, contract, stipulate, bargain. **7.** concede, grant, allow, let, permit, approve.
—Ant. disagree.
agreement, *n.* **1.** bargain, compact, contract, covenant, treaty, pact, settlement. **2.** unanimity, harmony, concord.
—Ant. disagreement.
—Syn. Study. AGREEMENT, BARGAIN, COMPACT, CONTRACT all suggest an arrangement between two or more parties. AGREEMENT ranges in meaning from a mutual understanding to a binding obligation: *an agreement to meet next week; a tariff agreement.* BARGAIN applies particularly to agreements about buying and selling; it suggests haggling: *We made a bargain that I would do the work if they supplied the materials.* COMPACT applies to treaties or alliances between nations or to solemn personal pledges: *a compact to preserve the peace.* CONTRACT is used esp. in law and business for such agreements as are legally enforceable: *a contract to sell a house.*
aid, *v.* **1.** support, help, succor, assist. **2.** promote, facilitate, ease, simplify. **3.** be of help, give help *or* assistance. —*n.* **4.** help, support, succor, assistance, service, relief, charity. **5.** assistant, helper, supporter, servant, aide, right hand, cohort, ally, comrade.
—Ant. hinder, obstruct; obstacle, obstruction.
—Syn. Study. See HELP.
ailing, *adj.* sickly, sick, ill, unwell, not well, failing, weak, flagging, languishing, abed, indisposed, infirm, diseased, unhealthy, troubled, afflicted, suffering, in distress, distressed, in pain, hurting, bothered, disabled, under the weather, feeling poorly, in poor health, prostrate, infected, laid up, bedridden.
—Ant. healthy, well.
ailment, *n.* disorder, infirmity, affliction, indisposition, malaise, malady, disease, sickness, complaint, ill, debility, disability, handicap, defect.
aim, *v.* **1.** direct, point, give direction to. **2.** strive, seek, try. —*n.* **3.** direction, sighting. **4.** end, object, goal, target, purpose, intent, intention, ambition, desire, aspiration, objective, plan, point.
—Syn. Study. AIM, END, OBJECT all imply something that is the goal of one's efforts. AIM implies a direct effort toward a goal, without diversion from it: *Her aim is to be an astronaut.* END emphasizes the goal as separate from the effort: *unscrupulous means to achieve noble ends.* OBJECT emphasizes the goal of a specific effort: *the object of my research.*
air, *n.* **1.** atmosphere, ambience, aura, climate, mood, sense, feeling, quality. **2.** breeze, breath, zephyr, wind. **3.** character, appearance, impression, aspect, look, mien; manner, demeanor, attitude, conduct, behavior, deportment, bearing. **4.** (plural) pretension, pretense, show, hauteur, arrogance, affectation, haughtiness. —*v.* **5.** ventilate. **6.** expose, display, show off, parade, exhibit, reveal, disclose.
—Syn. Study. See WIND.
alarm, *n.* **1.** fear, apprehension, fright, consternation, terror, panic, dismay, trepidation, dread, anxiety, distress, uneasiness, excitement. **2.** warning, alert, danger *or* distress signal, notification, siren. —*v.* **3.** terrify, frighten, scare, startle, appall, shock, panic.
—Ant. calm, comfort.
alert, *adj.* **1.** attentive, vigilant, watchful, aware, wide-awake, on guard, on one's toes, wary, observant. **2.** nimble, brisk, lively, quick, active, agile, sprightly, spirited. —*v.* **3.** prepare for action, warn, alarm, signal, notify, advise, caution.
—Ant. asleep, listless.
alien, *n.* **1.** stranger, foreigner, immigrant, outsider, *Auslander,* nonnative, newcomer. **2.** extraterrestrial, *E.T.* —*adj.* **3.** strange, foreign; exotic, unfamiliar. **4.** adverse, hostile, opposed.
—Ant. native; friendly.
—Syn. Study. See STRANGER.
alive, *adj.* **1.** existing, living, breathing, quick. **2.** unextinguished, operative, functioning. **3.** lively, active, alert, vivacious, animated, spirited, spry, sprightly, energetic, vigorous. **4.** swarming, thronged, aswarm, crowded, ahum, humming, buzzing, jumping, astir, packed, bustling.
—Ant. dead.
allay, *v.* quiet, appease, moderate, soothe, soften, assuage, alleviate, lighten, lessen, mitigate, relieve, ease.
—Ant. aggravate.
allege, *v.* declare, affirm, attest, state, assert, aver, avow, say, depose, claim, accuse.
—Ant. deny.
allegiance, *n.* duty, obligation, faithfulness, loyalty, fealty, fidelity.
—Ant. treason, treachery.
alleviate, *v.* ease, lessen, diminish, quell, abate, mitigate, lighten, relieve, assuage, allay, mollify.
—Ant. aggravate, intensify.
alliance, *n.* **1.** league, confederation, union, association, coalition, combination, bloc, partnership, affiliation, federation, confederacy. **2.** treaty, pact, compact, bond. **3.** marriage, intermarriage, relation, relationship. **4.** affinity, unity.
—Syn. Study. ALLIANCE, LEAGUE, CONFEDERATION, UNION refer to the joining of states for mutual benefit or for the joint exercise of functions. ALLIANCE refers to a combination of states for the promotion of common interests: *a trade alliance.* LEAGUE usu. suggests a closer, more formal combination or a more definite purpose: *The League of Nations was formed to promote world peace.* CONFEDERATION applies to a fairly permanent combination for the exercise in common of certain governmental functions: *a confederation of Canadian provinces.* UNION implies an alliance so close and permanent that the separate states become essentially one: *the union of England and Scotland to form Great Britain.*
allot, *v.* **1.** divide, distribute, parcel out, apportion, assign, share, deal out, dole out, mete out, deal, dispense, measure out. **2.** appropriate, allocate, set apart, appoint, earmark.
—Syn. Study. See ASSIGN.
allow, *v.* **1.** permit, let, grant. **2.** grant, yield, cede, relinquish, give, consent to, agree to, authorize. **3.** admit, acknowledge, concede, own, confess. **4.** bear, suffer, tolerate, put up with, stand for, brook, sanction, permit, countenance.
—Ant. forbid, prohibit; refuse.
—Syn. Study. ALLOW, PERMIT, LET imply granting or conceding the right of someone to do something. ALLOW suggests passivity or even oversight; it points to the absence of an attempt or intent to hinder: *The baby-sitter allowed the children to run around the house.* PERMIT implies a more positive or willing consent; it is often used of a formal authorization: *Bicycle riding is not permitted in this park.* LET is a familiar, conversational term used in a similar sense: *My parents let me stay up late.*
allowance, *n.* **1.** allotment, stipend, pin *or* pocket money, ration, allocation. **2.** deduction, discount, rebate, reduction, credit. **3.** acceptance, admission, concession, acknowledgment. **4.** sanction, tolerance, leave, permission, license, permit, authorization, approval.
ally, *v.* **1.** unite, unify, join, confederate, combine, connect, league, associate, affiliate, collaborate, band together, team up. —*n.* **2.** comrade, collaborator, coconspirator, associate, partner, friend, confederate, aide, accomplice, accessory, assistant, abettor; colleague.
—Ant. enemy, foe, adversary.
almost, *adv.* nearly, somewhat, about, approximately, practically, virtually, bordering on, on the brink *or* verge of, barely, hardly, scarcely, not quite, all but, close to.
alone, *adj.* **1.** apart, single, solitary, unaccompanied, solo, unescorted, by oneself, unattended, unassisted, on one's own, singlehanded, individual, singular, unique. **2.** lone, lonesome, desolate, abandoned.
—Ant. together, accompanied.
also, *adv.* in addition, too, further, likewise, besides, moreover, furthermore.
alter, *v.* modify, change, revise, transform; adjust, adapt, convert, redo.
—Ant. preserve, keep.
—Syn. Study. See ADJUST, CHANGE.
alternate, *v.* **1.** take turns, rotate, change, exchange, interchange. —*n.* **2.** substitute, stand-in, variant, alternative, backup, understudy, pinch hitter, surrogate.
alternative, *n.* **1.** choice, option, alternate, variant, substitute, surrogate. —*adj.* **2.** mutually exclusive, different, variant, additional, substitute.
—Syn. Study. See CHOICE.
always, *adv.* **1.** all the time, uninterruptedly, perpetually, in perpetuity, unendingly, ever after, till the end of time, everlastingly, eternally, forever, continually, ever. **2.** every time, each time, at all times, again and again, without exception; often, usually, as a rule.
—Ant. never.
amateur, *n.* lay person, dabbler, beginner, nonexpert, dilettante, tyro, novice, nonprofessional, neophyte.
—Ant. professional, expert.
amaze, *v.* astound, surprise, astonish, stagger, stupefy, bewilder, confuse, perplex, daze, dumbfound, awe, stun, floor, take aback, dazzle, nonplus, confound, flabbergast, knock one's socks off, make one gasp.
ambiguous, *adj.* **1.** equivocal, doubtful, dubious, unclear, uncertain, vague, indistinct, indeterminate. **2.** difficult, obscure, unclassifiable, anomalous. **3.** puzzling, enigmatic, problematic, cryptic, mysterious, confusing.
—Ant. explicit, clear.
—Syn. Study. AMBIGUOUS, EQUIVOCAL both refer to words or expressions that are not clear in meaning. AMBIGUOUS describes that which is capable of two or more contradictory interpretations, usu. unintentionally so: *an ambiguous line in a poem; an ambiguous smile.* EQUIVOCAL also means susceptible of contradictory interpretations, but usu. by a deliberate intent to mislead or mystify: *an equivocal response to an embarrassing question.*
ambition, *n.* **1.** goal, object, aim, hope, desire, dream, wish, objective, purpose; appetite, craving, aspiration, enterprise, yearning, longing. **2.** energy, initiative, drive, enterprise, enthusiasm, zeal.
—Ant. satisfaction; sloth, laziness.
ambitious, *adj.* enterprising, aspiring, hopeful, enthusiastic, energetic, vigorous, zealous, eager.
—Ant. apathetic; humble.
—Syn. Study. AMBITIOUS, ENTERPRISING describe a person who wishes to rise above his or her present position or condition. An AMBITIOUS person strives for worldly success; such efforts may be admired or frowned on by others: *an ambitious college graduate; an ambitious social climber.* An ENTERPRISING person is characterized by energy and daring in undertaking projects: *This company needs an enterprising new manager.*
ambivalent, *adj.* undecided, uncertain, equivocal, vacillating, irresolute, hesitant; (*informal*) on the fence.
ameliorate, *v.* improve, better, amend, raise, elevate, promote, reform.
—Ant. aggravate.
—Syn. Study. See IMPROVE.
amiable, *adj.* gracious, agreeable, well-disposed, warm, genial, congenial, winning, affable, pleasant, obliging, approachable, goodnatured, affectionate, friendly, amicable.
—Ant. hostile.
amid, *prep.* among, in the middle *or* center of, surrounded by, in the thick of.
among, *prep.* amid, between, surrounded by.
amorous, *adj.* **1.** loving, tender. **2.** enamored, in love, fond of, ardent, tender, passionate, impassioned, erotic, lustful, libidinous, lecherous, on the make, horny, hot.
—Ant. indifferent, cold.
ample, *adj.* **1.** large, spacious, expansive, wide-ranging, extensive, vast, great, capacious, roomy, broad, wide. **2.** liberal, generous, free, abundant, copious, abounding, unrestricted, rich, lavish, inexhaustible, plenteous, plentiful.
—Ant. insufficient, meager, scanty, sparse.
—Syn. Study. See PLENTIFUL.
amplify, *v.* **1.** enlarge, extend, expand, widen, broaden, develop, augment, increase, supplement, lengthen. **2.** exaggerate, overstate,

blow up, magnify, stretch, embellish, embroider, elaborate on.
　—Ant. abridge, abbreviate.

amuse, *v.* divert, entertain, please, occupy, interest, beguile, charm.
　—Ant. bore.
　—Syn. Study. AMUSE, DIVERT, ENTERTAIN mean to occupy the attention with something pleasant. That which AMUSES is usu. playful or humorous and pleases the fancy. DIVERT implies turning the attention from serious thoughts or pursuits to something light, amusing, or lively. That which ENTERTAINS usu. does so because of a plan or program that engages the attention by being pleasing and sometimes instructive.

amusing, *adj.* **1.** entertaining, diverting, pleasing, charming, cheering, lively. **2.** comical, comic, funny, droll, laughable, delightful, hilarious, farcical, ludicrous, ridiculous, absurd.
　—Ant. boring, tedious.
　—Syn. Study. AMUSING, COMICAL, DROLL describe that which causes mirth. That which is AMUSING is quietly humorous or funny in a gentle, good-humored way: *The baby's attempts to talk were amusing.* That which is COMICAL causes laughter by being incongruous, witty, or ludicrous: *His huge shoes made the clown look comical.* DROLL adds to COMICAL the idea of strangeness or peculiarity, and sometimes that of sly or waggish humor: *a droll imitation.*

ancestral, *adj.* hereditary, inherited, patrimonial.

ancestry, *n.* **1.** pedigree, descent, stock, genealogy, heritage. **2.** family, house, line, lineage, forebears.
　—Ant. posterity, descendants.

ancient, *adj.* old, primeval, primordial, stone-age, Neanderthal, neolithic; aged, antique, antiquated, obsolescent, obsolete, archaic, timeworn, venerable, outmoded, unfashionable, out-of-date; antediluvian.
　—Ant. new, modern.
　—Syn. Study. ANCIENT, ANTIQUATED, ANTIQUE refer to something dating from the past. ANCIENT implies existence or first occurrence in the distant past: *an ancient custom.* ANTIQUATED connotes something that is outdated or no longer useful: *antiquated methods; antiquated ideas.* ANTIQUE suggests a curious or pleasing quality in something old: *antique furniture.*

anger, *n.* **1.** indignation, rage, fury, choler, bile, spleen, irritation, vexation, annoyance, irritability, outrage. —*v.* **2.** vex, irritate, exasperate, infuriate, enrage, incense, madden, provoke, outrage, make one's blood boil.
　—Ant. patience, delight; calm, gladden, cheer.
　—Syn. Study. ANGER, INDIGNATION, RAGE, FURY describe deep and strong feelings aroused by injury, injustice, etc. ANGER is the general term for sudden violent displeasure accompanied by an impulse to retaliate: *insults that provoked a burst of anger.* INDIGNATION, a more formal word, implies deep and justified anger, often directed at something unworthy: *The scandal aroused public indignation.* RAGE is vehement, uncontrolled anger: *rage at being fired from a job.* FURY is rage so great that it resembles insanity: *He smashed his fist against the wall in a drunken fury.*

angry, *adj.* irate, incensed, enraged, wrathful, fuming, livid, infuriated, furious, mad, provoked, indignant, exasperated, aggravated.
　—Ant. patient, calm.

anguish, *n.* **1.** pain, suffering, misery, grief, woe, anxiety, angst, agony, torment, torture, rack. —*v.* **2.** agonize, afflict, trouble, beset, torment.
　—Ant. comfort.

animal, *n.* **1.** creature, being, organism, mammal. **2.** beast, brute, monster, savage, ogre, Neanderthal. —*adj.* **3.** living, sentient. **4.** crude, beastly, brutal, bestial, subhuman.
　—Syn. Study. See CARNAL.

animate, *v.* **1.** revitalize, activate, breathe life into, vivify, enliven, vitalize, quicken. **2.** invigorate, encourage, inspire, hearten, energize, fortify, stimulate, motivate, spur, rouse, arouse, waken. **3.** refresh, exhilarate, buoy up, excite.
　—Ant. thwart, discourage, dishearten.

animation, *n.* liveliness, vivacity, spirit, life, vigor, vitality, verve, pep, energy; enthusiasm, ardor, exhilaration, cheerfulness, sprightliness, buoyancy.
　—Ant. sluggishness, torpor.

announce, *v.* proclaim, declare, report, promulgate, broadcast, air, make public or known, tell, reveal, divulge, propound.
　—Ant. suppress.
　—Syn. Study. ANNOUNCE, PROCLAIM, PUBLISH mean to communicate something in a formal or public way. TO ANNOUNCE is to give out news, often of something expected in the future: *to announce a lecture series.* TO PROCLAIM is to make a widespread and general announcement of something of public interest: *to proclaim a holiday.* TO PUBLISH is to make public in an official way, now esp. by printing: *to publish a book.*

annoy, *v.* harry, hector, badger, tease, irk, pester, harass, bother, irritate, nag, plague, bedevil, needle, hassle, bug, get in someone's face.
　—Ant. comfort, soothe.
　—Syn. Study. See BOTHER.

answer, *n.* **1.** reply, response, rejoinder, retort, riposte. **2.** solution. **3.** defense, plea. —*v.* **4.** reply, respond, rejoin. **5.** be responsible or liable or accountable. **6.** reply to, respond to. **7.** serve, suit, satisfy, fulfill.
　—Ant. ask, question; differ.
　—Syn. Study. ANSWER, REPLY, RESPONSE, REJOINDER, RETORT all refer to words used to meet a question, proposal, charge, etc. An ANSWER is something said or written in return: *an answer giving the desired information.* A REPLY is usually somewhat more formal or detailed: *a courteous reply to a letter.* A RESPONSE is often a reaction to an appeal, suggestion, etc.: *an enthusiastic response to a plea for cooperation.* A REJOINDER is a quick, usually clever answer to another person's reply or comment: *a rejoinder that silenced the opposition.* A RETORT is a keen, prompt answer, usually to a charge or criticism: *The false accusation provoked a sharp retort.*

antagonist, *n.* opponent, adversary, rival, competitor, competition, opposition, enemy, foe.
　—Ant. ally, friend.
　—Syn. Study. See ADVERSARY.

anticipate, *v.* **1.** foresee, expect, foretaste, forecast, foretell, prophesy, prophesize, predict. **2.** expect, look forward to, prepare for, count on, await.

antipathy, *n.* repugnance, dislike, aversion, disgust, abhorrence, hatred, detestation.
　—Ant. attraction, sympathy, love.

antique, *adj.* **1.** ancient, old, archaic, venerable, medieval, Neanderthal. **2.** antiquated, old-fashioned, out-of-date, obsolescent, obsolete, passé, outmoded, old hat, dated, out of

fashion, unfashionable, out of vogue, stale, timeworn, secondhand. —*n.* **3.** heirloom, collectible, collector's item, antiquity, museum piece, classic, work of art, artwork, showpiece, objet d'art, rarity.
　—Ant. modern, new.
　—Syn. Study. See ANCIENT.

antisocial, *adj.* unfriendly, asocial, unsociable, standoffish, aloof, distant, unapproachable, solitary, reclusive, hermitlike, withdrawn, misanthropic.
　—Ant. social, sociable, friendly, gregarious.

anxiety, *n.* **1.** apprehension, fear, dread, angst, agita, nervousness, foreboding; uneasiness, disquietude. **2.** solicitous desire, eagerness, solicitude, concern, longing, ache.
　—Ant. security, calmness, equanimity.

anxious, *adj.* concerned, worried, apprehensive, uneasy, troubled, disquieted, apprehensive, tense, distressed, disturbed, nervous, fretful, edgy, on edge, perturbed, restless, upset, wary.
　—Ant. secure, certain, sure, confident.

apathetic, *adj.* unfeeling, passionless, emotionless, indifferent, unconcerned, impassive, stoical, cool, cold, uninterested, phlegmatic, dull, lifeless, flaccid, obtuse, sluggish, torpid.
　—Ant. alert, emotional, passionate, ardent, animated.

ape, *v.* imitate, mimic, counterfeit, copy, affect, emulate, follow, mirror.

apex, *n.* tip, point, vertex, summit, top, pinnacle, zenith; acme, climax.

apology, *n.* **1.** excuse, plea, explanation, reparation. **2.** defense, justification, vindication. **3.** poor substitute, makeshift.

appall, *v.* horrify, dismay, alarm, discomfit, repel, disgust, daunt.
　—Ant. reassure, comfort.

apparel, *n.* clothes, clothing, togs, duds, gear, threads, glad rags, dress, garb, attire, costume, garments.

apparent, *adj.* **1.** plain, clear, open, evident, obvious, marked, conspicuous, patent, unquestionable, unmistakable, manifest. **2.** seeming, ostensible, specious, illusory. **3.** visible, open, in sight, perceptible, detectable, discernible.
　—Ant. concealed, obscure; real.
　—Syn. Study. APPARENT, EVIDENT, OBVIOUS all refer to something easily perceived. APPARENT applies to that which can readily be seen or perceived: *an apparent effort.* EVIDENT applies to that which facts or circumstances make plain: *Your innocence was evident.* OBVIOUS applies to that which is unquestionable, because of being completely manifest or noticeable: *an obvious change of method.*

appeal, *n.* **1.** entreaty, request, petition, prayer, call, supplication, invocation. **2.** application, suit, solicitation. **3.** attraction, lure, allurement, charm, fascination, interest. —*v.* **4.** entreat, supplicate, petition, ask, beseech, beg, implore, pray.

appear, *v.* **1.** become visible, come into sight or view, emerge, crop up, materialize, enter the picture, manifest, show up. **2.** seem, look, show. **3.** be obvious or manifest or clear.
　—Ant. disappear.
　—Syn. Study. See SEEM.

appearance, *n.* **1.** aspect, guise, mien, air, look. **2.** form, apparition; arrival, coming, advent.
　—Syn. Study. APPEARANCE, ASPECT, GUISE refer to the way in which something outwardly presents itself to view. APPEARANCE refers to the outward look: *the shabby appearance*

of the car. ASPECT refers to the appearance at some particular time or in special circumstances; it often has emotional implications, either ascribed to the object itself or felt by the beholder: *In the dusk the forest had a terrifying aspect.* GUISE suggests a misleading appearance, assumed for an occasion or a purpose: *an enemy in friendly guise.*

appease, *v.* **1.** pacify, quiet, soothe, calm, placate, mollify, alleviate, mitigate, temper, allay, assuage. **2.** satisfy, fulfill, propitiate. **3.** conciliate, propitiate, win over.
　—Ant. aggravate, perturb; dissatisfy.
　—Syn. Study. APPEASE, CONCILIATE, PROPITIATE imply trying to overcome hostility or win favor. TO APPEASE is to make anxious overtures and often undue concessions to satisfy someone's demands: *Chamberlain tried to appease Hitler at Munich.* TO CONCILIATE is to win over an enemy or opponent by friendly gestures and a willingness to cooperate: *to conciliate an opposing faction.* TO PROPITIATE is to soften the anger of a powerful superior who has been offended: *Offerings were made to propitiate the gods.*

appetite, *n.* **1.** hunger, desire, longing, craving, thirst; demand. **2.** liking, relish, gusto, zest, zeal, passion, enthusiasm, keenness, hankering, longing, yearning.
　—Ant. renunciation, apathy.

applause, *n.* hand-clapping, cheering, cheers, shouting; approval, acclamation, approbation, acclaim, plaudits, laurels, éclat, commendation, praise, kudos.
　—Ant. disapproval, condemnation.

apple-polish, *v.* fawn, toady, flatter, kowtow, truckle, blandish, butter up, bootlick; (*slang*) suck up to, brown-nose.

applicable, *adj.* fit, suitable, suited, relevant, apt, fitting, befitting, proper, apropos, germane, pertinent, pointed, appropriate, relevant, apposite, right, seemly.
　—Ant. inept.

application, *n.* **1.** applying, utilization, use, practice, employment, operation, exercise. **2.** relevance, aptness, aptitude, suitability, pertinence. **3.** request, petition, solicitation, appeal, claim. **4.** attention, effort, assiduity, industry, persistence, perseverance, diligence, dedication, commitment. **5.** software program.
　—Ant. inattention, laziness.
　—Syn. Study. See EFFORT.

apply, *v.* **1.** lay on, place on or upon. **2.** use, employ, put to use, effect, utilize. **3.** devote, dedicate, commit, focus, concentrate, address, pay attention; credit, assign, appropriate, allot. **4.** have a bearing, refer, be pertinent. **5.** ask, petition, sue, entreat, solicit, appeal, request.

appoint, *v.* **1.** nominate, assign, name, select, choose; designate, point out, allot. **2.** equip, rig, outfit, accouter, furnish, supply; decorate.
　—Ant. dismiss; strip.
　—Syn. Study. See FURNISH.

appointment, *n.* **1.** nomination, selection, assignment, appointing, designating. **2.** office, post, station, sinecure, position, job, situation, place, assignment. **3.** engagement, agreement, arrangement. **4.** assignation, rendezvous, tryst, meeting, date.

apportion, *v.* divide, allot, distribute, assign, allocate, appoint, partition, measure, mete, dole out, deal, dispense, parcel out.

appreciate, *v.* **1.** esteem, value, prize, rate highly, cherish, enjoy, admire, treasure, respect, honor. **2.**

be aware *or* conscious of, detect, understand, comprehend, recognize, perceive, know. **3.** rise *or* increase in value *or* worth.
—Ant. disparage; scorn.
—Syn. Study. APPRECIATE, ESTEEM, VALUE, PRIZE imply holding a person or thing in high regard. To APPRECIATE is to exercise wise judgment, delicate perception, and keen insight in realizing worth: *to appreciate fine workmanship.* To ESTEEM is to feel respect combined with a warm, kindly sensation: *to esteem one's former teacher.* To VALUE is to attach importance because of worth or usefulness: *I value your opinion.* To PRIZE is to value highly and cherish: *to prize a collection of rare books.*

apprehension, *n.* **1.** anxiety, misgiving, dread, fear, angst, alarm; worry, uneasiness, suspicion, distrust, mistrust. **2.** understanding, intelligence, reason. **3.** view, opinion, idea, belief, sentiment. **4.** arrest, seizure, capture.
—Ant. confidence, composure; release.

apprise, *v.* inform, tell, advise, give notice to, notify, warn, acquaint.

appropriate, *adj.* **1.** fitting, fit, right, suitable, apt, befitting, meet, felicitous, proper, apropos. **—***v.* **2.** set apart, apportion, allocate, earmark, allot. **3.** seize, expropriate, annex, usurp, steal, pilfer, adopt, take as one's own.
—Ant. inappropriate, inept.

approve, *v.* **1.** commend, praise, recommend, appreciate, value, esteem, prize. **2.** sanction, authorize, confirm, endorse, ratify, validate, uphold, support, sustain; countenance, condone, permit, allow, accept, assent to, tolerate.
—Ant. disapprove.

apt, *adj.* **1.** inclined, disposed, prone, liable. **2.** likely. **3.** clever, bright, intelligent, brilliant, ingenious; adroit, handy, dexterous, skillful, expert. **4.** appropriate, suited, pertinent, relevant, fit, fitting, apropos.
—Ant. inapt, indisposed, malapropos.
—Syn. Study. APT, RELEVANT, PERTINENT all refer to something suitable or fitting. APT means to the point and particularly appropriate: *an apt comment.* RELEVANT means pertaining to the matter in hand: *a relevant question.* PERTINENT means directly related to and important to the subject: *pertinent information.*

aptitude, *n.* **1.** proclivity, inclination, bent; gift, ability, capability, facility, capacity, skillfulness, flair, genius, talent, knack, faculty. **2.** readiness, intelligence, cleverness, talent; understanding, ability, aptness. **3.** fitness, suitability, applicability, relevance, appropriateness.

arbitrary, *adj.* **1.** discretionary. **2.** capricious, uncertain, unreasonable, willful. **3.** uncontrolled, unlimited, unrestrained; absolute, despotic, dictatorial, totalitarian, tyrannical, imperious, overbearing, peremptory, domineering; authoritarian, highhanded.
—Ant. systematic, rational, fair, certain.

archaic, *adj.* old, ancient, antiquated, antique, old-fashioned, out-of-date, passé, outmoded, obsolete, obsolescent, superseded, superannuated, dated.
—Ant. modern, up-to-date.

archetype, *n.* model, form, pattern, prototype, example, ideal, standard, epitome, quintessence, exemplar, embodiment, personification, paradigm.

ardent, *adj.* passionate, fervent, fervid, keen, avid, intense, eager, sanguine, enthusiastic, zealous; vehement, impassioned, hot, burning, fiery, warm.
—Ant. cool, apathetic.

ardor, *n.* **1.** warmth, fervor, fervency, eagerness, zeal, passion, enthusiasm, desire, keenness. **2.** fire, burning, heat, warmth.
—Ant. indifference.

arduous, *adj.* **1.** laborious, hard, difficult, tough, backbreaking, toilsome, onerous, burdensome. **2.** tiring, exhausting, formidable, taxing, grueling, fatiguing. **3.** severe, unendurable, harsh, daunting.
—Ant. easy.

argue, *v.* **1.** debate, discuss, reason, wrangle. **2.** contend, dispute, bicker, quarrel, squabble, remonstrate, spar, fight, disagree. **3.** contest, debate, discuss, dispute. **4.** maintain, say, assert, hold, claim, insist, contend.
—Ant. agree.

argument, *n.* **1.** controversy, dispute, debate, discussion, disagreement, quarrel, altercation, conflict. **2.** reasoning, reason, proof, point, position, logic, plea, claim. **3.** fact, statement; theme, thesis, topic, subject, matter.
—Ant. agreement.
—Syn. Study. ARGUMENT, CONTROVERSY, DISPUTE imply the expression and discussion of differing opinions. An ARGUMENT usu. arises from a disagreement between two persons, each of whom advances facts supporting his or her point of view: *an argument over a debt.* A CONTROVERSY is usu. a public expression of contrary opinions; it may be dignified and of some duration: *a political controversy.* A DISPUTE is an oral contention, usu. brief, and often of an angry or undignified character: *a heated dispute between neighbors.*

arid, *adj.* **1.** dry, sere, moistureless, parched; barren. **2.** dull, lifeless, uninteresting, dry, empty, jejune.
—Ant. wet, damp.
—Syn. Study. See DRY.

aroma, *n.* **1.** perfume, odor, scent, fragrance, bouquet, redolence, smell, savor. **2.** subtle quality, spirit, essence, characteristic, aura, atmosphere, air; suggestion, hint, flavor.
—Ant. stench.
—Syn. Study. See PERFUME.

arouse, *v.* **1.** animate, stir, rouse, awaken; inspirit, inspire, excite, incite, provoke, instigate, stimulate. **2.** awaken, get up, arise, stir, wake up.
—Ant. calm, mitigate.

arrange, *v.* **1.** order, place, adjust, array, group, sort, dispose, organize, systematize, line up, align, classify. **2.** settle, determine, establish, adjust. **3.** prepare, plan, contrive, devise, concoct, organize. **4.** orchestrate, score, interpret, adapt, adjust. **5.** settle, agree, come to terms. **6.** prepare, adjust, adapt, make preparations *or* plans.
—Ant. disarrange, disorder, disturb.

arrest, *v.* **1.** seize, apprehend, capture, detain, take into custody, take prisoner. **2.** stop, check, bring to a standstill, stay, slow, retard, hinder, deter, obstruct, delay, interrupt, restrain, hold, withhold. **—***n.* **3.** detention, custody, imprisonment, apprehension, capture, seizure; (*slang*) collar, bust. **4.** stoppage, halt, stay, check, obstruction, deterrent, detention, restraint, delay, interruption.
—Ant. release; activate, animate; continue.
—Syn. Study. See STOP.

arrival, *n.* **1.** advent, coming, appearance. **2.** reaching, attainment, success. **3.** newcomer; passenger, traveler, tourist.
—Ant. departure.

arrive, *v.* come, make an appearance, appear, turn up, show up; prosper, get ahead, make the grade, make it.
—Ant. depart; fail.

arrogance, *n.* haughtiness, pride, insolence, disdain, effrontery, superciliousness, scorn, self-glorification, presumptuousness, nerve, gall, loftiness, hubris, pomposity, pompousness, pretension, pretentiousness, braggadocio, bluster, snobbery, brazenness, imperiousness, highhandedness, uppitiness, superiority, airs, immodesty, conceit, egotism, hauteur.
—Ant. humility.

arrogant, *adj.* presumptuous, haughty, imperious, proud, insolent, scornful, overbearing, dictatorial, highhanded, lordly, immodest, self-important, vain, snobbish, high and mighty, (*Brit.*) swell-headed, on one's high horse, cocky, high-flown, ostentatious.
—Ant. humble, self-effacing.

art, *n.* trade, craft; skill, adroitness, dexterity, talent, expertise, aptitude, ingenuity, knack, cleverness.

artifice, *n.* **1.** ruse, device, subterfuge, wile, machination, expedient, trick, stratagem. **2.** craft, trickery, guile, deception, deceit, cunning, fraud, duplicity, double-dealing.
—Syn. Study. See TRICK.

artificial, *adj.* **1.** unreal, inauthentic, fabricated, manmade, unnatural, synthetic, manufactured, imitation, plastic, made-up, concocted, phony, fashioned, mock, false, fake, imitation, spurious, ersatz, pretend, counterfeit, simulated, sham, bogus. **2.** affected, put-on, insincere, pretentious, assumed, feigned, deceitful, disingenuous.
—Ant. real, genuine, authentic.

artless, *adj.* natural, simple, guileless, open, frank, plain, unaffected, candid, honest, sincere, innocent, genuine, direct, straightforward, aboveboard, uncomplicated, unpretentious, unassuming, ingenuous, naive, unsophisticated, humble, ordinary, true, truthful, trusting, trustful, unsuspicious, unsuspecting; unskillful, rude, crude, inexpert, primitive, incompetent, clumsy, bungling, awkward.
—Ant. cunning, sly, crafty.

ascend, *v.* **1.** mount, rise, climb *or* go upward, soar, climb, arise. **2.** climb, scale.
—Ant. descend; fall.

ascertain, *v.* determine, establish, pinpoint, verify; learn, find out, discover, uncover.
—Ant. guess, assume.
—Syn. Study. See LEARN.

ascribe, *v.* attribute, impute, refer, assign, charge.
—Syn. Study. See ATTRIBUTE.

ashamed, *adj.* abashed, humiliated, mortified, embarrassed, red-faced, chagrined, sheepish, struck dumb, crushed, sorry, penitent, humbled, abased, dashed, bowed down, crestfallen.
—Ant. proud.

ask, *v.* **1.** interrogate, question, inquire of, quiz. **2.** inquire, seek information. **3.** request, solicit, petition, sue, appeal, seek, beseech, implore, beg, supplicate, entreat.
—Ant. answer.

askance, *adv.* suspiciously, dubiously, doubtfully, skeptically, mistrustfully.

aspect, *n.* **1.** feature, attribute, characteristic, facet, element. **2.** countenance, expression, mien, visage; air. **3.** view, viewpoint, outlook, prospect.
—Syn. Study. See APPEARANCE.

aspire, *v.* desire, long, yearn, covet, pine for, hanker after, be eager for, aim for, hope, wish, aim, dream of, have ambitions, be ambitious, strive for.

assail, *v.* assault, set *or* fall upon, attack; abuse, impugn, maltreat, malign.
—Syn. Study. See ATTACK.

assassinate, *v.* murder, kill, slay, butcher, slaughter, do away with, put to death, execute, (*slang*) put a hit on, hit, waste.

assault, *n.* **1.** assailing, attack, invasion, aggression, charge, offensive, blitzkrieg, strike, raid, incursion, sortie. **2.** beating, battering, violation, molestation, abuse. **—***v.* **3.** attack, assail, storm, charge, invade, beset, hit, strike, batter, maul, molest, abuse.
—Syn. Study. See ATTACK.

assemble, *v.* **1.** bring together, gather, congregate, collect, convene, convoke, summon, muster, marshal, call together. **2.** put together, manufacture, construct, erect, fabricate, make, piece together, connect, set up. **3.** meet, convene, congregate, gather, gather together, come together, unite, amass.
—Ant. disperse.
—Syn. Study. See GATHER.

assembly, *n.* **1.** company, assemblage, throng, mob, gathering, convention, congress, convocation, meeting, group, body, congregation, flock, crowd, multitude, host, horde. **2.** congress, legislature, parliament, lower house, conclave, synod, council, diet.
—Syn. Study. See CONVENTION.

assent, *v.* **1.** acquiesce, accede, concur, agree, consent. **—***n.* **2.** agreement, concurrence, acquiescence, consent, approval, accord.
—Ant. refuse, deny, dissent.

assert, *v.* **1.** declare, affirm, maintain, aver, say, pronounce, allege, avow. **2.** maintain, defend, uphold, support, vindicate, claim, emphasize. **3.** press, make felt, emphasize.
—Ant. controvert, contradict, deny.
—Syn. Study. See DECLARE.

assertion, *n.* allegation, statement, contention, pronouncement, insistence, proclamation, avowal, declaration, claim, affirmation.
—Ant. denial, contradiction.

assign, *v.* **1.** allocate, allot, apportion, consign. **2.** appoint, designate, order, nominate, elect, select, choose, specify.
—Syn. Study. ASSIGN, ALLOCATE, ALLOT mean to apportion or measure out. To ASSIGN is to distribute things to specific persons: *to assign duties.* To ALLOCATE is to earmark or set aside parts of things available or expected in the future, each for a specific purpose: *to allocate income to various types of expenses.* To ALLOT implies restricting an amount, size, purpose, etc., and then apportioning or assigning: *to allot spaces for parking.*

assist, *v.* help, support, aid, sustain, benefit, abet, back.
—Ant. impede, obstruct, hinder.
—Syn. Study. See HELP.

associate, *v.* **1.** connect, link. **2.** join, affiliate, (*informal*) team up with. **3.** unite, combine, couple. **4.** fraternize, consort, keep company. **—***n.* **5.** acquaintance, comrade, fellow, companion, friend, peer, equal; confederate, accomplice, ally, partner, colleague.
—Ant. dissociate, alienate; adversary, opponent.
—Syn. Study. See ACQUAINTANCE.

association, *n.* **1.** organization, alliance, group, sisterhood, brotherhood, team, society, club, fraternity, sorority. **2.** companionship, relationship, camaraderie, friendship. **3.** connection, combination, link, affiliation, conjunction, bond, tie. **4.** company, corporation, firm.

assume, *v.* **1.** presume, believe, think, surmise, guess, suppose, presuppose, take for granted, infer. **2.** accept, adopt, appropriate, acquire, undertake. **3.** pretend, feign, affect, simulate, counterfeit, put on, sham, fake.
—**Syn. Study.** See PRETEND.

assurance, *n.* **1.** declaration, avowal. **2.** pledge, promise, guarantee, commitment, vow, word of honor, warranty, surety, guaranty, oath. **3.** certainty, confidence, trust. **4.** courage, bravery, self-confidence. **5.** boldness, impudence, presumption, arrogance, effrontery, rudeness, impertinence, nerve, cheek, audacity, insolence, brazenness.
—**Ant.** denial; distrust, uncertainty; cowardice, diffidence.
—**Syn. Study.** See CONFIDENCE.

astonish, *v.* amaze, strike with wonder, surprise, astound, shock, dumbfound, bowl over, floor, flabbergast, fill with awe, awe, startle, daze, stun, stupefy, confound, stagger, overwhelm.

astute, *adj.* keen, shrewd, cunning, artful, crafty, sly, wily, penetrating, eagle-eyed, sharp, quick, perspicacious, ingenious, intelligent, sagacious, discerning, subtle, clever, adroit, calculating, canny, perceptive, observant, alert, quick-witted, wise, insightful, knowledgeable.
—**Ant.** ingenuous, naive, candid, unsophisticated; dull.

asylum, *n.* **1.** hospital, institute, retreat, sanitarium. **2.** refuge, haven, sanctuary, shelter, retreat, safe house, harbor.

atheist, *n.* agnostic, infidel, disbeliever, nonbeliever, skeptic, doubter.
—**Ant.** believer.
—**Syn. Study.** ATHEIST, AGNOSTIC, INFIDEL refer to persons not inclined toward religious belief. An ATHEIST denies the existence of a deity or of divine beings. An AGNOSTIC believes it is impossible to know whether there is a God without sufficient evidence. An INFIDEL is an unbeliever, esp. one who does not accept Christianity or Islam; the word is usu. applied pejoratively.

atom, *n.* iota, jot, dot, whit, tittle, scintilla, mote; indivisible particle.

atrocious, *adj.* **1.** wicked, cruel, iniquitous, villainous, fiendish, abominable, inhuman, savage, barbaric, brutal, barbarous, ruthless, heinous, monstrous, horrifying, horrible, dreadful, awful. **2.** bad, tasteless, execrable, detestable, abominable, awful, terrible, rotten, horrid, appalling, horrendous, frightful, lousy, third-rate.
—**Ant.** kind, benevolent; tasteful, praiseworthy.

attach, *v.* **1.** fasten to, affix, join, cement, connect, append, secure, pin, rivet, add, tack on, annex. **2.** associate, attribute, assign, ascribe, pin, apply, put, place, fix, affix. **3.** adhere, pertain, belong, cleave, stick to.
—**Ant.** detach, separate; repel.

attachment, *n.* **1.** affection, friendship, regard, admiration, fondness, liking, love, devotion; fidelity, faithfulness, affinity, partiality; bent, predilection. **2.** tie, fastening, connection, link, bond.
—**Ant.** detachment, separation.
—**Syn. Study.** See ADDITION.

attack, *v.* **1.** assail, assault, molest, threaten, storm, charge, engage in battle, set upon. **2.** criticize, impugn, censure, blame, abuse, berate, revile, inveigh against, denounce,

condemn, malign, vilify, denigrate, disparage, deprecate, slander. —*n.* **3.** onslaught, assault, offense, onset, encounter, aggression, invasion.
—**Ant.** defend; defense.
—**Syn. Study.** ATTACK, ASSAIL, ASSAULT all mean to set upon someone with hostile intent. ATTACK is a general word that applies to the beginning of any planned aggressive action, physical or verbal: *to attack an enemy from ambush; to attack a candidate's record.* ASSAIL implies a vehement, sudden, and usu. repeated attack that aims to weaken an opponent: *assailed by gunfire; assailed by gossip.* ASSAULT implies a violent physical or verbal attack: *an elderly couple assaulted by a mugger; a reputation assaulted by the press.*

attain, *v.* reach, achieve, accomplish, effect, secure, gain, procure, acquire, get, obtain, win; arrive at, reach.
—**Ant.** lose.
—**Syn. Study.** See GAIN.

attempt, *v.* **1.** try, undertake, seek, make an effort, endeavor, strive, venture. —*n.* **2.** trial, effort, endeavor, enterprise. **3.** attack, assault.
—**Ant.** accomplish, attain.
—**Syn. Study.** See TRY.

attend, *v.* **1.** be present at, frequent. **2.** accompany, go with, escort, squire, usher, follow. **3.** minister to, serve, wait on. **4.** tend, take charge of. **5.** heed, listen to, pay attention to, respect.
—**Syn. Study.** See ACCOMPANY.

attendant, *n.* **1.** escort, companion, comrade. **2.** servant, waiter, valet, lackey, flunky, menial, slave. **3.** concomitant, accompaniment, consequence. —*adj.* **4.** present, in attendance, accompanying, concomitant, consequent.

attention, *n.* **1.** concentration, care, consideration, observation, heed, regard, mindfulness, notice, watchfulness, alertness. **2.** civility, courtesy, homage, deference, respect, politeness, regard. **3.** attentions, regard, court, courtship, suit, wooing. **4.** notice, acclaim, notoriety, publicity, prominence, limelight.
—**Ant.** inattention.

attentive, *adj.* **1.** observant, intent, mindful, thoughtful, alive, alert, awake. **2.** polite, courteous, gallant, gracious, accommodating, considerate, solicitous, civil, respectful, deferential.
—**Ant.** inattentive; discourteous.

attitude, *n.* **1.** position, disposition, manner, bearing, stance, carriage, demeanor, mien, pose. **2.** opinion, feeling, viewpoint, point of view, approach, inclination, position, posture.
—**Syn. Study.** See POSITION.

attract, *v.* cause to approach, magnetize; draw, pull, invite, allure, win, engage, captivate, endear, enamor, charm, absorb, transfix, enthrall, enrapture, cast a spell over, beguile, fascinate, hypnotize, mesmerize, entrance, bewitch, intrigue, entice, lure, appeal to, fascinate.
—**Ant.** repel, repulse.

attribute, *v.* **1.** ascribe, impute, assign, charge, credit, trace to. —*n.* **2.** quality, character, characteristic, property, feature, trait, virtue, mark; peculiarity, quirk, eccentricity, idiosyncrasy, singularity, uniqueness.
—**Syn. Study.** ATTRIBUTE, ASCRIBE, IMPUTE, as verbs, mean to assign something to a definite cause. Possibly because of an association with *tribute,* ATTRIBUTE often has a complimentary connotation: *to attribute one's success to a friend's encouragement.* ASCRIBE is used in a similar sense, but has a neutral implication: *to ascribe an accident to carelessness.*

IMPUTE usu. means to attribute something dishonest to a person; it implies blame: *to impute an error to a new employee.* See also QUALITY.

audacious, *adj.* **1.** bold, daring, spirited, adventurous, fearless, intrepid, brave, courageous, dauntless, venturesome, undaunted, valiant, confident. **2.** bold, impudent, presumptuous, assuming, shameless, flagrant, insolent, impertinent, brazen, forward, defiant, rude, disrespectful.
—**Ant.** cowardly, feckless; shy, retiring, humble, subservient, craven, timid, timorous, abject, servile.

aura, *n.* atmosphere, mood, feeling, air, ambiance, climate.

austere, *adj.* **1.** harsh, hard, stern, strict, forbidding, severe, formal, stiff, inflexible. **2.** grave, sober, serious. **3.** simple, severe, without ornament, plain, Spartan, spare. **4.** rough, harsh, sour, astringent, acerbic, bitter.
—**Ant.** soothing, flexible; kind; sweet.

austerity, *n.* severity, harshness, strictness, asceticism, rigor, rigidity, rigorousness, stiffness, inflexibility.
—**Ant.** lenience, flexibility.

authentic, *adj.* **1.** reliable, trustworthy, veritable, true, accurate, actual, factual, legitimate, undisputed, verifiable, authoritative. **2.** genuine, real, true, bona fide, unadulterated, pure, uncorrupted.
—**Ant.** unreliable, inaccurate; sham, fraudulent, corrupt.

authoritative, *adj.* **1.** official, conclusive, unquestioned, authentic, valid, documented, certified, validated, legitimate, sanctioned. **2.** sound, verifiable, accurate, factual, dependable, true, trustworthy, truthful, reliable; scholarly, learned. **3.** impressive, positive. **4.** peremptory, dogmatic, authoritarian, dictatorial, imperious, autocratic.
—**Ant.** unofficial; unreliable; conciliatory.

authority, *n.* **1.** control, influence, command, rule, jurisdiction, dominion, right, prerogative, hegemony, sway, power, supremacy. **2.** expert, specialist, scholar. **3.** statute, law, rule. **4.** warrant, justification, permit, permission, sanction, authorization.
—**Syn. Study.** AUTHORITY, CONTROL, INFLUENCE denote a right to direct the actions of others. AUTHORITY is a power that exists because of rank, to issue commands and to punish for violations: *to have authority over subordinates.* CONTROL is either power or influence applied to the manipulation of persons or things: *to be in control of a project.* INFLUENCE is a personal and unofficial power derived from deference of others to one's character, ability, or station; it may be exerted unconsciously or may operate through persuasion: *to have influence over one's friends.*

authorize, *v.* **1.** empower, commission, allow, permit, let. **2.** sanction, approve, countenance, endorse, license, entitle, green-light. **3.** establish, entrench. **4.** warrant, justify, legalize, support, back.
—**Ant.** forbid, prohibit.

automatic, *adj.* **1.** self-moving, self-acting, mechanical, robotic, automated. **2.** involuntary, uncontrollable, reflex, unconscious, instinctive, instinctual, natural, spontaneous, impulsive, (*informal*) knee-jerk, unavoidable.
—**Ant.** manual; deliberate, intentional.

auxiliary, *adj.* **1.** supporting, helping, helpful, accessory, supplementary, aiding, assisting, abetting. **2.**

subsidiary, subordinate, secondary, ancillary, extra. —*n.* **3.** helper, aide, ally, assistant, confederate, deputy.
—**Ant.** chief, main.

available, *adj.* **1.** accessible, ready, at one's disposal, present, obtainable, nearby, on tap, within reach, at hand, handy, usable, of use or service. **2.** valid, efficacious, profitable, advantageous.
—**Ant.** unavailable; unbecoming; invalid, unprofitable.

avenge, *v.* revenge, take vengeance, exact satisfaction for, get even, settle the score, punish, exact reprisals.
—**Ant.** forgive, pardon.

average, *n.* **1.** mean, norm, standard, median. —*adj.* **2.** common, usual, customary, general, typical, regular, mean, medial, normal, intermediate, middle. **3.** mediocre, middling, ordinary, passable, tolerable, satisfactory, run-of-the-mill, commonplace, undistinguished, unexceptional, so-so.

averse, *adj.* disinclined, reluctant, unwilling, loath, opposed, resistant, anti, against, contrary, hostile.
—**Ant.** inclined, disposed.
—**Syn. Study.** See RELUCTANT.

aversion, *n.* repugnance, disgust, antipathy, antagonism, animosity, hostility, odium, horror, loathing, detestation, hate, hatred, abhorrence; dislike, distaste, objection, disinclination, unwillingness, reluctance.
—**Ant.** predilection, liking; favor.

avoid, *v.* keep away from or clear of, shun, evade, escape, elude, eschew, leave alone, steer clear of, refrain from, dodge, circumvent, sidestep, fly from, shrink from.
—**Ant.** confront, face.

await, *v.* **1.** wait for, look for, expect. **2.** attend, be in store for, be ready for.

aware, *adj.* cognizant or conscious (of), informed, mindful, apprised, knowledgeable, knowing, in the know, enlightened, *au courant,* hip to, wise to, acquainted with, privy to, (*slang*) down.
—**Ant.** unaware, oblivious.
—**Syn. Study.** See CONSCIOUS.

awe, *n.* **1.** reverence, respect, veneration; dread, fear, terror. —*v.* **2.** solemnize; daunt, cow, frighten, intimidate.
—**Ant.** contempt, irreverence; scorn.

awkward, *adj.* **1.** clumsy, bungling, unskillful, inexpert, gauche, inept, maladroit, (*informal*) all thumbs. **2.** inelegant, ungraceful, ungainly, gawky, unrefined, unpolished. **3.** hazardous, dangerous, perilous, risky, precarious. **4.** trying, embarrassing, touchy, sensitive, uncomfortable, delicate, unpleasant, ticklish, sticky.
—**Ant.** deft, adroit, adept; graceful, refined, polished.

B

babble, *v.* **1.** gibber, blabber, gabble, jabber, blather, prattle. **2.** talk, chat, gossip, chatter, natter, palaver, gab, jaw, schmooze. —*n.* **3.** nonsense, gibberish, twaddle, prattle, mumbo jumbo, drivel, blather, rubbish, garbage.

back, *n.* **1.** rear, posterior, end, hind. —*v.* **2.** support, sustain, second, uphold, promote, encourage, sponsor, underwrite, bankroll, invest in, aid, abet, favor, assist; countenance, allow, side with, endorse, stand by.
—**Ant.** front, fore, face.

—**Syn. Study.** BACK, HIND, POSTERIOR, REAR refer to something situated behind something else. BACK means the opposite of front: *a back window.* HIND, and the more formal word POSTERIOR, refer to the rearmost of two or more, often similar objects: *hind wings; posterior lobe.* REAR is used of buildings, conveyances, etc., and in military language it is the opposite of fore: *the rear end of a truck; rear echelon.*

backward, *adv.* **1.** rearward, in reverse, regressively, back foremost, retrogressively, behind. —*adj.* **2.** reversed, returning. **3.** behind, late, slow, tardy. **4.** shy, reticent, diffident, retiring, unwilling, loath, chary, averse, reluctant, hesitant, bashful, wavering, disinclined, timid. **5.** slow, retarded, undeveloped, underdeveloped.
—**Ant.** forward; precocious.

backwater, *n.* back country, hinterland, outback, backwoods, Podunk, sticks, boondocks, boonies, middle of nowhere.

bad, *adj.* **1.** evil, wicked, ill, corrupt, base, depraved, unprincipled, vicious, vile, wrong, unspeakable, nefarious, debauched, amoral, immoral; disingenuous, rascally, mischievous, naughty, unruly, ill-behaved, rowdy, misbehaving, disobedient, wild, disorderly; sinful, criminal, dishonest, villainous; deleterious, pernicious. **2.** defective, worthless, poor, inferior, imperfect; wretched, miserable, egregious, execrable, substandard, incompetent, ill-qualified, inadequate. **3.** incorrect, faulty. **4.** invalid, unsound. **5.** sick, ill. **6.** regretful, sorry, apologetic, rueful, sad, conscience-stricken, remorseful, contrite, wretched, upset. **7.** unfavorable, unfortunate, adverse, unpropitious, inauspicious. **8.** offensive, disagreeable, mean, abominable. **9.** vile, wretched, shabby, scurvy. **10.** severe, serious, distressing, grave, terrible, awful, painful. **11.** rotten, decayed, putrid, contaminated, spoiled, tainted. **12.** (*slang*) good.
—**Ant.** good.

bag, *n.* **1.** container, case, receptacle, pouch, sack, sac, poke, reticule, packet, pocket. **2.** luggage, baggage, suitcase, duffel, duffel bag, carry-on, overnight bag, overnighter, backpack, knapsack, rucksack, haversack, satchel, saddlebag, valise, grip, carryall, traveling bag. **3.** purse, handbag, pocketbook, shoulder bag, clutch purse, change purse, wallet, evening bag, briefcase, tote bag, portfolio, schoolbag, attache case, cosmetic bag, kit, fanny pack, flight bag, garment bag, holdall, book bag. —*v.* **4.** catch, net, trap, entrap, kill, ensnare, snare, capture, land, shoot.

bailiwick, *n.* domain, field, sphere, purview, territory, province, department, jurisdiction, realm, terrain, precinct.

balance, *n.* **1.** equilibrium, symmetry, harmony, proportion, equipoise, equality. **2.** poise, composure, self-control, equilibrium, equipoise, self-possession. —*v.* **3.** weigh, compare, estimate. **4.** counterpoise, counterbalance, offset, counteract, neutralize, compensate, allow for, make up for. **5.** proportion, equalize, square, adjust.
—**Syn. Study.** See SYMMETRY.

ban, *v.* **1.** prohibit, interdict, outlaw, forbid, proscribe, bar, disallow, debar, embargo. —*n.* **2.** prohibition, interdiction, interdict, taboo, proscription.
—**Ant.** permit, allow; permission, blessing.

band, *n.* **1.** company, party, troop, crew, gang, group, platoon, corps,

horde, pack, bunch, team, ensemble, assemblage, body. **2.** clique, coterie, set, association. **3.** musical group, group, orchestra, (*Variously*) rock band, jazz band.

banish, *v.* exile, expel, deport, ostracize, outlaw, extradite, reject, cast out.
—**Ant.** admit, receive.

bankrupt, *v.* **1.** impoverish, pauperize, ruin. —*adj.* **2.** impoverished, pauperized, insolvent, indigent, impecunious, destitute; (*slang*) broke, stone-broke, flat broke. **3.** ruined, worn out, exhausted, uninformed, insipid.

banter, *n.* **1.** badinage, raillery, repartee, kidding (around), ribbing, joking, jesting. —*v.* **2.** tease, twit, make fun of; ridicule, deride, mock.

bar, *n.* **1.** obstruction, hindrance, deterrent, stop, impediment, obstacle, barrier. **2.** pub, brewpub, saloon, café, bistro, nightclub, cocktail lounge. —*v.* **3.** hinder, obstruct, deter, stop, impede. **4.** exclude, shut out, block.
—**Ant.** suffer, allow, permit.

barbarian, *n.* **1.** savage, philistine, alien, brute, boor, ruffian, yahoo, Neanderthal, redneck, lowbrow. —*adj.* **2.** rude, uncivilized, savage, primitive, barbaric, barbarous, rough, crude, coarse. **3.** untutored, ignorant, uncultivated, unlettered, philistine, uncivil, ill-mannered.
—**Ant.** refined, civilized, cultivated; humane.

bare, *adj.* **1.** naked, nude, uncovered, unclothed, undressed; exposed, unprotected, unsheltered, unshielded, open. **2.** unfurnished, undecorated, plain, stark, Spartan, monastic, ascetic. **3.** basic, literal, straightforward, direct, unvarnished, plain, simple, sheer, mere. —*v.* **4.** disclose, denude, lay open, expose, unfold, unmask, divulge, reveal, uncover.
—**Ant.** covered, dressed.

bargain, *n.* **1.** compact, agreement, stipulation, arrangement, contract, convention, understanding, covenant, pact, settlement, deal, treaty, stipulation, transaction. **2.** good deal, buy, item on sale. —*v.* **3.** contract, agree, stipulate. **4.** trade, sell, transfer. **5.** haggle, negotiate, barter, dicker, wrangle.
—**Syn. Study.** See AGREEMENT.

barren, *adj.* **1.** sterile, unprolific, childless, dry, unfruitful, infertile, unproductive, poor, bare. **2.** uninteresting, dull, stupid; uninstructive, unsuggestive, ineffectual, ineffective.
—**Ant.** fertile; interesting, effectual.

barrier, *n.* bar, obstruction, hindrance, barricade, block, stop, impediment, obstacle, restraint; fence, railing, stockade, palisade, wall; limit, boundary.

base, *n.* **1.** bottom, stand, rest, pedestal, understructure, substructure, foot, basis, foundation, ground, groundwork; principle. **2.** fundamental part, ingredient, or element. **3.** station, goal, starting-point, point of departure. —*adj.* **4.** low, despicable, contemptible. **5.** mean, sorry, tacky, shoddy, common, poor, inferior, cheap, tawdry, worthless. **6.** unrefined, plebeian, vulgar, lowly, humble, unknown. **7.** scandalous, shameful, disreputable, disgraceful, discreditable, dishonorable, infamous, notorious. —*v.* **8.** found, rest, establish, ground, secure, build.
—**Ant.** top, peak; moral, virtuous; good, valuable; refined, pure; honorable.
—**Syn. Study.** BASE, BASIS, FOUNDATION refer to anything upon which a structure is built and upon which it rests. BASE usu. refers to a physical

supporting structure: *the base of a statue.* BASIS more often refers to a figurative support: *the basis of a report.* FOUNDATION implies a solid, secure understructure: *the foundation of a skyscraper; the foundation of a theory.*

bashful, *adj.* diffident, shy, abashed, timid, timorous, coy, sheepish, retiring, meek, nervous, self-conscious, reticent, awkward, modest, self-effacing; embarrassed, shamefaced, ashamed.
—**Ant.** arrogant, immodest, forward, brazen.

basics, *n.* fundamentals, essentials, rudiments, principles, grammar, rules, guidelines, ABC's.

basis, *n.* bottom, base, foundation, ground, principle, underpinning, infrastructure, heart, core, footing.
—**Syn. Study.** See BASE.

batter, *v.* **1.** hit, strike, clout, pummel, bash, thrash, clobber, beat, pound, belabor, smite. **2.** attack, assault, bombard. **3.** abuse, mistreat, maltreat, violate, harm, maul, bruise, mangle, disfigure.

battle, *n.* **1.** action, skirmish, campaign, contest, conflict, engagement, military engagement *or* encounter. **2.** warfare, combat, war, fight. —*v.* **3.** strive, struggle, fight, combat, war, contest, conflict, contend with.

beach, *n.* **1.** coast, seashore, littoral, shore, strand, sands, margin, rim. —*v.* **2.** put ashore, strand, run aground.

beam, *n.* **1.** ray, pencil, streak, gleam, suggestion, hint, glimmer. —*v.* **2.** shine, gleam, glisten, glitter, radiate. **3.** smile, grin, brighten.

bear, *v.* **1.** support, hold up, uphold, sustain. **2.** carry, transport, convey, waft; conduct, guide, take. **3.** yield, afford, produce. **4.** transmit, utter, spread, broadcast, advertise, exhibit, show, demonstrate. **5.** stand, endure, suffer, undergo, tolerate, brook, abide, put up with. **6.** maintain, keep up, carry on. **7.** give birth to, bring forth.
—**Syn. Study.** BEAR, STAND, ENDURE refer to supporting the burden of something distressing. BEAR is the general word and suggests merely being able to put up with something: *She is bearing the disappointment quite well.* STAND is an informal equivalent, but with an implication of stout spirit: *I couldn't stand the pain.* ENDURE implies continued resistance over a long period of time: *to endure torture.*

bearing, *n.* **1.** carriage, posture, manner, stance, attitude, presence, demeanor. **2.** connection, relationship, correlation, pertinence, relevance.

beastly, *adj.* **1.** bestial, animalistic, animal, brutish, brutal, primitive, barbaric, base, inhuman. **2.** unkind, cruel, uncivil, mean, ruthless, merciless, pitiless. **3.** inclement, stormy, severe, miserable, abominable, execrable, horrid, ghastly, foul, vile, nasty, rotten.

beat, *v.* **1.** hit, pound, strike, thrash, batter, knock, thump, maul, pummel, thwack, whack, punch, scourge, bludgeon, club, bash, pelt, clout, manhandle, cudgel, cane, whip, flog, lash, buffet. **2.** conquer, subdue, overcome, vanquish, overpower, defeat. **3.** excel, outdo, surpass. **4.** throb, pulsate, palpitate, pound, thump. —*n.* **5.** stroke, blow. **6.** pulsation, throb, tattoo, rhythm.
—**Syn. Study.** BEAT, HIT, POUND, STRIKE, THRASH refer to the giving of blows. BEAT implies the giving of repeated blows: *to beat a rug.* To HIT is usu. to give a single blow, definitely directed: *to hit a ball.* To POUND is

to give heavy and repeated blows, often with the fist: *to pound the table.* To STRIKE is to give one or more forceful blows suddenly or swiftly: *to strike a gong.* To THRASH implies inflicting repeated blows as punishment, to show superior strength, or the like: *to thrash an opponent.*

beautiful, *adj.* handsome, comely, attractive, lovely, gorgeous, exquisite, good-looking, stunning, dazzling, pretty, fair, fine, elegant, beauteous, (*informal*) to die for.
—**Ant.** ugly; inelegant, ungraceful.
—**Syn. Study.** BEAUTIFUL, HANDSOME, LOVELY, PRETTY refer to a pleasing appearance. BEAUTIFUL is used of a person or thing that gives intense pleasure to the senses; it may refer to a woman but rarely to a man: *a beautiful landscape; a beautiful actress.* HANDSOME often implies stateliness or pleasing proportions and symmetry; it is used of a man and sometimes a woman: *a handsome sofa; a handsome man.* That which is LOVELY is beautiful in a warm and endearing way: *a lovely smile.* PRETTY usu. suggests a moderate beauty in persons or things that are small or feminine: *a pretty blouse; a pretty child.*

beautify, *v.* embellish, adorn, ornament, decorate, elaborate, garnish, bedeck, enhance, prettify, glamorize.
—**Ant.** uglify, despoil, mar, deface, vandalize.

beauty, *n.* **1.** loveliness, elegance, grace, gracefulness, good looks, allure, comeliness, fairness, attractiveness. **2.** belle, knockout, stunner, siren, dream, dish. **3.** grace, charm, excellence, attraction, elegance, refinement.
—**Ant.** ugliness; gracelessness.

becoming, *adj.* **1.** attractive, neat, pretty, graceful, fetching, chic, stylish, fashionable, tasteful. **2.** fit, proper, apt, suitable, appropriate, fitting, seemly.
—**Ant.** unbecoming, ugly, inappropriate.

bedlam, *n.* hubbub, din, confusion, racket, noise, clamor, chaos, agitation, riot, pandemonium, babel, tumult, uproar, hullabaloo, ruckus, rumpus, commotion, turmoil, furor, madhouse.
—**Ant.** calm, tranquility, peace, serenity.

beg, *v.* **1.** ask for, entreat, crave, implore, beseech, importune, plead with, wheedle, cajole, supplicate, sue for. **2.** solicit, sponge, cadge, scrounge, panhandle.

begin, *v.* **1.** commence, start, initiate, inaugurate, institute. **2.** originate, open, launch, establish, found, set up, create.
—**Ant.** end, conclude, die.
—**Syn. Study.** BEGIN, COMMENCE, INITIATE, START (when followed by noun or gerund) refer to setting into motion something that continues for some time. BEGIN is the common term: *to begin knitting a sweater.* COMMENCE is a more formal word, often suggesting a prolonged or elaborate beginning: *to commence proceedings in court.* INITIATE implies an ingenious first act in a new field: *to initiate a new procedure.* START means to set out on a course of action: *to start paving a street.*

beginner, *n.* amateur, tyro, neophyte, novice, pupil, student, newcomer.

beginning, *n.* **1.** initiation, inauguration, inception, dawning, birth, genesis, origin, creation, get-go, start, commencement. **2.** source, birth, origin, rise.

begrudge, *v.* envy, grudge, covet, resent, be spiteful.

beguile, *v.* **1.** mislead, swindle, dupe, hoodwink, bamboozle, con, trick, hoax, defraud, cheat, deceive, fool. **2.** charm, please, distract, engage; fascinate, mesmerize, enchant, entrance, enrapture.

behave, *v.* conduct oneself, act, deport *or* comport oneself, act properly, be obedient *or* good.
—Ant. misbehave.

behavior, *n.* demeanor, conduct, manners, deportment, bearing, comportment.

belief, *n.* **1.** opinion, view, tenet, doctrine, dogma, creed, idea, conviction, principle, persuasion. **2.** certainty, faith, assurance, confidence.
—Syn. Study. BELIEF, CONVICTION refer to acceptance of an alleged fact as true without positive knowledge or proof. BELIEF is such acceptance in general: *belief in astrology.* CONVICTION is a settled, belief that something is right: *a conviction that a decision is just.*

beneficial, *adj.* healthful, healthy, wholesome; favorable, good, serviceable, useful, helpful, profitable, advantageous.
—Ant. unwholesome, unfavorable, disadvantageous.

benevolent, *adj.* kind, kindly, well-disposed, kindhearted, gracious, humane, humanitarian, sympathetic, compassionate, unselfish, generous, liberal, obliging, benign, altruistic, magnanimous, open-handed; beneficial, helpful, salutary.
—Ant. cruel, selfish.

bent, *adj.* **1.** curved, crooked, hooked, bowed, flexed, deflected. **2.** determined, set on, decided, intent, resolute, resolved, fixed on. **—*n.* 3.** inclination, leaning, bias, tendency, propensity, proclivity, penchant, predilection. **4.** ability, aptitude, talent, gift, flair, knack.
—Ant. straight; undecided; disinclination.

bequeath, *v.* leave, will, pass on, pass along, hand down.

beseech, *v.* **1.** implore, beg, entreat, pray, petition, supplicate, importune, adjure. **2.** solicit, ask, entreat, beg, implore.

beset, *v.* assail, harass, besiege.

besides, *adv.* **1.** moreover, in addition, furthermore, else, otherwise, too, also, yet, further. **—*prep.* 2.** over and above, in addition to, except, other than, save, distinct from.

best, *adj.* **1.** finest, first, paramount, superlative, preeminent, unexcelled, unsurpassed, unrivaled, superb, excellent, A-one, first-rate, top, foremost. **—*v.* 2.** beat, conquer, win out over, surpass, overpower, get the better of, defeat, vanquish, trounce, rout, crush, outdo, overwhelm, overcome, outwit, master, subdue.

bet, *v.* gamble, wager, risk, stake, hazard, play, take a chance *or* flier, venture, speculate, try one's luck, count on.

betray, *v.* be unfaithful to, be a traitor to, deceive, be disloyal to, cheat on, stab in the back, sell down the river.
—Ant. protect, safeguard.

better, *adj.* **1.** superior; more useful, more valuable; more suitable, more appropriate, more fit, more applicable. **2.** larger, greater, bigger. **—*v.* 3.** improve, amend, ameliorate, emend; advance, promote; reform, correct, rectify. **4.** surpass, exceed, outdo, excel.
—Ant. worse; worsen.
—Syn. Study. See IMPROVE.

bewilder, *v.* confuse, perplex, puzzle, mystify; nonplus, astonish, daze, stagger, befog, muddle, befuddle, baffle, flabbergast.

bewitch, *v.* cast a spell over, charm, enchant, captivate, spellbind, entrance, beguile, enrapture, fascinate, hypnotize, mesmerize.

bias, *n.* **1.** prejudice, preconception, predilection, proclivity, propensity, proneness, partiality, predisposition, bent, leaning, tendency. **—*v.* 2.** prejudice, predispose, bend, influence, incline, dispose, sway, color, taint, distort.
—Ant. justness, impartiality.
—Syn. Study. BIAS, PREJUDICE mean a preconceived opinion about something or someone. A BIAS may be favorable or unfavorable: *bias in favor of or against an idea.* PREJUDICE implies a preformed judgment even more unreasoning than BIAS, and usu. implies an unfavorable opinion: *prejudice against a race.*

bid, *v.* **1.** command, order, direct. **2.** offer, propose, tender, proffer. **—*n.* 3.** offer, proposal.
—Ant. forbid, prohibit, enjoin.

big, *adj.* **1.** large, great, huge, bulky, massive, immense, colossal, jumbo, gargantuan, elephantine, enormous. **2.** important, significant, outstanding, major, momentous.
—Ant. small; trivial.

bigoted, *adj.* intolerant, narrow-minded, closed-minded, one-sided, partial, small-minded, parochial, biased, prejudiced.
—Ant. tolerant, broad-minded, open-minded, generous.

bill, *n.* account, reckoning, score, charge, invoice, statement.

bind, *v.* **1.** band, bond, tie, fasten, secure, attach. **2.** engage, obligate, oblige.
—Ant. untie, unbind.

birth, *n.* **1.** act of bearing, bringing forth, delivery, parturition. **2.** lineage, heritage, parentage, descent, ancestry. **3.** origin, beginning, creation, emergence.
—Ant. death, end.

bit, *n.* particle, speck, grain, mite, crumb, iota, jot, atom, trace, touch, hint, suggestion, suspicion, scintilla, tittle, whit, fragment, morsel, piece, scrap, shred.

bitter, *adj.* **1.** harsh, acrid, biting, acerbic, sharp, caustic, mordant. **2.** grievous, distasteful, painful, miserable, dispiriting, distressing, calamitous. **3.** harsh, sarcastic, caustic, cutting, vicious, acrimonious.
—Ant. sweet.

black, *adj.* **1.** dark, dusky, sooty, inky, jet-black, raven, ebony, sable, swarthy. **2.** gloomy, sad, dismal.
—Ant. white; clean, pure, undefiled.

blame, *v.* **1.** reproach, reprove, censure, condemn, find fault, criticize, disapprove, upbraid. **—*n.* 2.** censure, reprehension, condemnation, stricture, disapproval, disapprobation, reproach, reproof, animadversion, finger-pointing. **3.** guilt, culpability, fault, wrong, misdeed, misdoing, shortcoming, sin, defect, reproach.
—Ant. credit, honor.

blameless, *adj.* irreproachable, guiltless, unimpeachable, innocent, inculpable, not guilty.
—Ant. guilty, culpable.

blanch, *v.* whiten, bleach, pale, fade, lose color, turn white, go pale, be aghast.
—Ant. darken; blush.

bland, *adj.* **1.** gentle, agreeable, affable, friendly, kindly, mild, amiable; mild-mannered. **2.** soft, mild, balmy, soothing, nonirritating. **3.** dull, flavorless, insipid, boring, uninteresting.
—Ant. cruel, unfriendly; boorish, crude; irritable, irksome.

blank, *adj.* **1.** unmarked, void, empty, unadorned, plain, bare, undistinguished. **2.** spacey, passive, impassive, emotionless, expressionless, vacant, vacuous, mindless, unexpressive, **—*n.* 3.** space, line, form; void, vacancy, emptiness.
—Ant. distinguished, marked.

blarney, *n.* **1.** flattery, blandishment, cajolery; (*informal*) sweet talk, soft soap. **2.** nonsense, rubbish, blather, humbug.

blasé, *adj.* **1.** worldly-wise, sophisticated, knowing, worldly. **2.** jaded, disillusioned, world-weary. **3.** unconcerned, indifferent, uninterested, nonchalant, cool, emotionless, unimpressed, bored, phlegmatic, apathetic, insouciant.

blasphemy, *n.* profanity, cursing, iniquity, irreverence, oath, impiety, swearing, impiousness, sacrilege.
—Ant. reverence, piety.

blast, *n.* **1.** wind, squall, gust, gale, storm. **2.** blare, sound, noise, roar, din, racket. **3.** explosion, detonation, outburst, discharge. **—*v.* q 4.** defame, discredit, denounce, criticize, attack. **5.** explode, burst, blow up, dynamite.
—Syn. Study. See WIND.

blaze, *n.* **1.** fire, flame, holocaust, inferno. **—*v.* 2.** burn, shine, flame, flare up, flicker.

bleach, *v.* whiten, blanch, etiolate, pale, lose color.
—Ant. darken, dye.

blemish, *v.* **1.** stain, sully, spot, taint, injure, tarnish; mar, damage, scar, disfigure, deface, impair. **—*n.* 2.** stain, defect, blot, spot, speck, disfigurement, flaw, taint, fault, imperfection, scar, mark, impairment.
—Ant. purify; purity, immaculateness.
—Syn. Study. See DEFECT.

blend, *v.* **1.** mingle, combine, coalesce, mix, meld, intermingle, commingle, amalgamate, unite, compound. **—*n.* 2.** mixture, combination, amalgamation.
—Ant. separate.
—Syn. Study. See MIX.

blind, *adj.* **1.** sightless, stone-blind, purblind, unsighted. **2.** ignorant, imperceptive, obtuse, insensitive.
—Ant. discerning, enlightened.

bliss, *n.* happiness, gladness, joy, delight, felicity, glee, enjoyment, pleasure, gaiety, exhilaration.
—Ant. misery, unhappiness, dejection.

blithe, *adj.* **1.** joyous, merry, glad, cheerful, happy, mirthful, blissful, delighted, jubilant, lighthearted, buoyant, lively, animated, elated, vivacious, joyful. **2.** carefree, unconcerned, happy-go-lucky, insouciant, blasé.
—Ant. unhappy, miserable, cheerless.

block, *n.* **1.** obstacle, hindrance, impediment, obstruction, deterrent, bar, stumbling block, barrier. **—*v.* 2.** prevent, bar, hamper, frustrate, obstruct, hinder, deter, arrest, stop.
—Ant. encourage, advance, continue.

bloody, *adj.* **1.** bloodstained, sanguinary, gory. **2.** murderous, cruel, bloodthirsty, savage, barbarous.

bloom, *n.* **1.** flower, blossom, efflorescence. **2.** freshness, glow, flush, vigor, prime. **—*v.* 3.** flourish, thrive, effloresce; glow.

blot, *n.* **1.** spot, stain, blotch, splotch. **2.** blemish, reproach, stain, taint, dishonor, disgrace, spot. **—*v.* 3.** spot, stain, bespatter; sully, disfigure, deface. **4.** darken, dim, obscure, eclipse, hide, overshadow.

blow, *n.* **1.** stroke, buffet, thump, thwack, rap, slap, cuff, box, beat, knock. **2.** shock, surprise, bombshell, jolt, revelation. **3.** calamity, disaster, misfortune, affliction. **—*v.* 4.** pant, puff, wheeze, breathe, exhale.

blowhard, *n.* braggart, boaster, braggadocio, blusterer, showoff, bigmouth, loudmouth, windbag, gasbag.
—Ant. introvert, milquetoast, shrinking violet.

blue, *adj.* **1.** depressed, dismal, unhappy, morose, gloomy, downhearted, down in the mouth *or* dumps, doleful, melancholy, dispirited, dejected, sad, glum. **2.** obscene, lewd, lascivious, licentious, indecent, risqué, ribald, adult, X-rated, pornographic, vulgar, smutty.
—Ant. happy, mirthful; moral, clean, proper.

blueprint, *n.* plan, outline, scheme, design, schema, master plan, ground plan, diagram, program, model, paradigm, pattern, original, game plan, strategy.

bluff, *n* **1.** fraud, deceit, lie, dissembling. **—*v.* 2.** mislead, defraud, deceive, lie, dissemble, fake.
—Ant. suave, diplomatic, tactful; gradual; plain.

blunder, *n.* **1.** mistake, error, faux pas, gaffe, lapse, slip, misstep, slipup, miscue, impropriety, indiscretion;(*slang*) boner, howler, blooper, goof, boo-boo. **—*v.* 2.** bungle, botch, bobble, err, make an error, bumble, mess up, goof up.
—Syn. Study. See MISTAKE.

blunt, *adj.* **1.** rounded, worn, not sharp, dull. **2.** abrupt, brusque, curt, short, obtuse, plainspoken, direct, candid, frank, undiplomatic. **—*v.* 3.** soften, mitigate, mollify, soothe, weaken, dim, blur, obscure.
—Ant. sharp, acute; courteous, civil, polite.
—Syn. Study. BLUNT, BRUSQUE, CURT characterize manners and speech. BLUNT suggests a lack of regard for the feelings of others: *blunt and tactless remarks.* BRUSQUE connotes a sharpness that borders on rudeness: *a brusque denial.* CURT applies esp. to disconcertingly concise language: *a curt reply.*

boast, *v.* **1.** exaggerate, brag, swagger, crow, bluster, bloviate, blow one's own horn. **—*n.* 2.** bluster, bragging, swaggering, braggadocio.
—Ant. deprecate, belittle.
—Syn. Study. BOAST, BRAG imply vocal self-praise. BOAST usu. refers to a particular ability, possession, etc., that may justify a good deal of pride: *He boasts of his ability as a singer.* BRAG, a more informal term, usu. suggests a more exaggerated boasting but less well-founded: *He brags loudly about his marksmanship.*

body, *n.* **1.** carcass, corpse, remains, cadaver. **2.** trunk, torso. **3.** consistency, density, substance, thickness. **4.** substance, essence, core, heart, matter.
—Ant. spirit, soul.
—Syn. Study. BODY, CARCASS, CORPSE, CADAVER all refer to a physical organism, usu. human or animal. BODY denotes the material substance of a human or animal, either living or dead: *the muscles in a horse's body; the body of an accident victim.* CARCASS means the dead body of an animal, unless applied humorously or contemptuously to the human body: *a sheep's carcass; Save your carcass.* CORPSE usu. refers to the dead body of a human being: *preparing a corpse for burial.* CADAVER refers to a dead body, usu. a human one used for scientific study: *dissection of cadavers in anatomy classes.*

bogus, *adj.* false, sham, counterfeit, inauthentic, mock, phony, spurious, pseudo, imitation, fraudulent, specious, fake, ersatz.

—**Ant.** genuine, real, true, authentic.

bohemian, *adj.* **1.** free-living, free-spirited. —*n.* **2.** nonconformist, free spirit, beatnik, hippie.
—**Ant.** conformist, conservative, straight arrow.

boil, *v.* bubble, seethe, foam, froth, churn, stew, simmer, rage.
—**Syn. Study.** BOIL, SEETHE, SIMMER, STEW are used figuratively to refer to agitated states of emotion. To BOIL suggests being very hot with anger: *He was boiling when the guests arrived late.* To SEETHE is to be violently agitated: *a mind seething with conflicting ideas.* To SIMMER means to be at the point of bursting out or boiling over: *to simmer with curiosity; to simmer with anger.* To STEW means to be in a restless state of anxiety: *to stew over one's troubles.*

boisterous, *adj.* rough, noisy, loud, unrestrained, wild, tumultuous, turbulent, tempestuous, rambunctious, rowdy, unruly.
—**Ant.** calm, serene, pacific.

bold, *adj.* **1.** fearless, courageous, brave, intrepid, daring, dauntless, valorous, valiant, heroic. **2.** forward, brazen, brassy, presumptuous, insolent. **3.** pronounced, outstanding, striking, vivid, prominent.
—**Ant.** cowardly, timorous, timid; backward, shy; inconspicuous.
—**Syn. Study.** BOLD, BRAZEN, FORWARD, PRESUMPTUOUS refer to manners that break the rules of propriety. BOLD suggests immodesty: *a bold stare.* BRAZEN suggests the same, together with a defiant manner: *a brazen liar.* FORWARD implies bringing oneself to notice with too much assurance: *The forward young man challenged the speaker.* PRESUMPTUOUS implies taking too much for granted: *It was presumptuous of her to think she could defeat the champion.*

bondage, *n.* slavery, servitude, serfdom, thralldom, subjugation, enslavement, captivity, imprisonment.
—**Ant.** freedom.
—**Syn. Study.** See SLAVERY.

bonus, *n.* bounty, premium, reward, honorarium, gift, subsidy, extra, tip, emolument, dividend, perquisite, perk.
—**Syn. Study.** BONUS, BOUNTY, PREMIUM refer to an additional payment. A BONUS is a gift to reward performance, paid either by an employer or by a government: *a bonus based on salary; a soldier's bonus.* A BOUNTY is a public reward offered to stimulate interest in a specific undertaking and to encourage performance: *a bounty for killing wolves.* A PREMIUM is usu. something additional given as an inducement to buy or produce: *a premium received with a magazine subscription.*

border, *n.* **1.** side, edge, margin; periphery, circumference. **2.** frontier, boundary. —*v.* **3.** bound, limit, abut, touch, be adjacent.

bore, *v.* weary, fatigue, tire, annoy, wear out, exhaust, jade, leave cold.
—**Ant.** amuse.

bother, *v.* **1.** annoy, pester, plague, tease, harass, irritate, hector, hound, nag, pick on, needle, hassle, bully, abuse. **2.** bewilder, confuse, perplex, puzzle, perturb, upset, disconcert, discomfit.
—**Ant.** solace, comfort.
—**Syn. Study.** BOTHER, ANNOY, PLAGUE imply persistent interference with someone's comfort or peace of mind. To BOTHER is to cause irritation, esp. by repeated interruptions in the midst of pressing duties: *Don't bother me while I'm working.* To ANNOY is to cause mild irritation, as by repetition of an action that

displeases: *The dog's constant barking annoyed the neighbors.* To PLAGUE is to trouble or bother, but usu. connotes severe mental distress: *The family was plagued by lack of money.*

bottom, *n.* **1.** base, foot. **2.** underside. **3.** foundation, base, basis, substructure. **4.** seat, buttocks, rear end, derrière, behind, backside, butt, buns, duff, tush, keister, fanny, can, gluteus maximus. —*adj.* **5.** fundamental, basic, elementary. **6.** undermost, lowest.
—**Ant.** top; superficial, superfluous.

bounty, *n.* **1.** generosity, munificence, charity, liberality, philanthropy, unselfishness, goodness, kindness, beneficence. **2.** gift, award, present, benefaction. **3.** reward, premium, bonus, award, gratuity.
—**Syn. Study.** See BONUS.

bow, *v.* **1.** stoop, bend. **2.** yield, submit, capitulate, bend, give in. **3.** weigh down, burden, overload, subdue, crush.

brag, *v.* boast, bluster, crow, talk big, swagger, bluster, gloat, exaggerate.
—**Ant.** depreciate, be modest.
—**Syn. Study.** See BOAST.

brains, *n.* understanding, intelligence, mind, intellect, sense, thought, perspicacity, perceptiveness, wisdom, sagacity, wit, acumen, discernment, knowledge.
—**Ant.** stupidity.

branch, *n.* **1.** bough, limb, arm, offshoot, ramification. **2.** section, subdivision, department. —*v.* **3.** divide, subdivide, diverge, ramify.

bravado, *n.* boasting, swaggering, braggadocio, pretense, boldness, machismo, arrogance, bluster, bombast.
—**Ant.** shame, modesty.

brave, *adj.* **1.** courageous, valiant, fearless, gallant, spunky, plucky, valorous, intrepid, daring, dauntless, bold, heroic, stouthearted. —*v.* **2.** face, defy, challenge, meet, confront, pit oneself against; endure, bear, suffer, tolerate.
—**Ant.** cowardly, fearful; craven, pusillanimous.
—**Syn. Study.** BRAVE, COURAGEOUS, VALIANT, FEARLESS refer to facing danger with moral strength. BRAVE is a general term that suggests fortitude, daring, and resolve: *a brave pioneer.* COURAGEOUS implies a nobler kind of bravery, esp. as resulting from an inborn quality of spirit: *courageous leaders.* VALIANT implies an inner strength manifested by brave deeds, often in battle: *a valiant knight.* FEARLESS implies coolness in the face of danger: *a fearless firefighter.*

brawl, *n.* **1.** quarrel, squabble, argument, spat, wrangle, feud, disagreement, dispute, row, fray, fight, affray, altercation, melee, riot. —*v.* **2.** quarrel, squabble, argue, wrangle, feud, disagree, dispute, fight, bicker.

brazen, *adj.* **1.** brassy, barefaced, brash, outspoken, candid, open, unabashed, shameless. **2.** bold, forward, impudent, insolent, defiant, rude, saucy, fresh, cheeky.
—**Ant.** shy, diffident, modest.
—**Syn. Study.** See BOLD.

breach, *n.* **1.** break, rupture, fracture, crack, split, fissure, rift, rent, opening, chasm. **2.** infraction, violation, infringement. **3.** falling out, misunderstanding; split, rift, schism, disagreement, difference, quarrel, dispute.
—**Ant.** observance.
—**Syn. Study.** BREACH, INFRACTION, VIOLATION all denote an act of breaking a legal or moral code. BREACH is most often used of a legal offense, but it may refer to the breaking of any code of conduct:

breach of contract; breach of etiquette. INFRACTION most often refers to the breaking of clearly formulated rules or laws: *an infraction of regulations.* VIOLATION often suggests a willful, forceful refusal to obey: *done in violation of instructions.*

break, *v.* **1.** fracture, rupture, fragment, crack, shatter, splinter. **2.** dissolve, annul, negate, dismiss. **3.** lacerate, wound, cut, injure, harm, hurt. **4.** interrupt, suspend, disrupt, stop. **5.** exceed, outdo, surpass, beat. **6.** reveal, announce, tell, make public, disclose. **7.** ruin, bankrupt, make bankrupt. **8.** tame, make obedient. **9.** dissolve, separate, split. —*n.* **10.** disruption, separation, rent, tear, rip, rift, schism, severance, split; breach, gap, fissure, crack, chasm, rupture, fracture. **11.** suspension, stoppage, stop, caesura, hiatus, interruption, lacuna, pause.
—**Ant.** repair.

breed, *v.* **1.** beget, bear, bring forth, conceive, give birth to, produce, engender, father, mother. **2.** propagate, procreate, originate, create, beget. **3.** raise, rear, bring up, nurture, train, educate. **4.** grow, develop, flourish, arise, rise. —*n.* **5.** race, lineage, strain, family, pedigree. **6.** sort, kind, species, class.

breeze, *n.* wind, air, blow, zephyr, breath, puff, draft, gust.
—**Ant.** calm.
—**Syn. Study.** See WIND.

brevity, *n.* conciseness, compactness, condensation, succinctness, pithiness; terseness, curtness, economy.
—**Ant.** lengthiness.
—**Syn. Study.** BREVITY, CONCISENESS refer to the use of few words in speaking. BREVITY emphasizes the short duration of speech: *reduced to extreme brevity.* CONCISENESS emphasizes compactness of expression: *clear in spite of great conciseness.*

brief, *adj.* **1.** short, short-lived, fleeting, momentary, passing, evanescent, fugitive, transitory, ephemeral, transient, temporary. **2.** concise, succinct, pithy, condensed, compact, laconic; curt, short, terse, abrupt. —*n.* **3.** outline, précis, synopsis, summary, abstract, abridgment, digest, condensation, extract. —*v.* **4.** advise, informt, enlighten, fill in, explain.
—**Ant.** long, tendentious.
—**Syn. Study.** See SHORT. See also SUMMARY.

bright, *adj.* **1.** radiant, radiating, resplendent, effulgent, lucent, lustrous, glowing, beaming, lambent, brilliant, shining, gleaming, luminous; vivid, light, sunny, fulgent. **2.** quick-witted, intelligent, keen, discerning, acute, gifted, talented, expert, ingenious, creative. **3.** lively, animated, cheerful, merry, happy, sprightly, lighthearted, gay, vivacious, genial, pleasant.
—**Ant.** dull; opaque, dense; undistinguished, ignominious; slow, stupid; laconic, doleful, melancholy.

brilliance, *n.* **1.** brightness, shine, splendor, luster, radiance, sparkle, glitter, glister, gleam. **2.** excellence, distinction, eminence, renown, prominence, preeminence, singularity, fame, illustriousness.
—**Ant.** dullness; notoriety, oblivion.

brim, *n.* rim, edge, border, margin, periphery, circumference, bound, brink, lip.
—**Ant.** center.
—**Syn. Study.** See RIM.

bring, *v.* take along, conduct, convey, escort, transport, carry.
—**Ant.** remove, withdraw.

brisk, *adj.* **1.** active, lively, energetic, busy, vigorous; animated, sprightly,

pert, quick, nimble, agile, alert, spry. **2.** sharp, invigorating, refreshing, bracing.
—**Ant.** slow, lethargic; dull.

brittle, *adj.* fragile, frail, breakable, frangible, weak, delicate.
—**Ant.** supple, flexible, elastic.
—**Syn. Study.** See FRAIL.

broad, *adj.* **1.** wide. **2.** large, extensive, expansive, vast, spacious, ample. **3.** diffused, diffuse, open, full. **4.** liberal, large, big, tolerant, open-minded, hospitable. **5.** main, general, rough, approximate, sweeping, unspecific. **6.** plain, clear, bold, obvious, evident, explicit.
—**Ant.** narrow; stingy.

broad-minded, *adj.* tolerant, open-minded, liberal, progressive, generous, charitable, forbearing, unbigoted, unparochial, ecumenical.
—**Ant.** narrow-minded, bigoted, close-minded.

brood, *n.* **1.** offspring, litter, young, progeny, issue, babies, children. **2.** breed, kind, sort, lineage, stock, family, strain, species, class. —*v.* **3.** incubate, sit, hatch, set. **4.** dwell on, ponder, ruminate over, meditate on, think about. **5.** sulk, obsess, anguish over, mope, pout, pine, eat one's heart out, fret, worry, agonize, despair, be sullen.

brook, *n.* **1.** stream, rivulet. —*v.* **2.** bear, suffer, tolerate, allow, stand, endure, abide, put up with, submit to, withstand, countenance.

brother, *n.* fellow man, countryman, kinsman, associate, friend, sibling, (slang) bro.

brush, *n.* **1.** touch; encounter, meeting; collision, action, fight, battle, skirmish. **2.** undergrowth, brambles, underbrush, thicket, copse, shrubs, bracken.

brusque, *adj.* abrupt, blunt, rough, unceremonious, bluff, gruff, churlish, terse, brash, undiplomatic, tactless.
—**Ant.** courteous, courtly, polished, refined, gentle.
—**Syn. Study.** See BLUNT.

brutal, *adj.* **1.** savage, cruel, inhuman, ruthless, barbarous, brutish, barbaric. **2.** crude, coarse, gross, harsh, rude, rough. **3.** bestial, beastly, animal, carnal.
—**Ant.** kind, sensitive.

brute, *n.* **1.** beast, quadruped, animal. **2.** barbarian, savage, heathen, Neanderthal, lout, boor, oaf, ogre. —*adj.* **3.** animal, brutish, irrational, unreasoning. **4.** savage, cruel, brutal. **5.** sensual, carnal, physical.
—**Ant.** human; kind; spiritual.

bubbly, *adj.* **1.** frothy, foamy, effervescent, sparkling, carbonated. **2.** high-spirited, vivacious, animated, lively, energetic, sprightly, effervescent, perky, pert, cheerful, ebullient, buoyant.
—**Ant.** flat, colorless.

building, *n.* edifice, structure, construction.

bulk, *n.* **1.** size, magnitude, mass, volume, dimensions. **2.** greater part, majority, most; body, mass. —*v.* **3.** grow, swell, bulge, expand, enlarge, aggrandize.

bulky, *adj.* massive, ponderous, large, voluminous, ungainly, awkward, unwieldy, clumsy, cumbersome; great, big, large, huge, vast.
—**Ant.** small, delicate.

bunch, *n.* cluster; bundle, batch, clump, crowd, knot, gathering, assortment, mass, group, lot, bundle, batch, collection.

burden, *n.* **1.** load, weight. **2.** encumbrance, impediment, trouble, grievance, onus, albatross, millstone, cross. **3.** substance, core, point, essence, epitome, central

idea, tenor, drift. —*v.* **4.** load, overload, oppress, weigh down, tax, encumber, saddle with.
—**Ant.** unload, lighten, help.

burn, *v.* **1.** flame, blaze, flare, smolder, ignite, be on fire. **2.** tingle, be hot, glow. **3.** consume, scorch, sear, overcook, blacken, singe, char, toast. **4.** desire, wish, long, yearn, pine, itch, ache.

burst, *v.* **1.** explode, crack, blow up, split, rupture, shatter. **2.** rend, tear, break. —*n.* **3.** explosion. **4.** spurt, outpouring, gust.
—**Ant.** implode.

bury, *v.* **1.** inter, entomb, lay to rest. **2.** sink, submerge, plunge, inundate. **3.** cover, hide, conceal, secrete, shroud, enshroud, obscure.
—**Ant.** disinter; rise; uncover.

business, *n.* **1.** occupation, trade, craft, metier, profession, calling, employment, vocation, pursuit, work. **2.** company, concern, enterprise, corporation, firm, dot-com. **3.** affair, matter, concern, transaction. **4.** commerce, trade, traffic. **5.** function, duty, office, position, role, responsibility, charge, obligation.

busy, *adj.* **1.** engaged, occupied, diligent, industrious, employed, engrossed, rapt, preoccupied, working, assiduous. **2.** active, brisk, bustling, hectic, lively, buzzing.
—**Ant.** indolent, unoccupied, lazy.

but, *conj.* **1.** however, nevertheless, yet, further, moreover, still. **2.** excepting, save, except. —*prep.* **3.** excepting, except, save, excluding. —*adv.* **4.** only, just, no more than.

butcher, *n.* **1.** murderer, slayer, killer, assassin, cutthroat, thug, (*slang*) hit man. —*v.* **2.** kill, slaughter, exterminate, liquidate, massacre, murder, assassinate. **3.** bungle, botch, foul up, make a mess *or* hash of.
—**Syn. Study.** See SLAUGHTER.

buy, *v.* purchase, acquire, obtain, get, procure.
—**Ant.** sell.

byword, *n.* slogan, motto, password, shibboleth, proverb, maxim, aphorism, saw, adage, saying, parable, epithet.

C

cabin, *n.* hut, shanty, shack, lean-to, bungalow, lodge, chalet, cottage, shed, hovel.

cadaverous, *adj.* deathly pale, deathly, ghastly, ghostly, ghostlike, spectral, corpselike, pallid, livid.
—**Ant.** robust, hearty, healthy.

cagey, *adj.* cunning, clever, shrewd, wily, calculating, conniving, scheming, designing, Machiavellian, manipulative, crafty, foxy, sharp, slick.

cajole, *v.* wheedle, coax, beguile, entice, inveigle, flatter, soft-soap, sweet-talk, blandish, seduce, persuade, butter up.

calamity, *n.* affliction, adversity, ill fortune, bad luck, trouble, evil, hardship, mischance, misadventure, mishap, blow, misfortune, disaster, catastrophe, cataclysm, devastation, tragedy.
—**Ant.** fortune, blessing, boon.
—**Syn. Study.** See DISASTER.

calculate, *v.* count, figure, reckon, estimate, weigh, assess, evaluate, gauge, determine, ascertain, compute, rate.
—**Ant.** assume, guess.

calculation, *n.* **1.** computation, figuring, reckoning, counting, determining, assessment, appraisal, estimate, estimation. **2.** forethought, planning, caution, wariness, foresight, discretion, prudence, deliberation.
—**Ant.** guess, assumption.

call, *v.* **1.** cry out, shout, yell, roar, bellow, hail. **2.** announce, proclaim. **3.** awaken, waken, rouse, wake up, arouse. **4.** summon, invite, send for, bid, gather, collect, rally. **5.** convoke, convene, call together, assemble, muster. **6.** name, give a name to, label, designate, dub, entitle. **7.** shout, cry, voice. **8.** visit, stop. —*n.* **9.** shout, cry, yell, whoop, outcry. **10.** summons, signal; invitation, bidding; appointment. **11.** need, occasion; demand, claim, requisition.

callous, *adj.* hard, hardened, inured, thick-skinned, heartless, hard-hearted, tough, cold, unfeeling, uncaring, hardboiled, emotionless, unemotional, indifferent, obtuse.
—**Ant.** soft; sensitive.

calm, *adj.* **1.** still, quiet, smooth, motionless, balmy, halcyon, even, placid, pacific, tranquil, unruffled, mild, peaceful. **2.** serene, collected, composed, cool, self-possessed, dispassionate, staid, impassive, cool-headed, stoical, unruffled, undisturbed, sedate, aloof. —*n.* **3.** stillness, serenity, calmness, quiet, smoothness, tranquility, peacefulness, aloofness, self-possession, composure, repose, equanimity. —*v.* **4.** still, quiet, tranquilize, pacify, hush, lull, sedate, smooth, appease, compose; allay, assuage, mollify, soothe, soften, placate.
—**Ant.** perturbed; tempestuous; excite, agitate.
—**Syn. Study.** CALM, COLLECTED, COMPOSED, COOL imply the absence of agitation. CALM implies an unruffled state in the midst of disturbance all around: *He remained calm throughout the crisis.* COLLECTED implies complete command of one's thoughts, feelings, and behavior, usu. as a result of effort: *The witness was remarkably collected during questioning.* COMPOSED implies inner peace and dignified self-possession: *pale but composed.* COOL implies clarity of judgment and absence of strong feeling or excitement: *cool in the face of danger.*

cancel, *v.* **1.** cross out, delete, erase, expunge, obliterate, blot out, efface, rub out. **2.** void, nullify, annul, countermand, revoke, rescind.
—**Ant.** ratify.

candid, *adj.* frank, open, outspoken, sincere, ingenuous, artless, honest, honorable, plain, guileless, straightforward, aboveboard, truthful, forthright, direct, unequivocal, plain-speaking, blunt, (*of an autobiography or the like*) tell-all.
—**Ant.** concealed, hidden, wily, deceitful.
—**Syn. Study.** See FRANK.

candor, *n.* frankness, honesty, forthrightness, directness, candidness, ingenuousness, straightforwardness, truthfulness, sincerity, openness, outspokenness, bluntness.
—**Ant.** evasiveness, deceitfulness.

cantankerous, *adj.* ill-natured, irritable, irascible, quarrelsome, fractious, cross, crotchety, captious, choleric, foul-tempered, mean-tempered, grumpy, ornery, testy, touchy, peevish, surly, petulant, snappish, waspish, crusty, contrary, grouchy, bilious, splenetic, curmudgeonly, crabby.
—**Ant.** sweet-natured, kindly, gracious.

capable, *adj.* **1.** able, competent, efficient, proficient, qualified, talented, skilled, adept, expert, masterful, skillful, ingenious. **2.** fitted, adapted, suited, qualified.
—**Ant.** incompetent, bungling, amateurish.

capacious, *adj.* spacious, roomy, ample, large, broad, comprehensive, wide, voluminous.
—**Ant.** confining, narrow.

capacity, *n.* **1.** ability, power, aptitude, potential, brains, acumen, bent, forte, leaning, propensity, ableness, talent, competence, capability. **2.** position, condition, character, place, role, job, function.
—**Ant.** incapacity, incompetence.

caper, *v.* **1.** skip, leap, spring, hop, gambol, frolic, frisk, play, romp, cavort, rollick. —*n.* **2.** escapade, prank, frolic, lark, antic, adventure, bit of mischief, stunt, high jinks, shenanigan.

capital, *n.* **1.** metropolis, major city, stronghold. **2.** wealth, principal, investment, worth, resources, assets, stock. —*adj.* **3.** chief, major, principal, first, main, central, paramount, preeminent, foremost, important, prime, primary, leading, cardinal, essential, vital. **4.** excellent, first-rate, splendid, fine, first-class, superior, outstanding, superb, extraordinary, great, super. **5.** fatal, serious.
—**Ant.** trivial, unimportant.
—**Syn. Study.** CAPITAL, CHIEF, MAJOR, PRINCIPAL apply to a leading representative of a kind. CAPITAL may suggest preeminence, importance, or excellence: *a capital idea.* CHIEF often means highest in office or power; it may mean most important: *the chief clerk; the chief problem.* MAJOR refers to someone or something greater in number, quantity, or importance: *a major resource; a major poet.* PRINCIPAL refers to the most influential or foremost person or thing: *a principal stockholder; the principal reason.*

capricious, *adj.* wayward, arbitrary, whimsical, quirky, unreliable, fanciful, wanton, inconstant, changeable, impulsive, unpredictable, fickle, temperamental, mercurial, volatile, unstable, erratic, chimerical, eccentric.
—**Ant.** predictable, stable, steady.

captivate, *v.* charm, enthrall, enchant, fascinate, hypnotize, mesmerize, enrapture, beguile, bewitch, enamor.
—**Ant.** repel, repulse.

captivity, *n.* bondage, servitude, enslavement, slavery, thralldom, serfdom, subjugation, subjection; imprisonment, confinement, incarceration, detention, arrest.
—**Ant.** freedom.

capture, *v.* **1.** seize, take prisoner, catch, arrest, snare, apprehend, collar, nick, place behind bars, trap, impound, grab, nab; imprison, incarcerate. —*n.* **2.** arrest, seizure, apprehension; imprisonment, incarceration, detention, captivity.
—**Ant.** release.

care, *n.* **1.** worry, anxiety, concern, anguish, angst, distress, grief, suffering, misery, tribulation, woe. **2.** heed, caution, attention, vigilance, carefulness, meticulousness, punctiliousness, mindfulness, solicitude, circumspection, alertness, watchfulness. **3.** charge, responsibility, protection, custody, safekeeping, guardianship, supervision. —*v.* **4.** have concern *or* regard, be solicitous *or* anxious, worry, be troubled, fret, mind. **5.** like, be inclined *or* disposed *or* interested, fancy.

careen, *v.* sway, lurch, lean, heel over, swing, roll, rock, wobble, reel, weave, waver, tip, veer, swerve, keel over.

careful, *adj.* **1.** cautious, discreet, wary, circumspect, watchful, wakeful, vigilant, guarded, prudent. **2.** painstaking, meticulous, discerning, exact, thorough, scrupulous, conscientious, attentive, assiduous, sedulous, heedful, thoughtful.
—**Ant.** careless.
—**Syn. Study.** CAREFUL, CAUTIOUS, DISCREET, WARY imply a watchful guarding against something. CAREFUL implies guarding against mistakes or bad consequences by paying close attention to details and by being concerned or solicitous: *He was careful not to wake the baby.* CAUTIOUS implies a fear of some unfavorable situation and investigation before acting: *cautious about investments.* DISCREET implies being prudent in speech or action: *discreet inquiries about his credit rating.* WARY implies a vigilant lookout for a danger: *wary of polite strangers.*

caregiver, *n.* protector, keeper, guardian, caretaker, attendant, custodian, warden, nurse, matron, fiduciary, nanny, au pair, babysitter, healthcare worker *or* aide.

careless, *adj.* **1.** inattentive, incautious, forgetful, remiss, negligent, neglectful, casual, indifferent, irresponsible, imprudent, absent-minded, heedless, reckless, indiscreet, thoughtless, unconcerned. **2.** negligent, remiss, reckless, slapdash, rash. **3.** inaccurate, inexact, imprecise, wrong, error-ridden, sloppy.
—**Ant.** careful.

carnal, *adj.* **1.** worldly, mundane, earthly, unregenerate. **2.** sensual, animal, fleshly, bodily, physical, sexual. **3.** lustful, impure, gross, lecherous, lascivious, salacious, libidinous, concupiscent, lewd, lubricious, wanton, sexual, erotic, licentious, prurient.
—**Ant.** spiritual, moral, intellectual.
—**Syn. Study.** CARNAL, SENSUAL, ANIMAL all refer to the physical rather than the rational or spiritual nature of human beings. CARNAL, although it may refer to any bodily need or urge, most often refers to sexuality: *carnal knowledge; the carnal sin of gluttony.* SENSUAL most often describes the arousal or gratification of erotic urges: *sensual eyes; sensual delights.* ANIMAL may describe any physical appetite, but is sometimes used of sexual appetite: *animal greediness; animal lust.*

carriage, *n.* **1.** vehicle, cart, wagon, conveyance; (*variously*) dogcart, brougham, hansom, victoria, buckboard, carryall, shay, sulky, surrey. **2.** bearing, posture, comportment, manner, mien, deportment, behavior, conduct, demeanor.

carry, *v.* move, bear, transport, convey, haul, lug, drag, cart, tote, schlep; take, bring, transfer.

case, *n.* **1.** instance, example, event, happening, occasion, illustration, occurrence. **2.** state, circumstance, situation, condition, contingency; plight, predicament. **3.** patient, victim, invalid. **4.** dispute, action, suit, lawsuit, cause, process, trial. **5.** receptacle, box, container, chest; folder, envelope, sheath.

cast, *v.* **1.** throw, fling, hurl, deposit, propel, put, toss, sling, pitch. **2.** throw out, send forth, hurl, toss. **3.** set aside, throw aside, discard, reject, dismiss, disband. **4.** bestow, confer. **5.** mold, form, found. **6.** compute, calculate, reckon; forecast, foretell. —*n.* **7.** throw, fling, toss. **8.** appearance, form, shape, mien, demeanor. **9.** sort, kind, style. **10.** tendency, inclination, turn, bent, trend, air. **11.** tinge, tint, hue, shade, touch; dash, trace, hint, suggestion.

caste, *n.* rank, class, status, social level, social stratum, order, level, standing, place, station, position.

castle, *n.* **1.** fortress, citadel, stronghold. **2.** palace, chateau, mansion, palazzo, hall, manor.

casual, *adj.* **1.** unexpected, unforeseen, chance, accidental, serendipitous, unpremeditated, unintentional, fortuitous. **2.** careless, negligent, unconcerned, indifferent, nonchalant, offhand, apathetic, cool, uninterested, informal. **3.** easygoing, natural, easy, relaxed, offhand, happy-go-lucky, devil-may-care, laid-back.
—**Ant.** premeditated, deliberate, calculated; careful; regular, routine.

cataclysm, *n.* disaster, calamity, catastrophe, debacle, crash, collapse, convulsion, meltdown; flood, deluge, inundation.
—**Syn. Study.** See DISASTER.

catalog, *n.* list, roll, roster, register, record, inventory.

catastrophe, *n.* disaster, mishap, cataclysm, calamity, misfortune, mischance, bad luck, tragedy, accident, fiasco, failure.
—**Ant.** triumph, good luck.
—**Syn. Study.** See DISASTER.

catch, *v.* **1.** seize, capture, restrain, stop, intercept, snatch, arrest, apprehend, grab, get hold of, grip, grasp, take prisoner, nab, nick, collar, pinch. **2.** trap, snare, net, ensnare, entrap, bag, net, round up. **3.** surprise, discover, detect, take unawares, find. **4.** captivate, attract, draw, charm, enchant, fascinate, win, bewitch, seduce, entice, allure, enthrall. —*n.* **5.** capture, seizure, arrest, apprehension. **6.** fastener, clasp, pin, hook, clip, bolt.
—**Ant.** release, let go.

catchword, *n.* slogan, catchphrase, byword, password, shibboleth, motto, watchword, maxim, household word, tag line, battle cry, rallying cry.

cause, *n.* **1.** occasion, origin, source, root, agent, genesis, wellspring, prime mover, reason, ground, grounds, basis. **2.** purpose, object, aim, end. —*v.* **3.** bring about, effect, determine, produce, create, induce, generate, provoke, promote, originate, occasion, give rise to, result in, precipitate, engender.
—**Syn. Study.** See REASON.

caustic, *adj.* corrosive, cutting, scathing, stinging, slashing, mordant, acid, trenchant, sharp, ironic, satiric, sarcastic, sardonic, critical, harsh.
—**Ant.** bland, harmless, innocuous.

caution, *n.* **1.** prudence, discretion, circumspectness, watchfulness, heed, care, wariness, vigilance, discretion. **2.** warning, admonition, advice, caveat, notice. —*v.* **3.** warn, admonish, advise, enjoin, counsel, forewarn, (*informal*) tip off.
—**Ant.** carelessness, imprudence.
—**Syn. Study.** See WARN.

cautious, *adj.* prudent, careful, heedful, watchful, discreet, wary, vigilant, alert.
—**Ant.** careless, heedless, indiscreet.
—**Syn. Study.** See CAREFUL.

caveat, *n.* warning, caution, admonition, recommendation, suggestion, tipoff.

cavity, *n.* hollow, hole, void, pit, opening, space, gap, crater.

cease, *v.* stop, desist, stay; terminate, end, finish, leave off, halt, break off; discontinue.
—**Ant.** start, begin; continue, persist.

cede, *v.* yield, resign, surrender, relinquish, abandon, renounce, abdicate, give up; turn over, grant, transfer, convey, give, hand over.
—**Ant.** persist, maintain.

celebrate, *v.* **1.** commemorate, keep, honor, observe. **2.** proclaim, announce. **3.** praise, extol, laud, glorify, honor, applaud, exalt, eulogize, lionize, commend. **4.** solemnize, ritualize, sanctify, consecrate, hallow, dedicate. **5.** have *or* give *or* throw a party, party, revel, rejoice, make merry, entertain, paint the town red, whoop *or* live it up, kill the fatted calf, enjoy oneself, frolic, carouse, have a rave, cut loose, go on a spree, have a ball.

celebrated, *adj.* famous, renowned, well-known, distinguished, illustrious, eminent, famed, prominent, noted, noteworthy, renowned, acclaimed.
—**Ant.** obscure, unknown.
—**Syn. Study.** See FAMOUS.

celebrity, *n.* **1.** notable, big name, personage, star, superstar, luminary, VIP, dignitary, personality, toast of the town, name, somebody, nabob, big shot, biggie, megastar, hot shot, big enchilada. **2.** fame, renown, celebrityhood, stardom, superstardom, name, acclaim, acclamation, recognition, eminence, prominence, prestige, popularity, notability, distinction, illustriousness, reputation, repute, éclat; notoriety.
—**Ant.** nobody, nonentity, has-been, wannabe.

celestial, *adj.* heavenly, ethereal, empyreal, empyrean, elysian, spiritual, godly, sublime, immortal, supernatural, otherworldly, transcendental, unearthly, divine, paradisial, paradisaic, supernal.
—**Ant.** earthly, mundane, terrestrial.

censure, *n.* **1.** condemnation, reproof, disapproval, disapprobation, blaming, criticism, blame, reproach, reprehension, rebuke, slap on the wrist, reprimand, stricture, animadversion. —*v.* **2.** criticize, disapprove, condemn, find fault with. **3.** reprove, rebuke, reprimand, reprehend, chide, blame, reproach, upbraid.
—**Ant.** praise, commend.
—**Syn. Study.** See ABUSE.

center, *n.* middle, midst, heart, core, midpoint, focus, nucleus, focal point; pivot, hub, point, axis.
—**Ant.** brim, edge, periphery.

ceremony, *n.* rite, ritual, formality, observance, solemnity, service, celebration, consecration, sanctification, hallowing.
—**Ant.** informality.

certain, *adj.* **1.** confident, sure, assured, convinced, satisfied, indubitable, indisputable, unquestionable, undeniable, incontestable, irrefutable, unquestioned, incontrovertible, absolute, positive, plain, patent, obvious, clear. **2.** sure, inevitable, infallible, unfailing. **3.** fixed, agreed upon, settled, prescribed, determined, determinate, constant, stated, given. **4.** definite, particular, special, especial. **5.** unfailing, reliable, trustworthy, dependable, trusty.
—**Ant.** uncertain; unclear, unsure; unsettled; indefinite; fallible, unreliable.

certainty, *n.* **1.** unquestionableness, inevitability, certitude, assurance, confidence, conviction. **2.** fact, truth, reality, actuality.
—**Ant.** doubt, uncertainty.

challenge, *v.* **1.** question, dispute, defy, contest, object to, call into doubt *or* question, impugn; dare, provoke; confront. —*n.* **2.** question, dispute, doubt. **3.** dare, provocation, confrontation, defiance, ultimatum. **4.** trial, test, problem, demand, stimulation.

champion, *n.* **1.** winner, victor, hero. **2.** defender, protector, vindicator, backer, advocate, guardian, supporter. **3.** fighter, warrior. —*v.* **4.** defend, support, maintain, fight for, advocate, protect, guard, back, stand up for, sustain, uphold, espouse.
—**Ant.** loser; oppose.

chance, *n.* **1.** fortune, fate, luck, accident, fortuity, serendipity. **2.** possibility, predictability, odds, prospect, likelihood, contingency, probability. **3.** opportunity, opening, occasion, time, turn. **4.** risk, hazard, peril, danger, jeopardy. —*v.* **5.** happen, occur, befall, take place. —*adj.* **6.** casual, accidental, fortuitous, unexpected, unpremeditated, unforeseen, serendipitous, unplanned, incidental, unintentional, inadvertant.
—**Ant.** necessity, inevitability; surety.

change, *v.* **1.** alter, make different, turn, transmute, transform, vary, modify. **2.** exchange, substitute, convert, shift, replace; barter, trade, commute. —*n.* **3.** variation, alteration, modification, deviation, transformation, transmutation, mutation, conversion, transition. **4.** substitution, exchange. **5.** variety, novelty, innovation, vicissitude.
—**Ant.** remain, endure; immutability.
—**Syn. Study.** CHANGE, ALTER both mean to make a difference in the state or condition of a thing. To CHANGE is to make a material or radical difference or to substitute one thing for another of the same kind: *to change a lock; to change one's plans.* To ALTER is to make some partial change, as in appearance, but usu. to preserve the identity: *to alter a garment; to alter a contract.*

chaotic, *adj.* confused, upset, tumultuous, turbulent, disordered, unruly, disorderly, anarchic, scattered, disarrayed, higgledy-piggledy, jumbled, helter-skelter, topsy-turvy, noisy, clamorous, uproarious, wild, frenzied, hectic, in pandemonium, at sixes and sevens.

character, *n.* **1.** individual, personality, person, personage. **2.** feature, trait, characteristic, quality, distinction, attribute, nature, disposition, mien, cast, mark, idiosyncrasy, peculiarity, singularity. **3.** name, reputation, repute, standing, status. **4.** morality, integrity, respectability, rectitude, honesty, goodness, honor, courage. **5.** symbol, mark, letter, figure, emblem, sign, label, rune, hieroglyph.
—**Syn. Study.** CHARACTER, PERSONALITY refer to the sum of the characteristics possessed by a person. CHARACTER refers esp. to the moral qualities and ethical standards that make up the inner nature of a person: *a man of sterling character.* PERSONALITY refers particularly to outer characteristics, as wittiness or charm, that determine the impression that a person makes upon others: *a pleasing personality.* See also REPUTATION.

characteristic, *adj.* **1.** typical, distinctive, discrete, special, peculiar, singular, representative, emblematic, symbolic, idiosyncratic, symptomatic. —*n.* **2.** feature, quality, trait, peculiarity, mark, attribute, property, idiosyncrasy, earmark, quiddity.
—**Syn. Study.** See FEATURE.

charge, *v.* **1.** command, enjoin, exhort, order, urge, bid, require. **2.** blame, accuse, indict, arraign, impeach, inculpate, incriminate, involve, inform against, betray. **3.** attack, assault, set on. —*n.* **4.** duty, responsibility, commission, office, trust, employment. **5.** care, custody, superintendence, ward, management. **6.** command, injunction, exhortation, order, direction, mandate, instruction, precept. **7.** accusation, indictment, imputation, allegation, crimination, incrimination. **8.** price, fee, cost; tax, lien, expense, encumbrance, outlay, expenditure, liability, debt. **9.** onset, attack, onslaught, assault, encounter.

charismatic, *adj.* alluring, attractive, fascinating, hypnotic, mesmerising, magnetic, captivating, spellbinding, beguiling, glamorous, entrancing, riveting, bewitching, prepossessing, unforgettable, irresistable, charming, seductive, magical.

charitable, *adj.* **1.** generous, openhanded, liberal, philanthropic, giving, altruistic, public-spirited, munificent, unselfish, big hearted, magnaminous, unsparing, beneficent, benign, kind, benignant, benevolent, bountiful, lavish. **2.** understanding, forgiving, mercfiful, forbearing, well-disposed, kind, tolerant, good, indulgent, compassionate, humane, sympathetic, broadminded, liberal, lenient, considerate, mild, kindly.
—**Ant.** mean, stingy; narrow minded, inconsiderate.
—**Syn. Study.** See GENEROUS.

charm, *n.* **1.** attractiveness, allurement, fascination, enchantment, appeal, allure, magnetism, charisma, desirability, elegance, urbanity, grace, sophistication, refinement, culture; bewitchment, spell, witchery, magic, sorcery. **2.** trinket, bauble, jewelry; amulet, talisman, fetish. —*v.* **3.** enchant, fascinate, captivate, catch, entrance, enrapture, transport, delight, please; attract, allure, enamor, bewitch; influence, control, subdue.
—**Ant.** revulsion; disgust.

chary, *adj.* **1.** careful, wary, discreet, guarded, prudent, cautious, circumspect. **2.** shy, bashful, modest, reticent, coy, reserved, private, self-effacing. **3.** fastidious, choosy, particular, finicky, fussy, meticulous, punctilious. **4.** sparing, stingy, frugal, economical, stinting, parsimonious.
—**Ant.** careless, indiscreet, imprudent, unreserved, lavish.

chaste, *adj.* virtuous, pure, moral, decent, undefiled, modest, celibate, abstinent, stainless, wholesome, virgin, virginal, intact, faithful, continent; clean, elevated, unsullied; unaffected, simple, subdued, austere, restrained, unadorned, severe, neat, straight, honest.
—**Ant.** sinful, impure, immodest; unrefined, coarse, inelegant.

chasten, *v.* discipline, punish, chastise, restrain, subdue, humble, scold, chide, admonish, upbraid, correct, castigate.
—**Ant.** indulge, reward.

cheap, *adj.* **1.** inexpensive, low-priced, bargain, discounted, on sale, reasonable, economy, budget. **2.** paltry, common, mean, low, lowly, poor, inferior, base, shoddy, shabby, tawdry, seedy, sleazy, tacky, trashy, second-rate, worthless, chintzy, cheapjack. **3.** stingy, miserly, frugal, penny-pinching, niggardly, tight-fisted, cheeseparing, parsimonious.
—**Ant.** dear, expensive, costly; exceptional, extraordinary, elegant.
—**Syn. Study.** CHEAP, INEXPENSIVE agree in their suggestion of low cost. CHEAP now often suggests shoddiness, inferiority, showy imitation, unworthiness, and the like: *a cheap fabric.* INEXPENSIVE emphasizes lowness of price (although more expensive than CHEAP) and suggests that the value is fully equal to the cost: *an inexpensive dress.* It is often

used as an evasion for the more pejorative CHEAP.

cheat, *n.* **1.** fraud, swindle, deception, trick, imposture, wile, deceit, artifice, chicanery, stratagem, hoax, imposition, snare, trap, pitfall, catch. **2.** swindler, imposter, trickster, sharper, cheater, dodger, charlatan, fraud, fake, phony, mountebank, rogue, con man, knave. *—v.* **3.** deceive, trick, victimize, defraud, mislead, dupe, gudgeon, cog, gull, cozen, outwit, bamboozle, delude, hoodwink, beguile, inveigle, swindle, con; entrap, hoax, ensnare, fool, cajole; dissemble.

—Syn. Study. CHEAT, DECEIVE, TRICK, VICTIMIZE refer to the use of fraud or artifice to obtain an unfair advantage or gain. CHEAT usu. means to be dishonest in order to make a profit for oneself: *to cheat customers by shortchanging them.* DECEIVE suggests misleading someone by false words or actions: *He deceived his parents about his whereabouts.* TRICK means to mislead by a ruse or stratagem, often of a crafty or dishonorable kind: *I was tricked into signing the note.* VICTIMIZE means to make a victim of; it connotes a particularly contemptible act: *to victimize a blind person.*

check, *v.* **1.** stop, halt, delay, arrest. **2.** curb, restrain, block, limit, retard, hamper, impede, thwart, control, repress, chain, bridle, hinder, hobble, obstruct, curtail. **3.** investigate, verify, assess, test, measure, examine, compare, authenticate, confirm, substantiate, validate, corroborate, inspect, monitor, study, scrutinize. **4.** agree, coincide, jibe, tally, conform, fit, mesh, correspond. **5.** pause, stop. *—n.* **6.** restraint, curb, bridle, bit, hindrance, obstacle, obstruction, impediment, control, bar, barrier, restriction, damper, interference, deterrent, repression. **7.** rebuff, arrest, stoppage, cessation, repulse, halt. **8.** bill, reckoning, tariff, tab, charge; ticket, receipt, coupon, tag, stub.

—Ant. continue, advance, foster, support.

—Syn. Study. CHECK, CURB, RESTRAIN refer to putting a control on movement, progress, action, etc. CHECK implies arresting suddenly, halting or causing to halt by means of drastic action: *to check a movement toward reform.* CURB implies slowing or stopping forward motion: *to curb inflation; to curb a horse.* RESTRAIN implies the use of force to put under control or hold back: *to restrain one's enthusiasm; to restrain unruly spectators.* See also STOP.

cheer, *n.* **1.** encouragement, comfort, solace, consolation. **2.** gladness, gaiety, happiness, bouyancy, liveliness, elation, blitheness, levity, animation, joy, mirth, glee, merriment, cheerfulness. *—v.* **3.** gladden, enliven, inspirit, exhilarate, animate, encourage. **4.** shout, applaud, acclaim, salute.

—Ant. derision; misery; discourage, deride; boo, hiss.

cheerful, *adj.* **1.** cheery, gay, blithe, happy, lively, lighthearted, all smiles, ebullient, glad, exuberant, merry, spirited, sprightly, joyful, joyous, mirthful, buoyant, gleeful, sunny, jolly. **2.** pleasant, bright, gay, winsome, gladdening, cheery, cheering, inspiring, animating.

—Ant. miserable; unpleasant.

cherish, *v.* **1.** foster, harbor, entertain, humor, encourage, indulge. **2.** nurse, nurture, nourish, tend, cultivate, preserve, support, sustain, comfort. **3.** treasure, cling to, hold dear, prize, value.

—Ant. abandon, scorn, disdain.

—Syn. Study. CHERISH, FOSTER, HARBOR imply the giving of affection, care, or shelter. CHERISH suggests regarding or treating something or someone as an object of affection or value: *to cherish a friendship.* FOSTER implies sustaining and nourishing something with care, esp. in order to promote, increase, or strengthen it: *to foster a hope.* HARBOR usu. suggests sheltering someone or entertaining something undesirable: *to harbor a criminal; to harbor a grudge.*

chief, *n.* **1.** head, leader, ruler, chieftain, commander, principal, superior, supervisor, boss, manager, ringleader, kingpin, head honcho, number one, numero uno, big cheese. *—adj.* **2.** principal, most important, prime, first, supreme, leading, paramount, key, foremost, primary, main, superior, premier, outstanding, greatest, great, grand, cardinal, master; vital, essential.

—Ant. follower, disciple; unimportant, trivial, trifling; secondary.

—Syn. Study. See CAPITAL.

chiefly, *adv.* mostly, principally, mainly, especially, particularly, above all, most of all, primarily, predominantly, largely, by and large, on the whole, generally, in general, usually, as a rule, preeminently, eminently.

—Ant. last, lastly.

childish, *adj.* infantile, childlike, puerile, babyish, juvenile, immature, naive, jejune, inexperienced, adolescent, undeveloped, backward, retarded, young, tender; weak, silly, simple, ingenuous, guileless, trusting, sophomoric.

—Ant. adult, sophisticated.

—Syn. Study. CHILDISH, INFANTILE, CHILDLIKE refer to characteristics or qualities of childhood. CHILDISH refers to characteristics that are undesirable and unpleasant: *childish selfishness.* INFANTILE usu. carries an even stronger idea of disapproval or scorn: *infantile temper tantrums.* CHILDLIKE refers to those characteristics that are desirable or merely neutral: *childlike innocence.*

chill, *n.* **1.** cold, coldness, frigidity, sharpness, nippiness, nip in the air, cold snap, coolness, rawness, artic air, iciness, frost. **2.** shivering, ague, cold, flu, influenza, grippe, sniffles. **3.** coolness, iciness, aloofness, unfriendliness, hostility, chilliness. *—adj.* **4.** chilly, cold, cool, numbing, raw, penetrating, icy, frigid, wintery, frosty, arctic, polar, glacial. **5.** indifferent, unsympathetic, cold blooded, cold, unfriendly, hostile, aloof; depressing, bleak, discouraging, standoffish, apathetic. *—v.* **6.** cool, freeze, refrigerate, ice. **7.** dampen, dispirit, discourage, dishearten, depress, deject, distress.

—Ant. warm; friendly; heartening.

chivalrous, *adj.* courteous, gallant, noble, courtly, gracious, helpful, thoughtful, considerate, unselfish, attentive, generous, giving, magnanimous, greathearted, benevolent, altruistic, kindhearted, kindly, polite.

—Ant. ill-bred, rude, selfish, self-centered, ungenerous.

choice, *n.* **1.** alternative, option, selection, choosing, election, preference. *—adj.* **2.** worthy, excellent, superior, fine, select, rare, uncommon, valuable, precious.

—Syn. Study. CHOICE, ALTERNATIVE, OPTION suggest the power of choosing between things. CHOICE implies the opportunity to choose freely: *Her choice for dessert was ice cream.* ALTERNATIVE suggests a chance to choose only one of a limited number of possibilities: *I had the alternative of going to the party or staying home alone.* OPTION emphasizes the right or privilege of choosing: *He had the option of taking the prize money or a gift.*

choose, *v.* select, elect, prefer, pick, cull, decide, determine, judge, opt, settle on.

chop, *v.* cut, cut up, mince, hack, dice, cube, hash, hew, lop off, crop, sever, cleave, dissever, whack, disjoin, separate, sunder, subdivide, saw, snip, split, splinter, chip, rive, rend, break up, slash, slice into pieces, carve up, quarter, dissect, dismember, anatomize, disconnect, take apart, divide, atomize, chew up, butcher, fragment, mangle, mutilate, shred.

chronic, *adj.* **1.** inveterate, constant, habitual, confirmed, hardened, dyed in the wool. **2.** perpetual, continuous, continuing, unending, neverending, everlasting, long standing, lingering, lasting, long-lived.

—Ant. fleeting, temporary.

chuckle, *v., n.* laugh, giggle, titter, chortle, crow, snigger.

—Ant. cry, sob.

chutzpah, *n.* audacity, pluck, self-confidence, self-assertiveness, brashness, boldness, temerity, temerariousness, aggressiveness, effrontery, presumption, presumptuousness, brazenness, impudence, impertinence, insolence, nerve, cheek, gall, face, crust, brass.

—Ant. timidity, modesty, self-effacement.

circle, *n.* **1.** ring, periphery, circumference, perimeter. **2.** ring, circlet, crown. **3.** compass, area, sphere, province, field, region, bounds, circuit. **4.** cycle, period, series. **5.** club, coterie, set, clique, society, company, class, fraternity. **6.** sphere, orb, globe, ball. *—v.* **7.** surround, encircle, encompass, round, bound, include. **8.** orbit, circuit, revolve, circumnavigate, go around, tour.

—Syn. Study. CIRCLE, CLUB, COTERIE refer to restricted social groups. A CIRCLE is a little group; in the plural it often suggests a section of society interested in one mode of life, occupation, etc.: *a sewing circle; theatrical circles.* CLUB implies an organized association with fixed requirements for membership: *an athletic club.* COTERIE suggests a small and exclusive group intimately associated because of similar backgrounds and interests: *a literary coterie.*

circuit, *n.* **1.** course, tour, journey, circle, round, ambit, lap, revolution, orbit. **2.** circumference, perimeter, periphery, girth, border, edge, limit, ambit, margin, outline, confines, pale, bound, boundary, compass.

circuitous, *adj.* indirect, roundabout, circular, wandering, meandering, crooked, devious, deviant, tortuous, serpentine, twisting, vagrant, oblique, errant, circumambulatory, circumlocutory.

—Ant. straight, straightforward, blunt.

circumstance, *n.* **1.** event, happening, occurence, incident, episode, affair, occasion. **2.** situation, state, state of affairs, condition, case.

civil, *adj.* courteous, polite, courtly, gracious, complaisant, cordial, formal, respectful, deferential, obliging; affable, urbane, debonair, chivalrous, gallant, suave; refined, well-mannered, well-bred, civilized, proper, polished.

—Ant. uncivil, discourteous; rude; ill-mannered, unrefined.

—Syn. Study. CIVIL, COURTEOUS, POLITE imply avoidance of rudeness toward others. CIVIL suggests only minimal observance of social amenities: *a civil reply.* COURTEOUS implies respectful, dignified, sincere, and thoughtful consideration for others: *a courteous thank-you note.* POLITE implies habitual courtesy, arising from a consciousness of one's training and the demands of good manners: *a polite young man.*

claim, *v.* **1.** demand, require, ask, call for, challenge, seek, exact, insist, command, be entitled to. **2.** assert, declare, allege, state, affirm, contend, maintain, uphold. *—n.* **3.** demand, request, requirement, requisition, call. **4.** right, title, privilege, pretension.

clannish, *adj.* exclusive, exclusionary, exclusory, select, selective, restricted, restrictive, cliquish, cliquey, snobbish, snobby, elite, elect, ethnocentric.

—Ant. open, unrestricted, all-embracing.

clash, *v.* **1.** clang, crash, clap, dash, clatter, clank. **2.** fight, battle, differ, argue, dispute, quarrel, squabble, feud, contend, conflict, struggle, disagree, interfere. *—n.* **3.** conflict, opposition, disagreement, interference, struggle, engagement, fight, battle, difference, argument, dispute, altercation, quarrel, squabble, contradiction.

—Ant. harmony, agreement.

clasp, *n.* **1.** brooch, pin, clip, hook, fastening, catch, hasp. **2.** hold, old in one's arms, clutch, enfold, grip, embrace, hug, grasp. *—v.* **3.** clip, fasten secure, close, hold, hook, pin, clamp. **4.** grasp, grip, clutch. **5.** embrace, hug, clutch, grasp, fold, envelop.

class **1.** rank, level, grade, order, stratum; status, caste, pedigree, birth, descent, extraction, stock. **2.** group, category, division, classification, genre, domain, realm; kind, type, sort. **3.** breeding, refinement, taste, savoir-faire, prestige, elegance, distinction, discernment, merit, excellence, importance. *—v.* **4.** rank, grade, rate, order, categorize, classify, arrange, sort, group, type.

clean, *adj.* **1.** unsoiled, unstained, clear, unblemished, pure, flawless, spotless, unsullied, neat, immaculate. **2.** pure, purified, unmixed, unadulterated, clarified. **3.** unsullied, undefiled, moral, decent, virtuous, respectable, good, blameless, innocent, upright, honorable, chaste. **4.** neat, trim, clean-cut, simple, definite, smooth, even, straight, tidy. **5.** complete, perfect, entire, whole, unabated, unimpaired. *—adv.* **6.** cleanly, neatly. **7.** wholly, completely, perfectly, entirely, altogether, fully, thoroughly, in all respects, out and out. *—v.* **8.** scour, launder, neaten, tidy up, straighten up, scrub, sweep, brush, wipe, mop, dust, wash, rinse, lave, cleanse, shower, sponge, vacuum, polish, bathe, disinfect, sanitize, purify, clear; decontaminate.

—Ant. dirty, soiled, impure, contaminated; immoral.

clear, *adj.* **1.** unclouded, light, bright, pellucid, limpid, diaphanous, crystalline, transparent, luminous. **2.** bright, shining, lucent. **3.** perceptible, understood, distinct, intelligible, orotund, comprehensible, lucid, plain, perspicuous, conspicuous, obvious. **4.** distinct, evident, plain, obvious, apparent, manifest, palpable, patent, unmistakable, unequivocal, unambiguous, indisputable, undeniable, unquestionable. **5.** innocent, pure, not guilty, unsullied, irreproachable, unblemished, clean, unspotted, unadulterated, moral, undefiled, virtuous, immaculate, spotless. **6.** serene, calm, untroubled, fair, cloudless, sunny. **7.** unobstructed, open, free, unimpeded, unhindered, unhampered, unencumbered, unentangled. **8.** smooth, clean, even, regular, unblemished.

9. emptied, empty, free, rid. **10.** limitless, unlimited, unqualified, unequivocal, boundless, free, open. *—v.* **11.** clarify, purify, refine, clean, cleanse. **12.** acquit, absolve, exonerate, vindicate, excuse, justify. **13.** extricate, disentangle, disabuse, rid, disencumber, disengage. **14.** liberate, free, emancipate, set free, disenthrall, loose, unchain, unfetter, let go.
—Ant. cloudy, dim, obscure; indistinct, unclear; guilty, culpable; troubled, disturbed, perturbed, obstructed; limited, confined.

clearly, *adv.* definitely, distinctly, evidently, plainly, understandably, obviously, certainly, surely, assuredly, entirely, completely, totally, apparently, manifestly, positively, without doubt, unequivocally, unquestionably, incontestably, undoubtedly, indubitably, demonstrably, absolutely, utterly.
—Ant. confusedly, indefinitely; partly.

clever, *adj.* **1.** bright, quick, able, apt, smart, intelligent, expert, gifted, talented, ingenious, quick witted, perceptive, discerning, wise, sage, sagacious, original, resourceful, inventive, creative, sharp, imaginative, shrewd, cunning, artful, crafty, sly, foxy, wily. **2.** skillful, adroit, dextrous, nimble, agile, handy, deft, adept.
—Ant. dull, slow, dimwitted; clumsy, awkward, maladroit.

climb, *v.* **1.** mount, ascend, scale, surmount. **2.** rise, arise. *—n.* **3.** ascent, climbing, scaling, rise.
—Ant. descend; descent.

close, *v.* **1.** stop, obstruct, shut, block, bar, stop up, clog, choke. **2.** enclose, cover in, shut in. **3.** end, terminate, finish, conclude, cease, complete. **4.** terminate, conclude, cease, end. *—adj.* **5.** shut, tight, closed, fast, confined. **6.** enclosed, shut in. **7.** heavy, unventilated, muggy, oppressive, uncomfortable, dense, thick. **8.** secretive, reticent, taciturn, close-mouthed, silent, uncommunicative, incommunicative, reserved, withdrawn. **9.** parsimonious, stingy, tight, closefisted, penurious, niggardly, miserly, mean. **10.** compact, condensed, dense, thick, solid, compressed, firm. **11.** near, nearby, adjoining, adjacent, neighboring, immediate. **12.** intimate, confidential, attached, dear, devoted. **13.** strict, searching, minute, scrupulous, exact, exacting, accurate, precise, faithful, nice. **14.** intent, fixed, assiduous, intense, concentrated, earnest, constant, unremitting, relentless, unrelenting. *—n.* **15.** end, finish, completion, conclusion, termination, cessation, culmination.
—Ant. open.

clothes, *n.* clothing, attire, apparel, wear, ensemble, dress, garments, habit, costume, garb, vestments, habiliments, accouterments, outfit, rags, glad rags, wardrobe.

cloud, *n.* **1.** fog, haze, mist, vapor. *—v.* **2.** becloud, bedim, shadow, confuse, blut, befog, muddle, muddy, overshadow, obscure, shade.

cloudy, *adj.* **1.** overcast, shadowy, clouded, murky, lowering, gloomy, cloudy, dismal, depressing, sullen. **2.** obscure, indistinct, dim, blurred, blurry, unclear, befogged, muddled, confused, dark, turbid, muddy, opaque.
—Ant. clear; distinct.

club, *n.* **1.** stick, cudgel, bludgeon, blackjack, billy, bat, mace, truncheon, baton, staff. **2.** society, organization, association, circle, set, coterie, clique, fraternity, sorority, sodality, brotherhood, sisterhood, alliance, union, league, confederation, federation, order, group.
—Syn. Study. See CIRCLE.

clumsy, *adj.* **1.** awkward, unskillful, ungainly, gawky, gauche, lumbering, ungraceful, lubberly. **2.** unhandy, maladroit, unskillful, inexpert, bungling, ponderous, heavy, heavy handed, inept, bumbling, cloddish, uncoordinated, oafish, butterfingers, ham-handed, hamfisted, all thumbs.
—Ant. adroit, clever, dexterous.

coarse, *adj.* **1.** low-quality, second-rate, shoddy, tawdry, trashy, kitschy, common, inferior, faulty, crude, rude, rough. **2.** indelicate, unpolished, uncivil, impolite, gruff, bluff, rude, loutish, uncouth, unrefined, impolite, boorish, churlish. **3.** gross, broad, indecent, vulgar, crass, ribald, lewd, lascivious, amoral, immoral, dirty, improper, obscene, smutty, filthy, foul, offensive, scurrilous, foulmouthed.
—Ant. pure, refined; civil, civilized, cultivated; decent, decorous.

coast, *n.* shore, seashore, strand, beach, seaside, seacoast, littoral, coastline, seaboard.

coax, *v.* wheedle, cajole, beguile, inveigle, persuade, flatter, urge, charm, manipulate.
—Ant. force, bully; deter.

coherence, *n.* cohesion, union, connection, congruity, consistency, correspondence, harmony, harmoniousness, orderliness, organization, agreement, unity, rationality, logic.
—Ant. incoherence, disorder.

cold, *adj.* **1.** chilly, chill, cool, frigid, gelid, frozen, freezing. **2.** unemotional, unenthusiastic, passionless, apathetic, unresponsive, unsympathetic, unaffected, stoical, affectless, dispassionate, phlegmatic, unfeeling, unsusceptible, unimpressible, unimpressed, cool, sluggish, torpid, indifferent, cold blooded, unconcerned, heartless, unperturbed, imperturbable. **3.** polite, formal, standoffish, aloof, distant, unapproachable, stonyhearted, reserved, unresponsive, unfriendly, inimical, hostile. **4.** calm, deliberate, depressing, dispiriting, disheartening, uninspiring, spiritless, unaffecting, dull. **5.** bleak, raw, cutting, keen, bitter, biting, numbing, glacial, Siberian, nippy, nipping, arctic, polar, frosty, icy, wintry, chill, chilly. *—n.* **6.** chill, shivers, ague, sniffles, grippe, flu.
—Ant. warm, hot.

collect, *v.* gather, assemble, amass, accumulate, aggregate, scrape together, compile, pile up, heap up, get together, rack up, hoard.
—Ant. strew, broadcast, spread.
—Syn. Study. See GATHER.

collection, *n.* set, accumulation, mass, heap, pile, hoard, store, gathering, assemblage, assembly, compilation, aggregation.

color, *n.* **1.** hue, tint, shade, tone, cast, tinge, tincture, pigmentation; pigment, dye, stain, paint. *—v.* **2.** affect, influence, distort, falsify, taint, twist, warp, bias, slant, twist; misrepresent, disguise, mask, conceal. **3.** blush, redden, flush, turn red.

colorless, **1.** pale, pallid, white, wan, ashen, sallow, sickly, washed out, blanched, bleached, etiolated, haggard. **2.** lifeless, boring, bland, dull, drab, insipid, uninteresting, vacuous, vapid, tedious, spiritless, dry, dreary, namby-pamby, lackluster, uninspired, monotonous, humdrum, run-of-the-mill, jejune, wearisome, tiresome.
—Ant. flushed; exciting, colorful.

combat, *v.* **1.** fight, contend, battle, oppose, struggle, contest, war, clash, duel, spar, strive against, defy, wrestle with, resist, withstand. *—n.* **2.** fight, skirmish, contest, battle, struggle, fracas, fray, affray, melee, donnybrook, brawl, conflict, war, brush, affair, encounter, engagement, duel, warfare, strife; altercation, feud, quarrel, dispute, row.
—Ant. support, defend.

combination, *n.* **1.** conjunction, association, union, grouping, set, array, connection, coalescence, blending. **2.** composite, compound, mixture, amalgamation, amalgam, alloy, aggregate, blend, emulsion, mix. **3.** alliance, confederacy, federation, union, league, organization, cartel, bloc, trust, syndication, consortium, coalition, association, society, club; cartel, combine, monopoly; conspiracy, cabal.

combine, *v.* unite, join, conjoin, associate, coalesce, blend, mix, incorporate, involve, compound, amalgamate, unify, connect, link, band, ally, mingle, commingle, consolidate, fuse, synthesize, bind, bond, put together, relate.
—Ant. dissociate, separate.
—Syn. Study. See MIX.

comfort, *v.* **1.** console, soothe, relieve, ease, cheer, pacify, calm, cheer, hearten, encourage, reassure, assuage, solace, gladden, refresh. *—n.* **2.** relief, consolation, solace, encouragement. **3.** luxury, ease, abundance, opulence, plenty; security.
—Ant. agitate, discommode, incommode; discomfort, discouragement.
—Syn. Study. COMFORT, CONSOLE, SOOTHE imply assuaging sorrow, worry, discomfort, or pain. COMFORT means to lessen someone's grief or distress by giving strength and hope and restoring a cheerful outlook: *to comfort a despairing friend.* CONSOLE, a more formal word, means to make grief or distress seem lighter by means of kindness and thoughtful attentions: *to console a bereaved parent.* SOOTHE means to pacify or calm: *to soothe a crying child.*

comical, *adj.* amusing, humorous, funny, comic, laugh-provoking, hilarious, mirthful, sidesplitting, jocular, silly, droll, risible, playful, clownish, ludic; laughable, ridiculous, ludicrous, absurd, foolish.
—Syn. Study. See AMUSING.

command, *v.* **1.** order, direct, bid, demand, charge, instruct, enjoin, require. **2.** govern, control, oversee, manage, rule, lead, preside over; dominate, overlook. **3.** exact, compel, secure, demand, require, claim. *—n.* **4.** order, direction, bidding, injunction, charge, mandate, behest, commandment, requisition, requirement, instruction, dictum. **5.** control, mastery, disposal, ascendancy, rule, sway, superintendence, power, management, domination.
—Ant. obey.
—Syn. Study. See DIRECT.

commence, *v.* begin, open, start, initiate, launch, establish, originate, inaugurate, enter upon *or* into.
—Ant. end, finish, terminate.
—Syn. Study. See BEGIN.

commendation, *n.* **1.** recommendation, praise, approval, approbation, applause; medal. **2.** eulogy, encomium, panegyric, praise.
—Ant. censure, blame.

comment, *n.* **1.** explanation, elucidation, expansion, criticism, critique, opinion, remark, view, reaction, observation, clarification, note, addendum, annotation, exposition, commentary. **2.** remark, observation, criticism. *—v.* **3.** remark, explain, annotate, criticize.

commerce, *n.* marketing, merchandising, interchange, traffic, trade, dealing, exchange, business, e-commerce, e-business, e-tailing.

common, *adj.* **1.** mutual, reciprocal, shared, joint. **2.** public, communal, community, general, collective, nonprivate, universal. **3.** widespread, general, ordinary, universal, prevalent, popular. **4.** familiar, usual, customary, frequent, habitual, run-of-the mill, stock, regular, conventional, standard, garden-variety, workaday, average, everyday. **5.** hackneyed, trite, stale, commonplace, overused, tired, banal, stereotyped, cliché. **6.** mean, low, base, mediocre, inferior. **7.** ordinary, vulgar, coarse, undistinguished, illbred, low-class, plebeian, unrefined.
—Ant. exceptional, singular, extraordinary, separate; unfamiliar, strange.
—Syn. Study. COMMON, ORDINARY, VULGAR refer, often with derogatory connotations, to what is usual or most often experienced. COMMON applies to what is widespread or unexceptional; it often suggests inferiority or coarseness: *common servants; common cloth.* ORDINARY refers to what is to be expected in the usual order of things; it suggests being average or below average: *a high price for something of such ordinary quality.* VULGAR means belonging to the people or characteristic of common people; it suggests low taste, coarseness, or ill breeding: *vulgar manners; vulgar speech.* See also GENERAL.

commotion, *n.* **1.** tumult, disturbance, perturbation, agitation, disorder, bustle, ado, turmoil, turbulence, riot, violence. **2.** sedition, insurrection, uprising, revolution.
—Ant. peace, calm, serenity.

communicate, *v.* **1.** impart, convey, transfer, transmit; give, bestow. **2.** divulge, announce, declare, disclose, reveal, make known, tell, spread, promulgate, publicize, broadcast, air.
—Ant. withhold, conceal.

community, *n.* **1.** hamlet, town, village, city. **2.** public, commonwealth, society. **3.** agreement, identity, similarity, likeness. *—adj.* **4.** common, joint, cooperative.

compact, *adj.* **1.** dense, solid, firm, tightly packed, condensed. **2.** concise, pithy, terse, laconic, short, sententious, succinct, brief, pointed, meaningful. *—v.* **3.** condense, consolidate, compress. **4.** stabilize, solidify. *—n.* **5.** covenant, pact, contract, treaty, agreement, bargain, entente, arrangement, convention, concordat.
—Ant. diverse, dispersed.
—Syn. Study. See AGREEMENT.

companion, *n.* **1.** associate, comrade, confederate, partner, fellow, mate, colleague, confrère, pal, buddy, intimate. **2.** assistant; nurse, governess, escort, chaperone, attendant, duenna.
—Syn. Study. See ACQUAINTANCE.

company, *n.* **1.** group, band, party, troop, assemblage, body, unit. **2.** companionship, fellowship, association, society. **3.** assembly, throng, group, ensemble, troop, flock, gathering, concourse, crowd, circle, set, coterie, retinue, entourage, followers, congregation. **4.** firm, partnership, corporation, concern, house, syndicate, association, business, establishment, enterprise, institution, dot-com.

compare, *v.* **1.** liken, contrast, associate, make an analogy with, refer, analogize. **2.** resemble, equal, correspond, match, parallel, approximate, rival, compete, be a match for, be on par with, vie with. **3.**

contrast, measure against, weigh, juxtapose, relate, correlate.

comparison, *n.* contrast, juxtaposition, balance, weighing; match, similarity, resemblance, likeness, relationship, commensurability, kinship.

compartment, *n.* division, section, apartment, cabin, roomette, room, berth, slot, cubby.

compassion, *n.* sorrow, pity, sympathy, feeling, mercy, commiseration, kindness, kindliness, tenderness, heart, tenderheartedness, clemency, empathy, solicitousness, solicitude, caring, consideration, concern, fellow feeling.
—**Ant.** mercilessness, indifference.
—**Syn. Study.** See SYMPATHY.

compassionate, *adj.* pitying, sympathetic, tender, kind, merciful, tenderhearted, kindly, clement, gracious, benignant, gentle, empathetic, understanding, caring, solicitous, comforting, consoling, supportive, responsive, considerate.
—**Ant.** merciless, pitiless, harsh, cruel, mean.

compel, *v.* **1.** impel, force, drive, coerce, constrain, oblige, commit, motivate, necessitate. **2.** subdue, subject, bend, bow, overpower.
—**Ant.** restrain.
—**Syn. Study.** COMPEL, IMPEL agree in the idea of forcing someone to be or do something. COMPEL implies an external force; it may be a persuasive urging from another person or a constraining reason or circumstance: *Bad health compelled him to resign.* IMPEL suggests an internal motivation deriving either from a moral constraint or personal feeling: *Guilt impelled him to offer money.*

compensate, *v.* **1.** counterbalance, counterpoise, offset, equalize, neutralize, square, even up, countervail, make up for. **2.** remunerate, reward, pay, recompense, reimburse. **3.** atone, make amends, expiate.

compensation, *n.* **1.** recompense, remuneration, payment, amends, reparation, indemnity, reward. **2.** atonement, requital, satisfaction, indemnification.

compete, *v.* contend, contest, rival, vie, emulate, oppose, dispute, conflict, fight, battle, clash, strive, cope, struggle.
—**Ant.** support.
—**Syn. Study.** COMPETE, CONTEND, CONTEST mean to strive or struggle. COMPETE emphasizes a sense of rivalry and of striving to do one's best: *to compete for a prize.* CONTEND suggests striving in opposition or debate as well as competition: *to contend against obstacles; to contend about minor details.* CONTEST implies struggling to gain or hold something in a formal competition or battle: *to contest with the incumbent for the nomination.*

competent, *adj.* fitting, suitable, sufficient, convenient, satisfactory, acceptable, O.K., all right, adequate; qualified, fit, apt, capable, proficient.
—**Ant.** incompetent, inapt.

competitor, *n.* opponent, contestant, rival, antagonist, foe, enemy, competition, opposition, adversary, contender.
—**Ant.** ally, friend.

complain, *v.* grumble, whine, growl, murmur, mutter, moan, wail, lament, bemoan, groan, grouse, carp, whimper, cry, gripe, squawk, kick, beef.
—**Syn. Study.** COMPLAIN, GRUMBLE, WHINE are terms for expressing dissatisfaction or discomfort. To COMPLAIN is to protest against or lament a condition or wrong: *to complain about high prices.* To GRUMBLE is to

utter surly, ill-natured complaints half to oneself: *to grumble about the service.* To WHINE is to complain in a meanspirited, objectionable way, using a nasal tone; it often suggests persistence: *to whine like a spoiled child.*

complement, *v.* **1.** complete, supplement, add to, round out, perfect, flesh out, top off, enhance. —*n.* **2.** supplement, completion, perfection, consummation, finishing touch.
—**Syn. Study.** COMPLEMENT, SUPPLEMENT both mean to make additions to something; a lack or deficiency is implied. To COMPLEMENT means to complete or perfect a whole; it often refers to putting together two things, each of which supplies what is lacking in the other: *Statements from different points of view may complement each other.* To SUPPLEMENT is to add something in order to enhance, extend, or improve a whole: *Some additional remarks supplemented the sales presentation.*

complete, *adj.* **1.** entire, intact, whole, full, unbroken, unimpaired, undivided, one, perfect, developed, unabated, undiminished, fulfilled. **2.** finished, ended, concluded, consummated, done, consummate, perfect, thorough; through-and-through, dyed-in-the-wool, rank, total, unqualified, unmitigated. —*v.* **3.** finish, end, conclude, consummate, perfect, accomplish, do, fulfill, achieve, effect, terminate, close, wrap up.
—**Ant.** incomplete; unfinished; begin, commence, initiate.
—**Syn. Study.** COMPLETE, ENTIRE, INTACT suggest that there is no lack or defect, nor has any part been removed. COMPLETE implies that a unit has all its parts, fully developed or perfected; it may also mean that a process or purpose has been carried to fulfillment: *a complete explanation; a complete assignment.* ENTIRE describes something having all its elements in an unbroken unity: *an entire book.* INTACT implies that something has remained in its original condition, complete and unimpaired: *a package delivered intact.*

complex, *adj.* **1.** compound, composite, complicated, mixed, mingled. **2.** involved, complicated, intricate, perplexing, tangled. —*n.* **3.** net, network, complication, web, tangle.
—**Ant.** simple; simplex.

compliment, *n.* **1.** praise, commendation, admiration, tribute, honor, eulogy, encomium, panegyric. **2.** regard, respect, civility; flattery. —*v.* **3.** commend, praise, honor, flatter, pay homage to *or* tribute to, laud. **4.** congratulate, felicitate.
—**Ant.** insult, injury; decry, disparage.

comply, *v.* acquiesce, obey, yield, conform, consent, assent, agree, accede, concede, concur, submit.
—**Ant.** refuse.

composed, *adj.* calm, tranquil, serene, undisturbed, collected, peaceful, cool, placid, pacific, unruffled, sedate, unperturbed, self-possessed, controlled, imperturbable, quiet, cool, unflappable, relaxed.
—**Ant.** upset, perturbed, disturbed, disquieted.
—**Syn. Study.** See CALM.

composure, *n.* serenity, calm, calmness, tranquility, equability, peacefulness, quiet, coolness, equanimity, self-possession.
—**Ant.** agitation.

comprehend, *v.* **1.** understand, conceive, know, grasp, see, discern, imagine, perceive, apprehend, realize, fathom, absorb, assimilate, appreciate. **2.** include, comprise, embrace,

take in, embody, contain.
—**Syn. Study.** See KNOW, INCLUDE.

comprehensive, *adj.* exhaustive, thorough, full, inclusive, broad, wide, large, extensive, sweeping, encyclopedic.
—**Ant.** limited.

comprise, *v.* include, comprehend, contain, embrace, embody; consist *or* be composed of.
—**Ant.** exclude.
—**Syn. Study.** See INCLUDE.

compulsory, *adj.* **1.** compelling, coercive, constraining. **2.** compelled, forced, obligatory, arbitrary, binding, necessary, unavoidable, inescapable, ineluctable.
—**Ant.** free, unrestrained, unrestricted.

compute, *v.* reckon, calculate, estimate, count, figure, determine, ascertain.

comrade, *n.* associate, companion, intimate, friend, fellow, partner, mate, colleague, confrere, cohort, compeer, crony, ally, sidekick, chum, buddy, pal, coworker, brother, bro, homeboy, homey.

conceal, *v.* **1.** hide, secrete, cover, put away, bury, screen, camouflage. **2.** keep secret, hide, disguise, dissemble.
—**Ant.** reveal.
—**Syn. Study.** See HIDE.

conceit, *n.* **1.** arrogance, hubris, cockiness, narcissism, pride, vainglory, self-esteem, vanity, amourpropre, egotism, complacency. **2.** fancy, imagination, whim, notion, vagary; thought, idea, belief, conception; metaphor, trope, figure, theme, image.
—**Ant.** humility, modesty.
—**Syn. Study.** See PRIDE.

conceited, *adj.* vain, proud, egotistical, self-important, self-centered, egocentric, self-satisfied, smug, complacent, self-sufficient, swell-headed, narcissistic, immodest, full of oneself, cocky, cocksure, snotty, arrogant, preening, in love with oneself, vainglorious, inflated, blind to one's own faults, stuck on oneself, stuck-up, supercilious, haughty, high and mighty, smug, superior.
—**Ant.** humble, modest, shy, retiring.

conceive, *v.* **1.** imagine, speculate, perceive, see, understand, realize, comprehend, envision, conjure up, hypothesize, postulate, posit, suppose, create, ideate, think. **2.** understand, apprehend, comprehend.

concentrate, *v.* **1.** focus, direct, center, consolidate. **2.** intensify, purify, clarify, reduce to an essence, reduce, condense, boil down, distill. **3.** think, focus one's thoughts, apply oneself.
—**Ant.** dissipate, disperse.

concern, *v.* **1.** affect, touch, interest, relate to, engage, involve, include. **2.** disquiet, trouble, disturb, worry, bother, perturb, unsettle, upset. —*n.* **3.** business, affair, problem, involvement, responsibility, interest, matter. **4.** care, worry, solicitude, anxiety, burden, responsibility. **5.** relation, bearing, appropriateness, consequence. **6.** firm, company, business, establishment, enterprise, organization, corporation, partnership, house.
—**Ant.** exclude; calm; unconcern, indifference.
—**Syn. Study.** CONCERN, CARE, WORRY connote an uneasy and burdened state of mind. CONCERN implies an anxious sense of interest in or responsibility for something: *concern over a friend's misfortune.* CARE suggests a heaviness of spirit caused by dread, or by the constant pressure of burdensome demands: *Poverty weighed them down with care.*

WORRY is a state of agitated uneasiness and restless apprehension: *distracted by worry over investments.*

conciseness, *n.* brevity, laconicism, summary, terseness, pithiness, directness, succinctness, cogency, compression, sententiousness, compactness, trenchancy.
—**Ant.** diversity.
—**Syn. Study.** See BREVITY.

conclusion, *n.* **1.** end, close, termination, finish, completion, ending, finale. **2.** summing up, summation. **3.** result, issue, outcome, aftermath, denouement. **4.** settlement, arrangement, wind-up. **5.** decision, judgment, determination. **6.** deduction, inference.
—**Ant.** beginning, commencement.

concur, *v.* **1.** agree, consent, coincide, harmonize. **2.** cooperate, combine, help, conspire, contribute.
—**Ant.** disagree.

condemn, *v.* **1.** blame, censure, disapprove, denounce, disparage, rebuke, scold, reprimand, upbraid, reprove, reproach, sit in judgment, judge, criticize. **2.** doom, find guilty, sentence, damn, convict.
—**Ant.** liberate, release, exonerate.

condense, *v.* compress, concentrate, consolidate, contract; abridge, epitomize, digest, shorten, abbreviate, abstract, reduce, diminish, curtail.
—**Ant.** expand.

condescend, *v.* deign, stoop, descend, humble *or* demean *or* degrade oneself, lower oneself, show noblesse oblige, come down off one's high horse.

condition, *n.* **1.** state, case, situation, circumstance, conjuncture, circumstances. **2.** requisite, prerequisite, requirement, contingency, consideration, proviso, provision, stipulation, sine qua non.

conduct, *n.* **1.** behavior, demeanor, action, actions, deportment, comportment, attitude, posture, bearing, carriage, mien, manners. **2.** direction, management, execution, guidance, leadership, administration, supervision, control, regulation, government. —*v.* **3.** behave, deport, act, bear, comport, acquit. **4.** direct, manage, carry on, supervise, regulate, administrate, administer, execute, guide, lead. **5.** lead, guide, escort, convoy, usher.

confederation, *n.* alliance, confederacy, league, federation, union, unity, society, state, unified group, association, combine, combination, coalition.
—**Syn. Study.** See ALLIANCE.

confer, *v.* **1.** bestow, give, donate, grant, award, present, vouchsafe, allow, promise. **2.** consult together, discuss, deliberate, discourse, parley, converse, advise, talk, meet, come to a decision.
—**Syn. Study.** See CONSULT. See also GIVE.

conference, *n.* meeting, interview, parley, colloquy, convention, consultation, congress, council, seminar, forum, colloquium, symposium, gathering, assembly.
—**Syn. Study.** See CONVENTION.

confess, *v.* acknowledge, avow, own, admit, disclose, divulge, tell the truth, make a confession, confide in, spill one's guts, testify, share one's secrets, accept responsibility, unburden oneself, reveal, come clean, grant, concede; declare, aver, confirm.
—**Syn. Study.** See ACKNOWLEDGE.

confidence, *n.* **1.** trust, belief, faith, reliance, dependence. **2.** assurance, self-reliance, boldness, intrepidity, self-confidence, courage, poise, aplomb, conviction, coolness.
—**Ant.** distrust, mistrust; modesty.

—**Syn. Study.** CONFIDENCE, ASSURANCE both imply a faith in oneself. CONFIDENCE usually implies a firm belief in oneself without a display of arrogance or conceit: *His friends admired his confidence at the party.* ASSURANCE implies even more sureness of one's own abilities, often to the point of offensive boastfulness: *She spoke with assurance but lacked the qualifications for the job.*

confident, *adj.* sure, bold, believing, assured, self-assured, secure, certain, positive, convinced; brave, intrepid, dauntless, cocksure, fearless.
—**Ant.** shy, modest, diffident.

confidential, *adj.* **1.** secret, restricted, private, classified, intimate, hush-hush. **2.** familiar, trusted, trusty, trustworthy, faithful, honorable, honest.
—**Syn. Study.** See FAMILIAR.

confine, *v.* **1.** enclose, bound, circumscribe, circle, encircle, limit, bind, restrict. **2.** immure, imprison, incarcerate, lock up, pen, jail, shut up, coop up. —*n.* **3.** (*usually plural*) bounds, boundary, perimeter, periphery, limits; frontiers, borders.

confirm, *v.* **1.** make certain *or* sure, assure, corroborate, verify, substantiate, authenticate. **2.** make valid *or* binding, ratify, sanction, approve, validate, bind. **3.** make firm, strengthen, settle, establish, fix, assure.

conflict, *v.* **1.** collide, clash, antagonize, oppose, vary with, interfere. **2.** contend, fight, combat, battle. —*n.* **3.** battle, struggle, encounter, contest, collision, fight, fray, war, combat, engagement, fracas, brawl, donnybrook, siege, strife; contention, controversy, opposition, variance, dispute, argument, wrangle, altercation, disagreement, feud, quarrel, row, squabble, tiff, spat, dust-up. **4.** interference, discord, disunity, disharmony, inconsistency, antagonism, clash.
—**Ant.** harmony, peace, friendliness.

conform, *v.* **1.** comply, yield, agree, assent, harmonize. **2.** tally, match, agree, correspond, square. **3.** adapt, adjust, accommodate.
—**Ant.** disagree, dissent.

confuse, *v.* **1.** jumble, disorder, disarrange, disturb, disarray. **2.** confound, mix, mix up, intermingle, mingle. **3.** perplex, mystify, nonplus, bewilder, astonish, surprise, disarm, shock, disconcert, embarrass, disturb. **4.** disconcert, abash, mortify, shame, confound, throw for a loop.
—**Ant.** enlighten.

confusion, *n.* **1.** perplexity, embarrassment, surprise, astonishment, shock, bewilderment, distraction. **2.** disorder, disarray, disarrangement, jumble, mess, turmoil, chaos, tumult, furor, commotion, ferment, agitation, stir. **3.** embarrassment, abashment, shamefacedness, shame, mortification.
—**Ant.** enlightenment; clarity.

congenial, *adj.* sympathetic, kindred, similar, friendly, amiable, amicable, *gemutleicheit*, propitious, favorable, genial; agreeable, pleasing, pleasant, complaisant, suited, adapted, well-suited, suitable, apt, proper.
—**Ant.** unsympathetic, disagreeable; unsuitable.

congress, *n.* meeting, assembly, conference, council, convention.

conjecture, *n.* **1.** hypothesis, theory, guess, surmise, opinion, supposition, inference, deduction. —*v.* **2.** conclude, suppose, assume, presume, suspect, surmise, hypothesize, theorize, guess.
—**Ant.** determine, ascertain.
—**Syn. Study.** See GUESS.

connect, *v.* join, unite, link, conjoin, couple, associate, network, affiliate, relate, tie, bind, attach, combine; cohere.
—**Ant.** disconnect, disjoin.
—**Syn. Study.** See JOIN.

connection, *n.* **1.** junction, conjunction, union, joining, association, alliance, dependence, interdependence. **2.** link, yoke, connective, bond, tie, coupling. **3.** association, relationship, affiliation, affinity. **4.** circle, set, coterie, acquaintanceship, network. **5.** relation, family member, relative, kinswoman, kinsman; kin, kith.
—**Ant.** disjunction, dissociation.

conquer, *v.* **1.** win, gain, be victorious, triumph. **2.** overcome, subdue, vanquish, overpower, overthrow, subjugate, defeat, master, subject, beat, rout, overrun, quash, gain the upper hand, crush, reduce. **3.** surmount, overcome, overwhelm.
—**Ant.** surrender, submit, give up, yield.
—**Syn. Study.** See DEFEAT.

conquest, *n.* **1.** captivation, seduction, enchantment. **2.** vanquishment, victory, triumph, win. **3.** subjugation, overthrow, defeat, mastery, subjection, rout.
—**Ant.** surrender.
—**Syn. Study.** See VICTORY.

conscientious, *adj.* just, upright, honest, principled, fair, moral, ethical, righteous, right-minded, upright, honorable, straightforward, incorruptible, faithful; careful, particular, painstaking, scrupulous, assiduous, sedulous, diligent, persevering, meticulous, punctilious, rigorus, thorough, attentive, serious, exacting, demanding; devoted, dedicated.
—**Ant.** dishonest, corrupt, unscrupulous.
—**Syn. Study.** See PAINSTAKING.

conscious, *adj.* **1.** aware, cognizant, awake, sentient, alert, knowing, percipient, intelligent. **2.** sensible, sensitive, felt; rational, reasoning. **3.** deliberate, intentional, purposeful, willful, studied.
—**Ant.** unconscious.
—**Syn. Study.** CONSCIOUS, AWARE, COGNIZANT refer to a realization or recognition of something about oneself or one's surroundings. CONSCIOUS usually implies sensing or feeling certain facts, truths, conditions, etc.: *to be conscious of an extreme weariness; to be conscious of one's own inadequacy.* AWARE implies being mentally awake to something on a sensory level or through observation: *aware of the odor of tobacco; aware of gossip.* COGNIZANT, a more formal term, usually implies having knowledge about some object or fact through reasoning or through outside sources of information: *to be cognizant of the drawbacks of a plan.*

consecrate, *v.* **1.** sanctify, hallow, venerate, elevate. **2.** devote, dedicate.
—**Ant.** desecrate.
—**Syn. Study.** See DEVOTE.

consecutive, *adj.* successive, continuous, regular, uninterrupted, one after another, succeeding, following.
—**Ant.** alternate, random.

consent, *v.* **1.** agree, assent, permit, allow, let, concur, yield, give in, submit, cede, concede, comply, accede, acquiesce. —*n.* **2.** assent, acquiescence, permission, compliance, concurrence, agreement. **3.** accord, concord, agreement, consensus.
—**Ant.** refuse, disagree; dissent.

consequence, *n.* **1.** effect, result, outcome, issue, upshot, sequel, aftermath, denouncement, event, end. **2.** importance, significance, moment, weight, concern, interest. **3.** distinction, importance, singularity, weight.
—**Syn. Study.** See EFFECT. See also IMPORTANCE.

conservative, *n.* **1.** reactionary, right-winger, rightist, tory, fundamentalist, old fogey, traditionalist, conformist, Neanderthal. —*adj.* **2.** reactionary, right, nonprogressive, tory, right-wing; unprogressive, backward, orthodox, traditional, hidebound, conventional, standard, fundamentalist, dyed-in-the-wool; prudent, stable, staid, sober, old-world, cautious, temperate, old-fashioned, sober-sided.

consider, *v.* **1.** contemplate, meditate, reflect, ruminate, ponder, muse on, brood over, deliberate, weigh, revolve, study, think about. **2.** think, suppose, assume, presume. **3.** regard, respect, honor.
—**Ant.** ignore.
—**Syn. Study.** See STUDY.

considerate, *adj.* thoughtful, kind, charitable, patient, concerned, helpful, friendly, neighborly, gracious, obliging, accommodating, generous, unselfish, sympathetic, compassionate, solicitous, well-disposed, respectful, civil, polite, well-bred, chivalrous, genteel.
—**Ant.** inconsiderate.

consideration, *n.* **1.** thought, meditation, reflection, cogitation, study, examination, rumination, deliberation, contemplation, attention, advisement, regard. **2.** recompense, payment, remuneration, fee, reward, honorarium, emolument, tip, gratuity, compensation, pay. **3.** thoughtfulness, sympathy, solicitude, respect, caring, regard, attentiveness, kindness, kindliness, patience, concern. **4.** importance, consequence, weight, significance, moment, interest.

consistent, *adj.* **1.** agreeing, concordant, compatible, congruous, consonant, harmonious, suitable, apt, conformable, conforming. **2.** constant, faithful, assiduous, unwavering, stable, devoted, perseverant, sedulous, immutable, persistent.
—**Ant.** inconsistent.

consolation, *n.* comfort, solace, relief, encouragement, reward.
—**Ant.** discomfort, discouragement.

console, *v.* comfort, solace, cheer, encourage, soothe, relieve, calm.
—**Ant.** aggravate, agitate, disturb.
—**Syn. Study.** See COMFORT.

consonant, *adj.* in agreement, concordant, consistent, harmonious, compatible, congruous, conformant, suitable, fitting, predictable.
—**Ant.** discordant, inconsistent.

conspicuous, *adj.* **1.** visible, manifest, noticeable, clear, marked, salient, discernible, perceptible, plain, open, apparent, ostentatious, showy, evident, public. **2.** prominent, outstanding, obvious, striking, noteworthy, attractive, eminent, distinguished, noted, celebrated, illustrious, notorious, renowned, well-known.
—**Ant.** unclear, imperceptible; undistinguished, trifling.

conspire, *v.* **1.** plot, intrigue, cabal, contrive, devise. **2.** combine, concur, cooperate, agree.

constancy, *n.* firmness, fortitude, resolution, determination, inflexibility, decision, tenacity, steadfastness, faithfulness, fidelity, fealty, devotion, loyalty; regularity, stability, immutability, uniformity, permanence, sameness.
—**Ant.** randomness, faithlessness, irregularity, instability.

constant, *adj.* **1.** invariable, uniform, stable, unchanging, fixed, immutable, invariable, unvarying, permanent. **2.** perpetual, unremitting, uninterrupted, continual, 24/7, recurrent, assiduous, unwavering, unfailing, persistent, persevering, determined. **3.** steadfast, faithful, loyal, dependable, staunch, true, tried and true, true-blue, trusty, devoted, steady, resolute, firm, unshaking, unshakable, unwavering, unswerving, determined.
—**Ant.** inconstant, variable, random, unstable, changeable; sporadic; unsteady, wavering.
—**Syn. Study.** See FAITHFUL.

consternation, *n.* amazement, dread, dismay, bewilderment, awe, alarm, terror, fear, panic, fright, horror.
—**Ant.** composure, equanimity.

constrain, *v.* **1.** force, compel, oblige, coerce. **2.** confine, check, bind, restrain, curb.
—**Ant.** liberate, free.

constrict, *v.* compress, contract, shrink, cramp, squeeze, bind, tighten.
—**Ant.** unbind, untie.

construct, *v.* build, frame, form, devise, erect, make, fabricate, raise, assemble, fashion, shape, forge, invent, put together.
—**Ant.** raze.

consult, *v.* confer, deliberate, discuss with, interview, seek the opinion of, take the advice of, meet with, counsel, converse, come to a mutual decision, offer advice, advise, talk over with, question, look up.
—**Syn. Study.** CONSULT, CONFER imply talking over a situation or a subject with someone. To CONSULT is to seek advice, opinions, or guidance from a presumably qualified person or source: *to consult with a financial analyst.* To CONFER is to exchange views, ideas, or information in a discussion: *The partners conferred about the decline in sales.*

consume, *v.* **1.** destroy, expend, use up, use, exhaust, spend, waste, deplete, drain, dissipate, squander, eat up, devour. **2.** absorb, engross, occupy one's attention, obsess, preoccupy, distract, keep one busy.

consummate, *v.* **1.** complete, perfect, fulfill, accomplish, achieve, climax, attain, end, realize, finish, effect, execute, do. —*adj.* **2.** complete, perfect, done, finished, effected, fulfilled, excellent, supreme.
—**Ant.** imperfect, unfinished, base.

contain, *v.* hold, accommodate, include, embody, embrace, bear, carry, have inside, admit, encompass.
—**Syn. Study.** CONTAIN, HOLD, ACCOMMODATE express the idea that something is so designed that something else can exist or be placed within it. CONTAIN refers to what is actually within a given container. HOLD emphasizes the idea of keeping within bounds; it refers also to the greatest amount or number that can be kept within a given container. ACCOMMODATE means to contain comfortably or conveniently, or to meet the needs of a certain number. A plane that ACCOMMODATES fifty passengers may be able to HOLD sixty, but at a given time may CONTAIN only thirty.

contaminate, *v.* defile, pollute, sully, stain, soil, tarnish, taint, corrupt, befoul, besmirch, infect, poison, vitiate, rot, infect, spoil, debase, adulterate.

contemplate, *v.* **1.** look at, view, observe, regard, survey, behold, scrutinize, inspect. **2.** consider, reflect on, meditate on, study, ponder, deliberate, think about, revolve in one's mind, muse, ruminate, mull over, cogitate, brood over, chew on, study, examine. **3.** intend, mean, purpose, design, plan.

contempt, *n.* **1.** scorn, disdain, derision, contumely, disgust; loathing, abhorrence, odium, hatred, hate. **2.** dishonor, disgrace, shame.
—**Ant.** respect, reverence; honor.
—**Syn. Study.** CONTEMPT, DISDAIN, SCORN imply strong feelings of disapproval and aversion toward what seems base, mean, or worthless. CONTEMPT is disapproval tinged with disgust: *to feel contempt for a weakling.* DISDAIN is a feeling that a person or thing is beneath one's dignity and unworthy of one's notice, respect, or concern: *a disdain for crooked dealing.* SCORN denotes open or undisguised contempt often combined with derision: *He showed only scorn for those who were not as ambitious as himself.*

contemptible, *adj.* despicable, mean, low, miserable, base, vile, scurvy, inferior, abject, shabby, shameful, nefarious, infamous, villianous.
—**Ant.** splendid, admirable.

contemptuous, *adj.* disdainful, scornful, sneering, insolent, arrogant, supercilious, haughty, derisive, insulting, snide.
—**Ant.** humble, respectful.

contend, *v.* **1.** struggle, strive, fight, battle, combat, vie, compete, rival. **2.** debate, dispute, argue, wrangle. **3.** assert, maintain, claim, aver, theorize, argue, postulate.
—**Syn. Study.** See COMPETE.

content, *adj.* **1.** satisfied, contented, sanguine, happy, comfortable, sated, pleased with the status quo, appeased, gratified, uncomplaining, O.K., blasé, blithe, unambitious, smug, self-satisfied. **2.** assenting, acceding, resigned, willing, agreeable. —*v.* **3.** appease, gratify, satisfy. —*n.* **4.** substance, material, matter, information, subject matter, subject, topic, theme; stuff.
—**Ant.** dissatisfied, malcontent, miserable.

contention, *n.* **1.** struggling, struggle, strife, discord, dissension, quarrel, disagreement, squabble, feud; rupture, break, falling out; opposition, combat, conflict, competition, rivalry, contest. **2.** disagreement, dissension, debate, wrangle, altercation, dispute, argument, controversy.
—**Ant.** agreement.

contentment, *n.* happiness, satisfaction, content, ease, satiety, comfort, pleasure, gratification, tranquility, serenity, peace.
—**Ant.** misery.

contest, *n.* **1.** struggle, conflict, battle, combat, war, fight, encounter. **2.** competition, contention, rivalry, match, tournament, tourney, rivalry, meet, game. **3.** strife, dispute, controversy, debate, argument, altercation, quarrel, contention. —*v.* **4.** struggle, fight, compete, contend, vie, combat, battle. **5.** argue against, dispute, controvert, counter, confute, object to, refute, litigate, debate, oppose, contend against. **6.** doubt, question, challenge, dispute. **7.** rival, strive, compete, vie, contend for.
—**Syn. Study.** See COMPETE.

continual, *adj.* unceasing, incessant, ceaseless, uninterrupted, unremitting, constant, continuous, 24/7, unbroken, successive, perpetual, unending, habitual, permanent, everlasting, eternal; recurrent, recurring, frequentative, repeated, repetitious, repetitive.
—**Ant.** periodic, sporadic.

continue, *v.* **1.** keep on, go onward or forward, persist, persevere, pursue, proceed with. **2.** endure, persist, last, remain. **3.** remain, abide, tarry, stay, rest. **4.** persist in, extend, perpetuate, prolong, carry on, maintain, retain; carry over, postpone, adjourn.
—**Ant.** cease, interrupt.
—**Syn. Study.** CONTINUE, ENDURE, PERSIST, LAST imply existing uninterruptedly for an appreciable length of time. CONTINUE implies duration or existence without break or interruption: *The rain continued for two days.* ENDURE, used of people or things, implies persistent continuance despite influences that tend to weaken, undermine, or destroy: *The temple has endured for centuries.* PERSIST implies steadfast and longer than expected existence in the face of opposition: *to persist in an unpopular belief.* LAST implies remaining in good condition or adequate supply: *I hope the cake lasts until the end of the party.*

contract, *n.* **1.** agreement, compact, bargain, covenant, understanding, deal, commitment, obligation, arrangement, pact, convention, concordat, treaty, stipulation. —*v.* **2.** draw together, compress, concentrate, condense, reduce, lessen, diminish, squeeze, constrict, decrease, shorten, narrow, shrivel, shrink.
—**Ant.** disperse, spread.
—**Syn. Study.** See AGREEMENT.

contradict, *v.* deny, gainsay, dispute, controvert, impugn, challenge, assail, oppose, argue against, defy.
—**Ant.** corroborate, support.

contradictory, *adj.* contrary, opposed, opposite, opposing, antagonistic, incongruous, conflicting, incompatible, discrepant, irreconcilable, paradoxical, inconsistent, contrary.
—**Ant.** corroborative.

contrary, *adj.* **1.** opposite, opposed, contradictory, conflicting, discordant, counter, opposing. **2.** untoward, unfavorable, adverse, unfriendly, hostile, oppugnant, antagonistic, disagreeable, irreconcilable. **3.** perverse, self-willed, intractable, obstinate, refractory, headstrong, stubborn, pigheaded, contumacious.
—**Ant.** obliging, compliant, tractable.

contrast, *v.* **1.** oppose, compare, differentiate, juxtapose, discriminate, distinguish, set off. —*n.* **2.** opposition, comparison, differentiation, difference, discrimination, contrariety, juxtaposition.

contrive, *v.* plan, devise, invent, design, hatch, brew, concoct, form, make; plot, complot, conspire, scheme; manage, effect.

control, *v.* **1.** dominate, command, manage, govern, rule, direct, reign over. **2.** check, curb, hinder, restrain, bridle, constrain. —*n.* **3.** regulation, domination, command, management, direction, government, rule, reign, sovereignty, mastery, superintendence.
—**Syn. Study.** See AUTHORITY.

controversy, *n.* dispute, contention, debate, disputation, disagreement, confrontation, questioning, altercation; quarrel, wrangle, argument, squabble, spat.
—**Ant.** concord, agreement, accord.
—**Syn. Study.** See ARGUMENT.

convene, *v.* **1.** assemble, meet, congregate, collect, gather. **2.** convoke, summon, call to order.
—**Ant.** disperse, adjourn.

convenient, *adj.* **1.** suitable, opportune, expedient, suited, fit, appropriate, suitable, adapted, serviceable, well-suited, favorable, easy, comfortable, agreeable, helpful, advantageous, useful. **2.** at hand, accessible, handy, nearby, within reach, at one's fingertips, close at hand, available, ready.
—**Ant.** inconvenient.

convention, *n.* **1.** assembly, conference, convocation, meeting. **2.** agreement, consent. **3.** custom, precedent.
—**Syn. Study.** CONVENTION, ASSEMBLY, CONFERENCE, CONVOCATION refer to meetings for particular purposes. CONVENTION usually suggests a formal meeting of members or delegates of a political, social, or professional group: *an annual medical convention.* ASSEMBLY usually implies a regular meeting for a customary purpose: *an assembly of legislators; a school assembly in the auditorium.* CONFERENCE suggests a meeting for consultation or discussion: *a sales conference.* CONVOCATION usually refers to an ecclesiastical or academic meeting whose participants were summoned: *a convocation of economic experts.*

conventional, *adj.* accepted, usual, habitual, customary, regular, common, traditional, normal, standard, orthodox, established, ordinary, everyday, old-fashioned, formal, stuffy, stodgy, old hat.
—**Ant.** unconventional, unusual.

conversant, *adj.* **1.** familiar, versed, learned, skilled, practiced, well-informed, proficient. **2.** acquainted, associating.
—**Ant.** unfamiliar, ignorant.

converse, *v.* **1.** talk, chat, speak, discuss, confabulate, hold a dialouge. —*n.* **2.** discourse, talk, conversation, discussion, colloquy. **3.** opposite, reverse, transformation.

convert, *v.* **1.** change, transmute, transform, modify, alter, mutate, metamorphose, remodel, switch, change over, redo, remake; proselyte, proselytize. —*n.* **2.** proselyte, neophyte, disciple.
—**Ant.** renegade, recreant.
—**Syn. Study.** See TRANSFORM.

convey, *v.* **1.** carry, transport, bear, bring, transmit, lead, conduct. **2.** communicate, impart.

convince, *v.* persuade, satisfy, sway, influence, win over, talk into.

convulsion, *n.* seizure, frenzy, paroxysm, fit, spasm, attack, outburst, outbreak, irruption, upheaval, eruption, storm, tumult, furor.

cool, *adj.* **1.** chilly, unheated, cold, refreshing. **2.** calm, unexcited, serene, levelheaded, unflappable, relaxed, under control, imperturbable, phlegmatic, unmoved, deliberate, composed, collected, self-possessed, unruffled, sedate, undisturbed, placid, quiet, dispassionate, unimpassioned. **3.** frigid, distant, aloof, standoffish, snobbish, stuck-up, frosty, superior, chilling, freezing, apathetic, repellent. **4.** indifferent, lukewarm, tepid, unconcerned, cold-blooded. **5.** audacious, impudent, bold, brazen, overconfident, presumptuous, impertinent, insolent, shameless. —*v.* **6.** allay, calm, moderate, quiet, temper, assuage, abate, dampen.
—**Ant.** warm, tepid, lukewarm, hot.
—**Syn. Study.** See CALM.

copy, *n.* **1.** reproduction, replica, likeness, double, twin, transcript, imitation, carbon, duplicate, facsimile, fax, Xerox, photocopy. **2.** original, manuscript, pattern, model, archetype. —*v.* **3.** imitate, ape, mimic, follow in someone's footsteps, mime, impersonate, emulate, parrot, echo; duplicate, transcribe.
—**Ant.** original.

core, *n.* **1.** center, middle, heart, nucleus, inside, focus. **2.** heart, pith, gist, essence, marrow, quintessence. **3.** pit, seed.

corpse, *n.* body, remains, carcass, cadaver, stiff.
—**Syn. Study.** See BODY.

correct, *v.* **1.** set right, rectify, amend, emend, reform, remedy, repair, fix, cure. **2.** admonish, warn, rebuke, discipline, chasten, berate, scold, punish, castigate. —*adj.* **3.** accurate, precise, factual, truthful, proper, exact, faultless, perfect, right, true, valid, fitting, apt, suitable, appropriate, unimpeachable.
—**Ant.** ruin, spoil; incorrect, wrong.
—**Syn. Study.** CORRECT, ACCURATE, PRECISE imply conformity to fact, standard, or truth. A CORRECT statement is one free from error, mistakes, or faults: *The student gave a correct answer in class.* An ACCURATE statement is one that, as a result of an active effort to comprehend and verify, shows careful conformity to fact, truth, or spirit: *The two witnesses said her account of the accident was accurate.* A PRECISE statement shows scrupulously strict and detailed conformity to fact: *The chemist gave a precise explanation of the experiment.*

correspond, *v.* **1.** conform, agree, harmonize, accord, match, tally, concur, coincide, fit, suit. **2.** communicate, write, be in touch, keep in contact.
—**Ant.** differ, diverge.

corrupt, *adj.* **1.** dishonest, venal, false, untrustworthy, bribable, degenerate, degraded. **2.** debased, depraved, base, perverted, wicked, sinful, evil, dissolute, profligate, abandoned, reprobate. **3.** putrid, impure, putrescent, rotten, contaminated, adulterated, tainted, corrupted, spoiled, infected. —*v.* **4.** bribe, lure, entice, suborn, buy off, lead astray. **5.** pervert, deprave, debase, vitiate, debauch. **6.** infect, taint, pollute, contaminate, adulterate, spoil, defile, putrefy, poison.
—**Ant.** honest; honorable; pure, unspoiled, unadulterated; purify.

corruption, *n.* **1.** perversion, depravity, abandon, dissolution, sinfulness, evil, immorality, wickedness, profligacy, debauchery, degradation. **2.** dishonesty, baseness, bribery. **3.** decay, rot, putrefaction, putrescence, foulness, pollution, defilement, contamination, adulteration.
—**Ant.** righteousness; honesty; purity.

cosmetic, *n.* **1.** makeup, greasepaint, cover-up, paint, rouge, foundation, pancake, war paint. —*adj.* **2.** beautifying, decorative, enhancing, improving, corrective. **3.** superficial, surface, shallow, cursory, passing, slapdash, skin-deep, lick and a promise, once over lightly.

cost, *n.* **1.** price, charge, expense, expenditure, outlay. **2.** sacrifice, loss, penalty, damage, detriment, suffering, pain.

costly, *adj.* valuable, dear, high-priced, high, exorbitant, outrageous, overpriced, top-dollar, at a premium; exclusive, sumptuous, expensive, precious, rich, splendid.
—**Ant.** cheap.

coterie, *n.* society, association, set, circle, clique, club, brotherhood, fraternity, sisterhood, sorority, in crowd.
—**Syn. Study.** See CIRCLE.

cottage, *n.* cabin, lodge, hut, shack, shanty, chalet, bungalow, lean-to, snuggery, retreat.
—**Ant.** palace, castle.

counsel, *n.* **1.** advice, opinion, judgment, guidance, exhortation, direction, instruction, suggestion, recommendation, caution, warning, admonition. **2.** consultation, deliberation, discussion, consideration, forethought. **3.** purpose, plan, design, scheme. **4.** lawyer, solicitor, barrister, advocate, counselor, adviser, guide.
—**Syn. Study.** See ADVICE.

countenance, *n.* **1.** aspect, appearance, look, expression, mien. **2.** face, visage, physiognomy. **3.** favor, encouragement, aid, assistance, support, patronage, sanction, approval, approbation. —*v.* **4.** favor, encourage, support, aid, abet, patronize, sanction, approve.
—**Ant.** condemn, prohibit.
—**Syn. Study.** See FACE.

counteract, *v.* neutralize, counterbalance, annul, countervail, offset, contravene, thwart, oppose, resist, hinder, check, frustrate, defeat.
—**Ant.** cooperate, promote.

counterfeit, *adj.* **1.** spurious, false, fraudulent, forged, fake, imitation, bogus, phony, funny. **2.** sham, pretended, feigned, simulated, fraudulent, false, mock, fake, unreal, ersatz, make-believe, pretend, insincere, artificial, meretricious, pseudo, factitious, synthetic. —*n.* **3.** imitation, forgery, falsification, sham. —*v.* **4.** imitate, forge, copy, fake, falsify. **5.** resemble, simulate, feign, sham, pretend, dissemble.
—**Ant.** genuine.
—**Syn. Study.** See FALSE.

couple, *n.* **1.** pair, twosome, duo, duet; yoke, brace, two, span. —*v.* **2.** fasten, link, join, unite, associate, pair, conjoin, connect, combine, wed.
—**Ant.** separate, disjoin.

courage, *n.* fearlessness, dauntlessness, intrepidity, fortitude, pluck, spirit, heroism, daring, audacity, bravery, mettle, valor, hardihood, bravado, gallantry, chivalry, boldness, dauntlessness, nerve, grit, guts, spunk, moxie.
—**Ant.** cowardice.

course, *n.* **1.** advance, tack, direction, bearing. **2.** path, way, run, orbit, route, channel, way, road, track, passage. **3.** progress, passage, process. **4.** process, career, race. **5.** conduct, behavior, deportment. **6.** method, mode, procedure. **7.** sequence, succession, order, turn, regularity.

courteous, *adj.* civil, polite, well-mannered, well-bred, urbane, debonair, affable, gracious, courtly, respectful, obliging, well-behaved, formal, ceremonious, tactful, polished, urbane, civilized, proper, decorous, considerate, diplomatic, gentlemanly, ladylike, chivalrous, considerate.
—**Ant.** discourteous, rude, curt, brusque.
—**Syn. Study.** See CIVIL.

cover, *v.* **1.** overlay, overspread, envelop, enwrap, clothe. **2.** shelter, protect, shield, guard, defend. **3.** hide, screen, cloak, disguise, secrete, veil, shroud, mask, enshroud. **4.** include, comprise, provide for, take in, embrace, contain, embody, comprehend. **5.** suffice, defray, offset, compensate for, counterbalance. —*n.* **6.** lid, top, case, covering, integument. **7.** protection, shelter, asylum, refuge, concealment, guard, defense. **8.** veil, screen, disguise, mask, cloak.
—**Ant.** uncover; exposure.

coward, *n.* sissy, mouse, baby, spineless, jellyfish, invertebrate, milksop, mama's boy, Scaramouche, chicken, yellowbelly, milquetoast,

Caspar Milquetoast, candyass, crybaby, shirker, scaredy cat, recreant, quitter, yellowbellied sapsucker, sneak, cur, girlie-man, shrinking violet, slacker, milksop, mollycoddle, weak sister, weakling, wuss, wimp, pantywaist, gutless wonder, doormat.

cowardice, *n.* fearfulness, baseness, cold feet, yellow streak, spinelessness, cravenness, faint-heartedness, cowardliness, pusillanimity, timidity.
—**Ant.** boldness, bravery, temerity.

cowardly, *adj.* shy, spineless, frightened, namby-pamby, craven, pusillanimous, recreant, timid, timorous, faint-hearted, white-livered, lily-livered, chicken-hearted, yellow, fearful, afraid, scared.
—**Ant.** brave, bold, valiant.

coy, *adj.* retiring, diffident, shy, self-effacing, bashful, modest, self-conscious, sheepish, unassuming, unpretentious, reserved, shrinking, timid, demure; evasive, reluctant, recalcitrant.
—**Ant.** bold, pert, brazen, arch.

cozy, *adj.* comfortable, snug, secure, safe, warm, easeful, comforting, intimate, close, homespun, homelike, homey, soft, comfy, gemutleicheit, down-home, restful, relaxing, easy.
—**Ant.** cold, unwelcoming.

crack, *v.* **1.** break, snap, fracture, rupture, shiver, shatter, smash, split; crackle, craze. —*n.* **2.** snap, report. **3.** break, flaw, split, fissure, cleft, chink, breach, crevice, fracture, rift, gap, slit, rupture, breach, cranny, interstice.

crackpot, *n.* **1.** eccentric, crank, character, oddity, odd duck, oddball, queer fish, crackbrain, screwball, nut case. **2.** fanatic, zealot, maniac, faddist, believer, true believer. —*adj.* **3.** impractical, crazy, lunatic, visionary, quixotic.

craft, *n.* **1.** skill, ingenuity, dexterity, talent, deftness, cleverness, mastery, know-how, expertise, flair, genius, ability, aptitude, expertness. **2.** skill, art, artfulness, craftiness, subtlety, artifice; cunning, deceit, guile, shrewdness, deceitfulness, deception, fraud, trickery, duplicity, foxiness, craftiness. **3.** handicraft, trade, art, vocation, metier, calling, occupation, profession, work.

crafty, *adj.* skillful, sly, cunning, deceitful, artful, wily, insidious, treacherous, two-faced, duplicitous, tricky, designing, scheming, plotting, arch, shrewd, foxy, clever, canny, calculating, sneaky, shifty, dodgy.
—**Ant.** gullible, naive.

cram, *v.* stuff, crowd, pack, compress, squeeze, overcrowd, gorge, jam, fill, glut, press.

cranky, *adj.* **1.** ill-tempered, cross, crotchety, cantankerous, testy, tetchy, touchy, grouchy, crabby, surly, gruff, choleric, peevish, contentious, petulant, querulous, splenetic, churkish, curmudgeonly, waspish, perverse. **2.** eccentric, queer, odd, strange, peculiar, curious.
—**Ant.** amiable, good-natured; rational.

crave, *v.* **1.** long for, desire, want, yearn *or* hunger for. **2.** require, need. **3.** beg for, beseech, entreat, implore, solicit, supplicate.
—**Ant.** relinquish, renounce.

crazy, *adj.* **1.** demented, insane, mad, deranged, lunatic, cracked, unbalanced, non compos mentis, certifiable, crackers, gaga, goofy, loony, off one's rocker, screwy, batty, bats, bonkers, out of one's gourd, screwy, nuts, nutty as a fruitcake, loco, bananas, out to lunch, meshuga, psycho, schizzy, schizoid, mental, out

of one's mind, cuckoo, crackers, ditzy, crackbrained, a few bricks shy of a load, not playing with a full deck, off one's nut, flipped out, have a screw loose, have bats in one's belfry, mad as a hatter, unhinged, gone round the bend, wild-eyed, queer in the head, addled, berserk, not all there, wacky, off one's rocker, not having all one's marbles. **2.** silly, stupid, absurd, moronic, foolish, nonsensical, inane, preposterous, ridiculous, laughable, ludicrous, asinine, moronic, idiotic, harebrained, crackpot, screwball, crackbrain, cockamamie, fatuous, daffy, cockeyed. **3.** ill-considered, impractical, imprudent, unsound, pointless, irrational, rash, reckless, quixotic, wild, visionary. **4.** avid, zealous, excited, keen, eager, enthusiastic. **5.** infatuated, stuck on, wild *or* mad about, nuts, nutty, ape, besotted, sweet on, enamored, gaga for.
—**Ant.** sane, well-balanced; firm; strong.

create, *v.* make, form, bring into being, conceive, engender, generate, think up, frame, forge, fashion, fabricate, develop, manufacture, design, contrive, devise, initiate, start, dream up, begin, give birth to, produce, originate, invent, cause, occasion.

credible, *adj.* believable, trustworthy, reliable, satisfactory; probable, possible.

credit, *n.* **1.** belief, trust, confidence, faith, reliance, credence. **2.** influence, authority, power. **3.** trustworthiness, credibility, reliability, reputability. **4.** repute, estimation, character; reputation, name, esteem, regard, standing, position, rank, condition; notoriety. **5.** commendation, honor, merit. **6.** acknowledgment, ascription. —*v.* **7.** believe, trust, confide in, have faith in, rely upon.
—**Ant.** discredit.

credulous, *adj.* believing, trusting, trustful, unsuspecting, gullible, trustful, simple, silly, superstitious, impressionable, wide-eyed, easily fooled, naive, innocent.
—**Ant.** incredulous, cautious, wary.

crime, *n.* offense, wrong, sin; infraction, violation, breach, misdemeanor, tort, felony: trespassing, breaking and entering, theft, robbery, assault, battery, statutory rape, rape, embezzlement, slander, libel, treason, manslaughter, murder.
—**Syn. Study.** CRIME, OFFENSE, SIN agree in referring to a breaking of law. CRIME usu. refers to any serious violation of a public law: *the crime of treason.* OFFENSE is used of a less serious violation of a public law, or of a violation of a social or moral rule: *a traffic offense; an offense against propriety.* SIN means a breaking of a moral or divine law: *the sin of envy.*

criminal, *adj.* **1.** felonious, unlawful, illegal, lawless, illicit, dishonest, crooked; evil, bad, corrupt, vile, black, immoral, amoral, villainous, depraved, disgraceful, reprehensible, nefarious, flagitious, iniquitous, wicked, sinful, wrong. —*n.* **2.** convict, malefactor, evildoer, wrongdoer, lawbreaker, outlaw, miscreant, villain, desperado, mafioso, transgressor, sinner, culprit, delinquent, offender, felon; crook, hoodlum, gangster, thug, tough, mobster, hood.
—**Syn. Study.** See ILLEGAL.

cripple, *v.* disable, maim, weaken, impair, break down, ruin, destroy, lame, handicap, damage, debilitate.

crisis, *n.* climax, juncture, exigency, strait, pinch, nail-biter, crunch

time, emergency, disaster, catastrophe, calamity, danger.

criterion, *n.* standard, rule, principle, measure, parameter, touchstone, test, proof, sine qua non.
—**Syn. Study.** See STANDARD.

critic, *n.* **1.** reviewer, appraiser, commentator, censor, judge, connoisseur, maven, expert. **2.** censurer, carper, faultfinder, caviler.

critical, *adj.* **1.** captious, carping, censorious, faultfinding, caviling, severe. **2.** discriminating, tasteful, judicial, fastidious, nice, exact, precise. **3.** decisive, climacteric, crucial, determining, defining, momentous, important. **4.** dangerous, perilous, risky, suspenseful, hazardous, precarious, ticklish.
—**Ant.** unimportant, superficial, trivial.

criticism, *n.* **1.** censure, disparagement, disapproval, condemnation, faultfinding, stricture, animadversion, reflection. **2.** review, critique, comment, judgment, appraisal, analysis, assessment, evaluation.

crooked, *adj.* **1.** bent, curved, winding, devious, sinuous, tortuous, serpentine. **2.** deformed, misshapen, disfigured, twisted, awry, askew, crippled. **3.** criminal, dishonest, illicit, wrong, unscrupulous, knavish, tricky, fraudulent, dishonorable, unlawful, illegal, deceitful, insidious, crafty, treacherous.
—**Ant.** straight; honest, upright.

cross, *n.* **1.** trouble, misfortune, misery, burden. —*v.* **2.** oppose, thwart, frustrate, baffle, contradict, foil. **3.** interbreed, cross-breed, hybridize, blend, combine, mongrelize. —*adj.* **4.** irate, piqued, annoyed, surly, choleric, grouchy, splenetic, huffy, pettish, in a pet, grumpy, crusty, querulous, short-tempered, petulant, fractious, irascible, waspish, crabbed, cranky, curmudgeonly, churlish, sulky, cantankerous, ill-natured, peevish, sullen, ill-tempered, intemperate, impatient, complaining, snappish, irritable, fretful, moody, touchy, testy, unpleasant, unkind, mean, angry, spiteful, resentful, gloomy, glowering, morose, sour, vexed.
—**Ant.** aid, support; complaisant, amenable, agreeable, sweet.

crowd, *n.* **1.** multitude, swarm, throng, mass, mob, flock, company, host, horde, herd. **2.** masses, proletariat, plebians, rabble, mob, people, populace, hoi polloi, plebs, proles, citizenry. —*v.* **3.** assemble, throng, swarm, flock together, herd. **4.** push, shove, cram, pack, press, squeeze, cramp, force.
—**Syn. Study.** CROWD, MULTITUDE, SWARM, THRONG refer to large numbers of people. CROWD suggests a jostling, uncomfortable, and possibly disorderly company: *A crowd gathered to listen to the speech.* MULTITUDE emphasizes the great number of persons or things but suggests that there is space enough for all: *a multitude of people at the market.* SWARM as used of people is usu. contemptuous, suggesting a moving, restless, often noisy, crowd: *A swarm of dirty children played in the street.* THRONG suggests a company that presses together or forward, often with some common aim: *The throng pushed forward to see the cause of the excitement.*

crude, *adj.* **1.** unrefined, natural, unprocessed, original, unfinished, unprepared, coarse, raw. **2.** rudimentary, primitive, unripe, immature, undeveloped, unpolished, unfinished, incomplete. **3.** rustic, coarse, boorish, uncouth, rough, rude, clumsy, awkward. **4.** undisguised, blunt, bare, rough, direct.
—**Ant.** refined; aged, mature, ripe;

complete, perfect; indirect, subtle.
—**Syn. Study.** See RAW.

cruel, *adj.* **1.** barbarous, bloodthirsty, sanguinary, ferocious, fell, hard-hearted, harsh, heartless, callous, beastly, vicious, sadistic, fiendish, satanic, atrocious, barbaric, remorseless, uncaring, conscienceless, unsympathetic, merciless, unmerciful, relentless, implacable, pitiless, ruthless, truculent, brutal, savage, inhuman, brutish, barbarian, unmoved, unfeeling, unrelenting. **2.** severe, hard, bitter.
—**Ant.** kind, benevolent, beneficial.

crush, *v.* **1.** squeeze, press, bruise, crumple, rumple, wrinkle, compress. **2.** break, shatter, pulverize, granulate, powder, mash, smash, crumble, disintegrate. **3.** put down, quell, overpower, subdue, overwhelm, overcome, quash, conquer, oppress.

cry, *v.* **1.** lament, grieve, weep, bawl, sorrow, sob, shed tears, bewail, bemoan, squall, blubber, whimper, keen, snivel, moan, groan, mewl, pule, wail. **2.** call, shout, yell, yowl, scream, exclaim, ejaculate, clamor, roar, shriek, howl, bellow, vociferate. **3.** yelp, bark, bellow, hoot. —*n.* **4.** shout, scream, wail, shriek, screech, yell, yowl, roar, whoop, bellow, clamor. **5.** exclamation, outcry, clamor, ejaculation. **6.** weeping, lament, lamentation, tears.
—**Ant.** laugh.

crying, *adj.* **1.** weeping, wailing, in tears, shedding tears, bawling, sobbing, blubbering. **2.** flagrant, notorious, demanding, urgent, important, great, enormous.
—**Ant.** laughing; nugatory, trifling.

cunning, *n.* **1.** ability, skill, adroitness, expertness, expertise, cleverness, genius, talent, art, aptitude, deftness, handiness, skillfulness, finesse. **2.** craftiness, shrewdness, artfulness, wiliness, trickery, intrigue, artifice, guile, craft, deceit, deceitfulness, slyness, deception. —*adj.* **3.** ingenious, skillful, expert, apt, deft, adroit, talented, able, handy. **4.** artful, wily, tricky, foxy, crafty, sly, intriguing, duplicitous, double-dealing.
—**Ant.** stupidity, inability; dullness; naive, gullible, dull.

curb, *n.* **1.** restraint, check, control, bridle, rein. —*v.* **2.** control, restrain, check, bridle, repress, suppress, contain, subdue, reduce, diminish, hold down.
—**Ant.** encourage, further, foster.
—**Syn. Study.** See CHECK.

cure, *n.* **1.** course of treatment, therapy, medication, medicine, drug, prescription, remedy, restorative, specific, antidote. —*v.* **2.** remedy, restore, heal, make well *or* whole, mend, repair, correct, rectify, fix.

cure-all, *n.* remedy, cure, relief, nostrum, elixir, panacea, magic bullet, sovereign remedy, universal remedy, theriac, catholicon.

curious, *adj.* **1.** inquisitive, inquiring, prying, spying, peeping, snooping, interfering, intrusive, nosy, meddlesome, interested. **2.** strange, novel, unusual, singular, rare, foreign, exotic, queer, extraordinary, unique, odd, peculiar, eccentric, outré, offbeat, weird, bizarre, freakish, erratic, pixilated, quaint, outlandish, grotesque, abnormal, kinky.
—**Ant.** blasé; common, commonplace, usual, customary.

current, *adj.* **1.** contemporary, contemporaneous, ongoing, known, in circulation, in the air, present-day, present, prevailing, prevalent, general, common, circulating, widespread, popular, rife. **2.** accepted, stylish, fashionable, modish, latest, up-to-date, trendy, chic, voguish, in

vogue, à la mode, du jour. —*n.* **3.** stream, river, tide, flow, undercurrent; course, progress, progression, drift, mainstream, trend.
—**Ant.** outmoded, uncommon, unpopular.

curse, *n.* **1.** imprecation, execration, fulmination, blasphemy, profanity, damnation, malediction, oath, denunciation, anathema, ban. **2.** evil, misfortune, calamity, trouble, vexation, annoyance, affliction, torment, bane, thorn, harm, cross to bear, hex, disaster, trial, plague, scourge. —*v.* **3.** blaspheme, swear, imprecate, execrate, fulminate, damn, denunciate, accurse, maledict, anathematize, condemn, profane, excommunicate. **4.** doom, destroy, plague, scourge, afflict, trouble, vex, annoy, burden, saddle, handicap.
—**Ant.** blessing, benediction.

curt, *adj.* **1.** short, shortened, brief, abbreviated, concise, laconic, blunt, terse. **2.** rude, snappish, abrupt, dry, brusque, gruff.
—**Ant.** long, drawn-out, lengthy; courteous, courtly.
—**Syn. Study.** See BLUNT.

curtail, *v.* lessen, diminish, decrease, dock, shorten, abbreviate, blunt, abridge, reduce, cut.
—**Ant.** extend, expand.
—**Syn. Study.** See SHORTEN.

cushion, *v.* absorb, insulate, lessen, diminish, check, slow, alleviate, meliorate, soften, mitigate, buffer, mollify.

custody, *n.* **1.** keeping, guardianship, care, custodianship, charge, safekeeping, watch, preserving, protection, preservation; possession, ownership, mastery, holding. **2.** imprisonment, confinement, detention, incarceration.

custom, *n.* habit, practice, usage, procedure, rule, convention, form, observance, formality.
—**Syn. Study.** CUSTOM, HABIT, PRACTICE mean an established way of doing things. CUSTOM, applied to a community or to an individual, implies a more or less permanent way of acting reinforced by tradition and social attitudes: *the custom of giving gifts at Christmas.* HABIT, applied particularly to an individual, implies such repetition of the same action as to develop a natural, spontaneous, or rooted tendency or inclination to perform it: *He has an annoying habit of interrupting the speaker.* PRACTICE applies to a regularly followed procedure or pattern in conducting activities: *It is his practice to verify all statements.*

customary, *adj.* usual, habitual, wonted, accustomed, conventional, common, regular, normal, routine, everyday, ordinary.
—**Ant.** unusual, rare, uncommon, irregular.
—**Syn. Study.** See USUAL.

cut, *v.* **1.** gash, slash, slit, lance, pierce, penetrate, incise, wound. **2.** wound, hurt, move, touch, slight, insult. **3.** divide, sever, carve, cleave, sunder, bisect, chop, hack, hew, fell, saw, lop off, crop. **4.** reap, mow, harvest. **5.** clip, shear, pare, prune. **6.** abridge, edit, shorten, abbreviate, curtail. **7.** lower, lessen, reduce, diminish. **8.** dissolve, dilute, thin, water, water down. —*n.* **9.** incision, wound, slash, gash, slit; channel, passage, strait. **10.** style, fashion, mode, kind, sort.

cutting, *adj.* **1.** sharp, keen, incisive, trenchant, piercing. **2.** mordant, mordacious, caustic, biting, acid, wounding, sarcastic, sardonic, bitter, severe.
—**Ant.** dull; kind.

cynical, *adj.* distrustful, pessimistic,

sarcastic, sardonic, satirical, unbelieving, disbelieving, sneering, contemptuous, derisive, cutting, scornful, ridiculing, censorious, captious, waspish, world-weary, jaded, supercilious, misanthropic, withering, biting, trenchant, hypercritical, ill-tempered, ill-natured, crusty, cantankerous, curmudgeonly.
—**Ant.** innocent, trustful, credulous, naive, optimistic, hopeful; good-natured, pleasant.

D

dabbler, *adj.* **1.** nonprofessional, amateur, dilettante, putterer, tinkerer, Sunday painter. **2.** beginner, tyro, starter, novice, neophyte, abecedarian, tenderfoot, greenhorn, raw recruit.
—**Ant.** professional, expert, adept.

dainty, *adj.* **1.** delicate, beautiful, charming, exquisite, fine, elegant, graceful, neat. **2.** choice, appetizing, tasty, toothsome, delicious, savory, palatable, tender, juicy, delectable, luscious. **3.** particular, fastidious, scrupulous, sensitive, overrefined, mincing, genteel, finicky, squeamish, finical, overnice.
—**Ant.** clumsy, inelegant; disgusting, distasteful; sloppy.
—**Syn. Study.** See DELICATE.

damage, *n.* **1.** injury, harm, hurt, detriment, mischief, impairment, mutilation, destruction, devastation, vandalism, loss. —*v.* **2.** injure, harm, hurt, impair, mar, wound, mutilate, disfigure, deface, ruin, spoil, wreck.
—**Ant.** improvement; improve, better.

damn, *v.* **1.** doom, condemn, sentence, excommunicate, consign to hell, banish, expel. **2.** condemn, attack, denounce, castigate, blast, blame, find fault with, criticize, upbraid, berate, reprove, reprimand, censure, repudiate. **3.** curse at, swear at, execrate, imprecate, vituperate, anathematize, fulminate, thunder against, blaspheme against.

damp, *adj.* **1.** moist, humid, dank, steamy, wet, clammy. —*n.* **2.** moisture, humidity, dankness, wet, wetness, dampness, fog, vapor, steam, clamminess. **3.** dejection, depression, dispiritedness, chill, discouragement.
—**Ant.** dry, arid.

danger, *n.* hazard, risk, peril, threat, insecurity, imperilment, endangerment, uncertainty, jeopardy, liability, exposure; injury, evil.
—**Ant.** security, safety.
—**Syn. Study.** DANGER, HAZARD, PERIL imply harm that one may encounter. DANGER is the general word for liability to injury or harm, either near at hand and certain, or remote and doubtful: *to be in danger of being killed.* HAZARD suggests a danger that one can often foresee but cannot avoid: *A mountain climber is exposed to many hazards.* PERIL usually denotes great and imminent danger: *The passengers on the disabled ship were in great peril.*

dappled, *adj.* multicolored, multihued, varicolored, mottled, motley, spotted, polka-dot, flecked, maculate, freckled, freckly, pied, brindled, bespeckled, stippled, shadowed, shadowy.

dare, *v.* venture, hazard, risk, brave, challenge, defy, endanger, provoke, gamble, make bold, imperil, stake, try.

daredevil, *adj.* daring, rash, adventurous, risk-taking, reckless, heedless, foolhardy, wild, devil-may-care, venturesome, nervy, temerarious,

gutsy, death-defying, impulsive, impetuous, madcap, audacious, intrepid, brave, imprudent, bold, fearless.

daring, *n.* **1.** courage, adventurousness, boldness, bravery, derring-do, pluck, mettle, spunk, guts, valor, grit, audacity, intrepidity, heroism. —*adj.* **2.** courageous, venturesome, adventurous, bold, brave, audacious, dauntless, undaunted, intrepid, fearless, valiant, valorous, gallant, chivalrous, doughty, hardy, rash, reckless, unafraid, plucky, gutsy, heroic.
—**Ant.** cowardice; timid, cowardly, pusillanimous, fearful.

dark, *adj.* **1.** dim, gloomy, murky, umbrageous, shadowy, tenebrous, penumbral, dusky, unilluminated, unlit, sunless, shady, black, stygian, inky, jet-black, pitch-dark, pitchy, Cimmerian. **2.** gloomy, cheerless, dismal, dreary, dull, drab, bleak, mournful, dour, somber, grim, sad, morose, morbid, disheartening, discouraging. **3.** sullen, frowning, sulky, morose, dour, funereal, grim, somber, brooding, glum, moody, lugubrious, sour, depressed, grumpy, dyspeptic, glaring, threatening. **4.** unenlightened, ignorant, untaught, untutored, uneducated, unlettered, benighted, in the dark. **5.** obscure, recondite, abstruse, dim, deep, profound, cryptic, incomprehensible, unintelligible, occult, cabalistic, mysterious, puzzling, enigmatic, enigmatical, mystic, mystical. **6.** hidden, secret, concealed. **7.** infernal, wicked, sinful, nefarious, flagitious, foul, infamous, hellish, devilish, evil, bad, satanic, vile, base, iniquitous, sinister, villainous.
—**Ant.** light, fair; cheerful; pleasant; intelligent, educated; clear, intelligible; open, revealed; heavenly, godly.

dash, *v.* **1.** strike, break; throw, thrust; splash, splatter. **2.** rush, dart, bolt, fly. —*n.* **3.** pinch, bit, suggestion, soupçon, hint, touch, tinge, smack, sprinkle, sprinkling. **4.** vigor, spirit, élan, flourish, éclat, bravado.

daunt, *v.* **1.** intimidate, overawe, subdue, dismay, frighten, appall. **2.** discourage, dispirit, dishearten, thwart, frustrate.
—**Ant.** encourage, actuate.

dauntless, *adj.* fearless, bold, undaunted, intrepid, brave, courageous, daring, indomitable, unconquerable, valiant, valorous, unafraid, unflinching, stalwart, audacious, gallant, stouthearted, plucky, heroic, chivalrous, doughty, undismayed.
—**Ant.** fearful, cowardly, timid, timorous.

dawdle, *v.* idle, linger, loiter, tarry, lag, poke along, dally, dilly-dally, loll, laze, lallygag, take one's time, procrastinate, temporize, put off, straggle, lie about, waste time.
—**Ant.** hasten, hurry.
—**Syn. Study.** See LOITER.

dawn, *n.* **1.** daybreak, sunrise, sunup, break of day, first light, crack of dawn, cockcrow, dawning. —*v.* **2.** appear, open, begin, break, arise, emerge, unfold, begin, originate.
—**Ant.** sunset; disappear.

daydream, *v.* **1.** imagine, fantasize, dream, muse, pipe-dream, woolgather, build castles in the air. —*n.* **2.** reverie, dream, fantasy, imagining, woolgathering, fancy, musing, castle in Spain.

daze, *v.* **1.** stun, stupefy, blind, dazzle, bedazzle, shock, stagger, startle, astonish, astound, amaze, surprise, overcome, overpower, dumbfound, benumb, paralyze, floor, flabbergast, bowl over, blow one's mind. **2.** confuse, bewilder, befuddle, puzzle, mystify, baffle, perplex, nonplus.

—*n.* **3.** confusion, flurry, whirl, spin, perplexity, bemusement, bewilderment, fog, state of shock, shell-shock, paralysis, spaciness, cloud, stupefaction.

dazzle, *v.* **1.** bedazzle, blind, daze, bedaze. **2.** astonish, amaze, stun, stupefy, overwhelm, astound, confound, flabbergast.

dead, *adj.* **1.** deceased, lifeless, extinct, inanimate, defunct, departed. **2.** insensible, numb, unfeeling, indifferent, cool, cold, callous, obtuse, frigid, affectless, phlegmatic, unemotional, unsympathetic, apathetic, lukewarm. **3.** infertile, barren, sterile. **4.** still, motionless, inert, inoperative, useless, dull, inactive, unemployed. **5.** smothered, extinguished, out. **6.** complete, absolute, utter, entire, total. **7.** straight, direct, unerring, exact, precise, sure.
—**Ant.** alive, live, animate; fervid, eager, warm, animated; fertile; partial; crooked, indirect, devious.

deadly, *adj.* **1.** fatal, lethal, mortal. **2.** implacable, truculent, sanguinary, murderous, bloodthirsty, remorseless, ruthless.
—**Syn. Study.** See FATAL.

deal, *v.* **1.** act, behave. **2.** trade, do business, traffic. **3.** distribute, dole, mete, dispense, apportion, allot, give, assign. —*n.* **4.** bargain, arrangement, pact, contract, transaction, negotiation, understanding.
—**Ant.** gather, collect.

dear, *adj.* **1.** beloved, loved, precious, darling, esteemed, adored, cherished, prized, valued, pet, treasured, favorite, admired, honored. **2.** expensive, high-priced, costly, valuable, high; exorbitant, overpriced, outrageous.
—**Ant.** hateful; cheap.

death, *n.* **1.** decease, demise, passing, dying, end, departure. **2.** stop, cessation, termination, extinction, obliteration, annihilation, destruction, decimation, finish, surcease, end, finale.
—**Ant.** life.

debase, *v.* **1.** adulterate, corrupt, vitiate, contaminate, pollute, taint, mar, spoil, poison, defile, foul, befoul. **2.** lower, depress, reduce, impair, deteriorate, degrade, abase, demean, devalue, depreciate, demote, belittle, diminish.
—**Ant.** purify; elevate, raise, exalt.

debate, *n.* **1.** discussion, argument, controversy, disputation, wrangle, polemic, one-on-one, dispute, contention. **2.** deliberation, consideration, reflection, cogitation, thought. —*v.* **3.** discuss, dispute, argue, contend, hold. **4.** deliberate, consider, discuss, argue.
—**Ant.** agreement.

debt, *n.* liability, obligation, duty, due, debit, responsibility, encumbrance.

debut, *n.* **1.** introduction, appearance, arrival, coming out, introduction, inauguration, induction, initiation, unveiling, launching, installation, premiere. —*v.* **2.** come out, appear, arrive, enter, launch, premiere, make a debut.

decadence, *n.* decline, degeneration, retrogression, decay, fall, deterioration; corruption, dissolution, immorality, debauchery, dissipation, degeneracy, indulgence.
—**Ant.** flourishing, progress; morality, improvement.

decay, *v.* **1.** deteriorate, decline, retrogress, degenerate, fall, fall away, wither, perish. **2.** decompose, disintegrate, rot, putrefy. —*n.* **3.** decline, deterioration, degeneration, decadence, weakening, wasting, atrophy, collapse, downfall, impairment, dilapidation. **4.** decomposition, putrefaction, rotting, rot.

—**Ant.** flourish, grow; progress.
—**Syn. Study.** DECAY, DECOMPOSE, DISINTEGRATE, ROT imply a deterioration or falling away from a sound condition. DECAY implies either entire or partial deterioration by progressive natural changes: *Teeth decay.* DECOMPOSE suggests the reducing of a substance to its component elements: *Moisture makes some chemical compounds decompose.* DISINTEGRATE emphasizes the breaking up, going to pieces, or wearing away of anything, so that its original wholeness is impaired: *Rocks disintegrate.* ROT is applied esp. to decaying vegetable matter, which may or may not emit offensive odors: *Potatoes rot.*

deceit, *n.* **1.** deceiving, guile, duplicity, fraud, concealment, fraudulence, dishonesty, dissimulation, deception, cheating, hypocrisy, craftiness, slyness, insincerity, disingenuousness. **2.** trick, stratagem, artifice, wile, trickery, subterfuge, ploy, ruse, maneuver, hoax, double-cross, con, sham, chicanery, device, cozenage. **3.** falseness, duplicity, treachery, perfidy.
—**Ant.** honesty, forthrightness.
—**Syn. Study.** DECEIT, GUILE, DUPLICITY, FRAUD refer either to practices designed to mislead or to the qualities in a person that prompt such behavior. DECEIT is intentional concealment or misrepresentation of the truth: *Consumers are often victims of deceit.* GUILE is crafty or cunning deceit; it suggests subtle but treacherous tactics: *The agent used guile to gain access to the documents.* DUPLICITY is doing the opposite of what one says or pretends to do; it suggests hypocrisy or pretense: *the duplicity of a friend who does not keep a secret.* FRAUD refers to deceit or trickery by which one may derive benefit at another's expense; it often suggests illegal or dishonest practices: *an advertiser convicted of fraud.*

deceitful, *adj.* **1.** dishonest, underhanded, lying, crafty, sly, cunning, duplicitous, hypocritical, scheming, insincere, disingenuous, false, hollow, empty, deceiving, fraudulent, designing, tricky, wily, two-faced. **2.** misleading, fraudulent, deceptive, counterfeit, illusory, fallacious, crooked, phony.
—**Ant.** sincere, honest, forthright; genuine.

deceive, *v.* mislead, delude, cheat, cozen, dupe, gull, fool, hoax, cheat, swindle, betray, con, two-time, take for a ride, bamboozle, hoodwink, trick, double-cross, defraud, outwit, entrap, ensnare, betray.
—**Syn. Study.** See CHEAT.

decent, *adj.* **1.** fitting, appropriate, suited, suitable, apt, proper, fit, seemly, becoming. **2.** tasteful, modest, seemly, proper, decorous, respectable, clean, polite, dignified.
—**Ant.** indecent, indecorous, improper, unfit, unsuitable.

deception, *n.* **1.** deceiving, gulling, fraudulence, dupery, dissimulation, hanky-panky, dishonesty, chicanery, trickery, double-dealing, underhandedness, duplicity, deceit, intrigue, hypocrisy, sophistry. **2.** artifice, sham, cheat, imposture, treachery, subterfuge, stratagem, ruse, hoax, fraud, trick, wile, maneuver, imposture, pretense.

deceptive, *adj.* deceiving, misleading, delusive, fallacious, specious, false, deceitful, illusory, unreliable.
—**Ant.** genuine, authentic.

decide, *v.* resolve, determine, settle, purpose, conclude, arbitrate, judge, make up one's mind.
—**Ant.** waver, hesitate, vacillate.

—**Syn. Study.** DECIDE, RESOLVE, DETERMINE imply settling something in dispute or doubt. To DECIDE is to make up one's mind after consideration: *I decided to go to the party.* To RESOLVE is to settle conclusively with firmness of purpose: *She resolved to ask for a promotion.* To DETERMINE is to settle after investigation or observation: *It is difficult to determine the best course of action.*

decided, *adj.* **1.** unambiguous, unquestionable, definite, unmistakable, undeniable, indeniable, indisputable, indubitable, certain, sure, emphatic, pronounced, absolute, unequivocal, categorical, incontrovertible. **2.** fixed, firm, adamant, stony, assertive, resolute, determined, resolved, unwavering, unhesitating, unfaltering.
—**Ant.** undecided, ambiguous, indefinite; irresolute, hesitant.

decipher, *v.* decode, decrypt, unravel, break, crack, solve, figure out, translate, unriddle, work out, dope out, puzzle out, explain, elucidate, analyze, interpret, resolve.
—**Ant.** encode, encipher, obscure, hide.

decisive, *adj.* incontrovertible, firm, resolute, determined, conclusive, final, finishing, irreversible, critical, crucial, mortal.
—**Ant.** indecisive, irresolute, vacillating, wavering.

declaim, *v.* orate, perorate, hold forth, elocute, lecture, preach, sermonize, harangue, speechify, rant, rave, thunder, trumpet, shout, tubthump, mouth off.
—**Ant.** mumble, mutter.

declare, *v.* **1.** announce, proclaim, pronounce, decree, rule, proclaim, promulgate, trumpet. **2.** affirm, assert, say, proclaim, avow, aver, protest, make known, state, utter. **3.** manifest, reveal, disclose, publish.
—**Ant.** deny, controvert; suppress.
—**Syn. Study.** DECLARE, AFFIRM, ASSERT imply making something known emphatically, openly, or formally. To DECLARE is to make known, sometimes in the face of actual or potential contradiction: *to declare someone the winner of a contest.* TO AFFIRM is to make a statement based on one's reputation for knowledge or veracity, or so related to a generally recognized truth that denial is not likely: *to affirm the necessity of high standards.* To ASSERT is to state boldly, usu. without other proof than personal authority or conviction: *to assert that the climate is changing.*

decline, *v.* **1.** refuse, avoid, reject, deny. **2.** stoop, condescend, lower oneself, abase, debase. **3.** fail, weaken, deteriorate, pale, diminish, degenerate, decay, languish. —*n.* **4.** failing, loss, enfeeblement, deterioration, degeneration, enervation, weakening, decay, diminution, lessening, retrogression.
—**Ant.** agree; rise; improve, increase; strengthening.
—**Syn. Study.** See REFUSE.

decorate, *v.* adorn, bedeck, beautify, ornament, embellish, deck, deck out, dress, dress up, trim, spruce up, smarten, appoint, garnish, pretty up, titivate, accouter, furbish, dandify, prettify, doll up, gussy up.
—**Ant.** simplify, streamline, strip.

decorous, *adj.* proper, decent, seemly, becoming, sedate, conventional, fitting, fit, suitable, seemly, dignified, correct, mannerly, refined, elegant, polite, genteel, demure.
—**Ant.** indecorous, indecent, unseemly, unbecoming, unfit.

decorum, *n.* etiquette, gentility, good form, courtliness, punctilio,

correctness, protocol, politeness, politesse, manners, manner, behavior, comportment, deportment, decency, propriety, dignity.
—**Ant.** indecency, impropriety.

decrease, *v.* **1.** diminish, lessen, abate, fall off, decline, contract, dwindle, shrink, wane, ebb, subside, go south. —*n.* **2.** abatement, diminution, reduction, decline, wane, subsidence, falling off, contraction, shrinking, dwindling, lessening, ebb, ebbing.
—**Ant.** increase.
—**Syn. Study.** DECREASE, DIMINISH, DWINDLE, SHRINK imply becoming smaller or less in amount. DECREASE commonly implies a sustained reduction in stages, esp. of bulk, size, volume, or quantity, often from some imperceptible cause or inherent process: *The swelling decreased daily.* DIMINISH usu. implies the action of some external cause that keeps taking away: *Disease caused the number of troops to diminish steadily.* DWINDLE implies an undesirable reduction by degrees, resulting in attenuation: *His followers dwindled to a mere handful.* SHRINK esp. implies contraction through an inherent property under specific conditions: *Many fabrics shrink in hot water.*

decree, *n.* **1.** order, directive, edict, command, commandment, dictum, injunction, mandate, proclamation, declaration, directive, instruction, prescription, prescript, ruling, fiat, ukase, pronunciamento, diktat. —*v.* **2.** order, direct, command, dictate, rule, require, prescribe, direct, enjoin, bid, mandate, instruct, pronounce, ordain.

decrepit, *adj.* weak, feeble, enfeebled, infirm, aged, superannuated, effete, broken down, falling apart, frail, worn-out, wasted away, unfit, debilitated, enervated, disabled, crippled, doddering, dilapidated, deteriorating, crumbling, decaying, antiquated, tumbledown, ramshackle, rickety, derelict, creaky, run-down.
—**Ant.** sturdy, strong, trim, in good shape, new.

decry, *v.* denigrate, deprecate, disparage, censure, belittle, discredit, condemn, put down, criticize, attack, denounce, impugn, blast, lambaste, repudiate, reject, oppugn.
—**Ant.** praise, laud, commend.
—**Syn. Study.** DECRY, DENIGRATE, DEPRECATE involve the expression of censure or disapproval. DECRY means to denounce or to express public disapproval of: *to decry all forms of discrimination.* DENIGRATE means to defame or to sully the reputation or character of: *to denigrate the memory of a ruler.* DEPRECATE means to express regretful disapproval of or to plead against: *to deprecate a new policy.*

deduce, *v.* conclude, infer, reason, gather, assume, presume, judge, make out, conjecture, speculate, guess, reckon, suppose, surmise, think, understand, dope out.

deed, *n.* act, performance, exploit, achievement, action, feat, accomplishment.

deem, *v.* judge, regard, think, consider, hold, believe, account, count, suppose.

deep, *adj.* **1.** recondite, abstruse, abstract, difficult, profound, arcane, esoteric, inscrutable, occult, weighty; mysterious, obscure, unfathomable. **2.** grave, serious, grievous, intense, poignant, heartfelt, profound. **3.** absorbing, absorbed, involved, intense, heartfelt, great, extreme. **4.** penetrating, intelligent, bright, cunning, sagacious, wise, learned, erudite, knowledgeable,

knowing, perspicacious, insightful, sharp-witted, acute, discerning, astute, shrewd, artful.
—**Ant.** shallow.

deface, v. mar, disfigure, vandalize, mutilate, blemish, deform, spoil, soil, injure, harm; blot out, efface, obliterate, erase, eliminate.
—**Ant.** beautify.

defeat, v. **1.** overcome, conquer, overwhelm, vanquish, beat, subdue, trounce, whip, crush, best, do in, thrash, overthrow, subjugate, suppress, rout, check. **2.** frustrate, thwart, foil, baffle, disconcert, unnerve, balk, foil, check, end, finish. —n. **3.** overthrow, vanquishment, downfall, rout, setback, Waterloo. **4.** frustration, bafflement.
—**Ant.** yield, surrender, submit.
—**Syn. Study.** DEFEAT, CONQUER, OVERCOME, SUBDUE imply gaining victory or control over an opponent. DEFEAT usu. means to beat or frustrate in a single contest or conflict: *Confederate forces were defeated at Gettysburg.* CONQUER means to finally gain control over by physical, moral, or mental force, usu. after long effort: *to conquer poverty; to conquer a nation.* OVERCOME emphasizes perseverance and the surmounting of difficulties: *to overcome opposition; to overcome a bad habit.* SUBDUE means to conquer so completely that resistance is broken: *to subdue a rebellious spirit.*

defect, n. **1.** blemish, flaw, fault, shortcoming, imperfection, mar, blotch, scar, blot, foible, weakness. **2.** deficiency, want, lack. —v. **3.** desert, abandon, revolt, rebel, betray, go over to the other side.
—**Ant.** sufficiency, perfection; support.
—**Syn. Study.** DEFECT, BLEMISH, FLAW refer to faults, both literal and figurative, that detract from perfection. DEFECT is the general word for any kind of shortcoming, imperfection, or deficiency, whether hidden or visible: *a birth defect; a defect in a plan.* A BLEMISH is usu. a surface defect that mars the appearance; it is also used of a moral fault: *a skin blemish; a blemish on his reputation.* A FLAW is usu. a structural defect or weakness that mars the quality or effectiveness: *a flaw in a diamond; a flaw in Hamlet's character.*

defective, adj. imperfect, incomplete, faulty, deficient, insufficient, flawed, broken, out of order, on the blink, on the fritz, inadequate; (euphemism, applied to humans) challenged.
—**Ant.** perfect, complete, adequate.

defend, v. **1.** guard, garrison, fortify, shield, shelter, screen, preserve, protect, keep watch over, safeguard, secure. **2.** uphold, champion, argue for, back, support, maintain, assert, justify, plead, espouse, vindicate, stick up for, go to bat for.
—**Ant.** attack.

defer, v. delay, postpone, put off, prevent, adjourn; procrastinate.
—**Ant.** speed, expedite.
—**Syn. Study.** DEFER, DELAY, POSTPONE imply keeping something from occurring until a future time. To DEFER is to decide to do something at a more convenient time in the future; it often suggests avoidance: *to defer making a payment.* DELAY is sometimes equivalent to DEFER, but it usu. suggests a hindrance, obstacle, or dilatory tactic: *Completion of the building was delayed by bad weather.* To POSTPONE is to put off to a particular time in the future, often to wait for new information or developments: *to postpone a trial.*

deference, n. **1.** homage, honor, veneration, reverence, obeisance,

tribute, respect, esteem, appreciation, admiration. **2.** submission, subjection, submissiveness, compliance, acquiescence.
—**Ant.** disrespect, insolence.

defiant, adj. antagonistic, insubordinate, contumacious, obstinate, unruly, headstrong, disobedient, stubborn, refractory, recalcitrant, rebellious, insolent, resistant, in-your-face; daring, courageous, brave, bold, audacious.
—**Ant.** friendly, amiable; cowardly.

definite, adj. **1.** defined, determined, specific, particular, exact, explicit, pronounced, fixed, precise, determinate. **2.** certain, clear, express, sure, positive, assured, fixed, settled, confirmed.
—**Ant.** indefinite, undetermined, indeterminate; uncertain, unclear.

deformed, adj. malformed, misshapen, crippled, lame, disfigured, distorted, twisted, grotesque, contorted, abnormal, warped, bent, perverted.

defy, v. challenge, resist, dare, brave, flout, face, confront, stand up to, thumb one's nose at, scorn, despise.
—**Ant.** encourage, support, help.

degradation, n. humiliation, disgrace, debasement, dishonor, disrepute, discredit, shame, ignominy, abasement; degeneration, decline, decadence, degeneracy, perversity, depravity, turpitude, immorality, deterioration, corruption, baseness, debauchery, profligacy, prodigality.
—**Ant.** exaltation.

degrade, v. **1.** demote, depose, downgrade, lower, break, cashier, bust. **2.** debase, deprave, lower, abase, vitiate, deteriorate. **3.** humiliate, dishonor, disgrace, discredit, humble, shame, mortify, belittle, deprecate, cheapen, reduce, lower.
—**Ant.** exalt.
—**Syn. Study.** See HUMBLE.

dejected, adj. depressed, dispirited, disheartened, pouting, dour, low-spirited, discouraged, despondent, downhearted, sad, unhappy, miserable, lugubrious, glum, gloomy, grim, wretched, sullen, brooding, sulky, downcast, down, low, crestfallen, melancholy, blue, forlorn, disconsolate, sorrowful, morose, heartbroken, down in the dumps or mouth.
—**Ant.** happy, cheerful, lighthearted.

delay, v. **1.** put off, defer, postpone, procrastinate, defer, suspend, shelve, put on hold, put on ice, put on the back burner, table. **2.** impede, slow, retard, hinder, detain, stop, arrest. **3.** linger, loiter, tarry, wait, hesitate, lag behind, dawdle, stall, dally, mark time, drag one's feet, shilly-shally, dilly-dally. —n. **4.** wait, holdup, delaying, procrastination, loitering, tarrying, dawdling, stay, setback, stop. **5.** deferment, postponement, respite, deferring, interlude, hiatus, lull, interruption, suspension, stoppage, gap, lacuna.
—**Ant.** expedite, hasten, speed.
—**Syn. Study.** See DEFER.

delegate, n. **1.** representative, deputy, envoy, ambassador, legate, agent. —v. **2.** depute, entrust, commission, appoint, designate, name, assign, nominate, empower, authorize, accredit, mandate.

delete, v. cancel, strike or take out, erase, expunge, eradicate, remove, efface, blot out, obliterate.

deliberate, adj. **1.** intentional, voluntary, weighed, considered, studied, purposive, purposeful, premeditated, willful, planned, calculated, conscious, prearranged, preconceived, cold-blooded. **2.** careful,

slow, unhurried, leisurely, methodical, thoughtful, circumspect, cautious, wary, measured, regular, even, sure, steady, unhesitating, unfaltering. —v. **3.** weigh, consider, ponder over, reflect, study, think, ruminate, meditate. **4.** consult, confer.
—**Ant.** haphazard, unintentional; careless, unwary, incautious.
—**Syn. Study.** DELIBERATE, INTENTIONAL, VOLUNTARY refer to something not happening by chance. DELIBERATE is applied to what is done not hastily but with full realization of what one is doing: *a deliberate attempt to evade justice.* INTENTIONAL is applied to what is definitely intended or done on purpose: *an intentional omission.* VOLUNTARY is applied to what is done by a definite exercise of the will and not because of outside pressures: *a voluntary enlistment.* See also SLOW.

delicacy, n. **1.** tenderness, sensitivity, tact, diplomacy, feeling, sensibility, consideration, thoughtfulness, solicitude, solicitousness. **2.** refinement, finesse, dexterity, skill, deftness, facility, artistry, artfulness, adroitness, grace. **3.** frailty, unhealthiness, fragility, feebleness, weakness, debility, valetudinarianism. **4.** treat, rare treat, tidbit, morsel, choice morsel, dainty, goody, luxury, savory.

delicate, adj. **1.** dainty, exquisite, fine, nice, fragile, graceful, elegant, choice. **2.** faint, gradual, nice, precise, muted, soft, subdued, slight, subtle. **3.** tender, fragile, frail, dainty, slight, weak, slender, sensitive, frangible. **4.** critical, precarious, dangerous, ticklish, sensitive, sticky, tricky, touchy, hairy. **5.** scrupulous, careful, painstaking, exact, exacting, precise, accurate; discriminating, fastidious, demanding.
—**Ant.** rude, crude; blunt; rough, insensitive, unbreakable; careless.
—**Syn. Study.** DELICATE, DAINTY, EXQUISITE imply beauty or subtle refinement such as might belong in rich surroundings. DELICATE suggests something fragile, soft, light, or fine: *a delicate carving.* DAINTY suggests a smallness, gracefulness, and beauty that forbids rough handling: *a dainty handkerchief;* of persons, it refers to fastidious sensibilities: *a dainty eater.* EXQUISITE suggests an outstanding beauty and elegance that appeals to the most refined taste: *an exquisite tapestry.*

delicious, adj. pleasing, luscious, palatable, savory, dainty, delicate, delectable, ambrosial, mouthwatering, toothsome, choice, flavorful, tasty, appetizing, scrumptious, yummy.
—**Ant.** unpleasant, bitter, acrid, unpalatable.

delight, n. **1.** enjoyment, pleasure, transport, delectation, gratification, bliss, joy, rapture, ecstasy. —v. **2.** please, satisfy, transport, enrapture, enchant, charm, ravish, gratify, gladden, cheer, tickle, amuse, entertain, excite, thrill, captivate, entrance, fascinate.
—**Ant.** disgust, revulsion, displeasure; displease.

delightful, adj. pleasing, pleasant, pleasurable, enjoyable, charming, enchanting, agreeable, delectable, rapturous, joyful, lovely, amusing, entertaining, diverting, exciting, thrilling; attractive, winning, winsome, engaging, fascinating, captivating, ravishing, congenial, compatible.
—**Ant.** unpleasant, disagreeable, revolting, repellent.

deliver, v. **1.** give up, surrender, hand over, transfer, give over, yield, resign, cede, grant, relinquish. **2.** give forth, emit, cast, direct, deal,

discharge. **3.** utter, pronounce, announce, proclaim, declare, communicate, publish, impart, promulgate, advance. **4.** set free, liberate, release, free, emancipate. **5.** redeem, rescue, save, release, extricate, disentangle.
—**Ant.** limit, confine.

delude, v. mislead, deceive, beguile, cozen, cheat, dupe, gull, defraud, trick, con, lead down the garden path, take in, fool.
—**Ant.** enlighten.

deluge, n. inundation, flood, downpour, rainstorm, torrent, monsoon, overflow, cataclysm, catastrophe.

delusion, n. deception, trick, stratagem, artifice, ruse, pretense; illusion, misconception, fancy, fallacy, error, mistake, hallucination.

demand, v. **1.** claim, require, exact, ask for, call for, challenge, clamor for, need, want, necessitate, cry out for, insist on. **2.** ask, inquire. —n. **3.** claim, requisition, requirement, bid, behest, order, insistence, outcry, want, need, desire. **4.** inquiry, question, asking, interrogation.
—**Ant.** waive, relinquish.

demolish, v. ruin, destroy, put an end to, lay waste, raze, level, smash, topple, devastate, annihilate, crush, quash, dispose of.
—**Ant.** construct, build, create.
—**Syn. Study.** See DESTROY.

demonstrate, v. **1.** show, explain, explicate, expound, spell out, illustrate, make clear, make plain, make evident, prove, establish, show and tell. **2.** exhibit, manifest, display, evidence, evince, present, disclose, divulge, expose. **3.** protest, object, march, rally, boycott, strike, picket, parade.

demure, adj. **1.** prudish, prim, overmodest, priggish, fastidious, dainty, delicate, squeamish, proper, Victorian, puritanical. **2.** sober, modest, serious, sedate, decorous, coy.
—**Ant.** licentious, immodest; indecorous.
—**Syn. Study.** See MODEST.

denounce, v. **1.** condemn, assail, censure, attack, stigmatize, decry, repudiate, oppose, oppugn, reject, criticize, impugn, revile, vilify, shame, pillory, slur, scorn, blame, brand, label. **2.** inform against, accuse, denunciate, give away, betray, report, reveal, incriminate, implicate, complain about, charge.
—**Ant.** commend, exonerate.

dense, adj. **1.** thick, solid, heavy, close, compact, condensed, composed, impenetrable. **2.** crowded, tight, packed, impassable. **3.** stupid, foolish, dim, dim-witted, slow, slow-witted, dull, obtuse, stolid, cloddish, thick, dumb, oafish, cloddish.

deny, v. **1.** dispute, controvert, oppose, refute, negate, gainsay, contradict. **2.** turn down, forbid, decline, disallow, reject, renounce, abjure, disavow. **3.** refuse, repudiate, disown, disavow, renounce, disclaim, forswear.
—**Ant.** concede, agree, concur; accept; receive.

depart, v. **1.** go away, start, set out, leave, quit, retire, withdraw, absent, go, retreat, exit, decamp, abscond, flee, skip, cut and run, disappear, vanish, evaporate, shove off, hit the road, split. **2.** turn aside, diverge, deviate, vary, change, abandon, stray, veer. **3.** die, pass on or away.
—**Ant.** arrive; converge.

depict, v. **1.** represent, portray, paint, limn, delineate, design, outline, sketch, reproduce, draw. **2.** describe, characterize, give an account of, recount, relate, bring to life, tell tales of, reveal.

deplore, v. grieve, regret, lament,

bemoan, bewail, mourn.
—**Ant.** boast.

deposit, *v.* **1.** place, put, lay down, lay. **2.** throw down, drop, precipitate. **3.** entrust, leave, lodge, consign, keep, place, put; bank, save, store, hoard; secure. —*n.* **4.** sediment, deposition, precipitate; silt, mud, slime, sand, alluvium. **5.** coating; lode, vein, ore.

depraved, *adj.* corrupt, perverted, corrupted, immoral, wicked, evil, sinful, iniquitous, profligate, debased, dissolute, reprobate, indecent, unprincipled, unscrupulous, unregenerate, debauched, dirty, low, shameless, loose, wanton, libertine, lecherous, libidinous, lustful, carnal, concupiscient, degenerate, licentious, lascivious, lewd.
—**Ant.** upright, honest; honorable, decorous, modest.

depress, *v.* **1.** dispirit, deject, oppress, dishearten, grieve, cast a pall over, burden, weigh down, discourage, dampen, chill, sadden. **2.** reduce, weaken, dull, debilitate, enervate, sap; diminish, reduce, bring down, lower. **3.** devalue, cheapen, depreciate, reduce, devaluate. **4.** humble, humiliate, abase, debase, degrade, abash, shame, bring low.
—**Ant.** inspirit, encourage; elevate; gladden.

depressed, *adj.* dejected, downcast, sad, unhappy, miserable, morose, saddened, blue, despondent, melancholy, gloomy, morbid, in despair, desperate, hopeless, grieving, angst-ridden, moody, somber, in poor *or* low spirits, sullen, brooding, funereal, lugubrious, dour, grim, sulky, down, low, singing the blues, wretched, down in the mouth, discouraged, disheartened, melancholic, anguished, distraught, despairing, down in the dumps, disconsolate, desolate, glum, woebegone, forlorn, heartbroken, crestfallen, downhearted, dispirited, in low spirits, heavy-hearted.
—**Ant.** happy, cheerful.

deprive, *v.* dispossess, bereave, strip, divest, disallow, deny, withhold, refuse, withdraw, remove, expropriate, take away.
—**Ant.** endow.

deprived, *adj.* poor, impoverished, destitute, poverty-stricken, badly off, needy, in need, in want, wanting, underprivileged, disadvantaged, impecunious, low-born, pauperized, insolvent, indigent, penniless, poor as a church mouse, in straitened circumstances, pinched, down and out, broke, stony broke, hard up, born on the wrong side of the tracks.

depth, *n.* **1.** deepness, extent, measure, profoundness, profundity. **2.** obscurity, abstruseness, reconditeness, intricacy, complexity **3.** profundity, wisdom, sagacity, understanding, perception, perspicacity, acuteness, acuity, astuteness, insight, acumen, penetration. **4.** intensity, profundity, strength, vividness, brilliance, richness. **5.** deep, chasm, abyss, pit, bottomless pit, nadir.

derelict, *adj.* **1.** deserted, abandoned, neglected; ruined, rundown, tumbledown, dilapidated. **2.** neglectful, negligent, remiss, delinquent, careless, heedless, lax, slack, irresponsible, slipshod, sloppy, slovenly. —*n.* **3.** tramp, vagrant, outcast, pariah, loafer, good-for-nothing, vagabond, slacker, hobo, bum, street person, homeless person, skell, bag lady, parasite on society, ne'er-do-well, panhandler.

derogatory, *adj.* disparaging, belittling, demeaning, derogative, depreciatory, deprecatory, depreciative, slighting, uncomplimentary, insulting, disdainful, scornful, contemptuous, spiteful, abusive, pejorative, defamatory, malicious, maligning, critical, censorious, negative, abasing, debasing, lowering, minimizing, denigrating, diminishing, detracting, offensive.
—**Ant.** flattering, complimentary.

descent, *n.* **1.** falling, fall, sinking, descending. **2.** inclination, declination, slope, slant, dip, drop, plunge, plummet, declivity, grade, decline. **3.** extraction, lineage, derivation, parentage, genealogy.
—**Ant.** ascent, rise.

describe, *v.* narrate, account, recount, recite, report, chronicle, tell, relate; delineate, portray, characterize, limn, represent, depict, identify, label, style.

desert, *n.* **1.** waste, wilderness, Sahara, barrens, infertile land, heath, tundra, wild, dust bowl. —*adj.* **2.** desolate, barren, forsaken, wild, uninhabited, lonely, arid, bare, vacant, empty, uncultivated. —*v.* **3.** abandon, forsake, leave behind, give up, relinquish, leave, quit, renounce, maroon, strand, abscond.

design, *v.* **1.** plan, devise, project, contrive, invent, create, conceive, originate, think up, develop, form, organize, frame, fashion, forge, mold, make. **2.** intend, purpose, mean, propose. **3.** sketch, draw, delineate. —*n.* **4.** plan, scheme, proposal, proposition, project, conception, study, undertaking, enterprise. **5.** sketch, plan, drawings, blueprint, outline, draft, pattern, layout, diagram, map, model, prototype. **6.** end, intention, purpose, intent, aim, object, goal, point, target.
—**Ant.** achieve, execute, accomplish; execution; accident, fortuity, chance.

designing, *adj.* contriving, scheming, sly, artful, cunning, tricky, wily, crafty, deceitful, treacherous, arch, Machiavellian, astute, unscrupulous.
—**Ant.** open, candid, frank, honest, guileless, artless, naive.

desire, *v.* **1.** wish *or* long for, crave, want, wish, covet, fancy. **2.** ask, importune, request, solicit. —*n.* **3.** craving, longing, yearning, hankering, yen, ache, wish, need, hunger, appetite, thirst. **4.** request, wish, aspiration. **5.** lust, libido, sex drive, lasciviousness, concupiscence, sexual appetite, sexuality, sensuality, prurience, libidinousness, lustfulness, horniness, randiness, the hots, hot pants.
—**Ant.** abominate, loathe, abhor.
—**Syn. Study.** DESIRE, CRAVING, LONGING, YEARNING suggest feelings that impel a person to the attainment or possession of something. DESIRE is a strong wish, worthy or unworthy, for something that is or seems to be within reach: *a desire for success.* CRAVING implies a deep and compelling wish for something, arising from a feeling of (literal or figurative) hunger: *a craving for food; a craving for companionship.* LONGING is an intense wish, generally repeated or enduring, for something that is at the moment beyond reach but may be attainable in the future: *a longing to visit Europe.* YEARNING suggests persistent, uneasy, and sometimes wistful or tender longing: *a yearning for one's native land.*

desolate, *adj.* **1.** barren, laid waste, devastated, ravaged, scorched, destroyed. **2.** deserted, empty, bleak, remote, uninhabited, desert; lonely, alone, lone, solitary, forsaken, lonesome. **3.** miserable, wretched, unhappy, sad, woeful, woebegone, disconsolate, inconsolable, forlorn, lost, cheerless, joyless, comfortless, down, sorrowful, mournful, gloomy, dejected, downcast, depressed, hopeless, dreary, dismal. —*v.* **4.** lay waste, devastate, ravage, ruin, sack, destroy, despoil. **5.** depopulate. **6.** sadden, depress, dismay, dishearten, daunt, dispirit, discourage. **7.** forsake, abandon, desert.
—**Ant.** fertile; populous, crowded; happy, delighted; cultivated; build, create; cheer.

despair, *n.* desperation, despondency, hopelessness, discouragement, gloom, disheartenment, misery, melancholy, woe, anguish, grief, distress.
—**Ant.** encouragement, hope, optimism.
—**Syn. Study.** DESPAIR, DESPERATION, DESPONDENCY refer to a state of mind caused by circumstances that seem too much to cope with. DESPAIR suggests total loss of hope, usu. accompanied by apathy and low spirits: *He sank into despair after the bankruptcy.* DESPERATION is a state in which loss of hope drives a person to struggle against circumstances, with utter disregard of consequences: *In desperation, they knocked down the door.* DESPONDENCY is a state of deep gloom due to loss of hope and a sense of futility and resignation: *despondency after a serious illness.*

desperate, *adj.* **1.** reckless, foolhardy, impetuous, wild, mad, rash, headlong, frantic. **2.** urgent, pressing, compelling, acute, critical, serious, grave; precarious, perilous, life-threatening, hazardous, tenuous, dangerous. **3.** wretched, forlorn, hopeless, desolate, frantic, at one's wit's end, at the end of one's rope *or* tether. **4.** extreme, excessive, great, heroic, prodigious.
—**Ant.** careful; hopeful.

despicable, *adj.* contemptible, vile, base, worthless, detestable, scurvy, sordid, wretched, miserable, ignoble, ignominious, shabby, shameful, reprehensible, mean, abject, low, pitiful.
—**Ant.** lovable, likable, worth.

despise, *v.* scorn, disdain, spurn, sneer at, look down on, be contemptuous of; hate, detest, abhor, loathe.
—**Ant.** love, like, admire.

despite, *prep.* notwithstanding, in spite of, undeterred by, regardless of, without considering, ignoring, without regard for.

despondency, *n.* depression, dejection, discouragement, melancholy, gloom, desperation, despair, sadness, blues, grief, anguish, sorrow, misery, low spirits, blue meanies.
—**Ant.** elation, joy, happiness.
—**Syn. Study.** See DESPAIR.

despondent, *adj.* depressed, dejected, discouraged, dour, wretched, heartbroken, spiritless, moody, somber, morose, sorrowful, unhappy, down, downcast, miserable, gloomy, grim, sullen, brooding, sulking, desolate, forlorn, disconsolate, disheartened, downhearted, melancholy, sad, blue, dispirited, hopeless, low-spirited, low, down in the mouth, down in the dumps.
—**Ant.** elated, joyful, happy.

destiny, *n.* fate, karma, kismet, lot, fortune, future, doom, destination, end, outcome, disposition.
—**Syn. Study.** See FATE.

destitute, *adj.* needy, poor, indigent, penniless, impoverished, in want, insolvent, down-and-out, hard up, broke, stony broke, poverty-stricken, bankrupt, down on one's luck, down at the heels, on one's uppers, badly off.
—**Ant.** affluent, rich, opulent.

destroy, *v.* **1.** smash, demolish, raze, spoil, consume, level, wreck, crush, wipe out, tear down, break up, trash, ruin, waste, ravage, devastate, desolate, lay waste. **2.** end, terminate, finish, do away with, bring to an end, exterminate, extinguish, extirpate, annihilate, eradicate, slay, kill, uproot. **3.** nullify, invalidate, counteract, neutralize, cancel, reverse, annul, stop.
—**Ant.** create; originate, start.
—**Syn. Study.** DESTROY, DEMOLISH, RAZE imply completely ruining or doing away with something. To DESTROY is to reduce something to nothingness or to take away its powers and functions so that restoration is impossible: *Disease destroys tissues.* To DEMOLISH is to destroy something organized or structured by smashing it to bits or tearing it down: *The evidence demolished the attorney's case.* To RAZE is to level a building or other structure to the ground: *to raze a fortress.*

destruction, *n.* **1.** extinction, extermination, desolation, havoc, laying waste, rack and ruin, devastation, ruin, eradication. **2.** killing, liquidation, assassination, slaying, holocaust, annihilation, murder, slaughter, death, massacre, genocide. **3.** plague, pandemic, deluge, catastrophe, calamity.
—**Ant.** birth, origin; creation.

destructive, *adj.* ruinous, harmful, injurious, baneful, poisonous, unwholesome, damaging, detrimental, dangerous, hurtful, toxic, noxious, baleful, pernicious, mischievous, deleterious, fatal, deadly, lethal; extirpative, eradicative.
—**Ant.** salutary; creative.

detain, *v.* **1.** delay, arrest, retard, stop, slow, stay, check, keep. **2.** impound, lock up, put away, hold, restrain, confine, arrest. **3.** keep back, withhold, retain.
—**Ant.** promote, encourage; advance.

detect, *v.* discover, catch, expose, find, find out, ascertain, uncover, locate, determine, dig up, unearth, learn, hear of, hear; note, notice, spot, observe, perceive, identify, discern, feel, catch, scent, smell.
—**Syn. Study.** See LEARN.

deter, *v.* discourage, restrain, dissuade, hinder, prevent, stop, inhibit, intimidate, daunt, obstruct, check, impede, frighten off.
—**Ant.** encourage, further, continue.

determine, *v.* **1.** settle, decide, conclude, judge. **2.** conclude, infer, learn, find out, discover, ascertain, verify, check, certify. **3.** affect, act on, shape, govern, regulate, dictate, fix, decide, establish, condition, influence, resolve. **4.** impel, induce, lead, incline.
—**Syn. Study.** See DECIDE.

determined, *adj.* staunch, resolute, unflinching, firm, inflexible, rigid, rigorous, unfaltering, unwavering, dogged, strong-willed, tenacious, intent, fixed, persistent, persevering, steady, stubborn, obstinate, adamant, single-minded, unflinching, unhesitating, unyielding.
—**Ant.** irresolute, vacillating, wavering, faltering, flexible.

detest, *v.* abhor, hate, loathe, abominate, execrate, despise, scorn, hold in contempt, revile, disdain, sneer at, look down on.
—**Ant.** love, like.
—**Syn. Study.** See HATE.

detestable, *adj.* abominable, hateful, execrable, loathsome, vile, odious, abhorred, abhorrent, despicable, contemptible, beneath contempt, sordid, miserable, scurvy, vile, shabby, ignoble, mean, base, low, reprehensible, ignominious,

shameful.
—**Ant.** lovable, likable.

detriment, *n.* loss, damage, injury, hurt, harm, ill, impairment, disadvantage, prejudice, drawback, liability.
—**Ant.** advantage, profit.

devastate, *v.* ravage, lay waste, desolate, destroy, strip, pillage, plunder, sack, spoil, despoil, raze, ruin, wreck, demolish, obliterate.
—**Ant.** build, erect, create.

development, *n.* **1.** expansion, growth, elaboration, progress, increase, enlargement, increment, advance, improvement. **2.** opening, disclosure, developing, unfolding, maturing, maturation, evolution, maturity.
—**Ant.** deterioration, decadence, degeneration.

deviate, *v.* digress, diverge, depart, swerve, part, wander, veer, err, stray, drift, turn aside *or* away.
—**Ant.** converge.
—**Syn. Study.** DEVIATE, DIGRESS, DIVERGE imply turning or going aside from a path. To DEVIATE is to stray from a usual or established standard, course of action, or route: *Fear caused him to deviate from the truth.* To DIGRESS is to wander from the main theme in speaking or writing: *The speaker digressed to relate an amusing anecdote.* To DIVERGE is to differ or to move in different directions from a common point or course: *Their interests gradually diverged.*

device, *n.* **1.** invention, contrivance, gadget, mechanism, machine, implement, utensil, apparatus, instrument, appliance, tool, contraption, widget. **2.** plan, scheme, project, design, expedient. **3.** wile, ruse, artifice, shift, trick, stratagem, evasion, maneuver. **4.** design, figure, emblem, trademark, badge, logotype, colophon, symbol, crest, seal; motto, slogan, legend.

devilish, *adj.* satanic, diabolic, diabolical, demonic, demoniac, infernal, Mephistophelian, fiendish, hellish, villainous, sinister, wicked, evil, sinful, heinous, malign, malevolent, cruel; impish, naughty, mischievous, prankish.
—**Ant.** good, fine, upstanding, righteous, godly.

devise, *v.* order, arrange, plan, think out, contrive, invent, prepare, concoct, scheme, project, design, make up, conceive, dream up, formulate, create, frame.
—**Ant.** disorder, disarrange.

devote, *v.* dedicate, consecrate, assign, apply, consign, give up, commit, allocate, set aside, appropriate, pledge.
—**Ant.** resign, relinquish.
—**Syn. Study.** DEVOTE, DEDICATE, CONSECRATE share the sense of assigning or committing someone or something to a particular activity, function, or end. DEVOTE is the most general of these terms, although it carries overtones of religious commitment: *He devoted his evenings to mastering the computer.* DEDICATE implies a more solemn or noble purpose and carries an ethical or moral tone: *We are dedicated to the achievement of equality for all.* CONSECRATE, even in nonreligious contexts, implies an intense and sacred commitment: *consecrated to the service of humanity.*

devotion, *n.* **1.** dedication, consecration. **2.** attachment, fondness, loyalty, allegiance, affection, love. **3.** devotedness, zeal, fervor, intensity, fanaticism, enthusiasm, willingness, ardor, eagerness, earnestness. **4.** religion, religiousness, piety, faith, devoutness, sanctity, saintliness, godliness, reverence, holiness, spirituality.

devout, *adj.* **1.** churchgoing, staunch, dedicated, faithful, reverent, pious, devoted, religious, worshipful, holy, saintly. **2.** earnest, sincere, hearty, serious, honest, genuine, heartfelt, zealous.
—**Ant.** atheistic, agnostic; insincere, scornful.
—**Syn. Study.** See RELIGIOUS.

dexterous, *adj.* adroit, deft, skillful, supple, lithe, agile, handy, nimble, clever, expert, apt, ready, quick, able, keen, sharp, artful.
—**Ant.** clumsy, awkward, maladroit, unapt.
—**Syn. Study.** DEXTEROUS, ADROIT, DEFT imply facility and ease in performance. DEXTEROUS most often refers to physical, esp. manual, ability but can also refer to mental ability: *a dexterous woodcarver; dexterous handling of a delicate situation.* ADROIT usu. implies mental cleverness and ingenuity but can refer to physical ability: *an adroit politician; an adroit juggler.* DEFT suggests a light and assured touch in physical or mental activity: *a deft magician; deft handling of the reporters after the tragedy.*

dialect, *n.* **1.** provincialism, idiom, localism, jargon, patois, variant, vernacular, cant, slang, argot. **2.** language, tongue, speech.
—**Syn. Study.** See LANGUAGE.

diction, *n.* phraseology, wording, expression, terminology, word choice, vocabulary, style, usage, grammar, language; distinctness, enunciation, pronunciation.

die, *v.* **1.** decease, pass away *or* on, perish, expire, depart. **2.** cease, stop, end, vanish, disappear. **3.** weaken, fail, subside, fade, sink, faint, decline, wither, decay.
—**Syn. Study.** DIE, PERISH mean to relinquish life. To DIE is to cease to live from any cause or circumstance; it is used figuratively of anything that has once displayed activity: *He died of cancer. Her anger died.* PERISH, a more literary term, implies death under harsh circumstances such as hunger or violence; figuratively, it connotes permanent disappearance: *Hardship caused many pioneers to perish. Ancient Egyptian civilization has perished.*

difference, *n.* discrepancy, disparity, dissimilarity, inconsistency, unlikeness, variation, diversity, imbalance, disagreement, inequality, dissimilitude, divergence, contrast, contrariety; discrimination, distinction.
—**Ant.** similarity; agreement.

different, *adj.* **1.** differing, unlike, diverse, discrete, conflicting, dissimilar, disparate, distinct, opposite, separate, distinguishable, divergent, altered, changed, contrary, contrasted, deviant, deviating, variant. **2.** sundry, divers, miscellaneous, various, manifold, assorted, multifarious, numerous, abundant, varied, many, several. **3.** unusual, peculiar, unique, odd, singular, distinctive, extraordinary, special, remarkable, bizarre, strange, weird, rare, unconventional, original, new, novel, out of the ordinary, exceptional.
—**Ant.** similar, like; uniform, identical.
—**Syn. Study.** See VARIOUS.

differentiate, *v.* **1.** modify, specialize, transform, convert, adapt, adjust, alter, change. **2.** distinguish, oppose, set off, tell apart, discriminate, separate, contrast.
—**Ant.** group together.
—**Syn. Study.** See DISTINGUISH.

difficult, *adj.* **1.** hard, arduous, tough, strenuous, onerous, laborious, burdensome, toilsome. **2.** obscure, complex, intricate, puzzling, enigmatic, thorny, baffling, profound, abstruse, perplexing. **3.** intractable, recalcitrant, contrary, refractory, stubborn, obstinate, unmanageable, austere, rigid, reserved, forbidding, unaccommodating. **4.** fastidious, particular, fussy, demanding, finicky, nitpicking, critical, troublesome.
—**Ant.** easy, simple; clear, plain; accommodating; careless, sloppy.

difficulty, *n.* **1.** dilemma, predicament, quandary, fix, exigency, hardship, obstacle, distress, pitfall, snag, hindrance, strain, tribulation, emergency, trouble, problem. **2.** reluctance, unwillingness, obstinacy, stubbornness.
—**Ant.** ease; willingness.

diffident, *adj.* shy, self-conscious, self-effacing, bashful, abashed, embarrassed, timid, sheepish, modest.
—**Ant.** forward, bold, unabashed.

digest, *v.* **1.** understand, assimilate, study, ponder, consider, comprehend, take in, grasp, study, think over, meditate on, contemplate, ruminate over, reflect on. **2.** arrange, systematize, classify, codify. —*n.* **3.** summary, epitome, abstract, synopsis, abridgment, brief, conspectus, condensation, précis, resume, abbreviation.
—**Ant.** expand.
—**Syn. Study.** See SUMMARY.

dignify, *v.* ennoble, exalt, uplift, glorify, honor, elevate, grace, build up, raise, promote, magnify, distinguish, enhance, improve, better, upgrade.
—**Ant.** demean, humble.

digress, *v.* deviate, diverge, wander, maunder, expatiate, go off on a tangent, detour, ramble, stray.
—**Syn. Study.** See DEVIATE.

dilate, *v.* expand, spread out, enlarge, engross, widen, extend, swell, distend.
—**Ant.** shrink, constrict.

dilemma, *n.* predicament, problem, question, quandary, difficulty, strait, plight, trouble; double bind, catch-22, impasse, deadlock, stalemate, bind, fix, jam, spot, pickle.
—**Syn. Study.** See PREDICAMENT.

dilettante, *n.* **1.** amateur, dabbler, Sunday painter, trifler, nonprofessional, tyro, putterer. **2.** connoisseur, aesthete, expert, authority, specialist, collector, maven.

diligence, *n.* persistence, effort, application, industry, assiduity, industriousness, steadiness, steadfastness, focus, concentration, perseverance, assiduousness, sedulousness, constancy, devotion, earnestness, conscientiousness, constancy, thoroughness, scrupulousness, meticulousness, punctilio.
—**Ant.** carelessness, laziness.

diligent, *adj.* industrious, assiduous, sedulous, occupied, busy, intent, steady, steadfast, focused, concentrating, constant, attentive, persistent, painstaking, persevering, indefatigable, untiring, tireless, unremitting, hard-working, thorough, meticulous, scrupulous, punctilious.
—**Ant.** lazy, careless; remiss.

dim, *adj.* **1.** obscure, dark, shadowy, fuzzy, tenebrous, gloomy, dusky, nebulous, hazy, cloudy, foggy, misty, murky, crepuscular. **2.** indistinct, unclear, ill-defined, blurred, vague, faint, imperceptible, weak, indiscernible, confused, indefinite. **3.** dull, slow, stupid, obtuse, doltish, foolish, dense, thick, dumb. —*v.* **4.** darken, cloud, obscure, dull. **5.** blur, dull, fade.
—**Ant.** clear, bright, distinct; definite.

diminish, *v.* lessen, reduce, decrease, subside, ebb, dwindle, shrink, decline, lower, curtail, cut down, truncate, abbreviate, shorten, abridge, compress, condense, make smaller *or* shorter, abate, contract, shrivel up.
—**Ant.** increase.
—**Syn. Study.** See DECREASE.

diminutive, *adj.* little, small, tiny, dwarf, dwarflike, dwarfish, minute, microscopic, submicroscopic, miniature, petite, minuscule, undersized, pygmy, midget, Lilliputian, teeny-weeny, itsy-bitsy.
—**Ant.** large, immense.

dip, *v.* **1.** immerse, plunge, dive, duck, submerge, douse, bathe, dunk. **2.** sink, drop, incline, decline, slope downward, fall, go down, descend, sag, subside, slump, lower.
—**Ant.** rise.
—**Syn. Study.** DIP, IMMERSE, PLUNGE refer to putting something into liquid. To DIP is to put down into a liquid quickly or partially and lift out again: *to dip a finger into water to test the temperature.* IMMERSE denotes a lowering into a liquid until covered by it: *to immerse meat in salt water.* PLUNGE adds a suggestion of force or suddenness to the action of dipping: *to plunge a lobster into boiling water.*

diplomatic, *adj.* politic, tactful, artful, discreet, prudent, wise, considerate, sensitive, courteous, polite, thoughtful, discerning, perceptive, perspicacious, shrewd, knowing.
—**Ant.** tactless, rude.
—**Syn. Study.** DIPLOMATIC, POLITIC, TACTFUL imply ability to avoid offending others, esp. in situations where this is important. DIPLOMATIC suggests a smoothness and skill in handling others, usually in such a way as to attain one's own ends and yet avoid any unpleasantness or opposition: *diplomatic inquiries about the stockbroker's finances.* POLITIC emphasizes expediency or prudence in looking out for one's own interests, thus knowing how to treat people of different types in delicate situations: *a truth which it is not politic to insist on.* TACTFUL suggests a nice touch in the handling of delicate matters or situations; it often involves a sincere desire not to hurt the feelings of others: *a tactful way of correcting someone.*

direct, *v.* **1.** guide, advise, regulate, conduct, manage, control, handle, run, administer, supervise, operate, dispose, lead, govern, rule. **2.** order, command, instruct, require, tell, charge, dictate, enjoin. **3.** point, focus, train, level, aim. —*adj.* **4.** straight, undeviating. **5.** immediate, personal, unbroken, simple, evident. **6.** straightforward, downright, plain, categorical, unequivocal, unambiguous, express, open, sincere, outspoken, plain-spoken, candid, honest, blunt, uninhibited, unreserved, frank, earnest, ingenuous, obvious, naive.
—**Ant.** divert, mislead; crooked; devious; ambiguous, sly.
—**Syn. Study.** DIRECT, ORDER, COMMAND mean to issue instructions. DIRECT suggests also giving explanations or advice; the emphasis is on steps necessary to accomplish a purpose: *He directed me to organize the files.* ORDER connotes a more personal relationship and instructions that leave no room for refusal: *She ordered him out of the class.* COMMAND suggests greater formality and a more fixed authority: *The officer commanded the troops to advance.*

dirty, *adj.* **1.** soiled, foul, unclean, filthy, squalid, defiled, grimy,

dingy. **2.** dirtying, soiling, befouling, besmirching. **3.** vile, mean, base, vulgar, low, groveling, scurvy, shabby, contemptible, despicable. **4.** indecent, obscene, nasty, lascivious, lewd, lecherous, licentious, immoral, amoral, risqué, off-color, prurient, salacious, coarse, blue, lubricious, bawdy, earthy, libidinous, smutty, ribald, scabrous, X-rated, pornographic, adult.
—**Ant.** clean; elevated, exalted; decent, moral.

disability, *n.* handicap, impairment, defect, infirmity; incapacity, disqualification, inability, incompetence, impotence, incapability, unfitness, helplessness.
—**Ant.** ability, capacity, capability.

disable, *v.* weaken, damage, ruin, impair, harm, hurt, destroy, cripple, incapacitate, enfeeble, paralyze; disqualify, incapacitate, eliminate.
—**Ant.** strengthen; qualify; include.

disadvantage, *n.* **1.** drawback, inconvenience, hindrance, deprivation, flaw, defect, handicap, liability, shortcoming, weakness, weak spot, fault. **2.** detriment, hurt, harm, damage, injury, loss, disservice.
—**Ant.** advantage.

disappear, *v.* fade, vanish, cease, pass away, end, evaporate, vaporize, evanesce, become extinct, perish, die.
—**Ant.** appear.
—**Syn. Study.** DISAPPEAR, FADE, VANISH mean that something or someone passes from sight or existence. DISAPPEAR is used of whatever suddenly or gradually goes away: *We watched them turn down a side street and disappear.* FADE suggests a complete or partial disappearance that proceeds gradually and often by means of a blending into something else: *Dusk faded into darkness.* VANISH suggests complete, generally rapid disappearance: *The sun vanished behind clouds.*

disappointment, *n.* **1.** setback, loss, blow, fiasco, calamity, disaster, dissatisfaction, fizzle, washout, failure, defeat, frustration, unfulfillment. **2.** dejection, depression, discouragement, distress, regret, disenchantment, sorrow, letdown, mortification, frustration, chagrin.
—**Ant.** fulfillment, victory; consummation.

disapprove, *v.* object to, criticize, condemn, censure, decry, put down, deplore, deprecate, belittle, look down on, frown on, knock, look down one's nose at, reproach, take exception to, find disfavor with, disdain, scorn, repudiate, oppugn, oppose.

disaster, *n.* calamity, catastrophe, cataclysm, mischance, mishap, accident, misadventure, blow, debacle, trouble, act of God, adversity, misfortune, affliction.
—**Ant.** luck, fortune.
—**Syn. Study.** DISASTER, CALAMITY, CATASTROPHE, CATACLYSM refer to adverse happenings usu. occurring suddenly and unexpectedly. DISASTER may be caused by negligence, bad judgment, or the like, or by natural forces, as a hurricane or flood: *a railroad disaster that claimed many lives.* CALAMITY suggests great affliction, either personal or general; the emphasis is on the grief or sorrow caused: *the calamity of losing a child.* CATASTROPHE refers esp. to the tragic outcome of a personal or public situation; the emphasis is on the destruction or irreplaceable loss: *the catastrophe of a defeat in battle.* CATACLYSM, physically a sudden and violent change in the earth's surface, also refers to a personal or

public upheaval of unparalleled violence: *a cataclysm that turned our lives in a new direction.*

disband, *v.* break up, disorganize, demobilize, dissolve, disperse, dismiss, scatter, separate, retire.
—**Ant.** organize, unite.

discern, *v.* **1.** perceive, see, recognize, notice, apprehend, discover, descry, espy, come upon, behold. **2.** discriminate, distinguish, differentiate, judge.
—**Syn. Study.** See NOTICE.

discharge, *v.* **1.** unload, disburden, relieve, unburden. **2.** remove, send forth, get rid of, expel, eject, emit. **3.** fire, shoot, set off, detonate. **4.** relieve, release, absolve, exonerate, clear, acquit, liberate, set free, free. **5.** fulfill, perform, execute, observe. **6.** dismiss, cashier, fire, remove, expel, break. **7.** pay, honor, disburse, make good on, liquidate, dissolve, settle. —*n.* **8.** emission, ejection, expulsion, removal, evacuation, voiding. **9.** detonation, firing, shooting. **10.** fulfillment, execution, performance, observance.
—**Ant.** load, burden.
—**Syn. Study.** See RELEASE.

disciple, *n.* follower, adherent, apostle, devotee, votary; partisan, fan, aficionado, supporter; pupil, student, scholar, apprentice, proselyte, learner.
—**Ant.** leader; rebel.

discipline, *n.* **1.** training, drill, exercise, instruction, practice, regimen, inculcation, indoctrination, schooling. **2.** penalty, punishment, chastisement, castigation, correction. **3.** subjection, direction, rule, order, control, regulation, subjugation, government. **4.** rules, regulations. —*v.* **5.** train, exercise, drill, practice, instruct, teach, condition, coach, break in, indoctrinate, educate. **6.** punish, correct, chastise, castigate, reprove, reprimand, rebuke, scold.

disclose, *v.* **1.** reveal, make known, make public, publicize, impart, report, inform, divulge, show, tell, unveil, communicate. **2.** uncover, lay open, expose, bare, bring to light; muckrake.
—**Ant.** conceal, hide; cover.

disconcert, *v.* disturb, confuse, perturb, ruffle, discompose, discomfort, make uneasy, put off, fluster, agitate, upset, unsettle, baffle, puzzle, rattle, shake up, discombobulate, perplex, bewilder, frustrate, embarrass, abash; disarrange, disorder.
—**Ant.** calm; order, arrange.

disconsolate, *adj.* inconsolable, unhappy, desolate, forlorn, heartbroken, sad, melancholy, dejected, gloomy, miserable, cheerless, sorrowful, depressed, blue, wretched, downhearted, in low spirits, morose, dour, sullen, brooding, anxious, hopeless.
—**Ant.** happy, cheerful, delighted.

discontent, *n.* discontentment, dissatisfaction, uneasiness, inquietude, restlessness, unhappiness, distaste, malaise, agitation, restiveness, displeasure.
—**Ant.** contentment; satisfaction, pleasure, ease, restfulness.

discontinue, *v.* put an end to, interrupt, stop, cease, quit, desist, drop, suspend, break off, give up, terminate.
—**Ant.** continue, further.

discourage, *v.* **1.** dishearten, dismay, intimidate, dispirit, daunt, depress, deject, overawe, cow, awe, subdue, abash, embarrass, frighten. **2.** dissuade, deter, hinder, prevent, obstruct, throw cold water on, inhibit, suppress, stop, hamper, oppose, prevent.
—**Ant.** encourage, hearten, embolden.

—**Syn. Study.** DISCOURAGE, DISMAY, INTIMIDATE mean to dishearten or frighten a person so as to prevent some action. To DISCOURAGE is to dishearten by expressing disapproval or by suggesting that a contemplated action will probably fail: *He was discouraged from going into business.* To DISMAY is to dishearten, shock, or bewilder by sudden difficulties or danger: *a prosecutor dismayed by disclosures of new evidence.* To INTIMIDATE is to deter by making timid: *The prospect of making a speech intimidates me.*

discouragement, *n.* **1.** depression, dejection, hopelessness, despair, frustration, dismay, disappointment, disenchantment, chagrin, intimidation. **2.** deterrent, damper, wet blanket, cold water, impediment, obstacle, obstruction, setback, barrier, opposition, hindrance.
—**Ant.** encouragement.

discover, *v.* **1.** learn of, ascertain, unearth, determine, track down, identify, locate, smoke out, ferret out, dig up; find out, detect, espy, descry, discern, see, notice. **2.** originate, bring to light, invent, conceive of, devise, contrive, pioneer, stumble on.
—**Ant.** conceal.
—**Syn. Study.** See LEARN.

discreet, *adj.* wise, judicious, prudent, circumspect, tactful, sensitive, thoughtful, politic, artful, diplomatic, cautious, careful, heedful, considerate, wary, guarded, watchful.
—**Ant.** indiscreet, careless, imprudent; incautious, inconsiderate.
—**Syn. Study.** See CAREFUL.

discrepancy, *n.* gap, disparity, lacuna, dissimilarity, deviation, divergence, incompatibility, difference, inconsistency, incongruity, disagreement, discordance, contrariety, variance, variation.
—**Ant.** similarity, congruity, consistency, concord, accord, agreement.

discriminate, *v.* **1.** distinguish, separate, discern, make out, differentiate. **2.** favor, disfavor, segregate, set apart, show prejudice, be biased, be intolerant.
—**Ant.** group, unite; indiscriminate, undistinguished.
—**Syn. Study.** See DISTINGUISH.

discuss, *v.* examine, reason, deliberate, argue, debate, talk over, sift, consider, converse about, chat, review, consult on, thrash out.

disdain, *v.* **1.** sneer, mock, jeer at, snub, deride, insult, taunt, ridicule, lord it over, look down one's nose at, ignore, repudiate, reject, abhor, loathe, execrate, despise, scorn, spurn. —*n.* **2.** contempt, derision, superiority, mockery, dismissal, ridicule, rejection, repudiation, scorn, contumely, contemptuousness, haughtiness, arrogance, superciliousness, hauteur.
—**Ant.** accept, like, love; love, admiration, regard.
—**Syn. Study.** See CONTEMPT.

disdainful, *adj.* contemptuous, scornful, haughty, arrogant, derisive, sneering, superior, pompous, proud, snobbish, lordly, jeering, mocking, insolent, insulting, hoity-toity, stuck-up, highfalutin, high and mighty, swaggering, aloof, standoffish, supercilious, contumelious.
—**Ant.** friendly, amiable, considerate, attentive.

disease, *n.* morbidity, illness, sickness, ailment, complaint, affection, disorder, malady, abnormality, derangement, distemper, indisposition, infirmity, affliction, infection,

cancer, plague.
—**Ant.** health, salubriety.

disfigure, *v.* mar, deface, injure, deform, spoil, ruin, blemish, damage, scar, mutilate, impair, distorted.
—**Ant.** beautify.

disgrace, *n.* **1.** dishonor, ignominy, infamy, shame, dishonor, disfavor, humiliation, embarrassment, degradation, debasement, discredit, vilification, mortification, disapproval, disapprobation, disparagement, stain, taint, notoriety, baseness. **2.** odium, obloquy, degradation, opprobrium, scandal, blemish, aspersion, slur, stigma, smirch, black mark. —*v.* **3.** shame, dishonor, defame, disfavor, humiliate, disapprove, discredit, degrade, debase, stain, sully, taint, tarnish, reproach.
—**Syn. Study.** DISGRACE, DISHONOR, IGNOMINY, INFAMY imply a very low position in the opinion of others. DISGRACE implies being excluded and held in strong disfavor by others: *to bring disgrace to one's family by not paying debts.* DISHONOR suggests a loss of honor or honorable reputation; it usu. relates to one's own conduct: *He preferred death to dishonor.* IGNOMINY is disgrace that invites public contempt: *the ignominy of being caught cheating.* INFAMY is shameful notoriety, or baseness of action or character that is widely known and recognized: *The children never outlived their father's infamy.*

disgust, *v.* **1.** sicken, nauseate, turn one's stomach. **2.** offend, displease, repel, repulse, revolt. —*n.* **3.** distaste, nausea, loathing, hatred, abhorrence, disrelish. **4.** dislike, detestation, repugnance, aversion, dissatisfaction, antipathy, contempt, hatred, odium, animus, animosity, enmity, antagonism.
—**Ant.** please, delight, attract; relish, liking, love; satisfaction.

disgusting, *adj.* offensive, offending, loathsome, sickening, nauseous, nauseating, sick-making, fulsome, off-putting, repellant, obnoxious, gross, vile, nasty, repulsive, revolting, odious, hateful, repugnant, foul, abominable, abhorrent, distasteful, detestable.
—**Ant.** delightful, delectable, attractive, beautiful.

dishonest, *adj.* unprincipled, immoral, duplicitous, unreliable, untrustworthy, underhanded, dishonorable, unfair, cheating, lying, double-dealing, unprincipled, hypocritical, crooked, shady, unscrupulous, conniving, corrupt, knavish, thievish, deceitful, treacherous, perfidious; false, fraudulent, counterfeit, fake, bogus, artificial, phony.
—**Ant.** honest, upright.

dishonorable, *adj.* **1.** ignoble, base, depraved, debased, inglorious, degrading, disgraceful, shameful, shameless, false, fraudulent. **2.** infamous, notorious, unscrupulous, unprincipled, corrupt, traitorous, perfidious, dishonest, two-faced, duplicitous, despicable, reprehensible, heinous, villainous, low, mean, scurvy, vile, disreputable, disgraceful, scandalous, ignominious, discreditable, flagitious, contemptible, unchivalrous.
—**Ant.** honorable.

disintegrate, *v.* reduce to particles or fragments, break up, decay, rot, fall apart, separate, shatter, crumble, decompose, molder.
—**Ant.** integrate.
—**Syn. Study.** See DECAY.

disinterested, *adj.* objective, neutral, just, detached, unbiased, unprejudiced, unselfish, impartial, fair, generous, liberal, open-minded, equitable, dispassionate, evenhanded, impersonal, altruistic.

—Ant. biased, prejudiced, illiberal, bigoted, selfish, partial.
—Syn. Study. See FAIR.

dislike, v. disrelish, disgust, distaste, repugnance, antipathy, loathing, aversion, antagonism, displeasure, disfavor, disaffection, hatred, animus, animosity, enmity, detestation, contempt, ill will, hostility.
—Ant. like; relish, delight, delectation.

disloyal, adj. unfaithful, faithless, untrue, untrustworthy, deceitful, double-dealing, two-faced, cheating, unreliable, fickle, false, perfidious, treacherous, traitorous, treasonable, subversive, disaffected, unpatriotic.
—Ant. loyal, faithful, true, honest.

dismay, v. 1. discourage, dishearten, daunt, appall, terrify, horrify, frighten, scare, intimidate, disconcert, put out, alarm, paralyze. —n. 2. consternation, terror, horror, panic, fear, alarm.
—Ant. encourage, hearten, embolden; security, confidence.
—Syn. Study. See DISCOURAGE.

dismiss, v. release, let go, discharge, discard, reject, set or put aside; fire, depose, replace, remove, give the old heave-ho, show someone the door, oust, give the boot, cashier, pink-slip, can, sack, down-size.
—Ant. hire, employ.
—Syn. Study. See RELEASE.

disobedient, adj. insubordinate, naughty, mischievous, bad, ill-behaved, obstreperous, unmanageable, fractious, wayward, intractable, undutiful, contrary, perverse, willful, headstrong, recalcitrant, mutinous, mulish, pigheaded, contumacious, defiant, refractory, unruly, rebellious, obstinate, stubborn, unsubmissive, uncompliant.
—Ant. obedient.

disobey, v. transgress, violate, disregard, defy, infringe, flout, ignore, resist, oppose, violate, overstep, break, contravene, be insubordinate, thumb one's nose at, be unruly, rebel, refuse to comply, be fractious, act up.
—Ant. obey.

disorder, n. 1. disorderliness, disarray, jumble, mess, litter, clutter, chaos, untidiness, muddle, jumble, shambles, hodgepodge, disarrangement, confusion, irregularity, disorganization, derangement. 2. disturbance, tumult, brawl, uproar, fight, unrest, quarrel, bustle, clamor, riot, turbulence, pandemonium, upheaval, ferment, fuss, hubbub, hullaballoo, commotion, turmoil, bedlam, rumpus, free-for-all, fracus, donnybrook, scuffle, melee, breach of the peace. 3. ailment, malady, derangement, illness, complaint, sickness, disease, indisposition. —v. 4. disarrange, disarray, mess up, disorganize, unsettle, disturb, derange, discompose, upset, confuse, confound.
—Ant. order.

disparity, n. dissimilarity, inequality, difference, distinction, dissimilitude, gap, discrepancy, imbalance, incongruity, contrast, unevenness, inconsistency.
—Ant. similarity, equality, similitude.

dispense, v. deal, distribute, apportion, allot, dole, mete out, furnish, supply, provide, parcel, disburse, issue, assign.

disperse, v. 1. scatter, dissipate, separate. 2. spread, diffuse, disseminate, broadcast, sow, scatter; dispel. 3. vanish, disappear, evanesce.
—Ant. unite, combine; appear.
—Syn. Study. See SCATTER.

displace, v. 1. misplace, move, dislocate, transfer, shift, relocate, disturb, disarrange, disorder, unsettle. 2. replace, remove, depose, oust, dismiss, expel, unseat, eject, evict, exile, banish, discharge, fire, sack, kick out.

display, v. 1. show, exhibit, manifest, demonstrate, make visible, evince. 2. reveal, uncover, betray, unveil, disclose, demonstrate. 3. unfold, open out, spread out. 4. show, flourish, flaunt, parade, show off. —n. 5. show, exhibition, manifestation. 6. parade, ostentation, flourish, flaunting, spectacle, show, pageantry, pomp, splash, éclat.
—Ant. conceal, hide; cover.
—Syn. Study. DISPLAY, EXHIBIT, MANIFEST mean to show or bring to the attention of another or others. To DISPLAY is literally to spread something out so that it may be most completely and favorably seen: to display goods for sale. To EXHIBIT is to display something to the public for inspection or appraisal: to exhibit orchids at a flower show. They may both refer to showing or revealing one's qualities or feelings: to display wit; to exhibit surprise. MANIFEST means to show feelings or qualities plainly or clearly: He manifested his anger with a scowl.

displeasure, n. dissatisfaction, annoyance, disapprobation, disapproval, distaste, dislike; anger, ire, wrath, indignation, annoyance, irritation, chagrin, exasperation, vexation; offense.
—Ant. pleasure, satisfaction, approval, delight; calm, peace.

disposition, n. 1. temper, temperament, nature, character, humor, attitude, personality, makeup, spirit, frame of mind. 2. inclination, willingness, bent, tendency, proneness, bias, predisposition, proclivity. 3. arrangement, order, grouping, location, placement. 4. settlement, outcome, finale, result, fate, end, upshot, aftermath, consequence, issue, dispensation. 5. regulation, appointment, management, control, direction.
—Ant. indisposition, unwillingness.

dispute, v. 1. argue, discuss, debate, agitate. 2. wrangle, contest, quarrel, bicker, spat, squabble, spar, brawl. 3. oppose, decry, gainsay, controvert, contradict, deny, impugn. —n. 4. argumentation, argument, disagreement, conflict, discord, strife, feud, contention, debate, controversy, disputation, altercation, quarrel, wrangle, bickering, spat, squabble, tiff, row.
—Ant. agree, concur; agreement, concurrence.
—Syn. Study. See ARGUMENT.

disregard, v. 1. ignore, neglect, overlook, disobey, pay no attention or heed or regard to, take no notice of. 2. slight, insult, snub, disparage, disdain, cut, give the cold shoulder, reject, spurn. —n. 3. neglect, inattention, inattentiveness, oversight. 4. disrespect, slight, indifference, contempt, disdain, aloofness.
—Ant. regard, view, notice, note; attention; respect.
—Syn. Study. See SLIGHT.

disrespectful, adj. discourteous, impolite, rude, crude, uncivil, insulting, flippant, outspoken, offensive, naughty, impudent, impertinent, irreverent, ill-mannered, insolent, pert, indecorus, saucy, forward, fresh, cheeky.
—Ant. respectful, courteous, polite, civil, reverent.

dissatisfaction, n. discontent, displeasure, dislike, disappointment, disapproval, disapprobation, uneasiness, unhappiness, frustration, discomfort, disquiet, malaise.
—Ant. satisfaction, approval, approbation.

dissent, n. difference, dissidence, disagreement, dissatisfaction, opposition, nonconformity, separation, friction, discord, contention, strife, conflict.
—Ant. agreement, concurrence, satisfaction, unity.

dissipate, v. 1. scatter, disperse, dispel, disintegrate. 2. waste, squander, run through, exhaust, throw away, fritter away. 3. scatter, disappear, vanish, disintegrate. 4. debauch, revel, carouse, party, sow wild oats, go on a spree, burn the candle at both ends.
—Ant. integrate, unite; appear; join.
—Syn. Study. See SCATTER.

dissolve, v. 1. sever, loose, loosen, free, disunite, break up; dismiss, disperse, adjourn. 2. destroy, dispel, ruin, disintegrate, break down, terminate, end; perish, crumble, die, expire.
—Ant. solidify; unite; meet; integrate; originate.

distaste, n. dislike, disinclination, disfavor, antipathy, revulsion, nausea, horror, aversion, repugnance, disgust, displeasure, dissatisfaction, disrelish.
—Ant. taste, delectation, liking, love, satisfaction; relish.

distasteful, adj. 1. disagreeable, displeasing, offensive, repugnant, repulsive, obnoxious, off-putting, objectionable, nasty, foul, unpleasant. 2. unpalatable, unsavory, nauseating, loathsome, revolting, sick-making, fulsome, vile, disgusting, sickening.
—Ant. tasteful, agreeable, pleasant, inoffensive; attractive, delightful.

distinct, adj. 1. distinguished, distinguishable, different, individual, separate, detached, discrete, sui generis, singular, various, varied, dissimilar. 2. definite, well-defined, sharp, perceptible, understandable, vivid, precise, exact, noticeable, recognizable, obvious, unambiguous, clear-cut, explicit, marked, evident, apparent, unequivocal, clear, plain, unmistakable, unconfused.
—Ant. indistinct, blurred, same; similar; indefinite, unclear, confused.
—Syn. Study. See VARIOUS.

distinction, n. 1. difference, contrast, separation, distinctiveness, differentiation, discrimination. 2. honor, credit, prominence, greatness, uniqueness, excellence, merit, quality, worth, prestige, consequence, glory, reputation, repute, name, fame, celebrity, renown, importance, note, account, eminence, superiority.
—Ant. indifference; similarity; disrepute, dishonor.

distinguish, v. 1. mark, characterize, identify, indicate, separate, set apart. 2. discriminate, differentiate, separate, divide, classify, categorize. 3. discern, recognize, perceive, know, tell. 4. make prominent or conspicuous or eminent.
—Syn. Study. DISTINGUISH, DIFFERENTIATE, DISCRIMINATE mean to note the difference between two or more similar things. To DISTINGUISH is to recognize differences based on characteristic features or qualities: to distinguish a light cruiser from a heavy cruiser. To DIFFERENTIATE is to find and point out the exact differences in detail: The symptoms of both diseases are so similar that it is hard to differentiate one from the other. To DISCRIMINATE is to note fine or subtle distinctions and to judge their significance: to discriminate prejudiced from unprejudiced testimony.

distinguished, adj. 1. conspicuous, marked, extraordinary. 2. noted, eminent, famed, famous, celebrated, renowned, illustrious, respected, noteworthy, preeminent, prominent, honored.
—Ant. undistinguished, common; infamous; unknown; unrefined, coarse.

distress, n. 1. pain, anxiety, sorrow, grief, agony, anguish, misery, adversity, hardship, trial, tribulation, suffering, trouble, affliction, sorrow, woe, ache, torment, angst, chagrin. 2. need, necessity, want, privation, deprivation, destitution, poverty, indigence. —v. 3. trouble, worry, disturb, perturb, upset, vex, harass, harry, oppress, afflict, bother, grieve, pain, make miserable or unhappy.
—Ant. comfort; fulfillment, opulence; console, mitigate, delight.

distribute, v. 1. deal out, deal, allot, apportion, assign, mete, dole, dispense, give. 2. disperse, spread, scatter, strew, diffuse, disseminate. 3. divide, separate, classify, categorize, dispose, sort, arrange, group, order.
—Ant. collect, keep; unite.

distrust, v. 1. doubt, suspect, mistrust, question, be skeptical of, be wary of, discredit, disbelieve, be leery of, smell a rat. —n. 2. doubt, suspicion, mistrust, misgiving, doubtfulness, uncertainty, skepticism, disbelief, incredulity, hesitation, wariness, qualm.
—Ant. trust, depend.
—Syn. Study. See SUSPICION.

disturbance, n. 1. perturbation, agitation, commotion, disorder, disruption, disarray, upheaval, upset, confusion, derangement. 2. disorder, tumult, riot, uproar, violence, trouble, outburst, turmoil, turbulence, brouhaha, brawl, melee, fray, fracas, donnybrook.
—Ant. order, organization; calm, serenity.

diverge, v. 1. branch off, separate, fork, bifurcate, divide, split, radiate, ramify, spread apart. 2. differ, deviate, disagree, vary.
—Ant. converge, unite; agree, concur.
—Syn. Study. See DEVIATE.

diverse, adj. 1. unlike, dissimilar, separate, different, disagreeing. 2. various, divers, varied, multiform, manifold, variant, divergent, assorted, mixed, miscellaneous, heterogeneous.
—Ant. similar, like.
—Syn. Study. See VARIOUS.

divert, v. 1. turn aside, deflect, switch, redirect, change, alter, avert, shift, sidetrack. 2. draw aside or away, turn aside, distract. 3. distract, entertain, amuse, delight, gratify, exhilarate, beguile, interest, engage, occupy.
—Ant. fix; weary, bore, tire.
—Syn. Study. See AMUSE.

divest, v. 1. strip, unclothe, denude, disrobe, undress. 2. strip, dispossess, deprive, relieve, rid, get rid, disencumber.
—Ant. invest.

divide, v. 1. separate, sunder, cut off, sever, shear, cleave, part. 2. apportion, share, deal out, partition, distribute, portion. 3. set at odds, sow dissension among, split, disaffect, alienate, disunite, cause to disagree, estrange. 4. classify, sort, arrange, distribute, categorize, grade, group, order, rank, organize, assort, arrange.
—Ant. unite; keep, retain; disarrange.

division, n. 1. partition, dividing, separation, apportionment, allotment, distribution, sharing. 2. mark, boundary, partition, demarcation. 3. section, part, compartment, partition, segment. 4. disagreement,

dissension, difference, variance, rupture, disunion, strife, upset, conflict, discord, breach, rift, estrangement, alienation, feud.
—Ant. agreement, union, accord.

do, v. **1.** perform, act. **2.** execute, finish, carry out, conclude, end, terminate, complete. **3.** accomplish, finish, achieve, attain, effect, bring about, execute, carry out. **4.** exert, put forth. **5.** behave, proceed, act, fare, manage.

doctrine, n. tenet, dogma, theory, precept, belief, canon, conviction, creed, credo, opinion, idea, concept, proposition, thesis, postulate, article of faith, principle; teachings.

dodge, v. equivocate, quibble, evade, be evasive, elude, sidestep, duck, hedge, double-talk, waffle.

dominant, adj. predominant, paramount, ruling, governing, controlling, most influential, prevailing, prevalent, common, principal, leading, reigning, supreme, superior, preeminent, outstanding, important, first, chief, main, primary, ascendant.
—Ant. secondary.
—**Syn. Study.** DOMINANT, PREDOMINANT, PARAMOUNT describe something outstanding or supreme. DOMINANT applies to something that exerts control or influence: *the dominant powers at an international conference.* PREDOMINANT applies to something that is foremost at a specific time: *English is one of the world's predominant languages.* PARAMOUNT refers to something that is first in rank or order: *Safety is of paramount importance.*

donation, n. gift, contribution, offering, grant, benefaction, boon, award, bequest, bestowal, alms, giving, largess, present, gratuity.

doom, n. **1.** fate, destiny, lot, karma, kismet, fortune. **2.** ruin, death, downfall, destruction, extinction, annihilation, end. **3.** judgment, decision, sentence, condemnation. —v. **4.** destine, predestine, foreordain, decree. **5.** condemn, sentence, ordain.

dormant, adj. **1.** asleep, inactive, torpid, quiescent, slumbering, at rest, quiet, still, comatose, torpid, hibernating, somnolent, lethargic, dull, sluggish. **2.** quiescent, inoperative, in abeyance, latent, potential, inert, suspended, hidden, unexpressed, concealed.
—Ant. awake, active; operative; kinetic.
—**Syn. Study.** See INACTIVE.

doubt, v. **1.** distrust, mistrust, suspect, question, disbelieve, discredit, have misgivings. **2.** hesitate, waver, vacillate, fluctuate, scruple, be uncertain, have doubts or reservations. —n. **3.** undecidedness, indecision, uncertainty, faltering, irresolution, hesitation, hesitancy, vacillation, misgiving, suspense; mistrust, distrust, suspicion, reservations, qualms, anxiety, worry.
—Ant. trust; decision, certainty, conviction.

doubtful, adj. **1.** uncertain, unsure, ambiguous, equivocal, indeterminate, undecided, fifty-fifty. **2.** undetermined, unsettled, indecisive, enigmatic, problematic, puzzled. **3.** dubious, incredulous, skeptical, hesitating, hesitant, wavering, irresolute, vacillating.
—Ant. certain, sure, unambiguous, decided; settled; unhesitating, resolute.
—**Syn.** DOUBTFUL, DUBIOUS, INCREDULOUS, SKEPTICAL all involve a reluctance to be convinced. DOUBTFUL implies a strong feeling of uncertainty or indecision about something or someone: *to be doubtful*

about the outcome of a contest. DUBIOUS usu. implies vacillation or hesitation caused by mistrust or suspicion: *dubious about the statements of a witness.* INCREDULOUS suggests an unwillingness or reluctance to believe: *incredulous at the good news.* SKEPTICAL implies a general disposition to doubt or question: *skeptical of human progress.*

dowdy, adj. badly dressed, frumpy, shabby, old-fashioned, chintzy, frowzy, seedy, slovenly, sloppy, messy, drab, dull, unbecoming, unfashionable, tacky, cheapjack.
—Ant. fashionable, chic, modish, à la mode.

downhearted, adj. dejected, discouraged, depressed, downcast, despondent, disheartened, sad, sorrowful, unhappy, dispirited, crestfallen, blue, low-spirited, wretched, woebegone.
—Ant. happy, elated.

downright, adj. utter, absolute, complete, outright, positive, perfect, arrant, out-and-out, thoroughgoing, flat-out, unqualified, unmitigated, direct, straightforward, plain, frank, open, candid, blunt, brash, unambiguous, outright, categorical, unequivocal, explicit.

drag, v. **1.** draw, pull, haul, trail, tug. **2.** trail, linger, loiter, dawdle, lag, straggle, poke along.
—Ant. drive, push; speed, expedite.

draw, v. **1.** drag, haul, pull, tug, tow, lead. **2.** attract, lure, elicit, magnetize. **3.** delineate, sketch, depict, trace. **4.** frame, formulate, compose, write, draw up, prepare, form. **5.** get, derive, deduce, infer, understand. **6.** produce, bring in, bear. **7.** draw or pull out, attenuate; extend, stretch, lengthen.
—Ant. drive, push.

dread, n. **1.** terror, fear, apprehension, angst, fright, trepidation, uneasiness, anticipation, alarm, nervousness, dismay, worry, anxiety, consternation, distress, perturbation, disquiet, aversion, horror, panic, cold feet, butterflies, heebie-jeebies. **2.** awe, reverence, veneration. —adj. **3.** frightful, dire, terrible, dreadful, horrible, feared, terrifying.
—Ant. intrepidity, bravery; pleasant, delightful.

dreary, adj. **1.** gloomy, dismal, drear, cheerless, chilling, chill, depressing, comfortless, somber, bleak, doleful, wretched, funereal, glum, morose. **2.** monotonous, tedious, wearisome, dull, boring, uninteresting, tiresome, lifeless, colorless, drab, arid, dry, dead, prosaic, humdrum, ordinary, vapid, run-of-the-mill, unexciting.
—Ant. cheerful, comforting; interesting, engaging.

drench, v. steep, wet, soak, ret, saturate, flood, drown, inundate.
—Ant. dry.

dress, n. **1.** costume, frock, gown; clothing, garb, attire, apparel, garments, vestments, clothes, suit, habit, habiliment; regalia, array, panoply. —v. **2.** attire, robe, garb, clothe, array, accouter, apparel, rig, deck out. **3.** trim, ornament, adorn, decorate.
—Ant. undress.

drive, v. **1.** push, force, impel, propel, send. **2.** overwork, overtask, overburden, overtax. **3.** urge, constrain, impel, compel, force. **4.** go, travel, ride. —n. **5.** vigor, pressure, effort, energy, impetus, vim, spunk, enterprise, ambition, determination, industry, initiative, zeal, enthusiasm, get-up-and-go, pep, zip, push.
—Ant. curb, restrain.

droll, adj. queer, odd, risible, eccentric, ridiculous, diverting, amusing, comical, waggish, witty, funny.

—Ant. serious.
—Syn. Study. See AMUSING.

droop, v. sink, bend, hang down, dangle, flag, languish, fail, weaken, decline, faint, wilt, wither, fade, slump, sag.
—Ant. rise.

drunk, adj. **1.** drunken, intoxicated, inebriated, besotted, tipsy, crapulent, crapulous, under the influence, under the weather, in one's cups, soused, pickled, high as a kite, boozy, boozed up, tight, lit, three sheets to the wind, under the table, loaded, stoned, stewed to the gills, bombed out of one's mind, plastered, crocked, sloshed, smashed, blotto, befuddled, tanked, polluted, stinko, juiced up, on a bender or jag. **2.** delirious, excited, exhilarated, exuberant, animated, ecstatic, flushed, fevered, inflamed, in high spirits.
—Ant. sober; sedate.

drunkard, n. toper, sot, tippler, drinker, inebriate, dipsomaniac, alcoholic, problem drinker, wino, boozer, lush, souse, alky, rummy, juicer, juicehead.
—Ant. teetotaler, dry.

dry, adj. **1.** arid, parched, dehydrated, desiccated, waterless, barren, bare, sere, moistureless, thirsty. **2.** plain, bald, unadorned, unembellished. **3.** dull, uninteresting, dreary, tiresome, boring, tedious, jejune, barren, monotonous, prosaic, stale, commonplace, uninspired, wearisome, vapid. **4.** sarcastic, biting, sardonic, keen, sharp, pointed, sly, witty, droll, wry, cynical, cutting, keen, ironic.
—Ant. wet, drenched; interesting, fascinating.
—Syn. Study. DRY, ARID both mean without moisture. DRY is the general word indicating absence of water or freedom from moisture, which may be favorable or unfavorable: *a dry well; a dry bath towel.* ARID suggests intense dryness in a region or climate, resulting in bareness or in barrenness: *arid tracts of desert.*

dubious, adj. **1.** doubtful, undecided, indeterminate, uncertain, unsure, inconclusive, dubitable, fluctuating, wavering. **2.** questionable, equivocal, ambiguous, obscure, unclear, misleading, vague, cryptic, mysterious, enigmatical.
—Ant. definite, incisive, certain; unquestionable, unequivocal, clear.
—Syn. Study. See DOUBTFUL.

dull, adj. **1.** slow, obtuse, stupid, blunted, unimaginative, sluggish, dense, bovine, cloddish, backward, dumb, dim, unintelligent, stolid. **2.** insensible, unfeeling, insensate, apathetic, numb, unresponsive, hard, inured, phlegmatic, unimpassioned, lifeless, callous, dead. **3.** listless, spiritless, torpid, inactive, lifeless, inert, inanimate. **4.** boring, depressing, monotonous, uninspired, unoriginal, humdrum, tedious, uninteresting, tiresome, dreary, vapid, wearisome, dry, jejune. —v. **5.** blunt, deaden, desensitize, narcotize, stupefy, paralyze, obtund, benumb. **6.** depress, dishearten, discourage, dispirit, sadden, deject.
—Ant. bright, imaginative, quick; sensitive; spirited, active, animated; interesting; encourage, inspirit, hearten.

dumb, adj. **1.** mute, speechless, silent, voiceless, quiet, taciturn, mum, wordless; inarticulate. **2.** stupid, dull.
—Ant. voluble, talkative, loquacious.

duplicate, adj. **1.** double, twofold; identical, twin, matching. —n. **2.** facsimile copy, replica, clone, dead ringer, Xerox copy, photocopy, fax, reproduction, transcript. —v. **3.**

copy, replicate, reproduce, repeat, double, imitate, photocopy, clone, match, Xerox.
—Ant. original.

duplicity, n. deceitfulness, deceit, double-dealing, deception, guile, cheating, delusion, cunning, hoax, victimization, trickery, hypocrisy, dissimulation, chicanery, artifice, fraud, dishonesty, perfidy, treachery, flimflam.
—Ant. naiveté, honesty, openness, simplicity.
—Syn. Study. See DECEIT.

durable, adj. lasting, enduring, stable, constant, permanent, heavy-duty, indestructible, substantial, sturdy, tough, stout, strong, sound, dependable, reliable, long-wearing.
—Ant. unstable, temporary, temporal.

dusky, adj. dim, shadowy, murky, cloudy, dark, shady, obscure, clouded, penumbral, unilluminated, unlit, gloomy, tenebrous, crepuscular.
—Ant. fair, blond, light; clear, unclouded.

dutiful, adj. respectful, docile, submissive, deferential, reverential, polite, considerate, yielding, obedient; compliant, willing, obliging, faithful, reliable, responsible, diligent, conscientious.
—Ant. disrespectful, disobedient, irreverent.

duty, n. **1.** obligation, responsibility, burden, onus, task, assignment, job, occupation, calling, function, role, part, bit, charge. **2.** office, function, responsibility, service, business. **3.** homage, respect, deference, reverence; loyalty, fidelity, faithfulness, allegiance.
—Syn. Study. DUTY, OBLIGATION refer to something a person feels bound to do. A DUTY often applies to what a person performs in fulfillment of the permanent dictates of conscience, piety, right, or law: *one's duty to tell the truth; a parent's duty to raise children properly.* An OBLIGATION is what is expected at a particular time in fulfillment of a specific and often personal promise, contract, or agreement: *social or financial obligations.*

dwarf, n. **1.** midget, pygmy, homunculus, manikin, Lilliputian, runt. —adj. **2.** diminutive, tiny, small, little, Lilliputian, stunted, dwarfed, undersized. —v. **3.** stunt; overshadow, diminish, dominate, minimize.
—Ant. giant, colossus; huge, gigantic, immense, colossal.
—Syn. Study. DWARF, MIDGET, PYGMY are terms for a very small person. A DWARF is someone checked in growth or stunted, or in some way not normally formed. A MIDGET (not in technical use) is someone normally proportioned, but diminutive. A PYGMY is properly a member of one of certain small-sized peoples of Africa and Asia, but the word is often used imprecisely to mean dwarf or midget. DWARF is a term often used to describe very small plants. PYGMY is used to describe very small animals.

dwell, v. **1.** abide, reside, lodge, remain, rest, have quarters, stay, live, inhabit. **2.** continue, perpetuate, linger, emphasize.
—Ant. leave, depart; cease, end, terminate, stop.

dwindle, v. diminish, lessen, decline, decrease, wane, shrink, waste away, reduce, fade, peter out, ebb, taper off, shrivel away, degenerate, sink, decay.
—Ant. increase, grow, wax.
—Syn. Study. See DECREASE.

E

eager, *adj.* avid, ardent, enthusiastic, zealous, keen, hot, hungry, passionate, energetic, excited, itchy, breathless, impatient, anxious, atingle, chomping at the bit, raring to go.
—**Ant.** reluctant, disinclined, hesitant.

earn, *v.* **1.** gain, acquire, win, get, obtain, secure, procure, collect, make, receive, reap. **2.** merit, deserve, warrant, rate, qualify for, be worthy of.
—**Syn. Study.** See GAIN.

earnest, *adj.* **1.** resolute, serious, sincere, zealous, ardent, eager, fervent, fervid, determined, purposeful. **2.** deep, firm, stable, intent, steady, faithful, true.
—**Ant.** insincere, apathetic; faithless, unfaithful, wavering.
—**Syn. Study.** EARNEST, RESOLUTE, SERIOUS, SINCERE imply having qualities of steady purposefulness. EARNEST implies having a purpose and being steadily and soberly eager in pursuing it: *an earnest student.* RESOLUTE adds a quality of determination: *resolute in defending the rights of others.* SERIOUS implies having depth and a soberness of attitude that contrasts with gaiety and frivolity; it may include the qualities of both earnestness and resolution: *serious and thoughtful.* SINCERE suggests genuineness, trustworthiness, and absence of superficiality: *a sincere interest in a person's welfare.*

earth, *n.* **1.** globe, world, planet, terra firma. **2.** ground, soil, turf, sod, dirt, loam.
—**Ant.** heaven; sky.

earthly, *adj.* **1.** terrestrial, worldly, mundane, physical, material, earthy. **2.** possible, conceivable, imaginable, feasible.
—**Ant.** spiritual; impossible, inconceivable.
—**Syn. Study.** EARTHLY, TERRESTRIAL, WORLDLY, MUNDANE refer to that which is concerned with the earth literally or figuratively. EARTHLY now almost always implies a contrast to that which is heavenly: *earthly pleasures; our earthly home.* TERRESTRIAL applies to the earth as a planet or to land as opposed to water: *the terrestrial globe; terrestrial areas.* WORLDLY is commonly used in the sense of being devoted to the vanities, cares, advantages, or gains of physical existence to the exclusion of spiritual interests or the afterlife: *worldly success; worldly standards.* MUNDANE is a formal equivalent of WORLDLY and suggests that which is bound to the earth, is not exalted, and therefore is commonplace: *mundane pursuits.*

earthy, *adj.* **1.** plain, simple, unadorned, down-to-earth, unpretentious, matter-of-fact, unsophisticated, uncomplicated, direct, practical, pragmatic, clear-eyed. **2.** unrefined, impolite, rude, crude, vulgar, scatological, obscene, blue, gross, risqué, dirty, wanton, ribald, bawdy, coarse, shameless, uninhibited, abandoned, lusty, rough, indecent.
—**Ant.** refined, elevated, delicate.

ease, *n.* **1.** comfort, relaxation, rest, repose, well-being, leisure, effortlessness, contentment, happiness. **2.** tranquility, serenity, calmness, quiet, quietude, peace. **3.** informality, unaffectedness, naturalness, lightness, flexibility, freedom. —*v.* **4.** comfort, relieve, disburden, relax, soothe, tranquilize, pacify, calm,

still. **5.** tranquilize, soothe, allay, alleviate, mitigate, abate, assuage, lighten, lessen, reduce. **6.** facilitate, expedite, simplify, smooth, further, clear, assist, aid, help, advance, forward, oil the works.
—**Ant.** discomfort, effort; disturbance, perturbation; affectation; burden; increase.

easy, *adj.* **1.** facile, light, unstrained, unhurried, leisurely, gentle, moderate. **2.** tranquil, untroubled, comfortable, contented, satisfied, quiet, at rest. **3.** easygoing, compliant, submissive, complying, accommodating, agreeable, yielding, docile, pliant, tractable, amenable, soft. **4.** lenient, light, undemanding, flexible, indulgent, tolerant. **5.** informal, unrestrained, unconstrained, unembarrassed, smooth, down-to-earth, unceremonious.
—**Ant.** difficult, hard, immoderate; troubled, disturbed, uncomfortable, disagreeable, unyielding; restrained, embarrassed.

easygoing, *adj.* relaxed, placid, calm, serene, tranquil, even-tempered, permissive, tolerant, casual, mellow, carefree, poised, composed, collected, easy, unruffled, self-possessed, imperturbable, nonchalant, insouciant, laid-back, cool.
—**Ant.** tense, rigid, demanding.

ebb, *n.* **1.** reflux, regression, regress, retrogression. **2.** decline, decay, deterioration, degeneration, wane. —*v.* **3.** subside, abate, recede, retire. **4.** decline, sink, wane, decrease, decay, waste *or* fade away.
—**Ant.** flow, neap; wax; increase, swell, well; rise.

eccentric, *adj.* **1.** off-center, uncentered, off-balance, unbalanced. **2.** odd, unusual, peculiar, unconventional, strange, curious, bizarre, sui generis, idiosyncratic, unorthodox, unique, quirky, far-out, kinky, queer, aberrant, weird, freakish, offbeat, off-the-wall, oddball, bizzarre. —*n.* **3.** character, oddity, original, strange one, crank, individualist, nonconformist, crackpot, freak, oddball, odd duck, card, weirdo, loner.

economical, *adj.* thrifty, frugal, saving, provident, sparing; stingy, tight, penurious, parsimonious, cheap, miserly, tightfisted, mean, penny-pinching, scrimping.
—**Ant.** lavish, spendthrift.
—**Syn. Study.** ECONOMICAL, THRIFTY, FRUGAL imply careful and efficient use of resources. ECONOMICAL implies prudent planning in the disposition of resources so as to avoid unnecessary waste or expense: *It is economical to buy in large quantities.* THRIFTY adds the idea of industry and successful management: *a thrifty shopper looking for bargains.* FRUGAL suggests saving by denying oneself luxuries: *so frugal that he never takes taxis.*

economy, *n.* **1.** frugality, thriftiness, thrift, saving, conservatism, restraint, control. **2.** briefness, brevity, succinctness, terseness, conciseness, concision, compactness, curtness.
—**Ant.** lavishness.

ecstatic, *adj.* overjoyed, joyful, elated, bursting, rapturous, exhilarated, thrilled, blissful, euphoric, rhapsodic, excited, delighted, gleeful, happy, glad, orgasmic, delirious, exultant, jubilant, transported, on cloud nine, in seventh heaven, beside oneself, happy as a lark.
—**Ant.** glum, dispirited, downhearted.

edge, *n.* **1.** border, rim, lip, margin, boundary, verge, brink, side, brim, fringe, limit, perimeter, periphery. —*v.* **2.** inch, sidle, crawl, creep,

steal, worm, work one's way.
—**Ant.** center.

edify, *v.* enlighten, educate, illuminate, improve, better, transform, uplift, raise, boost, lift, elevate.

educate, *v.* teach, instruct, school, drill, indoctrinate, edify, tutor, inform, enlighten, coach, prepare, ready, rear, cultivate, civilize, train, discipline.
—**Syn. Study.** See TEACH.

education, *n.* **1.** teaching, schooling, cultivation, upbringing, drilling, instruction, tuition, training. **2.** learning, knowledge, enlightenment, culture, lore, erudition.
—**Ant.** illiteracy.

eerie, *adj.* fearful, awesome, weird, uncanny, strange, ghostly, spectral, unearthly, mysterious, scary, creepy, spooky.
—**Ant.** common, ordinary.
—**Syn. Study.** See WEIRD.

effect, *n.* **1.** consequence, result, upshot, aftermath, end, outcome, issue. **2.** power, efficacy, force, validity, weight. **3.** operation, execution; accomplishment, fulfillment. **4.** purport, intent, tenor, significance, signification, meaning, import. —*v.* **5.** bring about, accomplish, cause, make happen, achieve, do, perform, complete, consummate, realize, secure, obtain, execute, produce, create.
—**Ant.** cause.
—**Syn. Study.** EFFECT, CONSEQUENCE, RESULT refer to something produced by an action or a cause. An EFFECT is that which is produced, usu. more or less immediately and directly: *The drug had the effect of producing sleep.* A CONSEQUENCE, something that follows naturally or logically, as in a train of events or sequence of time, is less intimately connected with its cause than is an effect: *One consequence of a recession is a rise in unemployment.* A RESULT may be near or remote, and often is the sum of effects or consequences as making an end or final outcome: *The English language is the result of the fusion of many different elements.*

effective, *adj.* **1.** effectual, efficacious, efficient, capable, competent, productive, useful, serviceable, able, functional. **2.** operative, in force, active, functioning, real, actual, basic, essential.
—**Ant.** ineffective, incompetent, inefficient, ineffectual; inactive, inoperative.
—**Syn. Study.** EFFECTIVE, EFFECTUAL, EFFICACIOUS, EFFICIENT refer to that which produces or is able to produce an effect. EFFECTIVE is applied to something that produces a desired or expected effect, often a lasting one: *an effective speech.* EFFECTUAL usually refers to something that produces a decisive outcome or result: *an effectual settlement.* EFFICACIOUS refers to something capable of achieving a certain end or purpose: *an efficacious remedy.* EFFICIENT, usually used of a person, implies skillful accomplishment of a purpose with little waste of effort: *an efficient manager.*

effort, *n.* application, endeavor, exertion, attempt, struggle, strain, labor, pains, energy, toil, trouble, work, elbow grease, striving.
—**Ant.** ease.
—**Syn. Study.** EFFORT, APPLICATION, ENDEAVOR, EXERTION imply energetic activity and expenditure of energy. EFFORT is an expenditure of physical or mental energy to accomplish some objective: *He made an effort to control himself.* APPLICATION is continuous effort plus careful attention and diligence: *application to one's*

studies. ENDEAVOR means a continued and sustained series of efforts to achieve some end, often worthy and difficult: *an endeavor to rescue survivors.* EXERTION is vigorous action or effort, frequently without an end in view: *out of breath from exertion.*

effusive, *adj.* demonstrative, extravagant, gushing, profuse, enthusiastic, emotional, exuberant, rhapsodic, ebullient, lavish, voluble, outgoing, unrestrained, unrepressed, expansive, unreticent, talkative.
—**Ant.** taciturn, laconic.

egocentric, *adj.* self-centered, self-referencing, conceited, egotistic, egotistical, egomaniacal, selfish, spoiled, narcissistic, self-loving, self-absorbed, vain, vainglorious, stuck-up, stuck on oneself.
—**Ant.** modest, self-effacing, humble.

egotism, *n.* self-love, egoism, selfishness, conceit, narcissism, solipsism, self-importance, self-indulgence, egocentricity, self-absorption, pride, vainglory, braggadocio, swellheadedness, egomania, amour-propre.
—**Ant.** altruism, modesty.
—**Syn. Study.** EGOTISM, EGOISM refer to preoccupation with one's ego or self. EGOTISM is the common word for a tendency to speak or write about oneself too much; it suggests selfishness and an inordinate sense of one's own importance: *His egotism alienated most of his colleagues.* EGOISM, a less common word, emphasizes the moral justification of a concern for one's own welfare and interests, but carries less of an implication of boastful self-importance: *a healthy egoism that stood him well in times of trial.*

elaborate, *adj.* **1.** meticulous, thorough, complete, exhaustive, minute, precise, exact, painstaking, labored, studied, fancy, extravagant, showy, Byzantine, decorated, baroque, rococo, detailed, ornate, intricate, complicated, complex. —*v.* **2.** ornament, decorate, embellish, complicate, adorn; develop, cultivate, enhance, enrich, improve, enlarge, expand, refine.
—**Ant.** simple; simplify.

elate, *v.* cheer, cheer up, excite, exhilarate, inspirit, exalt, lift, uplift, elevate, delight, overjoy, thrill, transport, tickle.
—**Ant.** depress, discourage.

elect, *v.* **1.** select, choose, prefer, pick, vote, determine, designate, name, usher in. —*adj.* **2.** select, chosen, choice, first-rate, superior, elite, of the first water.
—**Ant.** refuse, reject; second-rate.

elegant, *adj.* tasteful, fine, luxurious, sumptuous, grand, opulent, swank, fancy, ritzy, plush; refined, polished, cultivated, debonair, polished, suave, soigné, to the manner born, well-bred, aristocratic, chic, fashionable, grand, posh, dignified, artistic, genteel, courtly, graceful; choice, nice, superior; excellent.
—**Ant.** inelegant, distasteful; unrefined, disgraceful; inferior.

element, *n.* **1.** component, constituent, ingredient, unit, part, essential, fundamental, segment, piece, feature, factor, detail. **2.** rudiment, principle, basis, basic. **3.** habitat, environment, medium, milieu, atmosphere, locale, sphere, domain.
—**Ant.** whole, nonessential; compound.
—**Syn. Study.** ELEMENT, COMPONENT, CONSTITUENT, INGREDIENT refer to units that are parts of whole or complete substances, systems, compounds, or mixtures. ELEMENT denotes a fundamental, ultimate part:

the elements of matter; the elements of a problem. COMPONENT refers to one of a number of separate parts: Iron and carbon are components of steel. CONSTITUENT refers to an active and necessary part: The constituents of a molecule of water are two atoms of hydrogen and one of oxygen. INGREDIENT is most frequently used in non-scientific contexts to denote any part that is combined into a mixture: the ingredients of a cake; the ingredients of a successful marriage.

elementary, adj. primary, rudimentary, basic, fundamental, rudimental; easy, straightforward, clear, understandable, plain, simple, uncomplicated.
—**Ant.** advanced, secondary; complex, complicated.

elevate, v. enhance, exalt, heighten, raise, lift up, hallow, sanctify, increase, intensify, promote, advance, improve, enhance, dignify, refine, animate, cheer, elate, liven, inspirit, uplift.
—**Ant.** lower, debase, decrease; depress.
—**Syn. Study.** ELEVATE, ENHANCE, EXALT, HEIGHTEN mean to raise or make higher in some respect. To ELEVATE is to raise up to a higher level, position, or state: to elevate the living standards of a group. To ENHANCE is to add to the attractions or desirability of something: Landscaping enhances the beauty of the grounds. To EXALT is to raise very high in rank, character, estimation, mood, etc.: A king is exalted above his subjects. To HEIGHTEN is to increase the strength or intensity: to heighten one's powers of concentration.

elevation, n. loftiness, grandeur, dignity, nobility, nobleness, refinement, exaltation, sublimity.
—**Ant.** valley; depths.
—**Syn. Study.** See HEIGHT.

eligible, adj. suitable, qualified, acceptable, fitted, fit, worthy, admissible, desirable, proper, appropriate.
—**Ant.** unsuitable, ineligible.

eliminate, v. get rid of, expel, remove, exclude, reject, omit, ignore, cut, delete, erase, dismiss, elide, take away, kick out, kill, destroy, excommunicate, banish, scorn, repudiate, disdain, drop, dispose of, cancel, terminate, dispose of, annihilate, eradicate, expunge, obliterate, bury, waste.
—**Ant.** include, accept.

elude, v. **1.** avoid, escape, evade, slip away from, shun, dodge. **2.** puzzle, bewilder stump, baffle, confound, foil, thwart, confuse, frustrate, disconcert.
—**Ant.** grasp.
—**Syn. Study.** See ESCAPE.

emanate, v. emerge, issue, proceed, come forth, originate, arise, spring, flow, ooze, exude, radiate, emit.
—**Syn. Study.** See EMERGE.

embarrass, v. disconcert, abash, make uncomfortable, confuse, upset, shame, mortify, humble, humiliate, fluster, discombobulate, disgrace, distress, discomfit, discompose, chagrin.
—**Ant.** comfort, console.

embarrassment, n. **1.** bashfulness, awkwardness, clumsiness, uneasiness, disconcertment, abashment, perplexity, confusion, discomposure, discomfort, mortification, chagrin. **2.** trouble, annoyance, vexation, distress, harassment, hindrance, deterrent, difficulty, mess, predicament, dilemma, problem.
—**Ant.** comfort, composure; encouragement.
—**Syn. Study.** See SHAME.

embellish, v. **1.** beautify, ornament, adorn, decorate, garnish, bedeck,

improve, trick out, enrich, gild, embroider. **2.** enhance, embroider, exaggerate about, elaborate, overdo, dress up.
—**Ant.** strip down, simplify.

emblem, n. token, sign, symbol, figure, image, badge, device, representation, insigne, seal, crest, trademark, mark.

embrace, v. **1.** clasp, hug, grasp, hold, enfold, cuddle. **2.** accept, adopt, espouse, welcome, receive, seize. **3.** encircle, surround, enclose, contain. **4.** include, contain, comprise, comprehend, cover, embody, incorporate, encompass.
—**Ant.** exclude, reject.

emerge, v. emanate, issue, come forth, spread, stream; appear, surface, develop, transpire, happen, evolve.
—**Ant.** hide.
—**Syn. Study.** EMERGE, EMANATE, ISSUE mean to come forth from a place or source. EMERGE is used of coming forth from concealment, obscurity, or something that envelops: The sun emerged from behind the clouds. EMANATE is used of intangible or immaterial things, as light or ideas, spreading from a source: Rumors often emanate from irresponsible persons. ISSUE is most often used of a number of persons, a mass of matter, or a volume of smoke, sound, or the like, coming forth through any outlet or outlets: The crowd issued from the building.

emergency, n. crisis, straits, urgency, turning point, exigency, necessity, extremity, pinch, dilemma, quandary, danger, predicament, difficulty.

eminence, n. repute, distinction, prominence, celebrity, renown, importance, preeminence, superiority, greatness, conspicuousness, note, fame, rank, position, esteem, exaltation, respect, reverence, illustriousness.
—**Ant.** disrepute, obscurity.

eminent, adj. distinguished, signal, notable, noteworthy, noted, esteemed, respected, revered, honored, dignified, important, preeminent, great, superior, famous, celebrated, well-known, prominent, celebrated, renowned, outstanding, illustrious, conspicuous, exalted.
—**Ant.** disreputable, commonplace, ordinary; low, debased; inconspicuous.

emit, v. send or give forth, discharge, eject, vent, exhale, exude, emanate, issue, radiate, send out, put forth, give off, expel.
—**Ant.** inspire, inhale, accept.

emotion, n. feeling, passion, sentiment, sensation, fervor; compassion, sympathy, empathy.
—**Ant.** apathy.
—**Syn. Study.** See FEELING.

empathy, n. compassion, understanding, responsiveness, concern, consideration, tender-heartedness, caring, sensitivity, identification, involvement, sharing, fellow feeling, perceptiveness, perceptivity, sympathy.
—**Ant.** callousness, indifference.
—**Syn. Study.** See SYMPATHY.

emphasize, v. stress, accent, accentuate, italicize, bring out, underline, underscore, play up, highlight, feature, mark, spotlight, single out, punctuate, point up, call attention to.
—**Ant.** deemphasize, play down, underplay, ignore.

emphatic, adj. significant, marked, striking, positive, energetic, express, insistent, categorical, resolute, explicit, assertive, intense, forcible,

forceful, pronounced, strong, decided, unequivocal, definite, dynamic.
—**Ant.** insignificant, uncertain, unsure.

employ, v. **1.** use, engage, hire, retain, occupy, enlist, recruit, enroll, sign up, take on, commission. **2.** use, apply, make use of.

employee, n. worker, servant, agent, clerk, wage earner, staff member, hand, underling, minion, helper, aide, assistant.
—**Ant.** employer, boss.

empower, v. **1.** enable, enfranchise, inspire, actualize, self-actualize. **2.** authorize, sanction, entitle, warrant, license.
—**Ant.** disenfranchise, marginalize.

empty, adj. **1.** void, hollow, unfilled, bare, barren, blank; vacant, unoccupied, uninhabited. **2.** unsatisfactory, meaningless, superficial, trivial, insincere, worthless, valueless, idle, hollow, delusive, vain, ineffectual, ineffective, unsatisfying. **3.** frivolous, foolish, vacuous, inane, stupid. —v. **4.** clear, remove, eject, vacate; unload, unburden, pour out, evacuate, drain, discharge, exhaust, drain.
—**Ant.** full, replete; occupied, inhabited; satisfactory, effectual; serious.

enchant, v. fascinate, cast a spell over, spellbind, mesmerize, hypnotize, beguile, enthrall, entrance, attract, allure, captivate, charm, enrapture, transport, bewitch, delight, seduce, entice.
—**Ant.** bore.

encircle, v. surround, ring, confine, hem in, wreathe, circle, compass, encompass, environ, gird, enfold, enclose.

enclose, v. surround, encircle, encompass, circumscribe, shut in, pen, confine, bound, envelop, wall in, immure.
—**Ant.** set free.

encounter, v. **1.** meet, confront, face, experience. **2.** contend against, engage with, attack, cope with, compete with. —n. **3.** meeting. **4.** battle, combat, conflict, confrontation, engagement, contest, competition, brush, struggle, fight, clash, struggle, skirmish, altercation, dispute, duel, quarrel, disagreement, wrangle.

encourage, v. **1.** inspirit, embolden, hearten, stimulate, incite; reassure, assure, console, comfort. **2.** urge, abet, second, support, favor, countenance, advance, foster, promote, aid, help, foment.
—**Ant.** discourage, dispirit.

encumber, v. **1.** impede, hamper, retard, embarrass, obstruct, complicate, involve, entangle, handicap, hinder, inconvenience, trammel, slow down. **2.** load, oppress, overload, burden, weigh down, strain, saddle, tax.
—**Ant.** disencumber; unload, unburden.

end, n. **1.** extremity, extreme. **2.** limit, bound, boundary, termination, tip, terminus. **3.** close, termination, conclusion, finish, outcome, issue, consequence, result, completion, attainment. **4.** finale, conclusion, peroration. **5.** purpose, aim, object, objective, goal, intention, design, intent, drift. —v. **6.** terminate, conclude, wind up, finish, complete, close. **7.** stop, cease, discontinue, conclude.
—**Ant.** beginning, start; begin, commence, open; continue.
—**Syn. Study.** See AIM.

endeavor, v. **1.** attempt, essay, try, make an effort, strive, struggle, labor; seek, aim. —n. **2.** effort, pains, undertaking, enterprise, exertion,

struggle, essay, attempt, trial.
—**Syn. Study.** See TRY. See also EFFORT.

endless, adj. limitless, unlimited, vast, illimitable, immeasurable, unending, boundless, infinite, interminable, incessant, unceasing, eternal, continuous, perpetual, everlasting, nonstop.
—**Ant.** limited, finite.
—**Syn. Study.** See ETERNAL.

endow, v. equip, invest, enrich; confer, bestow, give, grant, present.
—**Ant.** divest.

endowment, n. gift, grant, bequest, largess, bounty, present; capacity, talent, faculties, quality, power, ability, aptitude, capability, genius.
—**Ant.** incapacity.

endure, v. **1.** sustain, hold out against, undergo, bear, support, suffer, experience. **2.** experience, stand, tolerate, bear, brook, allow, permit, submit. **3.** continue, last, persist, remain.
—**Ant.** fail, subside; refuse; die, perish, fail.
—**Syn. Study.** See BEAR. See also CONTINUE.

enemy, n. foe, adversary, opponent, antagonist, rival, competitor, contestant, contender, the opposition, the other side.
—**Ant.** friend, ally.

energetic, adj. **1.** lively, dynamic, animated, spirited, tireless, indefatigable, sprightly, spry, vital, high-powered, peppy, zippy, full of beans, forcible, vigorous, active. **2.** powerful, effective, effectual, strong, efficacious, potent.
—**Ant.** lazy, inactive; ineffective, impotent, weak.

energy, n. **1.** activity, exertion, power, force, operation, dynamism, vigor, potency, zeal, push, spirit, animation, life, vitality, vivacity, liveliness, spirit, drive, verve, dash, élan, pep, zip, zing, get-up-and-go. **2.** force, power, might, efficacy, strength, intensity.
—**Ant.** inertia, inactivity; weakness.

engender, v. **1.** produce, cause, give rise to, originate, beget, create, occasion, excite, stir up, incite, generate, breed. **2.** procreate, beget, create, generate, breed.
—**Ant.** terminate; kill.

enigma, n. puzzle, riddle, problem, question, conundrum, mystery, poser.

enjoyment, n. delight, delectation, pleasure, gratification, happiness, joy, relish, zest, recreation, entertainment, diversion.
—**Ant.** detestation, abhorrence, displeasure, boredom.

enlarge, v. extend, augment, amplify, dilate, increase, aggrandize, magnify, expand, greaten, swell, spread, wax, widen, stretch, inflate, broaden, lengthen.
—**Ant.** limit, decrease, lessen, abate.

enlighten, v. illumine, edify, teach, inform, instruct, educate, inform, apprise, advise, counsel, make aware.
—**Ant.** confuse.

enliven, v. **1.** invigorate, animate, inspirit, vivify, stimulate, pep up, jump-start, energize, vitalize, inspire, rouse, kindle, spark off, quicken. **2.** exhilarate, gladden, cheer, brighten, inspire, delight, buoy up, uplift.
—**Ant.** dispirit, slow; depress.

enormous, adj. **1.** huge, immense, vast, colossal, mammoth, gigantic, prodigious, elephantine, gargantuan, titanic, tremendous, Brobdingnagian, massive, monstrous. **2.** outrageous, atrocious, flagitious, depraved, wicked, flagrant, scandalous, egregious.
—**Ant.** small, diminutive, tiny;

honorable.
—**Syn. Study.** See HUGE.

enrage, *v.* incense, infuriate, anger, inflame, provoke, madden, exasperate, aggravate, inflame, make someone's blood boil, tick someone off, make someone see red.
—**Ant.** tranquilize, calm, assuage.
—**Syn. Study.** ENRAGE, INCENSE, INFURIATE imply stirring to violent anger. To ENRAGE or to INFURIATE is to provoke wrath: *They enrage (infuriate) her by their deliberate and continual harassment.* To INCENSE is to inflame with indignation or anger: *to incense a person by making insulting remarks.*

entangle, *v.* **1.** complicate, ensnare, enmesh, tangle, knot, mat. **2.** mix up, embarrass, confuse, perplex, bewilder, involve, ensnare, embroil.
—**Ant.** simplify.

enterprise, *n.* **1.** project, plan, undertaking, venture, adventure, effort, scheme, program. **2.** boldness, daring, mettle, audacity, zeal, drive, vigor, ambition, readiness, spirit, energy, resolve, purpose, gumption, guts.

enterprising, *adj.* ambitious, ready, resourceful, adventurous, venturesome, dashing, bold, energetic, spirited, eager, zealous, resolute, determined, hard-working, industrious, purposeful, goal-oriented, diligent, assiduous, persevering, tireless, indefatigable, aggressive.
—**Ant.** phlegmatic, lazy.
—**Syn. Study.** See AMBITIOUS.

entertain, *v.* **1.** divert, amuse, please. **2.** receive, consider, admit. **3.** harbor, cherish, hold, tolerate, allow, maintain, sustain, support.
—**Ant.** bore; refuse, reject; expel.
—**Syn. Study.** See AMUSE.

enthusiasm, *n.* eagerness, earnestness, sincerity, interest, warmth, avidity, gusto, relish, exuberance, excitement, keenness, fervor, zeal, ardor, passion, devotion.
—**Ant.** coolness.

enthusiast, *n.* zealot, devotee, fan, aficionado, admirer, supporter, promoter, champion, adherent, disciple, booster.

enthusiastic, *adj.* ardent, zealous, eager, fervent, passionate, vehement, fervid, burning, impassioned, keen, hearty, avid, energetic, vigorous, devoted, exuberant, fanatical.
—**Ant.** blasé, dispassionate, cool, unenthusiastic.

entice, *v.* allure, inveigle, excite, lure, attract, decoy, tempt, seduce, coax, cajole, wheedle, persuade, draw, beguile, blandish, wheedle.
—**Ant.** discourage, deter, dissuade.

entire, *adj.* **1.** whole, complete, unbroken, perfect, unimpaired, intact, undiminished, undivided, continuous. **2.** full, complete, thorough, unqualified, unrestricted, unmitigated.
—**Ant.** partial, imperfect, divided; restricted, incomplete.
—**Syn. Study.** See COMPLETE.

entitle, *v.* **1.** empower, qualify, allow, permit, make eligible, authorize, fit, enfranchise. **2.** name, designate, call, title, dub, label, term.
—**Ant.** disqualify.

entrance, *n.* **1.** entry, ingress, access, entree. **2.** entry, door, portal, gate, doorway, passage, inlet. **3.** admission, entry, admittance. —*v.* **4.** fascinate, captivate, bewitch, beguile, spellbind, enthrall, overpower, mesmerize, hypnotize, enrapture, enchant, charm, delight, transport.
—**Ant.** exit; disenchant.

entreat, *v.* appeal, implore, beg, beseech, supplicate, crave, solicit, pray, importune, petition, sue.

enumerate, *v.* count, name, list, itemize, specify, detail, spell out, catalogue, take stock of, quote, recite, relate, narrate, recount, recapitulate, rehearse, cite.

envelop, *v.* wrap, cover, enfold, hide, conceal, surround, enclose, encompass, shroud, swathe, swaddle, embrace.

envy, *n.* **1.** jealousy, enviousness, grudge, covetousness. —*v.* **2.** covet, begrudge, resent.
—**Ant.** generosity.
—**Syn. Study.** ENVY and JEALOUSY are very close in meaning. ENVY denotes a longing to possess something awarded to or achieved by another: *to feel envy when a friend inherits a fortune.* JEALOUSY, on the other hand, denotes a feeling of resentment that another has gained something that one more rightfully deserves: *to feel jealousy when a coworker receives a promotion.* JEALOUSY also refers to anguish caused by fear of losing someone or something to a rival: *a husband's jealousy of other men.*

epicure, *n.* gastronome, gourmet, epicurean, voluptuary, sensualist, glutton, gourmand, hedonist, sybarite, bon vivant, Lucullus, foodie.

episode, *n.* occurrence, event, incident, happening, experience.
—**Syn. Study.** See EVENT.

equable, *adj.* even, uniform, tranquil, steady, regular, even-tempered, temperate, easygoing, serene, calm, placid, composed, cool, unruffled, levelheaded, unflappable.
—**Ant.** uneven, irregular, turbulent, intemperate.

equal, *adj.* **1.** proportionate, commensurate, balanced, coordinate, correspondent, equivalent, tantamount, like, alike. **2.** uniform, even, regular, unvarying, invariant. **3.** adequate, sufficient, competent, suitable, fit. —*n.* **4.** peer, match, mate, fellow. —*v.* **5.** match, meet, even, square with, correspond to, parallel, rival, be commensurate with.
—**Ant.** unequal, disproportionate, incommensurate, dissimilar; uneven, irregular, variable; inadequate, insufficient, unsuitable.

equip, *v.* furnish, provide, supply, stock, attire, dress, deck out, fit out, outfit, rig, array, accouter.
—**Syn. Study.** See FURNISH.

equipment, *n.* apparatus, paraphernalia, gear, accouterments.

equivocal, *adj.* **1.** ambiguous, uncertain, vague, hazy, indefinite, unclear, indistinct, doubtful, questionable, dubious, indeterminate. **2.** evasive, misleading, roundabout, hedging, oblique, circumlocutory, ambivalent, waffling, wishy-washy.
—**Ant.** unequivocal, certain; definite, unquestionable.
—**Syn. Study.** See AMBIGUOUS.

eradicate, *v.* remove, destroy, extirpate, abolish, obliterate, uproot, exterminate, annihilate.
—**Ant.** insert, add; originate, create.

erase, *v.* efface, expunge, cancel, obliterate, delete, scratch, wipe out.
—**Ant.** create.

erect, *adj.* **1.** upright, standing, vertical, perpendicular, plumb. —*v.* **2.** build, raise, construct, upraise. **3.** set up, found, establish, institute.
—**Ant.** horizontal; raze, destroy; dissolve, liquidate.

erroneous, *adj.* mistaken, incorrect, inaccurate, false, wrong, untrue, invalid, fallacious, faulty, flawed, botched.
—**Ant.** correct, accurate, true.

error, *n.* **1.** mistake, inaccuracy, fault, flaw, gaffe, goof, foul-up, boner, blunder, slip, oversight. **2.** offense, wrongdoing, fault, sin, transgression, trespass, misdeed, iniquity.
—**Syn. Study.** See MISTAKE.

escape, *v.* **1.** flee, abscond, decamp, fly, steal away, run away. **2.** shun, fly, elude, evade, avoid. —*n.* **3.** flight; getaway, departure, decampment, bolt, breakout.
—**Syn. Study.** ESCAPE, ELUDE, EVADE mean to keep free of something. To ESCAPE is to succeed in keeping away from danger, pursuit, observation, etc.: *to escape punishment.* To ELUDE is to slip through an apparently tight net, thus avoiding, often by a narrow margin, whatever threatens; it implies using adroitness or slyness to baffle or foil: *The fox eluded the hounds.* To EVADE is to turn aside from or go out of reach of a person or thing, usually by directing attention elsewhere: *to evade the police.*

escort, *n.* **1.** convoy, guard, guide, protection, safeguard, guidance. —*v.* **2.** conduct, usher, guard, guide, convoy, accompany, attend, shepherd, squire, conduct, watch over.
—**Syn. Study.** See ACCOMPANY.

especially, *adv.* particularly, chiefly, principally, unusually, specifically, conspicuously, uniquely, notably, strikingly, noticeably, mainly, predominantly, primarily, first of all, above all, significantly, prominently, signally, specially, markedly.

essential, *adj.* **1.** indispensable, necessary, vital, requisite, required, imperative, quintessential, elemental, principal, primary, key, main, leading, chief, fundamental, rudimentary, elementary, basic, inherent, intrinsic, important. —*n.* **2.** necessity, basic, element.
—**Ant.** dispensable, unnecessary, unimportant.
—**Syn. Study.** ESSENTIAL, INHERENT, INTRINSIC refer to that which is in the natural composition of a thing. ESSENTIAL suggests that which is in the very essence or constitution of a thing: *Quiet is essential in a public library.* INHERENT means inborn or fixed from the beginning as a permanent quality or constituent of a thing: *properties inherent in iron.* INTRINSIC implies belonging to the nature of a thing itself and comprised within it, without regard to external considerations or accidentally added properties: *the intrinsic value of diamonds.* See also NECESSARY.

establish, *v.* **1.** set up, found, institute, form, organize, create, fix, settle, install. **2.** verify, substantiate, prove, confirm, certify, affirm, show, authenticate, validate, support, demonstrate, substantiate, back up. **3.** appoint, ordain, fix, enact, decree.
—**Ant.** liquidate, dissolve; disprove.

esteem, *v.* **1.** prize, value, honor, revere, respect, appreciate, treasure, cherish, hold dear, admire, look up to, venerate, estimate, regard. —*n.* **2.** respect, regard, favor, admiration, honor, reverence, veneration. **3.** estimation, valuation, estimate, appreciation, opinion.
—**Ant.** disregard; disrespect, disfavor; deprecation.
—**Syn. Study.** See APPRECIATE. See also RESPECT.

estimable, *adj.* respectable, reputable, worthy, deserving, meritorious, good, excellent, honored, praiseworthy, laudable.
—**Ant.** disreputable, unworthy, bad, inferior.

estimate, *v.* **1.** judge, compute, reckon, gauge, count, assess, approximate, determine, guess, calculate, conjecture, value, evaluate, appraise. —*n.* **2.** judgment, calculation, valuation, estimation, opinion, computation, approximation, assessment, appraisal, viewpoint.

estimation, *n.* judgment, opinion, appreciation, regard, honor, veneration, esteem, respect, reverence.

eternal, *adj.* **1.** endless, everlasting, perpetual, infinite, unending, neverending, interminable, unceasing, ceaseless, incessant, constant, nonstop, relentless, permanent. **2.** timeless, immortal, deathless, undying, imperishable, indestructible.
—**Ant.** transitory, ephemeral; perishable, mortal.
—**Syn. Study.** ETERNAL, ENDLESS, EVERLASTING, PERPETUAL imply lasting or going on without ceasing. That which is ETERNAL is, by its nature, without beginning or end: *God, the eternal Father.* That which is ENDLESS never stops but goes on continuously as if in a circle: *an endless succession of years.* That which is EVERLASTING will endure through all future time: *a promise of everlasting life.* PERPETUAL implies continuous renewal far into the future: *perpetual strife between nations.*

ethical, *adj.* moral, virtuous, principled, high-principled, honest, law-abiding, licit, legitimate, civilized, upright, decent, honorable, conscientious, righteous, right-minded, right-thinking, upstanding, just, scrupulous, proper, open, fair, good, straightforward, noble.
—**Ant.** unethical, immoral.

etiquette, *n.* decorum, propriety, code of behavior, convention, form, ceremony, formalities, protocol, rules, customs, politeness, courtesy, good manners, seemliness, civility.
—**Ant.** impropriety, indignity.

eulogize, *v.* praise, extol, laud, commend, panegyrize, applaud, honor, flatter, compliment.
—**Ant.** criticize, condemn.

evade, *v.* **1.** escape, elude, escape from, circumvent, shirk, avoid, shun, sidestep, dodge. **2.** baffle, foil, elude. **3.** prevaricate, equivocate, quibble, fence, hedge, maneuver, fudge, waffle, cop out.
—**Ant.** face, confront.
—**Syn. Study.** See ESCAPE.

evaporate, *v.* **1.** vaporize, dehydrate, dry. **2.** disappear, fade, vanish, evanesce, melt away, dissolve, disperse.
—**Ant.** condense, sublimate.

evasion, *n.* **1.** avoidance, dodging, escape. **2.** prevarication, equivocation, quibbling, subterfuge, sophistry, deception, deceit, chicanery, artifice, trickery, excuse, fudging, waffling, double-talk.

even, *adj.* **1.** level, flat, smooth, plane. **2.** parallel, flush, level. **3.** regular, equable, uniform, steady, well-balanced, in equilibrium, conforming, standard. **4.** commensurate, equal; square, balanced. **5.** calm, placid, tranquil, even-tempered, temperate, composed, sedate, peaceful. **6.** fair, just, equitable, impartial. —*adv.* **7.** still, yet; just; fully, quite, completely; indeed. —*v.* **8.** level, smooth; balance, equilibrate, counterpoise.
—**Ant.** uneven, irregular; unsteady; unequal, incommensurate; agitated, intemperate; unfair, unjust, prejudiced, biased.

evening, *n.* eventide, dusk, twilight, gloaming, nightfall, eve, even, sundown, sunset, p.m.
—**Ant.** dawn, sunrise.

event, *n.* **1.** occurrence, episode, incident, happening, affair, case, occasion, experience, circumstance. **2.** result, issue, consequence, outcome, upshot, end.
—**Syn. Study.** EVENT, EPISODE, INCIDENT refer to a happening. An

EVENT is usu. an important happening, esp. one that comes out of and is connected with previous happenings: *historical events.* An EPISODE is one of a series of happenings, frequently distinct from the main course of events but arising from them and having an interest of its own: *an episode in her life.* An INCIDENT is usu. a minor happening that is connected with an event or series of events of greater importance: *an amusing incident in a play.*

ever, *adv.* **1.** continuously, eternally, perpetually, constantly, always, forever, yet, still, at all times, endlessly, forever and a day, till the end of time, till the cows come home. **2.** by any chance, at all, at any time.
—Ant. never.

evidence, *n.* **1.** ground, grounds, proof, testimony. **2.** indication, sign, signal. **3.** information, deposition, affidavit, exhibit, testimony, proof. —*v.* **4.** make clear, show, manifest, demonstrate.

evident, *adj.* plain, clear, obvious, manifest, palpable, patent, unmistakable, apparent, discernible, noticeable, conspicuous.
—Ant. concealed, hidden.
—Syn. Study. See APPARENT.

evil, *adj.* **1.** wicked, bad, immoral, amoral, sinful, iniquitous, flagitious, depraved, vicious, corrupt, perverse, wrong, base, vile, nefarious, malicious, malignant, malevolent. **2.** harmful, injurious, wrong, bad, pernicious, destructive, mischievous. **3.** unfortunate, disastrous, miserable, unlucky, inauspicious, dire, ominous. —*n.* **4.** wickedness, depravity, iniquity, unrighteousness, sin, corruption, baseness, badness. **5.** harm, mischief, misfortune, disaster, calamity, misery, pain, woe, suffering, sorrow.
—Ant. good.

exact, *adj.* **1.** accurate, correct, precise, literal, faithful, close. **2.** strict, rigorous, rigid, unbending, exacting, demanding, severe, scrupulous. **3.** methodical, careful, punctilious, accurate, critical, nice, regular, precise, orderly. —*v.* **4.** call for, demand, require, force, compel. **5.** extort, wrest, wring, extract.
—Ant. inexact, inaccurate, imprecise, unfaithful, free; disorderly.

exalt, *v.* **1.** elevate, promote, dignify, raise, ennoble. **2.** praise, extol, glorify, bless, honor, idolize, dignify, revere, venerate, celebrate. **3.** elate, make proud, please.
—Ant. lower, debase; damn, condemn; displease.
—Syn. Study. See ELEVATE.

examination, *n.* **1.** inspection, scrutiny, inquiry, observation, investigation, study, analysis, probe, search, exploration, research, survey, appraisal, assessment, scanning, inquisition. **2.** test, trial, quiz, exam.
—Syn. Study. EXAMINATION, INSPECTION, SCRUTINY refer to a looking at something. An EXAMINATION is an orderly attempt to test or to obtain information about something, often something presented for observation: *an examination of merchandise for sale.* An INSPECTION is usu. a formal and official examination: *An inspection of the plumbing revealed a defective pipe.* SCRUTINY implies a critical and minutely detailed examination: *His testimony was given close scrutiny.*

examine, *v.* **1.** inspect, scrutinize, search, probe, explore, study, investigate, test. **2.** catechize, quiz, interrogate, question, test, crossexamine, grill, pump.

example, *n.* sample, specimen, representative, illustration, case, pattern, model, instance, prototype, standard, archetype, exemplar, pattern, norm, criterion, benchmark.

exasperate, *v.* irritate, annoy, vex, infuriate, exacerbate, anger, incense, provoke, nettle, needle, enrage, inflame, rile, embitter, irk, bother, harass, pique, gall, rankle, torment, badger, bug, peeve, get under someone's skin, get someone's goat, rub someone the wrong way.
—Ant. calm, assuage, tranquilize.

exceed, *v.* overstep, transcend, surpass, cap, top, outdo, excel, outstrip, beat, overtake, be superior to, go beyond, overwhelm, better, outdistance, pass, eclipse, overextend.

excel, *v.* surpass, outdo, exceed, transcend, outstrip, eclipse, beat, win over, cap, top, dominate, outrank, overshadow, eclipse; shine, be preeminent.

excellence, *n.* superiority, eminence, preeminence, transcendence, supremacy, prominence, greatness, finesse, distinction; merit, virtue, purity, goodness, uprightness.
—Ant. baseness; inferiority.

excellent, *adj.* superb, outstanding, exceptional, matchless, peerless, nonpareil, supreme, superlative, capital, first-class, select, distinguished, noteworthy, splendid, remarkable, marvelous, extraordinary, great, super, terrific, good, choice, worthy, fine, first-rate, estimable, superior, better, admirable, prime, *(slang)* def, phat.
—Ant. bad, inferior, base.

except, *prep.* but, save, excepting, excluding, barring, not counting, apart from, other than, saving.
—Ant. including.

exceptional, *adj.* unusual, extraordinary, special, uncommon, irregular, peculiar, rare; strange, unnatural, anomalous, abnormal, aberrant.
—Ant. customary, common, usual, normal, regular, natural.

excess, *n.* **1.** superfluity, superabundance, nimiety, redundancy, overflow, surfeit, glut, overabundance, overkill. **2.** surplus, remainder. **3.** immoderation, intemperance, overindulgence, dissipation, prodigality, extravagance, dissolution, debauchery.
—Ant. lack, need, want.

excessive, *adj.* immoderate, extravagant, extreme, exorbitant, inordinate, outrageous, unreasonable, disproportionate, undue, extortionate, unjustifiable, enormous.
—Ant. reasonable, proportionate.

excitable, *adj.* emotional, passionate, fiery, quick-tempered, volatile, jumpy, nervous, restive, restless, fidgety, edgy, touchy, high-strung, mercurial, testy, hot-blooded, feverish, hysterical, hot-tempered, hasty, irascible, irritable, choleric.
—Ant. unemotional, cool, calm, serene, tranquil.

excite, *v.* **1.** stir, arouse, rouse, awaken, stimulate, animate, kindle, spur, move, motivate, animate, galvanize, electrify, spark, light a fire under, inflame, incite. **2.** stir up, provoke, disturb, agitate, irritate, discompose.
—Ant. pacify, calm, soothe.

excited, *adj.* ruffled, discomposed, stormy, perturbed, aroused, disturbed, upset, worked up, overwrought, nervous, edgy, uneasy, flustered, frantic, frenetic, beside oneself, jittery, impassioned, stimulated, brisk, agitated, stirred up, agog, eager, enthusiastic, stoked, passionate, animated, lively, spirited, fervent.
—Ant. calm, unruffled, composed, pacific.

excitement, *n.* agitation, commotion, ado, to-do, perturbation, upset, restlessness, disquiet, tension, unrest, malaise, stir, disturbance, activity, ferment, furor, turmoil, tumult, hubbub, brouhaha.
—Ant. serenity, peace.

exclamation, *n.* outcry, ejaculation, interjection, cry, complaint, call, utterance, yell, bellow, protest, vociferation, shout, clamor.

exclude, *v.* **1.** bar, restrain, keep out, shut out. **2.** debar, eliminate, expel, eject, reject, prohibit, withhold, except, omit, preclude; proscribe, prevent.
—Ant. include; accept.

exclusive, *adj.* **1.** incompatible, inimical, excluding, barring, restricted, limited. **2.** restrictive, closed, private, cliquish, snobbish, fastidious, select, narrow, clannish, snobbish, selfish, illiberal, narrow, narrow-minded, uncharitable; fashionable, chic, aristocratic, choice, upper-class, elegant, stylish, trendy.
—Ant. inclusive, including; liberal; poor.

excursion, *n.* journey, tour, trip, jaunt, junket, outing, cruise, airing, expedition, voyage, ramble, stroll, walk, hike, trek, drive, ride, sail.

excuse, *v.* **1.** forgive, pardon, overlook, acquit, absolve, exonerate, exculpate. **2.** apologize for, exonerate, exculpate, clear, vindicate. **3.** condone, allow, permit, warrant, mitigate, extenuate, palliate, justify. **4.** release, disoblige, free, liberate, disencumber. —*n.* **5.** plea, apology, absolution, justification, explanation, story, reason, defense, vindication. **6.** pretext, pretense, subterfuge, evasion, makeshift, loophole.
—Ant. condemn; oblige, shackle.
—Syn. Study. EXCUSE, FORGIVE, PARDON imply being lenient or giving up the wish to punish. EXCUSE means to overlook some (usu.) slight offense, because of circumstance, realization that it was unintentional, or the like: *to excuse rudeness.* FORGIVE is applied to excusing more serious offenses; the person wronged not only overlooks the offense but harbors no ill feeling against the offender: *to forgive and forget.* PARDON often applies to an act of leniency or mercy by an official or superior; it usu. involves a serious offense or crime: *The governor was asked to pardon the condemned criminal.*

execute, *v.* **1.** carry out, accomplish, do, perform, implement, achieve, effect, consummate, finish, complete. **2.** kill, put to death, garrote, remove, murder, butcher, slay. **3.** enforce, effectuate, administer; sign, seal, and deliver.

exemption, *n.* immunity, impunity, privilege, freedom, exception.
—Ant. culpability.
—Syn. Study. EXEMPTION, IMMUNITY, IMPUNITY imply special privilege or freedom from requirements imposed on others. EXEMPTION implies release or privileged freedom from sharing with others some duty or legal requirement: *exemption from military service.* IMMUNITY implies freedom from a penalty or from some natural or common liability, esp. one that is disagreeable or threatening: *immunity from prosecution; immunity from disease.* IMPUNITY (limited mainly to the expression *with impunity*) suggests freedom from punishment: *The police force was so inadequate that crimes could be committed with impunity.*

exercise, *n.* **1.** exertion, labor, toil, work, action, activity. **2.** drill, calisthenics, workout, practice, training, schooling, discipline. **3.** practice, use, application, employment, performance, operation. **4.** ceremony, ritual, procedure, observance, service. —*v.* **5.** discipline, drill, train, school. **6.** practice, use, apply, employ, effect, exert. **7.** discharge, perform. **8.** harass, irritate, vex, harry, distress, agitate, worry, annoy, make uneasy, try, burden, trouble, pain, afflict.
—Ant. laziness, sloth.

exertion, *n.* effort, action, activity, endeavor, struggle, attempt, strain, trial, striving, work, toil, drive, industry.
—Syn. Study. See EFFORT.

exhaust, *v.* **1.** empty, drain, void. **2.** use up, expend, consume, waste, squander, dissipate, spend, fritter away. **3.** enervate, tire, prostrate, wear out, fatigue, weaken, cripple, debilitate.
—Ant. fill; use; innervate, invigorate, strengthen.

exhaustion, *n.* tiredness, debilitation, enervation, weariness, lassitude, weakness, fatigue.
—Ant. energy, exhilaration, strength.

exhibit, *v.* **1.** expose, present, display, show, demonstrate, offer. **2.** manifest, display, show, betray, reveal, express, disclose, indicate, evince. —*n.* **3.** exhibition, showing, show, display, demonstration, offering, exposition, manifestation.
—Ant. conceal, hide.
—Syn. Study. See DISPLAY.

exhilarate, *v.* make cheerful *or* merry, cheer, gladden, enliven, inspirit, animate, inspire, elate, excite, transport, enrapture.
—Ant. depress, sadden, deject.

exorbitant, *adj.* extraordinary, outrageous, immoderate, extortionate, extreme, disproportionate, preposterous, undue, unjustifiable, excessive, inordinate, extravagant, unreasonable, unconscionable, enormous.
—Ant. reasonable, inexpensive.

expand, *v.* increase, extend, swell, enlarge, dilate, distend, inflate, bloat, aggrandize, spread *or* stretch out, unfold, develop.
—Ant. contract, shrink.
—Syn. Study. See INCREASE.

expect, *v.* look forward to, anticipate, await, hope for, wait for, count on, rely on, envision, foresee, contemplate.

expectation, *n.* confidence, watchfulness, apprehension, suspense, expectancy, anticipation, hope, trust, prospect.

expedient, *adj.* **1.** advantageous, win-win, fit, suitable, profitable, advisable, proper, right, correct, pertinent, applicable, fitting, apropos, appropriate, desirable. —*n.* **2.** device, contrivance, means, resource, shift, resort.
—Ant. unsuitable, inapt, undesirable.

expedite, *v.* speed up, hasten, quicken, speed, step up, push, accelerate, hurry, precipitate; dispatch.
—Ant. slow.

expedition, *n.* **1.** excursion, journey, voyage, mission, exploration, field trip, trek, trip, junket, safari. **2.** promptness, speed, haste, quickness, dispatch, alacrity, swiftness, dispatch.
—Ant. sloth.
—Syn. Study. See TRIP.

expel, *v.* drive *or* force away, drive *or* force out, discharge, eject; dismiss, oust, banish, exile, expatriate, deport.
—Ant. accept, invite.

expend, *v.* **1.** use, employ, consume, spend, exhaust, use up. **2.** pay, disburse, spend, lay out.
—Ant. save, husband, conserve.

expense, *n.* **1.** cost, charge, price,

outlay, expenditure. **2.** loss, injury, harm, debit, detriment, sacrifice, impairment, ruin, destruction.

expensive, *adj.* costly, dear, high-priced, up-market, valuable, precious, priceless, extravagant, at a premium.
—**Ant.** inexpensive, cheap, tawdry.

experience, *n.* **1.** incident, event, happening, affair, episode, occurrence, circumstance, adventure, encounter. **2.** knowledge, know-how, sophistication, skill, judgment, common sense, wisdom, sagacity. —*v.* **3.** meet with, undergo, feel, encounter, live through, know, observe; endure; suffer.
—**Ant.** inexperience, naiveté.

experienced, *adj.* skilled, expert, veteran, practiced, accomplished, proficient, knowledgeable, knowing, wise, sage, versed, qualified, adroit, adept, shrewd, prepared, masterly, professional, competent, efficient, capable, au fait.
—**Ant.** inexperienced, inexpert, naive, artless, unqualified.

experiment, *n.* **1.** test, trial, examination, proof, assay, procedure, experimentation, research, investigation. —*v.* **2.** try, test, examine, prove, assay.

expert, *n.* **1.** specialist, authority, connoisseur, master, scholar, pundit, maven, virtuoso, wizard, champion. —*adj.* **2.** trained, skilled, skillful, experienced, practiced, knowledgeable, learned, qualified, adept, polished, capable, masterly, superior, first-rate, adept, au fait, accomplished, excellent, superb, wonderful, proficient, dexterous, adroit, clever, apt, quick.
—**Ant.** butcher, shoemaker, dolt; untrained, inexperienced, maladroit.
—**Syn. Study.** See SKILLFUL.

explain, *v.* **1.** elucidate, expound, interpret, explicate, clarify, throw light on, make plain *or* manifest. **2.** account for, justify, excuse, rationalize, legitimize, extenuate.
—**Ant.** confuse.
—**Syn. Study.** EXPLAIN, ELUCIDATE, EXPOUND, INTERPRET imply making the meaning of something clear or understandable. To EXPLAIN is to make plain, clear, or intelligible something that is not known or understood: *to explain a theory.* To ELUCIDATE is to throw light on what before was dark and obscure, usu. by illustration and commentary and sometimes by elaborate explanation: *They asked her to elucidate her statement.* To EXPOUND is to give a methodical, detailed, scholarly explanation of something, usu. Scriptures, doctrines, or philosophy: *to expound the doctrine of free will.* To INTERPRET is to give the meaning of something by paraphrase, by translation, or by an explanation based on personal opinion: *to interpret a poem.*

explanation, *n.* **1.** clarification, elucidation, explication, exposition, definition, interpretation, description. **2.** meaning, interpretation, solution, key, answer, definition, account, justification.

explicit, *adj.* **1.** clear, unequivocal, express, unambiguous, precise, definite, exact, categorical, determinate. **2.** open, outspoken, candid, frank, direct, forthright, straightforward, definite, unashamed, unabashed.
—**Ant.** unclear, equivocal, ambiguous, indefinite; clandestine, concealed.

exploit, *n.* **1.** deed, feat, attainment, accomplishment, achievement. —*v.* **2.** use, profit from, capitalize on, manipulate, utilize, take advantage of.

expose, *v.* **1.** lay open, subject, risk,

endanger, imperil, jeopardize. **2.** bare, uncover; exhibit, display. **3.** make known, betray, uncover, unveil, disclose, reveal, unmask, bring to light; muckrake.
—**Ant.** conceal, hide.

exposition, *n.* **1.** exhibit, exhibition, show, demonstration, display. **2.** explanation, elucidation, commentary, treatise, critique, interpretation, exegesis, explication.

exposure, *n.* **1.** disclosure, unmasking, presentation, display, divulgement, revelation, exposé. **2.** aspect, orientation, view, outlook, setting, location.
—**Ant.** hiding, concealment.

express, *v.* **1.** utter, declare, state, word, speak, assert, articulate, verbalize, phrase, voice, say, tell, communicate. **2.** show, manifest, reveal, expose, indicate, exhibit, represent. **3.** indicate, signify, designate, denote, show, demonstrate, reveal, betoken, convey. **4.** press *or* squeeze out, expel, extract, wring out. —*adj.* **5.** clear, distinct, definite, explicit, plain, obvious, positive, unambiguous, categorical; unsubtle. **6.** special, particular, singular, signal. **7.** quick, speedy, prompt, immediate, swift, direct, fast, rapid, nonstop.
—**Ant.** conceal.

expression, *n.* **1.** utterance, verbalization, announcements, declaration, assertion, statement. **2.** phrase, term, idiom. **3.** language, diction, phraseology, wording, phrasing, presentation. **4.** manifestation, sign, indication, token, symbol, representation. **5.** look, countenance, aspect, air, mien, intonation, tone.
—**Ant.** silence.

expressive, *adj.* **1.** meaning, allusive, eloquent, revealing, significant, suggestive, meaningful, indicative. **2.** striking, telling, lively, vivid, strong, emphatic.
—**Ant.** expressionless, meaningless.

exquisite, *adj.* **1.** dainty, beautiful, elegant, rare, delicate, appealing, charming. **2.** fine, admirable, consummate, perfect, matchless, complete, valuable, precious. **3.** intense, acute, keen, poignant. **4.** sensitive, responsive. **5.** rare, select, choice, excellent, precious, valuable, priceless; vintage. **6.** refined, elegant, delicate, discriminating, polished, debonair.
—**Ant.** ugly, hideous; imperfect, valueless, worthless; dull; vacuous, vapid; common, ordinary; poor, inferior; boorish.
—**Syn. Study.** See DELICATE.

extemporaneous, *adj.* impromptu, unstudied, spontaneous, unrehearsed, unplanned, unscripted, ad-lib, extempore, improvised, unpremeditated, offhand, off the cuff.
—**Ant.** prepared, premeditated.
—**Syn. Study.** EXTEMPORANEOUS, IMPROMPTU are used of expression that is not planned. EXTEMPORANEOUS may refer to a speech given without any advance preparation: *extemporaneous remarks.* IMPROMPTU is also used of a speech, but often refers to a poem, song, etc., delivered without preparation and at a moment's notice: *She entertained the guests with some impromptu rhymes.*

extend, *v.* **1.** stretch *or* draw out, attenuate. **2.** lengthen, prolong, protract, continue. **3.** expand, spread out, dilate, enlarge, widen, diffuse, fill out. **4.** hold forth, offer, bestow, grant, give, impart, yield.
—**Ant.** shorten, abbreviate; discontinue; shrink, curtail.
—**Syn. Study.** See LENGTHEN.

extensive, *adj.* **1.** wide, broad, large, extended, spacious, ample, vast. **2.** far-reaching, comprehensive, thorough; inclusive.

extent, *n.* space, degree, magnitude, measure, amount, scope, compass, range, expanse, stretch, reach, size; length, area, volume.

exterior, *adj.* **1.** outer, outside, outward, external, surface, superficial. **2.** outlying, extraneous, foreign, extrinsic. —*n.* **3.** outside, face, facing, surface, covering, coating, front, skin, shell, facade. **4.** appearance, mien, aspect, face.
—**Ant.** interior, inner; important; interior, inside.

exterminate, *v.* extirpate, annihilate, destroy, eradicate, abolish, eliminate, obliterate, wipe out, root out, deracinate.
—**Ant.** create, generate, originate.

extinct, *adj.* **1.** extinguished, quenched, out, put out. **2.** obsolete, dated, outmoded, old-fashioned, antiquated, passé, out-of-date, antediluvian, ancient, old hat, archaic. **3.** ended, terminated, over, dead, gone, vanished.
—**Ant.** extant; modern; begun, initiated.

extol, *v.* praise, laud, eulogize, commend, glorify, exalt, celebrate, applaud, panegyrize, acclaim, pay tribute *or* homage to.
—**Ant.** condemn, damn.

extract, *v.* **1.** draw forth *or* out, get, pull *or* pry out. **2.** deduce, divine, understand. **3.** extort, exact, evoke, educe, draw out, elicit, wrest, wring, bleed. **4.** derive, withdraw, distill. —*n.* **5.** excerpt, quotation, citation, selection. **6.** decoction, distillate, solution.

extraneous, *adj.* external, extrinsic, foreign, alien, strange, out of place, off *or* beside the point, adventitious; inappropriate, not germane, not pertinent, nonessential, superfluous, peripheral, incidental, irrelevant, inappropriate, needless.
—**Ant.** internal, intrinsic; appropriate, pertinent, essential, vital.

extraordinary, *adj.* exceptional, special, inordinate, uncommon, singular, signal, rare, phenomenal, unique, curious, peculiar, odd, bizarre, strange, abnormal, nonpareil, amazing, marvelous, fantastic, incredible, fabulous, drop-dead, miraculous, far-out, unreal, remarkable, unusual, egregious, unheard of.
—**Ant.** ordinary, common, usual, customary.

extravagant, *adj.* **1.** imprudent, wasteful, lavish, profligate, reckless, spendthrift, prodigal, immoderate, excessive, inordinate, exorbitant. **2.** unreasonable, fantastic, wild, foolish, absurd, outrageous, preposterous.
—**Ant.** prudent, thrifty, moderate; reasonable, thoughtful, sensible.

extreme, *adj.* **1.** utmost, greatest, rarest, highest; superlative. **2.** outermost, endmost, ultimate, last, uttermost, remotest. **3.** extravagant, immoderate, excessive, fanatical, uncompromising, radical, outré, unreasonable. **4.** unusual, exceptional, uncommon, outstanding, notable, noteworthy, abnormal, extraordinary. —*n.* **5.** farthest, furthest, remotest. **6.** acme, limit, end; extremity.
—**Ant.** reasonable.

extremity, *n.* **1.** terminal, limit, end, termination, extreme, verge, limit, edge, margin, periphery, frontier, border, boundary, bounds. **2.** utmost, extreme, maximum, limits.

exuberance, *n.* cheerfulness, joy, exhilaration, buoyancy, animation, liveliness, spirit, enthusiasm, excitement, zest, energy, vigor; superabundance, excess, copiousness, profusion, luxuriance, lavishness, superfluity, redundancy, overflow.

—**Ant.** dejection, somberness, melancholy, lassitude; paucity, lack, need, want.

F

fable, *n.* **1.** legend, myth, tale, parable, allegory, story, romance, fancy, tradition, saga, epic, folk tale, fairy tale. **2.** lie, untruth, falsehood, fib, fiction, invention, fabrication, tall tale, cock-and-bull story, whopper.
—**Ant.** truth, gospel.
—**Syn. Study.** See LEGEND.

fabricate, *v.* **1.** construct, build, frame, erect, make, manufacture, raise, fashion, form, produce, assemble, put together. **2.** devise, invent, coin, create, originate, concoct, imagine, hatch, design, think up. **3.** forge, fake, falsify, counterfeit, feign, trump up, cook up.
—**Ant.** destroy, raze.

fabulous, *adj.* **1.** unbelievable, incredible, amazing, astonishing, fantastic, marvelous, wonderful, miraculous, phenomenal, astounding. **2.** untrue, unreal, unrealistic, invented, fabled, fictional, fictitious, fabricated, coined, made up, imaginary, mythical, legendary, storied, fanciful, storybook, fairytale.
—**Ant.** commonplace; real, natural.

face, *n.* **1.** countenance, visage, front, features, look, expression, physiognomy, look, appearance, aspect, mien; sight, presence. **2.** show, pretense, pretext, exterior. —*v.* **3.** meet face to face, confront, encounter, meet, meet with, brave, deal *or* cope with.
—**Ant.** back; interior.
—**Syn. Study.** FACE, COUNTENANCE, VISAGE refer to the front of the (usu. human) head. FACE is used when referring to physical features: *a pretty face with high cheekbones.* COUNTENANCE, a more formal word, denotes the face as it is affected by or reveals a person's state of mind; hence, it often signifies the look or expression on the face: *a thoughtful countenance.* VISAGE, still more formal, refers to the face as seen in a certain aspect, esp. as revealing a person's character: *a stern visage.*

facet, *n.* aspect, side, angle, position, posture, phase, view, viewpoint, feature, light, slant, particular, detail.

facile, *adj.* **1.** effortless, easy, adroit, deft, dexterous, fluent, flowing, smooth, graceful, elegant. **2.** superficial, glib, slick, surface, shallow, slight.
—**Ant.** labored, laborious, profound.

faction, *n.* side, bloc, camp, cabal, cadre, splinter group, circle, clique, set, pressure group, junta, ring, gang, group, party, sect, interest, division, wing, denomination, order, school, society, body.

factory, *n.* manufactory, mill, workshop, plant, works.

factual, *adj.* actual, real, true, demonstrable, provable, evidential, evidentiary, verifiable, de facto, genuine, certain, undoubted, unquestioned, valid, authentic, bona fide.
—**Ant.** imaginary, groundless, illusory.

faculty, *n.* ability, capacity, aptitude, capability, knack, turn, talent, skill, potential, flair, gift, genius, cleverness, dexterity.
—**Ant.** inability, incapacity.
—**Syn. Study.** See ABILITY.

fade, *v.* **1.** wither, droop, languish, decline, decay, die out, perish, ebb, wane, wilt, waste away, languish, deteriorate, shrivel, peter out. **2.**

blanch, etiolate, bleach, pale. **3.** disappear, vanish, die out, pass away, evanesce.
—**Ant.** flourish; flush; appear.
—**Syn. Study.** See DISAPPEAR.

fail, *v.* **1.** come short, fall short, disappoint, miscarry, misfire, falter, abort, founder, run aground, come to nothing, go wrong, flop, fizzle, (*slang*) tank. **2.** fall off, dwindle, pass *or* die away, decline, fade, weaken, sink, wane, give out, cease, disappear. **3.** desert, forsake, disappoint, let down, abandon.
—**Ant.** succeed.

failing, *n.* shortcoming, weakness, foible, deficiency, defect, frailty, imperfection, fault, flaw, blemish, blind spot.
—**Ant.** success, sufficiency; strength.
—**Syn. Study.** See FAULT.

failure, *n.* **1.** unsuccessfulness, miscarriage, abortion, failing. **2.** neglect, omission, dereliction, nonperformance, deficiency, insufficiency, defectiveness. **3.** loser, nonstarter, incompetent, nonentity, also-ran, flop, dud, lemon, washout, dead duck. **4.** decline, decay, deterioration, loss. **5.** bankruptcy, insolvency, failing, bust, downfall, ruin.
—**Ant.** success; adequacy, sufficiency, effectiveness.

faint, *adj.* **1.** indistinct, ill-defined, dim, faded, dull. **2.** feeble, half-hearted, faltering, irresolute, weak, languid, drooping. **3.** giddy, vertiginous, unsteady, woozy, lightheaded, dizzy, swooning. **4.** cowardly, timorous, pusillanimous, fearful, timid, dastardly, fainthearted. —*v.* **5.** swoon, pass out, black out. —*n.* **6.** swoon, unconsciousness, blackout, collapse.
—**Ant.** strong; distinct; brave, bold.

fair, *adj.* **1.** impartial, disinterested, unbiased, equitable, just, honest, unprejudiced. **2.** reasonable, passable, tolerable, average, middling. **3.** bright, sunny, cloudless; fine. **4.** unobstructed, open, clear, distinct, unencumbered, plain. **5.** clean, spotless, pure, untarnished, unsullied, unspotted, unblemished, unstained. **6.** beautiful, lovely, comely, pretty, attractive, pleasing, handsome. **7.** courteous, civil, polite, gracious. —*n.* **8.** exhibit, exhibition, festival, kermis, bazaar, show.
—**Ant.** unfair.
—**Syn. Study.** FAIR, IMPARTIAL, DISINTERESTED refer to lack of bias in opinions, judgments, etc. FAIR implies the treating of all sides alike, justly and equitably: *a fair compromise.* IMPARTIAL also implies showing no more favor to one side than another, but suggests particularly a judicial consideration of a case: *an impartial judge.* DISINTERESTED implies a fairness arising from lack of desire to obtain a selfish advantage: *a disinterested concern that the best person win.*

fairy, *n.* fay, pixy, pixie, leprechaun, nix, nixie, brownie, elf, sprite.

faith, *n.* **1.** sureness, certitude, conviction, confidence, trust, reliance, credit, credence, assurance. **2.** belief, doctrine, tenet, creed, dogma, religion, persuasion.
—**Ant.** discredit, distrust.

faithful, *adj.* **1.** constant, loyal, stable, dependable, steadfast, staunch. **2.** strict, thorough, true, devoteed. **3.** true, reliable, trustworthy, trusty. **4.** credible, creditable, believable, trustworthy, reliable. **5.** strict, rigid, accurate, precise, exact, conscientious, close.
—**Ant.** unfaithful, faithless.
—**Syn. Study.** FAITHFUL, CONSTANT, LOYAL imply qualities of stability, dependability, and devotion. FAITHFUL implies enduring fidelity to what one is bound to by a pledge, duty, or obligation: *a faithful friend.* CONSTANT suggests lack of change in affections or loyalties: *a constant companion through thick and thin.* LOYAL implies firm support and defense of a person, cause, institution, or idea considered to be worthy: *a loyal citizen.*

faithless, *adj.* **1.** disloyal, false, inconstant, fickle, perfidious, treacherous. **2.** unreliable, untrustworthy, untrue. **3.** untrusting; unbelieving, doubting. **4.** skeptical, freethinking, atheistic, agnostic, heathen, infidel.
—**Ant.** faithful.

fake, *adj.* **1.** fraudulent, false, unreal, forged, fabricated, counterfeit, bogus, phony, sham, spurious, pretend, pinchbeck. —*n.* **2.** fraud, hoax, imposture, deception, counterfeit, forgery, imitation, sham, phony. —*v.* **3.** pretend, feign, affect, counterfeit, sham, simulate, act, make-believe, affect.

false, *adj.* **1.** erroneous, incorrect, amiss, faulty, flawed, unfactual, imprecise, inexact, inaccurate, invalid, unsound, unreal, imaginary, spurious, mistaken, wrong, untrue, improper. **2.** untruthful, lying, mendacious, untrue, concocted, meretricious, fallacious, fabricated, fictitious. **3.** deceitful, treacherous, faithless, insincere, hypocritical, disingenuous, disloyal, unfaithful, two-faced, inconstant, recreant, perfidious, traitorous. **4.** deceptive, deceiving, misleading, fallacious. **5.** sham, counterfeit, spurious, artificial, bogus, phony, forged, ersatz, unreal, fake, feigned, imitation, fraudulent, factitious, make-believe, synthetic, mock, unnatural. **6.** substitute, ersatz, supplementary, stand-in.
—**Ant.** true; genuine.
—**Syn. Study.** FALSE, SHAM, COUNTERFEIT agree in referring to something that is not genuine. FALSE is used mainly of imitations of concrete objects; it sometimes implies an intent to deceive: *false teeth; false hair.* SHAM is rarely used of concrete objects and usu. has the suggestion of intent to deceive: *sham title; sham tears.* COUNTERFEIT always has the implication of cheating; it is used particularly of spurious imitation of coins and paper money.

falsehood, *n.* lie, fib, untruth, distortion, fabrication, fiction, misstatement, prevarication, distortion, cock-and-bull story.
—**Ant.** truth.

fame, *n.* reputation, acclaim, prominence, cachet, brilliance, repute, renown, eminence, celebrity, honor, illustriousness, superiority, preeminence, stardom, name, glory; notoriety.
—**Ant.** infamy, disrepute.

familiar, *adj.* **1.** common, well-known, frequent, everyday, ordinary, current, usual, routine, customary, habitual, traditional. **2.** well-acquainted, conversant, well-versed. **3.** easy, informal, unceremonious, unconstrained, free. **4.** confidential, intimate, close, friendly, affable, social, sociable, relaxed, free-and-easy, amicable. **5.** presuming, presumptive, unreserved, disrespectful, bold, forward, insolent, impudent.
—**Ant.** unfamiliar, unknown.
—**Syn. Study.** FAMILIAR, CONFIDENTIAL, INTIMATE suggest a friendly relationship between persons, based on frequent association, common interests, etc. FAMILIAR suggests an easygoing and unconstrained relationship between persons who are well-acquainted: *on familiar terms with one's neighbors.* CONFIDENTIAL implies a sense of mutual trust that extends to the sharing of confidences and secrets: *a confidential adviser.* INTIMATE connotes a very close and warm relationship characterized by empathy and sharing of private thoughts: *intimate letters to a friend.*

familiarity, *n.* **1.** acquaintance, grasp, experience, knowledge, understanding. **2.** intimacy, friendliness, affability, sociability, ease, informality, closeness, naturalness. **3.** disrespect, boldness, presumption, impudence, insolence, impertinence, impropriety.
—**Ant.** unfamiliarity.

famous, *adj.* celebrated, renowned, popular, noted, prominent, public, well-known, famed, notable, eminent, distinguished, illustrious, honored, venerable, lionized; notorious.
—**Ant.** unknown, undistinguished.
—**Syn. Study.** FAMOUS, CELEBRATED, RENOWNED, NOTORIOUS refer to someone or something widely known. FAMOUS is the general word for a person or thing that receives wide public notice, usu. favorable: *a famous lighthouse.* CELEBRATED refers to a famous person or thing that enjoys wide public praise or honor for merit, services, etc.: *a celebrated poet.* RENOWNED usu. implies wider, greater, and more enduring fame and glory: *a renowned hospital.* NOTORIOUS means widely known and discussed because of some bad or evil quality or action: *a notorious criminal.*

fanatical, *adj.* zealous, enthusiastic, visionary, frenzied, rabid, extreme, maniacal, mad, frenzied, frantic, frenetic, fervent, obsessive, compulsive, monomaniacal, passionate, agog, immoderate, excessive, fiendish, hysterical, single-minded, hotheaded, quixotic.

fancy, *n.* **1.** imagination, fantasy, hallucination, illusion, dream, pipe dream, mirage, phantasm, phantom, figment. **2.** image, conception, idea, thought, notion, impression. **3.** caprice, whim, vagary, quirk, humor, crotchet. **4.** preference, liking, inclination, fondness. —*adj.* **5.** fine, elegant, choice. **6.** ornamental, decorated, ornate. **7.** fanciful, capricious, whimsical, irregular, extravagant. —*v.* **8.** picture, envision, conceive, imagine. **9.** like, be pleased with, take a fancy to, favor, prefer, be attracted to, want, have an appetite for.
—**Ant.** plain; regular, ordinary; dislike, abhor.

fascinate, *v.* bewitch, charm, enchant, entrance, enrapture, spellbind, intrigue, beguile, transfix, engross, absorb, enthrall, hypnotize, mesmerize, attract, seduce, cast a spell over, entice, captivate, allure, infatuate, enamor.
—**Ant.** repel, disgust.

fashion, *n.* **1.** custom, style, vogue, mode, trend, look, taste, fad, rage, craze. **2.** custom, style, conventionality, conformity. **3.** haut monde, beau monde, in crowd, jet set, high society, society. **4.** manner, way, mode, method, attitude, approach. **5.** make, form, figure, shape, stamp, mold, pattern, model, cast. **6.** kind, sort. —*v.* **7.** make, shape, frame, construct, model, style, create, work, manufacture, mold, form. **8.** accommodate, adapt, suit, fit, adjust.

fashionable, *adj.* stylish, chic, in vogue, in fashion, in style, smart, trendy, du jour, voguish, exclusive, inside, swank, tony, au courant, à la mode, soigné, soignée, all the rage, hip, with it, in, jiggy.
—**Ant.** unfashionable, dowdy.

fast, *adj.* **1.** quick, swift, rapid, fleet. **2.** energetic, active, alert, quick. **3.** dissolute, dissipated, profligate, unmoral, wild, reckless, extravagant, prodigal. **4.** strong, resistant, impregnable. **5.** immovable, fixed, secure, steadfast, staunch, firm. **6.** tied, knotted, fastened, fixed, tight, close. **7.** permanent, lasting, enduring, eternal. **8.** loyal, faithful, steadfast. —*adv.* **9.** tightly, fixedly, firmly, securely, tenaciously. **10.** quickly, swiftly, rapidly, speedily. **11.** energetically, recklessly, extravagantly, wildly, prodigally.
—**Ant.** slow, lethargic; upright, moral; weak, defenseless; feeble; temporary; disloyal, faithless.
—**Syn. Study.** See QUICK.

fasten, *v.* make fast, fix, secure, anchor, attach, pin, rivet, bond, bind, stick, affix, tie, connect, link, hook, clasp, clinch, clamp, tether.
—**Ant.** loosen, loose, untie.

fat, *adj.* **1.** bulky, overfed, overweight, heavy, rotund, tubby, flabby, fleshy, plump, corpulent, obese, adipose, stout, portly, chubby, pudgy, potbellied, beefy, broad in the beam, big-boned, paunchy. **2.** oily, fatty, unctuous, greasy, pinguid. **3.** rich, profitable, remunerative, lucrative. **4.** fertile, rich, fruitful, productive. **5.** plentiful, copious, abundant.
—**Ant.** thin, skinny, cadaverous; poor; scarce, scanty; barren.

fatal, *adj.* **1.** deadly, lethal, mortal, toxic, terminal; destructive, disastrous, ruinous, pernicious, calamitous, catastrophic. **2.** fateful, inevitable, doomed, predestined, foreordained, damned, decreed, inescapable.
—**Ant.** lifegiving, constructive; indeterminate.
—**Syn. Study.** FATAL, DEADLY, LETHAL, MORTAL apply to something that has caused or is capable of causing death or dire misfortune. FATAL may refer to the future or the past; in either case, it emphasizes inevitability or inescapable consequences: *a fatal illness; fatal errors.* DEADLY refers to the future, and suggests something that causes death by its very nature, or has death as its purpose: *a deadly disease; a deadly poison.* LETHAL is usu. used in technical contexts: *Carbon monoxide is a lethal gas.* MORTAL refers to death that has actually occurred or to the fact that living beings die: *He received a mortal blow. We are all mortal.*

fate, *n.* **1.** destiny, fortune, luck, lot, chance, karma, kismet, providence, doom. **2.** death, destruction, ruin, doom, downfall, undoing, disaster, collapse, nemesis, end, finish. —*v.* **3.** predetermine, destine, predestine, foreordain, preordain.
—**Syn. Study.** FATE, DESTINY refer to a predetermined and usu. inescapable course or outcome of events. The two words are frequently interchangeable. FATE stresses the irrationality and impersonal character of events: *It was Napoleon's fate to be exiled.* The word is often used lightly: *It was my fate to meet her that very afternoon.* DESTINY is often used of a favorable or exalted lot in life: *It was her destiny to save her people.*

fatherly, *adj.* paternal, parental, protecting, protective; kind, tender, benign.

fault, *n.* **1.** defect, imperfection, blemish, flaw, failing, frailty, foible, deficiency, peccadillo, weakness, shortcoming, vice. **2.** error, mistake, slip, blunder, lapse, failure, oversight, gaffe, offense. **3.** misdeed, sin, transgression, trespass, misdemeanor, offense, wrong, delinquency, indiscretion, culpability.
—**Ant.** strength.

—**Syn. Study.** FAULT, FOIBLE, WEAKNESS, FAILING, VICE refer to human shortcomings or imperfections. FAULT refers to any ordinary shortcoming; condemnation is not necessarily implied: *Of his many faults the greatest is vanity.* FOIBLE suggests a weak point that is slight and often amusing, manifesting itself in eccentricity rather than in wrongdoing: *the foibles of an artist.* WEAKNESS suggests that a person is unable to control a particular impulse or response, and gives way to it: *a weakness for ice cream.* FAILING is particularly applied to humanity at large, suggesting common, often venial, shortcomings: *Procrastination is a common failing.* VICE is the strongest term and designates a habit that is detrimental, immoral, or evil: *to succumb to the vice of compulsive gambling.*

faulty, *adj.* defective, imperfect, incomplete, flawed, unsound, damaged, impaired, broken, bad.
—**Ant.** perfect, complete, consummate.

favor, *n.* **1.** courtesy, gesture, service, good turn, kindness, goodwill, benefit, good deed. **2.** partiality, bias, patronage, prejudice. **3.** gift, present. —*v.* **4.** prefer, encourage, patronize, approve, countenance, allow. **5.** facilitate, ease; propitiate, conciliate, appease. **6.** encourage, benefit, help, aid, help, support, assist.
—**Ant.** cruelty; disfavor; disapprove, disallow, discourage.

favorite, *adj.* **1.** preferred, chosen, pet, best-liked, best-loved, fair-haired, popular, beloved, loved, prized, treasured, dearest, precious, adored, esteemed, dearly beloved. —*n.* **2.** preference, pet, darling, chosen one, apple of one's eye, fair-haired one, ideal, flavor of the month.

fear, *n.* **1.** apprehension, consternation, dismay, alarm, qualms, timidity, cowardice, second thoughts, trepidation, dread, terror, fright, horror, panic. **2.** anxiety, solicitude, angst, foreboding, distress, misgiving, worry, unease, concern. **3.** awe, respect, reverence, veneration. —*v.* **4.** be afraid of, shudder at, quiver, tremble at, shrink from, apprehend, dread. **5.** revere, venerate, reverence, respect.
—**Ant.** boldness, bravery, intrepidity; security, confidence.

fearless, *adj.* brave, intrepid, bold, courageous, heroic, valorous, valiant, dauntless, plucky, gallant, daring, reckless.
—**Ant.** cowardly.
—**Syn. Study.** See BRAVE.

feasible, *adj.* **1.** practicable, workable, viable, doable, applicable, possible. **2.** suitable, suited, usable, practical, practicable. **3.** likely, probable, realistic.
—**Ant.** unfeasible, impractical, impossible; unsuitable, unsuited; unlikely, improbable.
—**Syn. Study.** See POSSIBLE.

feast, *n.* **1.** celebration, anniversary, commemoration, ceremony, banquet, fête, entertainment, carousal, revelry, sumptuous repast, spread, blowout. —*v.* **2.** eat, gourmandize, glut *or* stuff *or* gorge oneself, wine and dine, overindulge. **3.** gratify, delight, please, cheer, gladden.

feat, *n.* achievement, accomplishment, deed, action, act, exploit, attainment, tour de force.

feature, *n.* characteristic, peculiarity, trait, property, mark, attribute, hallmark, quality, aspect, facet, quirk, peculiarity, idiosyncrasy.
—**Syn. Study.** FEATURE, CHARACTERISTIC, PECULIARITY refer to a distinctive trait of an individual or of a class. FEATURE suggests an outstanding or marked property that attracts attention: *A large art exhibit was a feature of the convention.* CHARACTERISTIC means a distinguishing mark or quality always associated in one's mind with a particular person or thing: *A fine sense of humor is one of his characteristics.* PECULIARITY means a distinctive and often unusual property exclusive to one individual, group, or thing: *A blue-black tongue is a peculiarity of the chow chow.*

feeble, *adj.* **1.** weak, feckless, ineffective, ineffectual. **2.** infirm, sickly, debilitated, enervated, declining, frail. **3.** faint, dim, weak, obscure, imperceptible, indistinct.
—**Ant.** strong, effective, effectual; healthy; clear.

feed, *v.* **1.** nourish, sustain, purvey, provision, cater, supply, maintain, nurture. **2.** satisfy, minister to, gratify, please.
—**Ant.** starve.
—**Syn. Study.** FEED, FODDER, FORAGE, PROVENDER mean food for animals. FEED is the general word; however, it most often applies to grain: *chicken feed.* FODDER is applied to coarse feed that is fed to livestock: *Cornstalks are good fodder.* FORAGE is feed that an animal obtains (usu. grass, leaves, etc.) by grazing or searching about for it: *Lost cattle can usually live on forage.* PROVENDER denotes dry feed for livestock, such as hay, oats, or corn: *a supply of provender in the haymow.*

feeling, *n.* **1.** consciousness, perception, impression; emotion, passion, sentiment, sensibility; sympathy, empathy, compassion. **2.** tenderness, sensitivity, sentiment, sentimentality, susceptibility, pity. **3.** intuition, idea, notion, inkling, suspicion, sense, belief, hunch, theory, presentiment, impression, view, sentiment, opinion, tenor. —*adj.* **4.** sentient, emotional, sensitive, tender; sympathetic. **5.** emotional, impassioned, passionate.
—**Ant.** apathy, coolness; unemotional, insensitive, unsympathetic; cool.
—**Syn. Study.** FEELING, EMOTION, PASSION, SENTIMENT refer to pleasurable or painful sensations experienced when one is stirred to sympathy, anger, fear, love, grief, etc. FEELING is a general term for a subjective point of view as well as for specific sensations: *to be guided by feeling rather than by facts; a feeling of pride, of dismay.* EMOTION is applied to an intensified feeling: *agitated by emotion.* PASSION is strong or violent emotion, often so overpowering that it masters the mind or judgment: *stirred to a passion of anger.* SENTIMENT is a mixture of thought and feeling, esp. refined or tender feeling: *Recollections are often colored by sentiment.*

feign, *v.* **1.** invent, concoct, devise, fabricate, forge, counterfeit. **2.** simulate, pretend, counterfeit, affect; emulate, imitate, mimic. **3.** make believe, pretend, imagine.
—**Syn. Study.** See PRETEND.

female, *n.* **1.** woman, girl. —*adj.* **2.** feminine, delicate, womanly, soft, gentle, maternal, nurturing.
—**Ant.** male; masculine, manly.
—**Syn. Study.** FEMALE, FEMININE, EFFEMINATE describe women and girls or whatever is culturally attributed to them. FEMALE classifies individuals on the basis of their genetic makeup or their ability to produce offspring in sexual reproduction. It contrasts with MALE in all uses: *her oldest female relative; the female parts of the flower.* FEMININE refers to qualities and behavior deemed especially appropriate to or ideally associated with women and girls. In American and Western European culture, these have traditionally included such features as charm, gentleness, and patience: *to dance with feminine grace; a feminine sensitivity to moods.* FEMININE is sometimes used of physical features too: *small, feminine hands.* EFFEMINATE is most often applied derogatorily to men or boys, suggesting that they have traits culturally regarded as appropriate to women and girls rather than to men: *an effeminate speaking style.* See also WOMAN, WOMANLY.

ferocious, *adj.* fierce, savage, wild, cruel, violent, ravenous, vicious, feral, brutal, bestial, merciless, ruthless, pitiless, inhuman, barbaric, bloodthirsty, predatory, fiendish, monstrous, rapacious.
—**Ant.** mild, tame, calm.
—**Syn. Study.** See FIERCE.

fertile, *adj.* productive, prolific, fecund, fruitful, rich, teeming, bounteous, abundant, copious, plenteous, luxuriant.
—**Ant.** sterile, barren.
—**Syn. Study.** See PRODUCTIVE.

fervent, *adj.* fervid, ardent, earnest, warm, heated, hot, burning, glowing, fiery, inflamed, eager, zealous, vehement, impassioned, passionate, enthusiastic, intense, fanatical, excited, frantic, frenzied, emotional, heartfelt, ecstatic.
—**Ant.** cool, apathetic.

fervor, *n.* ardor, intensity, earnestness, eagerness, enthusiasm, fervency, warmth, zeal, gusto, ebullience, spirit, verve, passion, fire, heat, vehemence.
—**Ant.** coolness, apathy.

feud, *n.* hostility, quarrel, argument, difference, falling out, dispute, conflict, vendetta, strife, enmity, animosity, antagonism, rivalry, discord, grudge, bad blood, hard feelings, dissension.

fiction, *n.* **1.** novel, fantasy, story, fable, tale, legend, myth. **2.** fabrication, figment, unreality, lie, falsehood, prevarication, invention, falsity.
—**Ant.** nonfiction, fact; reality.

fictitious, *adj.* **1.** imaginary, illusory, fanciful, fancied, invented, created, concocted, made-up, dreamed up, unreal, visionary, chimerical, mythical. **2.** artificial, bogus, fake, mock, ungenuine, deceptive, counterfeit, factitious, synthetic.
—**Ant.** real, genuine.

fidelity, *n.* **1.** loyalty, faithfulness, devotion, fealty, dependability, resolve, allegiance, trustworthiness, reliability, constancy, steadfastness, staunchness, firmness, steadiness, stability, dedication. **2.** accuracy, precision, faithfulness, exactness, closeness.
—**Ant.** disloyalty, unfaithfulness; inaccuracy.

fierce, *adj.* **1.** ferocious, wild, vehement, violent, savage, cruel, fell, feral, bestial, inhuman, sanguinary, dangerous, brutal, bloodthirsty, murderous, homicidal. **2.** truculent, barbarous, intractable, angry, hostile, aggressive, stormy, violent, tempestuous, tumultuous, raging, merciless, remorseless, ruthless, uncontrollable, frenzied, untamed, furious, passionate, turbulent, impetuous.
—**Ant.** tame, domesticated; calm; civilized; cool, temperate.
—**Syn. Study.** FIERCE, FEROCIOUS, TRUCULENT suggest vehement hostility and unrestrained violence. FIERCE implies an aggressive, savage, or wild temperament and appearance: *the fiercest of foes; a fierce tribe.* FEROCIOUS implies merciless cruelty or brutality, esp. of a bloodthirsty kind: *a ferocious tiger.* TRUCULENT implies an intimidating or menacing fierceness: *a truculent bully.*

fiery, *adj.* **1.** hot, flaming, heated, fervent, fervid, burning, afire, glowing. **2.** fervent, fervid, vehement, inflamed, impassioned, spirited, ardent, impetuous, passionate, fierce, zealous, excited, eager, hot-headed.
—**Ant.** cool, cold; dispassionate.

fight, *n.* **1.** battle, war, combat, encounter, conflict, contest, scrimmage, bout, clash, hostilities, duel, brawl, donnybrook, fracas, riot, engagement, fray, affray, action, skirmish, affair, struggle. **2.** melee, struggle, scuffle, tussle, riot, row, fray. —*v.* **3.** contend, strive, battle, combat, conflict, contest, engage, struggle, clash, feud, take up arms, joust, confront, oppose, encounter, make war, brawl, strive against, cross swords, exchange blows, grapple, wrestle; dispute, defy, resist, protest, withstand, oppugn; argue, quarrel, wrangle, squabble, disagree.

filthy, *adj.* **1.** dirty, foul, unclean, defiled, squalid, nasty, vile, scummy, slimy, grungy, shabby, sordid, soiled, grimy, unkempt, slovenly. **2.** obscene, vile, dirty, pornographic, licentious, lascivious, indecent, impure, smutty, X-rated, gross, offensive, bawdy, ribald, blue, foul-mouthed, immoral, taboo.
—**Ant.** clean, spotless, immaculate.

final, *adj.* **1.** last, latest, ultimate; ending, concluding, terminal, closing, drop-dead. **2.** conclusive, decisive, definitive.
—**Ant.** prime, primary.

fine, *adj.* **1.** superior, high-grade, choice, excellent, admirable, elegant, superb, magnificent, exceptional, first-rate, quality, marvelous, prime, choice, great, supreme, peachy, exquisite, finished, consummate, perfect, refined, select, delicate. **2.** powdered, pulverized, minute, small, little. **3.** keen, sharp, acute. **4.** outstanding, masterly, masterful, virtuoso, skilled, accomplished, brilliant.
—**Ant.** inferior, poor, bad, unfinished; dull; unskilled, maladroit.

finish, *v.* **1.** bring to an end, end, cease, stop, terminate, conclude, close. **2.** use up, complete, consume. **3.** complete, perfect, consummate, polish. **4.** accomplish, achieve, execute, complete, perform, do. —*n.* **5.** end, conclusion, termination, close. **6.** polish, elegance, refinement.
—**Ant.** begin, start, commence; originate, create; beginning.

finished, *adj.* **1.** ended, completed, consummated, over, done, done with; complete, consummate, perfect. **2.** polished, refined, elegant, perfected; trained, experienced, practiced, qualified, accomplished, proficient, skilled, gifted, talented.
—**Ant.** begun; incomplete, imperfect; unrefined, inelegant; inexperienced, unqualified, unskilled, maladroit.

firm, *adj.* **1.** hard, solid, stiff, rigid, inelastic, compact, condensed, compressed, dense. **2.** steady, unshakable, rooted, fast, fixed, stable, secure, immovable. **3.** fixed, settled, unalterable, established, confirmed. **4.** steadfast, unwavering, determined, immovable, resolute, staunch, constant, steady, reliable. —*n.* **5.** company, partnership, association, business, concern, house, corporation, dot-com.
—**Ant.** flabby, flaccid, elastic, soft; unsteady, unstable; wavering, irresolute, inconstant, unreliable.

fitness, *n.* **1.** condition, physical

condition, conditioning, tone, vigor, well-being, shape, fettle, health, healthfulness, trim, repair, order, salubrity, salubriousness. **2.** appropriateness, suitability, applicability, aptness, cogency, propriety, competence, pertinence, seemliness, adequacy.

fix, *v.* **1.** make fast, fasten, pin, attach, tie, secure, stabilize, establish, set, plant, implant. **2.** settle, determine, establish, define, limit. **3.** repair, mend, correct, emend, remedy, rectify, doctor, straighten out. —*n.* **4.** difficulty, quandary, straits, corner, predicament, dilemma, plight, spot, double bind, pickle, jam, bind, pinch.
—**Ant.** loosen, loose, detach; unsettle; break.

flame, *n.* **1.** blaze, conflagration, holocaust, inferno, fire. **2.** heat, ardor, zeal, passion, fervor, warmth, enthusiasm. —*v.* **3.** burn, blaze. **4.** glow, burn, warm; shine, flash. **5.** inflame, fire.

flash, *n.* **1.** flame, outburst, flare, gleam, glare. **2.** instant, split second, moment, twinkling, wink. **3.** ostentation, display. —*v.* **4.** glance, glint, glitter, scintillate, gleam.

flat, *adj.* **1.** horizontal, level, even, equal, plane, smooth. **2.** low, recumbent, outstretched, reclining, supine, prone, prostrate. **3.** unqualified, downright, positive, outright, peremptory, absolute. **4.** uninteresting, dull, tedious, lifeless, boring, spiritless, prosaic, unanimated; insipid, vapid, tasteless, stale, dead, unsavory.
—**Ant.** vertical, upright, perpendicular; doubtful, dubious; spirited, animated; tasteful, savory; pointed.

flatter, *v.* apple-polish, fawn, toady, kowtow, truckle, blandish, praise, compliment, court, play up to, curry favor with, cajole, wheedle, coax, beguile, entice, inveigle, flatter, soft-soap, honey, sweet-talk, butter up, bootlick, suck up to, brown-nose.
—**Ant.** insult, affront, offend.

flavor, *n.* **1.** taste, savor, tang, piquancy, zest. **2.** seasoning, extract, flavoring. **3.** characteristic, essence, quality, spirit, soul, nature, quality, property, style, mark, feel, feeling. **4.** smell, odor, aroma, perfume, fragrance.

flaw, *n.* defect, imperfection, blot, blemish, spot, fault; crack, crevice, breach, break, cleft, fissure, rift, fracture.
—**Syn. Study.** See DEFECT.

fleet, *adj.* swift, fast, quick, rapid, speedy, expeditious, fleet-footed, nimble-footed, hasty, express, snappy.
—**Ant.** slow, sluggish.

flexible, *adj.* **1.** pliable, pliant, flexile, limber, plastic, elastic, supple. **2.** adaptable, tractable, compliant, yielding, gentle.
—**Ant.** inflexible, rigid, solid, firm; intractable, unyielding.

flock, *n.* bevy, covey, flight, gaggle; brood, hatch, litter; shoal, school; swarm; pride; drove, herd, pack; group, company, body, band, pack, bunch, troop, assembly, congregation, collection, mass, mob, throng, gang, host, horde, crowd.

flood, *n.* **1.** deluge, inundation, overflow, flash flood, freshet, tidal wave, tide, torrent, stream. **2.** abundance, surge, rush, flow, glut, surfeit, profusion, plethora, excess, superfluity. —*v.* **3.** inundate, submerge, overflow, swamp, immerse, drown. **4.** overwhelm, glut, saturate, choke; swarm, surge, rush, crowd, pour; permeate, fill, engulf, cover.

flourish, *v.* **1.** thrive, prosper, be

successful, grow, increase, develop, bloom, blossom, thrive, burgeon, boom, succeed. **2.** brandish, wave, parade, flaunt, display, show off, be ostentatious, boast, brag, vaunt. —*n.* **3.** parade, fanfare, display, ostentation, show, display, dash. **4.** decoration, ornament, adornment, embellishment, elaboration, frill, floweriness, floridness.
—**Ant.** decline, die, fail; disfigure, mar.
—**Syn. Study.** See SUCCEED.

flow, *v.* **1.** gush, spout, stream, spurt, jet, discharge. **2.** proceed, run, pour, roll on. **3.** overflow, abound, teem, pour. —*n.* **4.** current, flood, stream. **5.** stream, river, rivulet, rill, streamlet. **6.** outpouring, discharge, overflowing.

fluctuate, *v.* waver, vacillate, change, vary, alternate, seesaw, swing, waver, shift, undulate, oscillate.

fluent, *adj.* flowing, articulate, eloquent, well-spoken, facile, easy, graceful, natural, effortless, ready, polished, slick, expressive, glib, voluble, copious, smooth.
—**Ant.** terse, curt, silent.
—**Syn. Study.** FLUENT, GLIB, VOLUBLE may refer to an easy flow of words or to a person able to communicate with ease. FLUENT suggests the easy and ready flow of an accomplished speaker or writer; it is usually a term of commendation: *a fluent orator.* GLIB implies an excessive fluency and lack of sincerity or profundity; it suggests talking smoothly and hurriedly to cover up or deceive: *a glib salesperson.* VOLUBLE implies the copious and often rapid flow of words characteristic of a person who loves to talk and will spare the audience no details: *a voluble gossip.*

fly, *v.* **1.** take wing, soar, hover, flutter, flit, wing, flap. **2.** hasten, hurry, run, race, dash, sprint, scoot. **3.** elapse, pass, glide, slip by, expire.

foe, *n.* enemy, opponent, adversary, antagonist, competition, opposition, contestant.
—**Ant.** friend, ally, associate.

fog, *n.* **1.** cloud, mist, haze, pea soup, soup; smog. **2.** cloud, confusion, obfuscation, dimming, blurring, darkening. —*v.* **3.** befog, becloud, obfuscate, dim, blur, darken. **4.** daze, bewilder, befuddle, muddle.
—**Ant.** clarity; clear, brighten; clarify.

foible, *n.* weakness, fault, failing, frailty, defect, imperfection, infirmity, shortcoming, flaw, peculiarity, idiosyncrasy, quirk.
—**Ant.** strength, perfection.
—**Syn. Study.** See FAULT.

follow, *v.* **1.** succeed, ensue. **2.** conform, obey, heed, comply, observe. **3.** accompany, attend. **4.** pursue, chase, trail, track, trace. **5.** ensue, succeed, result, come next, arise, proceed.
—**Ant.** lead; order.
—**Syn. Study.** FOLLOW, ENSUE, RESULT, SUCCEED imply coming after something else, in a natural sequence. FOLLOW is the general word: *We must wait to see what follows. A detailed account follows.* ENSUE implies a logical sequence, what might be expected normally to come after a given act, cause, etc.: *When the power lines were cut, a paralysis of transportation ensued.* RESULT emphasizes the connection between a cause or event and its effect, consequence, or outcome: *The accident resulted in injuries to those involved.* SUCCEED implies coming after in time, particularly coming into a title, office, etc.: *Formerly the oldest son succeeded to his father's title.*

follower, *n.* **1.** adherent, partisan, disciple, protégé, student, pupil. **2.** attendant, servant; supporter, retainer, companion, associate. **3.** supporter, devotee, fan, aficionado, promoter, enthusiast, advocate, proponent, booster, rooter, groupie.
—**Ant.** leader, teacher; enemy, foe.
—**Syn. Study.** FOLLOWER, ADHERENT, PARTISAN refer to someone who demonstrates allegiance to a person, doctrine, cause, or the like. FOLLOWER often has an implication of personal relationship or of deep devotion to authority or to a leader: *a follower of Gandhi.* ADHERENT, a more formal word, suggests active championship of a person or point of view: *an adherent of monetarism.* PARTISAN suggests firm loyalty, as to a party, cause, or person, that is based on emotions rather than on reasoning: *a partisan of the conservatives.*

food, *n.* provisions, rations, nutrition, nutriment, nourishment, aliment, bread, sustenance, victuals; meat, viands; diet, regimen, fare, menu.

fool, *n.* **1.** simpleton, dolt, dunce, blockhead, airhead, nincompoop, ninny, numbskull, ignoramus, booby, sap, idiot, ass, jackass, silly, featherbrain, loon, goose, dimwit, nitwit, halfwit, imbecile, moron, clod, oaf, birdbrain, dumbbell, fathead, chump, schmuck, nit, twit, twerp, jerk, dope, retard, space cadet, mental midget. **2.** jester, buffoon, harlequin, zany, clown, merry-andrew. —*v.* **3.** impose on, trick, deceive, delude, hoodwink, cozen, cheat, gull, gudgeon, hoax, dupe. **4.** joke, jest, play, toy, trifle, dally, idle, banter, tease, twit, kid, fiddle, monkey.
—**Ant.** genius.

foolish, *adj.* **1.** silly, senseless, stupid, dull, vacant, fatuous, inane, vapid, slow, asinine, simple, witless. **2.** ill-considered, unwise, thoughtless, irrational, imprudent, unreasonable, absurd, ridiculous, nonsensical, preposterous, foolhardy.
—**Ant.** bright, brilliant, clever, intelligent; wise, sage, sagacious.
—**Syn. Study.** FOOLISH, FATUOUS, INANE imply weakness of intellect and lack of judgment. FOOLISH implies lack of common sense or good judgment or, sometimes, weakness of mind: *a foolish decision; a foolish child.* FATUOUS implies being not only foolish, dull, and vacant in mind, but complacent and highly self-satisfied as well: *a fatuous grin.* INANE suggests a lack of content, meaning, or purpose: *inane conversation about the weather.*

forbid, *v.* outlaw, proscribe, disallow, inhibit, prohibit, taboo, interdict, prevent, preclude, stop, obviate, deter, discourage, ban, hinder, veto, debar.
—**Ant.** allow, permit, encourage.

forbidding, *adj.* hostile, stern, harsh, unfriendly, ugly, bad, ominous, dangerous, offensive, unpleasant, unappealing, dismaying, grim, disagreeable, rebarbative, off-putting, menacing, threatening, minatory.
—**Ant.** attractive, appealing.

force, *n.* **1.** strength, power, impetus, intensity, might, vigor, energy. **2.** coercion, violence, compulsion, constraint, enforcement, pressure. **3.** efficacy, effectiveness, effect, efficiency, validity, potency, potential. —*v.* **4.** compel, constrain, oblige, coerce, necessitate. **5.** drive, propel, impel. **6.** overcome, overpower, violate, ravish, rape.
—**Ant.** weakness, frailty; ineffectiveness, inefficiency.

forecast, *v.* **1.** predict, augur, foretell, foresee, anticipate, prophesize, be prescient, see the future, read tea leaves. **2.** prearrange, plan, contrive, project. **3.** conjecture, guess, estimate. —*n.* **4.** prediction, augury, conjecture, guess, estimate, foresight, prophecy, prevision, anticipation, forethought, prescience.
—**Syn. Study.** See PREDICT.

foreigner, *n.* alien, stranger, nonnative, outsider, outlander, immigrant, newcomer, new arrival, *Auslander.*
—**Ant.** native.
—**Syn. Study.** See STRANGER.

foresight, *n.* **1.** prudence, forethought, prevision, care, anticipation, insight, circumspection, perspicacity, precaution; forecast. **2.** prescience, prevision, foreknowledge, prospect, expectation, perception.

forgive, *v.* pardon, excuse, allow, indulge, overlook, ignore, disregard; clear, acquit, absolve, exonerate, exculpate, spare, let off; cancel, waive, abolish, void, nullify, erase.
—**Ant.** blame, condemn, censure.
—**Syn. Study.** See EXCUSE.

forlorn, *adj.* **1.** abandoned, deserted, forsaken, desolate, alone, neglected, outcast, shunned, friendless, bereft, lonesome, lost, solitary. **2.** desolate, dreary, unhappy, miserable, wretched, pitiable, pitiful, helpless, woebegone, disconsolate, comfortless, pathetic, woeful, melancholy, glum, depressed, dejected, mournful, inconsolable, lugubrious.
—**Ant.** accompanied; happy, cheerful.

form, *n.* **1.** shape, figure, outline, mold, appearance, cast, cut, configuration. **2.** mold, model, pattern. **3.** manner, style, arrangement, sort, kind, order, type. **4.** figure, body, shape, build, physique, anatomy. **5.** ceremony, ritual, formula, formality, conformity, rule, convention. **6.** document, paper, application, business form, blank. **7.** method, procedure, system, mode, practice, formula, approach. —*v.* **8.** construct, frame, shape, model, mold, fashion, outline, cast. **9.** fabricate, forge, shape, fashion, turn out, manufacture, make, produce. **10.** compose, make up, serve for, constitute. **11.** order, arrange, organize, systematize, dispose, combine. **12.** frame, invent, devise, conceive, contrive, create, originate, dream up, compose, formulate, concoct, coin, imagine.

formal, *adj.* **1.** standard, customary, established, prescribed, proper, academic, conventional, conformal, conforming, conformist. **2.** ceremonial, ceremonious, ritual, conventional. **3.** ceremonious, stiff, prim, precise, punctilious, starched, dignified, stuffy, strait-laced, stodgy. **4.** perfunctory, external. **5.** official, express, explicit, strict, rigid, definite, authorized, spelled-out, formalized, legal, rigorous. **6.** rigorous, methodical, regular, set, fixed, rigid, stiff, exacting, strict, formulaic, unbending, systematic, orderly.

formidable, *adj.* dreadful, appalling, threatening, menacing, fearful, terrible, frightful, horrible, alarming, awesome, intimidating, daunting; mind-boggling, incredible, prodigious, impressive; arduous, staggering, overwhelming, difficult, challenging, onerous.
—**Ant.** pleasant, friendly, amiable.

forsake, *v.* **1.** quit, leave, desert, abandon. **2.** give up, renounce, forswear, relinquish, recant, drop, forgo, yield, repudiate, surrender, resign, abdicate, deny, turn one's back on.

fortunate, *adj.* lucky, happy, propitious, favorable, advantageous, providential, opportune, well-timed, timely, auspicious; successful, prosperous, blessed, fortuitous, favored.
—**Ant.** unlucky, unfortunate.
—**Syn. Study.** FORTUNATE, LUCKY, HAPPY refer to persons who enjoy, or events that produce, good fortune. FORTUNATE implies that the success is obtained by the operation of favorable circumstances more than by direct effort: *fortunate in one's choice of a wife; a fortunate investment.* LUCKY, a more colloquial word, is applied to situations that turn out well by chance: *lucky at cards; my lucky day.* HAPPY emphasizes a pleasant ending or something that happens at just the right moment: *By a happy accident I was home when your package arrived.*

forward, *adv.* **1.** onward, ahead, up ahead, in advance, frontward. **2.** out, forth, to the fore, into view, into the open. —*adj.* **3.** well-advanced, up front, ahead. **4.** ready, prompt, eager, willing, sincere, earnest, zealous. **5.** pert, bold, presumptuous, assuming, confident, impertinent, impudent, brazen, flippant, disrespectful, cheeky, saucy, pushy, fresh. **6.** radical, extreme, unconventional, progressive.
—**Ant.** backward.

foster, *v.* **1.** promote, encourage, further, favor, patronize, forward, advance, stimulate, cultivate, back, help, assist. **2.** bring up, rear, breed, nurse, nourish, sustain, support; care for, cherish.
—**Ant.** discourage.
—**Syn. Study.** See CHERISH.

foul, *adj.* **1.** offensive, gross, disgusting, loathsome, repulsive, repellent, noisome, fetid, putrid, stinking. **2.** filthy, dirty, unclean, squalid, polluted, sullied, soiled, tarnished, stained, tainted, impure. **3.** stormy, unfavorable, rainy, tempestuous. **4.** abominable, wicked, vile, base, shameful, infamous, sinful, scandalous. **5.** scurrilous, obscene, smutty, profane, vulgar, low, coarse. **6.** unfair, dishonorable, underhanded, cheating. —*v.* **7.** soil, defile, sully, stain, dirty, besmirch, smut, taint, pollute, poison. **8.** defile, dishonor, disgrace, shame, taint, blacken, denigrate, debase, degrade, demean, defame, devaluate, belittle, discredit.
—**Ant.** delightful, attractive, pleasant; pure; saintly, angelic; fair, honorable; clean, purify; clear; honor.

foundation, *n.* **1.** base, basis, substructure, underpinning, fundamental, principle, grounds, groundwork, rationale, footing. **2.** establishment, founding, institution, creation, inauguration, setting up, origination, organization, organizing, settlement; endowment.
—**Ant.** superstructure.
—**Syn. Study.** See BASE.

fragrant, *adj.* perfumed, odorous, redolent, sweet-smelling, sweet-scented, aromatic, odoriferous, balmy.
—**Ant.** noxious.

frail, *adj.* brittle, fragile, breakable, frangible; delicate, weak, dainty, thin, slight; infirm, feeble, decrepit, sickly, puny, scrawny; ailing, unwell, ill, poorly, wasting away, consumptive.
—**Ant.** strong, pliant, elastic, unbreakable; healthy.
—**Syn. Study.** FRAIL, BRITTLE, FRAGILE imply a delicacy or weakness of substance or construction. FRAIL applies particularly to health and immaterial things: *a frail constitution; frail hopes.* BRITTLE implies a hard material that snaps or breaks to pieces

easily: *brittle as glass.* FRAGILE implies that the object must be handled carefully to avoid breakage or damage: *fragile bric-a-brac.*

frank, *adj.* **1.** candid, open, outspoken, unreserved, unrestrained, unrestricted, nonrestrictive, sincere, free, bold, truthful, uninhibited. **2.** artless, ingenuous, guileless, innocent, on the level, naive. **3.** undisguised, avowed, downright, outright, direct.
—**Ant.** secretive, restrained, restricted; sly, artful, dissembling.
—**Syn. Study.** FRANK, CANDID, OPEN, OUTSPOKEN imply a freedom and boldness in speaking. FRANK implies a straightforward, almost tactless expression of one's real opinions or sentiments: *He was frank in his rejection of the proposal.* CANDID suggests sincerity, truthfulness, and impartiality: *a candid appraisal of her work.* OPEN implies a lack of reserve or of concealment: *open antagonism.* OUTSPOKEN suggests free and bold expression, even when inappropriate: *an outspoken and unnecessary show of disapproval.*

fraud, *n.* deceit, trickery, duplicity, treachery, swindling, double-dealing, chicanery, fraudulence; breach of confidence, trick, deception, guile, artifice, ruse, stratagem, wile, hoax, humbug, scam, flimflam, gyp, rip-off.
—**Ant.** honesty.
—**Syn. Study.** See DECEIT.

free, *adj.* **1.** unfettered, independent, at liberty, unrestrained, unrestricted; self-governing, autonomous, democratic, sovereign. **2.** unregulated, unrestricted, unimpeded, open, unobstructed. **3.** clear, immune, exempt, uncontrolled, decontrolled. **4.** easy, firm, swift, unimpeded, unencumbered. **5.** loose, unattached, unfastened, untied, lax. **6.** frank, open, unconstrained, unceremonious, familiar, informal, easy, relaxed, casual, natural. **7.** loose, licentious, ribald, lewd, immoral, libertine. **8.** liberal, lavish, generous, bountiful, unstinted, munificent, charitable, unsparing, openhanded. —*v.* **9.** liberate, set free, release, unchain, rescue, redeem, emancipate, manumit, deliver, disenthrall. **10.** rid, relieve, disengage, clear, unburden, disencumber.
—**Ant.** dependent, restrained, restricted; close, obstructed; difficult; unfamiliar; moral, upright; stingy, niggardly; confine, enthrall.
—**Syn. Study.** See RELEASE.

freedom, *n.* **1.** liberty, independence, self-determination, autonomy, self-government. **2.** release, deliverance, liberation, emancipation; exemption, relief, immunity, franchise, privilege. **3.** range, latitude, scope, play, noninterference, margin; ease, license, facility, permission, right, privilege, authority, authorization, carte blanche. **4.** frankness, honesty, candor, naturalness, unrestraint, openness, ingenuousness. **5.** familiarity, license, looseness, laxity; boldness, audacity, brass, nerve, gall.
—**Ant.** dependence; restriction; difficulty; secrecy; unfamiliarity, restraint.

frenzy, *n.* agitation, excitement, paroxysm, enthusiasm, turmoil, passion, distraction, seizure, outburst, bout, fit; rage, fury, raving, mania, insanity, delirium, derangement, aberration, lunacy, madness, fever, furor, transport.
—**Ant.** calm, coolness; sanity, judgment.

frequently, *adv.* often, many times, repeatedly, regularly, continually,

over and over, time and again, habitually, commonly, usually, customarily, ordinarily, generally.
—**Ant.** seldom.
—**Syn. Study.** See OFTEN.

fresh, *adj.* **1.** new, recent, novel, modern, up-to-date, original, unconventional, different, alternative, unorthodox. **2.** youthful, healthy, robust, vigorous, well, hearty, hardy, strong. **3.** refreshing, pure, cool, unadulterated, sweet, invigorating. **4.** inexperienced, artless, untrained, immature, raw, green, uncultivated, unskilled, unsophisticated, untested, naive, wet behind the ears.
—**Ant.** stale, old; impure, contaminated; experienced, skilled.
—**Syn. Study.** See NEW.

fret, *v.* **1.** worry, fume, rage, agonize, lose sleep, grieve, brood, whine, fuss, complain, whimper, stew, be upset *or* anxious. **2.** torment, worry, harass, annoy, irritate, vex, taunt, goad, tease, nettle, needle.

fretful, *adj.* irritable, peevish, petulant, querulous, touchy, testy, tetchy, temperamental, vexed, edgy, cross, irascible, choleric, crabby, moody, grumpy, sulky, disagreeable, impatient, abrupt, cranky, waspish, pettish, splenetic, captious, snappish, short-tempered, ill-tempered.
—**Ant.** calm, even-tempered, temperate, easy-going.

friction, *n.* discord, disaccord, disharmony, conflict, dissension, disagreement, contention, dispute, controversy, dissent, bickering, argument, wrangling, ill will, bad blood, animosity, rivalry, hostility, strife, antagonism, strain, incompatibility, contentiousness, enmity.
—**Ant.** friendliness, amity, cooperation.

friend, *n.* **1.** companion, crony, chum, acquaintance, intimate, partner, comrade, alter ego, ally, playmate, pal, chum, confidant. **2.** well-wisher, patron, supporter, backer, encourager, advocate, defender. **3.** ally, associate, confrère, confederate, fellow, colleague, coworker, cohort.
—**Ant.** enemy, foe, adversary.
—**Syn. Study.** See ACQUAINTANCE.

friendly, *adj.* **1.** kind, kindly, amicable, fraternal, amiable, cordial, sociable, congenial, convivial, simpatico, neighborly, genial, well-disposed, benevolent, affectionate, kindhearted, demonstrative, affable, approachable, familiar, chummy. **2.** helpful, favorable, advantageous, propitious.
—**Ant.** unfriendly, inimical; unfavorable.

fright, *n.* dismay, consternation, terror, fear, alarm, panic, dread, horror, trepidation, shock, apprehension.
—**Ant.** bravery, boldness.

frighten, *v.* scare, terrify, alarm, appall, shock, dismay, intimidate, panic, startle, petrify, unnerve, distress, daunt, cow, scare out of one's wits, make one's hair stand on end.

frightful, *adj.* dreadful, terrible, alarming, terrific, fearful, awful, shocking, dread, dire, horrid, horrible, hideous, ghastly, gruesome, atrocious, abhorrent, loathsome, grisly, lurid, macabre, horrifying, horrendous, unspeakable, vile, repugnant.
—**Ant.** delightful, attractive, beautiful.

frivolous, *adj.* **1.** unimportant, trifling, petty, paltry, trivial, flimsy, inconsequential, nugatory, insignificant, minor, niggling, superficial, worthless, two-bit, penny-ante. **2.** silly, foolish, childish, puerile, scatterbrained, birdbrained, irresponsible, flighty, giddy, airy-fairy.

—**Ant.** important, vital; mature, adult, sensible.

frugal, *adj.* prudent, provident, saving, conservative, moderate, economical, thrifty, chary, provident, saving, sparing, careful; parsimonious, stingy, penurious, mean, miserly.
—**Ant.** lavish, wasteful.
—**Syn. Study.** See ECONOMICAL.

fruitful, *adj.* prolific, fertile, fecund, productive, profitable; plentiful, abundant, rich, copious, bountiful, luxurious, flourishing.
—**Ant.** barren, scarce, scanty, unprofitable, fruitless.
—**Syn. Study.** See PRODUCTIVE.

fruitless, *adj.* **1.** useless, worthless, bootless, pointless, unrewarding, to no avail, unavailing, profitless, ineffectual, unprofitable, vain, idle, futile, abortive. **2.** barren, sterile, unfruitful, unproductive, infecund, unprolific.
—**Ant.** fruitful, useful, profitable, effectual; abundant, fertile.

frustrate, *v.* defeat, nullify, baffle, disconcert, foil, balk, check, thwart, stymie, block, counter, forestall, prevent, stop, halt, hamper, hinder, cripple, impede; upset, exasperate, discourage, disappoint.
—**Ant.** encourage, foster.

fulfill, *v.* **1.** carry out, consummate, execute, discharge, accomplish, achieve, complete, effect, realize, perfect. **2.** perform, do, obey, observe, discharge. **3.** satisfy, meet, answer, fill, comply with. **4.** complete, end, terminate, bring to an end, finish, conclude.
—**Ant.** fail; dissatisfy; create, originate.

full, *adj.* **1.** filled, replete, brimming, jampacked, loaded, bursting, chock-full, jammed, crammed, crowded, stuffed; gorged, saturated, satiated, sated. **2.** complete, thorough, total, comprehensive, broad, extensive, exhaustive. **3.** complete, entire, whole, uncut, intact, unshortened. **4.** wide, broad, ample, generous, copious. **5.** utmost, greatest, maximum, top, extreme, highest.

fume, *n.* **1.** smoke, vapor, exhalation, gas. **2.** rage, fury, agitation, storm. —*v.* **3.** smoke, vaporize. **4.** seethe, smolder, rant, explode, get steamed up, chafe, fret, rage, rave, flare up, bluster, storm, fly off the handle, blow a gasket.

fun, *n.* merriment, enjoyment, pleasure, amusement, divertissement, glee, jollity, mirth, cheer, high spirits, delight, frolic, recreation, entertainment, pastime, joy, sport, diversion, joking, jesting, playfulness, gaiety, frolic.
—**Ant.** misery, melancholy.

fundamental, *adj.* **1.** basic, underlying, principal, main, central, rudimentary, prime, cardinal, quintessential, inherent, intrinsic, important, crucial, critical, chief, essential, primary, elementary, necessary, indispensable. **2.** original, first. —*n.* **3.** principle, rule, basic law, essence, essential.
—**Ant.** superficial, superfluous, dispensable; last, common; nonessential.

funny, *adj.* amusing, diverting, comical, farcical, absurd, ridiculous, comic, risible, waggish, sidesplitting, hilarious, uproarious, jocular, merry, slapstick, zany, entertaining, hysterical, droll, witty, facetious, humorous, laughable, ludicrous, incongruous, foolish; peculiar, odd, unusual, curious, strange, queer, mysterious, weird, bizarre, eccentric, off the wall.
—**Ant.** sad, melancholy, humorless.

furnish, *v.* **1.** provide, supply; purvey, cater. **2.** appoint, equip, fit up, rig, deck out, decorate, outfit, fit out.

—**Syn. Study.** FURNISH, APPOINT, EQUIP refer to providing something necessary or useful. FURNISH often refers to providing necessary or customary objects or services that increase living comfort: *to furnish a bedroom with a bed, desk, and chair.* APPOINT, a more formal word, now usu. used in the past participle, means to supply completely with all requisites or accessories, often in an elegant style: *a well-appointed hotel; a fully appointed suite.* EQUIP means to supply with necessary materials or apparatus for a particular action, service, or undertaking; it emphasizes preparation: *to equip a vessel; to equip a soldier.*

fury, *n.* **1.** passion, furor, frenzy, rage, ire, anger, choler, rancor, wrath. **2.** violence, turbulence, fierceness, impetuousness, impetuosity, vehemence. **3.** shrew, virago, termagant, vixen, nag, hag, maenad, spitfire, hellcat, she-devil, witch, bitch.
—**Ant.** calm, serenity.
—**Syn. Study.** See ANGER.

fuss, *n.* activity, ado, bustle, bother, dither, flurry, fret, excitement, furor, agitation, unrest, trouble, disquiet, stir, uproar, hubbub, brouhaha, flap, stink, hoopla, to-do, stir, commotion.
—**Ant.** inactivity, quiet, serenity.

futile, *adj.* **1.** ineffectual, useless, unsuccessful, vain, unavailing, idle, profitless, unprofitable, bootless, worthless, valueless, fruitless, unproductive. **2.** trivial, frivolous, minor, nugatory, unimportant, trifling.
—**Ant.** effective, effectual, successful; profitable, worthy; basic, important, principal, major.
—**Syn. Study.** See USELESS.

G

gadget, *n.* device, tool, appliance, implement, instrument, utensil, mechanism, contrivance, contraption, invention, creation, doohickey, dingus, thingumabob, gizmo, thingamajig, doodad, widget, whatchamacallit.

gaiety, *n.* **1.** merriment, mirth, glee, jollity, joyousness, liveliness, levity, exhilaration, elation, bouyancy, blitheness, delight, exultation, mirthfulness, jubilation, high spirits, happiness, felicity, pleasure, joie de vivre, sportiveness, hilarity, vivacity, life, cheerfulness, joviality, animation, spirit. **2.** showiness, finery, gaudiness, brilliance, glitter, flashiness, flash, cheeriness, brightness, garishness.
—**Ant.** sadness, melancholy, misery.

gain, *v.* **1.** obtain, secure, procure, get, acquire, attain, earn, win, achieve, capture, net, reap, glean, garner, collect. **2.** reach, get to, arrive at, attain. **3.** improve, better, progress, advance, forward; near, approach. —*n.* **4.** profit, increase, yield, return, benefit, income, advantage, advance; profits, winnings, earnings, proceeds, revenue.
—**Ant.** lose; worsen; retreat; losses.
—**Syn. Study.** GAIN, ATTAIN, EARN, WIN imply obtaining a reward or something advantageous. GAIN suggests the expenditure of effort to get or reach something desired: *After battling the blizzard, we finally gained our destination.* ATTAIN suggests a sense of personal satisfaction in having reached a lofty goal: *to attain stardom.* EARN emphasizes a deserved reward for labor or services:

to earn a promotion. WIN stresses attainment in spite of competition or opposition: *to win support in a campaign.*

gall, *v.* **1.** irritate, annoy, irk, vex, nettle, peeve, provoke, bother, harass, plague, goad, nag, needle, rankle, aggravate, exasperate, get one's goat. —*n.* **2.** overconfidence, impertinence, forwardness, temerity, effrontery, brazenness, brashness, impudence, insolence, nerve, cheek, crust, brass, guts, chutzpah, moxie.

gallant, *adj.* **1.** brave, high-spirited, valorous, valiant, chivalrous, courageous, bold, intrepid, fearless, daring. **2.** majestic, stately, grand, imposing, glorious, magnificent, splendid, fine. **3.** polite, courtly, chivalrous, noble, attentive, thoughtful, considerate, well-bred, courteous.
—**Ant.** cowardly, fearful; tawdry; impolite, discourteous.

game, *n.* **1.** amusement, pastime, diversion, divertissement, play, fun, sport, contest, competition. **2.** scheme, artifice, strategy, stratagem, plan, plot, undertaking, venture, adventure. —*adj.* **3.** plucky, brave, bold, spirited, daring, devil-may-care, unflinching, gutsy, resolute, intrepid, dauntless, valorous, fearless, heroic, gallant.

gang, *n.* band, group, crew, crowd, company, party, set, clique, coterie, horde, pack, mob, ring; squad, shift, team.

garb, *n.* **1.** fashion, mode, style, cut. **2.** clothes, clothing, dress, costume, attire, apparel, habiliments, habit, garments, raiment, vesture. —*v.* **3.** dress, clothe, attire, array, apparel.

garish, *adj.* glaring, loud, showy, tawdry, gaudy, flashy, cheap, florid, vulgar, harsh, meretricious, tasteless, trashy, glitzy.
—**Ant.** elegant.

garnish, *v.* **1.** adorn, decorate, ornament, embellish, grace, enhance, beautify, trim, bedeck, bedizen, set off. —*n.* **2.** decoration, ornamentation, ornament, adornment, garniture, garnishment.
—**Ant.** strip.

garrulous, *adj.* talkative, loquacious, prating, prattling, wordy, diffuse, babbling, verbose, prolix.
—**Ant.** taciturn, silent, reticent.
—**Syn. Study.** See TALKATIVE.

gasp, *v.* pant, puff, blow, snort, huff, gulp for air, wheeze.

gather, *v.* **1.** get together, collect, aggregate, assemble, muster, marshal, bring *or* draw together. **2.** learn, infer, understand, deduce, assume, conclude. **3.** accumulate, amass, garner, hoard. **4.** pluck, garner, reap, harvest, glean, cull, crop. **5.** grow, increase, accrete, collect, thicken, condense.
—**Ant.** separate, disperse; decrease.
—**Syn. Study.** GATHER, ASSEMBLE, COLLECT, MUSTER, MARSHAL imply bringing or drawing together. GATHER expresses the general idea usu. with no implication of arrangement: *to gather seashells.* ASSEMBLE is used of persons, objects, or facts brought together in a specific place or for a specific purpose: *to assemble data for a report.* COLLECT implies purposeful accumulation to form an ordered whole: *to collect evidence.* MUSTER, primarily a military term, suggests thoroughness in the process of collection: *to muster all one's resources.* MARSHAL, another chiefly military term, suggests rigorously ordered, purposeful arrangement: *to marshal facts for effective presentation.*

gathering, *n.* assembly, meeting, assemblage, crowd, mob, flock, swarm, multitude, convocation, congregation, company, throng,

horde, host, group, body, association, conclave.

gaudy, *adj.* showy, tawdry, garish, brilliant, loud, flashy, conspicuous, obvious, vulgar, unsubtle, ostentatious, tinselly, trashy, tatty, crude, tasteless, shoddy, honky-tonk, tacky, chintzy, glitzy.
—**Ant.** elegant, refined, subtle.

gaunt, *adj.* thin, emaciated, haggard, lean, spare, skinny, scrawny, bony, skeletal, wasted, starved, cadaverous, pinched, underweight, hollow-cheeked, spindly, lanky, lank, angular, rawboned, meager.
—**Ant.** obese, fat.

gay, *adj.* **1.** joyous, gleeful, jovial, glad, happy, lighthearted, lively, convivial, vivacious, animated, frolicsome, sportive, hilarious, jolly, carefree, debonair, jubilant, high-spirited, bubbly, effervescent, sparkling, in high spirits, joyful, merry, good-humored, expansive, cheerful, sprightly, blithe, airy. **2.** bright, showy, fine, brilliant.
—**Ant.** unhappy, miserable; dull.

general, *adj.* **1.** common, popular, universal, public, widespread, shared, extensive, global, world-wide, inclusive, comprehensive, overall, catholic. **2.** normal, common, usual, prevalent, customary, regular, ordinary, popular, habitual, everyday, familiar, accustomed, run-of-the-mill, nonexclusive, widespread, prevailing. **3.** miscellaneous, unrestricted, mixed, assorted, heterogeneous, diversified, encyclopedic, blanket, sweeping, across-the-board, unspecialized, nonspecific. **4.** vague, lax, indefinite, ill-defined, inexact, imprecise, broad, loose, approximate.
—**Ant.** special, partial; uncommon, unusual, extraordinary; specific; definite, exact, precise.
—**Syn. Study.** GENERAL, COMMON, POPULAR, UNIVERSAL agree in the idea of being nonexclusive and widespread. GENERAL means pertaining to or true of all or most of a particular class or body, irrespective of individuals: *a general belief.* COMMON means shared or experienced frequently or by a majority of group members: *a common problem.* POPULAR means belonging to or favored by the people or the public generally, rather than a particular class: *a popular misconception.* UNIVERSAL means found everywhere with no exception: *a universal need.*

generally, *adv.* usually, commonly, ordinarily, often, in general, normally, typically, on average, as a rule, by and large, mostly, mainly, for the most part, on the whole, roughly, broadly, loosely, largely, in the main, principally.
—**Ant.** rarely.
—**Syn. Study.** See OFTEN.

generosity, *n.* kindness, liberality, lavishness, benevolence, philanthropy, unselfishness, good nature, beneficence, humanity, big-heartedness, largesse, munificence, charity, bounteousness, magnanimity.
—**Ant.** stinginess, niggardliness, parsimony.

generous, *adj.* **1.** charitable, liberal, munificent, bountiful, unselfish, unstinting, openhanded, beneficent. **2.** noble, high-minded, magnanimous; large, big. **3.** ample, plentiful, abundant, flowing, overflowing, copious, lavish, handsome, full.
—**Ant.** stingy, tightfisted, selfish, niggardly; small, parsimonious; scarce, scanty, barren.
—**Syn. Study.** GENEROUS, CHARITABLE, LIBERAL, MUNIFICENT all describe giving or sharing something of value. GENEROUS stresses the warm and sympathetic nature of the

giver: *a retired executive, generous with her time.* CHARITABLE stresses the goodness and kindness of the giver and the indigence or need of the receiver: *a charitable contribution to a nursing home.* LIBERAL emphasizes the large size of the gift and the openhandedness of the giver: *a liberal bequest to the university.* MUNIFICENT refers to a gift or award so strikingly large as to evoke amazement or admiration: *a lifetime income, a truly munificent reward for his loyalty.*

genial, *adj.* **1.** affable, amiable, warm, congenial, good-natured, neighborly, sociable, hospitable, easygoing, convivial, cheerful, sympathetic, cordial, friendly, pleasant, agreeable, kindly, well-disposed, hearty, encouraging. **2.** enlivening, lively, warm, mild, conducive, gentle.
—**Ant.** unsympathetic, unpleasant, discouraging; cool.

genius, *n.* **1.** intelligence, brilliance, ingenuity, wit, brains, judgment, acumen, insight, capacity, ability, talent, gift, aptitude, faculty, bent. **2.** intellect, mastermind, master, virtuoso, maestro, expert, adept, brain, brainiac, Einstein, brain surgeon, rocket scientist, whiz kid, wunderkind, prodigy, walking encyclopedia.
—**Ant.** inability, incapacity.

gentle, *adj.* **1.** soft, bland, peaceful, clement, moderate, pacific, soothing, kind, tender, humane, lenient, merciful, meek, mild, kindly, amiable, submissive, gentle-hearted, kindhearted. **2.** gradual, moderate, temperate, tempered, light, mild. **3.** wellborn, noble, highborn. **4.** honorable, respectable, refined, cultivated, polished, well-bred, polite, elegant, courteous, courtly. **5.** manageable, tractable, tame, docile, trained, peaceable, quiet.
—**Ant.** immoderate, turbulent, unkind, cruel, heartless; sudden, abrupt; unrefined, unpolished, impolite; intractable, wild, noisy.

genuine, *adj.* authentic, real, true, bona fide, verifiable, veritable, legitimate, proper, original, echt, factual, provable, honest-to-God, the real McCoy.
—**Ant.** false, counterfeit.

get, *v.* **1.** obtain, acquire, procure, secure, gain. **2.** earn, win, gain. **3.** learn, understand, fathom, see, perceive, follow, comprehend, appreciate, take in, work out, apprehend, grasp. **4.** capture, seize, arrest, apprehend, pick up, bag, nab, pinch. **5.** prevail on *or* upon, persuade, induce, influence, coax, cajole, wheedle, sway, cause, dispose.
—**Ant.** lose.
—**Syn. Study.** GET, OBTAIN, ACQUIRE, PROCURE, SECURE imply gaining possession of something. GET suggests gaining possession in any manner, either voluntarily or without effort: *to get a copy of a book.* OBTAIN suggests putting forth effort to gain possession of something wanted: *to obtain information.* ACQUIRE often suggests possessing something after a prolonged effort: *to acquire a fortune in the oil business.* PROCURE stresses the use of special means or measures to get something: *to procure a rare etching from an art dealer.* SECURE suggests obtaining something and making possession safe and sure: *to secure benefits for striking workers.*

ghastly, *adj.* **1.** dreadful, horrible, frightful, hideous, grisly, dismal, awful, horrid, gruesome, terrifying, grim, loathsome, ugly, terrible, shocking. **2.** pale, deathly, white, wan, cadaverous, haggard, pallid, drawn, livid, pasty-faced, ashen.

—Ant. lovely, attractive, beautiful; ruddy, robust, healthy.

ghost, *n.* **1.** apparition, phantom, spirit, phantasm, wraith, revenant, shade, spook, specter, supernatural being, illusion, banshee, ghoul, hallucination, vision, haint, poltergeist, doppelganger, zombie. **2.** shadow, hint, suggestion, trace, scintilla, glimmer, soupçon.

giant, *adj.* **1.** oversize, outsize, huge, enormous, great, grand, king-size, gigantic, mammoth, jumbo, colossal, gargantuan, immense, massive, monstrous, monster, vast, Brobdingnagian, Bunyanesque, elephantine, humongous. —*n.* **2.** superhuman, ogre, Cyclops, leviathan, whale, gorilla, King Kong, mammoth, colossus, titan, Atlas, Goliath, amazon, behemoth, monster.

—**Ant.** Lilliputian, tiny.

giddy, *adj.* **1.** lightheaded, light, dizzy, faint, vertiginous, swimming, reeling, spacey, seeing double, groggy, confused. **2.** silly, frivolous, lighthearted, merry, playful, whimsical, pixilated, foolish, goofy, wacky. **3.** emptyheaded, flighty, featherbrained, witless, spacey, scatterbrained, capricious, irresponsible, fickle, volatile, mecurical, reckless, whimsical. **4.** high, tipsy, tiddly, pixilated, intoxicated, inebriated, addled, muddled, befuddled, stupefied.

—**Ant.** sober.

gift, *n.* **1.** donation, present, contribution, offering, boon, alms, favor, handout, honorarium, giveaway, bonus, charity, gratuity, tip, benefaction, grant, largess, subsidy, allowance, endowment, bequest, legacy, dowry, inheritance, bounty. **2.** talent, strength, endowment, power, faculty, ability, capacity, forte, capability, genius, bent, aptitude, flair, knack, facility, power.

gigantic, *adj.* huge, enormous, tremendous, colossal, mammoth, massive, giant, stupendous, towering, staggering, gargantuan, Brobdingnagian, jumbo, super-duper, monstrous, elephantine, immense, prodigious, herculean, titanic, cyclopean, vast, extensive, infinite, humongous.

—**Ant.** small, tiny, infinitesimal, microscopic.

—**Syn. Study.** GIGANTIC, COLOSSAL, MAMMOTH are used of whatever is physically or metaphorically of great magnitude. GIGANTIC refers to the size of a giant, or to anything that is of unusually large size: *a gigantic country.* COLOSSAL refers to the awesome effect and extraordinary size or power of a colossus or of something of similar size, scope, or effect: *a colossal mistake.* MAMMOTH refers to the size of the animal of that name and is used esp. of anything large and heavy: *a mammoth battleship.*

gingerly, *adj.* **1.** cautious, careful, circumspect, mindful, heedful, wary, chary, fastidious, dainty, squeamish, tentative, nervous, canny, timid, shy, prudent, discreet, guarded, politic. —*adv.* **2.** cautiously, carefully, heedfully, warily, charily, delicately, daintily, tentatively.

give, *v.* **1.** deliver, bestow, hand over, offer, vouchsafe, impart, accord, furnish, provide, supply, donate, contribute, afford, spare, accommodate with, confer, grant, cede, relinquish, yield, turn over, assign, present, award. **2.** set forth, issue, show, present, offer. **3.** afford, yield, produce. **4.** issue, put forth, emit, publish, utter, give out (with), pronounce, render, communicate, impart, divulge. **5.** draw back, recede, retire, relax, cede, yield, give over, give away, sink, give up.

—**Ant.** receive.

—**Syn. Study.** GIVE, CONFER, GRANT, PRESENT mean that something concrete or abstract is bestowed on one person by another. GIVE is the general word: *to give someone a book.* CONFER usu. means to give as an honor or as a favor; it implies courteous and gracious giving: *to confer a medal.* GRANT is usu. limited to the idea of acceding to a request or fulfilling an expressed wish; it often involves a formal act or legal procedure: *to grant a prayer; to grant immunity.* PRESENT, a more formal word than GIVE, usu. implies a certain ceremony in the giving: *to present an award.*

glad, *adj.* **1.** delighted, pleased, elated, inspirited, jubilant, triumphant, exhilarated, gratified, contented. **2.** cheerful, joyous, joyful, happy, merry, cheery, animated, lighthearted, blithe, exuberant, on cloud nine, in high spirits.

—**Ant.** miserable, unhappy, sad.

glamour, *n.* allure, allurement, glam, attraction, seductiveness, appeal, charm, charisma, fascination, magnetism, exoticism, star quality, sophistication, urbanity, elegance.

—**Ant.** ordinariness, dowdiness.

glance, *v.* **1.** reflect, glint, shimmer, twinkle, sparkle, flicker, glitter, flash, glimpse, gleam, glisten, scintillate, shine. **2.** glimpse, look, peek, peep, scan. —*n.* **3.** glitter, gleam; glimpse, look, gander.

glare, *n.* **1.** dazzle, flare, glitter, luster, brilliance, sparkle, flash. **2.** showiness, ostentation, garishness, gaudiness, flashiness. **3.** frown, stare, dirty look, black look, scowl, glower. —*v.* **4.** shine, dazzle, gleam. **5.** glower, scowl, look daggers at, frown.

gleam, *n.* **1.** ray, flash, beam, glimmer, glimmering. —*v.* **2.** shine, glimmer, flash, glitter, sparkle, beam.

glee, *n.* joy, exultation, delight, exuberance, cheer, exhilaration, elation, joy, rapture, enjoyment, high spirits, jubilation, merriment, jollity, hilarity, mirth, joviality, gaiety, liveliness, verve, life.

—**Ant.** misery, sadness, melancholy.

glib, *adj.* **1.** fluent, voluble, talkative, garrulous, ready. **2.** slippery, smooth, facile, artful, slick, unctuous, fast-talking, superficial.

—**Ant.** taciturn, silent, quiet; artless, guileless.

—**Syn. Study.** See FLUENT.

glide, *v.* slide, slip, flow, coast, skate, sail, stream, float, soar.

—**Ant.** stick.

glisten, *v.* reflect, glint, twinkle, wink, blink, glow, glimmer, shimmer, sparkle, shine, gleam, glitter.

gloom, *n.* **1.** darkness, dimness, shadow, shade, obscurity, gloominess, murkiness, dusk, cloudiness, blackness, dullness. **2.** melancholy, sadness, depression, dejection, despondency, doldrums, moroseness, woe, desolation, blues.

—**Ant.** brightness, effulgence; joy, glee, happiness.

gloomy, *adj.* **1.** dark, shaded, obscure, shadowy, dim, dusky; dismal, lowering. **2.** depressed, dejected, sad, melancholy, despondent, downcast, crestfallen, downhearted, glum, dispirited, disheartened, morose, lugubrious, dismal, moody, doleful, forlorn, sullen, dreary, blue, saturnine, in the dumps.

—**Ant.** bright, effulgent, dazzling; happy, delighted, gleeful.

glorious, *adj.* **1.** admirable, delightful, superb, splendid, brilliant, superior, excellent. **2.** famous, renowned, noted, celebrated, famed, eminent, distinguished, illustrious.

—**Ant.** horrible; unknown; notorious.

glory, *n.* **1.** praise, honor, distinction, renown, fame, prestige, repute, eminence, celebrity. **2.** resplendence, splendor, magnificence, grandeur, pomp, brilliance, effulgence. —*v.* **3.** revel, relish, delight, pride oneself, crow, gloat, exult, rejoice, triumph.

—**Ant.** infamy, dishonor; gloom.

gloss, *n.* **1.** luster, sheen, polish, glaze, shine. **2.** show, mask, front, mien, appearance, pretext, facade, surface, veneer, disguise, camouflage, pretense. **3.** explanation, exegesis, critique, comment, note, interpretation, analysis, annotation, commentary. —*v.* **4.** polish, shine, glaze, varnish. **5.** annotate, explain, interpret, analyze.

—**Syn. Study.** See POLISH.

glossy, *adj.* **1.** lustrous, shiny, shining, glazed, smooth, sleek. **2.** slick, artificial, simulated, feigned, pseudo, false, unreal, imitation, fraudulent, counterfeit, specious, plausible.

gluttonous, *adj.* greedy, devouring, voracious, ravenous, grasping, insatiable, ravening, hoggish, piggish, piggy, avid, rapacious.

—**Ant.** abstinent, abstemious, restrained.

godly, *adj.* God-fearing, moral, pure, reverent, pietistic, blessed, pious, saintly, devout, religious, holy, righteous, good.

—**Ant.** sinful, heathen, atheistic.

good, *adj.* **1.** moral, righteous, religious, pious, pure, virtuous, conscientious, meritorious, worthy, exemplary, upright, upstanding, right-thinking, principled, ethical, godly, law-abiding. **2.** commendable, adroit, efficient, proficient, able, skillful, expert, ready, dexterous, clever, capable, qualified, fit, suited, suitable, convenient. **3.** satisfactory, excellent, exceptional, valuable, precious, capital, admirable, commendable. **4.** well-behaved, dutiful, respectful, submissive, acquiescent, tractable, obedient, heedful. **5.** kind, beneficent, friendly, kindly, benevolent, humane, favorable, well-disposed, gracious, obliging. **6.** honorable, worthy, deserving, fair, unsullied, immaculate, unblemished, innocent, unimpeached. **7.** reliable, safe, trustworthy, honest, competent. **8.** genuine, sound, valid. **9.** agreeable, pleasant, genial, cheering. **10.** satisfactory, advantageous, favorable, auspicious, propitious, fortunate, profitable, useful, serviceable, beneficial. —*n.* **11.** profit, worth, advantage, benefit, usefulness, utility, gain. **12.** excellence, merit, righteousness, kindness, virtue. **13.** (*plural*) property, belongings, effects, chattel, furniture. **14.** (*plural*) wares, merchandise, stock, commodities.

—**Ant.** bad.

—**Syn. Study.** See PROPERTY.

goodness, *n.* **1.** virtue, morality, integrity, honesty, uprightness, godliness, honor, rectitude, decency, nobility, ethicality, highmindedness, piety, purity, innocence, character, respectability, trustworthiness, probity, righteousness, good. **2.** kindness, benevolence, charity, unselfishness, graciousness, goodwill, compassion, beneficence, warmth, tolerance, patience, mercy, justice, generosity, kindliness, benignity, humanity. **3.** excellence, worth, value, quality, merit, superiority, distinction.

—**Ant.** evil.

—**Syn. Study.** GOODNESS, VIRTUE, MORALITY refer to qualities of character or conduct that entitle the possessor to approval and esteem. GOODNESS is the simple word for a general quality recognized as an inherent part of one's character: *Many could tell of her goodness and honesty.* VIRTUE is a rather formal word, and usually suggests GOODNESS that is consciously or steadily maintained, often in spite of temptations or evil influences: *a man of unassailable virtue.* MORALITY implies conformity to the recognized standards of right conduct: *a citizen of the highest morality.*

gorgeous, *adj.* sumptuous, magnificent, splendid, rich, grand, glorious, exquisite, beautiful, breathtaking, to die for, radiant, showy, colorful, marvelous, regal, elegant, lustrous, resplendent, brilliant, glittering, dazzling, superb, bodacious.

—**Ant.** poor; ugly.

gossip, *n.* **1.** scandal, small talk, hearsay, palaver, idle talk, tittle-tattle, rumor, information, word, chitchat, grapevine, inside dope, scuttlebutt, dish, newsmongering. **2.** chatterer, babbler, gabber, Nosy Parker, scandalmonger, busybody, tattletale, telltale, yenta, quidnunc, bigmouth, chatterbox, blabbermouth. —*v.* **3.** bruit, chatter, prattle, prate, palaver, tattle, whisper behind someone's back, spread rumors, blab.

govern, *v.* **1.** rule, reign, hold sway, control, command, sway, influence, have control, lead, sit on the throne, wield the scepter, run the show, be in power, exercise *or* wield power, be in the driver's seat. **2.** direct, guide, restrain, check, conduct, manage, supervise, superintend, oversee, command, look after.

—**Ant.** obey; follow.

grace, *n.* **1.** attractiveness, charm, gracefulness, comeliness, ease, elegance, symmetry, beauty; polish, refinement. **2.** favor, kindness, kindliness, love, goodwill, benignity, benevolence, friendliness. **3.** mercy, clemency, pardon, leniency, forgiveness. **4.** sanctity, holiness, devoutness, devotion, piety, piousness, blessedness. —*v.* **5.** adorn, embellish, beautify, enhance, deck, decorate, ornament; honor, dignify.

—**Ant.** ugliness; disfavor; condemnation; hate, abhorrence; dishonor, disgrace.

graceful, *adj.* **1.** flowing, fluid, facile, smooth, willowy, supple, limber, lithe, lissome, nimble, athletic, pliant, agile, sprightly, airy, dextrous, deft, light, spry; adroit, skillful, adept, artful, accomplished, gifted, proficient, talented. **2.** elegant, refined, tasteful, artistic, exquisite, urbane, debonair, soigné, dapper, polished, suave, savvy, well-mannered, polite, courteous, mannerly, tactful, diplomatic.

—**Ant.** clumsy, maladroit; oafish, loutish, boorish, tasteless.

gracious, *adj.* **1.** kind, kindly, benevolent, benign, courteous, chivalrous, well-mannered, mannerly, polite, courtly, friendly, well-disposed, favorable. **2.** compassionate, tender, merciful, lenient, clement, mild, gentle. **3.** indulgent, beneficent, accommodating, considerate, thoughtful, forbearing, welcoming, affable, sociable, amiable, agreeable, cordial, tolerant, accepting, patient, lenient, understanding, obliging.

—**Ant.** ungracious, unkind, impolite; cool, cruel.

gradual, *adj.* slow, by degrees, little by little, step by step, moderate, gentle, easy, even, regular, steady, piecemeal.

—**Ant.** sudden, precipitous, abrupt, immoderate.

—**Syn. Study.** See SLOW.

grand, *adj.* **1.** imposing, stately, august, majestic, dignified, exalted, elevated, eminent, princely, regal, kingly, royal, great, illustrious. **2.** lofty, magnificent, great, large, palatial, splendid, brilliant, superb, glorious, sublime, noble, fine. **3.** main, principal, chief, head, leading, foremost, highest. **4.** complete, comprehensive, inclusive, all-inclusive, total, sum.

—**Ant.** base, undignified; ignoble; secondary; incomplete.

grandeur, *n.* magnificence, splendor, grandness, resplendence, magnitude, sweep, amplitude, scope, loftiness, nobility, stateliness, majesty, sublimity, luxuriousness, pomp.

—**Ant.** insignificance, nullity.

grant, *v.* **1.** bestow, confer, award, bequeath, give. **2.** agree *or* accede to, admit, allow, concede, accept, cede, yield. —*n.* **3.** gift, present, endowment, bequest, subsidy, award, donation, contribution, allowance, aid.

—**Ant.** receive.

—**Syn. Study.** See GIVE.

graphic, *adj.* **1.** distinct, well-defined, detailed, explicit, clear, lucid, plain, unmistakable, precise, photographic, descriptive, realistic, true-to-life, lifelike, vivid, picturesque, striking, telling. **2.** diagrammatic, well-delineated, detailed.

grasp, *v.* **1.** seize, hold, clasp, grip, clutch, grab, catch. **2.** lay hold of, seize upon, fasten on; concentrate on, comprehend, understand. —*n.* **3.** grip, hold, clutches. **4.** hold, possession, mastery. **5.** reach, comprehension, compass, scope.

—**Ant.** loose, loosen; misunderstand.

grateful, *adj.* **1.** appreciative, thankful, obliged, indebted. **2.** pleasing, agreeable, welcome, refreshing, pleasant, gratifying, satisfying, satisfactory.

—**Ant.** ungrateful; unpleasant, disagreeable, unsatisfactory.

gratify, *v.* please, indulge, humor, satisfy, refresh, fulfill, delight, reward, cheer, gladden, sate, satiate.

—**Ant.** displease, dissatisfy.

grave, *n.* **1.** crypt, vault, mausoleum, burial ground, cemetery plot, final resting place, eternal rest, place of interment, tomb, sepulcher, pit, excavation. —*adj.* **2.** sober, solemn, serious, dignified, sedate, earnest, staid, thoughtful, unsmiling, somber, dour, gloomy, grim. **3.** weighty, momentous, important, serious, consequential, critical, vital, urgent, pressing, pivotal, perilous.

—**Ant.** undignified, thoughtless; unimportant, trivial, trifling.

—**Syn. Study.** GRAVE, SOBER, SOLEMN refer to the condition of being serious in demeanor or appearance. GRAVE indicates a dignified seriousness due to heavy responsibilities or cares: *The jury looked grave while pondering the evidence.* SOBER implies a determined but sedate and restrained manner: *a wise and sober judge.* SOLEMN suggests an impressive and earnest seriousness marked by the absence of gaiety or mirth: *The minister's voice was solemn as he announced the text.*

great, *adj.* **1.** immense, enormous, huge, gigantic, vast, ample, grand, large, big. **2.** numerous, countless. **3.** considerable, important, momentous, serious, weighty. **4.** notable, remarkable, noteworthy. **5.** distinguished, famous, famed, eminent,

noted, prominent, celebrated, illustrious, grand, renowned. **6.** consequential, important, vital, critical. **7.** chief, principal, main, grand, leading. **8.** noble, lofty, grand, exalted, elevated, dignified, majestic, august.

—**Ant.** small; insignificant; paltry; infamous, notorious; trivial; secondary.

greed, *n.* desire, avidity, avarice, cupidity, covetousness, greediness, voracity, ravenousness, rapacity, selfishness, gluttony, insatiability.

—**Ant.** generosity.

greedy, *adj.* **1.** grasping, rapacious, selfish, avaricious, acquisitive, materialistic, money-hungry. **2.** gluttonous, voracious, ravenous, starved, insatiable, piggish, hoggish. **3.** desirous, covetous, eager, anxious.

—**Ant.** generous, unselfish.

greet, *v.* address, welcome, receive, usher in, meet; hail, accost, salute, address.

grief, *n.* suffering, distress, sorrow, regret, anguish, heartache, agony, torment, desolation, heartbreak, remorse, tribulation, ordeal, bitterness, curse, dejection, trauma, affliction, wretchedness, woe, misery, sadness, melancholy, moroseness.

—**Ant.** joy, happiness, glee, delight.

grieve, *v.* **1.** lament, weep, mourn, sorrow, suffer, bewail, regret, rue, deplore, mope, eat one's heart out, bemoan. **2.** distress, sadden, depress, agonize, break one's heart, pain.

—**Ant.** delight in.

grievous, *adj.* **1.** distressing, sad, sorrowful, painful, lamentable, regrettable. **2.** deplorable, lamentable, calamitous, heinous, egregious, awful, monstrous, appalling, shocking, intolerable, unbearable, outrageous, flagrant, atrocious, flagitious, dreadful, gross, shameful, iniquitous. **3.** severe, heavy, painful, grave, serious, acute, distressing, damaging, hurtful, wounding.

—**Ant.** delighted, happy, joyful; delightful, pleasant, favorable.

grim, *adj.* **1.** stern, unrelenting, merciless, uncompromising, harsh, unyielding. **2.** sinister, ghastly, repellent, frightful, horrible, dire, appalling, horrid, grisly, gruesome, hideous, dreadful. **3.** severe, hard, fierce, forbidding, ferocious, cruel, savage, ruthless.

—**Ant.** merciful, lenient, sympathetic; wonderful, delightful, pleasant; amenable, genial, congenial, amiable.

grit, *n.* spirit, pluck, fortitude, courage, valor, bravery, resolve, toughness, mettle, nerve, backbone, gameness, dauntlessness, tenacity, determination, hardihood, staunchness, stalwartness, doughtiness, guts, gutsiness, spunk, chutzpah, moxie, stick-to-itiveness, resolution.

groggy, *adj.* confused, muddled, dazed, addled, befuddled, stupefied, stunned, reeling, in a stupor, unsteady, shaky, wobbly, weak-kneed, numb, faint, punch-drunk, spacey, foggy, befogged, muzzy, dopey, woozy, punchy, slap-happy.

—**Ant.** clear-headed, alert.

gross, *adj.* **1.** whole, entire, total, overall, aggregate. **2.** glaring, flagrant, outrageous, shameful, heinous, grievous. **3.** coarse, indelicate, indecent, low, animal, sensual, vulgar, broad, lewd. **4.** fat, obese, corpulent, overweight, heavy, ponderous, large, big, bulky, massive, great. **5.** disgusting, repulsive, repellent, revolting, nauseating, sickening, gruesome, lurid.

—**Ant.** partial, incomplete; delicate, decent; small, dainty, slim.

grouchy, *adj.* cantankerous, irritable, irascible, fractious, cross, crabby, crotchety, choleric, foul-tempered,

mean-tempered, grumpy, ornery, curmudgeonly, splenetic, bilious, tetchy, testy, touchy, peevish, surly, vinegary.

—**Ant.** even-tempered, gracious.

ground, *n.* **1.** land, earth, soil, mold, turf, sod, terra firma, loam, dirt. **2.** (*often plural*) foundation, basis, base, premise, motive, reason, cause, consideration, factor, account. —*v.* **3.** found, fix, settle, establish, base, set. **4.** instruct, prepare, train, teach, coach, tutor, inform, initiate.

grow, *v.* **1.** increase, swell, enlarge, dilate, greaten, expand, extend, flourish, develop, thicken, spread, thrive, prosper. **2.** sprout, germinate; arise, issue, stem, spring up, originate. **3.** swell, wax, extend, mature, ripen, advance, improve. **4.** raise, cultivate, produce, propagate, plant, sow, breed.

—**Ant.** decrease, shrink; wane, deteriorate.

growth, *n.* **1.** development, evolution, cultivation, nurturing, extension, proliferation, flowering, advance, success, progress, increase, augmentation, expansion. **2.** product, outgrowth, result; produce.

—**Ant.** failure, stagnation.

grudge, *n.* **1.** malice, ill will, spite, resentment, bitterness, rancor, hard feelings, grievance, pique, aversion, venom, vendetta, vengefulness, animosity, animus, odium, vindictiveness, malevolence, enmity, hatred. —*v.* **2.** begrudge, envy, resent, mind, covet.

—**Ant.** good will, amiability.

grudging, *adj.* reluctant, unenthusiastic, unwilling, begrudging; apathetic, indifferent, perfunctory, lukewarm, tepid; ungenerous, mean-spirited, resentful, bitter, rancorous.

—**Ant.** enthusiastic, generous.

guarantee, *n.* **1.** guaranty, warrant, pledge, assurance, promise, surety, security, bond, obligation, word of honor. —*v.* **2.** guaranty, secure, ensure, insure, warrant, promise.

guard, *v.* **1.** protect, keep safe, preserve, save, watch over, shield, defend, shelter. **2.** hold, check, watch, be careful. —*n.* **3.** protector, guardian, sentry, watchman, defender, sentinel. **4.** defense, protection, shield, bulwark, security, aegis, safety.

—**Ant.** attack, assault; ignore; danger.

guardian, *n.* **1.** guard, protector, defender, champion, paladin. **2.** trustee, warden, keeper, custodian.

—**Ant.** assailant.

guess, *v.* **1.** conjecture, surmise, hazard, suppose, fancy, believe, imagine, think. **2.** estimate, solve, answer, penetrate. —*n.* **3.** notion, judgment, conclusion, conjecture, surmise, supposition, estimate, hypothesis, speculation, assumption, feeling, suspicion, postulate, theory, shot in the dark.

—**Ant.** know.

—**Syn. Study.** GUESS, CONJECTURE, SURMISE imply attempting to form an opinion as to the probable. To GUESS is to risk an opinion regarding something one does not know about, or, wholly or partly by chance, to arrive at the correct answer to a question: *to guess the outcome of a game.* TO CONJECTURE is to make inferences in the absence of sufficient evidence to establish certainty: *to conjecture the circumstances of the crime.* SURMISE implies making an intuitive conjecture that may or may not be correct: *to surmise the motives that led to the crime.*

guide, *v.* **1.** lead, pilot, steer, conduct, direct, show *or* point the way, escort, instruct, induce, influence,

regulate, manage, govern, rule. —*n.* **2.** leader, counselor, adviser, guru, mentor, teacher, master, director, conductor. **3.** model, criterion, exemplar, standard, ideal, example, illustration. **4.** beacon, light, landmark, lodestar; mark, sign, signal, indication, key, clue.

—**Ant.** follow.

guile, *n.* cunning, treachery, deceit, artifice, duplicity, deception, trickery, fraud, craft, artfulness, chicanery, shrewdness.

—**Ant.** ingenuousness, honesty.

—**Syn. Study.** See DECEIT.

guileless, *adj.* artless, honest, sincere, open, candid, frank, truthful, ingenuous, naive, unsophisticated, simpleminded.

—**Ant.** cunning, sly, deceitful, artful, treacherous.

guilt, *n.* guiltiness, culpability, criminality, blame, responsibility, crime, sinfulness, misconduct, wrongdoing, reproach, shamefulness, condemnation.

—**Ant.** exoneration, innocence.

guiltless, *adj.* innocent, spotless, blameless, immaculate, pure, unsullied, unpolluted, untarnished, sinless.

—**Ant.** culpable, guilty.

guilty, *adj.* **1.** wrong, culpable, responsible, at fault, blameworthy, sinful, answerable, criminal, malfeasant, delinquent, offending, reprehensible. **2.** sorry, regretful, remorseful, contrite, apologetic, repentant, rueful, penitent, conscience-stricken; ashamed, embarrassed, sheepish, mortified, red-faced.

—**Ant.** innocent, blameless; unrepentant; proud.

guise, *n.* appearance, aspect, semblance, look, image, likeness, mien, air, disguise, front, facade, pretense; behavior, bearing, demeanor; form, shape, fashion, mode, manner.

—**Syn. Study.** See APPEARANCE.

guru, *n.* teacher, guide, instructor, tutor, coach, trainer, handler, preceptor, master, docent, expert, mentor, Svengali.

—**Ant.** student, acolyte, follower.

gush, *v.* **1.** pour, stream, spurt, flow, spout, flood, cascade, rush, jet, burst, run. **2.** bubble over, overflow, effervesce, be effusive, prate, babble, jabber, blather, chatter, make a fuss, run off at the mouth, run one's mouth.

H

habit, *n.* **1.** disposition, tendency, bent, wont, inclination, predisposition, second nature, attitude, penchant, proclivity, frame of mind. **2.** custom, practice, routine, convention, policy, pattern, mode, rule, way, usage, wont, manner.

—**Syn. Study.** See CUSTOM.

habitat, *n.* home, locality, haunt, environment, turf, locale, site, domain, bailiwick, realm, terrain, element, sphere of activity, neighborhood, precincts, range, territory, surroundings, environs, vicinity, stamping ground, home ground, milieu.

habitual, *adj.* confirmed, inveterate, accustomed, customary, established, chronic, hardened, ingrained, persistent, constant; usual, common, regular, familiar, ordinary, set, standard, routine, normal, natural, traditional, fixed, settled, ritual.

—**Ant.** rare, unaccustomed, unusual, uncommon, irregular.

—**Syn. Study.** See USUAL.

habituate, *v.* accustom, familiarize,

acclimate, acclimatize, train, inure, harden, make used (to).

hack, *v.* **1.** cut, notch, chop, hew, mangle, lacerate, gash, slash, butcher, mutilate, damage. *—n.* **2.** cut, notch, gash. *—adj.* **3.** hackneyed, trite, clichéd, overdone, old, banal, used, worn-out, commonplace, stale, stereotyped; old-hat.
—Ant. novel, new.

hackneyed, *adj.* trite, clichéd, stale, timeworn, overused, tired, routine, stereotyped, tedious, mediocre, humdrum, moldy, run-of-the-mill, well-worn, unoriginal, bromidic, platitudinous, commonplace, pedestrian, worn-out, banal, cornball, bathetic, stock, set, old-hat, warmed-over, motheaten, threadbare, corny.
—Ant. original, inventive.

haggard, *adj.* careworn, gaunt, emaciated, drawn, anemic, weak, feeble, spent, exhausted, ghastly, cadaverous, run-down, weary, withered, hollow-cheeked, hollow-eyed, meager, spare, worn, wasted.
—Ant. hale, hearty, robust.

haggle, *v.* bargain, negotiate, bicker, deal, squabble, dicker, disagree, wrangle, dispute, cavil, argue.

hale, *adj.* robust, healthy, vigorous, sound, strong, hearty, fit as a fiddle, able-bodied, hardy, wholesome, flourishing, in fine fettle, in the pink.
—Ant. haggard, weak, feeble.

halfhearted, *adj.* unenthusiastic, indifferent, uninterested, cold, cool, lukewarm, nonchalant, phlegmatic, lackadaisical, insouciant, uncaring, perfunctory, curt, abrupt, discouraging.
—Ant. enthusiastic, eager, encouraging.

hallowed, *adj.* sacred, consecrated, holy, blessed, sacrosanct, inviolable; honored, revered.
—Ant. profane; despised.
—Syn. Study. See HOLY.

hallucination, *n.* illusion, delusion, aberration, phantasm, vision, fantasy, mirage, daydream, dream, chimera, phantom, figment of the imagination, apparition, specter, ghost, doppelganger, wraith, haint.
—Ant. reality.

halt, *v.* hold, stop, cease, desist, quit, end, terminate, check, curb, stem, discontinue, conclude, shut down, come to a standstill.
—Ant. continue, persist.
—Syn. Study. See STOP.

hamper, *v.* impede, hinder, hold back, encumber, prevent, obstruct, restrain, clog, slow, balk, delay, retard, inhibit, block, interfere with, frustrate, restrict, curb, limit, handicap, trammel, bar, curtail, lessen, diminish, reduce.
—Ant. promote, further, encourage, speed.
—Syn. Study. See PREVENT.

handsome, *adj.* **1.** comely, fine, admirable, good-looking, hunky, dishy, attractive, well-made. **2.** liberal, considerable, ample, large, generous, magnanimous, sizable, substantial.
—Ant. ugly, unattractive.
—Syn. Study. See BEAUTIFUL.

handy, *adj.* **1.** convenient, useful, practical, functional, serviceable. **2.** near, nearby, at hand, close, adjacent, convenient, close by, near at hand, close at hand. **3.** adept, dexterous, skilled, skillful, artful, adroit, deft, clever, proficient.

hang, *v.* **1.** suspend, dangle, hover, swing. **2.** execute, lynch, string up, kill, garrote. **3.** drape, decorate, adorn, furnish. **4.** depend, rely, rest; hold fast, cling, adhere. **5.** be doubtful *or* undecided, waver, hesitate, demur, halt. **6.** loiter, linger, hover, float. **7.** impend, be imminent.

happen, *v.* come to pass, take place, occur, develop, materialize, transpire, prove, chance; befall, betide.

happiness, *n.* good fortune, pleasure, contentment, gladness, bliss, content, contentedness, beatitude, blessedness, delight, joy, enjoyment, gratification, satisfaction, felicity, jubilation, cheerfulness, cheeriness, elation, exuberance, exhilaration, high spirits, ecstasy, rapture.
—Ant. misery, dissatisfaction.

happy, *adj.* **1.** joyous, joyful, glad, blithe, merry, cheerful, contented, gay, blissful, delighted, satisfied, pleased, gladdened, elated, ecstatic, euphoric, exultant, overjoyed, jubilant. **2.** favored, lucky, fortunate, propitious, advantageous, successful, prosperous. **3.** appropriate, fitting, apt, felicitous, opportune, befitting, pertinent.
—Ant. unhappy, sad, cheerless, melancholy; unlucky, luckless, unfortunate; inappropriate, inapt.

harangue, *n.* **1.** diatribe, tirade, oration, declamation, philippic, screed, exhortation, vituperation, rodomontade, address, speech, bombast. *—v.* **2.** preach, lecture, sermonize, pontificate, vituperate, rant and rave, rant, declaim, address.
—Syn. Study. See SPEECH.

harass, *v.* trouble, harry, raid, molest, disturb, distress; plague, vex, worry, badger, pester, annoy, torment, torture.

harbor, *n.* **1.** port, haven. **2.** shelter, refuge, asylum, protection, cover, sanctuary, retreat. *—v.* **3.** shelter, protect, lodge. **4.** conceal, hide, secrete. **5.** entertain, indulge, foster, cherish.
—Syn. Study. HARBOR, PORT, HAVEN refer to a shelter for ships. A HARBOR is a natural or an artificially constructed shelter and anchorage for ships: *a fine harbor on the eastern coast.* A PORT is a harbor viewed esp. with reference to its commercial activities and facilities: *a thriving port.* HAVEN is a literary word meaning refuge, although occasionally referring to a natural harbor that can be utilized by ships as a place of safety: *to seek a haven in a storm.* See also CHERISH.

hard, *adj.* **1.** solid, firm, inflexible, rigid, unyielding, resistant, resisting, adamantine, flinty, impenetrable, compact. **2.** difficult, toilsome, burdensome, wearisome, exhausting, laborious, arduous, onerous, fatiguing, wearying. **3.** difficult, complex, intricate, complicated, perplexing, tough, puzzling. **4.** vigorous, severe, violent, stormy, tempestuous, inclement. **5.** oppressive, harsh, rough, cruel, severe, unmerciful, grinding, unsparing, unrelenting. **6.** severe, harsh, stern, austere, strict, exacting, callous, unfeeling, unsympathetic, impassionate, insensible, unimpressible, insensitive, indifferent, unpitying, inflexible, relentless, unyielding, cruel, obdurate, adamant, hardhearted. **7.** unfriendly, unkind; harsh, unpleasant. **8.** unsympathetic, unsentimental, shrewd, hardheaded, callous. *—adv.* **9.** energetically, vigorously, violently. **10.** earnestly, intently, incessantly. **11.** harshly, severely, gallingly, with difficulty.
—Ant. soft; easy; fair; merciful; sympathetic; kind.

harden, *v.* **1.** solidify, indurate, ossify, petrify. **2.** strengthen, confirm, fortify, steel, brace, nerve, toughen, inure; habituate, accustom, season, train, discipline.

hardship, *n.* want, deprivation, misery, distress, adversity, unhappiness, bad luck, difficulty, trial, oppression, privation, need, austerity, trouble, affliction, burden, suffering, misfortune, grievance.

hardy, *adj.* **1.** vigorous, hearty, sturdy, hale, robust, stout, strong, sound, healthy, rugged, tough, durable, stalwart, red-blooded. **2.** bold, daring, courageous, brave, intrepid.
—Ant. weak, feeble, unsound, unhealthy; cowardly, pusillanimous.

harm, *n.* **1.** injury, damage, hurt, abuse, misfortune, wound, molestation, ill-treatment, mischief, detriment. **2.** wrong, evil, wickedness, wrongdoing, iniquity. *—n.* **3.** injure, hurt, damage; maltreat, molest, abuse, wound.
—Ant. good.

harmful, *adj.* injurious, detrimental, hurtful, deleterious, pernicious, mischievous, destructive, damaging, dangerous; unhealthy, noisome, noxious, toxic, poisonous, venomous.
—Ant. beneficial.

harmonious, *adj.* **1.** amicable, congenial, sympathetic, agreeable, compatible, in accord, simpatico. **2.** consonant, congruous, concordant, consistent, correspondent, symmetrical. **3.** melodious, tuneful, agreeable, concordant, sweet-sounding.
—Ant. unsympathetic; discordant, incongruous, asymmetrical; cacophonous, noisy.

harmony, *n.* **1.** agreement, concord, unity, unanimity, rapport, peace, amity, friendship, accord, unison. **2.** balance, orderliness, closeness, togetherness, parallelism, congruity, consonance, conformity, correspondence, consistency, congruence, fitness, suitability. **3.** melody, melodiousness, concord, euphony, tunefulness.
—Ant. discord, disagreement; nonconformity, unfitness; cacophony, noise.
—Syn. Study. See SYMMETRY.

harrowing, *adj.* trying, stressful, distressing, painful, agonizing, vexing, alarming, unnerving, heart-rending, traumatic, nerve-wracking, disquieting, dismaying, horrible, torturous, frightening, excruciating, harsh, hairy.
—Ant. pleasant, relaxing.

harry, *v.* **1.** harass, torment, worry, molest, plague, trouble, vex, hector, gall, fret, disturb, harrow, chafe, annoy, pester. **2.** ravage, devastate, plunder, strip, rob, pillage.
—Ant. help, support, succor.

harsh, *adj.* **1.** unpleasant, severe, austere, bleak, dour, spartan; stringent, Draconian, tyrannical, abusive, punishing, punitive, inhuman, merciless, ruthless, pitiless; disagreeable, impolite, discourteous, uncivil, rude, nasty, curt, abrupt, bluff, gruff, curmudgeonly, brusque, rough, hard, unfeeling, unkind, brutal, cruel, stern, acrimonious, bad-tempered, ill-natured, crabbed, choleric, splenetic, surly, sullen, irascible, churlish, peevish, grouchy, bilious, cross, sarcastic, acerbic. **2.** jarring, unaesthetic, inartistic, discordant, dissonant, unharmonious.
—Ant. gentle, pleasant, kind, good-natured; aesthetic, harmonious.
—Syn. Study. See STERN.

haste, *n.* **1.** swiftness, quickness, urgency, briskness, celerity, alacrity, quickness, rapidity, dispatch, speed, expedition, promptitude. **2.** need, hurry, flurry, hustle, bustle, ado, precipitancy, precipitation, rush, rashness, recklessness.
—Ant. sloth.

hasten, *v.* hurry, accelerate, urge, press, expedite, quicken, speed, precipitate, dispatch; rush, fly, sprint, race, bolt, dash, scurry, scamper.

hasty, *adj.* **1.** speedy, quick, hurried, swift, rapid, fast, fleet, brisk, prompt, immediate, instantaneous. **2.** precipitate, rash, foolhardy, reckless, indiscreet, thoughtless, impetuous, careless, headlong, unthinking.
—Ant. slow, deliberate; discreet, thoughtful.

hatch, *v.* **1.** incubate, breed, brood. **2.** contrive, devise, plan, plot, formulate, originate, invent, dream up, cook up, fabricate, produce, concoct, design, scheme, project.

hate, *v.* **1.** abhor, detest, loathe, despise, scorn, recoil from, execrate, abominate, dislike intensely. *—n.* **2.** hatred, abhorrence, loathing, odium, animosity, antipathy, animus, aversion, hostility, antagonism, malice, detestation, enmity, malevolence, spite, scorn, vindictiveness, contempt.
—Ant. like, love.
—Syn. Study. HATE, ABHOR, DETEST imply feeling intense dislike or aversion toward something. HATE, the simple and general word, suggests passionate dislike and a feeling of enmity: *to hate autocracy.* ABHOR expresses a deep-rooted horror and a sense of repugnance or complete rejection: *to abhor cruelty.* DETEST implies intense, even vehement, dislike and antipathy, besides a sense of disdain: *to detest a combination of ignorance and arrogance.*

hateful, *adj.* detestable, odious, abominable, execrable, loathsome, abhorrent, repugnant, invidious, obnoxious, offensive, disgusting, nauseating, revolting, vile, repulsive, horrid, horrible, despicable, scurvy, heinous, foul, contemptible; malignant, malevolent, malicious, evil, spiteful, contemptuous, mean, nasty, ugly.
—Ant. lovable, appealing, attractive, likable.
—Syn. Study. HATEFUL, ODIOUS, OFFENSIVE, OBNOXIOUS refer to something that provokes strong dislike or aversion. HATEFUL implies causing dislike along with hostility and ill will: *a hateful task.* ODIOUS emphasizes a disgusting or repugnant quality: *odious crimes.* OFFENSIVE is a general term that stresses the resentment or displeasure aroused by something that is insulting or unpleasant: *an offensive remark; an offensive odor.* OBNOXIOUS implies causing annoyance or discomfort by objectionable qualities: *His constant bragging is obnoxious.*

hatred, *n.* aversion, animosity, hate, detestation, loathing, abomination, odium, horror, repugnance, revulsion.
—Ant. attraction, love, favor.

haughty, *adj.* disdainful, proud, arrogant, supercilious, snobbish, lordly, contemptuous, superior, self-important, smug, self-satisfied, complacent, pretentious, conceited, egotistical, overbearing, overweening, patronizing, vain, condescending, disdainful, scornful, highfalutin, hoity-toity, stuck-up, swell-headed, high and mighty, on one's high horse, la-di-da, snooty, uppity.
—Ant. humble, shy, self-effacing.

have, *v.* **1.** hold, occupy, possess, own, keep, contain. **2.** get, receive, take, obtain, acquire, gain, secure, procure. **3.** experience, enjoy, suffer, undergo. **4.** permit, allow.

havoc, *n.* devastation, ruin, destruction, desolation, waste, damage.

hazard, *n.* **1.** danger, peril, jeopardy, risk. **2.** chance, accident, luck, fortuity, fortuitousness, uncertainty. *—v.* **3.** venture, dare, gamble, stake, risk, jeopardize, endanger, imperil, threaten.
—Ant. safety, security; certainty,

surety.
—Syn. Study. See DANGER.

haze, *n.* **1.** vapor, dust, mist, cloud, fog, smog. **2.** obscurity, dimness, cloud, vagueness, blur, nebulousness, fuzziness, muddle.
—Ant. clearness, clarity.

head, *n.* **1.** command, authority. **2.** commander, director, chief, chieftain, leader, principal, commander in chief, master. **3.** top, summit, acme. **4.** culmination, crisis, conclusion. **5.** source, origin, rise, fountainhead, wellspring, font, beginning, headwaters. —*adj.* **6.** front, leading, topmost, chief, principal, main, cardinal, foremost, first. —*v.* **7.** lead, direct, supervise, oversee, control, guide, manage, administer, command, rule, govern.

headlong, *adj.* rushed, precipitate, precipitous, hasty, abrupt, hurried, impetuous, sudden, impulsive, reckless.

headstrong, *adj.* willful, stubborn, obstinate, intractable, self-willed, dogged, pigheaded, tenacious, contrary, mulish.
—Ant. amenable, tractable, genial, agreeable.
—Syn. Study. See WILLFUL.

heal, *v.* **1.** cure, remedy, restore, repair, renew, revitalize, rejuvenate; mend, recover, recuperate, improve. **2.** amend, settle, harmonize, compose, soothe, reconcile, patch up, put right, set straight.
—Ant. discompose; soil, pollute, infect.

healthy, *adj.* **1.** hale, sound, hearty, well, robust, vigorous, strong. **2.** healthful, wholesome, nutritious, nourishing, salubrious, salutary, hygienic, invigorating, bracing, beneficial, tonic.
—Ant. unhealthy, ill, sick, weak; unwholesome, enervating.
—Syn. Study. HEALTHY, HEALTHFUL, WHOLESOME refer to physical, mental, or moral health and well-being. HEALTHY most often applies to what possesses health, but may apply to what promotes health: *a healthy child; a healthy climate.* HEALTHFUL is usu. applied to something conducive to physical health: *a healthful diet.* WHOLESOME, connoting freshness and purity, applies to something that is physically or morally beneficial: *wholesome food; wholesome entertainment.*

heap, *n.* **1.** mass, stack, pile, mound, hoard, store, mountain, stockpile, supply, accumulation, collection. —*v.* **2.** pile or heap up, amass, accumulate. **3.** bestow, confer, cast, shower.

hear, *v.* **1.** listen to, perceive, attend to, pay attention to, understand, catch, heed, harken to **2.** understand, learn, find out, discover, gather, get wind of, pick up on, ascertain, be told or advised or informed.

heat, *n.* **1.** warmth, fever, fire, fieriness, torridness, hotness. **2.** warmth, intensity, ardor, fervor, zeal, flush, fever, excitement, impetuosity, vehemence, violence. —*v.* **3.** stimulate, warm, stir, animate, arouse, excite, rouse, intensify, impassion, inflame, kindle, ignite, quicken, awaken, activate, hot up.
—Ant. coolness; phlegm; cool, discourage.

heathen, *n.* **1.** pagan, gentile, barbarian, savage, Philistine, nonbeliever, infidel, idolater, atheist, skeptic, heretic. —*adj.* **2.** gentile, pagan, heathenish, irreligious, unenlightened, barbarous, savage, Philistine.
—Ant. civilized, religious.
—Syn. Study. HEATHEN, PAGAN are both applied to peoples who are not Christian, Jewish, or Muslim;

these terms may also refer to irreligious peoples. HEATHEN is often used of those whose religion is unfamiliar and therefore regarded as primitive, unenlightened, or uncivilized: *heathen idols; heathen rites.* PAGAN is most frequently used of the ancient Greeks and Romans who worshiped many deities: *a pagan civilization.*

heave, *v.* **1.** raise, lift, hoist, elevate. **2.** pant, exhale, breathe. **3.** vomit, retch. **4.** rise, swell, dilate, bulge, expand.

heavenly, *adj.* **1.** blissful, beautiful, divine, seraphic, cherubic, angelic, saintly, sainted, holy, beatific, blessed, beatified, glorified. **2.** celestial, unearthly, extraterrestrial, otherworldly, ultramundane.
—Ant. hellish, satanic, diabolical, devilish.

heavy, *adj.* **1.** weighty, ponderous, massive. **2.** burdensome, harsh, oppressive, depressing, onerous, distressing, severe, grievous, cumbersome. **3.** broad, thick, coarse, blunt. **4.** serious, intense, momentous, weighty, important, pithy, concentrated. **5.** trying, difficult. **6.** downhearted. **7.** ponderous, dull, tedious, tiresome, wearisome, burdensome, boring, lifeless. **8.** dense.
—Ant. light.

hectic, *adj.* **1.** frantic, busy, rushed, overactive, bustling, furious, frenzied, frenetic, perfervid, hysterical, hyper. **2.** feverish, fevered, febrile, hot, heated, burning, flushed.
—Ant. calm. cool.

heed, *v.* **1.** pay or give attention to, consider, regard, notice, mark, follow, listen to, observe, obey. —*n.* **2.** attention, notice, observation, consideration, care, caution, heedfulness, watchfulness, vigilance.
—Ant. disregard, ignore.

height, *n.* **1.** altitude, elevation; stature, tallness. **2.** hill, peak, crag, tor, cliff, bluff, promontory, headland, prominence, mountain. **3.** top, peak, pinnacle, apex, eminence, acme, summit, zenith, culmination.
—Ant. depth, abyss.
—Syn. Study. HEIGHT, ALTITUDE, ELEVATION refer to distance above a level. HEIGHT denotes extent upward (as from foot to head) as well as any measurable distance above a given level: *The tree grew to a height of ten feet. They looked down from a great height.* ALTITUDE usually refers to the distance, determined by instruments, above a given level, commonly mean sea level: *The airplane flew at an altitude of 30,000 feet.* ELEVATION implies a distance to which something has been raised or uplifted above a level: *a hill's elevation above the surrounding country.*

hell, *n.* **1.** Gehenna, Tartarus, inferno, Abaddon, Avernus, Hades, Erebus, pandemonium, abyss, limbo, underworld, infernal regions, nether regions, bottomless pit, lower world. **2.** damnation, perdition, ruin, downfall, destruction; punishment, misery, wretchedness, torture.
—Ant. heaven.

help, *v.* **1.** aid, assist, succor, encourage, befriend, support, second, uphold, cooperate, back, abet, save. **2.** further, facilitate, promote, ease, foster. **3.** relieve, ameliorate, alleviate, remedy, cure, heal, restore, improve, better. **4.** refrain from, avoid, forbear. —*n.* **5.** support, backing, aid, assistance, relief, succor.
—Ant. discourage, attack, undermine.
—Syn. Study. HELP, AID, ASSIST, SUCCOR agree in the idea of furnishing someone with something that is needed. HELP implies furnishing anything that furthers one's efforts or satisfies one's needs: *I helped her*

plan the party. AID and ASSIST, somewhat more formal, imply a furthering or seconding of another's efforts. AID suggests an active helping; ASSIST suggests less need and less help: *to aid the poor; to assist a teacher in the classroom.* To SUCCOR, still more formal and literary, is to give timely help and relief to someone in difficulty or distress: *Succor him in his hour of need.*

helper, *n.* aid, assistant, supporter, auxiliary, ally, colleague, amanuensis, right hand, henchman, sidekick, cohort, partner, deputy, subordinate, underling, employee.

helpful, *adj.* useful, convenient, beneficial, advantageous, serviceable, practical, pragmatic, utilitarian, valuable, constructive, supportive, sensible, profitable.
—Ant. useless, inconvenient, disadvantageous, uncooperative.

herd, *n.* **1.** drove, flock, clutch, crowd, group, pack, bunch, cluster, multitude, host, horde, throng, mass, swarm, press, crush, gathering. —*v.* **2.** flock, assemble, associate, keep company, gather, congregate, collect.

heritage, *n.* inheritance, estate, patrimony, birthright, legacy, bequest.

heroic, *adj.* intrepid, dauntless, gallant, valorous, brave, courageous, bold, daring, fearless, valiant, noble, plucky, stouthearted, chivalrous, audacious, honorable, virtuous, steadfast, staunch, stalwart.
—Ant. cowardly, fearful.

hesitate, *v.* **1.** waver, vacillate, falter, equivocate, dither, fluctuate, alternate, yo-yo, shilly-shally, fumble, tergiversate, waffle, falter, stumble, hem and haw, blow hot and cold, change one's mind. **2.** demur, delay, pause, wait, hang back, dilly-dally, temporize, think twice, balk, boggle at, shrink from, stall.
—Ant. resolve, decide.

hew, *v.* **1.** cut, chop, hack. **2.** make, shape, fashion, form. **3.** sever, cut down, fell.

hide, *v.* conceal, secrete, screen, mask, cloak, veil, shroud, cover, disguise, withhold, suppress, cache, squirrel away, camouflage, keep secret, obscure, repress, hush up, silence, eclipse, blot out, block.
—Ant. open, reveal.
—Syn. Study. HIDE, CONCEAL, SECRETE mean to keep something from being seen or discovered. HIDE is the general word: *A rock hid them from view.* CONCEAL, somewhat more formal, usually means to intentionally cover up something: *He concealed the evidence of the crime.* SECRETE means to put away carefully, in order to keep secret: *The spy secreted the important papers.*

hideous, *adj.* horrible, frightful, ugly, grotesque, lurid, grisly, grim, revolting, repellent, repulsive, nauseating, detestable, odious, monstrous, dreadful, appalling, terrifying, terrible, ghastly, macabre, shocking.
—Ant. beautiful, lovely, attractive.

high, *adj.* **1.** lofty, tall, elevated, towering, skyscraping. **2.** intensified, energetic, intense, strong. **3.** expensive, costly, dear, high-priced. **4.** exalted, elevated, eminent, prominent, preeminent, distinguished. **5.** shrill, sharp, acute, high-pitched, strident. **6.** chief, main, principal, head. **7.** consequential, important, grave, serious, capital, extreme. **8.** lofty, haughty, arrogant, snobbish, proud, lordly, supercilious. **9.** elated, merry, hilarious, happy; giddy, pixilated, intoxicated, inebriated.
—Ant. low.

hilarity, *n.* laughter, gaiety, joviality,

exuberance, cheerfulness, boisterousness, jubilation, elation, revelry, vivacity, conviviality, exhilaration, high spirits, glee, mirth, merriment, levity, jollity, hilariousness, hysterics, joy, jocularity.

hill, *n.* elevation, prominence, eminence, mound, rise, highland, knoll, hillock, foothill, mount, hummock, height, butte.
—Ant. valley, dale, glen, hollow, depth.

hinder, *v.* **1.** interrupt, check, retard, impede, encumber, delay, hamper, obstruct, trammel. **2.** block, thwart, prevent, obstruct.
—Ant. encourage, disencumber.
—Syn. Study. See PREVENT.

hindrance, *n.* impediment, deterrent, hitch, encumbrance, obstruction, check, restraint, hobble, obstacle, snag, barrier, drawback, stumbling block, curb, limitation.
—Ant. help, aid, support.
—Syn. Study. See OBSTACLE.

hint, *n.* **1.** suggestion, implication, intimation, allusion, insinuation, innuendo, reminder, inkling. —*v.* **2.** imply, intimate, insinuate, suggest, mention.
—Syn. Study. HINT, INTIMATE, INSINUATE, SUGGEST denote the conveying of an idea to the mind indirectly or without full or explicit statement. To HINT is to convey an idea covertly or indirectly, but in a way that can be understood: *She hinted that she would like a bicycle for her birthday.* To INTIMATE is to give a barely perceptible hint, often with the purpose of influencing action: *He intimated that a conciliation was possible.* To INSINUATE is to hint artfully, often at what one would not dare to say directly: *Someone insinuated that the defendant was guilty.* SUGGEST denotes recalling something to the mind or starting a new train of thought by means of association of ideas: *Her restlessness suggested that she wanted to leave.*

hire, *v.* **1.** engage, employ; let, lease, rent, charter. —*n.* **2.** rent, rental; pay, stipend, salary, wages, remuneration.
—Syn. Study. HIRE, CHARTER, RENT refer to paying money for the use of something. HIRE is most commonly applied to paying money for a person's services, but is also used in reference to paying for the temporary use of something: *to hire a gardener; to hire a convention hall.* CHARTER is applied to hiring a vehicle for the exclusive use of a group or individual: *to charter a boat.* RENT, although used in the above senses, is most often applied to paying a set sum at regular intervals for the use of a dwelling or other property: *to rent an apartment.*

history, *n.* record, chronicle, account, annals, story, relation, narrative, description, depiction, portrayal, representation, recital, narration.

hit, *v.* **1.** strike, knock, smack, whack, bash, bang, thump, punch, buffet, slap, swat, beat, pummel, batter, whip, sock. **2.** reach, attain, gain, win, accomplish, achieve. **3.** touch, suit, fit, befit, affect. **4.** find, come upon, meet with, discover, happen upon. **5.** collide, strike, clash. —*n.* **6.** blow, stroke; success.
—Syn. Study. See BEAT.

hitch, *v.* **1.** couple, join, link, fix, make fast, fasten, connect, hook, tether, attach, tie, unite, harness, yoke. —*n.* **2.** halt, obstruction, hindrance, catch, impediment, snag, difficulty, trouble, problem, handicap, mishap.
—Ant. loose, loosen, untie.

hoarse, *adj.* husky, throaty, guttural,

gruff, harsh, grating, raucous, rough.

hold, *v.* **1.** have, keep, retain, possess, own, occupy. **2.** bear, sustain, hold up, support, maintain, keep (up), continue, carry on. **3.** engage in, observe, celebrate, preside over, carry on, pursue. **4.** hinder, restrain, keep back; confine, detain, imprison, impound, incarcerate, coop up. **5.** contain, admit, accommodate, include, comprise. **6.** think, believe, embrace, espouse, entertain, have, regard, consider, esteem, judge, deem. **7.** continue, persist, last, endure, remain. **8.** adhere, cling, remain, stick. **—*n.*** **9.** grasp, grip. **10.** control, influence.

—Syn. Study. See CONTAIN.

hole, *n.* **1.** aperture, opening, cavity, excavation, pit, hollow, crater, depression, breach, fissure, orifice, slit, slot, crack, concavity. **2.** burrow, lair, den, retreat, cave.

holy, *adj.* **1.** blessed, sacred, consecrated, hallowed, dedicated, sacrosanct, inviolable, religious, sanctified, venerated, heavenly, celestial. **2.** saintly, godly, divine, pious, devout, spiritual, pure, virtuous, pietistic, religious, God-fearing, blessed, incorruptible, chaste, unsullied, sinless, immaculate, reverent, reverential, faithful.

—Ant. unholy, desecrated, impious, piacular, sinful, impure, corrupt.

—Syn. Study. HOLY, SACRED, HALLOWED refer to something that is the object of worship or veneration. HOLY refers to the divine, that which has its sanctity directly from God or is connected with Him: *Remember the Sabbath day to keep it holy.* Something that is SACRED is usually dedicated to a religious purpose by human authority: *a sacred shrine.* Something that is HALLOWED has been made holy by being worshiped or venerated: *The church graveyard is hallowed ground.*

homage, *n.* **1.** respect, reverence, deference, obeisance, honor, tribute. **2.** fealty, allegiance, faithfulness, fidelity, loyalty, devotion. **3.** devotion, worship, adoration.

—Ant. disrespect, irreverence, dishonor; faithlessness, disloyalty.

home, *n.* **1.** house, apartment, residence, household, abode, dwelling, domicile, habitation. **2.** refuge, retreat, institution, asylum, hospice, shelter. **3.** hearth, fireside, family; rightful place.

—Syn. Study. See HOUSE.

homely, *adj.* plain, simple, unpretentious, modest, unassuming, informal, homespun, familiar, friendly, gemütlichkeit, congenial, folksy, down-home; unattractive, coarse, inelegant, uncomely, ugly, ill-favored.

—Ant. beautiful.

honest, *adj.* **1.** honorable, upright, fair, just, incorruptible, trusty, law-abiding, ethical, principled, reputable, aboveboard, straight, fair, just, on the level, decent, reliable, creditable, proper, trustworthy, truthful, virtuous, moral. **2.** open, sincere, candid, straightforward, frank, unreserved, ingenuous.

—Ant. dishonest; corrupt, disingenuous, untrustworthy, secretive.

honesty, *n.* **1.** uprightness, probity, integrity, justice, fairness, trustworthiness, virtue, virtuousness, morality, righteousness, character, reliability, propriety, rectitude, honor. **2.** truthfulness, sincerity, candor, frankness, truth, veracity, earnestness, openness, guilelessness.

—Ant. dishonesty, inequity; deceit, insincerity.

—Syn. Study. See HONOR.

honor, *n.* **1.** esteem, fame, glory, repute, reputation, credit. **2.** credit, distinction, dignity. **3.** respect, deference, homage, reverence, veneration, consideration, distinction. **4.** privilege, favor, distinction, joy, pleasure, delight. **5.** honesty, integrity, sincerity, character, principle, probity, uprightness, nobleness. **6.** purity, chastity, virginity, virtue, innocence. **—*v.*** **7.** revere, esteem, venerate, respect, adore, worship, hallow.

—Ant. dishonor, disrepute, discredit; indignity; disfavor; indecency; execrate, abominate.

—Syn. Study. HONOR, HONESTY, INTEGRITY, SINCERITY refer to the highest moral principles. HONOR denotes a fine sense of, and a strict conformity to, what is considered morally right or due: *The soldier conducted himself with honor.* HONESTY denotes moral virtue and particularly the absence of deceit or fraud: *known for her honesty in business dealings.* INTEGRITY indicates a soundness of moral principle that no power or influence can impair: *a judge of unquestioned integrity.* SINCERITY particularly implies the absence of deceit and a strong adherence to the truth: *Your sincerity was evident in every word.*

honorable, *adj.* **1.** upright, honest, noble, highminded, just, fair, trusty, trustworthy, true, virtuous. **2.** dignified, distinguished, noble, illustrious, great. **3.** creditable, reputable, estimable, right, proper, equitable.

—Ant. ignoble, untrustworthy, corrupt; undignified; disreputable.

hope, *n.* **1.** expectation, wish, yearning, hankering, craving, dream, fancy, ambition, longing, desire. **2.** confidence, prospect, promise, anticipation, assumption, conviction, belief, trust, reliance, faith. **—*v.*** **3.** trust, expect, anticipate, await, wish, want, desire, long for, pray, dream, set one's sights on, hold one's breath, wait with bated breath, cross one's fingers.

—Ant. hopelessness.

hopeful, *adj.* **1.** expectant, sanguine, optimistic, confident, assured. **2.** encouraging, bright, rosy, promising, heartening, auspicious, propitious.

—Ant. hopeless.

hopeless, *adj.* **1.** desperate, despairing, despondent, forlorn, gloomy, disconsolate. **2.** irremediable, remediless, incurable, irreperable, beyond saving *or* repair. **3.** futile, vain, pointless, worthless, unavailing, useless, bootless.

—Ant. hopeful.

horrendous, *adj.* terrible, overwhelming, frightful, fearful, horrific, gruesome, lurid, macabre, awful, grotesque, dreadful, ghastly, terrifying, stupefying, dire, atrocious.

horrible, *adj.* **1.** horrendous, terrible, horrid, dreadful, awful, appalling, frightful, hideous, grim, ghastly, shocking, revolting, repulsive, repellent, dire, formidable, horrifying, harrowing. **2.** appalling, disgraceful, foul, abhorrent, unspeakable, monstrous, scandalous, outrageous, loathsome, deplorable, shocking, abominable, odious.

—Ant. attractive, delightful, beautiful; welcome, fine.

horror, *n.* **1.** fear, abhorrence, terror, dread, dismay, consternation, panic, alarm. **2.** aversion, repugnance, loathing, antipathy, detestation, revulsion, distaste, aversion, antipathy, animosity, hatred, abomination.

—Ant. calm, serenity; attraction, delight, love.

hostile, *adj.* opposed, adverse, averse, unfriendly, inimical, antagonistic, contrary, warlike, oppugnant, antipathetic.

—Ant. friendly, amiable, amicable.

hostility, *n.* **1.** enmity, antagonism, animosity, animus, ill will, unfriendliness, antipathy, malevolence, malice, opposition, hatred. **2.** (*plural*) war, warfare, fighting, conflict, combat, bloodshed.

—Ant. friendliness, good will, love; peace, truce.

hot, *adj.* **1.** heated, torrid, sultry, burning, fiery, white-hot, red-hot, piping hot, blistering, scorching, sizzling, searing, scalding, boiling, sweltering. **2.** pungent, piquant, sharp, acrid, spicy, peppery, biting, blistering. **3.** ardent, fervent, fervid, angry, furious, vehement, intense, excited, excitable, irascible, animated, violent, passionate, impetuous.

—Ant. cold.

hotheaded, *adj.* reckless, rash, incautious, headstrong, impetuous, emotional, hot-tempered, passionate, fiery, headlong, volatile, hasty, wild, foolhardy, heedless, daredevil, devil-may-care, madcap, thoughtless.

—Ant. cool, serene, phlegmatic.

house, *n.* **1.** home, residence, dwelling, abode, domicile, homestead, household. **2.** firm, company, partnership, business, establishment. **—*v.*** **3.** accommodate, board, put up, take in, lodge, harbor, shelter, reside, dwell.

—Syn. Study. HOUSE, HOME, RESIDENCE, DWELLING are terms applied to a place in which people live. HOUSE is generally applied to a structure built for one or two families or social units: *a ranch house in the suburbs.* HOME may be used of an apartment or a private house; it retains connotations of domestic comfort and family ties: *Their home is full of charm and character.* RESIDENCE is characteristic of formal usage and often implies spaciousness and elegance: *the private residence of the prime minister.* DWELLING is a general and neutral word (*a houseboat is a floating dwelling*) and therefore commonly used in legal, scientific, and other technical contexts, as in a lease or in the phrases *multiple dwelling, single-family dwelling.*

household, *n.* **1.** family, ménage, people, brood, folks, occupants, dwellers, home, homestead, hearth, fireside, hearth and home. **—*adj.*** **2.** domestic, family, home, domiciliary, residential. **3.** simple, ordinary, common, commonplace, plain, prosaic, everyday, garden-variety, homespun, plain-Jane. **4.** familiar, well-known, public, famous, unmistakable, notorious.

hubbub, *n.* noise, tumult, uproar, clamor, din, racket, disorder, confusion, disturbance, riot, hurly-burly, excitement, whirl, activity, ferment, agitation, ado, rumpus, commotion, bedlam, fracas, pandemonium, ruckus.

—Ant. serenity, calm.

—Syn. Study. See NOISE.

huge, *adj.* enormous, tremendous, immense, large, extensive, mammoth, vast, gigantic, colossal, stupendous, bulky, humongous, oversized, outsized, great, massive, gargantuan, prodigious, monumental, titanic, elephantine, leviathan, jumbo, Brobdingnagian, Cyclopean.

—Ant. tiny, small, infinitesimal, microscopic.

—Syn. Study. HUGE, ENORMOUS, TREMENDOUS, IMMENSE imply great magnitude. HUGE, when used of concrete objects, usually adds the idea of massiveness, bulkiness, or even lack of shape: *a huge mass of rock.* ENORMOUS applies to what exceeds a norm or standard in extent, magnitude, or degree: *an enormous iceberg.* TREMENDOUS suggests something so large as to be astonishing or to inspire awe: *a tremendous amount of equipment.* IMMENSE, literally not measurable, is particularly applicable to what is exceedingly great, without reference to a standard: *immense buildings.* All of these terms are used figuratively: *a huge success; enormous curiosity; tremendous effort; immense joy.*

humane, *adj.* **1.** merciful, kind, kindly, kindhearted, tender, human, benevolent, sympathetic, compassionate, gentle, accommodating, understanding, sensitive, magnanimous, philanthropic, tolerant, patient, forbearing, just, beneficent, humanitarian, benignant, charitable. **2.** refining, polite, cultivating, elevating, humanizing, spiritual.

—Ant. inhumane, cruel, ruthless, merciless; boorish, degrading.

humble, *adj.* **1.** low, lowly, lowborn, inferior, mean, ignoble, ordinary, plebeian, simple, obscure, unprepossessing, unimportant, plain, common, poor; meek, modest, submissive, self-effacing, servile, obsequious, subservient, unassuming, unpresuming, unpretending, unpretentious. **2.** respectful, reserved, deferential, polite, courteous, courtly. **—*v.*** **3.** degrade, humiliate, lower, abase, debase, chasten, demean, lose face, chagrin, reduce, mortify, shame, subdue, abash, crush, break, make (someone) eat humble pie, take (someone) down a peg.

—Ant. haughty, immodest, snobbish, conceited, pretentious; impolite, discourteous; raise, elevate.

—Syn. Study. HUMBLE, DEGRADE, HUMILIATE suggest a lowering in self-respect or in the estimation of others. HUMBLE most often refers to a lowering of pride or arrogance, but may refer to a lessening of power or importance: *humbled by failure; to humble an enemy.* DEGRADE literally means to demote in rank or standing, but commonly refers to a bringing into dishonor or contempt: *You degrade yourself by cheating.* To HUMILIATE is to make another feel inadequate or unworthy, esp. in a public setting: *humiliated by criticism.*

humbug, *n.* **1.** trick, hoax, fraud, imposture, deception, con game, swindle, imposition. **2.** falseness, deception, sham, pretense, hypocrisy, charlatanism. **3.** cheat, impostor, swindler, charlatan, pretender, confidence man, deceiver, quack.

humid, *adj.* damp, dank, wet, moist, muggy, clammy, sticky, steamy, sultry, soggy.

—Ant. dry.

humiliate, *v.* mortify, degrade, debase, dishonor, disgrace, abash, abase, chasten, demean, lower, chagrin, embarrass, discredit, shame, humble, crush, break, put down, subdue.

—Ant. honor, elevate, exalt.

—Syn. Study. See HUMBLE.

humiliation, *n.* mortification, shame, abasement, degradation, chagrin, disgrace, ignominy, indignity, discredit, embarrassment, humbling, dishonoring, belittling, depreciation, disparagement, derogation, obloquy.

—Ant. honor, elevation.

—Syn. Study. See SHAME.

humility, *n.* lowliness, meekness, humbleness, submissiveness, modesty, shyness, timidity, bashfulness,

mildness, diffidence, servility, self-effacement, self-abasement, unpretentiousness.
—Ant. haughtiness.

humor, *n.* **1.** wit, fun, facetiousness, pleasantry, comedy, drollery, waggishness, raillery, banter, jokes, jests. **2.** disposition, tendency, temperament, temper, nature, spirits, frame of mind, mood; whim, caprice, fancy, vagary. —*v.* **3.** indulge, gratify, placate, soothe, please, mollify, appease, baby, spoil.
—**Syn. Study.** HUMOR, WIT refer to an ability to perceive and express a sense of the clever or amusing. HUMOR consists principally in the recognition and expression of incongruities or peculiarities present in a situation or character. It is frequently used to illustrate some fundamental absurdity in human nature or conduct, and is generally thought of as a kindly trait: *a genial and mellow type of humor.* WIT is a purely intellectual, often spontaneous, manifestation of cleverness and quickness in discovering analogies between things really unlike, and expressing them in brief, diverting, and often sharp observations or remarks: *biting wit.* See also SPOIL.

humorous, *adj.* amusing, funny, jocose, jocular, droll, comic, comical, witty, facetious, waggish, sportive, ludicrous, laughable, risible, farcical, side-splitting, hilarious, whimsical, playful.
—**Ant.** serious, sad, melancholy.

hunch, *n.* feeling, impression, presentiment, suspicion, premonition, intimation, gut sense, instinct, foreboding, funny feeling, intuition, guess.

hungry, *adj.* ravenous, famished, starved, starving, voracious, empty, hollow.
—**Ant.** sated.

hunt, *v.* **1.** chase, pursue, track, dog, hound, trail, trace, stalk, prey upon. **2.** search for, seek, scour, quest after, ransack, investigate, explore, examine, check out. —*n.* **3.** chase, pursuit, hunting; search.

hurry, *v.* **1.** rush, haste, hasten, be quick, move swiftly *or* quickly, speed, race, dash, hustle, scurry, tear, run, fly, scoot, shake a leg, step on it, get a move on, hotfoot it, skedaddle, get cracking. **2.** hasten, urge, forward, accelerate, quicken, expedite, hustle, dispatch. —*n.* **3.** bustle, haste, dispatch, celerity, speed, rush, urgency, eagerness, quickness, alacrity, promptitude, expedition. **4.** bustle, ado, precipitation, flurry, flutter, confusion, perturbation, dither, furor, frenzy, agitation, upset, fuss, to-do, turmoil.
—**Ant.** delay, slow.

hurt, *v.* **1.** injure, harm, damage, mar, maim, disable, handicap, impair. **2.** pain, ache, smart, sting, torment, throb, gripe, distress, bother, grieve, afflict, wound. —*n.* **3.** injury, harm, damage, detriment, disadvantage; bruise, wound; pang, distress, suffering, torment, agony, torture, anguish.

hut, *n.* cottage, cabin, shed, hovel, shack, shanty, lean-to, hole in the wall.

hypocrite, *n.* deceiver, pretender, dissembler, pharisee, double-dealer, two-face, Tartuffe, faker, phony, con artist, imposter, pretender, charlatan, liar, humbug, wolf in sheep's clothing.

hypocritical, *adj.* sanctimonious, pharisaical, Pecksniffian; insincere, deceiving, dissembling, pretending, false, hollow, empty, deceptive, misleading, deceitful, double-dealing,

untrustworthy, underhand, perfidious, treacherous.
—**Ant.** honest, direct, forthright, sincere.

I

icon, *n.* picture, image, symbol, idol, representation, sign.

iconoclast, *n.* unbeliever, disbeliever, doubter, questioner, challenger, heretic, nonconformist, rebel, trail-blazer.
—**Ant.** believer, supporter.

idea, *n.* **1.** thought, conception, notion, concept, construct, scheme, perception, mental image; impression, apprehension, fancy. **2.** opinion, view, belief, sentiment, judgment, supposition. **3.** intention, plan, object, objective, aim, design.
—**Syn. Study.** IDEA, THOUGHT, CONCEPTION, NOTION refer to a product of mental activity. IDEA refers to a mental representation that is the product of understanding or creative imagination: *She had an excellent idea for the party.* THOUGHT emphasizes the intellectual processes of reasoning, contemplating, reflecting, or recollecting: *I welcomed his thoughts on the subject.* CONCEPTION suggests imaginative, creative, and somewhat intricate mental activity: *The architect's conception of the building was a glass skyscraper.* NOTION suggests a fleeting, vague, or imperfect thought: *I had only a bare notion of how to proceed.*

ideal, *n.* **1.** example, model, conception, epitome, standard, pattern, paragon, paradigm, nonpareil, nonesuch. **2.** aim, object, intention, objective. —*adj.* **3.** perfect, consummate, complete. **4.** unreal, unpractical, impractical, imaginary, visionary, fanciful, fantastic, illusory, chimerical.

identical, *adj.* same, alike, twin, indistinguishable, exact, equal, selfsame, undifferentiated, duplicated, reduplicated, clonal, cloned, one and the same, same-old same-old.
—**Ant.** unique, nonpareil.

ideology, *n.* philosophy, belief, belief system, credo, creed, ethos, ethic, convictions, tenets, principles, dogma, doctrine, teachings, view, outlook, faith, religion, school, cult, Weltanschauung.
—**Ant.** nihilism.

idiosyncrasy, *n.* mannerism, quirk, tic, trait, habit, trick, peculiarity, characteristic, attribute, property, mark, hallmark, token, singularity, trademark, affectation.

idle, *adj.* **1.** unemployed, unoccupied, inactive. **2.** indolent, lazy, slothful, listless, lethargic, loafing, shiftless, lackadaisical, sluggish. **3.** worthless, unimportant, trivial, trifling, insignificant, useless, fruitless, vain, ineffective, unavailing, ineffectual, abortive, baseless, groundless. **4.** frivolous, vain, wasteful. —*v.* **5.** waste, fritter away, while away, kill time, laze about, loiter, loaf, lounge, mess around, putter, waste time, goof off, goldbrick.
—**Ant.** employed, occupied; active, energetic; worthy, important; thrifty.
—**Syn. Study.** IDLE, INDOLENT, LAZY, SLOTHFUL apply to a person who is not active. IDLE means to be inactive or not working at a job; it is not necessarily derogatory: *pleasantly idle on a vacation.* INDOLENT means naturally disposed to avoid exertion: *an indolent and contented fisherman.* LAZY means averse to exertion or work, and esp. to continued application; the word is usually

derogatory: *too lazy to earn a living.* SLOTHFUL denotes a reprehensible unwillingness to do one's share; it describes a person who is slowmoving and lacking in energy: *The heat made the workers slothful.* See also LOITER.

idol, *n.* **1.** image, icon, symbol, statue, false god. **2.** hero, heroine, superstar, celebrity, luminary.

if, *conj.* in case, provided, providing, granting, supposing, even though, though; whether.

iffy, *adj.* uncertain, unsure, doubtful.
—**Ant.** certain, sure.

ignoble, *adj.* mean, base, despicable, dishonorable, contemptible, vulgar, low.
—**Ant.** noble, honorable; superior.

ignominy, *n.* disgrace, dishonor, disrepute, humiliation, indignity, stigma, shame, infamy, notoriety.
—**Ant.** credit, honor, repute, fame, distinction.
—**Syn. Study.** See DISGRACE.

ignorant, *adj.* **1.** illiterate, unlettered, uneducated, untutored, unenlightened. **2.** unaware, unknowing, in the dark, uninformed, (*informal*) clueless.
—**Ant.** literate, lettered, educated.
—**Syn. Study.** IGNORANT, ILLITERATE, UNEDUCATED mean lacking in knowledge or training. IGNORANT may mean knowing little or nothing, or it may mean uninformed about a particular subject: *An ignorant person can be dangerous. I confess I'm ignorant of higher mathematics.* ILLITERATE most often means unable to read or write; however, it sometimes means not well-read or not well versed in literature: *classes for illiterate soldiers; an illiterate mathematician.* UNEDUCATED particularly refers to lack of schooling: *an intelligent but uneducated clerk.*

ignore, *v.* overlook, slight, disregard, neglect, turn one's back on, brush off, pass over, be blind to.
—**Ant.** notice, note, regard, mark.

ill, *adj.* **1.** unwell, sick, indisposed, unhealthy, ailing, diseased, unsound, infirm, under the weather. **2.** evil, wicked, bad, naughty. **3.** hostile, belligerent, malevolent, malicious, harsh, cruel, unkindly, unkind, unfavorable, adverse. —*n.* **4.** evil, wickedness, depravity, badness. **5.** harm, injury, hurt, pain, affliction.
—**Ant.** well, hale, healthy; good.
—**Syn. Study.** ILL, SICK mean being in bad health, not being well. ILL is the more formal word. In the U.S. the two words are used practically interchangeably except that SICK is always used when the word modifies the following noun: *He looks sick (ill); a sick person.* In England, SICK is not interchangeable with ILL, but usu. has the connotation of nauseous: *She got sick and threw up.* SICK, however, is used before nouns just as in the U.S.: *a sick man.*

illegal, *adj.* unlawful, illicit, criminal, unauthorized, illegitimate, unlicensed, prohibited, forbidden.
—**Ant.** legal, licit, authorized.
—**Syn. Study.** ILLEGAL, UNLAWFUL, ILLICIT, CRIMINAL describe actions not in accord with law. ILLEGAL refers to violation of statutes or, in games, codified rules: *an illegal seizure of property; an illegal block in football.* UNLAWFUL is a broader term that may refer to lack of conformity with any set of laws or precepts, whether natural, moral, or traditional: *an unlawful transaction.* ILLICIT most often applies to matters regulated by law, with emphasis on the way things are carried out: *the illicit sale of narcotics.* CRIMINAL refers to violation of a public law that

is punishable by a fine or imprisonment: *Robbery is a criminal act.*

ill-mannered, *adj.* impolite, uncivil, discourteous, rude, coarse, uncouth, unpolished, crude, rough, ill-bred, insulting, boorish.

ill-natured, *adj.* cross, cranky, petulant, testy, snappish, unkindly, sulky, ill-tempered, morose, sullen, dour, gloomy, sour, crusty, perverse, contrary, temperamental, crotchety, cantankerous.
—**Ant.** good-natured, kindly, pleasant, amiable, friendly.

illusion, *n.* delusion, hallucination, deception, fantasy, chimera, fancy, false impression, misconception, misapprehension, daydream, phantom, mirage, vision, figment of the imagination.
—**Ant.** fact, reality.

illustration, *n.* example, case, instance, sample, specimen, exemplar, exemplification, explication.

image, *n.* **1.** icon, idol, representation, statue, picture. **2.** reflection, likeness, figure, representation. **3.** idea, conception, mental picture. **4.** form, appearance, semblance. **5.** counterpart, duplicate, replica, clone, dead ringer, facsimile, copy.

imaginary, *adj.* fanciful, unreal, visionary, chimerical, hypothetical, conjectural, make-believe, made-up, mythical, notional, abstract, fancied, illusory, imagined.
—**Ant.** real.

imagine, *v.* **1.** conceive, image, picture, conceive of, realize, envisage, visualize, create, concoct. **2.** think, believe, fancy, assume, suppose, guess, conjecture, hypothesize, presume, infer, gather, surmise, suspect.

imitate, *v.* follow, mimic, ape, mock, impersonate, copy, parrot, emulate, echo, duplicate, reproduce, simulate, counterfeit.

immediate, *adj.* **1.** instant, without delay, present, instantaneous. **2.** present, next, near, close, proximate. **3.** pressing, urgent, present, existing, current.
—**Ant.** later.

immediately, *adv.* **1.** instantly, at once, promptly, right away, without hesitation, without delay, presently, directly, instantaneously, forthwith; *esp. in business contexts* ASAP. **2.** directly, closely, without intervention.
—**Ant.** later, anon.
—**Syn. Study.** IMMEDIATELY, INSTANTLY, DIRECTLY, PRESENTLY were once close synonyms, all denoting complete absence of delay or any lapse of time. IMMEDIATELY and INSTANTLY still almost always have that sense and usu. mean at once: *He got up immediately. She responded instantly to the request.* DIRECTLY is usu. equivalent to soon, in a little while rather than at once: *You go ahead, we'll join you directly.* PRESENTLY changes sense according to the tense of the verb with which it is used. With a present tense verb it usu. means now, at the present time: *The author presently lives in San Francisco. She is presently working on a new novel.* In some contexts, esp. those involving a contrast between the present and the near future, PRESENTLY can mean soon or in a little while: *She is at the office now but will be home presently.*

immense, *adj.* huge, great, vast, large, gargantuan, enormous, gigantic, massive, mammoth, colossal, titanic, jumbo, (*slang*) humongous.
—**Ant.** small, tiny, submicroscopic.
—**Syn. Study.** See HUGE.

immerse, *v.* **1.** plunge, dip, sink, dunk, douse, submerge, inundate. **2.**

involve, absorb, engage, engross, involve, occupy.
—**Syn. Study.** See DIP.

imminent, *adj.* impending, near, at hand, threatening, looming, approaching, forthcoming.
—**Ant.** delayed, far off.

immoderate, *adj.* excessive, extreme, exorbitant, inordinate, extravagant, intemperate.
—**Ant.** moderate, reasonable, temperate.

immoral, *adj.* debauched, indecent, wanton, libertine, lecherous, unregenerate, reprobate, unethical, abandoned, depraved, dissipated, licentious, dissolute, profligate, unprincipled, sinful, corrupt, amoral, wicked, evil, iniquitous, vile, degenerate, villainous, dishonest.
—**Ant.** moral, pious, good.

immortal, *adj.* undying, eternal, everlasting, deathless, enduring, imperishable, endless, unending, perpetual, permanent, never-ending.
—**Ant.** passing, ephemeral.

impair, *v.* weaken, cripple, damage, mar, injure; worsen, diminish, deteriorate, lessen.
—**Ant.** repair.
—**Syn. Study.** See INJURE.

impart, *v.* **1.** communicate, disclose, divulge, reveal, intimate, confide, tell, relate. **2.** give, bestow, grant.
—**Ant.** conceal, hide.

impartial, *adj.* unbiased, just, fair, unprejudiced, disinterested, equitable, objective, neutral, evenhanded, judicious.
—**Ant.** partial.
—**Syn. Study.** See FAIR.

impatient, *adj.* **1.** uneasy, restless, nervous, fidgety, agitated, fretful, eager, chafing, itchy, antsy. **2.** irritable, testy, fretful, violent, hot, snappish, short, querulous.
—**Ant.** patient, restful, quiet; calm, unperturbed.

impede, *v.* retard, slow, delay, hinder, hamper, prevent, encumber, obstruct, check, stop, block, thwart, interrupt, restrain.
—**Ant.** aid, encourage.
—**Syn. Study.** See PREVENT.

impediment, *n.* bar, barrier, block, restraint, restriction, hindrance, obstacle, obstruction, encumbrance.
—**Ant.** help, support, spur, stimulus.
—**Syn. Study.** See OBSTACLE.

impel, *v.* compel, drive, urge, press on, incite, constrain, force, push.
—**Ant.** restrain.
—**Syn. Study.** See COMPEL.

imperfect, *adj.* **1.** defective, faulty, deficient, flawed, blemished. **2.** rudimentary, undeveloped, underdeveloped, incomplete; immature.

impertinent, *adj.* intrusive, presumptuous, impudent, insolent, uncivil, discourteous, forward, disrespectful, impolite, brassy, rude, fresh, bold, arrogant, insulting, saucy, pert, brazen.
—**Ant.** polite, courteous, respectful.
—**Syn. Study.** IMPERTINENT, IMPUDENT, INSOLENT refer to bold and rude persons or behavior. IMPERTINENT, from its primary meaning of not pertinent and hence inappropriate or out of place, has come to imply an unseemly intrusion into the affairs of others; it may also refer to a presumptuous rudeness toward persons entitled to respect: *impertinent questions; an impertinent interruption.* IMPUDENT suggests a bold and shameless rudeness: *an impudent young rascal.* INSOLENT suggests the insulting or contemptuous behavior of an arrogant person: *The boss fired the insolent employee.*

impetuous, *adj.* impulsive, rash, precipitate, spontaneous, violent, reckless, headstrong, devil-may-care, hasty, furious, unpremeditated, spur-of-the-moment, hot-headed.
—**Ant.** planned, careful.
—**Syn. Study.** IMPETUOUS, IMPULSIVE both refer to persons who are hasty and precipitate in action, or to actions not preceded by thought. IMPETUOUS suggests great energy, overeagerness, and impatience: *an impetuous lover; impetuous words.* IMPULSIVE emphasizes spontaneity and lack of reflection: *an impulsive act of generosity.*

implacable, *adj.* unappeasable, inexorable, inflexible, intractable, uncompromising, unrelenting, remorseless, unbending, relentless, rancorous, merciless, ruthless, cruel, unforgiving, pitiless.
—**Ant.** flexible, merciful.

implicate, *v.* involve, concern, entangle, connect, incriminate.
—**Ant.** exonerate.

implore, *v.* call upon, supplicate, beseech, entreat, beg, importune.

impolite, *adj.* uncivil, rude, discourteous, disrespectful, insolent, ill-bred, coarse, insulting, offensive, unpolished, unrefined, boorish, ill-mannered, rough, crude, indecorous, vulgar.
—**Ant.** polite.

importance, *n.* consequence, significance, moment, weight, substance, import, momentousness, weightiness.
—**Ant.** unimportance, insignificance.
—**Syn. Study.** IMPORTANCE, CONSEQUENCE, SIGNIFICANCE, MOMENT refer to something valuable, influential, or worthy of note. IMPORTANCE is the most general of these terms, assigning exceptional value or influence to a person or thing: *the importance of Einstein's discoveries.* CONSEQUENCE may suggest personal distinction, or may suggest importance based on results to be produced: *a woman of consequence in world affairs; an event of great consequence for our future.* SIGNIFICANCE carries the implication of importance not readily or immediately recognized: *The significance of the discovery became clear many years later.* MOMENT, on the other hand, usu. refers to immediately apparent, self-evident importance: *an international treaty of great moment.*

impostor, *n.* pretender, deceiver, imitator, wolf in sheep's clothing, dissembler, swindler, shark, phony, faker, cheat, confidence man, con man, charlatan, mountebank.

impregnable, *adj.* unassailable, invincible, invulnerable, impenetrable, inviolable.
—**Ant.** vulnerable.
—**Syn. Study.** See INVINCIBLE.

improper, *adj.* **1.** inapplicable, unsuited, unfit, inappropriate, unsuitable. **2.** indecent, unbecoming, unseemly, indecorous, unfitting, immodest, suggestive. **3.** abnormal, irregular, faulty, mistaken.
—**Ant.** proper.
—**Syn. Study.** IMPROPER, INDECENT, UNBECOMING, UNSEEMLY are applied to that which is inappropriate or not in accordance with propriety. IMPROPER has a wide range, being applied to whatever is not suitable or fitting, and often specifically to what does not conform to the standards of conventional morality: *an improper diet; improper clothes; improper behavior in church.* INDECENT, a strong word, is applied to what is offensively contrary to standards of propriety and esp. of modesty: *indecent photographs.* UNBECOMING is applied to what is especially unfitting in the person concerned: *conduct unbecoming a minister.* UNSEEMLY is applied to whatever is unfitting or improper under the circumstances: *unseemly mirth.*

improve, *v.* **1.** ameliorate, better, amend, emend, upgrade, enhance. **2.** mend, gain, get better, convalesce, recuperate, recover, rally, revive.
—**Ant.** worsen, impair; fail, sink.
—**Syn. Study.** IMPROVE, AMELIORATE, BETTER imply bringing to a more desirable state. IMPROVE usu. implies remedying a lack or a felt need: *to improve a process.* AMELIORATE, a formal word, implies improving oppressive, unjust, or difficult conditions: *to ameliorate working conditions.* BETTER implies improving conditions that are adequate but could be more satisfactory: *to better a previous attempt; to better oneself by study.*

improvident, *adj.* **1.** incautious, unwary, thoughtless, careless, imprudent, heedless, without *or* lacking foresight. **2.** thriftless, wanton, spendthrift, extravagant, wasteful, prodigal.
—**Ant.** provident, cautious; thrifty.

improvised, *adj.* extemporaneous, impromptu, unpremeditated, ad hoc, offhand, off the cuff, unrehearsed, spontaneous.
—**Ant.** premeditated, rehearsed.

impudence, *n.* impertinence, effrontery, insolence, rudeness, brass, disrespect, audacity, cockiness, arrogance, brazenness, lip, boldness, presumption, presumptiveness, sauciness, pertness, flippancy, nerve, gall, chutzpah.
—**Ant.** politeness, courtesy, respectfulness.

impudent, *adj.* bold, brazen, brassy, presumptuous, forward, disrespectful, insolent, impertinent, insulting, rude, presumptive, saucy, pert, flippant, fresh, sassy, smart-mouthed.
—**Ant.** polite, courteous, well-behaved.
—**Syn. Study.** See IMPERTINENT.

impulsive, *adj.* emotional, impetuous, rash, unpredictable, snap, headlong, reckless, foolhardy, quick, hasty, unpremeditated.
—**Ant.** cool, cold, unemotional, premeditated.
—**Syn. Study.** See IMPETUOUS.

impute, *v.* attribute, charge, ascribe, refer, insinuate, imply.
—**Syn. Study.** See ATTRIBUTE.

inability, *n.* incapability, incapacity, disqualification, impotence, incompetence.
—**Ant.** ability.

inaccuracy, *n.* **1.** incorrectness, imprecision, erroneousness, inexactitude. **2.** error, blunder, mistake, slip, gaffe.
—**Ant.** accuracy.

inaccurate, *adj.* inexact, imprecise, off base, flawed, imperfect, unspecific; incorrect, wrong, erroneous, mistaken, false, fallacious, unsound, faulty, improper.
—**Ant.** accurate.

inactive, *adj.* dormant, inert, torpid, inanimate, unmoving, immobile, indolent, lazy, sluggish, passive, idle, slothful, dilatory.
—**Ant.** active; energetic.
—**Syn. Study.** INACTIVE, DORMANT, INERT, TORPID suggest lack of activity. INACTIVE describes a person or thing that is not acting, moving, functioning, or operating: *an inactive board member; inactive laws.* DORMANT suggests the quiescence or inactivity of that which sleeps or seems to sleep, but may be roused to action: *a dormant geyser.* INERT suggests something with no inherent power of motion or action; it may also refer to a person disinclined to move or act: *the inert body of an accident victim.* TORPID suggests a state of suspended activity, esp. of animals that hibernate: *Snakes are torpid in cold weather.*

inadequate, *adj.* inapt, incompetent, insufficient, incommensurate, defective, imperfect, incomplete; deficient, scarce, meager, scanty, sparse, skimpy.
—**Ant.** adequate.

inadvertent, *adj.* **1.** unintentional, accidental, unwitting, chance. **2.** heedless, inattentive, unintentional, thoughtless.
—**Ant.** intentional, purposive, purposeful.

inanimate, *adj.* **1.** lifeless, inorganic, inert, inactive, dormant, nonliving, motionless, immobile. **2.** dull, passive, torpid, unresponsive, listless, stagnant, slow, insensible, unconscious, lifeless, sluggish, inert, spiritless; dead, defunct.
—**Ant.** animate, alive; spirited.

inborn, *adj.* innate, inbred, native, natural, congenital, inherent, instinctive, inherited, hereditary.
—**Ant.** acquired, learned, conditioned, environmental.

incapable, *adj.* unable, incompetent, inefficient, impotent, unqualified.
—**Ant.** capable, competent, efficient, qualified.
—**Syn. Study.** INCAPABLE, INCOMPETENT are applied to a person or thing lacking in ability, preparation, or power for whatever is to be done. INCAPABLE usu. means inherently lacking in ability or power to meet and fill ordinary requirements: *a bridge incapable of carrying heavy loads; a worker described as clumsy and incapable.* INCOMPETENT, generally used only of persons, means unfit or unqualified for a particular task: *incompetent as an administrator.*

incentive, *n.* motive, inducement, incitement, enticement, stimulus, spur, impulse, goad, encouragement, prod, reward, perk.
—**Ant.** discouragement, disincentive.
—**Syn. Study.** See MOTIVE.

incessant, *adj.* uninterrupted, unceasing, ceaseless, continual, continuous, constant, unending, never-ending, unremitting, perpetual, eternal.
—**Ant.** interrupted, spasmodic, sporadic; temporary.

incident, *n.* event, occurrence, happening, circumstance, occasion, proceeding, fact, experience, episode.
—**Syn. Study.** See EVENT.

incidental, *adj.* fortuitous, chance, accidental, casual, contingent, serendipitous, unplanned.
—**Ant.** fundamental.

incisive, *adj.* **1.** penetrating, trenchant, biting, cutting, critical, stinging, sarcastic, sardonic, satirical, acid, severe, cruel. **2.** sharp, keen, acute, piercing, perceptive, trenchant.
—**Ant.** superficial, dull.

incite, *v.* urge on, rouse, provoke, stimulate, encourage, back, prod, push, spur, inspire, prompt, move, stir up, exhort, foment, egg on, goad, instigate, arouse, fire; induce.
—**Ant.** discourage.
—**Syn. Study.** INCITE, ROUSE, PROVOKE mean to goad or inspire an individual or group to take some action or express some feeling. INCITE means to induce activity of any kind, although it often refers to violent or uncontrolled behavior: *incited to greater effort; incited to rebellion.* ROUSE is used in a similar way, but has an underlying sense of awakening from sleep or inactivity: *to rouse an apathetic team.* PROVOKE

means to stir to sudden, strong feeling or vigorous action: *Kicking the animal provoked it to attack.*

inclination, *n.* bent, leaning, tendency, set, propensity, liking, preference, predilection, predisposition, proclivity, bias, penchant.
—Ant. dislike, antipathy.

include, *v.* contain, embrace, comprise, comprehend, embody, incorporate, cover, encompass, subsume, take in.
—Ant. exclude, preclude.
—Syn. Study. INCLUDE, COMPREHEND, COMPRISE, EMBRACE imply containing parts of a whole. INCLUDE means to contain as a part or member of a larger whole; it may indicate one, several, or all parts: *This anthology includes works by Sartre and Camus. The price includes appetizer, main course, and dessert.* COMPREHEND means to have within the limits or scope of a larger whole: *The plan comprehends several projects.* COMPRISE means to consist of; it usu. indicates all of the various parts serving to make up the whole: *This genus comprises 50 species.* EMBRACE emphasizes the extent or assortment of that which is included: *The report embraces a great variety of subjects.*

income, *n.* return, returns, receipts, revenue, profits, salary, wages, proceeds, take, bottom line, fees, pay, stipend, annuity, gain, earnings.
—Ant. expense, expenditure.

incompatible, *adj.* **1.** inconsistent, incongruous, unsuitable, unsuited, contradictory, irreconcilable. **2.** unsuited, clashing, jarring, conflicting, discordant, contrary, opposed, contradictory, inharmonious.
—Ant. compatible, consistent, appropriate; harmonious.

incompetent, *adj.* unqualified, unable, incapable, inadequate, unskillful, inept, maladroit, inexpert, awkward, bungling, inefficient, oafish, clumsy, unfit.
—Ant. competent, efficient, able, capable, adequate, fit.
—Syn. Study. See INCAPABLE.

incongruous, *adj.* **1.** unbecoming, inappropriate, incompatible, out of keeping, discrepant, absurd. **2.** inconsonant, dissonant, inharmonious, discordant. **3.** inconsistent, incoherent, illogical, unfitting, contrary, contradictory, paradoxical.
—Ant. congruous, becoming, appropriate, proper; harmonious; logical, consistent, coherent.

inconsistent, *adj.* incompatible, inharmonious, incongruous, unsuitable, irreconcilable, incoherent, discrepant, out of keeping, inappropriate.
—Ant. consistent, coherent, harmonious, suitable.

inconstant, *adj.* changeable, fickle, inconsistent, variable, moody, fluctuating, erratic, flighty, capricious, vacillating, wavering, mercurial, volatile, unsettled, unstable, mutable, uncertain.
—Ant. constant, steady, invariant, settled, staid.

incontrovertible, *adj.* undeniable, indisputable, incontestable, unquestionable, irrefutable.
—Ant. deniable, controvertible, disputable, questionable.

inconvenient, *adj.* burdensome, unwieldly, onerous, difficult, cumbersome, awkward, inopportune, disadvantageous, troublesome, annoying, untimely, incommodious.
—Ant. convenient, opportune, advantageous.

incorrect, *adj.* wrong, not valid, untrue, false, erroneous, mistaken, fallacious, faulty, improper, inexact,

inaccurate.
—Ant. correct.

increase, *v.* **1.** augment, add to, enlarge; extend, prolong. **2.** grow, dilate, swell, wax, distend, inflate, burgeon, spread, proliferate, snowball, heighten, broaden, widen, expand, enlarge, multiply. —*n.* **3.** growth, augmentation, enlargement, expansion, addition, extension, spread.
—Ant. decrease.

incredulous, *adj.* unbelieving, skeptical, doubtful, dubious, wary.
—Ant. credulous, trusting, susceptible.
—Syn. Study. See DOUBTFUL.

indecent, *adj.* offensive, distasteful, improper, unbecoming, unseemly, inappropriate, shameful, in bad taste, outrageous, vulgar, indelicate, coarse, rude, gross, immodest, unrefined, indecorous, obscene, filthy, lewd, licentious, lascivious, pornographic, bawdy, ribald, X-rated, prurient, smutty, debauched.
—Ant. decent.
—Syn. Study. See IMPROPER.

indefinite, *adj.* **1.** unlimited, unconfined, unrestrained, undefined, undetermined, indistinct, confused. **2.** vague, obscure, confusing, equivocal, dim, unspecific, doubtful, unsettled, uncertain.
—Ant. definite.

independence, *n.* freedom, liberty, emancipation, autonomy, self-determination, self-government, sovereignty, self-rule; self-sufficiency.
—Ant. dependence, reliance.

indifference, *n.* **1.** unconcern, listlessness, apathy, insensibility, nonchalance, insouciance, aloofness, detachment, coolness, insensitiveness, inattention. **2.** unimportance, triviality, insignificance.
—Ant. concern, warmth, sensibility.

indignation, *n.* consternation, annoyance, resentment, exasperation, wrath, anger, ire, fury, rage, choler.
—Ant. calm, serenity, composure.
—Syn. Study. See ANGER.

indignity, *n.* injury, slight, contempt, humiliation, affront, insult, outrage, scorn, obloquy, contumely, reproach, abuse, opprobrium, dishonor, disrespect.
—Ant. dignity; honor, respect.
—Syn. Study. See INSULT.

indiscriminate, *adj.* **1.** careless, random, uncritical, undiscriminating. **2.** confused, undistinguishable, mixed, haphazard, jumbled, unsystematic, unmethodical, erratic, higgledy-piggledy.
—Ant. discriminating; systematic, methodical.

indispensable, *adj.* crucial, vital, imperative, important, compelling, necessary, requisite, essential, needed.
—Ant. dispensable, disposable, unnecessary, nonessential.
—Syn. Study. See NECESSARY.

indisposed, *adj.* **1.** sick, ill, unwell, ailing, out of sorts, under the weather. **2.** disinclined, unwilling, reluctant, averse, loath, hesitant, resistant.
—Ant. well, healthy, hardy, hale; eager, willing.

indisputable, *adj.* incontrovertible, incontestable, unquestionable, undeniable, indubitable; evident, apparent, obvious, certain, manifest, sure, definite.
—Ant. questionable, dubitable, dubious; uncertain.

indolent, *adj.* idle, lazy, slothful, slow, inactive, sluggish, torpid, listless, inert.

—Ant. energetic, active, industrious.
—Syn. Study. See IDLE.

indomitable, *adj.* steadfast, staunch, tireless, unflagging, dauntless, fearless, intrepid, invincible, unconquerable, unyielding, unbeatable.
—Ant. yielding, weak, feeble.
—Syn. Study. See INVINCIBLE.

induce, *v.* **1.** persuade, influence, incentivize, move, actuate, prompt, instigate, incite, urge, impel, spur, prevail upon. **2.** bring about, produce, cause, effect, bring on.
—Ant. dissuade.
—Syn. Study. See PERSUADE.

inducement, *n.* lure, bait, impetus, incentive, motive, cause, stimulus, spur, incitement, carrot, come-on, perk.
—Ant. discouragement.
—Syn. Study. See MOTIVE.

indulge, *v.* yield to, satisfy, gratify, humor, pamper, favor; suffer, foster, allow; coddle, pamper, spoil.
—Ant. deny, forbid; discipline, punish.
—Syn. Study. See SPOIL.

industrious, *adj.* busy, hard-working, diligent, assiduous, conscientious, tireless, tenacious, sedulous, persistent, persevering.
—Ant. lazy, indolent.

ineffectual, *adj.* **1.** useless, unavailing, futile, nugatory, ineffective, fruitless, pointless, abortive, purposeless. **2.** powerless, impotent, feeble, weak, effete.
—Ant. effectual, efficacious, efficient.

inefficient, *adj.* incapable, ineffective, feeble, weak.
—Ant. efficient, effectual, efficacious.

inept, *adj.* **1.** clumsy, awkward, bungling, maladroit, ungainly, gauche, bumbling. **2.** inapt, unfitted, unfitting, unsuitable, unsuited, inappropriate, out of place, anomalous. **3.** absurd, foolish, stupid, inane, ridiculous.
—Ant. fit, suitable, apt, appropriate.

inert, *adj.* inactive, immobile, unmoving, lifeless, insensible, dead, passive, motionless, unresponsive, inanimate, still, quiescent.
—Ant. active, kinetic.
—Syn. Study. See INACTIVE.

inexpensive, *adj.* cheap, low-priced, economical, reasonable, budget, thrifty, discount, bargain-basement.
—Ant. expensive.
—Syn. Study. See CHEAP.

inexperienced, *adj.* naive, callow, unsophisticated, fledgling, unseasoned, raw, green, unpracticed, unschooled, untutored, uninformed, uninitiated, wet behind the ears, born yesterday.
—Ant. experienced, skilled, practiced.

infallible, *adj.* trustworthy, sure, certain, reliable, unfailing, foolproof, dependable.
—Ant. fallible, unreliable, uncertain.

infamous, *adj.* **1.** disreputable, ill-famed, notorious, dishonorable. **2.** detestable, shameful, bad, nefarious, odious, wicked, outrageous, shocking, vile, base, ignominious, evil, iniquitous, abominable, despicable, loathsome, foul, heinous, villainous.
—Ant. reputable, famed; honorable, good.

infamy, *n.* notoriety, disgrace, dishonor, discredit, shame, disrepute, obloquy, odium, opprobrium, scandal, debasement, abasement, ignominy, ill repute, stigma.
—Ant. honor, credit, repute.
—Syn. Study. See DISGRACE.

infantile, *adj.* babyish, childish, puerile, immature, weak, juvenile, jejune.
—Ant. mature, adult.
—Syn. Study. See CHILDISH.

inflame, *v.* kindle, excite, rouse, arouse, incite, fire, stimulate, ignite, provoke, excite, incense, anger, enrage, animate, motivate.
—Ant. discourage.
—Syn. Study. See KINDLE.

inflate, *v.* distend, swell, swell out, dilate, expand, puff up or out, bloat, blow up, balloon, dilate, enlarge, pump up; exaggerate, embellish, embroider.
—Ant. deflate.

inflexible, *adj.* rigid, stiff, inelastic, unbending, undeviating, unyielding, rigorous, implacable, relentless, unrelenting, inexorable, unremitting, immovable, resolute, steadfast, firm, stony, solid, persevering, stubborn, dogged, pigheaded, mulish, obstinate, refractory, willful, headstrong, intractable, obdurate, adamant, dyed in the wool.
—Ant. flexible, easygoing, malleable.

influence, *n.* **1.** sway, rule, authority, power, impact, force, effect, leverage, pull, clout, control, predominance. —*v.* **2.** modify, affect, sway, impress, bias, direct, control. **3.** move, impel, actuate, activate, incite, rouse, arouse, instigate, induce, persuade.
—Syn. Study. See AUTHORITY.

inform, *v.* enlighten, brief, impart, disclose, divulge, report, reveal, tip off, apprise, make known, advise, notify, tell.
—Ant. conceal, hide.

informal, *adj.* unconventional, natural, easy, unceremonious, casual, colloquial, unstilted, familiar, ordinary, everyday, relaxed, easygoing.
—Ant. formal, regular, customary, conventional.

information, *n.* knowledge, news, data, facts, circumstances, situation, intelligence, advice, report, lowdown, inside story.

infringe, *v.* **1.** violate, transgress, breach, break, overstep, disobey. **2.** trespass, encroach, invade, intrude, impinge.
—Ant. obey.
—Syn. Study. See TRESPASS.

infuriate, *v.* enrage, anger, incense, madden, provoke, inflame, rile, vex, irritate, outrage, nettle, raise (someone's) hackles, make (someone's) blood boil.
—Ant. calm, pacify.
—Syn. Study. See ENRAGE.

ingenious, *adj.* clever, skillful, adroit, bright, gifted, able, resourceful, inventive, shrewd, creative, imaginative, original.
—Ant. unskillful, maladroit.

ingenuous, *adj.* unreserved, unrestrained, frank, candid, free; simple, innocent, unsophisticated, childlike, trusting, open, guileless, artless, innocent, naive, straightforward, sincere, honest, unaffected.
—Ant. reserved, restrained; secretive, sly, insincere, jaded.

ingredient, *n.* constituent, element, component, part, factor.

inherent, *adj.* innate, inherited, native, natural, inborn, inbred, essential, intrinsic, congenital, hereditary, immanent, built-in, part and parcel.
—Ant. acquired.
—Syn. Study. See ESSENTIAL.

inheritance, *n.* heritage, patrimony, legacy, bequest, birthright.

inhibit, *v.* **1.** restrain, hinder, arrest, check, repress, obstruct, stop; discourage. **2.** prohibit, forbid, interdict, prevent.

—**Ant.** encourage, support, abet, promote.

initiate, *v.* **1.** begin, originate, set going, start, commence, introduce, inaugurate, open, launch. **2.** teach, instruct, indoctrinate, train. —*n.* **3.** new member, pledge, tyro, beginner, learner, amateur, freshman, novice, greenhorn, rookie, neophyte, newcomer, tenderfoot, fledgling, apprentice, recruit, novitiate, abecedarian, newbie.

—**Ant.** terminate, conclude, finish.

—**Syn. Study.** See BEGIN.

injure, *v.* **1.** damage, impair, harm, hurt, spoil, ruin, break, mar, handicap, wound. **2.** wrong, maltreat, mistreat, abuse, affront.

—**Syn. Study.** INJURE, IMPAIR mean to harm or damage something. INJURE is a general term referring to any kind or degree of damage: *to injure one's spine; to injure one's reputation.* To IMPAIR is to make imperfect in any way, often with a suggestion of progressive deterioration: *One's health can be impaired by overwork.*

injurious, *adj.* harmful, hurtful, damaging, ruinous, detrimental, pernicious, deleterious, inimical, adverse, destructive.

—**Ant.** beneficial, helpful, advantageous.

injury, *n.* **1.** harm, damage, ruin, detriment, wound, impairment, mischief, hurt, abuse, mistreatment, wrong, injustice. **2.** wrong, injustice, mistreatment, malfeasance.

innocent, *adj.* **1.** pure, untainted, sinless, virtuous, virginal. **2.** honest, in the clear, unimpeachable, irreproachable, above suspicion, faultless, guiltless, blameless. **3.** naive, simple, trusting, gullible, credulous, childlike, unworldly, unaffected, uninitiated, unsophisticated, artless, guileless, ingenuous.

—**Ant.** guilty, culpable; disingenuous, sophisticated, artful.

inquire, *v.* ask, question, query, investigate, examine, interrogate, probe.

—**Ant.** answer, reply.

inquiry, *n.* **1.** investigation, examination, study, scrutiny, probe, search, inspection, survey, inquest, exploration, research. **2.** inquiring, questioning, cross-examination, inquisition, interview, interrogation; query, question.

—**Ant.** answer, reply.

inquisitive, *adj.* inquiring, prying, nosy, curious, scrutinizing, questioning, probing, exploratory.

insane, *adj.* deranged, demented, lunatic, crazed, crazy, maniacal, unbalanced, unhinged, mental, not all there, *non compos mentis,* of unsound mind, mad; paranoiac, schizophrenic, delirious; foolish, senseless, stupid, thoughtless, asinine, idiotic, irrational, moronic, harebrained.

—**Ant.** sane.

insanity, *n.* **1.** derangement, dementia, lunacy, madness, mental illness *or* disorder, hysteria, craziness, mania, aberration; schizophrenia, paranoia, psychosis, neurosis. **2.** senselessness, foolhardiness, folly, foolishness, lunacy, nonsense, inanity, absurdity, stupidity, idiocy, irrationality, craziness, madness.

—**Ant.** sanity, probity.

inscrutable, *adj.* impenetrable, mysterious, incomprehensible, inexplicable, unexplainable, unfathomable, unknowable, baffling.

—**Ant.** clear, comprehensible, understandable.

—**Syn. Study.** See MYSTERIOUS.

insecure, *adj.* **1.** unsafe, exposed, unprotected, vulnerable, defenseless, pregnable. **2.** uncertain, unsure, risky, precarious, shaky.

—**Ant.** secure, safe; certain, sure.

insinuate, *v.* **1.** hint, suggest, intimate, impute; imply, whisper. **2.** instill, infuse, introduce, inject, inculcate.

—**Syn. Study.** See HINT.

insolent, *adj.* bold, rude, disrespectful, impudent, presumptuous, insubordinate, fresh, cheeky, sassy, impertinent, brazen, brassy, overbearing, contemptuous, insulting.

—**Ant.** polite, courteous, retiring; complimentary.

—**Syn. Study.** See IMPERTINENT.

inspection, *n.* examination, investigation, scrutiny, study, survey, scan, check, perusal, vetting.

—**Syn. Study.** See EXAMINATION.

instance, *n.* case, example, illustration, exemplification, exemplar, precedent; event, occurrence, episode, experience.

instant, *n.* moment, minute, second, twinkling, flash, jiffy, trice.

—**Syn. Study.** See MINUTE.

instruct, *v.* **1.** direct, command, order, prescribe, bid, require, tell, enjoin, charge, importune. **2.** teach, train, educate, tutor, coach, drill, discipline, indoctrinate, school, inform, enlighten, apprise, guide, edify.

—**Syn. Study.** See TEACH.

instruction, *n.* **1.** education, tutoring, coaching, training, drill, exercise, tuition, lessons, tutelage, edification, schooling, teaching. **2.** order, direction, mandate, command, directive.

instructor, *n.* teacher, trainer, coach, mentor, adviser, educator, scholastic, academician, lecturer, professor, master, guru, tutor, pedagogue, schoolmaster, preceptor.

—**Ant.** student, pupil.

instrument, *n.* tool, implement, utensil, device, gadget, apparatus, gizmo.

—**Syn. Study.** See TOOL.

insult, *v.* **1.** affront, offend, scorn, injure, slander, abuse, (*slang*) dis. —*n.* **2.** indignity, affront, slight, offense, contumely, scorn, outrage.

—**Ant.** compliment, dignify; dignity.

—**Syn. Study.** INSULT, INDIGNITY, AFFRONT, SLIGHT refer to acts or words that offend or demean. INSULT refers to a deliberately discourteous or rude remark or act that humiliates, wounds the feelings, and arouses anger: *an insult about her foreign accent.* INDIGNITY refers to an injury to one's dignity or self-respect: *The prisoners suffered many indignities.* AFFRONT implies open offense or disrespect, esp. to one's face: *Criticism of my book was a personal affront.* SLIGHT implies inadvertent indifference or disregard, but may also indicate ill-concealed contempt: *Not inviting me was an unforgivable slight.*

intact, *adj.* all in one piece, uninjured, unaltered, sound, whole, unimpaired, complete, undiminished, unbroken, entire.

—**Ant.** impaired, unsound, incomplete.

—**Syn. Study.** See COMPLETE.

integrity, *n.* **1.** uprightness, honesty, honor, morality, rectitude, right, righteousness, probity, principle, virtue, goodness. **2.** wholeness, entirety, completeness, totality.

—**Ant.** dishonesty, disrepute; part.

—**Syn. Study.** See HONOR.

intellect, *n.* mind, understanding, reason, sense, common sense, brains.

—**Ant.** inanity.

—**Syn. Study.** See MIND.

intellectual, *adj.* **1.** mental, cerebral; rational, reasoning, intelligent. **2.** literate, erudite, cultivated, cultured, highbrow, academic, scholarly, bookish, thoughtful, thought-provoking, brainy. —*n.* **3.** thinker, intellect, genius, highbrow, sage, wise man *or* woman, guru, pundit, polymath, expert, bluestocking, rocket scientist, brain, egghead, professor, mental giant, longhair, brainiac; geek.

—**Ant.** illiterate, untutored, ignorant; ignoramus, lowbrow, yahoo, know-nothing.

intelligence, *n.* **1.** intellect, capacity, brainpower, cleverness, astuteness, quickness, wit, sense, insight, perspicacity, perception, discernment, wisdom, sagacity, mind, understanding, discernment, reason, acumen, aptitude, penetration. **2.** knowledge, news, information, tidings, scoop, lowdown, inside story.

—**Ant.** stupidity.

intelligent, *adj.* **1.** understanding, gifted, knowledgeable, erudite, intellectual. **2.** astute, clever, quick, alert, bright, discerning, shrewd, smart, perspicacious, insightful, percipient, wise, sage, sagacious, enlightened, knowing, brainy, perceptive, sharp, canny, savvy, quick-witted, keen.

—**Ant.** stupid, unintelligent, slow; dull.

—**Syn. Study.** See SHARP.

intend, *v.* have in mind, mean, design, propose, contemplate, expect, meditate, project, aim for *or* at, purpose, plan, determine.

intensify, *v.* aggravate, deepen, quicken, strengthen; concentrate, focus, whet, reinforce.

—**Ant.** alleviate, lessen, weaken, dilute.

intent, *n.* **1.** intention, design, purpose, meaning, plan, plot, aim, goal, end, objective, object, mark. —*adj.* **2.** fixed, steadfast, bent, resolute, set, concentrated, unshakable, eager, focused.

—**Ant.** irresolute, apathetic.

intentional, *adj.* deliberate, purposeful, premeditated, designed, planned, intended, meant, willful, studied, preconceived.

—**Ant.** unintentional, purposeless, unpremeditated; involuntary.

—**Syn. Study.** See DELIBERATE.

interesting, *adj.* pleasing, attractive, gratifying, engaging, absorbing, exciting, fulfilling, entertaining, engrossing, compelling, intriguing, provocative, stimulating.

—**Ant.** uninteresting, dull, prosaic.

interpret, *v.* **1.** explain, explicate, elucidate, shed *or* cast light on, define, translate, decipher, decode. **2.** construe, understand, figure out.

—**Syn. Study.** See EXPLAIN.

interrupt, *v.* **1.** discontinue, suspend, cut short, disrupt, hold up, terminate. **2.** stop, cease, break off, disturb, hinder, interfere with, butt in.

—**Ant.** continue.

intimate, *adj.* **1.** close, closely associated, familiar, dear, confidential, cherished, bosom. **2.** private, personal, confidential, hidden, privy, secret. **3.** detailed, deep, cogent, exact, precise. **4.** inmost, deep within; intrinsic, inner, deep-rooted, deep-seated. —*n.* **5.** friend, associate, confidant, comrade, companion, alter ego, sidekick, chum, pal, buddy, bro, crony, familiar. —*v.* **6.** hint, suggest, insinuate, allude to, imply.

—**Ant.** open, public, known, blatant; enemy, foe; announce, proclaim.

—**Syn. Study.** See FAMILIAR.

intimidate, *v.* overawe, cow, subdue, dismay, frighten, daunt, abash, appall, browbeat, terrorize, tyrannize, alarm; discourage, dissuade.

—**Ant.** encourage, hearten.

—**Syn. Study.** See DISCOURAGE.

intolerable, *adj.* unbearable, unendurable, insufferable, insupportable.

—**Ant.** tolerable, bearable.

intolerant, *adj.* bigoted, illiberal, narrow, proscriptive, prejudiced, discriminatory, partial, close-minded, parochial, one-sided, opinionated, biased, totalitarian.

—**Ant.** tolerant, liberal, unprejudiced.

intractable, *adj.* stubborn, obstinate, unmanageable, perverse, fractious, refractory, headstrong, pigheaded, willful, dogged, unbending, inflexible, obdurate, adamant, stony, unyielding, contumacious.

—**Ant.** tractable, amiable, amenable, easygoing, flexible.

—**Syn. Study.** See UNRULY.

intrinsic, *adj.* essential, native, innate, inborn, inbred, natural, inherent, basic, fundamental, elemental, organic, congenital, immanent, underlying, true, real, genuine.

—**Ant.** extrinsic.

—**Syn. Study.** See ESSENTIAL.

introduce, *v.* **1.** present, announce, make known, acquaint. **2.** broach, suggest, offer, mention, propose, bring up, advance, set forth, put forward. **3.** originate, start, begin, establish, set up, launch, initiate, institute. **4.** add, insert, interpose, inject, interpolate.

—**Syn. Study.** INTRODUCE, PRESENT mean to bring persons into personal acquaintance with each other, as by announcement of names. INTRODUCE is the ordinary term, referring to making persons acquainted who are ostensibly equals: *to introduce a friend to one's sister.* PRESENT, a more formal term, suggests a degree of ceremony in the process, and implies (if only as a matter of compliment) superior dignity, rank, or importance in the person to whom another is presented: *to present a visitor to the president.*

intrude, *v.* trespass, obtrude, encroach, violate, infringe, interfere, interrupt, intervene, butt in, barge in, horn in.

—**Syn. Study.** See TRESPASS.

inundate, *v.* flood, deluge, overflow, overspread, overwhelm, glut.

invaluable, *adj.* priceless, precious, valuable, inestimable, incalculable, irreplaceable, treasured, incomparable.

—**Ant.** worthless.

invariable, *adj.* unalterable, unchanging, uniform, steady, stable, regular, set, rigid, unwavering, constant, invariant, changeless, unvarying; unchangeable, immutable, permanent, fixed.

—**Ant.** variable, changing, varying, mutable.

invent, *v.* **1.** devise, contrive, originate, discover, create, conceive, imagine, formulate, improvise, coin. **2.** produce, create, imagine, fancy, conceive, fabricate, concoct, make up, cook up.

inventory, *n.* roll, list, roster, listing, record, account, catalogue, register.

—**Syn. Study.** See LIST.

investigation, *n.* examination, inspection, inquiry, scrutiny, search, probe, inquest, interrogation, inquisition, research, exploration.

invigorate, *v.* animate, inspirit, enliven, strengthen, fortify, energize, quicken, vitalize, stimulate, rejuvenate, refresh, freshen.

—**Ant.** enervate, enfeeble, weaken, devitalize.

invincible, *adj.* unbeatable, mighty, unstoppable, unrivaled, unsurpassed, supreme, dominant, inexorable, matchless, undefeated, unconquerable, insuperable, impregnable, impenetrable, indomitable.

—Ant. weak, beatable, third-rate.
—**Syn. Study.** INVINCIBLE, IMPREGNABLE, INDOMITABLE suggest that which cannot be overcome or mastered. INVINCIBLE is applied to that which cannot be conquered in combat or war, or overcome or subdued in any manner: *an invincible army; invincible courage.* IMPREGNABLE is applied to a place or position that cannot be taken by assault or siege, and hence to whatever is proof against attack: *an impregnable fortress; impregnable virtue.* INDOMITABLE implies having an unyielding spirit, or stubborn persistence in the face of opposition or difficulty: *indomitable will.*

invite, *v.* **1.** call, request, ask, bid, summon, solicit. **2.** attract, appeal, capture, captivate, allure, lure, tempt, entice, draw, induce, beckon.

involuntary, *adj.* **1.** unintentional, reluctant, accidental, unwitting, unconscious, impulsive, unplanned. **2.** automatic, reflex, unwilled, instinctive, uncontrolled.
—**Ant.** voluntary, intentional, willed.

involve, *v.* **1.** include, embrace, contain, comprehend, comprise, entail, imply. **2.** entangle, implicate, connect, tie, bind.
—**Ant.** exclude, preclude.

irate, *adj.* angry, enraged, furious, infuriated, wrathful, livid, steaming, inflamed, incensed, mad as a wet hen, irked, aggravated, worked up, fuming, nettled, annoyed, exasperated, seeing red, splenetic, hopping *or* boiling mad, upset, livid, up in arms, hot under the collar, on the warpath, burned up, piqued, provoked, irritated, vexed.

irregular, *adj.* sporadic, uneven, random, fitful, haphazard, uncertain, occasional, casual, unmethodical, unsystematic, disorderly, capricious, erratic; eccentric, lawless, aberrant, devious, unconforming, nonconformist, unusual, abnormal, anomalous, peculiar, odd, singular, exceptional.
—**Ant.** regular.

irrepressible, *adj.* unrestrained, unconstrained, enthusiastic, effervescent, vivacious, uninhibited, exuberant, high-spirited, ebullient, buoyant.
—**Ant.** gloomy, depressive.

irritate, *v.* vex, annoy, chafe, fret, gall, nettle, ruffle, pique, incense, irk, anger, enrage, infuriate, exasperate, provoke, pester, bother, plague, worry, pick on, needle, hassle, peeve, get on (someone's) nerves, drive (someone) up the wall, burn (someone) up.
—**Ant.** please, delight.

isolation, *n.* solitude, loneliness; separation, disconnection, segregation, detachment.

issue, *n.* **1.** delivery, emission, sending, promulgation. **2.** point, crux; problem, question. **3.** product, effect, result, consequence, event, outcome, upshot, denouement, conclusion, end, consummation. —*v.* **4.** put out, deliver, circulate, publish, distribute. **5.** send out, discharge, emit. **6.** come forth, emerge, flow out. **7.** come, proceed, emanate, flow, arise, spring, originate, ensue.
—**Syn. Study.** See EMERGE.

J

jabber, *v.* prattle, chatter, babble, prate, run on, natter, palaver, gabble, blather, tittle-tattle, gibber, drivel, gab, gas, yap.

jaded, *adj.* **1.** world-weary, bored,

blasé, spoiled, sated, satiated, glutted, burned out. **2.** tired, weary, spent, exhausted, worn out, fatigued, enervated.
—**Ant.** fresh, bright-eyed, eager.

jam, *v.* **1.** push, stuff, press, shove, wedge, pack, crowd, ram, force, squeeze, bruise, crush, cram. —*n.* **2.** dilemma, quandary, predicament, trouble, difficulty, bind, fix, pickle, hot water, scrape, tight spot.

jargon, *n.* **1.** idiom, vocabulary, phraseology, language, vernacular, argot, patois, patter, lingo, cant, slang. **2.** mumbo-jumbo, nonsense, double-talk, gibberish.
—**Syn. Study.** See LANGUAGE.

jaunty, *adj.* **1.** spirited, lively, frisky, blithe, jovial, jubilant, sprightly, cheerful, lighthearted, buoyant, perky, carefree, breezy. **2.** chic, stylish, debonair, sporty, dashing, smart, natty, spruce, dapper.
—**Ant.** dull, drab.

jealous, *adj.* **1.** envious, resentful, bitter, grudging, covetous, green with envy. **2.** suspicious, distrustful, mistrustful; anxious, insecure, threatened, vulnerable.
—**Ant.** generous, open, trusting.

jeer, *v.* **1.** deride, scoff, gibe, mock, taunt, sneer at, ridicule, twit, rag. —*n.* **2.** sneer, scoff, gibe, derision, ridicule, taunt, hoot, hiss, boo, catcall.
—**Syn. Study.** See SCOFF.

jeopardy, *n.* hazard, risk, danger, peril, threat, menace, vulnerability.
—**Ant.** security.

job, *n.* position, situation, post, employment, work, livelihood, day job; assignment, duty, task, chore, function, role, mission, undertaking, project.
—**Ant.** unemployment.
—**Syn. Study.** See TASK.

join, *v.* **1.** connect, unite, link, couple, fasten, attach, conjoin, combine, associate, consolidate, amalgamate, bring together. **2.** adjoin, abut, touch, be adjacent to, border, meet, verge on.
—**Ant.** separate, divide.
—**Syn. Study.** JOIN, CONNECT, UNITE imply bringing two or more things together more or less closely. JOIN may refer to a connection or association of any degree of closeness, but often implies direct contact: *to join pieces of wood to form a corner.* CONNECT implies a joining as by a tie, link, or wire: *to connect two batteries.* UNITE implies a close joining of two or more things, so as to form one: *to unite layers of veneer sheets to form plywood.*

joke, *n.* witticism, quip, jest, trick, raillery, prank, bon mot, laugh, pun, story, anecdote, gag, wisecrack, crack, one-liner, routine.

jolly, *adj.* gay, glad, happy, spirited, jovial, merry, sportive, playful, cheerful, convivial, festive, joyous, mirthful, jocund, exuberant, jaunty, buoyant, blithe.
—**Ant.** serious, morose, mirthless.
—**Syn. Study.** See JOVIAL.

journey, *n.* **1.** excursion, trip, jaunt, tour, expedition, pilgrimage, voyage, outing, junket, cruise, odyssey, trek, travel. —*v.* **2.** travel, tour, peregrinate, roam, rove, voyage, go abroad, trek, wander, gad about, gallivant; go, proceed, fare.
—**Syn. Study.** See TRIP.

jovial, *adj.* jocular, jolly, merry, convivial, expansive, sportive, hilarious, gay, jocose, jocund, joyous, joyful, blithe, happy, glad, mirthful, lighthearted, in high spirits.
—**Ant.** serious, mirthless, cheerless, unhappy.
—**Syn. Study.** JOVIAL, JOCULAR, JOLLY refer to someone who is in good spirits. JOVIAL suggests a sociable

and friendly person, full of hearty good humor: *The jovial professor enlivened the party.* JOCULAR refers to an amusing person, given to joking or jesting in a playful way: *His jocular sister teased him about his haircut.* JOLLY suggests a cheerful person, full of fun and laughter: *a jolly Santa Claus.*

joy, *n.* satisfaction, exultation, gladness, delight, rapture, gratification, happiness, contentment, enjoyment, elation, exhilaration, gaiety, glee, cheerfulness, jubilation, lightheartedness, felicity, bliss, pleasure, ecstasy, transport.
—**Ant.** dissatisfaction, misery; unhappiness.

joyful, *adj.* glad, delighted, joyous, happy, blithe, buoyant, elated, cheerful, gleeful, pleased, gratified, ecstatic, exultant, overjoyed, jubilant, gay, merry, jocund, jolly, jovial, on cloud nine, in seventh heaven, tickled pink.
—**Ant.** sad, unhappy, melancholy, depressed.

joyless, *adj.* sad, cheerless, unhappy, gloomy, dismal, miserable.
—**Ant.** joyous.

judge, *n.* **1.** justice, magistrate; arbiter, arbitrator, umpire, referee, adjudicator, mediator, authority, expert. —*v.* **2.** try, pass sentence upon. **3.** estimate, consider, regard, esteem, reckon, deem. **4.** decide, determine, conclude, form an opinion, pass judgment, rule, decree, find.
—**Syn. Study.** JUDGE, REFEREE, UMPIRE indicate a person who is entrusted with decisions affecting others. JUDGE, in its legal and other uses, implies that the person has qualifications and authority for rendering decisions in matters at issue: *a judge appointed to the Supreme Court; a judge in a baking contest.* REFEREE refers to an officer who examines and reports on the merits of a case as an aid to a court; it is also used of a person who settles disputes, esp. in a game or sport: *a referee in bankruptcy; a basketball referee.* UMPIRE refers to a person who gives the final ruling when arbitrators of a case disagree; it is also used of a person who enforces the rules in a game: *an umpire to settle the labor dispute; a baseball umpire.*

judgment, *n.* **1.** ruling, finding, order, verdict, decree, decision, determination, conclusion, opinion, estimate. **2.** understanding, discrimination, discernment, perspicacity, sagacity, wisdom, intelligence, prudence, eye, brains, taste, penetration, discretion, common sense, judiciousness, acumen, perspicuity, shrewdness, acuity, insight, keenness, astuteness, practicality, diplomacy, sensibility, rationality, reasonableness.

judicial, *adj.* critical, analytical, keen, sharp, perceptive, perspicacious, discriminating, judicious; juridical, forensic.

judicious, *adj.* **1.** practical, expedient, discreet, prudent, politic, tactful, diplomatic, circumspect. **2.** wise, sensible, well-advised, rational, reasonable, sober, sound, well-informed, enlightened, sagacious, considered, common-sense.
—**Ant.** impractical, indiscreet, imprudent; silly, nonsensical, unsound, unreasonable.
—**Syn. Study.** See PRACTICAL.

jumble, *v.* **1.** mix, confuse, mix up, confound, shuffle, muddle. —*n.* **2.** medley, mixture, hodgepodge, muddle, mess, farrago, chaos, disorder, confusion, gallimaufry, potpourri, clutter, tangle, disarray.
—**Ant.** separate, isolate; order.

jump, *n.* leap, bound, spring, caper, vault, hop, skip, hurdle, pounce.

junction, *n.* combination, union, joining, meeting, confluence, conjunction, intersection, connection, linking, coupling, juncture; seam, welt, joint.
—**Syn. Study.** JUNCTION, JUNCTURE refer to a place, line, or point at which two or more things join. A JUNCTION is also a place where things come together: *the junction of two rivers.* A JUNCTURE is a line or point at which two bodies are joined, or a point of exigency or crisis in time: *the juncture of the head and neck; a critical juncture in a struggle.*

just, *adj.* **1.** unbiased, neutral, objective, equitable, fair, impartial, evenhanded, right. **2.** true, correct, accurate, exact, proper, regular, normal. **3.** rightful, legitimate, lawful, legal; deserved, merited, condign, suitable, apt, due. **4.** righteous, blameless, honest, upright, pure, conscientious, good, uncorrupt, virtuous, honorable, principled, decent.
—**Ant.** unjust.

justify, *v.* vindicate, exonerate, exculpate, absolve, acquit, defend, warrant, excuse, explain, rationalize.
—**Ant.** inculpate, convict, indict, accuse, condemn.

K

keen, *adj.* **1.** sharp, acute, honed, razor-sharp. **2.** sharp, cutting, biting, severe, bitter, poignant, caustic, acrimonious. **3.** piercing, penetrating, discerning, astute, sagacious, sharp-witted, quick, shrewd, clever, keen-eyed, keen-sighted, clear-sighted, clear-headed. **4.** ardent, eager, zealous, earnest, fervid, enthusiastic, avid, devoted, passionate, intense.
—**Ant.** dull.
—**Syn. Study.** See SHARP.

keep, *v.* **1.** retain, hold, hang on to, preserve, reserve, conserve, withhold, have, save. **2.** tend, care for, look after, protect, safeguard, feed, nourish, nurture, provide for. **3.** continue, persist, persevere, carry on, sustain, prolong. **4.** follow, obey, mind, regard, heed, abide by, adhere to, pay attention to, observe, defer to, agree to.
—**Ant.** lose, donate; cease.
—**Syn. Study.** KEEP, RETAIN, RESERVE, WITHHOLD refer to having or holding in one's possession, care, or control. KEEP means to continue to have or hold, as opposed to losing, parting with, or giving up: *to keep a book for a week.* RETAIN, a more formal word, often stresses keeping something in spite of resistance or opposition: *The dictator managed to retain power.* TO RESERVE is to keep for some future use, occasion, or recipient, or to hold back for a time: *to reserve a seat; to reserve judgment.* To WITHHOLD is generally to hold back altogether: *to withhold evidence.*

keeping, *n.* **1.** congruity, harmony, conformity, consistency, agreement. **2.** custody, protection, care, charge, guardianship, trust.
—**Ant.** incongruity, nonconformity, inconsistency.

kill, *v.* **1.** slaughter, slay, assassinate, massacre, butcher, execute, liquidate, dispatch, exterminate, annihilate, butcher, snuff out, waste, ice, murder; hang, electrocute, behead, guillotine, strangle, garrote. **2.** extinguish, exterminate, eradicate, obliterate, annihilate, destroy, do away with.
—**Ant.** create, originate.

killjoy, *n.* doomsayer, Cassandra,

pessimist, damper, crepehanger, worrywart, grump, malcontent, cynic, prophet of doom, spoilsport, wet blanket, grouch, sourpuss, grinch, drag, party pooper, gloomy Gus, dog in the manger. —Ant. optimist, positivist, enthusiast.

kind, *adj.* **1.** gracious, kindhearted, kindly, good, genial, amiable, cordial, pleasant, decent, gracious, hospitable, benevolent, benignant, beneficent, friendly, humane, generous, bounteous, charitable, humanitarian, giving, unselfish, forbearing, forgiving, helpful, accommodating; gentle, affectionate, loving, sweet, caring, thoughtful, considerate, understanding, solicitous, feeling, warm, tender, compassionate, sympathetic, tenderhearted, softhearted, good-natured. —*n.* **2.** sort, nature, character, manner, persuasion, stripe, description; genus, species, breed, set, class, type, variety, style, genre, race.

kindle, *v.* **1.** set fire to, ignite, inflame, fire, light. **2.** rouse, arouse, awaken, bestir, inflame, provoke, incite, stimulate, animate, foment, prompt, prick, goad, excite, agitate, jolt, inspire, energize, galvanize. —Ant. extinguish, quench. —**Syn. Study.** KINDLE, IGNITE, INFLAME literally mean to set something on fire. To KINDLE is to cause something gradually to begin burning; it is often used figuratively: *to kindle logs; to kindle someone's interest.* To IGNITE is to set something on fire with a sudden burst of flame; it also has figurative senses: *to ignite straw; to ignite dangerous hatreds.* INFLAME is most often used figuratively, meaning to intensify, excite, or rouse: *to inflame passions.*

kindness, *n.* **1.** service, favor, good turn. **2.** friendliness, graciousness, goodness, goodwill, humaneness, decency, gentleness, thoughtfulness, consideration, cordiality, hospitality, warmth, geniality, good nature, benevolence, beneficence, humanity, benignity, generosity, philanthropy, charity, sympathy, compassion, tenderness, amiability. —Ant. unkindness, malevolence.

kingdom, *n.* monarchy, realm, sovereignty, dominion, empire, domain, principality, province, sphere of influence.

kinship, *n.* relationship, affinity, connection, bearing, similarity, association, alliance, agreement, parallelism; consanguity, blood tie, family tie, lineage, common descent, flesh and blood.

knack, *n.* aptitude, aptness, facility, dexterity, skill, adroitness, skillfulness, expertness, genius, intuition, gift, talent, bent, ability, flair, capacity, proficiency.

knot, *n.* **1.** lump, knob. **2.** difficulty, perplexity, puzzle, conundrum, rebus; snarl, tangle.

knotty, *adj.* complicated, complex, involved, intricate, difficult, hard, tough, thorny, perplexing. —Ant. easy, uncomplicated.

know, *v.* **1.** perceive, understand, apprehend, comprehend, grasp, be familiar with, be acquainted with. **2.** recognize, identify, remember, recall, recollect. **3.** distinguish, discriminate, discern, differentiate. —**Syn. Study.** KNOW, COMPREHEND, UNDERSTAND refer to perceiving or grasping facts and ideas. To KNOW is to be aware of, sure of, or familiar with something through observation, study, or experience: *She knows the basic facts of the subject. I know*

that he agrees with me. To COMPREHEND is to grasp something mentally and to perceive its relationships to certain other facts or ideas: *to comprehend a difficult text.* To UNDERSTAND is to be fully aware not only of the meaning or nature of something but also of its implications: *I could comprehend everything you said, but did not understand that you were joking.*

knowledge, *n.* **1.** enlightenment, erudition, wisdom, science, information, learning, scholarship, lore. **2.** understanding, discernment, perception, apprehension, comprehension, judgment.

L

labor, *n.* **1.** toil, work, exertion, drudgery, travail, moil, sweat, effort, strain, pains, industry, slavery, donkey-work, grind, elbow grease. —*v.* **2.** work, toil, strive, drudge, moil, sweat, strain, struggle, slave, grind. —Ant. idleness, indolence, sloth. —**Syn. Study.** See WORK.

labored, *adj.* overdone, overworked, overwrought, ornate, unnatural, excessive, contrived.

laborious, *adj.* **1.** toilsome, arduous, onerous, burdensome, difficult, tiresome, wearisome, fatiguing, grueling, backbreaking, herculean, taxing, uphill, stiff, strenuous, tiring. **2.** diligent, hard-working, assiduous, industrious, sedulous, painstaking. —Ant. easy, simple.

lacerate, *v.* **1.** tear, mangle, cut, slash, rip, maim, rend, claw. **2.** hurt, injure, harm, wound, damage.

lack, *n.* **1.** deficiency, need, want, dearth, scarcity, paucity, shortcoming, absence, shortage, shortfall, deficit, scantiness, insufficiency, defectiveness. —*v.* **2.** want, need, require, be deficient in, fall short of. —Ant. sufficiency, copiousness, abundance. —**Syn. Study.** LACK, WANT, NEED, REQUIRE indicate the absence of something desirable, important, or necessary. LACK means to be without or to have less than a desirable quantity of something: *to lack courage; to lack sufficient money.* WANT stresses the urgency of fulfilling a desire or providing what is lacking: *The room wants some final touch to make it homey.* NEED suggests even more urgency, stressing the necessity of supplying something essential: *to need an operation.* REQUIRE has a similar sense, although it is used in formal or serious contexts: *The report requires some editing.*

lackadaisical, *adj.* listless, indolent, enervated, blasé, indifferent, languid, languorous, lazy, unconcerned, uninvolved, apathetic, nonchalant, lethargic, sluggish. —Ant. peppy, alert, energetic.

lackluster, *adj.* dull, ordinary, plain, pedestrian, routine, unexceptional, banal, colorless, prosaic, commonplace, mediocre, so-so, drab, lifeless, leaden. —Ant. brilliant, extraordinary, distinctive.

lag, *v.* **1.** fall behind *or* back, loiter, linger, delay, straggle, dawdle, trail, dally, hang back. —*n.* **2.** retardation, slowing, slowdown, decrease, diminution, abatement, ebb. —Ant. speed, quicken, expedite; expedition.

laggard, *n.* lingerer, dawdler, slowpoke, plodder, foot-dragger, procrastinator, delayer, dillydallier, straggler, idler, loiterer, slouch, sluggard, loafer, couch potato, snail.

laid-back, *adj.* relaxed, easygoing, at ease, casual, offhand, free and easy, dégagé, undemanding, loose, lax, nonchalant, blasé, flexible. —Ant. rigid, strict, severe.

lament, *v.* **1.** bewail, bemoan, deplore, grieve, weep, mourn *or* sorrow over *or* for. —*n.* **2.** lamentation, moan, wail, wailing, moaning. **3.** dirge, elegy, monody, threnody, requiem. —Ant. rejoice.

language, *n.* **1.** speech, communication, tongue. **2.** dialect, jargon, idiom, terminology, vernacular; lingo, lingua franca. **3.** speech, phraseology, jargon, style, expression, diction. —**Syn. Study.** LANGUAGE, DIALECT, JARGON, VERNACULAR refer to patterns of vocabulary, syntax, and usage characteristic of communities of various sizes and types. LANGUAGE is applied to the general pattern of a people or nation: *the English language.* DIALECT is applied to regionally or socially distinct forms or varieties of a language, often forms used by provincial communities that differ from the standard variety: *the Scottish dialect.* JARGON is applied to the specialized language, esp. the vocabulary, used by a particular (usu. occupational) group within a community or to language considered unintelligible or obscure: *technical jargon.* The VERNACULAR is the natural, everyday pattern of speech, usu. on an informal level, used by people indigenous to a community.

large, *adj.* **1.** big, huge, enormous, immense, gigantic, colossal, massive, vast, great, extensive, broad, sizeable, grand, spacious, ample, mammoth, gargantuan, elephantine, Brobdingnagian, jumbo, *(slang)* mondo. **2.** multitudinous; abundant, copious, ample, liberal, plentiful. —Ant. small, tiny; scanty, sparse, scarce, rare.

last, *adj.* **1.** final, ultimate, latest; concluding, conclusive, utmost, extreme, terminal, hindmost. —*v.* **2.** go on, continue, endure, perpetuate, remain, survive, persist, stay. —Ant. first; fail, die. —**Syn. Study.** See CONTINUE.

late, *adj.* **1.** tardy, slow, dilatory, delayed, belated, overdue, past due. **2.** continued, lasting, protracted. **3.** recent, modern, advanced. **4.** former, past, recent, previous, old, preceding; deceased, departed, dead. —Ant. early, fast.

latent, *adj.* hidden, concealed, covert, veiled; potential. —Ant. kinetic; open.

latitude, *n.* range, scope, extent, liberty, freedom, indulgence. —**Syn. Study.** See RANGE.

laud, *v.* praise, extol, applaud, celebrate, esteem, honor, commend, acclaim, glorify, exalt. —Ant. censure, condemn, criticize.

laugh, *v.* **1.** chortle, cackle, cachinnate, chuckle, hawhaw, guffaw, hoot, roar; giggle, snicker, snigger, titter. —*n.* **2.** chuckle, grin, smile; laughter, cachinnation, horse laugh. —Ant. cry, mourn, wail.

laughable, *adj.* funny, amusing, humorous, droll, comical; ludicrous, ridiculous, risible, absurd, foolish. —Ant. sad, serious.

lavish, *adj.* **1.** unstinted, extravagant, excessive, prodigal, profuse, abundant, liberal, bountiful, effusive, opulent, free, unstinting, openhanded; wasteful, improvident. —*v.* **2.** expend, shower, heap, pour, bestow, endow; waste, dissipate, squander, spend, sink. —Ant. stingy, niggardly; provident;

save. —**Syn. Study.** LAVISH, PRODIGAL, PROFUSE refer to that which exists in abundance and is poured out in great amounts. LAVISH suggests an unlimited, sometimes excessive generosity and openhandedness: *lavish hospitality.* PRODIGAL suggests wastefulness, improvidence, and reckless impatience: *He has lost his inheritance because of his prodigal ways.* PROFUSE emphasizes abundance, but may suggest exaggeration, emotionalism, or the like: *profuse thanks; profuse apologies.*

law, *n.* **1.** rule, regulation, statute, act, measure, ordinance, decree, edict, order, command, directive, injunction, commandment, mandate, canon, ukase. **2.** principle, theory, theorem, axiom, proposition, deduction, formula, corollary, postulate, conclusion, inference.

lawful, *adj.* **1.** legal, legitimate, valid, just, rightful, proper, licit, de jure, constitutional. **2.** sanctioned, allowed, permitted, permissible, justifiable, authorized. —Ant. illegal, illicit, illegitimate; forbidden.

lax, *adj.* **1.** loose, relaxed, slack, casual, easygoing, laid-back. **2.** negligent, careless, remiss, neglectful, heedless, slipshod, slovenly, permissive. —Ant. rigorous, responsible.

lay, *v.* **1.** place, put, deposit, set, locate. **2.** present, offer, submit, set forth, advance, put forward. **3.** wager, bet, stake, risk. **4.** impute, ascribe, attribute, charge. **5.** burden, penalize, assess, impose. —*n.* **6.** position, lie, site. **7.** song, lyric, musical poem, poem, ode, ballad. —*adj.* **8.** secular, unclerical, laic, laical. **9.** unprofessional, amateur, nonspecialist.

lazy, *adj.* idle, indolent, slothful, slow-moving, sluggish, inert, lethargic, shiftless, slack, inactive, torpid, laid-back. —Ant. industrious, quick. —**Syn. Study.** See IDLE.

lead, *v.* **1.** conduct, go before, precede, guide, direct, escort. **2.** guide, influence, induce, persuade, convince, draw, entice, lure, allure, seduce, lead on. **3.** excel, outstrip, surpass, exceed, outrun, outdo. —*n.* **4.** precedence, advance, vanguard, head. **5.** advantage, edge, supremacy, margin, preeminence. **6.** example, model, direction, guidance, pattern, precedent. —Ant. follow.

leading, *adj.* chief, principal, most important, foremost, major, prime, cardinal, paramount, primary; capital, ruling, governing; best, outstanding, preeminent, supreme, peerless, matchless, unrivaled, unequaled. —Ant. secondary, minor.

league, *n.* association, guild, society, band, fellowship, club, covenant, compact, alliance, confederation, combination, coalition, confederacy, union. —**Syn. Study.** See ALLIANCE.

lean, *v.* **1.** incline, slant, tend toward, bend, slope. **2.** repose, rest, rely, depend, trust, confide. —*adj.* **3.** skinny, thin, gaunt, emaciated, slim, slender, spare, wiry, bony, gangling, gangly, scrawny, lanky, lank, meager. **4.** sparse, barren, unfruitful, inadequate, deficient, jejune. —Ant. fat, obese; fertile, fruitful, adequate.

leap, *v., n.* jump, bound, spring, vault, hop, hurdle, skip.

learn, *v.* discover, ascertain, detect, hear, find out, understand, gather, determine, uncover; be taught, master, become proficient, acquire knowledge, memorize, commit to memory, study.

—**Syn. Study.** LEARN, DISCOVER, ASCERTAIN, DETECT imply adding to one's store of knowledge or information. To LEARN is to come to know by chance, or by study or other application: *to learn of a friend's death; to learn to ski.* To DISCOVER is to find out something previously unseen or unknown; it suggests that the new information is surprising to the learner: *I discovered that they were selling their house.* To ASCERTAIN is to find out and verify information through inquiry or analysis: *to ascertain the truth about the incident.* To DETECT is to become aware of something obscure, secret, or concealed: *to detect a flaw in reasoning.*

learning, *n.* erudition, lore, knowledge, scholarship, store of information, education, schooling.

—**Syn. Study.** LEARNING, ERUDITION, SCHOLARSHIP refer to facts or ideas acquired through systematic study. LEARNING usu. refers to knowledge gained from extensive reading and formal instruction: *Her vast learning is reflected in her many books.* ERUDITION suggests a thorough and profound knowledge of a difficult subject: *His erudition in languages is legendary.* SCHOLARSHIP suggests a high degree of mastery in a specialized field, along with an analytical or innovative ability suited to the academic world: *The author is renowned for several works of classical scholarship.*

leave, *v.* **1.** quit, vacate, abandon, forsake, desert, depart from, retire from, withdraw *or* escape from, relinquish, renounce. **2.** desist from, stop, forbear, cease, abandon, let alone. **3.** bequeath, will, devise, transmit. —*n.* **4.** permission, allowance, freedom, liberty, license, consent, authorization, sanction.

—**Ant.** arrive, gain.

legend, *n.* epic, saga, folk tale, romance, narrative, tradition, fiction, fairy tale, tall tale, fantasy, fable, myth, story, fiction.

—**Ant.** fact, history.

—**Syn. Study.** LEGEND, MYTH, FABLE refer to stories handed down from earlier times, often by word of mouth. A LEGEND is a story associated with a people or a nation; it is usu. concerned with a real person, place, or event and is popularly believed to have some basis in fact: *the legend of King Arthur.* A MYTH is one of a class of purportedly historical stories that attempt to explain some belief, practice, or natural phenomenon; the characters are usu. gods or heroes: *the Greek myth about Demeter.* A FABLE is a fictitious story intended to teach a moral lesson; the characters are usu. animals: *the fable about the fox and the grapes.*

legitimate, *adj.* **1.** legal, lawful, licit, statutory, authorized, permitted, sanctioned. **2.** reasonable, logical, sensible, common-sense, valid, warranted, called-for, correct, proper. —*v.* **3.** authorize, justify, legalize, sanction, warrant, validate, certify.

—**Ant.** illegitimate; unreasonable, incorrect, improper.

leisurely, *adj.* deliberate, slow, relaxed, languid, sluggish, lazy, laid-back, unhurried, easygoing.

—**Ant.** quick, hurried, hasty.

—**Syn. Study.** See SLOW.

lengthen, *v.* extend, stretch, prolong, protract, attenuate, elongate, draw out, continue, increase, drag out.

—**Ant.** shorten, abbreviate.

—**Syn. Study.** LENGTHEN, EXTEND,

PROLONG, PROTRACT agree in the idea of making longer. To LENGTHEN is to make longer, either in a material or immaterial sense: *to lengthen a dress; to lengthen human life.* To EXTEND is to lengthen beyond some original point or so as to reach a certain point: *to extend a railway line another fifty miles.* Both PROLONG and PROTRACT mean esp. to lengthen in time. To PROLONG is to continue beyond the desired, estimated, or allotted time: *to prolong an interview.* To PROTRACT is to draw out to undue length or to be slow in coming to a conclusion: *to protract a discussion.*

lenient, *adj.* mild, clement, kind, kindly, sparing, humane, patient, permissive, compassionate, forgiving, easygoing, magnanimous, tolerant, understanding, merciful, easy, gentle, soothing, tender, forbearing, long-suffering.

—**Ant.** harsh, cruel, brutal, merciless.

lessen, *v.* **1.** diminish, decrease, abate, dwindle, fade, shrink. **2.** diminish, decrease, depreciate, disparage, reduce, lower, degrade. **3.** decrease, diminish, abate, abridge, reduce.

—**Ant.** increase; raise; lengthen, enlarge.

let, *v.* **1.** allow, permit, sanction, authorize, license, give leave, enable, suffer, grant. **2.** lease, rent, sublet, hire, charter, contract to.

—**Ant.** prevent, disallow.

—**Syn. Study.** See ALLOW.

level, *adj.* **1.** even, flat, smooth, uniform, plain, flush. **2.** horizontal. **3.** equal, on a par, equivalent. **4.** even, equable, uniform. —*v.* **5.** even, equalize, smooth, flatten. **6.** raze, demolish, destroy.

—**Ant.** uneven; vertical; unequal.

liable, *adj.* **1.** subject, exposed, likely, open, susceptible, disposed, inclined. **2.** obliged, responsible, answerable, accountable, obligated.

—**Ant.** protected, secure.

liberal, *adj.* **1.** progressive, reform. **2.** tolerant, unbigoted, broadminded, impartial, dispassionate, fair, magnanimous, generous, honorable. **3.** generous, bountiful, beneficent, free, charitable, openhanded, munificent; abundant, ample, bounteous, unstinting, lavish, plentiful.

—**Ant.** illiberal; intolerant, prejudiced; stingy, parsimonious, niggardly.

liberate, *v.* set free, release, emancipate, free, disengage, unfetter, manumit, disenthrall, deliver, set loose, loose, let out, discharge.

—**Ant.** imprison, incarcerate; enthrall, enslave.

—**Syn. Study.** See RELEASE.

libertine, *n.* **1.** rake, roué, debauchee, lecher, sensualist, profligate, reprobate, womanizer, adulterer, whoremonger, philanderer, Don Juan, Casanova, lady-killer, old goat, satyr, dirty old man. —*adj.* **2.** amoral, licentious, lascivious, lewd, dissolute, depraved, corrupt, perverted, immoral, sensual, lecherous, prurient, salacious, carnal, bestial.

—**Ant.** prude; puritanical, prim, priggish.

liberty, *n.* freedom, liberation, independence; franchise, authorization, carte blanche, permission, leave, license, privilege, immunity.

lie, *n.* **1.** falsehood, prevarication, mendacity, untruth, fiction, misrepresentation, tall tale, whopper, story, falsification, fib. **2.** place, position, location, lay, site. —*v.* **3.** falsify, fabricate, misrepresent, perjure, invent, tell tales, prevaricate, fib. **4.** recline, be prostrate *or* recumbent.

—**Ant.** truth.

life, *n.* **1.** animation, vigor, vivacity, vitality, sprightliness, verve, dash, élan, brio, effervescence, sparkle, spirit, activity, energy, pep, zing, get-up-and-go. **2.** existence, being, viability, survival.

lifeless, *adj.* **1.** inanimate, unconscious, insensate, inert, unmoving, insensible, dead. **2.** dead, defunct, extinct. **3.** dull, inactive, inert, passive, sluggish, torpid, spiritless; tedious, flat, stale, vapid.

—**Ant.** alive, animate, live, organic; alive, extant; active, animated, spirited.

lift, *v.* raise, elevate, hold up, hoist, heave up; exalt, uplift; cheer up, stimulate, encourage, inspire, inspirit.

—**Ant.** lower; debase; dispirit, depress.

light, *n.* **1.** illumination, radiance, daylight; dawn, sunrise, daybreak. **2.** aspect, viewpoint, point of view, angle, approach. —*adj.* **3.** pale, whitish, blanched. **4.** undemanding, effortless, easy. **5.** shallow, humorous, slight, trivial, trifling, inconsiderable, unsubstantial, flimsy, insubstantial, gossamer, airy, flighty. **6.** airy, sprightly, spry, active, swift, nimble, agile. **7.** carefree, gay, cheery, cheerful, happy, lighthearted. **8.** frivolous, lightheaded, volatile, flighty. —*v.* **9.** alight, get *or* come down, descend, land, disembark. **10.** kindle, set fire to, ignite, set afire.

—**Ant.** darkness, sunset; difficult; deep, considerable, substantial; cheerless, sad; serious; board, embark, mount; quench.

lighten, *v.* **1.** illuminate, brighten, shine, illume. **2.** mitigate, relieve, alleviate, reduce, lessen, disencumber, unburden, ease. **3.** cheer, gladden.

—**Ant.** darken, adumbrate; intensify, aggravate; sadden.

lighthearted, *adj.* carefree, cheerful, buoyant, bright, gay, cheery, joyous, joyful, blithe, glad, happy, merry, jovial.

—**Ant.** heavy-hearted, cheerless, morose, sad, gloomy, melancholy.

like, *v.* **1.** value, esteem, enjoy, cherish, admire, respect, treasure, prize, appreciate, delight in, take pleasure in, be fond of, approve of, have a fondness *or* soft spot for, be partial to, take to, attracted to, relish, love, adore, worship, go for, prefer, have a penchant *or* predilection for, be sweet on, get a kick *or* charge *or* bang out of, take a shine to, dig, fancy. —*adv.* **2.** similar, comparable, equivalent, equal, identical, analogous, parallel, corresponding, homologous, of a piece, much the same as, along the same lines.

—**Ant.** despise, dislike; different, dissimilar.

likely, *adj.* apt, liable, probable, possible, suitable, appropriate.

—**Ant.** unlikely, improbable; unseemly, improper.

likeness, *n.* **1.** resemblance, similarity, agreement, correspondence, analogy, parallelism, equivalence, congruity, accord, conformity, coincidence, comparison, match, sameness. **2.** copy, replica, duplicate, reproduction, model, facsimile, representation, portrait, image.

—**Ant.** difference.

liking, *n.* preference, inclination, favor, disposition, bent, bias, leaning, propensity, capacity, proclivity, proneness, predilection, predisposition, tendency; partiality, fondness, affection, affinity, penchant.

—**Ant.** dislike, disfavor, disinclination.

limber, *adj.* pliant, flexible, supple,

pliable, lithe, springy, resilient, nimble, lissome, athletic.

—**Ant.** rigid, unbending, unyielding.

limelight, *n.* public eye *or* notice, cynosure, fame, celebrity, renown, stardom, glory, prominence, eminence, notoriety, publicity, réclame, acclaim, repute.

—**Ant.** reclusiveness, seclusion.

limit, *n.* **1.** bound, extent, boundary, confine, edge, perimeter, frontier, termination. **2.** restraint, restriction, constraint, check, hindrance. —*v.* **3.** restrain, restrict, confine, check, hinder, bound, circumscribe, narrow, curb, bridle.

linger, *v.* remain, stay on, persist, endure, hang around, pause, lag, idle, tarry, delay, dawdle, loiter.

link, *n.* **1.** bond, tie, connection, connective, copula, vinculum. —*v.* **2.** bond, join, unite, connect, league, conjoin, fasten, pin, bind, tie, couple, associate, relate.

—**Ant.** separation; separate, split, rive.

list, *n.* **1.** catalog, inventory, roll, roster, directory, index, record, laundry list, shopping list, schedule, series, register. **2.** leaning, tilt, tilting, careening. —*v.* **3.** register, catalogue, enlist, enroll, record, index, note, itemize, enumerate, tabulate, chronicle, book, enter, schedule. **4.** careen, incline, lean.

—**Syn. Study.** LIST, CATALOG, INVENTORY, ROLL imply a meaningful arrangement of items. LIST denotes a series of names, figures, or other items arranged in a row or rows: *a grocery list.* CATALOG adds the idea of an alphabetical or other orderly arranged list of goods or services, usu. with descriptive details: *a mail-order catalog.* INVENTORY refers to a detailed, descriptive list of goods or property, made for legal or business purposes: *The company's inventory consists of 2,000 items.* A ROLL is a list of names of members of a group, often used to check attendance: *The teacher called the roll.*

listen, *v.* hearken, hear, hark, attend, give ear, lend an ear, obey, heed, mind.

listless, *adj.* lethargic, weary, weak, enervated, tired, languid, lifeless, phlegmatic, inert, passive, impassive; unenthusiastic, indifferent, apathetic, insouciant, uncaring, inattentive, heedless.

—**Ant.** energetic, dynamic, active, lively; enthusiastic, eager.

litter, *n.* **1.** rubbish, debris, refuse, waste, trash, junk, fragments. **2.** untidiness, disorder, confusion, clutter, mess, disarray. —*v.* **3.** strew, scatter, mess up.

little, *adj.* **1.** small, diminutive, miniature, baby, petite, minuscule, Lilliputian, teeny-weeny, itsy-bitsy, minute, tiny, infinitesimal, wee. **2.** short, brief. **3.** weak, feeble, slight, inconsiderable, trivial, paltry, insignificant, unimportant, petty, scanty. **4.** mean, narrow, illiberal, paltry, stingy, selfish, small, niggardly. —*adv.* **5.** slightly, barely, just, hardly, scarcely.

—**Ant.** large, immense, huge; important; liberal, generous.

livelihood, *n.* maintenance, living, sustenance, support, subsistence, survival, keep, upkeep, daily bread.

lively, *adj.* **1.** energetic, active, vigorous, brisk, spry, frisky, perky, bouncy, peppy, vivacious, alert, nimble, agile, quick. **2.** animated, spirited, vivacious, bubbly, effervescent, sprightly, gay, blithe, blithesome, buoyant, gleeful. **3.** eventful, stirring, moving. **4.** strong, keen, distinct, vigorous, forceful, clear, piquant. **5.** striking, telling, effective.

6. vivid, bright, brilliant, fresh, clear, glowing, sparkling.
—**Ant.** inactive, torpid; leaden; uneventful; weak, dull, unclear; ineffective; dim, stale.

living, *adj.* **1.** alive, live, quick, existing; extant, surviving. **2.** active, lively, strong, vigorous, quickening. —*n.* **3.** livelihood, maintenance, sustenance, subsistence, support, upkeep, keep.
—**Ant.** dead.

load, *n.* **1.** burden, onus, weight, encumbrance, incubus, pressure. —*v.* **2.** weight, weigh down, burden, encumber, freight, oppress, saddle with, overwhelm.
—**Ant.** unload, lighten, disencumber.

loath, *adj.* reluctant, averse, unwilling, disinclined, indisposed; hesitant, wary, leery, cautious, chary, careful.
—**Ant.** eager, anxious, willing.
—**Syn. Study.** See RELUCTANT.

loathe, *v.* abominate, detest, hate, abhor, despise, execrate.
—**Ant.** adore, love.

loathing, *n.* disgust, dislike, aversion, abhorrence, hatred, hate, antipathy; animus, animosity, hostility.
—**Ant.** liking, love; friendship, regard.

loathsome, *adj.* disgusting, nauseating, sickening, repulsive, offensive, repellent, revolting, detestable, abhorrent, hateful, odious, despicable, abominable, execrable, contemptible, nasty, vile.
—**Ant.** attractive, delightful, lovable.

locale, *n.* place, location, site, spot, locality, setting, venue.

lodge, *n.* **1.** shelter, habitation, cabin, hut, cottage. **2.** club, association, society. —*v.* **3.** shelter, harbor, house, quarter, accommodate, board, put up, billet. **4.** place, put, set, plant, infix, deposit, lay, settle.

lofty, *adj.* **1.** high, elevated, towering, tall. **2.** exalted, elevated, majestic, noble, regal, imposing, august, stately, sublime. **3.** haughty, proud, arrogant, prideful.
—**Ant.** lowly; debased; humble.

loiter, *v.* linger, dally, dawdle, idle, loaf, delay, tarry, lag, lounge about, laze, lollygag.
—**Syn. Study.** LOITER, DALLY, DAWDLE, IDLE imply moving or acting slowly, stopping for unimportant reasons, and in general wasting time. To LOITER is to linger aimlessly: *to loiter outside a building.* To DALLY is to loiter indecisively or to delay as if free from care or responsibility: *to dally on the way home.* To DAWDLE is to saunter, stopping often, and taking a great deal of time, or to fritter away time working in a halfhearted way: *to dawdle over a task.* To IDLE is to move slowly and aimlessly, or to spend a great deal of time doing nothing: *to idle away the hours.*

lone, *adj.* **1.** alone, unaccompanied, solitary, lonely, secluded, apart, separate, separated; deserted, uninhabited, unoccupied, unpopulated, empty. **2.** isolated, solitary, sole, unique, lonely.
—**Ant.** accompanied, together; inhabited, occupied.

lonely, *adj.* lone, solitary, lonesome; sequestered, remote, dreary,.
—**Ant.** crowded, populous.

lonesome, *adj.* lonely, alone, secluded; desolate, isolated.

long, *adj.* **1.** lengthy, extensive, drawn out, attenuated, protracted, stretched, prolonged, extended. **2.** overlong, long-winded, tedious, boring, wordy, prolix. —*v.* **3.** crave, desire, yearn for, pine for, hanker for *or* after, wish, want, hunger.
—**Ant.** short, abbreviated; interesting; forgo.
—**Syn. Study.** See YEARN.

longing, *n.* craving, desire, hankering, yearning, aspiration, wish, hunger, lust.
—**Ant.** disinterest, apathy; satisfaction.

look, *v.* **1.** see, observe, consider, contemplate, view, regard, survey, scan, study, examine, read, inspect, scrutinize, notice, watch, witness, check out, stare, gaze, glance. —*n.* **2.** appearance, manner, looks, air, aspect, demeanor, behavior, mien, expression, face, countenance.
—**Syn. Study.** See SEEM.

loose, *adj.* **1.** free, unfettered, unbound, untied, unrestrained, unrestricted, released, unattached, unfastened, unconfined. **2.** disordered, unbound, disorganized, messy, scattered, uncombined. **3.** lax, slack, careless, negligent, heedless. **4.** wanton, libertine, unchaste, immoral, dissolute, licentious, debauched, abandoned, fast, profligate. **5.** general, vague, indefinite, inexact, imprecise, ill-defined, indeterminate, broad, nonspecific, indistinct. —*v.* **6.** loosen, free, set free, unfasten, undo, unlock, unbind, untie, unloose, release, liberate. **7.** relax, slacken, ease, loosen.
—**Ant.** bound, fettered; combined; tight, taut; moral, chaste; definite, specific; bind, commit; tighten.

loot, *n.* **1.** spoils, plunder, booty, prize, haul, boodle, swag. —*v.* **2.** plunder, rob, sack, rifle, raid, despoil, ransack, pillage, rape, ravage.

lordly, *adj.* **1.** grand, magnificent, majestic, royal, regal, kingly, aristocratic, dignified, noble, lofty. **2.** haughty, arrogant, lofty, imperious, domineering, overbearing, despotic, dictatorial, tyrannical.
—**Ant.** menial, servile; humble, obedient.

lore, *n.* **1.** learning, knowledge, erudition, culture, tradition, mythos, ethos. **2.** wisdom, counsel, advice, teaching, doctrine, lesson.

loss, *n.* **1.** detriment, disadvantage, damage, injury, harm, hurt, destruction. **2.** privation, deprivation, denial, sacrifice, forfeiture, bereavement.
—**Ant.** gain.

lost, *adj.* **1.** forfeited, vanished, gone, missing, missed. **2.** bewildered, nonplussed, asea, confused, perplexed, puzzled. **3.** wasted, misspent, squandered, dissipated. **4.** defeated, vanquished. **5.** destroyed, ruined, wrecked, demolished, devastated. **6.** depraved, abandoned, dissolute, corrupt, reprobate, profligate, licentious, shameless, hardened, irredeemable.
—**Ant.** found; pure, honorable, chaste.

loud, *adj.* **1.** earsplitting, blaring, thunderous, sonorous, fortissimo, noisy, clamorous, resounding, deafening, stentorian, boisterous. **2.** gaudy, flashy, showy, vulgar, blatant, tawdry, garish, tasteless, ostentatious, extravagant, splashy, glitzy.
—**Ant.** soft, quiet; sedate, tasteful.

loutish, *adj.* boorish, unrefined, uncouth, ill-bred, rough, oafish, cloddish, clumsy, crass, churlish, coarse, crude, brutish, beastly.
—**Ant.** refined, gracious, graceful.

love, *n.* **1.** affection, predilection, liking, inclination, regard, friendliness, kindness, tenderness, fondness, devotion, warmth, attachment, attraction, admiration, adulation, ardor, fervor, infatuation, crush, passion, adoration. —*v.* **2.** like, delight in, enjoy, relish, take pleasure in, be partial to, appreciate, value, have a taste *or* appetite *or* passion for, prefer, be taken with, get a kick *or* bang *or* charge out of, dig. **3.** have affection for, be enamored of, be in love with, adore, adulate, worship, lose one's heart to, idolize, dote on, cherish, admire, treasure, esteem, be infatuated with, be sweet on, hold dear, think the world of, be hung up on, have a crush on, be crazy *or* nuts *or* mad *or* wild about, be attracted to, be stuck on.
—**Ant.** hatred, dislike; detest, abhor, abominate, hate.

lovely, *adj.* beautiful, good-looking, pretty, handsome, attractive, comely, fair, fetching, engaging, captivating, alluring, bewitching, gorgeous, ravishing, pulchritudinous.
—**Ant.** ugly, unattractive, homely.
—**Syn. Study.** See BEAUTIFUL.

low, *adj.* **1.** short, squat, little, small, stubby, stunted. **2.** limited, sparse, scanty, inadequate, deficient. **3.** feeble, weak, exhausted, sinking, dying, expiring. **4.** depressed, dejected, dispirited, unhappy, sad, miserable. **5.** undignified, infra dig, lowly, dishonorable, disreputable, unbecoming, disgraceful. **6.** groveling, abject, sordid, mean, base, lowly, degraded, menial, servile, ignoble, vile. **7.** humble, lowly, meek, lowborn, poor, plain, plebeian, vulgar, base. **8.** coarse, vulgar, rude, crude. **9.** hushed, muted, muffled, indistinct, whispered, soft, subdued, gentle, quiet.
—**Ant.** high, upright.
—**Syn. Study.** See MEAN.

lower, *v.* **1.** reduce, decrease, diminish, lessen. **2.** soften, modulate, turn down, quiet down. **3.** degrade, humble, abase, humiliate, disgrace, debase. **4.** let down, drop, depress, take down, sink. **5.** darken, loom, menace, threaten; glower, frown, scowl.
—**Ant.** raise, increase; elevate, honor; brighten.

loyal, *adj.* faithful, true, patriotic, devoted, constant, dependable, trustworthy, steadfast, staunch, stable, reliable, dedicated, unswerving, unwavering, true-blue.
—**Ant.** faithless, disloyal, treacherous.
—**Syn. Study.** See FAITHFUL.

loyalty, *n.* faithfulness, allegiance, fealty, devotion, constancy, patriotism, fidelity, dependability.

lucid, *adj.* **1.** shining, bright, lucent, radiant, brilliant, resplendent, luminous. **2.** clear, transparent, pellucid, limpid, crystalline; intelligible, plain, unmistakable, obvious, distinct, evident, understandable; rational, sane, sober, sound, reasonable.
—**Ant.** dull; unclear, dull; unreasonable.

lucky, *adj.* fortunate, fortuitous, happy, favored, charmed, blessed; providential, timely, opportune, auspicious, propitious, favorable.
—**Ant.** unfortunate, unlucky.

ludicrous, *adj.* laughable, ridiculous, amusing, comical, funny, facetious, waggish, jocular, jocose, witty, droll; absurd, farcical, asinine, foolish, silly, zany, risible.
—**Ant.** miserable, serious, tragic.

lukewarm, *adj.* **1.** tepid, warmish, moderately warm, room-temperature. **2.** halfhearted, unenthusiastic, so-so, unimpassioned, apathetic, unresponsive, unmoved, indifferent, laodicean.
—**Ant.** dedicated, enthusiastic.

luminous, *adj.* **1.** bright, shining, luminescent, glowing, lucid, lucent, radiant, brilliant, lustrous, gleaming, shimmering, dazzling, sparkling, effulgent, resplendent. **2.** lighted, lit, illuminated. **3.** brilliant, bright, intelligent, smart, clever, enlightening. **4.** clear, intelligible, understandable, perspicacious, plain, lucid.
—**Ant.** dull; dark; stupid; unclear, unintelligible.

lunacy, *n.* **1.** madness, craziness, insanity, derangement, mental disorder, psychosis, mania, dementia, dementedness. **2.** folly, foolishness, foolhardiness, absurdity, silliness, irrationality.
—**Ant.** sanity, normalcy, sobriety.

lure, *n.* **1.** enticement, decoy, attraction, allurement, temptation, inducement, magnet, siren song, charm, come-on, bait. —*v.* **2.** allure, decoy, entice, draw, attract, tempt, seduce.

lurid, *adj.* **1.** vivid, glaring, sensational, shocking, melodramatic, graphic; gory, grisly, gruesome, macabre, appalling, shining, fiery, red, intense, fierce, terrible, unrestrained, passionate. **2.** wan, pale, pallid, sallow, ghastly; gloomy, murky, dismal, lowering.
—**Ant.** mild, controlled; cheery.

lurk, *v.* skulk, sneak, prowl, slink, steal; lie in wait, lie in ambush, lie hidden *or* concealed, hide.
—**Syn. Study.** LURK, SKULK, SNEAK, PROWL suggest avoiding observation, often because of a sinister purpose. To LURK is to lie in wait for someone or to move stealthily: *The thief lurked in the shadows.* SKULK has a similar sense, but usu. suggests cowardice or fear: *The dog skulked about the house.* SNEAK emphasizes the attempt to avoid being seen or discovered; it suggests a sinister intent or the desire to avoid punishment: *The children sneaked out the back way.* PROWL usu. implies seeking prey or loot; it suggests quiet and watchful roaming: *The cat prowled around in search of mice.*

luscious, *adj.* delicious, juicy, delectable, palatable, savory, mouthwatering, tasty, appetizing, ambrosial, succulent, scrumptious, yummy.
—**Ant.** unpalatable, disgusting.

lush, *adj.* tender, juicy, succulent, luxuriant, fresh, luxurious, sumptuous, opulent, rich.
—**Ant.** dry, tasteless; stringent, Spartan.

lust, *n.* **1.** desire, passion, appetite, craving, eagerness, cupidity. **2.** libido, libinousness, sex drive, horniness, desire, randiness, sexuality, sensuality, wantonness, sexual appetite, lechery, concupiscence, carnality, lubricity, salaciousness, licentiousness, lasciviousness, libertinism. —*v.* **3.** crave, desire, need, want, demand, hunger for, ache.

luster, *n.* **1.** gleam, glow, luminosity, radiance, effulgence, brilliance, shine, shimmer, sparkle, glitter, glisten, sheen, gloss. **2.** brilliance, brightness, radiance, luminosity, resplendence. **3.** illustriousness, glory, repute, renown, eminence, celebrity, dash, élan.
—**Ant.** dullness, tarnish; disrepute, dishonor.

lusty, *adj.* **1.** hearty, vigorous, strong, healthy, robust, energetic, lively, sturdy, stout. **2.** lecherous, amorous, libidinous, sexual, sensual, carnal, concupiscent, randy, horny, on the make.
—**Ant.** weak, frail, unhealthy.

luxurious, *adj.* **1.** splendid, grand, extravagant, magnificent, lavish, deluxe, fancy, elegant, palatial, royal, rich, sumptuous, ornate, opulent, well-appointed, swanky, ritzy, posh,

plush. **2.** voluptuous, sensual, self-indulgent, epicurean, sybaritic, hedonistic.
—**Ant.** poor, squalid. mean, Spartan.

lyrical, *adj.* melodic, musical, sweet, mellow, lilting, airy, graceful, lighthearted, buoyant, sunny; exuberant, rhapsodic, ecstatic, rapturous.
—**Ant.** sorrowful, elegiac.

M

macabre, *adj.* gruesome, horrible, grim, ghastly, morbid, weird, grisly, gory, ghoulish, dreadful, eerie, frightful, dire, terrifying, terrible, fearsome; deathly, cadaverous.
—**Ant.** delightful.

machination, *n.* manipulation, maneuver, stratagem, ploy, artifice, tactic, wile, device, trick, plot, cabal, intrigue, scheme, conspiracy, ruse, move, gambit.

machismo, *n.* manliness, virility, potency, boldness, courageousness, dominance, prepotency, primacy, arrogance, braggadocio, swagger, cockiness.

mad, *adj.* **1.** insane, lunatic, deranged, raving, distracted, crazy, crazed, maniacal, demented, unhinged, delirious, out of one's mind, psychotic, *non compos mentis,* of unsound mind, mentally unbalanced, mentally ill, touched, screwy, cuckoo, certifiable, not all there, cracked, nutty, nuts, loony, loopy, batty, loco, wacky, meshuga, off one's rocker, bananas, crazy as a bedbug *or* coot, crackers, bonkers. **2.** furious, exasperated, angry, enraged, raging, incensed, provoked, wrathful, irate, infuriated, fuming, berserk, irritated, exasperated. **3.** excited, frantic, frenzied, wild, rabid, ferocious. **4.** violent, furious, stormy. **5.** senseless, foolish, imprudent, impractical, ill-advised, excessive, reckless, unsound, unsafe, harmful, dangerous, perilous, unwise, rash, ill-considered, foolhardy. **6.** silly, childish, immature, puerile, nonsensical, madcap, heedless, absurd, indiscreet, extravagant, irrational, fatuous. **7.** infatuated, wild about, desirous, ardent, passionate, enthusiastic, eager, avid, zealous, fervent, fervid, fanatical, keen, hooked.
—**Ant.** sane; calm; serene; sensible, wise.

madden, *v.* infuriate, irritate, provoke, vex, annoy, enrage, anger, inflame, exasperate, incense, irk, pique; torment, plague, bedevil, rile, hassle.
—**Ant.** calm, mollify.

magic, *n.* enchantment, sorcery, necromancy, occultism, mysticism, spell, shamanism, wizardry, voodoo, vodun, conjuration, divination, black art, deviltry, thaumaturgy, miracle working, witchcraft; legerdemain, conjuring, sleight of hand, prestidigitation, hocus-pocus.

magician, *n.* sorcerer, necromancer, enchanter, conjuror, illusionist, wizard, magus, Merlin, Circe, Houdini, witch, warlock, thaumaturge, miracle worker, shaman.

magisterial, *adj.* **1.** dictatorial, dominating, dogmatic, doctrinaire, imperious, authoritarian, lordly. **2.** masterful, masterly, authoritative, commanding, expert.

magnificence, *n.* splendor, grandeur, impressiveness, sumptuousness, pomp, state, majesty, luxury, luxuriousness, éclat, brilliance, nobility, opulence, elegance, lavishness, augustness, sublimity, superiority, distinction.
—**Ant.** squalor, meanness.

magnificent, *adj.* **1.** splendid, fine, superb, august, stately, majestic, imposing, sumptuous, rich, royal, resplendent, opulent, lavish, luxurious, grand, gorgeous, beautiful, princely, impressive, glorious, awe-inspiring, commanding, dazzling, brilliant, radiant, excellent, exquisite, elegant, superior, extraordinary; showy, pretentious, flamboyant, flashy, ostentatious. **2.** noble, sublime, dignified, great, regal, distinguished, exalted, awesome.
—**Ant.** squalid, poor; base.

magnify, *v.* **1.** enlarge, augment, increase, add to, amplify, expand, inflate, heighten, boost, exacerbate, aggravate. **2.** exaggerate, overstate, dramatize, make a mountain out of a molehill, embellish, elaborate, stretch, embroider, lay it on thick.
—**Ant.** decrease, understate.

maim, *v.* mutilate, cripple, lacerate, mangle, injure, disable, lame, incapacitate, put out of commission, wound, deface, mar, impair, injure, damage.

main, *adj.* **1.** chief, cardinal, prime, paramount, primary, principal, first, foremost, preeminent, predominant, major, leading, capital. **2.** pure, sheer, utmost, direct, brute, utter, out-and-out, absolute, mere, plain.
—**Ant.** secondary, unimportant.

mainstay, *n.* support, backbone, spine, sine qua non, supporter, anchor, bulwark, buttress, linchpin, backer, champion, upholder, sustainer, pillar, brace, standby, prop, crutch.

maintain, *v.* **1.** keep, continue, preserve, retain, keep up, uphold, persevere, perpetuate, prolong, sustain, support. **2.** affirm, assert, aver, state, hold, allege, declare. **3.** contend, hold, claim, defend, vindicate, justify, advocate, champion, plead for, back, make a case for. **4.** provide for, support, sustain, keep up, nurture.
—**Ant.** discontinue.

maintenance, *n.* upkeep, care, preservation, conservation, support; subsistence, livelihood, living, allowance, sustenance, stipend, contribution, keep, daily bread.
—**Ant.** desuetude.

majestic, *adj.* regal, royal, princely, kingly, queenly, elevated, exalted, glorious, monumental, imperial, noble, lofty, stately, grand, august, dignified, imposing.
—**Ant.** base, squalid, unprepossessing, plebeian.

major, *adj.* greater, larger, capital, main, chief, important; vital, critical, crucial, principal, foremost, paramount, primary, prime, significant, outstanding.
—**Ant.** minor.
—**Syn. Study.** See CAPITAL.

make, *v.* **1.** form, build, assemble, produce, fabricate, create, contrive, design, construct, manufacture, fashion, mold, shape. **2.** cause, render, generate, create, produce. **3.** transform, convert, change, turn, alter, modify, metamorphose, transmute. **4.** give rise to, prompt, occasion. **5.** get, gain, acquire, obtain, secure, procure, earn, win. **6.** do, effect, bring about, perform, execute, accomplish, practice, act. **7.** cause, require, oblige, persuade, coerce, provoke, order, induce, compel, force. —*n.* **8.** style, form, build, shape, brand, kind, sort, type, trade name, construction, structure, constitution.
—**Ant.** destroy.

makeshift, *adj.* improvised, stopgap, provisional, expedient, tentative, standby, slapdash, surrogate, stand-in, temporary, substitute, reserve, spare, make-do, jerry-built.

malady, *n.* disease, illness, sickness, affliction, disorder, complaint, ailment, indisposition.

male, *adj.* masculine, manly, virile, manful, macho.
—**Ant.** female.
—**Syn. Study.** MALE, MASCULINE, VIRILE describe men and boys or whatever is culturally attributed to them. MALE classifies individuals on the basis of their genetic makeup or their ability to fertilize an ovum in bisexual reproduction. It contrasts with FEMALE in all uses: *his oldest male relative; the male parts of the flower.* MASCULINE refers to qualities or behavior deemed especially appropriate to or ideally associated with men and boys. In American and western European culture, this has traditionally included such traits as strength, aggressiveness, and courage: *a firm, masculine handshake; masculine impatience at indecision.* VIRILE implies the muscularity, vigor, and sexual potency of mature manhood: *a swaggering, virile walk.* See also MANLY.

malevolence, *n.* ill will, rancor, malignity, resentment, malice, maliciousness, spite, spitefulness, odium, hostility, meanness, evil, animosity, animus, bitterness, vindictiveness, treachery, deceit, grudge, hate, hatred, venom.
—**Ant.** benevolence, good will.

malevolent, *adj.* malicious, malignant, resentful, spiteful, begrudging, hateful, venomous, vicious, hostile, ill-natured, evil-minded, insidious, iniquitous, mean.
—**Ant.** benevolent, friendly, amiable.

malice, *n.* evil, cruelty, villainy, hostility, wickedness, beastliness, vileness, perversity, ill will, spite, spitefulness, animosity, animus, enmity, malevolence, grudge, venom, hate, hatred, bitterness, rancor.
—**Ant.** good will, benevolence.

malign, *v.* **1.** slander, libel, revile, abuse, slur, smear, decry, calumniate, defame, disparage, vilify, criticize, belittle, depreciate, denigrate, insult, derogate. —*adj.* **2.** evil, pernicious, baleful, injurious, unfavorable, baneful, malevolent.
—**Ant.** compliment, praise; good, favorable, benevolent.

malignant, *adj.* **1.** malicious, spiteful, malevolent, rancorous, bitter, malign, evil, vicious, invidious. **2.** dangerous, perilous, harmful, hurtful, virulent, pernicious, lethal, deadly, fatal.
—**Ant.** benevolent; benign.

malinger, *v.* shirk, slack, slack off, dodge, duck duty, get out of, goldbrick, goof off, loaf, vegetate.

malleable, *adj.* adaptable, plastic, bendable, ductile, moldable, pliant, pliable, supple, flexile, elastic, compliant.
—**Ant.** rigid, refractory.

maltreat, *v.* mistreat, abuse, injure, ill-treat, ill-use, misuse, damage.

manage, *v.* **1.** bring about, succeed, accomplish, arrange, contrive. **2.** conduct, handle, direct, govern, control, guide, regulate, engineer, rule, administer, supervise, superintend, micromanage. **3.** handle, wield, manipulate, control. **4.** dominate, influence; train, educate, handle.
—**Ant.** mismanage, bungle.

management, *n.* handling, direction, control, regulation, conduct, charge, supervision, manipulation, government, governance, stewardship, command, administration, superintendence, care, guidance, disposal, treatment, oversight, surveillance.
—**Ant.** mismanagement.

manager, *n.* administrator, executive, superintendent, supervisor, boss, director, overseer, governor, head, proprietor, chief.

mandate, *n.* command, order, fiat, decree, ukase, injunction, edict, ruling, commission.

maneuver, *n.* **1.** procedure, move; scheme, tactic, gambit, ploy, subterfuge, wile, machination, intrigue, plot, plan, design, stratagem, ruse, artifice, trick. —*v.* **2.** manipulate, handle, intrigue, trick, scheme, plot, plan, design, finesse, contrive, machinate, engineer.

mangle, *v.* cut, lacerate, crush, slash; disfigure, maim, ruin, spoil, butcher, deform, wreck, mar, deface, mutilate, destroy.

mania, *n.* **1.** excitement, enthusiasm, craze, fad, rage, passion. **2.** insanity, madness, aberration, derangement, dementia, frenzy, lunacy.
—**Ant.** phobia; rationality.

manifest, *adj.* **1.** evident, obvious, apparent, plain, clear, distinct, blatant, explicit, discernible, patent, open, palpable, visible, unmistakable, conspicuous. —*v.* **2.** show, display, reveal, disclose, exhibit, evidence, appear, present, indicate, betray, demonstrate, declare, express, make known.
—**Ant.** latent, hidden, inconspicuous; conceal.
—**Syn. Study.** See DISPLAY.

manifold, *adj.* **1.** various, many, numerous, multitudinous. **2.** varied, various, multifarious, multifaceted, diverse, diversified, assorted, miscellaneous, sundry.
—**Ant.** simple, singular.
—**Syn. Study.** See MANY.

manly, *adj.* **1.** manful, mannish, masculine, male, virile. **2.** strong, brave, honorable, courageous, bold, valiant, intrepid, undaunted, brave, valorous, plucky, daring, dauntless, fearless.
—**Ant.** feminine; weak, cowardly.
—**Syn. Study.** MANLY, MANFUL, MANNISH mean having traits or qualities considered typical of or appropriate to adult males. MANLY, a term of approval, suggests such admirable traits as maturity and steadiness: *a manly acceptance of responsibility.* MANFUL, also an approving term, stresses such qualities as courage and strength: *a manful effort to overcome great odds.* MANNISH is most often used, esp. derogatorily, in referring to the qualities or accouterments of a woman considered more appropriate to a man: *the mannish abruptness of her speech; She wore a severely mannish suit.* See also MALE.

manner, *n.* **1.** mode, fashion, style, way, habit, custom, method, technique, procedure, means, form. **2.** demeanor, deportment, bearing, behavior, carriage, conduct, comportment, attitude, mien, aspect, look, appearance. **3.** kind, sort.

manufacture, *v.* assemble, fabricate, make, construct, build, compose, create, produce, originate.
—**Ant.** destroy.

many, *adj.* numerous, multifarious, abundant, myriad, innumerable, manifold, sundry, various, varied, multitudinous.
—**Ant.** few.
—**Syn. Study.** MANY, NUMEROUS, INNUMERABLE, MANIFOLD imply the presence of a large number of units. MANY is a general word that refers

to a large but indefinite number of units or individuals: *many years ago; many friends and supporters.* NUMEROUS, a more formal word, stresses the individual and separate quality of the units: *to receive numerous letters.* INNUMERABLE denotes a number that is too large to be counted or, more loosely, that is very difficult to count: *the innumerable stars.* MANIFOLD implies that the number is large, but also varied or complex: *manifold responsibilities.*

mar, *v.* damage, impair, ruin, spoil, injure, blot, deface, disfigure, mutilate, scar, harm, hurt, deform, maim.

margin, *n.* border, edge, rim, limit, confine, bound, marge, verge, brink, perimeter, periphery, boundary, frontier.
—**Ant.** center.

mark, *n.* **1.** spot, blemish, stain, smudge, nick, scratch, splotch, trace, impression, line, cut, dent, bruise. **2.** badge, brand, sign, symbol, token, insigne, stamp, characteristic, hallmark, label, feature, attribute, trait, quality, property. **3.** note, importance, distinction, eminence, consequence. —*v.* **4.** label, tag. **5.** signify, specify, distinguish, indicate, designate, point out, brand, identify, imprint, impress, characterize. **6.** note, pay attention to, heed, notice, observe, regard, eye, spot, watch, see; mind, obey.

marriage, *n.* **1.** wedding, nuptials; wedlock, matrimony. **2.** union, alliance, association, confederation, affiliation, connection, coupling, merger, amalgamation.
—**Ant.** divorce; separation.

marshal, *v.* arrange, array, order, rank, dispose; gather, convoke.
—**Syn. Study.** See GATHER.

marvelous, *adj.* wonderful, wondrous, extraordinary, amazing, astonishing, astounding, miraculous, splendid, superb, glorious, spectacular, improbable, incredible, unbelievable, surprising, terrific, fantastic, fabulous, smashing, out of this world.
—**Ant.** terrible, ordinary, commonplace.

mask, *n.* **1.** face covering, veil, false face. **2.** disguise, concealment, pretense, guise, camouflage, show, semblance, coverup, cloak, veil; pretext, ruse, trick, subterfuge, evasion. —*v.* **3.** disguise, conceal, hide, veil, screen, cloak, shroud, cover.

mass, *n.* **1.** mountain, load, stack, mound, bunch, bundle, lot, batch, hoard, store, assortment, multitude, horde, host, crowd, throng, drove, swarm, aggregate, aggregation, assemblage, heap, congeries, collection, accumulation, conglomeration, pile, quantity. **2.** main body, bulk, majority. **3.** size, bulk, massiveness, magnitude, dimension. —*v.* **4.** assemble; collect, gather, marshal, amass, convoke; heap *or* pile up, aggregate.

massacre, *n.* **1.** killing, slaughter, carnage, extermination, annihilation, butchery, murder, genocide, blood bath, mass murder. —*v.* **2.** kill, butcher, slaughter, murder, slay, decimate, mow down.
—**Syn. Study.** See SLAUGHTER.

massive, *adj.* **1.** bulky, heavy, large, immense, huge, tremendous, hulking, mammoth, prodigious, colossal, oversized, enormous, gigantic, towering, vast, titanic, mighty, weighty, whopping, elephantine, humongous. **2.** solid, substantial, great, imposing, ponderous.
—**Ant.** diminutive; flimsy.

master, *n.* **1.** adept, expert, maestro, maven, past master, old hand, professional, pro, ace, virtuoso, cracker

jack. **2.** owner, head, leader, chief, commander, lord, governor, director, employer, boss, overseer, supervisor, taskmaster, ruler, slave driver, high muck-a-muck, kingpin, skipper, Pooh-Bah, the man, big wheel, big cheese, head honcho, big enchilada. **3.** teacher, instructor, guide, leader, tutor, mentor, guru, swami. —*adj.* **4.** chief, principal, head, leading, cardinal, primary, prime, main. **5.** dominating, predominant. **6.** skilled, adept, expert, skillful. —*v.* **7.** conquer, subdue, subject, subjugate, overcome, overpower. **8.** rule, direct, govern, manage, superintend, oversee.

matchless, *adj.* peerless, unrivaled, unequaled, inimitable, unparalleled, incomparable, unmatched, consummate.
—**Ant.** unimportant, unimpressive.

material, *n.* **1.** substance, matter, stuff, fabric. **2.** element, component, constituent. —*adj.* **3.** tangible, concrete, solid, real, substantive, substantial, palpable, physical, corporeal. **4.** important, essential, vital, consequent, momentous.
—**Ant.** spiritual; immaterial.

matter, *n.* **1.** substance, material, stuff. **2.** situation, issue, question, concern, thing, affair, business, question, subject, topic. **3.** consequence, importance, import, significance, moment. **4.** trouble, difficulty, problem. **5.** ground, reason, cause. —*v.* **6.** signify, be of importance, count, make a difference, be of consequence.
—**Ant.** insignificance; ease.

mature, *adj.* **1.** ripe, aged, complete, grown, adult, full-grown, fully-developed, maturated. **2.** developed, consummated, completed, perfected, elaborated, ready. —*v.* **3.** ripen, age, develop, mellow, season. **4.** perfect, complete.
—**Ant.** immature, childish, adolescent.

maxim, *n.* proverb, aphorism, saying, adage, apothegm, axiom, byword, saw, epigram, motto, slogan, witticism, truism, catchphrase.
—**Syn. Study.** See PROVERB.

meager, *adj.* scanty, paltry, skimpy, spare, puny, trifling, deficient, sparse, mean, insignificant; thin, lean, emaciated, spare, gaunt, skinny, lank, scrawny.
—**Ant.** abundant.
—**Syn. Study.** See SCANTY.

mean, *v.* **1.** plan, intend, purpose, contemplate, destine, foreordain, predestinate, design. **2.** signify, indicate, denote, imply, express. —*adj.* **3.** inferior, base, humble, common. **4.** common, humble, low, undignified, ignoble, plebeian, coarse, rude, vulgar. **5.** unimportant, unessential, insignificant, petty, paltry, little, poor, wretched, despicable, contemptible, low, base, vile, foul, disgusting, repulsive, repellent, depraved, immoral. **6.** unimposing, shabby, sordid, run-down, seedy, wretched, dismal, dreary, abysmal, sorry, squalid, poor. **7.** penurious, parsimonious, illiberal, cheap, stinting, penny-pinching, petty, money-grubbing, measly, stingy, miserly, tight, niggardly, selfish, mercenary. **8.** intermediate, middle, medium, average, moderate. —*n.plural.* **9.** agency, instrumentality, method, approach, mode, way. **10.** resources, backing, support. **11.** revenue, income, substance, wherewithal, property, wealth. **12.** (*sing.*) average, median, middle, midpoint, center, norm.
—**Ant.** exalted, dignified; important, essential; imposing, splendid, rich, generous; superior.
—**Syn. Study.** MEAN, LOW, BASE refer to characteristics worthy of dislike,

contempt, or disgust. MEAN suggests a petty selfishness or lack of generosity, and may describe spiteful, unkind, or even vicious behavior: *mean rumors; a mean bully.* LOW means dishonorable in purpose or character; it describes that which is morally reprehensible or vulgar: *low deeds; low company.* BASE suggests moral depravity, greed, and cowardice; it describes dishonorable or exploitative behavior: *base motives.*

meander, *v.* wander, stroll, amble, rove, mosey; ramble, zigzag, snake, twist, wind, turn.

meaning, *n.* **1.** sense, significance, purport, tenor, gist, trend, idea, signification, import, denotation, connotation, interpretation, content. **2.** intent, intention, aim, object, purpose, design, drift, spirit, implication.
—**Syn. Study.** MEANING, SENSE, SIGNIFICANCE, PURPORT denote that which is expressed or indicated by language or action. MEANING is a general word describing that which is intended to be, or actually is, expressed: *the meaning of a statement.* SENSE often refers to a particular meaning of a word or phrase: *The word "run" has many senses.* SENSE may also be used of meaning that is intelligible or reasonable: *There's no sense in what you say.* SIGNIFICANCE refers to a meaning that is implied rather than expressed: *the significance of a glance.* It may also refer to a meaning the importance of which is not immediately perceived: *We did not grasp the significance of the event until years later.* PURPORT usu. refers to the gist or essential meaning of something fairly complicated: *the purport of a theory.*

measureless, *adj.* limitless, boundless, immeasurable, immense, vast, endless, infinite, unending, unlimited, incalculable, indeterminate.
—**Ant.** limited, finite.

meddlesome, *adj.* prying, curious, interfering, intrusive, officious, nosy, inquisitive, eavesdropping.

mediate, *v.* intercede, interpose, arbitrate, reconcile, settle.

medicine, *n.* medication, medicament, remedy, drug, prescription, pharmaceutical, cure, nostrum.

mediocre, *adj.* indifferent, ordinary, common, commonplace, pedestrian, uninspired, tolerable, second-rate, third-rate, inferior, so-so, unexceptional, fair, medium, average, middling, passable, mean.
—**Ant.** superior.

meditate, *v.* **1.** contemplate, plan, reflect on, devise, scheme, plot, think over, dwell on. **2.** reflect, ruminate, contemplate, ponder, muse, cogitate, think, study.

meditative, *adj.* pensive, thoughtful, reflecting, engrossed, brooding, lost in thought, contemplative.
—**Syn. Study.** See PENSIVE.

medium, *n.* **1.** mean, average, mean proportion, mean average. **2.** means, agency, instrumentality, instrument. **3.** environment, atmosphere, ether, air, temper, conditions, influences. —*adj.* **4.** average, mean, ordinary, middling; mediocre.

meek, *adj.* humble, submissive, spiritless, tame, yielding, forbearing, docile, unassuming, shy, retiring, timid, weak, compliant, tractable, subdued, acquiescent, manageable, mild, peaceful, pacific, calm, gentle, modest.
—**Ant.** forward, unyielding, immodest.

meet, *v.* **1.** join, connect, intersect, cross, converge, come together, unite. **2.** encounter, bump into, see, rendezvous, get together, come

upon. **3.** encounter, compete with, battle, fight, confront, face, oppose. **4.** settle, discharge, fulfill, satisfy, answer, comply with. **5.** gather, assemble, congregate, convene, collect, muster. **6.** concur, agree, see eye to eye, unite, conjoin. —*n.* **7.** meeting, contest, competition, match.
—**Ant.** diverge; dissatisfy; scatter; disagree.

melancholy, *n.* **1.** gloom, depression, sadness, dejection, despondency, gloominess, blues. **2.** pensiveness, thoughtfulness, sobriety, seriousness. —*adj.* **3.** sad, depressed, dejected, gloomy, despondent, blue, dispirited, sorrowful, unhappy, disconsolate, inconsolable, miserable, dismal, doleful, lugubrious, moody, glum, down in the mouth, downhearted, downcast, low-spirited. **4.** sober, serious, thoughtful, pensive.
—**Ant.** cheer, happiness; cheerful, happy.

mellow, *adj.* **1.** ripe, full-flavored, soft, aged, mature. **2.** softened, muted, toned down, improved. **3.** soft, rich, mellifluous, dulcet, melodious, tuneful, sweet, smooth. **4.** genial, jovial, good-humored, good-natured, laid-back, casual, easygoing, gentle, amiable, agreeable, pleasant. —*v.* **5.** soften, ripen, develop, mature, improve, perfect, age, season, sweeten.
—**Ant.** immature.

melody, *n.* tune, song, air, descant, theme, strain, refrain.

melt, *v.* **1.** liquefy, fuse, dissolve, thaw. **2.** pass, dwindle, fade, fade out, blend. **3.** soften, gentle, mollify, relax.
—**Ant.** freeze.

memento, *n.* keepsake, remembrance, souvenir, token, reminder, relic, memorial, trophy, monument, favor, commemoration, testimonial, memento mori.

memorable, *adj.* notable, noteworthy, newsworthy, impressive, significant, remarkable, marked, signal, unforgettable, outstanding, standout, extraordinary, exceptional, indelible, haunting.

menace, *n.* **1.** threat, danger, peril, hazard, risk; intimidation. —*v.* **2.** threaten, intimidate, terrorize, terrify, frighten, scare, alarm, bare one's teeth.

mend, *v.* **1.** darn, patch, repair, renew, fix, restore, retouch. **2.** correct, rectify, make better, amend, emend, ameliorate, meliorate, improve, set right. **3.** heal, recover, improve, become better.
—**Ant.** ruin, destroy; die, languish.

menial, *adj.* **1.** servile, mean, base, low, subservient, slavish, demeaning, ignoble, degrading. —*n.* **2.** servant, domestic, attendant, footman, butler, valet, maid, maidservant, waiter; flunky, slave, underling, hireling, serf, minion, lackey.
—**Ant.** noble, dignified; master.

mental, *adj.* **1.** intellectual, cerebral, rational, reasoning, cognitive, psychological, psychic. **2.** neurotic, delusional, irrational, lunatic, mad, demented, unstable, deranged, nutty, loony, insane, psychotic, batty.

mention, *v.* **1.** refer to, allude to, name, specify, cite, speak of, make known, impart, disclose, divulge, communicate, declare, state, tell, aver. —*n.* **2.** reference, indirect reference, allusion.

mercenary, *adj.* venal, grasping, sordid, acquisitive, avaricious, greedy, predatory, money-grubbing, materialistic, covetous, stingy, tight, mean, niggardly.
—**Ant.** generous, unselfish, charitable, giving.

merciful, *adj.* compassionate, kind, clement, lenient, forgiving, benignant, beneficent, generous, tender, humane, kindhearted, tenderhearted, softhearted, sympathetic, forbearing.
—Ant. merciless.

merciless, *adj.* pitiless, cruel, hard, hardhearted, severe, ruthless, heartless, barbarous, barbaric, tough, callous, tyrannical, malevolent, relentless, unrelenting, unsympathetic, uncompassionate, unfeeling, inexorable.
—Ant. merciful.

mercurial, *adj.* **1.** sprightly, spirited, lively, animated, vivacious, ebullient, buoyant, frisky, energetic. **2.** flighty, fickle, changeable, volatile, moody, inconstant, temperamental, capricious, whimsical, erratic, restless.
—Ant. inactive, dispirited, phlegmatic; constant, steady.

mercy, *n.* compassion, pity, benevolence, forgiveness, indulgence, clemency, lenience, magnaminity, beneficence, tenderheartedness, softheartedness, leniency, forbearance, kindness, tenderness, mildness, gentleness.
—Ant. cruelty, pitilessness, harshness.

mere, *adj.* bare, scant, simple, pure, sheer, unmixed, entire.

merit, *n.* **1.** worth, excellence, value, desert, entitlement, due, credit. —*v.* **2.** deserve, be worthy of, earn, be entitled to, rate.

merriment, *n.* gaiety, mirth, hilarity, laughter, revelry, high spirits, joyfulness, jubilation, festivity, glee, fun, hilarity, enjoyment, frolicking, levity, cheerfulness, conviviality, jollity, joviality, jocularity.
—Ant. misery, melancholy.

merry, *adj.* jolly, gay, happy, jovial, joyful, joyous, mirthful, hilarious, gleeful, blithe, blithesome, frolicsome, cheery, cheerful, glad.

mess, *n.* **1.** dirtiness, untidiness, disarray, muss, clutter, pig sty, dump, sloppiness, upset. **2.** chaos, disorder, disarray, disorganization, shambles, clutter, tangle, mare's nest, mishmash, confusion, muddle, medley, farrago, hodgepodge, jumble; mixture, miscellany, mélange, salmagundi. **3.** unpleasantness, difficulty, predicament, plight, muddle, pickle. —*v.* **4.** muddle, confuse, mix, mix-up.
—Ant. tidiness; order, system; arrange.

metamorphosis, *n.* change, transformation, transmutation, mutation, alteration, transfiguration, transmogrification.

mete, *v.* distribute, apportion, parcel out, dole, allot, share, ration, assign, allocate, deal, measure.

method, *n.* **1.** mode, procedure, way, means, manner, fashion, approach, route, avenue, technique, process, course. **2.** order, system, arrangement, disposition, rule, structure, organization.
—Syn. Study. METHOD, MODE, WAY refer to the manner in which something is done. METHOD implies a fixed procedure, usu. following a logical and systematic plan: *the open-hearth method of making steel.* MODE, a more formal word, implies a customary or characteristic manner: *Kangaroos have an unusual mode of carrying their young.* WAY is a general word that may often be substituted for more specific words: *the best way to solve a problem; an attractive way of wearing the hair.*

meticulous, *adj.* careful, finical, finicky, solicitous, exact, precise, fastidious, scrupulous, thorough, particular, painstaking, punctilious,

fussy, demanding.
—Syn. Study. See PAINSTAKING.

middle, *adj.* **1.** central, equidistant, halfway, medial. **2.** intermediate, intervening. —*n.* **3.** center, midpoint, midst, heart, bull's-eye.
—Ant. end, final, initial.

midst, *n.* middle, center stage, arena, center, thick, heart, core.
—Ant. rim, edge.

might, *n.* power, ability, force, energy, muscle, potency, puissance, strength, efficacy.

mighty, *adj.* **1.** powerful, strong, vigorous, robust, sturdy, puissant, potent. **2.** sizable, huge, immense, enormous, vast, tremendous, bulky, massive, prodigious, monumental, towering.
—Ant. feeble, weak, impotent; small, negligible.

migrate, *v.* voyage, journey, go, travel, settle, relocate, expatriate, immigrate, emigrate, move, resettle.
—Ant. remain, stay.

mild, *adj.* **1.** amiable, gentle, temperate, kind, compassionate, indulgent, clement, equable, easygoing, mellow, affable. **2.** placid, peaceful, tranquil, pacific, calm. **3.** bland, emollient, mollifying, soothing, calming.
—Ant. intemperate, unkind, unpleasant; stormy, turbulent; piquant, biting, bitter.

milieu, *n.* environment, medium, locality, background, class, sphere, surroundings, element, climate, environs, setting, context.

mind, *n.* **1.** intellect, intelligence, wits, mentality, brainpower, wisdom, insight, shrewdness, understanding, reason, sense. **2.** brain, brains. **3.** sanity, reason, mental balance. **4.** disposition, temper, inclination, bent, intention, leaning, proclivity, bias. **5.** opinion, sentiments, belief, contemplation, judgment, consideration. **6.** purpose, intention, intent, will, wish, liking, desire, wont. **7.** remembrance, recollection, recall, memory. —*v.* **8.** pay attention, heed, obey, attend, attend to, mark, regard, notice, note. **9.** tend, take care of, watch, look after. **10.** be careful *or* cautious *or* wary. **11.** care, object.
—Syn. Study. MIND, INTELLECT, BRAIN refer to that part of a conscious being that thinks, feels, wills, perceives, or judges. MIND is a philosophical, psychological, and general term for the center of all mental activity, as contrasted with the body and the spirit: *His mind grasped the complex issue.* INTELLECT refers to reasoning power, as distinguished from the faculties of feeling: *a book that appeals to the intellect, rather than the emotions.* BRAIN is a physiological term for the organic structure that makes mental activity possible, but is often applied to mental ability or capacity: *a fertile brain.* These words may also refer to a person of great mental ability or capacity: *a great mind of our age; a fine scholar and intellect; the brain in the family.*

mindless, *adj.* **1.** inane, simple, unthinking, undemanding, silly, purposeless, unpurposeful, aimless, pointless, stupid, no-brain. **2.** heedless, careless, unmindful, thoughtless, inattentive, unthinking, unaware.
—Ant. aware; dutiful.

mingle, *v.* **1.** mix, blend, unite, commingle, intermix, join, conjoin, combine, intermingle, merge, marry, compound. **2.** participate, associate, socialize, circulate.
—Syn. Study. See MIX.

minor, *adj.* lesser, smaller, inferior,

secondary, subordinate, petty, inconsiderable, unimportant, small, insignificant, inconsequential, trifling, trivial, negligible, small-time, two-bit, minor-league, bush-league.
—Ant. major.

minute, *n.* **1.** moment, instant, flash, trice, blink of an eye, jiffy, second. **2.** (*plural*) note, log, memorandum, record, proceedings. —*adj.* **3.** small, tiny, little, infinitesimal, minuscule, diminutive, miniature, wee, microscopic, itty-bitty. **4.** detailed, exact, precise, thorough.
—Ant. tremendous, huge, large; general, inexact, rough.

miraculous, *adj.* **1.** marvelous, wonderful, wondrous, extraordinary, incredible, out of this world. **2.** supernatural, preternatural, magical, superhuman.
—Ant. prosaic, commonplace; natural.
—Syn. Study. MIRACULOUS, PRETERNATURAL, SUPERNATURAL refer to that which seems to transcend the laws of nature. MIRACULOUS refers to something that apparently contravenes known laws governing the universe: *a miraculous recovery.* PRETERNATURAL suggests the possession of supernormal qualities: *Dogs have a preternatural sense of smell.* It may also mean *supernatural: Elves are preternatural beings.* SUPERNATURAL suggests divine or superhuman properties: *supernatural aid in battle.*

mirth, *n.* joy, joyousness, gaiety, jollity, glee, merriment, amusement, high spirits, buoyancy, exuberance, joviality, laughter, hilarity, levity, high spirits, exhilaration.
—Ant. sadness, misery.

misadventure, *n.* mischance, mishap, ill fortune, ill luck, misfortune; accident, disaster, calamity, catastrophe.
—Ant. luck, fortune.

miscellaneous, *adj.* indiscriminate, promiscuous, mixed, diverse, motley, sundry, assorted, multifarious, diversified, varied, various, mingled, confused.
—Ant. specific, special, homogeneous.

mischief, *n.* **1.** harm, trouble, injury, damage, hurt, detriment, destruction, disadvantage. **2.** evil, malice, malicious mischief, vandalism; misfortune, trouble. **3.** misbehavior, naughtiness, impishness, roguishness, rascality, deviltry, mischievousness, monkey business, shenanigans.

miser, *n.* skinflint, tightwad, pinchpenny, hoarder, penny-pincher, Scrooge, cheapskate.

miserable, *adj.* **1.** wretched, unhappy, uneasy, uncomfortable, distressed, disconsolate, doleful, forlorn, depressed, dejected, despondent, mournful, despairing, distraught, afflicted, anguished, brokenhearted, heartbroken. **2.** poverty-stricken, poor, needy, destitute, penniless. **3.** contemptible, bad, wretched, mean, despicable, low, abject, worthless. **4.** deplorable, pitiable, lamentable, unfortunate, unlucky, ill-starred, star-crossed, luckless; calamitous, catastrophic, disastrous, cursed.

miserly, *adj.* penurious, niggardly, cheap, stingy, parsimonious, tightfisted, penny-pinching, close, mean, chintzy, mingy.
—Ant. generous, unselfish.
—Syn. Study. See STINGY.

misery, *n.* **1.** wretchedness, distress, tribulation, woe, trial, suffering, agony, anguish, torture. **2.** grief, anguish, woe, unhappiness, sorrow, torment, desolation, heartache.
—Ant. happiness, joy; delight.

misfortune, *n.* **1.** ill luck, bad luck,

ill fortune, hard luck, adversity. **2.** accident, disaster, calamity, catastrophe, reverse, affliction, mishap, mischance, adversity, distress, hardship, trouble, blow, contretemps, tragedy, shock.
—Ant. luck, fortune.

misgiving, *n.* apprehension, doubt, distrust, suspicion, mistrust, worry, concern, anxiety, qualm, scruple, disquiet, hesitation, uncertainty.

mislead, *v.* misguide, lead astray, delude, deceive, misinform, fool, trick, misdirect, give (someone) a bum steer, lead up the garden path.

misshapen, *adj.* distorted, deformed, malformed, contorted, warped, misproportioned, disproportionate, ill-formed, crooked, twisted, irregular.
—Ant. shapely, well-formed.

mist, *n.* cloud, fog, fogbank, haze, smog, soup, drizzle.

mistake, *n.* **1.** error, blunder, slip, inaccuracy, erratum, typo, misprint, fault, oversight, fumble, gaffe, misstep, flub, blooper, goof, boo-boo. **2.** misapprehension, misconception, misunderstanding. —*v.* **3.** misapprehend, misconceive, misunderstand, misjudge, err, get wrong, misread.
—Ant. accuracy; understanding.

mistaken, *adj.* erroneous, wrong, incorrect, misconceived, inaccurate, in error, wide of the mark, on the wrong track; faulty, false, fallacious.
—Ant. correct, accurate.

misunderstanding, *n.* **1.** mistake, misapprehension, error, misconception, false impression, wrong idea, misinterpretation. **2.** disagreement, dissension, discord, quarrel, dispute, argument, controversy, rift, falling out.
—Ant. understanding; agreement, concord.

mix, *v.* **1.** blend, combine, mingle, commingle, confuse, jumble, unite, compound, amalgamate, homogenize. **2.** consort, mingle, associate, join. —*n.* **3.** mixture, concoction.
—Syn. Study. MIX, BLEND, COMBINE, MINGLE concern the bringing of two or more things into more or less intimate association. MIX means to join elements or ingredients into one mass, generally with a loss of distinction between them: *to mix fruit juices.* BLEND suggests a smooth and harmonious joining, often a joining of different varieties to obtain a product of a desired quality: *to blend whiskeys.* COMBINE means to bring similar or related things into close union, usu. for a particular purpose: *to combine forces.* MINGLE usu. suggests a joining in which the identity of the separate elements is retained: *voices mingling at a party.*

mixture, *n.* **1.** blend, combination, compound, amalgamation. **2.** hodgepodge, gallimaufry, conglomeration, jumble, medley, melange, olio, potpourri, miscellany, farrago, salmagundi; variety, diversity.
—Ant. element, constituent.

moan, *n.* **1.** grumbling, groan, wail, lament, lamentation. —*v.* **2.** complain, grouse, whine, whimper, gripe, beef, bemoan, bewail, grieve, lament, mourn, deplore. **3.** sigh, mourn, weep, cry, keen, grieve.

mock, *v.* **1.** ridicule, deride, taunt, flout, gibe, scorn, abuse, sneer at, rag, rib, tease, jeer, chaff, scoff, banter, make sport of; mimic, ape, satirize, imitate, lampoon, parody, burlesque, spoof, roast. **2.** defy, challenge, dare, face. **3.** deceive, delude, disappoint, cheat, dupe, fool, defeat, mislead. —*n.* **4.** mockery, derision, ridicule, banter, sport, sneer. —*adj.* **5.** artificial, simulated, synthetic, imitation, ersatz, bogus, pseudo, phony, feigned, pretended,

counterfeit, sham, false, spurious, fake.
—**Syn. Study.** See RIDICULE.

mockery, *n.* **1.** ridicule, derision, taunting, disparagement, contempt, abuse, scorn, contumely. **2.** imitation, show, mimicry, caricature, parody, burlesque, lampoon, satire. **3.** travesty, pretense, pretext, sham, farce.

mode, *n.* **1.** method, way, manner, style, fashion. **2.** form, variety, degree, modification.
—**Syn. Study.** See METHOD.

model, *n.* **1.** standard, paragon, prototype, ideal, pattern, example, archetype, mold, original. **2.** representation, facsimile, copy, image, imitation. —*v.* **3.** form, plan, pattern, mold, shape, fashion, design.
—**Syn. Study.** See IDEAL.

moderate, *adj.* **1.** reasonable, temperate, judicious, just, fair, cool, steady, calm, peaceful. **2.** medium, average, usual. **3.** mediocre, fair. **4.** middle-of-the-road, conservative, temperate. —*n.* **5.** mugwump, middle-of-the-roader, conservative. —*v.* **6.** allay, meliorate, pacify, calm, assuage, sober, mitigate, soften, mollify, temper, qualify, appease, abate, lessen, diminish, reduce.
—**Ant.** immoderate; unusual; radical; disturb, increase, intensify.

modern, *adj.* recent, up-to-date, current, late, contemporary, today's, up-to-the-minute, present-day, latest, newfangled, present, new, novel, fresh; stylish, modish, in vogue, trendy, hip, hot.
—**Ant.** old, archaic, ancient, obsolete.
—**Syn. Study.** MODERN, RECENT, LATE apply to that which is near to or characteristic of the present as contrasted with any other time. MODERN, which is applied to those things that exist in the present age, sometimes has the connotation of up-to-date and, thus, good: *modern ideas.* That which is RECENT is separated from the present or the time of action by only a short interval; it is new, fresh, and novel: *recent developments.* LATE may mean nearest to the present moment: *the late reports on the battle.*

modest, *adj.* **1.** moderate, humble, unpretentious, decent, becoming, proper. **2.** inextravagant, unostentatious, retiring, unassuming, unobtrusive. **3.** decent, demure, prudish, chaste, pure, virtuous.
—**Ant.** immodest, immoderate, improper; extravagant.

modesty, *n.* **1.** unobtrusiveness, humility, diffidence, reticence, meekness. **2.** moderation, decency, propriety, simplicity, purity, chastity, prudery, prudishness.
—**Ant.** indecency, licentiousness.

modify, *v.* **1.** change, alter, vary, qualify, temper, adjust, tweak, restrict, limit, shape, reform. **2.** reduce, qualify, moderate, temper, abate, tone down, modulate, limit, restrict.

moist, *adj.* damp, humid, dank, wet, dewy, dank, clammy, muggy, moisture-laden.
—**Ant.** dry, arid.

molest, *v.* attack, assail; hearass, harry, disturb, trouble, annoy, vex, plague, tease, pester, torment, torture, hector, inconvenience, discommode, worry, bother.

moment, *n.* **1.** minute, instant, second, jiffy, trice, flash, twinkling, blink of an eye, trice. **2.** importance, consequence, significance, weight, gravity, seriousness, interest, import, consideration. **3.** momentum, force, power, impetus, drive.

—**Ant.** insignificance; inertia.
—**Syn. Study.** See IMPORTANCE.

momentous, *adj.* important, consequential, vital, weighty, serious, grave, decisive, crucial, critical, vital, pivotal.
—**Ant.** unimportant, trivial, trifling.

monetary, *adj.* pecuniary, financial, fiscal, capital, money, economic.

money, *n.* **1.** coin, cash, currency, specie, change, coin of the realm, legal tender, bills. **2.** funds, capital, assets, wealth. **3.** mazuma, long green, lettuce, dough, loot, bread, moolah, greenbacks, bucks, scratch, gelt, kale, cabbage, chump change.

mongrel, *n.* hybrid, mutt, half-breed, cur, mixed breed, crossbreed.
—**Ant.** purebred, thoroughbred.

monopolize, *v.* consume, possess, corner, control, dominate, appropriate, co-opt, engross, usurp, arrogate, preempt, take over, gobble up, grab, hog.
—**Ant.** share.

monotonous, *adj.* tedious, humdrum, tiresome, uniform, boring, soporific, wearisome, prosaic, routine, mechanical, run-of-the-mill, ordinary, commonplace, ho-hum, dull, unvaried, unvarying, one-note.

monster, *n.* **1.** ogre, giant, dragon, troll, bogeyman, Cyclops, griffin, gargoyle, sphinx, centaur, hippogriff. **2.** mooncalf, monstrosity, mutant, mutation, freak, deformity, eyesore. **3.** fiend, brute, miscreant, wretch, beast, villain, demon, devil.

monstrous, *adj.* **1.** huge, great, large, tremendous, gigantic, monster, prodigious, enormous, immense, vast, stupendous, colossal. **2.** frightful, hideous, revolting, shocking, repulsive, horrible, nightmarish, grotesque, ghoulish, freakish, atrocious, terrible, dreadful, horrendous, heinous, fiendish, barbaric, savage, inhuman, brutal, brutish, beastly.
—**Ant.** small, tiny; delightful, attractive.

mood, *n.* disposition, frame of mind, humor, temper, vein, attitude, inclination, nature, spirit.

moody, *adj.* gloomy, sullen, ill-humored, perverse, sulky, waspish, crotchety, crabby, crusty, cantankerous, cranky, petulant, temperamental, touchy, mercurial, erratic, fussy, changeable, flighty, fickle.
—**Ant.** amiable, temperate.

moral, *adj.* **1.** ethical, upright, honest, righteous, just, good, virtuous, honorable, idealistic, humane, high-minded, principled, scrupulous, incorruptible, noble. —*n.* **2.** (*plural*) ethics, integrity, standards, morality, scruples, ideals, principles, probity, rectitude.
—**Ant.** immoral, amoral.

morbid, *adj.* **1.** gloomy, lugubrious, glum, morose, somber, melancholy, depressed, sensitive, extreme. **2.** unwholesome, diseased, pathological, unhealthy, sick, sickly, tainted, corrupted, vitiated.
—**Ant.** cheerful; wholesome, salubrious.

moreover, *adv.* besides, further, furthermore, and, also, too, likewise, to boot, into the bargain, as well, what is more.

morose, *adj.* sullen, gloomy, depressed, despondent, melancholy, sad, dour, doleful, grim, funereal, cheerless, moody, sulky, churlish, splenetic, ill-humored, petulant.
—**Ant.** cheerful, happy, good-natured.

mortal, *adj.* **1.** human; transitory, fleeting, transient, ephemeral; bodily, corporeal, fleshly, perishable. **2.**

fatal, final, lethal, deadly, terminal. —*n.* **3.** human being, man, woman, person, individual, creature, earthling.
—**Ant.** immortal, god.
—**Syn. Study.** See FATAL.

mortify, *v.* shame, humiliate, humble, embarrass, abash, abase, subdue, restrain.

mostly, *adv.* in the main, generally, chiefly, especially, particularly, for the most part, customarily.

motion, *n.* **1.** movement, move, action, change, shift; agitation. **2.** gait, deportment, carriage, bearing, air. **3.** gesture, gesticulation, sign, movement, move.
—**Ant.** stasis.

motionless, *adj.* stable, fixed, unmoving, still, quiescent, stationary, immobile, quiet, stock-still.

motive, *n.* motivation, inducement, incentive, incitement, stimulus, spur, influence, reason, ground, cause, purpose.
—**Syn. Study.** MOTIVE, INDUCEMENT, INCENTIVE apply to something that moves or prompts a person to action. MOTIVE is usu. applied to an inner urge that moves a person; it may also apply to a contemplated goal, the desire for which moves the person: *Her motive was a wish to be helpful. Money was the motive for the crime.* INDUCEMENT is used mainly of opportunities offered by another person or by situational factors: *The salary they offered me was a great inducement.* INCENTIVE is usu. applied to something offered as a reward or to stimulate competitive activity: *Profit sharing is a good incentive for employees.*

mount, *v.* **1.** go up, ascend, climb, scale, get up on. **2.** raise, put into position, fix on. **3.** prepare, produce, make ready, ready.

mourn, *v.* grieve, lament, bewail, bemoan, sorrow for, regret, rue, deplore.
—**Ant.** laugh, rejoice.

move, *v.* **1.** stir, advance, budge, progress, make progress, proceed, move on, remove. **2.** turn, revolve, spin, gyrate, rotate, operate. **3.** act, bestir oneself, take action. **4.** stir, shake, agitate, excite, arouse, rouse; shift, transfer, propel. **5.** prompt, actuate, induce, influence, impel, activate, incite, rouse, instigate. **6.** affect, touch, stir, make an impression, have an effect, shake up.

movement, *n.* **1.** move, motion, change, repositioning, relocation, shift, transfer. **2.** motion, progress, advance, increase, activity, eventfulness.
—**Ant.** inertia, stasis.

multifarious, *adj.* numerous, various, many, abundant, multitudinous, manifold, diverse, sundry, multifold, legion, myriad, various and sundry.

multitude, *n.* host, crowd, throng, mass, army, swarm, collection, horde, mob.
—**Syn. Study.** See CROWD.

mundane, *adj.* **1.** worldly, earthly, terrestrial, terraqueous, secular, temporal. **2.** common, ordinary, banal.
—**Ant.** unearthly; extraordinary.
—**Syn. Study.** See EARTHLY.

murder, *n.* **1.** killing, assassination, homicide, manslaughter, slaying, slaughter, butchery. —*v.* **2.** kill, slay, assassinate, destroy, put an end to, put to death, wipe out, exterminate, eradicate, bump off, blow away, do in, rub out, waste, ice, snuff out, take for a ride, hit. **3.** spoil, mar,

ruin, destroy, wreck, mangle, butcher, mutilate.

murky, *adj.* dark, gloomy, cheerless, obscure, dim, cloudy, dusky, lowering, overcast, misty, hazy.
—**Ant.** bright, light, clear.

murmur, *n.* **1.** grumble, susurration, susurrus, drone, hum, whispering, mumble, complaint, plaint, whimper, mutter. —*v.* **2.** mumble, mutter, whisper. **3.** complain, grumble, grouse, moan, lament.

muscular, *adj.* brawny, sinewy, well-muscled, well-built, well-knit, rugged, robust, athletic, broad-shouldered, beefy, sturdy, burly, husky, hunky, strong, powerful, mighty, Bunyanesque, pumped up, (*slang*) buff.
—**Ant.** weak, feeble, underdeveloped.

muse, *v.* reflect, meditate, ponder, contemplate, think of or about, consider, chew over, weigh, evaluate, study, mull over, cogitate, deliberate, ruminate, brood; dream.

muster, *v.* call together, mobilize, round up, assemble, gather, summon, convoke, collect, marshal, convene.
—**Ant.** scatter, separate.

mutable, *adj.* **1.** changeable, alterable, variable, protean. **2.** fickle, changing, inconstant, unstable, vacillating, unsettled, wavering, unsteady, unpredictable, mercurial.
—**Ant.** immutable, invariable; stable, settled, motionless.

mute, *adj.* silent, dumb, speechless, still, voiceless, tightlipped, stifled, mum.
—**Ant.** loquacious, voluble, talkative.

mutilate, *v.* injure, disfigure, maim, damage, mar, cripple, mangle, spoil, ruin, deface, vandalize.

mutinous, *adj.* **1.** seditious, insurrectionary, revolutionary, insurgent. **2.** rebellious, refractory, insubordinate, unruly, defiant, disobedient, insubordinate, contumacious, turbulent, riotous.
—**Ant.** patriotic; obedient.

mutiny, *n.* **1.** revolt, rebellion, insurrection, revolution, uprising, insurgency, sedition. —*v.* **2.** revolt, rebel, rise up; disobey, subvert, agitate against.
—**Ant.** obedience.

mutual, *adj.* reciprocal, balanced, correlative, complementary, requited, common, interchangeable, communal, joint, shared.

mysterious, *adj.* secret, arcane, furtive, esoteric, occult, cryptic, inscrutable, mystical, obscure, puzzling, inexplicable, baffling, unexplainable, unintelligible, incomprehensible, enigmatic, impenetrable, recondite, hidden, concealed, dark, abstruse, cabalistic, unfathomable.
—**Syn. Study.** MYSTERIOUS, INSCRUTABLE, MYSTICAL, OBSCURE refer to that which is not easily comprehended or explained. That which is MYSTERIOUS, by being unknown or puzzling, excites curiosity, amazement, or awe: *a mysterious disease.* INSCRUTABLE applies to that which is impenetrable, so enigmatic that one cannot interpret its significance: *an inscrutable smile.* That which is MYSTICAL has a secret significance, such as that attaching to certain rites or signs: *mystical symbols.* That which is OBSCURE is discovered or comprehended dimly or with difficulty: *obscure motives.*

myth, *n.* legend, story, fiction, fable, allegory, parable, folk tale, fiction, tradition, epic, tale, tall tale.
—**Syn. Study.** See LEGEND.

N

nag, *v.* **1.** henpeck, pick on, find fault with, provoke, nettle, plague, torment, pester, harass, importune, irritate, annoy, vex. **—*n.* 2.** scold, harpy, fishwife, shrew, virago, pest, termagant, maenad.

naive, *adj.* unsophisticated, ingenuous, innocent, credulous, childlike, born yesterday, gullible, inexperienced, green, unworldly, trusting, simple-minded, simple, unaffected, natural, artless, guileless, candid, open, plain.
—Ant. sophisticated, disingenuous, artful, sly.

naked, *adj.* **1.** nude, bare, undressed, stripped, exposed, unclothed. **2.** bare, stripped, destitute, desert, denuded. **3.** unsheathed, exposed, bare. **4.** defenseless, unprotected, unguarded, exposed, unarmed, open. **5.** simple, plain, manifest, evident, unembellished, stark, mere, bare, sheer. **6.** plainspoken, blunt, direct, outspoken, unvarnished, uncolored, unexaggerated, plain.
—Ant. covered, dressed; protected; exaggerated, embellished.

namby-pamby, *adj.* **1.** insipid, bland, wishy-washy, insubstantial, overrefined, overnice, precious, jejune, goody-goody. **2.** weak, spineless, indecisive, wavering, wimpish, wimpy.
—Ant. strong, decisive.

name, *n.* **1.** appellation, title, label, tag, designation, epithet. **2.** reputation, repute, character. **3.** fame, repute, note, distinction, renown, eminence, honor, praise. **—*v.* 4.** call, title, entitle, dub, denominate. **5.** specify, mention, indicate, designate, identify, nominate.

nameless, *adj.* **1.** anonymous, unknown, obscure, undistinguished, unremarked, unnamed, untitled, unspecified, incognito. **2.** ineffable, unnamable, indescribable, inexpressible, unutterable, unspeakable.

narrate, *v.* recount, relate, tell, chronicle, reveal, retail, describe, detail, recite.

narrative, *n.* story, account, recital, history, chronicle, tale, description.

narrow-minded, *adj.* prejudiced, biased, bigoted, intolerant, illiberal, partial, opinionated, one-sided, parochial, stiff-necked, hidebound.
—Ant. liberal, broad-minded, tolerant, unprejudiced.

nasty, *adj.* **1.** filthy, dirty, disgusting, unclean, foul, impure, loathsome, polluted, defiled. **2.** nauseous, nauseating, disgusting, sickening, offensive, repulsive, repellent, objectionable. **3.** obscene, smutty, pornographic, lewd, licentious, lascivious, indecent, ribald, gross, indelicate, blue, vulgar, bawdy, risqué, off-color, suggestive, X-rated, raunchy. **4.** vicious, spiteful, ugly, badtempered, disagreeable, abusive, irascible, cruel, inconsiderate, rude, churlish, obnoxious, crotchety, crabby, cranky, cantankerous, curmudgeonly, mean.
—Ant. clean, pure, unpolluted; delightful; decent, honorable; amiable, agreeable.

nation, *n.* **1.** race, stock, ethnic group, population, clan, people, tribe. **2.** state, country, commonwealth, kingdom, realm, domain, land, political entity.

native, *adj.* **1.** inborn, inherent, inherited, natural, innate, inbred, hereditary, intrinsic, congenital. **2.** indigenous, autochthonous, aboriginal, natural, domestic, local, homegrown. **3.** unadorned, natural, real, genuine, original. **—*n.* 4.** inhabitant, aborigine, resident, citizen.
—Ant. acquired; imported; decorated; foreigner, alien.

nature, *n.* **1.** character, quality, attributes, properties, features, makeup, personality, temperament. **2.** kind, variety, description, class, category, genre, sort, character, type, species. **3.** universe, world, earth, cosmos, environment, macrocosm.

naughty, *adj.* **1.** ill-behaved, misbehaved, bad, disobedient, mischievous, roguish, devilish, unruly, obstreperous, rambunctious, undisciplined, wayward. **2.** risqué, improper, off-color, ribald, profane, dirty, vulgar, smutty.

nauseate, *v.* **1.** sicken, revolt, disgust. **2.** loathe, abhor, abominate, detest, reject.
—Ant. delight, enchant, attract; like, love, adore.

nauseous, *adj.* **1.** sickening, revolting, nasty, repellent, disgusting, repugnant, repulsive, foul, stomachturning, loathsome, abhorrent, detestable, despicable, nauseating, offensive. **2.** ill, sick to one's stomach, green around the gills, queasy, squeamish.

near, *adj.* **1.** close, nigh, at hand, nearby, adjacent, contiguous, touching, adjoining, bordering, abutting. **2.** imminent, impending, approaching, forthcoming, at hand. **3.** related, connected, intimate, familiar, allied, attached. **4.** faithful, close, accurate, literal.
—Ant. far.

nearly, *adv.* **1.** almost, approximately, well-nigh, about, not quite, all but, virtually, practically, as good as. **2.** intimately, identically, exactly, precisely, closely.

neat, *adj.* **1.** orderly, ordered, trim, tidy, spruce, smart, nice, neat as a pin. **2.** clever, effective, adroit, finished, well-planned, apt.
—Ant. disorderly, sloppy; maladroit, ineffective.

necessary, *adj.* essential, requisite, indispensable, required, compulsory, imperative, obligatory, of the essence, compelling, life-and-death, needed.
—Ant. unnecessary, dispensable.
—Syn. Study. NECESSARY, REQUISITE, INDISPENSABLE, ESSENTIAL indicate something that cannot be done without. NECESSARY refers to something needed for existence, for proper functioning, or for a particular purpose: *Food is necessary for life. Sugar is a necessary ingredient in this recipe.* REQUISITE refers to something required for a particular purpose or by particular circumstances: *She has the requisite qualifications for the job.* INDISPENSABLE means absolutely necessary to achieve a particular purpose or to complete or perfect a unit: *He made himself indispensable in the laboratory.* ESSENTIAL refers to something that is part of the basic nature or character of a thing and is vital to its existence or functioning: *Water is essential to life.*

necessity, *n.* **1.** needfulness, indispensability, need, indispensableness. **2.** requirement, requisite, demand, necessary, *sine qua non,* essential, prerequisite. **3.** compulsion, fate, destiny, kismet, karma, inevitability, inevitableness, unavoidability, irresistibility. **4.** poverty, neediness, indigence, necessitousness, need, want, destitution.
—Ant. dispensability; wealth.

need, *n.* **1.** requirement, want, necessity, exigency, emergency, urgency. **2.** want, necessity, lack, demand. **3.** destitution, poverty, neediness, want, deprivation, necessity, indigence, penury, distress, privation. **—*v.* 4.** require, want, lack.
—Ant. wealth, opulence.
—Syn. Study. See LACK.

neglect, *v.* **1.** disregard, ignore, slight, overlook, be remiss. **—*n.* 2.** disregard, dereliction, negligence, remissness, carelessness, failure, omission, default, inattention, heedlessness.
—Ant. regard, attend; regard, attention, care.

neglectful, *adj.* remiss, careless, negligent, inattentive, indifferent, heedless, thoughtless.
—Ant. regardful, careful, thoughtful.

negligible, *adj.* minor, unimportant, trivial, trifling, inconsequential, paltry, piddling, nugatory, petty, niggling, insignificant, slight, marginal, small, slender, slim, minuscule, outside, off.
—Ant. significant, important.

negotiate, *v.* **1.** arrange, arrange for, organize, orchestrate, execute, pull off, settle. **2.** bargain, deal, haggle, discuss, debate, transact, mediate, consult, come to terms.

nerve, *n.* **1.** strength, vigor, energy, power, force, might. **2.** courage, boldness, bravery, determination, pluck, mettle, tenacity, valor, daring, staunchness, steadfastness, fortitude, resolution, resoluteness, endurance. **3.** brashness, presumption, temerity, brass, brazenness, gall, effrontery, impertinence, impudence, insolence, audacity, chutzpah, crust.
—Ant. weakness, frailty, cowardice.

nervous, *adj.* excitable, uneasy, apprehensive, fearful, timid, timorous; high-strung, tense, agitated, overwrought, upset, edgy, on edge, fidgety, fretful, skittish, jumpy, jittery, in a dither, in a sweat, uptight, on pins and needles, rattled, strung out, jiggy.

new, *adj.* **1.** latest, contemporary, trendy, fashionable, experimental, recent, modern, up-to-date, novel, fresh. **2.** further, additional, fresh. **3.** unaccustomed, unused, fresh.
—Ant. old, stale.
—Syn. Study. NEW, FRESH, NOVEL describe things that have not existed or have not been known or seen before. NEW refers to something recently made, grown, or built, or recently found, invented, or discovered: *a new car; new techniques.* FRESH refers to something that has retained its original properties, or has not been affected by use or the passage of time: *fresh strawberries; fresh ideas.* NOVEL refers to something new that has an unexpected, strange, or striking quality, generally pleasing: *a novel experience.*

nice, *adj.* **1.** pleasing, pleasant, agreeable, delightful, good. **2.** kind, amiable, pleasant, cordial, winsome, likable, friendly. **3.** accurate, precise, skilled, delicate, fastidious, exact, exacting, critical, rigorous, strict, demanding, scrupulous. **4.** tactful, careful, discriminating, discerning, particular. **5.** minute, fine, subtle, refined. **6.** refined, well-mannered, well-spoken. **7.** suitable, proper, polite. **8.** neat, trim, fastidious, finical, finicky, dainty, fussy.
—Ant. unpleasant; unkind; inaccurate; tactless, careless; unrefined; improper, impolite; sloppy.

nickname, *n.* sobriquet, epithet, handle, nom de guerre, appellation, pet name, assumed name, alias, stage name, pen name, nom de plume, pseudonym.

nimble, *adj.* agile, quick, lively, spry, lithe, limber, sprightly, deft, dextrous; ready, alert, swift, quick-witted, on the qui vive.
—Ant. slow, clumsy, awkward.

noble, *adj.* **1.** highborn, aristocratic, high-class, upper-class, titled, lordly, patrician, blueblooded, to the manor born. **2.** high-minded, upright, righteous, virtuous, honest, incorruptible, principled, moral, decent, magnanimous, superior, elevated, exalted, worthy, lofty, honorable, great, large, generous. **3.** admirable, dignified, imposing, stately, impressive, grand, lordly, splendid. **—*n.* 4.** nobleman, noblewoman, patrician, blueblood, peer, aristocrat, lord, lady.
—Ant. lowborn; base; undignified; serf, slave.
—Syn. Study. NOBLE, HIGH-MINDED, MAGNANIMOUS suggest moral excellence and high ideals. NOBLE implies superior moral qualities and an exalted mind, character, or spirit that scorns the petty, base, or dishonorable: *a noble sacrifice.* HIGH-MINDED suggests exalted moral principles, thoughts, or sentiments: *a high-minded speech on social reform.* MAGNANIMOUS adds the idea of generosity, shown by a willingness to forgive injuries or overlook insults: *The magnanimous ruler granted amnesty to the rebels.*

noise, *n.* clamor, din, hubbub, racket, clatter, rattle, blare, uproar, outcry, crash, thunder, rumble, hullabaloo, tumult, ado.
—Ant. quiet, peace.
—Syn. Study. NOISE, CLAMOR, HUBBUB, DIN, RACKET refer to nonmusical or confused sounds. NOISE is a general word that usu. refers to loud, harsh, or discordant sounds: *noise from the street.* CLAMOR refers to loud noise, as from shouting or cries, that expresses feelings, desires, or complaints: *the clamor of an angry crowd.* HUBBUB refers to a confused mingling of sounds, usu. voices; it may also mean tumult or confused activity: *the hubbub on the floor of the stock exchange.* DIN is a very loud, continuous noise that greatly disturbs or distresses: *the din of a factory.* RACKET refers to a rattling sound or clatter: *to make a racket when doing the dishes.*

noiseless, *adj.* silent, quiet, still, inaudible, soundless, mute, hushed, muffled.
—Ant. noisy, clamorous, tumultuous.

noisy, *adj.* loud, deafening, earsplitting, piercing, resounding, cacophonous, thunderous, blaring, blasting, stentorian, clamorous, boisterous, tumultuous, riotous, vociferous, obstreperous, blustering, uproarious.
—Ant. quiet, silent, peaceful.

nominal, *adj.* titular, so-called, formal, in name only.

nonchalant, *adj.* unconcerned, indifferent, cool, apathetic, unexcited, calm, casual, dispassionate, detached, insouciant, aloof, blasé, unenthusiastic, laid-back.
—Ant. passionate, enthusiastic.

nondescript, *adj.* **1.** undistinguished, ordinary, commonplace, unremarkable, bland, everyday, colorless, drab, insipid, characterless, unexceptional. **2.** unclassifiable, amorphous, indescribable.

nonsense, *n.* twaddle, balderdash, senselessness, moonshine, absurdity, folly, trash, gobbledygook, gibberish, blather, bunk, poppycock, double-talk, mumbo jumbo, rot, hogwash, malarky, bilge, baloney, claptrap, hot air, applesauce, horse-feathers, tripe, bull, hooey, fiddlesticks, hokum, bushwa.

normal, *adj.* usual, ordinary, standard, regular, routine, average, conventional, common, general, typical, customary, everyday, traditional, habitual, accustomed, set.

notable, *adj.* **1.** noteworthy, noted, noticeable, remarkable, signal, distinctive, singular, striking, unparalleled, outstanding, distinguished, unusual, uncommon, extraordinary, great, memorable. **2.** prominent, important, eminent, distinguished, famed, famous, well-known, conspicuous, notorious. **3.** celebrity, personage, dignitary, luminary, VIP, name, big shot.
—**Ant.** common, ordinary; unimportant, undistinguished.

note, *n.* **1.** message, letter, e-mail, communication, correspondence, postcard, word, line; memo, memorandum, record, minute. **2.** comment, remark, commentary, observation, explanation, exegesis, gloss, criticism, critique, assessment, annotation, footnote. **3.** eminence, distinction, repute, celebrity, fame, renown, reputation, name. **4.** notice, heed, observation; consideration, regard. —*v.* **5.** mark down, jot down, record, make a note of, register. **6.** mention, designate, refer to, indicate, denote. **7.** notice, see, perceive, spot, remark, observe, regard, look at, mark, consider.

noted, *adj.* famous, celebrated, distinguished, famed, notable, renowned, eminent, illustrious, well-known, prominent, notorious.
—**Ant.** unknown, undistinguished; notorious, infamous.

noteworthy, *adj.* notable, significant, remarkable, newsworthy, impressive, signal, outstanding, standout, extraordinary, exceptional, great, major.
—**Ant.** insignificant, unremarkable.

notice, *n.* **1.** information, intelligence, advice, news bulletin, notification, mention, announcement. **2.** intimation, warning. **3.** sign, placard, poster, billboard, advertisement. **4.** observation, perception, attention, heed, note, cognizance. **5.** comment, mention, account, criticism, critique, review. —*v.* **6.** discern, perceive, see, become aware of, pay attention to, distinguish, discriminate, recognize, understand, regard, heed, note, observe, mark, remark.
—**Syn. Study.** NOTICE, PERCEIVE, DISCERN imply becoming aware of something through the senses or the intellect. NOTICE means to pay attention to something one sees, hears, or senses: *to notice a newspaper ad; to notice someone's absence; to notice one's lack of enthusiasm.* PERCEIVE is a more formal word meaning to detect by means of the senses; with reference to the mind, it implies realization, understanding, and insight: *to perceive the sound of hoofbeats; to perceive the significance of an event.* DISCERN means to detect something that is obscure or concealed; it implies keen senses or insight: *to discern the outlines of a distant ship; to discern the truth.*

notify, *v.* give notice to, inform, apprise, acquaint, make known to, advise, alert, tell, warn.

notion, *n.* **1.** conception, idea, concept, thought, image, impression. **2.** opinion, view, belief, sentiment, impression, judgment. **3.** whim, caprice, fancy, crotchet, whimsy, impulse, vagary, inclination, conceit, quirk.
—**Syn. Study.** See IDEA.

nourish, *v.* **1.** feed, maintain, keep, provide for, look after, care for, nurture, nurse, sustain, support, tend, attend. **2.** foster, cherish, harbor, cultivate, advance, promote, promulgate, foment, succor, aid, help, encourage.
—**Ant.** neglect.

novelty, *n.* **1.** originality, newness, innovation, uniqueness, freshness, inventiveness. **2.** fad, rage, wrinkle, craze. **3.** knickknack, curio, gimmick, bauble, toy, plaything, ornament, kickshaw, trinket, trifle, bibelot, whatnot, gewgaw, gimcrack, tchotchke.

now, *adv.* **1.** today, nowadays, currently, these days, at the moment, at present, in this day and age; for the time being. **2.** immediately, instantly, without delay, at once, right away, promptly, straightaway, as soon as possible, ASAP, in a jiffy, posthaste, forthwith, directly, without hesitation, pronto, instantaneously, in a second *or* minute, *tout de suite,* at the drop of a hat, before one can say "Jack Robinson."

noxious, *adj.* **1.** harmful, hurtful, unhealthy, unwholesome, injurious, mephitic, miasmatic, nocuous, detrimental, baneful, deleterious, pestilential, poisonous, destructive, deadly. **2.** corrupting, immoral, pernicious.
—**Ant.** harmless, wholesome, beneficial; moral.

nucleus, *n.* center, kernel, core, heart, pith, focus, hub.

nude, *adj.* uncovered, undressed, unclothed, undraped, naked, bare, exposed, denuded, stark-naked, *au naturel,* in the altogether, in the buff, in one's birthday suit.

nullify, *v.* invalidate, negate, annul, abrogate, quash, undo, cancel out, vitiate.
—**Ant.** confirm, establish.

number, *n.* **1.** sum, total, count, aggregate, collection. **2.** numeral, integer, digit, figure. **3.** quantity, collection, company, multitude, crowd, slew, bevy, swarm, legion, mob, host, mass, handful, few, several, loads, tons, horde, many, gazillion. —*v.* **4.** count, enumerate, calculate, compute, reckon, tally, figure, add up, sum up, total, tote up; account; include, consist of.

numberless, *adj.* innumerable, numerous, myriad, countless, uncounted, untold, infinite, incalculable, immeasurable.
—**Ant.** finite.

numerous, *adj.* many, numberless, copious, ample, plentiful, plenteous, plenty, abundant, surplus, multitudinous, myriad, profuse, innumerable, uncountable.
—**Ant.** few.
—**Syn. Study.** See MANY.

nurse, *v.* **1.** tend, take care of, minister to, look after, treat, attend. **2.** foster, cherish, succor, promote, foment, encourage, aid, abet, help. **3.** nourish, nurture, feed, rear, raise. **4.** suckle, feed, give suck to, breastfeed, wet-nurse.
—**Ant.** neglect.

nutrition, *n.* food, nutriment, aliment, nourishment, sustenance, subsistence.

nutritious, *adj.* healthful, healthy, wholesome, nutritive, nourishing, beneficial, salutary, alimentary.

O

oaf, *n.* **1.** simpleton, blockhead, dunce, dolt, fool, nincompoop, ninny, jackass, half-wit, numbskull, bonehead, pinhead, ignoramus,

dimwit, nitwit, booby, fathead, knucklehead, sap, dope, retard, idiot, imbecile, moron. **2.** lout, bungler, clumsy person, yahoo, bumpkin, clod, clodhopper, buffoon, lummox, galoot.
—**Ant.** genius.

oath, *n.* **1.** promise, vow, pledge, affirmation, word of honor. **2.** profanity, curse, blasphemy, malediction, imprecation, expletive, obscenity, swear word, dirty word, four-letter word.

obedient, *adj.* submissive, compliant, docile, tractable, yielding, agreeable, amenable, acquiescent, pliant, deferential, respectful, dutiful, subservient.
—**Ant.** disobedient, recalcitrant, refractory.

obese, *adj.* fat, stout, plump, pudgy, corpulent, portly, gross, fleshy, chubby, big, big-boned, huge, enormous, overweight, heavy, tubby, paunchy, rotund, pot-bellied, broad in the beam.
—**Ant.** thin, skinny, slender, slim.

object, *n.* **1.** thing, reality, fact, manifestation, phenomenon. **2.** focus, target, objective, goal, end, destination, aim. **3.** purpose, reason, idea, basis, base, target, goal, end, motive, intent, intention. —*v.* **4.** protest, disapprove, be averse, refuse, oppose, complain, remonstrate, take exception.
—**Ant.** approve.
—**Syn. Study.** See AIM.

objective, *n.* **1.** end, termination, object, destination, aim, target, goal, purpose, intent, intention, butt. —*adj.* **2.** unprejudiced, unbiased, impartial, fair, impersonal, just, judicious, neutral, equitable, disinterested, dispassionate, evenhanded, open-minded, detached.
—**Ant.** subjective, biased.

obligation, *n.* **1.** requirement, duty, responsibility, charge, burden, onus, demand, compulsion, liability, accountability, accountableness. **2.** agreement, contract, covenant, bond, stipulation, promise.
—**Syn. Study.** See DUTY.

oblige, *v.* **1.** require, constrain, compel, force, necessitate, bind, coerce, obligate. **2.** indulge, cater to, favor, accommodate, serve, please, benefit.
—**Ant.** disoblige, liberate, unfetter.
—**Syn. Study.** OBLIGE, ACCOMMODATE imply making a gracious and welcome gesture of some kind. OBLIGE emphasizes the idea of doing a favor (and often of taking some trouble to do it): *to oblige her with a loan.* ACCOMMODATE emphasizes providing a service or convenience: *to accommodate them with lodgings and meals.*

obliging, *adj.* helpful, accommodating, willing, amiable, friendly, outgoing, considerate, courteous, thoughtful, solicitous.
—**Ant.** unhelpful, selfish.

obliterate, *v.* erase, efface, do away with, expunge, rub out, delete, blot out, eradicate, wipe out, conceal, eliminate; destroy, annihilate, kill, exterminate, extirpate.
—**Ant.** construct, create, originate; restore.

oblivious, *adj.* **1.** unaware, unconscious, abstracted, forgetful, absentminded. **2.** heedless, disregardful, neglectful, careless, negligent.
—**Ant.** heedful, regardful, careful.

obnoxious, *adj.* revolting, repulsive, disgusting, nauseating, noisome, repellent, repugnant, objectionable, offensive, odious, hateful.
—**Syn. Study.** See HATEFUL.

obscene, *adj.* immodest, indecent, lewd, pornographic, coarse, ribald, smutty, offensive, filthy, immoral, indelicate, impure, unchaste, gross,

lubricious, off-color, risqué, vulgar, debauched, wanton, libertine, bawdy, blue, scabrous, erotic, sensual, carnal, dirty, libidinous, licentious, lecherous, lustful, lascivious, salacious, prurient, foul-mouthed, scurrilous, scatalogical, X-rated, adult.
—**Ant.** modest, decent, moral, pure, chaste.

obscure, *adj.* **1.** unclear, uncertain, doubtful, dubious, ambiguous, vague, hazy, enigmatic, perplexing, baffling, confusing; cryptic, esoteric, arcane, recondite, abstruse, complex, intricate, unfamiliar, mysterious. **2.** inconspicuous, unnoticeable, unnoticed, unknown, undistinguished. **3.** remote, retired, secluded. **4.** indistinct, blurred, blurry, imperfect, dim, veiled. **5.** dark, murky, dim, clouded, cloudy, gloomy, dusky, somber, shadowy, lurid.
—**Ant.** clear, certain, unambiguous, conspicuous, noted; distinct; bright.
—**Syn. Study.** See MYSTERIOUS.

observant, *adj.* **1.** attentive, watchful, heedful, mindful, vigilant, aware. **2.** perceptive, quick, alert, on the qui vive, keen-eyed, eagle-eyed, sharp, shrewd. **3.** careful, obedient, respectful.
—**Ant.** inattentive, careless; dull; disobedient.

observation, *n.* **1.** examination, inspection, survey, scrutiny, surveillance, noticing, perceiving, watching, regarding, attending. **2.** notice, observance, awareness, discovery, attention. **3.** information, record, memorandum. **4.** remark, comment, aside, reflection, opinion, sentiment, word, utterance.

observe, *v.* **1.** perceive, notice, see, discover, detect. **2.** regard, witness, mark, watch, note, view. **3.** remark, comment, mention; utter, say. **4.** obey, comply, conform, follow, fulfill. **5.** solemnize, celebrate, keep, commemorate, mark, keep holy, recognize.
—**Ant.** ignore.

obsession, *n.* fixed idea, *idée fixe,* fixation, compulsion, mania, passion, hang-up, preoccupation, domination, prepossession.

obsolete, *adj.* out-of-date, outdated, outmoded, passé, dead, antediluvian, old hat, superannuated, dated, superseded, antiquated, old-fashioned, ancient, old, archaic.
—**Ant.** modern, new, up-to-date.

obstacle, *n.* obstruction, hindrance, impediment, interference, check, block, barrier, hurdle, snag, hitch.
—**Syn. Study.** OBSTACLE, OBSTRUCTION, HINDRANCE, IMPEDIMENT refer to something that interferes with or prevents action or progress and must be removed, overcome, or bypassed. An OBSTACLE is something, material or nonmaterial, that stands in the way of progress: *an obstacle in a steeplechase; an obstacle to success.* An OBSTRUCTION is something that more or less completely blocks passage: *an obstruction in a drainpipe.* A HINDRANCE interferes and causes delay or difficulty: *Interruptions are a hindrance to my work.* An IMPEDIMENT slows down proper functioning or interferes with free movement: *Heavy rain was an impediment to our departure.*

obstinate, *adj.* mulish, obdurate, unyielding, recusant, stubborn, perverse, unbending, contumacious, inflexible, willful, headstrong, refractory, firm, intractable, resolute, pertinacious, persistent, dogged, tenacious, perverse, pigheaded, single-minded, contrary, recalcitrant, uncooperative, intransigent, adamant, set in one's ways, inexorable, stiff, rigid.

—**Ant.** submissive, flexible, tractable, irresolute.
—**Syn. Study.** See STUBBORN.

obstruct, *v.* block, stop, close, occlude, choke, clog, bar, hinder, barricade, dam up; arrest, halt, impede, prevent; retard, slow, check, arrest, interrupt, hamper, stall, delay, interfere with.
—**Ant.** encourage, help, support, further.

obstruction, *n.* **1.** obstacle, hindrance, barrier, occlusion, impediment, bar, check, stumbling block, hurdle. **2.** stopping, cessation, check.
—**Ant.** encouragement, furtherance; continuation.
—**Syn. Study.** See OBSTACLE.

obtain, *v.* get, acquire, procure, secure, gain, achieve, earn, win, attain, come by.
—**Ant.** lose, forgo.
—**Syn. Study.** See GET.

obtrusive, *adj.* **1.** meddlesome, meddling, intrusive, interfering, impertinent, invasive, interruptive, disruptive, presumptuous, officious, forward, prying, pushy, nosy. **2.** protruding, projecting; prominent, noticeable, conspicuous.

obvious, *adj.* plain, manifest, evident, clear, open, apparent, patent, palpable, perceptible, distinct, unmistakable, self-evident, conspicuous, visible, overt, prominent, glaring.
—**Ant.** concealed, hidden, indistinct, imperceptible.
—**Syn. Study.** See APPARENT.

occasion, *n.* **1.** occurrence, event, time, incident. **2.** opportunity, advantage, chance, convenience, opening. **3.** ground, reason, cause, motive, justification, inducement, influence. —*v.* **4.** bring about, cause, motivate, originate, create, move, give rise to, produce, effect, prompt, provoke, evoke, induce, generate, engender, impel.
—**Ant.** suppress.

occult, *adj.* **1.** mysterious, hidden, concealed, secret, undisclosed, unrevealed, unknown; mystical, recondite, cabalistic, veiled, shrouded. **2.** supernatural, metaphysical, preternatural, transcendental, magical.
—**Ant.** natural.

occupation, *n.* **1.** job, position, post, situation, appointment, line, field, career, work, calling, trade, business, profession, métier, vocation, employment, pursuit, craft; (*slang*) dodge. **2.** possession, tenure, use, occupancy. **3.** seizure, invasion, capture, conquest, takeover, appropriation.

occupy, *v.* **1.** take up, use, engage, employ, busy, absorb, monopolize, involve, engross, interest. **2.** possess, capture, seize, take hold of, conquer, invade, overrun, take over.

occur, *v.* **1.** come to pass, take place, happen, befall, arise, chance, develop, materialize, surface, transpire. **2.** appear, be met with, be found, arise, offer, meet the eye.

occurrence, *n.* event, incident, circumstance, affair, proceeding, transaction, happening.

odd, *adj.* **1.** different, extraordinary, unusual, strange, weird, atypical, exotic, anomalous, idiosyncratic, deviant, outlandish, uncanny, abnormal, freakish, offbeat, peculiar, singular, unique, queer, quaint, eccentric, uncommon, rare, fantastic, bizarre. **2.** occasional, casual, irregular, sporadic, random.
—**Ant.** ordinary, common, unexceptional, usual.

odious, *adj.* **1.** hateful, despicable, detestable, execrable, abominable, invidious. **2.** obnoxious, offensive,

disgusting, loathsome, repellent, repulsive, forbidding, vile, distasteful.
—**Ant.** attractive, lovable; inviting.
—**Syn. Study.** See HATEFUL.

odor, *n.* smell, aroma, fragrance, redolence, scent, perfume, bouquet; stench, stink, fetor.
—**Syn. Study.** ODOR, SMELL, SCENT, STENCH all refer to a sensation perceived by means of the olfactory nerves. ODOR refers to a relatively strong sensation that may be agreeable or disagreeable, actually or figuratively: *the odor of freshly roasted coffee; the odor of duplicity.* SMELL is used in similar contexts, although it is a more general word: *cooking smells; the sweet smell of success.* SCENT may refer to a distinctive smell, usu. delicate and pleasing, or to a smell left in passing: *the scent of lilacs; the scent of an antelope.* STENCH refers to a foul, sickening, or repulsive smell: *the stench of rotting flesh.*

offbeat, *adj.* unusual, unconventional, uncommon, unexpected, strange, bizarre, weird, peculiar, odd, queer, unorthodox, idiosyncratic, bohemian, outré, outlandish, deviant, out of the ordinary, special, eccentric, unique, far-out, off the wall, freaky, kinky.
—**Ant.** commonplace, conventional.

offend, *v.* **1.** irritate, annoy, vex, chafe, provoke, mortify, pique, needle, rankle, outrage, rile, anger, miff, gall, fret; displease, affront, insult, hurt, slight, snub, give offense, pain, chagrin, disgruntle. **2.** sin, transgress, err, stumble.
—**Ant.** please, delight, compliment.

offense, *n.* **1.** transgression, wrong, sin, trespass, misdemeanor, crime, fault, felony, violation, breach, infraction, wrongdoing, peccadillo, misdeed, infringement, dereliction, lapse. **2.** displeasure, unpleasantness, umbrage, resentment, wrath, indignation, anger, ire, annoyance, irritation, pique. **3.** attack, assault, onset, aggression.
—**Ant.** delight, pleasure; defense.
—**Syn. Study.** See CRIME.

offensive, *adj.* **1.** displeasing, irritating, annoying, vexing, vexatious, unpleasant, uncivil, discourteous, impolite, objectionable, rude, insolent, hateful, detestable, opprobrious, insulting, abusive. **2.** disagreeable, distasteful, disgusting, repulsive, obnoxious, unsavory, foul, vile, revolting, repellent, nauseating, nauseous, sickening, loathsome. **3.** repugnant, insulting, execrable, abominable, shocking, revolting. **4.** antagonistic, hostile, contentious, combative, fetid, rank, rancid, putrid, putrescent, rotten, unpalatable, unpleasant, provocative, threatening, aggressive, invading, attacking.
—**Ant.** pleasing, pleasant, polite, courteous; agreeable, tasteful, attractive; delightful; defensive.
—**Syn. Study.** See HATEFUL.

offer, *v.* **1.** present, proffer, tender, bid. **2.** propose, give, move, put forward, tender. **3.** volunteer, sacrifice, immolate, present. —*n.* **4.** pesentation, proposal, proposition, overture; bid.
—**Ant.** refuse; refusal, denial.
—**Syn. Study.** OFFER, PROFFER, TENDER mean to put something forward for acceptance or rejection. OFFER is the general word for presenting anything for acceptance, sale, consideration, or the like: *to offer help; to offer a cold drink.* PROFFER, chiefly a literary word, implies presenting something freely and unselfishly: *to proffer one's services.* TENDER is used in formal, legal, business, and polite social contexts: *to tender one's resignation; to tender payment.*

offhand, *adj.* **1.** casual, nonchalant, informal, unceremonious, relaxed, easygoing, unstudied, laid-back, blasé, insouciant. **2.** unpremeditated, spontaneous, impromptu, improvisatory, extemporaneous, impulsive, ad lib, spur of the moment, off the cuff, ad hoc.
—**Ant.** studied, formal.

office, *n.* **1.** business, department, firm, company, establishment, corporation, organization. **2.** position, post, station, situation. **3.** responsibility, charge, appointment, trust, obligation, commission, employment, occupation, assignment, chore, job, task, work, duty.

officious, *adj.* forward, obtrusive, forceful, direct, interfering, meddlesome, meddling, bold, aggressive, insistent, persistent, demanding.
—**Ant.** retiring, discreet, aloof.

often, *adv.* regularly, many times, habitually, commonly, ordinarily, continually, continuously, again and again, time and again, time after time, day in and day out, most of the time, mostly, frequently, generally, usually, repeatedly, customarily.
—**Ant.** seldom.
—**Syn. Study.** OFTEN, FREQUENTLY, GENERALLY, USUALLY refer to experiences that are habitual or customary. OFTEN and FREQUENTLY are used interchangeably in most cases, but OFTEN implies numerous repetitions: *We often go there;* whereas FREQUENTLY suggests repetition at comparatively short intervals: *It happens frequently.* GENERALLY emphasizes a broad or nearly universal quality: *It is generally understood. He is generally liked.* USUALLY emphasizes time, and means in numerous instances: *We usually have hot summers.*

ointment, *n.* unguent, emollient, salve, balm, lotion, demulcent.

old, *adj.* **1.** aged, elderly, aging, senior, advanced in years, gray, past one's prime, over the hill, superannuated. **2.** familiar, known. **3.** former, past, ancient, primeval, olden, primitive, antediluvian, antiquated, passé, antique, old-fashioned. **4.** deteriorated, dilapidated, worn, decayed. **5.** experienced, practiced, skilled, adroit, veteran, proficient, adept.
—**Ant.** new, modern.

old-fashioned, *adj.* outmoded, outdated, stale, tired, unfashionable, dead, obsolescent, stuffy, obsolete, antique, passé, antiquated, old, ancient, archaic, old-hat, timeworn, out.
—**Ant.** modern.

omen, *n.* sign, augury, foreboding, portent, token, indication, harbinger, premonition, foreshadowing, warning, forewarning, handwriting on the wall, presage, prognostication.
—**Syn. Study.** See SIGN.

ominous, *adj.* **1.** foreboding, fateful, dark, black, gloomy, lowering, menacing, sinister, threatening; unfavorable, ill-starred, inauspicious, unpropitious. **2.** significant, foreboding, portentous, prophetic, oracular, meaningful, indicative.
—**Ant.** favorable, propitious; insignificant, meaningless.
—**Syn. Study.** OMINOUS, PORTENTOUS, FATEFUL, THREATENING describe something that foretells a serious and significant outcome or consequence. OMINOUS suggests an evil or harmful consequence: *ominous storm clouds.* PORTENTOUS, although it may point to evil or disaster, more often describes something momentous or important: *a portentous change in foreign policy.* FATEFUL also stresses the great or decisive importance of what it describes: *a fateful encounter*

between two influential leaders. THREATENING may point to calamity or mere unpleasantness, but usu. suggests that the outcome is imminent: *a threatening rumble from a volcano.*

only, *adv.* **1.** alone, solely, just, exclusively. **2.** merely, barely, simply, but, just, no more than. **3.** singly, uniquely. —*adj.* **4.** sole, single, unique, solitary, lone. **5.** distinct, exclusive, alone. —*conj.* **6.** but, excepting or except that, however.

ooze, *v.* **1.** percolate, exude, seep, drip, drop, weep, secrete, leak, trickle. —*n.* **2.** mire, slime, mud, muck, sludge, slush, goo, gunk, glop.
—**Ant.** pour, flood.

open, *adj.* **1.** unclosed, uncovered, unenclosed. **2.** accessible, available, public, unrestricted, free. **3.** unfilled, unoccupied, vacant. **4.** undecided, unsettled, undetermined, debatable, disputable, arguable, moot, up in the air. **5.** liable, subject to, unprotected, bare, undefended, exposed. **6.** unreserved, candid, frank, ingenuous, artless, guileless, unconcealed, undisguised; sincere, honest, fair, aboveboard. **7.** expanded, extended, spread out, unclosed. **8.** generous, liberal, free, bounteous, bountiful, munificent, magnanimous, openhanded. **9.** obvious, evident, clear, apparent, plain. —*v.* **10.** unclose, unlock, unfasten, uncover, untie, undo. **11.** uncover, lay bare, bare, expose, reveal, divulge, disclose. **12.** expand, extend, spread out. **13.** begin, start, commence, initiate, inaugurate, launch, get the show on the road or the ball rolling.
—**Ant.** closed; close.
—**Syn. Study.** See FRANK.

opening, *n.* **1.** gap, hole, aperture, orifice, perforation; slit, slot, break, crack, crevice, chink, cranny, chasm, cleft, fissure, rent. **2.** beginning, start, birth, origin, outset, onset, launch, debut, presentation, commencement, initiation, dawn. **3.** vacancy, chance, opportunity, occasion, foothold, break, foot in the door.
—**Ant.** closing.

operate, *v.* **1.** work, run, use, act, function, perform, go, serve. **2.** manage, carry on, run, direct, conduct, control, handle, manipulate, drive.
—**Ant.** fail, break.

operation, *n.* **1.** action, process, procedure, manipulation, performance, proceeding. **2.** efficacy, influence, virtue, effect, force, action. **3.** undertaking, enterprise, project, venture, procedure, transaction, business, affair, maneuver.

operative, *adj.* operating, exerting, influencing, influential, effective, efficacious, efficient, effectual, serviceable.
—**Ant.** inoperative; ineffectual, inefficient.

opiate, *n.* narcotic, drug, anodyne, sedative, sedation, soporific, dope, downer.
—**Ant.** stimulant.

opinion, *n.* sentiment, view, point of view, conclusion, persuasion, belief, judgment, notion, conception, idea, impression, estimation, thought, conviction, perception, theory, viewpoint.
—**Syn. Study.** OPINION, SENTIMENT, VIEW are terms for one's conclusion about something. An OPINION is a belief or judgment that falls short of absolute conviction, certainty, or positive knowledge: *an opinion about modern art.* SENTIMENT refers to a rather fixed opinion, usu. based on feeling or emotion rather than reasoning: *sentiments on the subject of*

divorce. A VIEW is an intellectual or critical judgment based on one's particular circumstances or standpoint; it often concerns a public issue: *views on government spending.*

opinionated, *adj.* obstinate, stubborn, conceited, dogmatic, pigheaded, doctrinaire, inflexible, cocksure, obdurate, mulish, one-sided, partial, partisan, prejudiced, biased, bigoted.
—Ant. liberal, open-minded, unprejudiced.

opponent, *n.* adversary, antagonist, competitor, rival, disputant, contender, competition, contestant; enemy, foe, the opposition.
—Ant. ally, friend, associate.

opportune, *adj.* **1.** appropriate, favorable, advantageous, suitable, apt, suited, fit, fitting, fitted, fortunate, propitious, beneficial, helpful, profitable, lucky. **2.** convenient, timely, well-timed, lucky, felicitous, seasonable.
—Ant. inopportune, inappropriate; inconvenient.

opportunity, *n.* chance, occasion, time, opportune moment.

oppose, *v.* **1.** resist, withstand, counter, object to, defy, take a stand against, resist, contest, attack, counterattack, fight, grapple with, contend against, combat, thwart, confront, contravene, interfere with, oppugn. **2.** hinder, obstruct, prevent, check, bar, block, impede, stop, restrain, inhibit, restrict, obviate. **3.** offset, contrast, counterbalance, play off against, pit against. **4.** contradict, gainsay, deny, refuse.
—Ant. support, aid, help.
—**Syn. Study.** OPPOSE, RESIST, WITHSTAND imply holding out or acting against something. OPPOSE implies offensive action against the opposite side in a conflict or contest; it may also refer to attempts to thwart displeasing ideas, methods, or the like: *to oppose an enemy; to oppose the passage of a bill.* RESIST suggests defensive action against a threatening force or possibility; it may also refer to an inner struggle in which the will is divided: *to resist an enemy onslaught; hard to resist chocolate.* WITHSTAND generally implies successful resistance; it stresses the determination and endurance necessary to emerge unharmed: *to withstand public criticism; to withstand a siege.*

opposite, *adj.* **1.** facing, fronting, vis-à-vis. **2.** contrary, reverse, incompatible, irreconcilable, inconsistent, unlike, divergent, diverse, differing, different. **3.** opposed, adverse, refractory, hostile, antagonistic, inimical.
—Ant. compatible, consistent, like, same; friendly, amiable.

opposition, *n.* **1.** antagonism, hostility, resistance, disapproval, objection, conflict, defiance, antipathy. **2.** competition, enemy, foe, opponent, adversary, antagonist. **3.** offset, antithesis, contrast. **4.** contrariety, inconsistency, incompatibility, difference.
—Ant. help, support, furtherance; consistency, compatibility.

oppress, *v.* **1.** depress, weigh down, burden, afflict, trouble, overload, encumber, overwhelm, pressure. **2.** maltreat, harass, abuse, harry, persecute, wrong. **3.** overwhelm, crush, overpower, subdue, suppress, repress, subjugate, tyrannize.
—Ant. delight, liberate.

oppression, *n.* **1.** repression, suppression, subjection, subjugation, enslavement, maltreatment, abuse,

injury, pain, cruelty, injustice, tyranny, despotism, persecution, severity. **2.** hardship, affliction, wretchedness, woe, misery, suffering, calamity. **3.** depression, sadness, misery, torment, torture.

optimistic, *adj.* hopeful, upbeat, sanguine, full of hope, expectant, confident, sunny, rosy, cheerful, positive, buoyant, bullish, Pollyannaish, Panglossian.
—Ant. pessimistic, discouraged, doubtful, hopeless.

option, *n.* choice, selection, preference, alternative, opportunity, recourse.
—**Syn. Study.** See CHOICE.

opulent, *adj.* **1.** wealthy, rich, affluent, moneyed, prosperous, well-off, well-to-do, comfortable, well-heeled, flush, loaded, in the chips; lavish, deluxe, fancy, swanky, posh, ritzy, plush, sumptuous, luxurious. **2.** abundant, copious, plentiful, bountiful, prolific, profuse.
—Ant. poor, squalid; scarce.

oral, *adj.* verbal, spoken, mouthed, uttered, said, vocal, voiced, enunciated, articulated, viva voce.
—Ant. tacit, silent, taciturn.

oration, *n.* speech, address, lecture, discourse, declamation, harangue, declaration, recitation, monologue.
—**Syn. Study.** See SPEECH.

orbit, *n.* **1.** circuit, revolution, track, circle, round, cycle, ellipse, path, course. —*v.* **2.** revolve, go around, encircle, circle, circumvent.

ordain, *v.* **1.** appoint, call, nominate, elect, select, destine. **2.** decree, order, enact, prescribe, determine. **3.** predestine, predetermine, destine, fate.

ordeal, *n.* trial, test, tribulation, hardship, affliction, trouble, distress, misery, suffering, misfortune, disaster, calamity, adversity, tragedy, difficulty, ill fortune.

order, *n.* **1.** direction, injunction, mandate, law, ukase, dictate, edict, fiat, directive, command, instruction, rule, canon, prescription. **2.** succession, sequence. **3.** method, arrangement, harmony, regularity, symmetry. **4.** disposition, array, arrangement. **5.** class, kind, sort, genus, subclass; tribe, family. **6.** rank, status, importance, standing, position, grade, class, degree. **7.** fraternity, sorority, fellowship, association, guild, brotherhood, sisterhood, community. **8.** peace, calm, serenity, quiet, tranquility, discipline, lawfulness, peacefulness. —*v.* **9.** direct, command, instruct, bid, require; ordain. **10.** regulate, conduct, manage, run, operate, adjust, arrange, systematize, organize, classify, categorize, sort out, codify.
—**Syn. Study.** See DIRECT.

orderly, *adj.* **1.** regular, systematic, methodical. **2.** well-regulated, neat, trim, organized, well-organized. **3.** well-disciplined, well-trained, well-behaved, disciplined, law-abiding, peaceable, civil, decorous, well-mannered.
—Ant. irregular, unsystematic; sloppy, unregulated; undisciplined.
—**Syn. Study.** ORDERLY, SYSTEMATIC, METHODICAL characterize that which is efficient, thorough, and carefully planned. ORDERLY emphasizes neatness, harmony, and logical sequence or arrangement: *an orderly library.* SYSTEMATIC emphasizes an extensive, detailed plan and a relatively complex procedure designed to achieve some purpose: *a systematic search.* METHODICAL is similar in meaning, but stresses a carefully developed plan and rigid adherence to a fixed procedure: *methodical examination of the evidence.*

ordinary, *adj.* **1.** common, usual,

customary, regular, normal, routine, standard, conventional, traditional, typical, everyday, familiar, set, established, accustomed, habitual, frequent. **2.** inferior, second-rate, mean, midding, prosaic, commonplace, run-of-the-mill, average, workaday, passable, so-so, fair, undistinguished, pedestrian, garden-variety, mediocre, indifferent. **3.** plain, homely, common-looking, commonplace.
—Ant. uncommon, extraordinary, unusual; superior; beautiful.
—**Syn. Study.** See COMMON.

organic, *adj.* **1.** systematic, systematized, organized, coherent, integrated, consistent, orderly, structured. **2.** constitutional, structural, inherent, fundamental, essential, vital, integral, basic, elementary, innate.
—Ant. inorganic.

organize, *v.* **1.** coordinate, harmonize, unite, structure, standardize, arrange, classify, codify, catalogue, construct, form, dispose, constitute, make, shape, frame, systematize, order. **2.** establish, found, form, institute, create, originate, initiate, set up.
—Ant. destroy, ruin; disorder.

origin, *n.* **1.** source, rise, fountainhead, derivation, beginning, root, base, wellspring, fount, genesis, dawn, origination, start, commencement, inception, outset, launching, cradle, foundation, birthplace. **2.** parentage, birth, extraction, lineage, heritage, descent, ancestry, pedigree, genealogy, stock.

original, *adj.* **1.** primary, initial, first, earliest, basic; native, indigenous, primordial, primeval, primitive, aboriginal. **2.** new, fresh, novel, inventive, creative, innovative. —*n.* **3.** archetype, pattern, prototype, model, source.
—Ant. secondary; old, old-fashioned.

originate, *v.* **1.** arise, spring, rise, begin, emanate, flow, proceed, stem, issue, emanate, develop. **2.** initiate, invent, discover, create, author, engender, conceive, introduce, coin, devise, pioneer, design, concoct, mastermind, compose, formulate, generate, produce.
—Ant. terminate; follow.

ornament, *n.* **1.** accessory, detail, embellishment, adornment, enhancement, trimming, garnish, frill, frippery, bauble, trinket, decoration, ornamentation, design. —*v.* **2.** decorate, adorn, embellish, beautify, trim, garnish, grace, bedeck, enhance, accessorize, dress up.
—Ant. essential, necessity.

ornate, *adj.* elaborate, adorned, embellished, showy, splendid, flamboyant, sumptuous, elegant, decorated, florid, flowery, rococo, baroque, fancy, lavish, busy, fussy.
—Ant. simple, plain.

orthodox, *adj.* conventional, regular, customary, expected, accepted, recognized, approved, sanctioned, canonical, received, authoritative, doctrinaire, official, prevailing, prevalent, doctrinal, traditional, standard, conformable, conformist, conforming, correct, common, ordinary, popular, kosher, conservative, reactionary, die-hard, hidebound, pedantic.
—Ant. free-thinking, unconventional.

ostensible, *adj.* apparent, outward, superficial, patent, obvious; prominent, noticeable; professed, pretended, plausible.
—Ant. concealed, hidden, implausible.

ostentation, *n.* pretension, pretentiousness, semblance, exhibition,

flashiness, show, showiness, pretense, pretext, display, pageantry, pomp, pompousness, flourish, flamboyance, window dressing.

ostracize, *v.* banish, exile, expatriate, disenfranchise, excommunicate, expel, blackball, blacklist, boycott, isolate, segregate, exclude, avoid, shun, snub, cut.

outcome, *n.* end, result, consequence, issue, aftereffect, effect, upshot, development, aftermath, outgrowth, product, wake, payoff.

outdo, *v.* surpass, excel, exceed, beat, outstrip, outdistance, overcome, defeat, transcend, outshine, top, cap, trump.

outgoing, *adj.* friendly, sociable, approachable, open, gregarious, communicative, talkative, extroverted, demonstrative, expansive, effusive.
—Ant. restrained, shy, reserved.

outlaw, *n.* **1.** criminal, gangster, desperado, fugitive, renegade, pirate, mugger, mobster, mafioso, con artist, highwayman, holdup man, robber, thief, bandit, brigand. —*v.* **2.** forbid, ban, disallow, bar, interdict, proscribe, prohibit.

outline, *n.* **1.** contour, silhouette. **2.** plan, draft, drawing, rough, sketch, cartoon. —*v.* **3.** delineate, draft, draw, sketch, trace, profile, rough out, define, lay out.

outrage, *n.* **1.** violence, violation. **2.** affront, insult, offense, abuse, indignity. —*v.* **3.** shock, abuse, maltreat, injure, offend, ravish, rape.

outspoken, *adj.* frank, open, unreserved, candid, straightforward, plain-speaking.
—Ant. reserved, taciturn.
—**Syn. Study.** See FRANK.

outstanding, *adj.* **1.** renowned, famous, memorable, celebrated, distinguished, noteworthy, important, exceptional, first-rate, superb, extraordinary, super, prominent, eminent, conspicuous, striking. **2.** unsettled, unpaid, owing, due.
—Ant. inconspicuous; paid, settled.

overbearing, *adj.* domineering, dictatorial, bullying, highhanded, overweening, magisterial, despotic, haughty, arrogant, imperious, supercilious.
—Ant. humble, servile.

overcome, *v.* **1.** conquer, defeat, beat, triumph over, subjugate, suppress, subdue, vanquish, rout, crush. **2.** surmount. **3.** overpower, overwhelm, discomfit.
—**Syn. Study.** See DEFEAT.

overlook, *v.* **1.** omit, pass over, forget, fail to notice, slight, disregard, miss, neglect, ignore. **2.** excuse, forgive, pardon, condone, write off.
—Ant. regard, attend.
—**Syn. Study.** See SLIGHT.

overpower, *v.* overcome, overwhelm, vanquish, subjugate, subdue, conquer, master, rout, crush, defeat, beat, quell, prevail.

overrule, *v.* disallow, rescind, revoke, repeal, recall, repudiate, set aside, nullify, cancel, annul.
—Ant. allow, permit, approve.

oversee, *v.* supervise, direct, manage, superintend, survey, watch, overlook, administer, operate, run.

oversight, *n.* **1.** mistake, blunder, slip, error, erratum, omission, lapse, neglect, failure, dereliction, carelessness, fault, inattention. **2.** management, direction, control, superintendence, supervision, charge, surveillance, care, guidance, administration; protection, auspices, care, keeping.
—Ant. attention.

overt, *adj.* evident, clear, obvious, clear-cut, patent, visible, open, plain, manifest, showing, apparent, public.

—**Ant.** private, concealed, clandestine, secret.

overthrow, *v.* **1.** cast down, overcome, defeat, vanquish, beat, rout, depose, overwhelm, conquer, oust, unseat, topple, overturn, dethrone, overpower, subjugate, crush. **2.** upset, overturn. **3.** knock down, demolish, destroy, raze, level. **4.** subvert, ruin, destroy. —*n.* **5.** deposition, fall, displacement. **6.** defeat, destruction, ruin, rout, downfall, collapse, ouster, suppression, dispersion, demolition.
—**Ant.** support.

overture, *n.* **1.** approach, advance, tender, opening, proposal, proposition, offer. **2.** prelude, introduction; prologue.
—**Ant.** finale, termination, close, end, epilogue.

overturn, *v.* **1.** overthrow, destroy, vanquish, conquer, upset. **2.** upset, capsize, founder, invert, upend, tip over, turn turtle.

overwhelm, *v.* **1.** overpower, crush, overcome, overtax, stagger, subdue, suppress, quash, quell, conquer, beat, oppress, weigh down, subdue, defeat, vanquish. **2.** overload, overburden, cover, bury, sink, drown, inundate, submerge, flood, deluge, swamp.

own, *v.* **1.** have, hold, possess. **2.** acknowledge, admit, allow, confess, concede, avow; recognize.

P

pace, *n.* **1.** step, tempo, speed, velocity, clip, rate; gait. **2.** step, stride, walk, trot, jog, singlefoot, amble, rack, canter, gallop, run. —*v.* **3.** step, plod, trudge, walk, move, go, stride, tread.
—**Syn. Study.** PACE, PLOD, TRUDGE all mean to walk in a steady and monotonous way. PACE suggests steady, measured steps, as of someone lost in thought or impelled by some distraction: *to pace up and down the hall.* PLOD implies a slow, heavy, laborious walk: *The mail carriers plod their weary way.* TRUDGE implies a spiritless but usu. steady and doggedly persistent walk: *The farmer trudged to the village to buy supplies.*

pacific, *adj.* **1.** conciliatory, appeasing. **2.** peaceable, peaceful, calm, tranquil, at peace, quiet, unruffled, gentle, serene, still.
—**Ant.** hostile; agitated, perturbed.

pacify, *v.* **1.** quiet, calm, tranquilize, assuage, still, smooth, moderate, soften, ameliorate, mollify, meliorate, better, soothe. **2.** appease, conciliate.
—**Ant.** agitate, perturb, aggravate; anger, provoke.

pack, *n.* **1.** package, bundle, parcel, packet; knapsack, backpack, rucksack, duffel bag. **2.** set, gang, collection, crowd, throng, horde, mass, drove, mob, swarm, bevy, gathering, congregation, group, band, company, crew, squad. —*v.* **3.** stow, compress, compact, jam, stuff, fill. **4.** load, burden, lade.

package, *n.* bundle, parcel, packet, pack, bale, container, case, crate, carton, box.

pact, *n.* agreement, compact, contract, deal, arrangement, treaty, entente, understanding, deal, concord, bond, covenant, league, union, concordat, alliance, bargain.

pagan, *n.* **1.** heathen, idolater, gentile, unbeliever, polytheist. —*adj.* **2.** heathen, heathenish, gentile, irreligious, idolatrous, polytheistic.
—**Ant.** believer; pious, religious.
—**Syn. Study.** See HEATHEN.

pageant, *n.* **1.** spectacle, extravaganza, show, masque, tableau, ceremony, gala. **2.** display, show, procession, parade.

pain, *n.* **1.** suffering, distress, hurt, discomfort, soreness, spasm, cramp, affliction, woe, wretchedness, ordeal, torture, misery, anguish, agony, torment, throe, pang, ache, twinge, stitch. **2.** (*plural*) care, efforts, trouble, toil, labor. —*v.* **3.** afflict, torture, torment, distress, hurt, harm, injure, trouble, grieve, aggrieve, disquiet, discommode, incommode, inconvenience, displease, worry, tease, irritate, vex, annoy, wound, cut to the quick.
—**Ant.** joy, delight, pleasure; ease; please.

painful, *adj.* **1.** distressing, torturous, agonizing, tormenting, stinging, throbbing, burning, piercing, stabbing, raw, bitter, excruciating. **2.** laborious, difficult, arduous, severe.
—**Ant.** pleasant, soothing; easy, simple.

painstaking, *adj.* careful, assiduous, sedulous, strenuous, industrious, meticulous, thorough, exacting, demanding, rigorous, arduous.
—**Ant.** careless, frivolous.
—**Syn. Study.** PAINSTAKING, METICULOUS, CONSCIENTIOUS mean extremely careful or precise about details. PAINSTAKING stresses laborious effort and diligent attention to detail in achieving a desired objective: *the painstaking editing of a manuscript.* METICULOUS suggests a more extreme attention to minute details: *to be meticulous about matching shoes and clothing.* CONSCIENTIOUS stresses scrupulous effort to obey one's sense of moral obligation to perform tasks well: *a conscientious description of the facts.*

pair, *n.* **1.** twosome, matched set, duo, twins, double, dyad, couple, brace, span, yoke, two, tandem, team. —*v.* **2.** match, mate, couple, marry, join, pair off, partner, unite, yoke, twin, team, double.

palatable, *adj.* agreeable, appetizing, savory, tasty, gustatory, luscious, delicious, delectable, flavorsome, sapid, edible, yummy.
—**Ant.** unpalatable, tasteless, flavorless.
—**Syn. Study.** PALATABLE, APPETIZING, TASTY, SAVORY refer to tastes or aromas pleasing to the palate, and sometimes to the senses of sight and smell. PALATABLE usu. refers to food that is merely acceptable: *a barely palatable plate of vegetables.* APPETIZING suggests stimulation of the appetite by the smell, taste, or sight of food: *an appetizing display of meats and cheeses.* TASTY refers to food that has an appealing taste: *a tasty sausage.* SAVORY refers most often to well or highly seasoned food that is pleasing to the taste or smell: *a savory stew.*

palatial, *adj.* magnificent, grand, imposing, noble, stately, majestic, splendid, splendiferous, sumptuous, luxurious, deluxe, opulent, elegant, lavish, extravagant, swank, posh, ritzy.
—**Ant.** humble, simple.

pale, *adj.* **1.** pallid, wan, white, ashy, ashen, colorless, faded, washed out, sallow, pasty-faced, whey-faced, haggard, ghostly, bloodless, anemic, drained. **2.** dim, faint, feeble, obscure, weak.
—**Ant.** ruddy, hale, hearty; robust.
—**Syn. Study.** PALE, PALLID, WAN imply an absence of color, esp. from the human countenance. PALE implies a faintness or absence of color, which may be natural when applied to things (*the pale blue of a violet*), but when used to refer to the human face usu. means an unnatural and often temporary absence of color, as arising from sickness or sudden emotion: *pale cheeks.* PALLID, limited mainly to the human countenance, implies an excessive paleness induced by intense emotion, disease, or death: *the pallid lips of the dying man.* WAN implies a sickly paleness, as after a long illness: *wan and thin;* or it may suggest weakness: *a wan smile.*

pall, *n.* **1.** shroud, blanket, cover, covering, veil. —*v.* **2.** glut, satiate, fill, cloy, sate, surfeit, gorge. **3.** weary, tire, fatigue, wear on, jade.

palliate, *v.* moderate, abate, relieve, alleviate, ease, reduce, diminish, lessen, mitigate, soften, cushion.
—**Ant.** intensify, worsen.

pallid, *adj.* **1.** pale, faded, washed out, colorless, white, ashen, sallow, wan, pasty, ghastly, whey-faced. **2.** dull, colorless, insipid, anemic, unexciting, flat, lifeless, bland, nondescript, jejune, monotonous, humdrum.
—**Ant.** robust.
—**Syn. Study.** See PALE.

palpable, *adj.* **1.** obvious, evident, manifest, plain, unmistakable. **2.** tangible, material, real, bodily, substantial, objective, tactile, corporeal, physical, concrete.
—**Ant.** obscure, unclear; intangible, spiritual.

paltry, *adj.* trifling, petty, minor, trashy, mean, worthless, contemptible, insignificant, unimportant, trivial, inconsiderable, slight, small.
—**Ant.** important, major, significant, considerable, essential.
—**Syn. Study.** See PETTY.

pamper, *v.* indulge, gratify, humor, coddle, baby, cater to, spoil, pet.
—**Ant.** discipline.

pan, *v.* criticize, find fault, deprecate, censure, put down, fault, disparage, denigrate, disdain, excoriate, knock, rap, flame, flay, roast, trash.
—**Ant.** praise, extol.

panache, *n.* éclat, showiness, dash, flair, style, flamboyance, dazzle, showmanship, élan, verve, bravura, brilliance, virtuosity.

pang, *n.* **1.** pain, stab, stitch, twinge, prick, throe. **2.** qualm, scruple, compunction, scrupulousness, hesitation, misgiving, remorse, regret, contrition, guilt.

panic, *n.* **1.** terror, fright, alarm, hysteria, anxiety, nervousness, apprehension. —*v.* **2.** terrorize, frighten, alarm, unnerve.
—**Ant.** security; soothe, calm.

pant, *v.* **1.** gasp, breathe heavily, puff, huff, heave, wheeze, blow. **2.** long, yearn, thirst, crave, hanker, ache, pine, want, covet, hunger, desire.

paradigm, *n.* model, ideal, archetype, example, exemplar, standard, pattern, blueprint, criterion, classic example, locus classicus.

paragon, *n.* epitome, archetype, prototype, quintessence, standard, exemplar, criterion, model, ideal, pattern, nonesuch, masterpiece.

parallel, *adj.* **1.** corresponding, similar, analogous, like, resembling, correspondent. —*n.* **2.** match, counterpart, analogue, equivalent, equal. **3.** correspondence, analogy, similarity, resemblance, likeness. —*v.* **4.** match, resemble, repeat, echo, duplicate, correspond to, imitate. **5.** equal, be equivalent to.
—**Ant.** unique, unlike, singular, unusual; dissimilarity; differ.

paralyze, *v.* stun, shock, benumb, unnerve, deaden, stop in one's tracks, immobilize, freeze, disable, cripple, incapacitate, transfix.

paramount, *adj.* supreme, dominant, main, predominant, first, prime, primary, cardinal, essential, requisite, chief, principal.
—**Ant.** base, inferior, unimportant.
—**Syn. Study.** See DOMINANT.

paraphernalia, *n.* belongings, effects; equipment, apparatus, gear, appointments, appurtenances, accouterments, trappings, rig, equipage, stuff, junk.

paraphrase, *n.* **1.** rendering, version, translation, rewrite, rendition, rephrase. —*v.* **2.** restate, rephrase, reword, render, translate; explain, explicate, interpret.

parasite, *n.* yes-man, sycophant, leech, hanger-on, bloodsucker, toady, flatterer, flunky, freeloader, sponge, cadger, scrounger.

parcel, *n.* **1.** package, bundle, pack, packet. **2.** quantity, lot, group, batch, collection. **3.** lot, plot, tract, acreage, portion, land. —*v.* **4.** divide, distribute, mete out, apportion, deal out, allot, dole out, hand out, share, divvy up.

pardon, *n.* **1.** indulgence, allowance, excuse, forgiveness; remission, amnesty, reprieve, absolution. —*v.* **2.** forgive, absolve, remit, condone, excuse, overlook; acquit, clear, release, exonerate, exculpate.
—**Ant.** censure, blame.
—**Syn. Study.** PARDON, AMNESTY, REPRIEVE refer to the remission or delay of a penalty or punishment for an offense; these terms do not imply absolution from guilt. A PARDON is often granted by a government official; it releases the individual from any punishment due: *The governor granted a pardon to the prisoner.* AMNESTY is usu. a general pardon granted to a group of persons for offenses against a government; it often includes an assurance of no further prosecution: *to grant amnesty to the rebels.* A REPRIEVE is a delay of impending punishment, usu. for a specific period of time or until a decision can be made as to the possibility of pardon or reduction of sentence: *a last-minute reprieve, allowing the prisoner to file an appeal.* See also EXCUSE.

pare, *v.* **1.** peel; clip, cut, trim. **2.** diminish, lessen, clip, reduce, decrease.
—**Ant.** increase.

parentage, *n.* birth, descent, lineage, ancestry, origin, extraction, heritage, line, pedigree, family, stock, strain, bloodline, roots.

pariah, *n.* outcast, undesirable, untouchable, castaway, castoff, Ishmael, persona non grata, outsider.

parity, *n.* equality, equivalence, correspondence, similarity, analogy, parallelism, likeness, sameness, uniformity, par, congruity.
—**Ant.** inequality, dissimilarity, difference.

parley, *n.* **1.** conference, discussion, talk, conversation, discourse, dialogue, palaver, deliberation, meeting, colloquy, powwow, huddle. —*v.* **2.** confer, discuss, speak, converse, talk, discourse, negotiate.

parody, *n.* travesty, burlesque, imitation, caricature, lampoon, satire, mockery, mimicry, spoof, take-off.

paroxysm, *n.* fit, spasm, attack, access, seizure, throe, convulsion, spell, fugue, outburst, eruption, irruption, explosion, storm, flare-up.

parsimonious, *adj.* sparing, frugal, stingy, tight, tightfisted, close, niggardly, miserly, illiberal, mean, close-fisted, cheap, economical, thrifty, penurious.
—**Ant.** generous, open-handed, unsparing.
—**Syn. Study.** See STINGY.

part, *n.* **1.** portion, division, piece,

fragment, fraction, section, constituent, component, ingredient, element, member, organ. **2.** allotment, share, apportionment, portion, lot, dividend, concern, participation, interest, stock. **3.** (*usually plural*) region, quarter, neighborhood, area, corner, vicinity, neck of the woods, district, section. **4.** duty, function, role, office, responsibility, charge. **—*v.* 5.** divide, break, cleave, separate, sever, sunder, disunite, dissociate, dissever, disconnect, disjoin, detach. **6.** share, allot, portion, parcel out, apportion, distribute, deal out, mete out. **7.** depart, leave, go, quit; pass on *or* away, die, go to Glory, go to meet one's Maker.
—Ant. all, none, nothing, everything.

partial, *adj.* **1.** incomplete, unfinished, fragmentary, imperfect, limited. **2.** biased, prejudiced, one-sided, unfair, unjust, influenced, partisan.
—Ant. complete, perfect; unbiased, unprejudiced, just, fair.

partiality, *n.* **1.** bias, favor, prejudice, one-sidedness, injustice, unfairness, favoritism. **2.** fondness, liking, preference, bent, leaning, tendency, predilection, inclination, weakness, soft spot, penchant.
—Ant. justice, fairness; dislike, disfavor.

particle, *n.* mite, whit, jot, iota, tittle, bit, mote, grain, ace, scrap, scintilla, morsel, shred, sliver, smidgen, speck, molecule, atom.

particular, *adj.* **1.** special, specific, certain, peculiar, singular, isolated, individual, distinct, precise, express. **2.** one, individual, single, separate, distinct, discrete. **3.** noteworthy, marked, unusual, notable, extraordinary; peculiar, singular, odd, uncommon. **4.** exceptional, especial, characteristic, distinctive. **5.** certain, personal, special. **6.** detailed, descriptive, minute, circumstantial, critical, scrupulous, strict, careful, exact, precise. **7.** demanding, fussy, meticulous, hypercritical, critical, finical, finicky, discriminating, dainty, nice, fastidious, scrupulous. **—*n.* 8.** point, detail, circumstance, item, feature, particularity, specific.
—Ant. general, overall; common, ordinary; inexact, imprecise; undiscriminating, indiscriminate.

particularly, *adv.* **1.** exceptionally, especially, specially. **2.** specially, especially, individually, characteristically, uniquely, separately, discretely, unusually, specifically, singly. **3.** minutely, exactly, precisely, strictly.
—Ant. generally; commonly, usually, customarily.

partisan, *n.* **1.** adherent, supporter, follower, disciple, devotee, backer. **—*adj.* 2.** biased, partial, one-sided, sectarian, opinionated, prejudiced, parochial, myopic, shortsighted, narrowminded, limited.
—Ant. leader; unbiased, impartial.
—Syn. Study. See FOLLOWER.

partition, *n.* **1.** division, distribution, portion, share, allotment, apportionment. **2.** separation, division, split-up, partitioning, breakup, segmentation. **3.** part, section, division, segment, piece. **4.** barrier, wall, dividing wall, screen. **—*v.* 5.** divide, separate, apportion, portion, parcel out, deal out, mete out, share.
—Ant. unity; unite.

partner, *n.* **1.** sharer, partaker, associate, accessory, accomplice, ally, participant, colleague. **2.** husband, wife, spouse, lover, consort, companion, helpmate, helpmeet.

party, *n.* **1.** celebration, fête, gathering, function, reception, soirée, festivities, carousal, orgy, get-together, bash, blast, shindig, blowout, wingding, rave. **2.** group, gathering, assembly, assemblage, company. **3.** body, faction, circle, coterie, clique, set, combination, ring, league, alliance.

pass, *v.* **1.** go, move, proceed. **2.** disregard, pass over, skim over, skim, ignore. **3.** transcend, exceed, surpass. **4.** spend; circulate. **5.** convey, transfer, transmit, send, deliver. **6.** sanction, approve, okay, enact. **7.** leave, go away, depart. **8.** end, terminate, expire, cease. **9.** go on, happen, take place, occur. **10.** vanish, fade, die, disappear. **—*n.* 11.** notch, defile, ravine, gorge, gulch, canyon, channel. **12.** permission, license, ticket, passport, visa. **13.** stage, state, juncture, situation, condition.
—Ant. attend, regard, note, notice; disapprove; arrive, come; initiate, begin, start; appear.

passage, *n.* **1.** paragraph, verse, line, section, clause, text, extract, excerpt, selection, part, portion. **2.** way, route, avenue, channel, road, path, byway, lane, street, thoroughfare. **3.** movement, transit, transition, passing. **4.** voyage, trip, tour, excursion, journey. **5.** progress, course, advance, flow, march. **6.** passing, ratification, adoption, legalization, enactment.

passion, *n.* **1.** feeling, emotion, enthusiasm, zeal, ardor, eagerness, intensity, frenzy, fire, burning, fervor, transport, rapture, excitement; hope, fear, joy, grief, anger, love, attachment, affection, fondness, warmth. **2.** anger, ire, resentment, fury, wrath, rage, vehemence, indignation.
—Ant. coolness, apathy.
—Syn. Study. See FEELING.

passionate, *adj.* **1.** impassioned, emotional, ardent, vehement, excited, excitable, impulsive, fervent, fervid, zealous, enthusiastic, earnest, burning, fiery; animated, impetuous, violent. **2.** quick-tempered, irascible, short-tempered, temperamental, testy, touchy, choleric, hasty. **3.** sexual, erotic, sensual, amorous, lustful, lecherous, lusty, aroused, hot.
—Ant. dispassionate, cool, cold; calm, collected.

passive, *adj.* **1.** inactive, quiescent, inert, dormant, motionless, placid, phlegmatic, apathetic, listless, imperturbable, indifferent. **2.** suffering, receiving, submitting, submissive, compliant, unassertative, patient, resigned.
—Ant. active, energetic; hostile, resisting.

password, *n.* watchword, shibboleth, countersign, open sesame.

pastime, *n.* diversion, amusement, sport, entertainment, recreation, hobby, avocation, distraction.

patch, *v.* mend, repair, restore, fix, correct, emend; settle, smooth.
—Ant. break, crack, ruin, spoil.

patent, *adj.* open, manifest, evident, plain, clear, apparent, transparent, manifest, self-evident, unequivocal, explicit, tangible, obvious, palpable, unmistakable, conspicuous, unconcealed.
—Ant. concealed, hidden, unclear, dim.

path, *n.* way, walk, lane, trail, footpath, pathway, route, course, track, passage, road, avenue.

pathetic, *adj.* pitiable, touching, moving, affecting, tender, stirring, poignant, tragic, heartbreaking, wretched, sad, mournful, sorrowful, doleful, woeful, lamentable, pitiful.

patience, *n.* **1.** calmness, composure, endurance, fortitude, stoicism, stability, courage, self-possession, inner strength, submissiveness, submission, sufferance, resignation. **2.** perseverance, diligence, assiduity, sedulousness, indefatigability, persistence.
—Ant. impatience.

patient, *adj.* persevering, diligent, persistent, sedulous, assiduous, indefatigable, untiring; long-suffering, submissive, resigned, passive, composed; forbearing, tolerant, lenient, forgiving, accommodating.
—Ant. hostile, agitated; excited, perturbed.

pattern, *n.* **1.** model, original, prototype, archetype, ideal, standard. **2.** design, motif, figure, decoration, ornament, device. **3.** system, arrangement, order, plan, theme; repetition, regularity. **4.** plan, layout, diagram, drawing, blueprint, guide, mold, matrix, template. **5.** example, instance, sample, specimen, representation. **—*v.* 6.** imitate, copy, mimic, model on, follow.

pause, *n.* **1.** rest, wait, hesitation, suspension, lacuna, hiatus, interruption, delay, intermission, lull, breather, breathing space, break; stop, halt, cessation, stoppage. **—*v.* 2.** hesitate, waver, deliberate, wait, rest, interrupt, tarry, delay, mark time, suspend. **3.** cease, stop, arrest, halt, desist, forbear.
—Ant. continuity, continuousness.

pay, *v.* **1.** settle, liquidate, discharge. **2.** satisfy, compensate, reimburse, remunerate, recompense; reward; indemnify. **3.** yield, be profitable to, repay, requite. **4.** punish, repay, retaliate, requite, revenge. **5.** make amends, suffer, be punished, make compensation. **—*n.* 6.** payment, compensation, recompense, settlement, return, reward, gain, profit, consideration, wages, salary, income, stipend, remuneration, emolument, fee, allowance. **7.** requital, reward, punishment, just deserts.

payment, *n.* pay; expenditure, outlay, expense, contribution, disbursement, charge.

peace, *n.* **1.** agreement, treaty, armistice, truce, pact, accord, entente, entente cordiale, amity, harmony, concord. **2.** order, security. **3.** calm, quiet, tranquility, peacefulness, calmness, serenity.
—Ant. insecurity; agitation, disturbance.

peaceable, *adj.* pacific, peaceful, amicable, friendly, amiable, mild, dovish, nonviolent, temperate, gentle; calm, tranquil, serene, quiet.
—Ant. hostile, unfriendly; noisy.

peaceful, *adj.* tranquil, placid, serene, unruffled, calm, complacent; composed, mellow; unexcited, unagitated, pacific.
—Ant. perturbed, disturbed.
—Syn. Study. PEACEFUL, PLACID, SERENE, TRANQUIL refer to what is characterized by lack of strife or agitation. PEACEFUL is rarely applied to persons; it refers to situations, scenes, and activities free of disturbances or, occasionally, of warfare: *a peaceful afternoon; a peaceful protest.* PLACID, SERENE, TRANQUIL are used mainly of persons; when used of things (usu. elements of nature) there is a touch of personification. PLACID suggests an unruffled calm that verges on complacency: *a placid disposition; a placid stream.* SERENE is a somewhat nobler word; when used of persons it suggests dignity, composure, and graciousness; when applied to nature there is a suggestion of mellowness: *a serene summer landscape.* TRANQUIL implies a command of emotions that keeps one unagitated even in the midst of excitement or danger: *She remained tranquil despite the chaos around her.*

peak, *n.* point, top, crest, summit, acme, pinnacle, apex, culmination, apogee, zenith, crown, climax.
—Ant. base, bottom, abyss.

peaked, *adj.* pale, sickly, wan, drawn, haggard, pinched, emaciated, unhealthy, infirm, wasted, hollow-eyed, anemic, pallid, pasty, sallow, washed out, drained, gaunt, weak, feeble, sickly, unwell, ailing, waxen.
—Ant. hale, hearty, robust.

pearly, *adj.* opalescent, opaline, nacreous, lustrous, iridescent, mother-of-pearl, pale, whitish, light, snowy, dove-gray, pearl-gray.

peccadillo, *n.* petty sin *or* offense, slight crime, trifling fault, indiscretion, transgression, lapse, slip, error, misstep, shortcoming, weakness.

peculiar, *adj.* **1.** strange, odd, weird, queer, eccentric, bizarre, uncommon, unusual, extraordinary, singular, exceptional, anomalous, aberrant, deviant, outlandish, offbeat, unorthodox, quaint, sui generis, quirky, freakish. **2.** characteristic, appropriate, proper, individual, particular, select, especial, special, specific, unique, exclusive, distinctive.
—Ant. usual, common, ordinary; general, unspecific.

peculiarity, *n.* **1.** idiosyncrasy, abnormality, irregularity, quirk, kink, crotchet, caprice. **2.** singularity, oddity, rarity, eccentricity. **3.** distinction, feature, characteristic, property, quality, trait, attribute.
—Syn. Study. See FEATURE.

pedestrian, *n.* **1.** walker, stroller. **—*adj.* 2.** on foot, walking, afoot. **3.** commonplace, prosaic, dull, boring, banal, tiresome, mundane, run-of-the-mill, dry, humdrum, insipid, flat, trite.
—Ant. interesting, fascinating, engaging.

pedigree, *n.* genealogy, descent, family tree, family, heritage, ancestry, lineage, line, patrimony, birth, origin, extraction, strain, stock, blood, bloodline, parentage, roots.
—Syn. Study. PEDIGREE, GENEALOGY refer to an account of ancestry. A PEDIGREE is a table or chart recording a line of ancestors, either of persons or (more commonly) of animals, as horses, cattle, and dogs; in the case of animals, such a table is used as proof of superior qualities: *a detailed pedigree.* A GENEALOGY is an account of the descent of a person or family traced through a series of generations, usu. from the first known ancestor: *a genealogy that includes a king.*

peek, *v.* peep, peer, pry, glimpse, look, squint at, have a gander at.

peel, *v.* **1.** strip, skin, decorticate, pare, flay, flake off, shuck, hull, scale. **—*n.* 2.** skin, rind, bark, coating, peeling.
—Ant. cover.

peerless, *adj.* matchless, unequaled, unsurpassed, unique, incomparable, nonpareil, consummate, inimitable, *ne plus ultra,* superlative, unmatched, unrivaled, superior, the best.

peevish, *adj.* cross, querulous, fretful, vexatious, vexed, captious, discontented, petulant, testy, irritable, crusty, snappish, waspish, touchy, crabby, churlish, curmudgeonly, crotchety, grumpy, cantankerous, pettish, caviling, cranky, bilious, short-tempered, ill-tempered, ill-natured, nasty, out of sorts.
—Ant. good-natured, friendly, pleasant, amiable, agreeable.

pell-mell, *adv.* headlong, hurriedly, recklessly, agitatedly, frantically, frenziedly, wildly, higgledy-piggledy, helter-skelter, slapdash.

pelt, *v.* **1.** strike, bombard, shower,

bomb, pepper, strafe, shell, attack, assail, assault, pound, clobber, pummel, wallop, work over, beat, batter. —*n.* **2.** blow, whack, hit, smack, slap, bang, stroke. **3.** skin, hide, coat, fur, fleece.

penchant, *n.* liking, leaning, inclination, taste, fondness, bent, propensity, proclivity, affinity, preference, predilection, disposition, predisposition, prejudice, bias, partiality, soft spot, tendency.

penetrate, *v.* **1.** pierce, bore, probe, stab, puncture, enter; permeate, sink in, diffuse, suffuse, pervade. **2.** reach, get to, hit, strike, affect *or* impress deeply, touch. **3.** understand, discern, comprehend, fathom, sense, discover, grasp, unravel, perceive, figure out.
—**Syn. Study.** See PIERCE.

penetrating, *adj.* **1.** piercing, sharp, acute; shrill, strident, earsplitting, pervasive; pungent, harsh, biting, stinging. **2.** acute, discerning, critical, keen, shrewd, sharp, sharpwitted, intelligent, wise, sagacious, incisive, trenchant, searching, deep, perceptive, quick, discriminating, sensitive, clever, smart.
—**Ant.** blunt; uncritical, silly, stupid, undiscriminating.

penitent, *adj.* sorry, contrite, repentant, atoning, remorseful, regretful, sorrowful, rueful, griefstricken, sad, apologetic.

penniless, *adj.* poor, indigent, poverty-stricken, destitute, needy, impoverished, straitened, pinched, down and out, broke, hard-up, impecunious, necessitous, bankrupt, ruined, insolvent, wiped out, financially embarrassed, in reduced circumstances.
—**Ant.** rich, wealthy.
—**Syn. Study.** See POOR.

pensive, *adj.* serious, sober, grave, thoughtful, meditative, reflective, musing, cogitative, brooding, preoccupied, in a trance *or* reverie, dreamy, wistful, contemplative, thinking.
—**Ant.** frivolous, silly, unthinking, thoughtless, vapid.
—**Syn. Study.** PENSIVE, MEDITATIVE, REFLECTIVE suggest quiet modes of apparent *or* real thought. PENSIVE suggests dreaminess *or* wistfulness, and may involve little or no thought to any purpose: *a pensive, faraway look.* MEDITATIVE involves thinking of certain facts or phenomena, perhaps in the religious sense of "contemplation," without necessarily having a goal of complete understanding or of action: *a slow, meditative reply.* REFLECTIVE has a strong implication of orderly, perhaps analytic, processes of thought, usu. with a definite goal of understanding: *a reflective critic.*

penurious, *adj.* mean, parsimonious, stingy, tight, tightfisted, penny-pinching, cheap, ungenerous, thrifty, grudging, skinflinty, close-fisted, close, miserly, niggardly, chintzy.
—**Ant.** generous.

people, *n.* **1.** community, tribe, race, nation, clan, family, population, society. **2.** persons, human beings, humans, men and women, living souls, bodies, individuals, creatures, folks. **3.** populace, commonalty, public. —*v.* **4.** populate, colonize, settle, occupy.

perceive, *v.* **1.** see, discern, notice, note, discover, observe, descry, espy, distinguish, make out, catch sight of, glimpse, spot, mark, remark, detect, identify, take in. **2.** apprehend, understand, see, discern, appreciate, grasp, feel, sense, gather, comprehend, deduce, infer, conclude, determine, ascertain, figure

out, decipher.
—**Ant.** ignore.
—**Syn. Study.** See NOTICE.

perceptible, *adj.* noticeable, detectable, solid, concrete, appreciable, understandable, discernible, apparent, perceivable, evident, obvious, notable, manifest, plain, clear, prominent, palpable, patent, unmistakable, recognizable.
—**Ant.** undiscernible, concealed.

perception, *n.* **1.** appreciation, grasp, comprehension, perspective, cognition, recognition, perceiving, view, opinion, apprehension, understanding, discernment. **2.** intuition, insight, instinct, feeling, impression, idea, notion.
—**Ant.** misapprehension, misunderstanding.

perceptive, *adj.* astute, discerning, sensitive, responsive, keen, sharp, quick-witted, intelligent, acute, sensible, observant, bright, insightful, perspicacious, understanding, appreciative, sagacious, judicious, alert, attentive, on the ball.

perennial, *adj.* timeless, endless, unfailing, ceaseless, enduring, perpetual, perdurable, everlasting, permanent, imperishable, undying, deathless, eternal, immortal; lasting, durable, stable, lifelong, persistent, chronic, constant, incessant, continual.
—**Ant.** evanescent, temporary, flimsy, mortal; inconstant; sporadic.

perfect, *adj.* **1.** complete, finished, absolute, fulfilled, pure, entire, whole, ideal, completed, full, consummate. **2.** faultless, spotless, unblemished, excellent, exquisite. **3.** skilled, adept, adroit, expert, accomplished. **4.** typical, exact; thorough, sound, unqualified, pure, unmixed, unadulterated. —*v.* **5.** complete, finish, realize, fulfill, achieve, effect, execute, carry out, bring to perfection, consummate, accomplish.
—**Ant.** incomplete, unfinished; imperfect; maladroit.

perform, *v.* **1.** carry out, execute, do, discharge, transact. **2.** fulfill, accomplish, achieve, effect.

perfume, *n.* **1.** essence, attar, scent, extract, fragrance, cologne, toilet water; incense. **2.** redolence, scent, odor, smell, aroma, fragrance, bouquet, nose.
—**Ant.** stench, stink, noxiousness.
—**Syn.** PERFUME, FRAGRANCE, AROMA all refer to agreeable odors. PERFUME often indicates a strong, rich smell: *the perfume of flowers.* FRAGRANCE is usu. applied to a sweet, delicate, and fresh smell, esp. from growing things: *the fragrance of new-mown hay.* AROMA is usu. restricted to a distinctive, pervasive, somewhat spicy smell: *the aroma of coffee.*

perfunctory, *adj.* routine, automatic, businesslike, robotic, unspontaneous, formal, apathetic, removed, distant, offhand, cursory, fleeting, rushed, hasty, hurried, mechanical, indifferent, careless, superficial.
—**Ant.** careful, diligent, thoughtful.

peril, *n.* risk, jeopardy, danger, hazard, threat, exposure, vulnerability, susceptibility, uncertainty, insecurity.
—**Ant.** safety, security.
—**Syn. Study.** See DANGER.

period, *n.* interval, time, term, span, duration, spell, space, stretch, while; days, eon, years, age, era, epoch.
—**Syn. Study.** See AGE.

periphery, *n.* **1.** boundary, border, edge, rim, bound, margin, brim, ambit, circumference, perimeter. **2.** surface, outside, edge.
—**Ant.** center; inside.

perish, *v.* **1.** die, pass away, pass on, expire, decease. **2.** decay, age,

wither, shrivel, rot, molder, disappear, vanish, evanesce.
—**Ant.** survive.
—**Syn. Study.** See DIE.

perky, *adj.* jaunty, pert, brisk, lively, cheerful, cheery, bouncy, bright, peppy, spirited, frisky, animated, vivacious, effervescent, bubbly, buoyant, gay, vigorous, invigorated, bright-eyed and bushy-tailed.
—**Ant.** flaccid, retiring.

permanent, *adj.* lasting, unchanging, unchanged, changeless, unchangeable, fixed, persistent, unaltered, stable, immutable, invariant, invariable, constant; enduring, durable, abiding, perpetual, everlasting, remaining, perdurable, eternal, unending, endless, undying, indestructible, abiding, perennial, longlived.
—**Ant.** unstable, temporary, variable, inconstant; temporal.

permeate, *v.* pass through, penetrate, pervade, diffuse through, saturate, sink in, imbue, infiltrate, seep through, soak through, percolate through, spread throughout.

permission, *n.* liberty, license, enfranchisement, franchise, leave, permit, freedom, allowance, consent, assent, acquiescence, sufferance, tolerance, sanction, acceptance, authorization, approval, indulgence.
—**Ant.** refusal.

permit, *v.* **1.** allow, let, tolerate, agree to, endure, suffer, consent to, authorize, sanction, give leave, brook, admit, grant, enable, empower, enfranchise. —*n.* **2.** license, franchise, permission, authority, authorization.
—**Ant.** refuse, disallow.
—**Syn. Study.** See ALLOW.

pernicious, *adj.* **1.** ruinous, harmful, hurtful, detrimental, deleterious, injurious, destructive, damaging, baneful, noxious. **2.** virulent, toxic, poisonous, life-threatening, deadly, fatal, lethal. **3.** evil, wicked, malevolent, malicious, bad, iniquitous, villainous, nefarious, vicious, invidious.
—**Ant.** beneficial, salubrious, healthful; good.

perpendicular, *adj.* vertical, upright, standing, erect, plumb, straight up and down, at right angles to, at ninety degrees to.
—**Ant.** horizontal, parallel.

perpetrate, *v.* do, cause, effect, effectuate, commit, bring about, bring off, perform, carry out, pull off, accomplish, execute, be responsible for, practice.

perpetual, *adj.* everlasting, permanent, continuing, continuous, nonstop, recurrent, repetitive, enduring, constant, eternal, ceaseless, unceasing, incessant, never-ending, longlived, timeless, immutable, unending, endless, interminable, infinite.
—**Ant.** temporary, finite, impermanent; discontinuous.
—**Syn. Study.** See ETERNAL.

perplex, *v.* confuse, puzzle, bewilder, mystify, confound, distract, baffle, befuddle, disconcert, stump, stymie, nonplus, stupefy, stun, daze, dumbfound, flabbergast, throw for a loop.
—**Ant.** clarify.

persecute, *v.* **1.** oppress, harass, badger, molest, vex, afflict, irritate, trouble, annoy. **2.** punish, discriminate against, suppress, subjugate, abuse, outrage, victimize, tyrannize, torture, torment. **3.** importune, annoy, tease, bother, pester, harass, harry, plague, bully, hound.

perseverance, *n.* persistence, tenacity, pertinacity, resolution, resolve, staying power, stamina, grit, pluck,

patience, endurance, diligence, devotion, decisiveness, firmness, purposefulness, stubbornness, doggedness, determination, indefatigability.
—**Ant.** irresolution, impatience.
—**Syn. Study.** PERSEVERANCE, PERSISTENCE, TENACITY imply determined continuance in a state or in a course of action. PERSEVERANCE suggests effort maintained in spite of difficulties or long-continued application; it is used in a favorable sense: *The scientist's perseverance finally paid off in a coveted prize.* PERSISTENCE, which may be used in a favorable or unfavorable sense, implies steadfast, unremitting continuance in spite of opposition or protest: *an annoying persistence in a belief.* TENACITY is a dogged and determined holding on: *the stubborn tenacity of a salesman.*

persevere, *v.* persist, continue, keep on, last, stick it out, hold on, endure, sustain, resolve, decide, pursue doggedly, cling to.

persist, *v.* **1.** persevere, continue, last, linger, stay, endure, remain. **2.** insist, stand fast *or* firm, be staunch *or* steadfast, strive, toil, labor, work hard at.
—**Ant.** stop, discontinue.
—**Syn. Study.** See CONTINUE.

persistent, *adj.* **1.** persisting, persevering, enduring, indefatigable, pertinacious, tenacious, stubborn, pigheaded, immovable, obstinate, obdurate, inflexible, rigid, firm, fast, fixed, staunch, resolute, resolved, determined, unfaltering, unswerving, unflagging, tireless, dogged, unwavering, steadfast. **2.** continued, continual, continuous, continuing, unending, interminable, unrelenting, perpetual, incessant, unceasing, nonstop, repeated, constant, steady.
—**Ant.** amenable, obedient; inconstant, sporadic.
—**Syn. Study.** See STUBBORN.

person, *n.* human being, human, man *or* woman or child, living soul, mortal, body, somebody, individual, personage, one; character.

personality, *n.* character, nature, temperament, disposition, makeup, psyche, persona, constitution, features, attribute, temper, spirit, frame of mind, self, personal identity.
—**Syn. Study.** See CHARACTER.

persuade, *v.* **1.** prevail on, induce, urge, influence, exhort, importune, dispose, entice, impel, incline, prompt, sway, press, force, compel, seduce. **2.** win over, convince, satisfy, convert, talk into.
—**Ant.** dissuade, discourage.
—**Syn. Study.** PERSUADE, INDUCE imply influencing someone's thoughts or actions. They are used mainly in the sense of winning over a person to a certain course of action: *I persuaded her to call a doctor. I induced her to join the club.* They differ in that PERSUADE suggests appealing more to the reason and understanding: *I persuaded him to go back to work;* INDUCE emphasizes only the idea of successful influence, whether achieved by argument or promise of reward: *What can I say that will induce you to stay at your job?* Owing to this idea of compensation, INDUCE may be used in reference to the influence of factors as well as of persons: *The prospect of a raise in salary induced me to stay.*

pert, *adj.* bold, forward, impertinent, saucy, presumptuous, impudent, flippant, brash, brazen, cheeky, insolent, rude, impolite, fresh, out of line, brassy, big-mouthed.
—**Ant.** retiring, shy, bashful; polite, courteous.

pertinent, *adj.* pertaining, relating,

relevant, apt, germane, appropriate, apposite, fit, fitting, fitted, suited, suitable, applicable, proper.
—**Ant.** irrelevant, inappropriate, unsuited, unsuitable, improper.
—**Syn. Study.** See APT.

perturb, v. **1.** disturb, upset, fluster, ruffle, unsettle, disconcert, vex, worry, alarm, shake up, discompose, unnerve, discomfit, disquiet, agitate, stir up, trouble. **2.** disturb, derange, disorder, confuse, addle, muddle, disorganize.
—**Ant.** pacify, calm, tranquilize; clarify.

peruse, v. study, read, scrutinize, examine, survey, pore over, inspect, review, vet, scan, browse, run through, eyeball.
—**Ant.** skim.

pervade, v. permeate, diffuse, sink in, penetrate, pass through.

perverse, adj. **1.** wrongheaded, contradictory, improper, irregular, unfair, contrary, contumacious, disobedient, wayward, cantankerous, obstreperous, captious, fractious, irascible, sullen, surly, quarrelsome, churlish, curmudgeonly, bad-tempered, testy, cross, contentious, crabby, irritable, grouchy, cranky. **2.** willful, persistent, obstinate, stubborn, headstrong, pigheaded, dogged, intractable, unyielding, refractory.
—**Ant.** amiable, obedient; amenable, tractable.
—**Syn. Study.** See WILLFUL.

perverted, adj. deviant, deviate, abnormal, unnatural, warped, twisted, misguided, misapplied, distorted, wicked, amoral, immoral, profligate, dissolute, degraded, degenerate, debauched, evil, malign, malicious, malevolent, sinful, iniquitous, bad, base, foul, corrupt, corrupted, unprincipled, outrageous, perverse.

pessimistic, adj. cynical, gloomy, dark, foreboding, negative, hopeless, glum, despairing, depressed, dejected, despondent, melancholy, downhearted, heavy-hearted, defeatist, sad, sorrowful, blue, joyless, bleak, forlorn.
—**Ant.** optimistic, rosy, sanguine, positive, buoyant, cheerful, light-hearted, joyous.

pest, n. **1.** nuisance, annoyance, bother, vexation, irritant, nag, trial, gadfly, heckler, curse, thorn in one's side, pain in the neck, nudge. **2.** pestilence, plague, scourge, bane; epidemic, pandemic.

pester, v. harass, annoy, vex, torment, torture, molest, harry, hector, tease, trouble, plague, nettle, disturb, provoke, bother, worry, gall, badger, irritate, chafe, nag, irk, fret, heckle, needle, peeve, pique, exasperate, get on (someone's) nerves, try (someone's) patience, persecute, hassle, bug, drive (someone) up the wall, give (someone) a hard time.

pet, n. **1.** favorite, idol, apple of one's eye, fair-haired girl or boy, darling; lapdog. —v. **2.** fondle, indulge, baby, caress, stroke, pat, cuddle, pamper, humor, dote on, mollycoddle, spoil.

petition, n. **1.** request, supplication, suit, prayer, plea, entreaty, solicitation, appeal, application. —v. **2.** entreat, supplicate, beg, pray, request, ask, plead, appeal, solicit, sue, beseech, implore, importune.

petty, adj. **1.** unimportant, trifling, paltry, nugatory, trivial, minor, inferior, niggling, puny, piddling, measly, small-time, of no account, no big deal, inconsequential, unimportant, lesser, little, small, insignificant, negligible, inconsiderable. **2.** narrow, narrowminded, small. **3.** mean, ungenerous, stingy, miserly,

grudging, cheap, tightfisted, niggardly, parsimonious.
—**Ant.** important, considerable, significant; broadminded; generous.
—**Syn. Study.** PETTY, PALTRY, TRIVIAL, TRIFLING apply to something that is so insignificant as to be almost unworthy of notice. PETTY implies lack of significance or worth: petty quarrels. PALTRY applies to something that is contemptibly small or worthless: I was paid a paltry sum. TRIVIAL applies to something that is slight or insignificant, often being in contrast to something that is important: a trivial task. TRIFLING is often interchangeable with TRIVIAL; however, TRIFLING implies an even lesser, almost negligible, importance or worth: to ignore a trifling error.

petulance, n. irritability, peevishness, fretfulness, impatience, bad mood, ill temper, irascibility, churlishness, cholera, spleen, moodiness, sourness, huff, crabbiness, crossness, perversity, grouchiness, grumpiness, captiousness, pettishness, testiness, waspishness.

petulant, adj. irritable, peevish, fretful, vexatious, waspish, snappish, testy, short-tempered, hotheaded, hot-tempered, peppery, bilious, splenetic, choleric, moody, crabby, huffy, perverse, grumpy, pettish, touchy, cross, captious, sour, testy, cantankerous, curmudgeonly, crotchety.
—**Ant.** even-tempered, temperate, pleasant.

phantom, n. **1.** phantasm, apparition, specter, ghost, spirit, shade, wraith, vision, spook; illusion, delusion, figment of the imagination, chimera, hallucination, fancy, mirage. —adj. **2.** unreal, illusive, spectral, illusory, phantasmal; imaginary, hallucinatory.
—**Ant.** real, flesh-and-blood, material.

phenomenon, n. **1.** fact, occurrence, event, occasion, experience, happening, incident, circumstance. **2.** prodigy, marvel, wonder, miracle, curiosity, spectacle, sight, sensation, rarity, exception.

philander, v. flirt, trifle, dally, cheat, commit adultery, fool around, deceive, sleep around, play the field, traduce, betray.

philanderer, n. playboy, lover, flirt, roué, rake, lady-killer, skirt-chaser, Casanova, Lothario, Romeo, Don Juan, womanizer, wolf, stud, macho man, adulterer, cheat, deceiver.

phlegm, n. **1.** sluggishness, stoicism, apathy, lethargy, torpor, stolidness, listlessness, indolence, indifference. **2.** coolness, calm, self-possession, coldness, impassivity, impassiveness.

phobia, n. dread, fear, horror, terror, apprehension, qualm, loathing, revulsion, repugnance, distaste, antipathy, aversion, hatred.
—**Ant.** like, attraction, love.

phony, adj. **1.** false, sham, counterfeit, mock, pretend, make-believe, synthetic, artificial, fraudulent, imitation, bogus, ersatz, unreal, factitious, trumped-up, spurious, brummagem, pinchbeck, pseudo. —n. **2.** impostor, faker, mountebank, charlatan, pretender, fraud, humbug, bluffer, fourflusher, trickster, double-dealer, quack, deceiver, hypocrite, crook.
—**Ant.** genuine, authentic.

physical, adj. **1.** bodily, corporeal, corporal, mortal, fleshly, incarnate, carnal, earthly, natural, somatic; tangible, sensible. **2.** material, real, natural, palpable, concrete, actual, true, solid.
—**Ant.** mental, spiritual; unnatural, unreal.

—**Syn. Study.** PHYSICAL, BODILY, CORPOREAL, CORPORAL agree in pertaining to the body. PHYSICAL means connected with or pertaining to the animal or human body as a material organism: physical strength. BODILY means belonging to or concerned with the human body as distinct from the mind or spirit: bodily sensations. CORPOREAL, a more poetic and philosophical word, refers esp. to the mortal substance of which the body is composed, as opposed to spirit: our corporeal existence. CORPORAL is usu. reserved for reference to suffering inflicted on the human body: corporal punishment.

pick, v. **1.** choose, select, cull. **2.** criticize, find fault with. **3.** steal, rob, pilfer. **4.** pierce, indent, dig into, break up, peck. **5.** pluck, harvest, garner, gather, reap, collect, get, acquire. —n. **6.** choice, option, preference, election, selection; choicest part, best.

picture, n. **1.** painting, drawing, photograph, representation, portrait, depiction, illustration, sketch, portrayal, artwork. **2.** image, representation, similitude, semblance, likeness. **3.** description, account, representation. —v. **4.** imagine; depict, describe, delineate, portray, show, illustrate, display, paint, draw, represent.

picturesque, adj. **1.** striking, interesting, colorful, intriguing, unusual, unique, original, charming, idyllic, pretty, lovely, eye-catching, delightful, pleasing, scenic, beautiful. **2.** graphic, vivid, impressive; intense, lively.
—**Ant.** uninteresting, dull, colorless.

piece, n. **1.** portion, share, fraction, part, division, proportion, quantity, segment, section; bit, morsel, chunk, hunk, sliver, lump, particle, shard, remnant, scrap, shred, fragment. **2.** thing, example, instance, specimen. **3.** selection, work, composition, story, article, play.
—**Ant.** all, everything; none, nothing.

piecemeal, adv. **1.** gradually, bit by bit, inchmeal, inchwise, slowly, by degrees. **2.** separately, fractionally, disjointedly, spasmodically.

pierce, v. **1.** penetrate, enter, run through or into, perforate, stab, puncture, bore, drill, skewer, impale, thrust or poke into, lance, spear, spit, fix, transfix. **2.** affect, touch, move, rouse, thrill, excite, stir, pain, wound, cut to the quick.
—**Syn. Study.** PIERCE, PENETRATE suggest the action of one object passing through another or making a way through and into another. These terms are used both concretely and figuratively. TO PIERCE is to perforate quickly, as by stabbing; it suggests the use of a sharp, pointed instrument impelled by force: to pierce the flesh with a knife; a scream that pierced my ears. PENETRATE suggests a slow or difficult movement: No ordinary bullet can penetrate an elephant's hide; to penetrate the depths of one's ignorance.

piety, n. **1.** reverence, deference, dedication, dutifulness, loyalty, affection, regard, respect. **2.** godliness, devoutness, devotion, sanctity, grace, holiness, piousness, religiousness, veneration.
—**Ant.** irreverence, disrespect.

pile, n. **1.** assemblage, mound, stack, stockpile, supply, deposit, batch, hoard, aggregation, congeries, assortment, conglomeration, collection, mass, heap, accumulation. **2.** hair, down; wool, fur, pelage; nap.

—v. **3.** heap up, accumulate, assemble, amass, collect, stack, mound, hoard, aggregate, stockpile.

pilfer, v. steal, rob, thieve, plunder, embezzle, palm, snatch, misappropriate, appropriate, purloin, pinch, filch, lift, nick, pocket, swipe, rifle, shoplift, rip off, hook, snitch.

pilgrimage, n. journey, trip, excursion, tour, voyage, expedition, trek.
—**Syn. Study.** See TRIP.

pillage, v. **1.** rob, plunder, rape, despoil, sack, spoil. —n. **2.** booty, plunder, spoils. **3.** rapine, depredation, devastation, spoliation.

pillar, n. shaft, column, stele, post, upright, piling, pile, pilaster, obelisk, support, pier, prop.

pillory, v. mock, ridicule, deride, scorn, revile, sneer at, vilify, stigmatize, besmirch, smear, tarnish, blacken, skewer, crucify, tar and feather.
—**Ant.** praise, esteem.

pin, n. **1.** peg, fastening, bolt. **2.** brooch, clip. —v. **3.** fasten, fix, affix, attach, secure, tack, staple, clip, immobilize, tie down.

pine, v. **1.** yearn, long, ache, hunger, thirst, crave, itch, sigh. **2.** languish, fade, dwindle, wilt, droop, pine away.
—**Syn. Study.** See YEARN.

pinnacle, n. peak, eminence, culmination, tower, tip, crest, cap, crown, summit, apex, acme, zenith, top, climax, maximum, utmost, extreme.
—**Ant.** base.

pioneer, v. **1.** lead, precede, blaze a trail, break new ground, open up, kick off, guide, forerun. **2.** initiate, introduce, originate, institute, trigger, launch, develop, inaugurate, found, invent, create, dream up. —n. **3.** frontiersman, explorer, colonist, early settler; groundbreaker, predecessor, innovator, leader, trendsetter, pacesetter, forerunner, precursor, pathfinder, trailblazer, vanguard, bellwether, point man, point woman, point person.

pious, adj. **1.** devout, reverent, worshipful, reverential, dutiful, God-fearing, faithful, moral, spiritual, virtuous, saintly, angelic, seraphic, Christlike, godly, religious, holy. **2.** sanctimonious, hypocritical, self-righteous, pharisaical, goody-goody.
—**Ant.** impious, irreligious, unholy.
—**Syn. Study.** See RELIGIOUS.

piquant, adj. **1.** pungent, sharp, flavorsome, tart, spicy. **2.** stimulating, interesting, attractive, sparkling. **3.** smart, sharp, clever.
—**Ant.** insipid; uninteresting, unattractive; dull.

pique, v. **1.** offend, nettle, sting, irritate, chafe, vex; affront, wound, displease. **2.** interest, stimulate, excite, incite, stir; spur, prick.
—**Ant.** please, delight; compliment.

pit, n. **1.** hole, cavity, burrow, hollow. **2.** excavation, shaft, mine, ditch, trench, trough, well; pitfall, trap. **3.** hollow, depression, dent, indentation. **4.** stone, pip, seed.

piteous, adj. pathetic, pitiable, tearful, deplorable, wretched, miserable; affecting, distressing, moving, pitiful, lamentable, woeful, plaintive, grievous, heartbreaking, sorrowful, sad, mournful, morose, doleful, heart-rending, poignant.
—**Ant.** pleasant, cheerful.
—**Syn. Study.** See PITIFUL.

pithy, adj. terse, concise, brief, short, compact, epigrammatic, compressed, condensed, aphoristic, sententious, abridged, abbreviated, succinct, compendious, laconic, summary, to the point, short and sweet.
—**Ant.** expansive, lengthy, prolix, verbose.

pitiful, *adj.* **1.** pitiable, pathetic, piteous. **2.** small, insignificant, trifling, unimportant, beggarly, sorry, contemptible, deplorable, mean.
—**Syn. Study.** PITIFUL, PITIABLE, PITEOUS apply to that which arouses pity (with compassion or with contempt). That which is PITIFUL is touching and excites pity or is mean and contemptible: *a pitiful leper; a pitiful exhibition of cowardice.* PITIABLE may mean lamentable, or wretched and paltry: *a pitiable hovel.* PITEOUS refers only to that which exhibits suffering and misery, and is therefore heartrending: *piteous poverty.*

pitiless, *adj.* merciless, cruel, mean, unmerciful, ruthless, savage, brutal, harsh, tyrannical, stonyhearted, harsh, severe, cold, implacable, relentless, inexorable, hardhearted, heartless, inhumane, callous, malevolent, unsympathetic, indifferent, thoughtless.
—**Ant.** merciful, softhearted, kind, kindly.

pity, *n.* **1.** sympathy, compassion, commiseration, condolence, empathy, sorrow, kindness, tenderness, mercy. —*v.* **2.** commiserate, be *or* feel sorry for, sympathize with, empathize, weep for, feel for.
—**Ant.** apathy, cruelty, ruthlessness.
—**Syn. Study.** See SYMPATHY.

place, *n.* **1.** space, plot, spot, location, locale, locality, site, position, point, locus, area, scene, setting. **2.** condition, position, situation, circumstances. **3.** job, post, office, function, duty, berth, appointment, livelihood, charge, responsibility, employment, rank. **4.** region, area, section, sector. **5.** residence, dwelling, house, home, domicile, apartment, quarters, lodgings, digs, abode. **6.** stead, lien. **7.** opportunity, occasion, reason, ground, cause. —*v.* **8.** position, range, order, dispose, arrange, situate, put, set, locate, station, deposit, lay, seat, fix, establish. **9.** class, classify, sort, order, arrange, rank, group, categorize, regard, view, see, consider.
—**Ant.** misplace, displace.

placid, *adj.* calm, peaceful, unruffled, tranquil, serene, quiet, undisturbed, pacific, still; sedate, temperate, composed, poised, self-possessed, unexcitable, easygoing, unflappable.
—**Ant.** turbulent, tumultuous, perturbed.
—**Syn. Study.** See PEACEFUL.

plague, *n.* **1.** epidemic, pestilence, disease, Black Death, pandemic, holocaust, scourge. **2.** affliction, calamity, evil, curse, bane, blight, visitation, torment, torture. **3.** trouble, vexation, annoyance, nuisance, torment. —*v.* **4.** trouble, anguish, distress, torment, torture, molest, bother, incommode, discommode. **5.** vex, harry, hector, harass, fret, worry, pester, badger, annoy, tease, irritate, disturb, hound, nag, needle, exasperate, gall, irk, bug.
—**Syn. Study.** See BOTHER.

plain, *adj.* **1.** clear, distinct, lucid, unambiguous, unequivocal, intelligible, understandable, perspicuous, evident, manifest, simple, vivid, transparent, graphic, direct, crystal-clear, obvious, unmistakable, patent, apparent. **2.** downright, sheer, direct, transparent. **3.** unambiguous, candid, outspoken, blunt, direct, straightforward, forthright, sincere, frank, guileless, artless, ingenuous, open, unreserved, honest, openhearted. **4.** homely, unpretentious, homey, simple, basic, austere, stark, colorless, drab, bare, Spartan, unembellished, unadorned, frugal. **5.**

ugly, homely, unattractive. **6.** ordinary, common, commonplace, unostentatious. **7.** flat, level, plane, featureless, smooth, even. —*n.* **8.** grassland, pasture, meadowland, veldt, steppe, tundra, heath, moor, flatland, down, mesa, plateau, savanna, prairie, pampas.
—**Ant.** unclear, ambiguous, unintelligible; artful, sly, cunning, deceptive, insincere; beautiful, attractive; uncommon, extraordinary.

plan, *n.* **1.** scheme, plot, arrangement, program, pattern, layout, procedure, project, formula, method, system. **2.** drawing, sketch, floorplan, blueprint, draft, map, chart, diagram, representation. —*v.* **3.** arrange, outline, organize, map out, delineate, develop, scheme, plot, design, devise, contrive, invent, concoct, hatch.

platform, *n.* **1.** stage, dais, rostrum, pulpit; landing. **2.** principles, beliefs, tenets, policy, program, plank, party line.

platitude, *n.* cliché, commonplace, banality, bromide, truism, generalization, prosaicism, old saw, chestnut.
—**Ant.** witticism, mot.

plausible, *adj.* likely, believable, reasonable, credible, conceivable, probable, sound, sensible, rational, logical, acceptable.

play, *n.* **1.** drama, piece, show; comedy, tragedy, melodrama, farce. **2.** amusement, recreation, game, sport, diversion, pastime. **3.** fun, jest, trifling, frolic. **4.** action, activity, movement, exercise, operation, motion. **5.** freedom, liberty, scope, elbow room. —*v.* **6.** act, perform, enact, characterize, impersonate, personate. **7.** compete, contend with *or* against, engage. **8.** stake, bet, wager. **9.** represent, imitate, emulate, mimic. **10.** do, perform, bring about, execute. **11.** toy, trifle, sport, dally, caper, romp, disport, frolic, gambol, skip, revel, frisk, cavort, fool around.
—**Ant.** work.

playful, *adj.* high-spirited, cheerful, fun-loving, mischievous, devilish, frisky, coltish, antic, frolicsome, sportive, sprightly, prankish, puckish, impish, puppyish, kittenish, whimsical.
—**Ant.** somber, sober.

plead, *v.* **1.** entreat, appeal, beg, supplicate, request, petition, implore, beseech, solicit, importune, apply to. **2.** argue, persuade, reason. **3.** assert, maintain, declare, affirm, avow, swear, offer, allege, cite, make a plea, apologize, answer, make excuse.

pleasant, *adj.* **1.** pleasing, agreeable, enjoyable, pleasurable, acceptable, welcome, gratifying. **2.** companionable, sociable, engaging, winning, outgoing, welcoming, hospitable, gracious, charming, genteel, suave, debonair, well-bred, urbane, cultivated, delightful, congenial, polite, courteous, friendly, personable, amiable. **3.** fair, sunny, clear bright, cloudless, balmy, nice, fine. **4.** gay, sprightly, merry, cheery, cheerful, lively, sportive, vivacious. **5.** jocular, facetious, playful, humorous, witty, amusing.
—**Ant.** unpleasant, displeasing.

pleasing, *adj.* agreeable, pleasant, acceptable, pleasurable, charming, delightful, amusing, diverting, entertaining, enjoyable, delectable, interesting, engaging, attractive, winning, winsome.
—**Ant.** disagreeable, unpleasant, unacceptable.

pleasure, *n.* **1.** happiness, gladness, delectation, enjoyment, delight, joy,

well-being, satisfaction, gratification, fulfillment, contentment, comfort; amusement, diversion, entertainment, recreation, pastime, leisure. **2.** luxury, sensuality, voluptuousness. **3.** will, desire, choice, preference, purpose, wish, mind, inclination, predilection, option, fancy, discretion.
—**Ant.** displeasure, unhappiness; disinclination.

plentiful, *adj.* bountiful, profuse, bounteous, lavish, generous, unstinted, ample, plenteous, copious, abundant, full, rich; fertile, fruitful, productive, exuberant, luxuriant, thriving, prolific, bumper.
—**Ant.** scanty, barren, fruitless.
—**Syn. Study.** PLENTIFUL, AMPLE, ABUNDANT, BOUNTIFUL describe a more than adequate supply of something. PLENTIFUL suggests a large or full quantity: *a plentiful supply of fuel.* AMPLE suggests a quantity that is sufficient for a particular need or purpose: *an auditorium with ample seating for students.* ABUNDANT and BOUNTIFUL both imply a greater degree of plenty: *an abundant rainfall; a bountiful harvest.*

plenty, *n.* fullness, abundance, copiousness, plenteousness, plentifulness, profusion, wealth, bountifulness, lavishness, fertility, luxuriance, exuberance, affluence, extravagance, prodigality; superabundance, overfullness, plethora, excess.
—**Ant.** paucity, scarcity.

pliant, *adj.* pliable, ductile, plastic, clastic, malleable, workable, bendable; supple, flexible, lithe, limber; compliant, easily influenced, yielding, adaptable, manageable, tractable, facile, docile, impressionable, susceptible, responsive, receptive, easily led.
—**Ant.** inflexible; unyielding, rigid, intractable.

plight, *n.* condition, state, situation, predicament, circumstances, difficulty, quandary, straits, trouble, extremity, case, dilemma, hole, jam, pickle, fix, spot, scrape, hot water, fine kettle of fish, mess.
—**Syn. Study.** See PREDICAMENT.

plod, *v.* **1.** tramp, slog, drag, tread, lumber, stomp, galumph, walk heavily, pace, trudge. **2.** toil, moil, labor, drudge, sweat, work, slave, grind, grub, plug away.
—**Syn. Study.** See PACE.

plot, *n.* **1.** plan, scheme, intrigue, conspiracy, cabal, stratagem, machination. **2.** story, theme, thread, story line, chain of events, denouement, outline, scenario, skeleton. —*v.* **3.** devise, contrive, concoct, brew, hatch, frame, design, arrange, organize, dream up, cook up, calculate. **4.** conspire, scheme, contrive, plan, intrigue, machinate, collude.

ploy, *n.* stratagem, strategy, tactic, trick, maneuver, artifice, tactic, scheme, gimmick, dodge, wile, device, feint, gambit, ruse.

pluck, *v.* **1.** pull, jerk, yank, snatch, tug, tear, rip, grab, catch, clutch; pick, remove, withdraw, extract, draw out. —*n.* **2.** courage, grit, backbone, fortitude, resolution, spirit, bravery, boldness, determination, mettle, doughtiness, intrepidity, resolve, nerve, guts, moxie, chutzpah, spunk.

plump, *adj.* fleshy, fat, chubby, stout, portly, corpulent, obese, zaftig, pudgy, full-figured, Rubenesque, curvaceous, buxom, voluptuous, pneumatic, overweight, roly-poly, ample, full-bodied, tubby, rotund, chunky, beefy, broad in the beam, well-upholstered, round.
—**Ant.** thin, slender, skinny.

plunder, *v.* **1.** rob, despoil, fleece,

pillage, loot, ransack, rifle, ravage, rape, sack, vandalize, maraud, desolate, devastate, strip, lay waste. —*n.* **2.** pillage, rapine, spoliation, robbery, looting, depredation, vandalism, sack, theft, plundering. **3.** loot, booty, spoils, prizes, boodle.

plunge, *v.* **1.** immerse, submerge, dip. **2.** dive; rush, hasten; descend, drop, hurtle over. —*n.* **3.** leap, dive, rush, dash, dip, plummet, drop, descent, fall, pitch, nosedive.
—**Syn. Study.** See DIP.

poignant, *adj.* **1.** distressing, heartfelt, serious, intense, severe, bitter, tragic, heartbreaking, excruciating, pathetic, piteous, upsetting, moving, touching, emotional, dramatic, stirring, profound, deep, earnest, sincere. **2.** keen, strong, biting, mordant, caustic, acid, pointed. **3.** pungent, piquant, sharp, biting, acrid, stinging.

pointed, *adj.* **1.** sharp, piercing, acute, barbed, penetrating, epigrammatic, succinct, stinging, piquant, biting, mordant, sarcastic, caustic, severe, keen, incisive, pungent, telling, trenchant. **2.** directed, aimed, explicit, marked. **3.** marked, emphasized, accented, accentuated.
—**Ant.** blunt, dull, mild.

poise, *n.* **1.** balance, equilibrium, equipoise, counterpoise. **2.** composure, self-possession, steadiness, stability, aplomb, assurance, dignity, equanimity, sang-froid, presence of mind, reserve, serenity, coolheadedness, self-control, control. **3.** carriage, mien, demeanor, savoir-faire, sophistication, grace, polish, urbanity, breeding, behavior.
—**Ant.** instability, awkwardness.

poison, *n.* **1.** toxin, venom. —*v.* **2.** envenom, infect. **3.** defile, adulterate, debase, pervert, subvert, warp, corrupt, ruin, vitiate, contaminate, pollute, taint.
—**Syn. Study.** POISON, TOXIN, VENOM are terms for any substance that injures the health or destroys life when absorbed into the system. POISON is the general word: *a poison for insects.* A TOXIN is a poison produced by an organism; it is esp. used in medicine in reference to disease-causing bacterial secretions: *A toxin produces diphtheria.* VENOM is esp. used of the poisons injected by bite, sting, etc.: *snake venom; bee venom.*

policy, *n.* course *of* action, expediency, tactic, approach, game plan, design, scheme, program, method, system, conduct, behavior, strategy, tactics, principles, protocol, way, regulation, custom, practice, procedure, rule, management.

polish, *v.* **1.** brighten, smooth, burnish, shine, buff, rub, gloss, clean. **2.** finish, refine, improve, perfect, cultivate, enhance, ameliorate, fix, civilize, make elegant. —*n.* **3.** smoothness, gloss, shine, sheen, luster, glaze, sparkle, gleam, glow, radiance, brightness, brilliance. **4.** refinement, elegance, poise, grace, graciousness, savoir-faire, cultivation, suaveness, breeding, good manners, culture, politeness, politesse, propriety, dignity, smoothness, good taste, tastefulness, sophistication, urbanity, diplomacy, tactfulness, courteousness, civility.
—**Ant.** dullness.
—**Syn. Study.** POLISH, GLOSS, LUSTER, SHEEN refer to a smooth, shining, or bright surface from which light is reflected. POLISH suggests the smooth, bright reflection often produced by friction: *a lamp rubbed to a high polish.* GLOSS suggests a superficial, hard smoothness characteristic

of lacquered, varnished, or enameled surfaces: *a gloss on oilcloth.* LUSTER denotes the characteristic quality of the light reflected from the surfaces of certain materials, as pearls or freshly cut metals: *a pearly luster.* SHEEN sometimes suggests a glistening brightness such as that reflected from the surface of silk: *the sheen of a satin gown.*

polished, *adj.* **1.** smooth, glossy, burnished, shining, shiny, shined, lustrous, brilliant. **2.** refined, debonair, cultivated, graceful, sophisticated, urbane, soigné, courtly, genteel, civilized, well-bred, polite, cultured, finished, elegant, poised. **3.** accomplished, expert, proficient, skillful, adept, gifted, masterful, virtuoso, superlative, superb, superior; faultless, impeccable, flawless, excellent, perfect. —**Ant.** dull, dim; unrefined, impolite; inelegant; clumsy, amateurish, imperfect.

polite, *adj.* respectful, deferential, diplomatic, tactful, formal, proper, well-mannered, courteous, civil, well-bred, gracious, genteel, urbane, polished, poised, cultivated, refined, finished. —**Ant.** impolite, rude, discourteous, uncivil. —**Syn. Study.** See CIVIL.

politic, *adj.* **1.** sagacious, prudent, wise, tactful, diplomatic, discreet, judicious, provident, astute, wary. **2.** shrewd, artful, sly, cunning, underhanded, tricky, foxy, clever, subtle, Machiavellian, wily, intriguing, scheming, crafty, unscrupulous, strategic. **3.** expedient, judicious, political. —**Ant.** imprudent, indiscreet, improvident; artless, ingenuous, direct, open, honest. —**Syn. Study.** See DIPLOMATIC.

pollute, *v.* **1.** befoul, dirty, defile, adulterate, poison, blight, sully, soil, taint, tarnish, stain, contaminate, vitiate, corrupt, debase, deprave. **2.** desecrate, profane, violate, dishonor, defile. —**Ant.** purify; honor, revere, respect.

ponder, *v.* consider, meditate, reflect, cogitate, deliberate, ruminate, brood, mull over, chew over, muse, think, study; weigh, contemplate, examine. —**Ant.** forget, ignore.

ponderous, *adj.* **1.** heavy, massive, unwieldy, huge, awkward, clumsy, cumbersome, weighty, bulky. **2.** important, momentous, weighty, significant, consequential, grave, serious, critical, crucial. —**Ant.** light, weightless; unimportant.

poor, *adj.* **1.** needy, indigent, necessitous, straitened, insolvent, ruined, bankrupt, destitute, penniless, poverty-stricken, impecunious, impoverished, hard up, distressed, in want, badly off, pinched, down and out, broke, short, financially embarrassed, in reduced circumstances. **2.** deficient, insufficient, meager, lacking, incomplete. **3.** faulty, inferior, unsatisfactory, substandard, shabby, jerry-built, seedy, worthless, valueless. **4.** sterile, barren, unfertile, fruitless, unproductive. **5.** lean, emaciated, thin, skinny, meager, hungry, underfed, lank, gaunt. **6.** cowardly, abject, mean, base. **7.** scanty, paltry, meager, insufficient, inadequate. **8.** humble, unpretentious, unassuming, modest, inconsequential. **9.** unfortunate, hapless, unlucky, star-crossed, doomed, luckless, miserable, pitiable, piteous, pathetic, wretched. —**Ant.** rich, wealthy; sufficient, adequate, complete; superior; fertile;

well-fed; bold, brave; bold, pretentious; fortunate, lucky. —**Syn. Study.** POOR, IMPECUNIOUS, IMPOVERISHED, PENNILESS refer to those lacking money. POOR is the simple word for the condition of lacking the means to obtain the comforts of life: *a very poor family.* IMPECUNIOUS often suggests that the poverty is a consequence of unwise habits: *an impecunious actor.* IMPOVERISHED often implies a former state of greater plenty: *the impoverished aristocracy.* PENNILESS refers to extreme poverty; it means entirely without money: *The widow was left penniless.*

popular, *adj.* **1.** favorite, approved, accepted, received, liked. **2.** common, prevailing, current, general, prevalent, in vogue, faddish, dominant, predominant, customary, habitual, universal. —**Ant.** unpopular; uncommon, rare, unusual. —**Syn. Study.** See GENERAL.

populous, *adj.* crowded, filled, overcrowded, packed, jam-packed, crammed, teeming, swarming.

port, *n.* harbor, haven, refuge, anchorage, mooring; asylum. —**Syn. Study.** See HARBOR.

portent, *n.* indication, omen, augury, sign, warning, presage. —**Syn. Study.** See SIGN.

portion, *n.* **1.** part, section, segment, division, subdivision, parcel, hunk, chunk, lump, wedge, slice, sliver, fraction, piece, bit, morsel, fragment. **2.** share, allotment, quota, dole, dividend, division, apportionment, lot. **3.** serving, helping, ration. —*v.* **4.** divide, distribute, allot, apportion, deal or parcel out, mete, share. —**Ant.** all, everything; none, nothing.

portray, *v.* picture, delineate, limn, depict, paint, represent, sketch, show, render, characterize, describe; impersonate, pose as.

pose, *v.* **1.** sit, model; attitudinize. **2.** state, assert, propound. —*n.* **3.** attitude, posture, bearing, mien, stance, position; affectation, pretense, act, facade, show.

position, *n.* **1.** station, place, locality, spot, location, site, locale, placement, whereabouts, situation, post. **2.** situation, condition, state, circumstances. **3.** class, caste, station, importance, status, standing, rank, place. **4.** post, job, situation, place, employment. **5.** placement, disposition, array, arrangement. **6.** stance, bearing, mien, posture, attitude, pose. **7.** proposition, thesis, contention, principle, dictum, predication, assertion, doctrine. —*v.* **8.** put, place, site, settle, dispose, arrange, fix, set, situate. **9.** locate, fix, discover, establish, determine. —**Syn. Study.** POSITION, POSTURE, ATTITUDE, POSE refer to an arrangement or disposal of the body or its parts. POSITION is the general word for the arrangement of the body: *in a reclining position.* POSTURE is usu. an assumed arrangement of the body, esp. when standing: *a relaxed posture.* ATTITUDE is often a posture assumed for imitative effect or the like, but may be one adopted for a purpose (as that of a fencer or a tightrope walker): *an attitude of prayer.* A POSE is an attitude assumed, in most cases, for artistic effect: *an attractive pose.*

positive, *adj.* **1.** explicit, express, sure, certain, definite, precise, clear, unequivocal, categorical, unmistakable, direct. **2.** arbitrary, enacted, decided, determined, decisive, unconditional. **3.** incontrovertible,

substantial, indisputable, indubitable. **4.** stated, expressed, emphatic. **5.** confident, self-confident, self-assured, assured, convinced, unquestioning. —**Ant.** unsure, indefinite, unclear, equivocal; conditional; doubtful; tacit; tractable, self-effacing.

possess, *v.* **1.** have, hold, own, enjoy, be blessed or endowed with. **2.** occupy, hold, have, control, dominate; preoccupy, captivate, enchant, enthrall. —**Ant.** lose.

possession, *n.* **1.** custody, occupation, tenure. **2.** ownership, title, control, keeping, care, protection, guardianship, proprietorship.

possible, *adj.* feasible, practicable, likely, viable, workable, doable, attainable, potential; plausible, imaginable, conceivable, credible, thinkable, tenable, reasonable. —**Ant.** impossible, impractical, unlikely. —**Syn. Study.** POSSIBLE, FEASIBLE, PRACTICABLE refer to that which may come about or take place without prevention by serious obstacles. That which is POSSIBLE is naturally able or even likely to happen, other circumstances being equal: *He offered a possible compromise.* FEASIBLE refers to the ease with which something can be done and implies a high degree of desirability for doing it: *Which plan is the most feasible?* PRACTICABLE applies to that which can be done with the means at hand and with conditions as they are: *We ascended the slope as far as was practicable.*

post, *n.* **1.** column, pillar, pole, support, upright, stake, pale, picket, strut, prop, brace, pier, piling, pylon, leg, prop. **2.** position, office, situation, job, duty, role, function, employment, work, task, chore, assignment, appointment. **3.** station, round, beat, position. —*v.* **4.** announce, advertise, publicize, publish, proclaim, propagate; affix. **5.** station, place, set.

postpone, *v.* put off, defer, delay, procrastinate, adjourn, suspend, shelve, put on ice, table, put on the back burner. —**Syn. Study.** See DEFER.

posture, *n.* **1.** position, pose, attitude. **2.** position, condition, state, situation, disposition. —**Syn. Study.** See POSITION.

potent, *adj.* **1.** powerful, mighty, strong, vigorous, forceful, formidable, authoritative. **2.** cogent, influential, efficacious, effective, convincing, persuasive, compelling. —**Ant.** weak, impotent, powerless, feeble, frail; ineffectual.

potential, *adj.* **1.** possible, likely, implicit, implied, imminent, budding, embryonic, dormant, hidden, concealed, latent, passive, future. —*n.* **2.** possibility, potentiality, capacity, capability, aptitude, what it takes, the right stuff. —**Ant.** kinetic, impossible; impossibility.

pound, *v.* strike, beat, thrash, batter, pelt, hammer, pummel, bludgeon, maul, clobber, lambaste. —**Syn. Study.** See BEAT.

poverty, *n.* **1.** destitution, need, lack, want, privation, insolvency, pennilessness, bankruptcy, financial ruin, impoverishment, necessity, neediness, indigence, penury, distress. **2.** deficiency, sterility, barrenness, unfruitfulness. **3.** scantiness, jejuneness, sparingness, meagerness, scarcity, scarceness, lack, insufficiency, shortage, dearth, paucity, inadequacy. —**Ant.** wealth; abundance, fertility, fruitfulness.

power, *n.* **1.** ability, capability, capacity, faculty, competence, competency, might, strength, puissance. **2.** strength, might, muscle, brawn, vigor, force, energy. **3.** control, command, dominion, authority, sway, rule, ascendancy, influence, sovereignty, suzerainty, prerogative. —**Ant.** inability, incapacity, incompetence.

powerful, *adj.* **1.** mighty, potent, forceful, strong, vigorous, robust, energetic, sturdy, stalwart, tough. **2.** cogent, influential, convincing, effective, efficacious, effectual, strong, compelling, forceful, substantial, weighty, authoritative, important, impressive, persuasive, formidable, telling. —**Ant.** weak, frail, feeble; ineffective, ineffectual.

practicable, *adj.* possible, feasible, workable, performable, doable, achievable, attainable, viable, realizable, practical. —**Ant.** impracticable, impossible, unattainable. —**Syn. Study.** See POSSIBLE.

practical, *adj.* **1.** sensible, businesslike, pragmatic, efficient, useful, functional, realistic, reasonable, sound, utilitarian, applicable, serviceable, empirical. **2.** judicious, discreet, sensible, discriminating, balanced, reasoned, sound, shrewd, hard-nosed, expedient, down-to-earth. —**Ant.** impractical, inefficient. —**Syn. Study.** PRACTICAL, JUDICIOUS, SENSIBLE refer to good judgment in action, conduct, and the handling of everyday matters. PRACTICAL suggests the ability to adopt means to an end or to turn what is at hand to account: *to adopt practical measures for settling problems.* JUDICIOUS implies the possession and use of discreet judgment, discrimination, and balance: *a judicious use of one's time.* SENSIBLE implies the possession and use of reason and shrewd common sense: *a sensible suggestion.*

practice, *n.* **1.** custom, habit, wont, routine, convention, tradition, procedure, rule, way, style, mode. **2.** exercise, drill, experience, discipline, repetition, rehearsal, training, workout, application, study. **3.** performance, operation, action, process. —*v.* **4.** carry out, perform, do, drill, exercise, follow, observe. —**Syn. Study.** See CUSTOM.

praise, *n.* **1.** praising, commendation, acclamation, plaudit, compliment, acclaim, tribute, ovation, honor, homage, exaltation, laudation, approval, approbation, applause, kudos; enconium, eulogy, panegyric. —*v.* **2.** laud, approve, commend, admire, extol, celebrate, eulogize, panegyrize. **3.** glorify, magnify, exalt, worship, bless, adore, honor, revere, venerate, hallow. —**Ant.** condemnation, disapprobation, disapproval, criticism.

pray, *v.* importune, entreat, supplicate, beg, beseech, implore, sue, petition, invoke, appeal to, plead with, solicit, request, ask.

precarious, *adj.* **1.** uncertain, unstable, unsure, insecure, unsteady. **2.** delicate, ticklish, sensitive, slippery, touch-and-go, questionable, doubtful, dubious, unreliable, undependable, risky, perilous, hazardous, dangerous. **3.** groundless, unfounded, baseless. —**Ant.** certain, stable, sure, secure, independent, reliable, dependable; well-founded.

precaution, *n.* foresight, prudence, providence, wariness, forethought, vigilance, apprehension, circumspection, anticipation.

precious, *adj.* **1.** expensive, prized,

irreplaceable, high-priced, valuable, costly, dear, invaluable, priceless. **2.** esteemed, choice, adored, valued, revered, venerable, dear, beloved, darling, cherished. **3.** choice, fine, delicate, pretty, exquisite, chichi, dainty.
—**Ant.** inexpensive, cheap; worthless; ugly, unattractive.

precipitate, *v.* **1.** hasten, accelerate, hurry, speed up, expedite, speed, rush, quicken, dispatch, trigger, provoke, instigate, incite, facilitate, press, further. **2.** cast down, hurl *or* fling down, plunge. —*adj.* **3.** headlong, hasty, rash, reckless, indiscreet, impetuous, volatile, hotheaded, foolhardy. **4.** sudden, abrupt, unexpected.
—**Ant.** slow, retard; considered.

precipitous, *adj.* steep, abrupt, sheer, perpendicular, bluff.
—**Ant.** gradual, sloping.

precise, *adj.* **1.** definite, exact, defined, fixed, correct, strict, explicit, literal, specific, unerring, error-free, accurate. **2.** meticulous, scrupulous, careful, conscientious, rigorous, unbending, inflexible, severe, prim, absolute, fastidious, particular, finicky, fussy, exacting, critical, rigid, puritanical, demanding, crucial.
—**Ant.** indefinite, incorrect, inexact, lenient; flexible, tractable.
—**Syn. Study.** See CORRECT.

predatory, *adj.* predacious, plundering, ravaging, pillaging, rapacious, voracious, ravenous, greedy, larcenous, thieving.

predicament, *n.* dilemma, plight, difficulty, trial, emergency, crisis, impasse, imbroglio, quandary; situation, state, condition, position.
—**Syn. Study.** PREDICAMENT, PLIGHT, DILEMMA, QUANDARY refer to unpleasant or puzzling situations. PREDICAMENT and PLIGHT stress more the unpleasant nature, DILEMMA and QUANDARY the puzzling nature of a situation. PREDICAMENT, though often used lightly, may also refer to a crucial situation: *Stranded in a strange city without money, he was in a predicament.* PLIGHT, however, is usually used to refer to an unfortunate or distressing situation: *the plight of the homeless.* DILEMMA means a position of doubt or perplexity in which a person is faced by two equally undesirable alternatives: *the dilemma of a person who must support one of two friends in an election.* QUANDARY is the state of mental perplexity of one faced with a difficult situation: *We were in a quandary about plans for a vacation.*

predict, *v.* foretell, prophesy, foresee, forecast, presage, augur, prognosticate, portend, divine, forewarn, forebode.
—**Syn. Study.** PREDICT, PROPHESY, FORESEE, FORECAST mean to know or tell beforehand what will happen. To PREDICT is usu. to foretell with precision of calculation, knowledge, or shrewd inference from facts or experience: *Astronomers can predict an eclipse;* it may, however, be used without the implication of knowledge or expertise: *I predict it will be a successful party.* To PROPHESY is usu. to predict future events by the aid of divine or supernatural inspiration: *Merlin prophesied that two knights would meet in conflict;* this verb, too, may be used in a less specific sense: *I prophesy she'll be back in the old job.* FORESEE refers specifically not to the uttering of predictions but to the mental act of seeing ahead; there is often a practical implication of preparing for what will happen: *He was able to foresee their objections.* FORECAST means to predict by observation or study; however, it is most often used of phenomena that cannot be accurately predicted: *Rain is forecast for tonight.*

prediction, *n.* prophecy, forecast, augury, prognostication, foretoken, portent, divination, presage.

predilection, *n.* prepossession, favoring, partiality, predisposition, disposition, inclination, bent, preference, leaning, bias, prejudice, proclivity, fondness.
—**Ant.** disfavor, disinclination, dislike.

predominant, *adj.* ascendant, prevailing, prevalent, dominant, controlling, ruling, preeminent, superior, supreme, leading, paramount, main, chief, transcendant, important, primary, sovereign, telling, influential.
—**Ant.** rare, retrograde.
—**Syn. Study.** See DOMINANT.

predominate, *v.* preponderate, prevail, outweigh, overrule, surpass, dominate, control, rule, reign, overshadow, hold sway, lord it over.

preeminent, *adj.* eminent, surpassing, dominant, superior, over, above, distinguished, excellent, peerless, unequaled, inimitable, matchless, outstanding, unique, unrivaled, paramount, consummate, predominant, supreme, superb.
—**Ant.** undistinguished, inferior.

preface, *n.* introduction, foreword, preamble, prologue, prelude, preliminary, prolegomena.
—**Ant.** appendix, epilogue.

prefer, *v.* like better, favor, choose, elect, select, pick out, pick, incline *or* lean toward, opt for, embrace, espouse, esteem, approve, single out, fix upon, fancy.

preference, *n.* choice, selection, pick, predilection, favorite, desire, option, partiality, proclivity, fancy, predisposition, bent, inclination, leaning, prejudice, favoritism.

prejudice, *n.* **1.** preconception, bias, partiality, prejudgment, leaning, preconceived notion, jaundiced eye, predilection, predisposition, disposition; bigotry, unfairness, partisanship, favoritism, racism, discrimination, intolerance, apartheid, Jim Crow, sexism, male chauvinism, ageism. —*v.* **2.** bias, influence, warp, twist, poison, slant, distort.
—**Ant.** judgment, decision.
—**Syn. Study.** See BIAS.

preliminary, *adj.* advance, initial, opening, antecedent, premonitory, preceding, introductory, preparatory, prefatory, precursive, prior.
—**Ant.** resulting, concluding; conclusion, end, appendix, epilogue.
—**Syn. Study.** PRELIMINARY, INTRODUCTORY both refer to that which comes before the principal subject of consideration. That which is PRELIMINARY is in the nature of preparation or of clearing away details that would encumber the main subject or problem; it often deals with arrangements and the like that have to do only incidentally with the principal subject: *preliminary negotiations.* That which is INTRODUCTORY leads with natural, logical, or close connection directly into the main subject of consideration: *introductory steps.*

premeditate, *v.* consider, plan, deliberate, predetermine, prearrange.

premium, *n.* **1.** prize, door prize, bounty. **2.** bonus, gift, reward, recompense, extra, dividend, award, perquisite, perk; incentive, inducement, incitement, lure, bait, stimulus, goad, spur, come-on, freebie.
—**Syn. Study.** See BONUS.

preoccupied, *adj.* absorbed, engrossed, meditating, meditative, rapt, thoughtful, pensive, brooding, reflective, ruminative, pondering, musing, concentrating, inattentive, in a brown study, lost in thought, abstracted, faraway, oblivious, absent-minded, wrapped up, distracted, vague, spacey.
—**Ant.** unthinking, thoughtless.

prepare, *v.* **1.** contrive, devise, plan, plan for, anticipate, get *or* make ready, provide, arrange, order. **2.** manufacture, make, compound, fix, compose, fabricate, produce, fashion, forge, mold, build.
—**Ant.** destroy, ruin.

preposterous, *adj.* absurd, senseless, foolish, inane, asinine, ludicrous, laughable, risible, nonsensical, fatuous, mindless, crackbrained, mad, idiotic, incredible, outrageous, outlandish, outré, weird, bizarre, unreasonable, ridiculous, excessive, extravagant.
—**Ant.** rational, reasonable, sensible.
—**Syn. Study.** See ABSURD.

prerogative, *n.* right, privilege, precedence, license, franchise, immunity, freedom, liberty, advantage, claim, sanction, authority.
—**Syn. Study.** See PRIVILEGE.

presage, *n.* **1.** presentiment, foreboding, foreshadowing, indication, premonition, foreknowledge. **2.** portent, omen, sign, token, augury, warning, signal, prognostic. **3.** forecast, prediction, prophecy, prognostication, divination. —*v.* **4.** portend, foreshadow, forecast, predict.

prescribe, *v.* lay down, predetermine, appoint, ordain, order, rule, enjoin, direct, dictate, decree, establish, hand down, institute, demand, require, stipulate, command, instruct, define, specify.

presence, *n.* **1.** attendance, company. **2.** nearness, vicinity, neighborhood, proximity, vicinage, closeness. **3.** personality, aura, air, magnetism, charisma, attractiveness, bearing, carriage, mien, aspect, impression, appearance, poise, self-assurance, confidence, comportment, deportment, aplomb, sophistication.
—**Ant.** absence.

present, *adj.* **1.** current, contemporary, present-day, existing, extant; here, at hand, near, immediate, closest, adjacent, proximate, close, remaining. —*n.* **2.** now, nowadays, today, these days, the time being, this juncture, our times, the moment, the hour. **3.** gift, donation, offering, bounty, contribution, endowment, bonus, benefaction, largess, grant, gratuity, boon, tip. —*v.* **4.** give, endow, bestow, grant, confer, donate. **5.** afford, furnish, yield, offer, proffer. **6.** show, exhibit; introduce.
—**Ant.** absent; then; receive.
—**Syn. Study.** See GIVE. See also INTRODUCE.

presently, *adv.* by and by, in a little while, in due course, after a time, before long, in a minute, after a while, in a jiffy, at once, immediately, directly, right away, without delay, shortly, forthwith, soon.
—**Ant.** later.
—**Syn. Study.** See IMMEDIATELY.

preserve, *v.* **1.** keep, retain, conserve. **2.** guard, safeguard, shelter, shield, protect, defend, save. **3.** keep up, maintain, continue, uphold, sustain.
—**Ant.** forgo; lose.

prestige, *n.* reputation, influence, weight, importance, distinction, status, standing, rank, stature, significance, eminence, esteem, preeminence, primacy, superiority, supremacy, ascendancy, renown, fame, cachet, celebrity, glamour, stardom, charisma.
—**Ant.** disrepute, notoriety.

presume, *v.* **1.** assume, presuppose, suppose, take for granted, believe, surmise, gather, imagine, suspect, fancy, conjecture, guess. **2.** venture, undertake, dare, take the liberty.

presumptuous, *adj.* bold, impertinent, forward, arrogant, insolent, saucy, impudent, impertinent, forward, immodest, egotistical, audacious, rude, fresh, proud, brazen, brash, overweening.
—**Ant.** modest, polite.
—**Syn. Study.** See BOLD.

pretend, *v.* feign, affect, put on, assume, falsify, simulate, fake, sham, counterfeit, allege, profess; lie, make believe.
—**Syn. Study.** PRETEND, AFFECT, ASSUME, FEIGN imply an attempt to create a false appearance. To PRETEND is to create an imaginary characteristic or to play a part: *to pretend sorrow.* To AFFECT is to make a consciously artificial show of having qualities that one thinks would look well and impress others: *to affect shyness.* To ASSUME is to take on or put on a specific outward appearance, often with intent to deceive: *to assume an air of indifference.* To FEIGN implies using ingenuity in pretense, and some degree of imitation of appearance or characteristics: *to feign surprise.*

pretense, *n.* **1.** pretending, feigning, shamming, make-believe; subterfuge, fabrication, pretext, excuse. **2.** show, cover, cover-up, semblance, dissembling, pretension.

pretentious, *adj.* pompous, arrogant, inflated, high-flown, vain, vainglorious, affected, ostentatious, showy, la-di-da, highfalutin, mannered, precious, hoity-toity.
—**Ant.** earthy, plain.

pretty, *adj.* **1.** good-looking, appealing, lovely, cute, fetching, winsome, charming, fair, attractive, comely, pleasing, beautiful. **2.** fine, pleasant, excellent, splendid. —*adv.* **3.** moderately, fairly, somewhat, to some extent. **4.** very, quite.
—**Ant.** ugly; unpleasant; completely.
—**Syn. Study.** See BEAUTIFUL.

prevail, *v.* **1.** predominate, preponderate. **2.** win, succeed, triumph.
—**Ant.** lose.

prevailing, *adj.* **1.** prevalent, predominant, preponderating, dominant, preponderant. **2.** current, general, common. **3.** superior, influential, effectual, effective, efficacious, successful.
—**Ant.** rare, uncommon; inferior, ineffectual, ineffective, unsuccessful.

prevalent, *adj.* universal, catholic, frequent, ubiquitous, pervasive, omnipresent, usual, customary, established, widespread, current, common, prevailing, predominant, predominating, accepted, general.
—**Ant.** rare, unusual, uncommon.

prevent, *v.* hinder, stop, obstruct, hamper, impede, forestall, thwart, intercept, preclude, obviate, interrupt, avert, avoid, prohibit, ban, bar, forbid, enjoin, proscribe, foil, frustrate, abort, nip in the bud, check, block, balk, ward off, fend off, stave off, arrest, curb, restrain, inhibit, delay, retard, slow.
—**Ant.** encourage, aid, help, abet, support, continue.
—**Syn. Study.** PREVENT, HAMPER, HINDER, IMPEDE refer to different degrees of stoppage of action or progress. To PREVENT is to stop something effectually by forestalling action and rendering it impossible: *to prevent the sending of a message.* To HAMPER is to clog or entangle or put an embarrassing restraint upon: *to hamper preparations for a trip.* To HINDER is to keep back by delaying or stopping progress or action: *to*

hinder the progress of an expedition. To IMPEDE is to make difficult the movement or progress of anything by interfering with its proper functioning: *to impede a discussion by demanding repeated explanations.*

previous, *adj.* prior, earlier, former, preceding, foregoing, past, erstwhile, one-time, sometime.
—**Ant.** later, following.

price, *n.* charge, cost, expense, outlay, expenditure, payment, amount, fee; penalty, toll, sacrifice.

pride, *n.* conceit, self-esteem, egotism, hubris, overconfidence, self-love, vanity, arrogance, vainglory, self-importance; insolence, haughtiness, snobbishness, superciliousness, hauteur, presumption, smugness, snobbery.
—**Ant.** modesty; humility.
—**Syn. Study.** PRIDE, CONCEIT, EGOTISM, VANITY imply a favorable view of one's own appearance, advantages, achievements, etc., and often apply to offensive characteristics. PRIDE is a lofty and often arrogant assumption of superiority in some respect: *Pride must have a fall.* CONCEIT implies an exaggerated estimate of one's own abilities or attainments, together with pride: *blinded by conceit.* EGOTISM implies an excessive preoccupation with oneself or with one's own concerns, usu. but not always accompanied by pride or conceit: *Her egotism blinded her to others' difficulties.* VANITY implies self-admiration and an excessive desire to be admired by others: *His vanity was easily flattered.*

prim, *adj.* stiff, starched, formal, straitlaced, precise, proper; coy, demure, prudish, prissy, modest, puritanical, rigid, blue, priggish.
—**Ant.** flexible, informal; lewd, licentious, profligate.

primary, *adj.* **1.** first, highest, chief, principal, main, prime, leading, cardinal, preeminent, predominant. **2.** first, earliest, initial, primordial, embryonic, germinal, ultimate, primitive, original, primeval, aboriginal. **3.** elementary, essential, underlying, elemental, rudimentary, beginning, opening, fundamental, basic.
—**Ant.** last, final, ultimate; secondary.

primitive, *adj.* **1.** prehistoric, primal, primeval, prime, primary, primordial, original, aboriginal, pristine, first, antediluvian. **2.** uncivilized, uncultured, simple, unsophisticated, unrefined, raw, barbaric, barbarian, uncouth, savage.
—**Ant.** secondary; civilized, sophisticated, cultured.

principal, *adj.* first, highest, prime, paramount, capital, chief, primary, ranking, predominant, foremost, main, leading, cardinal, preeminent.
—**Ant.** ancillary, secondary.
—**Syn. Study.** See CAPITAL.

principally, *adv.* especially, chiefly, mainly, primarily, firstly, above all, in the main, mostly, for the most part, largely, predominantly, particularly, on the whole, in essence, essentially, basically.
—**Ant.** lastly.

principle, *n.* **1.** truth, given, precept, tenet, dictum, canon, rule, standard, test, parameter. **2.** theorem, assumption, truism, axiom, postulate, maxim, law, proposition. **3.** doctrine, tenet, credo, creed, ethic, dogma, idea, sentiment, belief, opinion. **4.** integrity, honesty, probity, righteousness, uprightness, rectitude, virtue, incorruptibility, goodness, trustworthiness, honor, morals, morality, conscience.

private, *adj.* **1.** individual, personal, singular, especial, special, particular, peculiar. **2.** confidential, secret, clandestine, hidden, concealed, covert, surreptitious, off the record, hush-hush, not for publication, top secret, eyes only. **3.** alone, secluded, cloistered, sequestered, solitary, retired, retiring, reclusive, withdrawn, reticent, antisocial, hermitic, reserved.
—**Ant.** public, general; known; open.

privation, *n.* hardship, deprivation, loss; destitution, want, need, necessity, distress, lack, indigence, poverty, penury, straits, misery.
—**Ant.** ease, wealth.

privilege, *n.* right, benefit, advantage, allowance, indulgence, consent, sanction, authority, immunity, leave, prerogative, advantage, license, freedom, liberty, permission, franchise, carte blanche.
—**Syn. Study.** PRIVILEGE, PREROGATIVE refer to a special advantage or right possessed by an individual or group. A PRIVILEGE is a right or advantage gained by birth, social position, effort, or concession. It can have either legal or personal sanction: *the privilege of paying half fare; the privilege of calling whenever one wishes.* PREROGATIVE refers to an exclusive right claimed and granted, often officially or legally, on the basis of social status, heritage, sex, etc.: *the prerogatives of a king; the prerogatives of management.*

prize, *n.* **1.** reward, premium, award, trophy, honor, accolade; winnings, jackpot, windfall, purse, receipts, haul, take. —*v.* **2.** value, esteem, treasure, cherish, hold dear.
—**Syn. Study.** See APPRECIATE.

probe, *v.* examine, explore, question, investigate, scrutinize, go into, search, sift, prove, test, study, delve into, plumb, dig into.
—**Ant.** overlook, ignore.

problem, *n.* question, doubt, uncertainty, puzzle, riddle, enigma, rebus, conundrum, poser; dilemma, quandary, difficulty, trouble, imbroglio.
—**Ant.** certainty, certitude, surety.

procedure, *n.* **1.** proceeding, conduct, management, operation, way, action, method, system, approach, strategy, scheme, policy, routine, tradition, practice, wont, modus operandi, methodology, course, process. **2.** act, deed, transaction, maneuver, goings on.

proceed, *v.* **1.** advance, go on, progress, move on, continue, make headway, forge ahead, press onward, pass on. **2.** go *or* come forth, issue, emanate, spring, arise, result, ensue, originate, stem, develop, derive, emerge.
—**Ant.** retreat.

process, *n.* course, procedure, operation, proceeding, system, approach, method, technique; activity, function, development.

proclaim, *v.* announce, declare, advertise, promulgate, publish, trumpet, circulate, broadcast, pronounce, make known, herald.
—**Syn. Study.** See ANNOUNCE.

procrastinate, *v.* temporize, play for time, stall, shelve, table, evade, delay, postpone, put off, defer, adjourn, prolong.

procure, *v.* **1.** acquire, gain, get, secure, win, obtain, appropriate. **2.** bring about, effect, cause.
—**Ant.** lose.
—**Syn. Study.** See GET.

prod, *v.* poke, jab, nudge, elbow; spur, urge, impel, egg on, push, thrust, stir, prompt, motivate, provoke, encourage, stimulate, needle, pester, harass, badger, nag, hound, carp at, goad, rouse, incite.

prodigal, *adj.* **1.** reckless, profligate, extravagant, lavish, wasteful, immoderate, intemperate, improvident, wanton. **2.** abundant, profuse, plenteous, copious, plentiful, bounteous, bountiful. —*n.* **3.** spendthrift, waster, wastrel, squanderer, carouser, playboy, profligate, big spender.
—**Ant.** cautious, provident, thrifty; scarce, scanty.
—**Syn. Study.** See LAVISH.

prodigious, *adj.* **1.** enormous, immense, huge, gigantic, tremendous, vast, immeasurable, colossal, mammoth, extensive, titanic. **2.** wonderful, marvelous, amazing, stupendous, astonishing, astounding, phenomenal, staggering, striking, mind-boggling, extraordinary, miraculous, wondrous, uncommon, unusual, strange. **3.** abnormal, monstrous, anomalous.
—**Ant.** small, tiny, infinitesimal; negligible, common; normal, usual.

produce, *v.* **1.** give rise to, cause, generate, occasion, originate, create, effect, make, manufacture, bring about. **2.** bear, bring forth, yield, furnish, supply, afford, give. **3.** exhibit, show, demonstrate, bring forward. —*n.* **4.** yield, product, crops, fruits, production.
—**Ant.** destroy, ruin; subdue, squelch; hide, conceal.

productive, *adj.* generative, creative; imaginative, inventive, resourceful; rich, fecund, prolific, fertile, fruitful.
—**Ant.** barren, unproductive.
—**Syn. Study.** PRODUCTIVE, FERTILE, FRUITFUL, PROLIFIC apply to the generative aspect of something. PRODUCTIVE refers to a generative source of continuing activity: *productive soil; a productive influence.* FERTILE applies to that in which seeds, literal or figurative, take root: *fertile soil; a fertile imagination.* FRUITFUL refers to that which has already produced and is capable of further production: *fruitful species; fruitful discussions.* PROLIFIC means highly productive: *a prolific farm; a prolific writer.*

profane, *adj.* **1.** irreverent, irreligious, blasphemous, sacrilegious, idolatrous, infidel, disrespectful, atheistic, sinful, piacular, wicked, impious, ungodly, godless, unredeemed, unredeemable. **2.** unconsecrated, secular, temporal. **3.** unholy, heathen, pagan, unhallowed, impure. **4.** common, low, mean, base, vulgar. —*v.* **5.** debase, misuse, defile, desecrate, violate, pollute, contaminate, degrade, pervert, corrupt.
—**Ant.** sacred, spiritual; pure, hallowed, holy; elevated, exalted.

profession, *n.* **1.** vocation, calling, occupation, trade, craft, business, employment, specialty, line, sphere, field, work, métier, (*slang*) dodge. **2.** confession, statement, affirmation, acknowledgment, admission, avowal, declaration, assertion.

proffer, *v.* offer, tender, volunteer, propose, suggest, hint.
—**Ant.** refuse.
—**Syn. Study.** See OFFER.

proficient, *adj.* skilled, adept, talented, gifted, expert, veteran, skillful, competent, practiced, experienced, qualified, trained, conversant, accomplished, finished, able, apt, capable, dextrous, polished, ace, topnotch, whiz-bang.
—**Ant.** unskilled, awkward, clumsy, untrained, unable, inept.

profit, *n.* **1.** gain, return, yield. **2.** returns, proceeds, revenue, dividend. **3.** advantage, benefit, gain, good, welfare, improvement, advancement. —*v.* **4.** gain, improve, advance, better, further, benefit, promote, aid, help, serve, avail, be advantageous.
—**Ant.** loss; lose.
—**Syn. Study.** See ADVANTAGE.

profound, *adj.* deep, intense, extreme, wise, learned, erudite, astute, analytical, penetrating, sagacious; abstruse, recondite arcane, esoteric, knotty, inscrutable, unfathomable, obscure, subtle, occult, secret, cabalistic, cryptic, enigmatic, puzzling, mysterious, mystifying.
—**Ant.** shallow, superficial.

profuse, *adj.* extravagant, abundant, copious, ample, plentiful, lavish, bountiful, prolific, luxuriant, exuberant, lush, thick, rich, generous, liberal, unsparing, unstinting.
—**Ant.** scarce, scanty.
—**Syn. Study.** See LAVISH.

profusion, *n.* abundance, plenty, copiousness, bounty, quantity, superabundance, wealth, glut, surplus, surfeit, plethora, superfluity, host, hoard, multitude, excess.
—**Ant.** scarcity, need, want.

progress, *n.* **1.** proceeding, advancement, advance, progression, headway. **2.** growth, development, improvement, increase, betterment. —*v.* **3.** advance, proceed; develop, improve, grow, increase, expand, evolve, mature, ripen, burgeon, spread.
—**Ant.** retrogression; recession; recede, decrease, diminish.

prohibit, *v.* **1.** forbid, interdict, disallow, bar, ban, outlaw, proscribe, taboo. **2.** prevent, hinder, preclude, obstruct, block, impede, hamper, inhibit, frustrate, foil, thwart, check, restrain.
—**Ant.** allow, permit; encourage, foster, further.

prohibition, *n.* interdiction, prevention, embargo, ban, restriction, taboo, proscription, injunction.
—**Ant.** permission.

project, *n.* **1.** plan, scheme, design, layout, proposal. **2.** activity, lesson, enterprise, assignment, obligation, undertaking, program, venture, commitment, engagement, occupation, job, work. —*v.* **3.** propose, contemplate, plan, contrive, scheme, plot, devise, concoct. **4.** throw, cast, toss, hurl, fling, launch, propel, shoot. **5.** extend, protrude, obtrude, jut out, stick out.

prolific, *adj.* **1.** fruitful, fertile, productive, teeming. **2.** abundant, copious, bountiful, profuse, plentiful, rich, lush, fecund.
—**Ant.** fruitless, unfruitful, barren, sterile; scarce.
—**Syn. Study.** See PRODUCTIVE.

prolong, *v.* lengthen, extend, protract, elongate, stretch, drag out, keep up, string out.
—**Ant.** abbreviate, shorten, curtail.
—**Syn. Study.** See LENGTHEN.

prominent, *adj.* **1.** conspicuous, noticeable, outstanding, manifest, obvious, evident, pronounced, eye-catching, striking, glaring, salient, flagrant, egregious, patent, unmistakable, discernible, principal, chief, important, main. **2.** projecting, jutting out, protuberant. **3.** important, leading, well-known, eminent, celebrated, famed, famous, distinguished, illustrious, renowned, acclaimed, honored, prestigious, notable, noteworthy.
—**Ant.** inconspicuous, unimportant; recessed; negligible, unknown.

promiscuous, *adj.* **1.** miscellaneous, hodgepodge, heterogeneous, random, chaotic, motley, scrambled, disorganized, disorderly, indiscriminate, confused, mixed, intermixed, intermingled, mingled. **2.** nonselective, indiscriminate, careless, heedless, haphazard, uncritical, unfussy, slipshod.
—**Ant.** pure, unmixed; selective, careful.

promise, *n.* **1.** word, pledge, assurance, vow, oath, bond, commitment, agreement, contract, covenant, compact. —*v.* **2.** pledge, agree, engage, assure, swear, vow, guarantee, take an oath.

promote, *v.* **1.** further, advance, encourage, forward, assist, aid, back, sanction, abet, boost, foster, develop, strengthen, stimulate, help, support. **2.** elevate, raise, exalt, upgrade, kick upstairs.
—**Ant.** discourage, obstruct; lower, debase.

prone, *adj.* **1.** inclined, disposed, liable, tending, bent, apt, likely, predisposed, of a mind, subject, given, leaning. **2.** prostrate, recumbent, reclining, face down, horizontal.
—**Ant.** averse; upright.

proof, *n.* **1.** evidence, testimony, certification, confirmation, verification, corroboration, validation, authentication, documentation, demonstration. **2.** test, trial, examination, measure, standard, touchstone, criterion.

propensity, *n.* inclination, bent, leaning, tendency, disposition, likelihood, proneness, predisposition.
—**Ant.** disinclination, aversion, distaste.

proper, *adj.* **1.** appropriate, fit, suitable, suited, apropos, convenient, fitting, befitting, correct, right, becoming, meet. **2.** correct, dignified, genteel, seemly, refined, punctilious, decorous, decent, respectable, polite, well-mannered. **3.** special, own, separate, distinct, particular, respective, distinctive, unique, specific, individual, peculiar. **4.** strict, accurate, precise, exact, just, formal, correct, orthodox, expected, accepted, normal, established, usual.
—**Ant.** improper.

property, *n.* **1.** possession, possessions, goods, effects, chattels, paraphernalia, gear, assets, means, resources, holdings, estate, belongings. **2.** land, real estate, acreage. **3.** ownership, right. **4.** attribute, quality, characteristic, feature, trait, mark, hallmark, oddity, idiosyncrasy, peculiarity, quirk.
—**Syn. Study.** PROPERTY, CHATTELS, EFFECTS, ESTATE, GOODS refer to what is owned. PROPERTY is the general word: *She owns a great deal of property. He said that the umbrella was his property.* CHATTELS is a term for pieces of personal property or movable possessions; it may be applied to livestock, automobiles, etc.: *a mortgage on chattels.* EFFECTS is a term for any form of personal property, including even things of the least value: *All my effects were insured against fire.* ESTATE refers to property of any kind that has been, or is capable of being, handed down to descendants or otherwise disposed of in a will: *He left most of his estate to his niece.* It may consist of personal estate (money, valuables, securities, chattels, etc.) or real estate (land and buildings). GOODS refers to household possessions or other movable property, esp. the stock in trade of a business: *The store arranged its goods on shelves.* See also QUALITY.

prophesy, *v.* foretell, predict, forecast, forewarn, augur, prognosticate, divine; presage, foreshadow, portend, bode, harbinger, herald.
—**Syn. Study.** See PREDICT.

proportion, *n.* **1.** relation, ratio, arrangement; comparison, analogy. **2.** size, extent, dimensions. **3.** percentage, division, quota, allotment, ration, portion, part, piece, share. **4.** symmetry, concord, suitableness, congruity, correspondence, correlation, harmony, agreement, balance, distribution, arrangement. —*v.* **5.** adjust, regulate, redistribute, arrange, balance, harmonize, modify, modulate, shape, fit, match, conform.
—**Ant.** disproportion.
—**Syn. Study.** See SYMMETRY.

proposal, *n.* plan, scheme, offer, bid, recommendation, outline, draft, suggestion, design, overture, approach, proposition, program, project, outline.

propose, *v.* **1.** offer, proffer, tender, suggest, recommend, present. **2.** nominate, name, suggest, introduce, submit, advance, put forward. **3.** plan, intend, design, mean, purpose. **4.** state, present, propound, pose, posit.

propriety, *n.* **1.** decorum, etiquette, protocol, good behavior, courtesy, punctili, dignity, gentility, decency, modesty. **2.** suitability, appropriateness, aptness, fitness, seemliness. **3.** rightness, correctness, accuracy.
—**Ant.** impropriety, immodesty, indecency; unseemliness.

prosaic, *adj.* stale, banal, clichéd, stereotyped, pedestrian, hackneyed, flat, stock, routine, ordinary, workaday, mediocre, bland, trite, threadbare, tired, dead, lifeless, jejune, boring, insipid, monotonous, ho-hum, run of the mill, commonplace, dull, matter-of-fact, humdrum, tedious, tiresome, wearisome, uninteresting.
—**Ant.** interesting, fascinating, beguiling.

prospect, *n.* **1.** anticipation, expectation, expectance, likelihood, intention, contemplation. **2.** view, scene, outlook, panorama, landscape, seascape, sight, spectacle, aspect, survey, vista, perspective. —*v.* **3.** search, explore, look for.
—**Syn. Study.** See VIEW.

prosper, *v.* succeed, thrive, flourish, progress, develop, grow rich, make good, make one's fortune, make it.
—**Ant.** fail, die.
—**Syn. Study.** See SUCCEED.

prosperous, *adj.* **1.** fortunate, successful, flourishing, thriving. **2.** affluent, wealthy, rich, well-to-do, well-off. **3.** favorable, propitious, fortunate, lucky, auspicious, golden, bright.
—**Ant.** unfortunate, unsuccessful; poor, impoverished; unfavorable.

prostitute, *n.* **1.** harlot, whore, strumpet, call girl, trollop, chippy, fallen *or* loose woman, hooker, lady of the night, ho, tart, hustler, streetwalker, courtesan. —*v.* **2.** degrade, demean, debase, lower, cheapen, defile, pervert, sell out, misapply, misuse, abuse.

protect, *v.* defend, guard, shield, cover, screen, shelter, save, harbor, house, secure, safeguard, preserve, conserve.
—**Ant.** attack, assail.

protection, *n.* **1.** preservation, guard, defense, shelter, screen, cover, security, refuge, safety, shield, barrier, immunity, bulwark, haven, sanctuary. **2.** aegis, patronage, sponsorship, care, custody, charge, safekeeping, keeping.
—**Ant.** attack.

protest, *n.* **1.** objection, disapproval, protestation, opposition, complaint, grievance, dissent, disagreement, demurral, disclaimer, denial, scruple, qualm, compunction, squawk, beef. —*v.* **2.** remonstrate, dissent, take exception, take issue with, demur, oppose, grumble, disapprove, disagree, scruple, gripe, grouse, beef, complain, object. **3.** declare, affirm, assert, avow, aver, testify, attest, announce, insist on, profess.
—**Ant.** approval; approve.

prototype, *n.* model, pattern, example, exemplar, original, archetype, first, precedent, mold, standard, paragon, epitome.

protract, *v.* draw out, lengthen, extend, prolong, continue, stretch, drag out.
—**Ant.** curtail, abbreviate, discontinue.
—**Syn. Study.** See LENGTHEN.

proud, *adj.* **1.** narcissistic, complacent, self-centered, boastful, bragging, self-satisfied, egotistical, vain, conceited. **2.** arrogant, overweening, haughty, overbearing, self-important, cocky, cocksure, high and mighty, snobbish, overconfident, disdainful, supercilious, snooty, imperious, presumptuous. **3.** honorable, creditable, estimable, illustrious, distinguished, eminent, reputable. **4.** stately, majestic, magnificent, noble, imposing, splendid, lofty, dignified, respected, august, grand.
—**Ant.** discontented, dissatisfied; humble, self-effacing; dishonorable; ignoble, base.

prove, *v.* **1.** demonstrate, show, confirm, authenticate, corroborate, validate, certify, affirm, manifest, establish, evidence, substantiate, verify, justify, ascertain, determine. **2.** try, test, examine, assay, check, analyze.
—**Ant.** disprove.

proverb, *n.* maxim, saying, adage, epigram, precept, truth, saw, axiom, aphorism, byword, apothegm; platitude, bromide, truism, cliché, commonplace, chestnut.
—**Syn. Study.** PROVERB, MAXIM are terms for short, pithy sayings. A PROVERB is such a saying popularly known and repeated, usu. expressing simply and concretely, though often metaphorically, a truth based on common sense or practical human experience: *A stitch in time saves nine.* A MAXIM is a brief statement of a general and practical truth, esp. one that serves as a rule of conduct: *It is wise to risk no more than one can afford to lose.*

provide, *v.* **1.** furnish, supply, afford, yield, produce, contribute, equip, outfit, accommodate, provision, purvey, give. **2.** prepare, get ready, procure, provide for, make provision for, arrange for, anticipate, forearm.
—**Ant.** deprive.

provoke, *v.* **1.** anger, enrage, exasperate, irk, vex, irritate, incense, gall, rile, distress, upset, disturb, perturb, outrage, insult, pique, madden, get on one's nerves, annoy, aggravate, exacerbate, infuriate, ire, nettle, affront. **2.** stir up, arouse, call forth, incite, stimulate, excite, fire, rouse, inflame, animate, inspirit, motivate, induce, encourage, goad, spur, impel, egg on. **3.** give rise to, induce, bring about, promote, foment, kindle, instigate.
—**Ant.** assuage, calm, propitiate.
—**Syn. Study.** See INCITE.

prowl, *v.* lurk, sneak, skulk, slink; scour, scavenge, patrol, cruise, cover, rove, roam, wander; prey, plunder, pillage, steal, stalk, hunt, track.
—**Syn. Study.** See LURK.

prudence, *n.* **1.** calculation, foresight, forethought, judgment, discretion, common sense, circumspection, caution, wisdom. **2.** providence, care, economy, frugality, carefulness, thrift.
—**Ant.** carelessness, imprudence, incaution.

prudent, *adj.* **1.** wise, judicious, cautious, discreet, tactful, sensible, discerning, politic, discriminating, reasonable, canny, shrewd, vigilant, guarded, sagacious, circumspect, careful, wary, provident. **2.** provident, frugal, sparing, economical, thrifty, saving, careful.
—**Ant.** imprudent, indiscreet, tactless, careless; improvident, prodigal.

prudish, *adj.* priggish, puritanical, prissy, prim, squeamish, fussy, strait-laced, stiff, rigid, overnice, formal, decorous, modest, proper, demure, pure, coy, reserved.
—**Ant.** immodest, indecent.
—**Syn. Study.** See MODEST.

prying, *adj.* curious, inquisitive, peeping, peering, peeking; nosy, meddlesome, interfering.
—**Ant.** uninterested, discreet.

pseudo, *adj.* sham, counterfeit, false, spurious, pretended, fake, phony, bogus, fraudulent, ersatz, make-believe, unreal, inauthentic, artificial, imitation, mock, dishonest, deceitful, hypocritical, forged.
—**Ant.** genuine, real.

publish, *v.* make public, put out, broadcast, air, announce, proclaim, promulgate, declare, disclose, divulge, reveal, impart, advertise, publicize, spread, makeknown, report, break the news, inform.
—**Ant.** conceal, hide.
—**Syn. Study.** See ANNOUNCE.

puerile, *adj.* **1.** immature, babyish, jejune, infantile, sophomoric, juvenile, childish, youthful. **2.** foolish, irrational, trivial, nugatory, silly, ridiculous, asinine, shallow, inconsequential, insignificant, irresponsible.
—**Ant.** mature, rational.

pulsate, *v.* beat, palpitate, pulse, pound, drum, thump, reverberate, hammer, throb; vibrate, oscillate.

pungent, *adj.* **1.** spicy, strong, penetrating, aromatic, highly seasoned, tangy, tasty, flavorful, biting, acrid, hot, peppery, piquant, sharp. **2.** poignant, distressing, upsetting, hurtful, piercing, intense, severe, acute, agonizing, oppressive, excruciating, consuming, racking, painful. **3.** caustic, biting, sarcastic, sardonic, mordant, penetrating, piercing, trenchant, cutting, severe, acrimonious, bitter, waspish. **4.** stimulating, acute, keen, sharp.
—**Ant.** mild, bland; painless; dull.

punish, *v.* correct, discipline, penalize, reprove, rebuke, take to task, dress down, admonish, teach a lesson, throw the book at, call onto the carpet, castigate, scold, berate, chastise, chasten, thrash, beat, spank; flog, whip, lash, scourge.
—**Ant.** praise, laud; forgive.

pupil, *n.* disciple, scholar, student, learner, schoolchild, apprentice; tyro, greenhorn, neophyte, novice, beginner, abecedarian, rookie.
—**Ant.** teacher, expert.

purchase, *v.* **1.** buy, acquire, get, obtain, procure. —*n.* **2.** buying, acquisition, procurement, obtaining, securing.
—**Ant.** sell, lose; sale.

pure, *adj.* **1.** unmixed, unadulterated, uncontaminated, unalloyed, clean, unsullied, untainted, unstained, undefiled, spotless, untarnished, immaculate, unpolluted, uncorrupted. **2.** unmodified, simple, homogeneous, genuine, faultless, perfect. **3.** thoroughbred, purebred, pedigreed. **4.** utter, sheer, unqualified, absolute. **5.** virginal, virgin, intact, guileless, moral, decent, decorous, sinless, innocent, chaste, undefiled, unsullied, modest, virtuous. **6.** honorable, principled, righteous, pious, worthy, ethical, above reproach, guiltless, innocent, true, honest, upright, sincere.
—**Ant.** impure.

purge, *v.* purify, cleanse, clear, clean, clarify, scour, wash out.

puritan, *n.* **1.** moralist, pietist, fanatic, purist, prude, zealot, stuffed shirt, killjoy, bluenose. —*adj.* **2.** prim, proper, prudish, strait-laced,

rigid, inflexible, stern, uncompromising, hard-line, moralistic, pietistic, stuffy, stiff, strict, severe, narrow-minded, narrow, austere, ascetic, Spartan, intolerant, hard-nosed, blue, uptight.
—Ant. libertine, immoralist, heathen; debauched, immoral, wanton, broad-minded, free-thinking, loose.

purport, v. **1.** profess, claim, mean, intend, signify. **2.** express, imply. —n. **3.** tenor, import, meaning, intention, claim, design, significance, signification, implication, drift, suggestion, gist.
—Ant. understand, see; infer; meaninglessness.
—Syn. Study. See MEANING.

purpose, n. **1.** object, intent, intention, determination, aim, end, design, view, goal, ambition, objective, target, point, rationale, reason. **2.** result, effect, advantage, consequence. —v. **3.** propose, design, intend, mean, contemplate, plan, aim, aspire, have in mind, consider.
—Ant. purposelessness.

push, v. **1.** shove, shoulder, thrust, drive, move, slide. **2.** press, urge, persuade, drive, impel. —n. **3.** attack, effort, onset.

put, v. **1.** place, lay, set, deposit, position, situate, station, stand, rest, settle, locate. **2.** set, levy, impose, inflict. **3.** express, state, utter, word, phrase, write.

puzzle, n. **1.** riddle, enigma, problem, rebus, paradox, conundrum, mystery, brainteaser, cipher, poser, maze, question. —v. **2.** bewilder, perplex, confound, mystify, confuse, baffle, nonplus, stymie, stump, flummox, throw for a loop.

Q

quagmire, n. **1.** swamp, marsh, fen, bog, mire, morass, slough. **2.** predicament, difficulty, dilemma, pickle, tight spot, fix, jam, corner, box, quandary.

quaint, adj. **1.** strange, odd, curious, bizarre, peculiar, queer, singular, eccentric, unorthodox, whimsical, offbeat, fanciful, outlandish, unconventional, fantastic, weird, unusual, extraordinary, unique, uncommon. **2.** picturesque, charming, old-fashioned, antiquated, antique, archaic, outdated, passé.
—Ant. common, usual, ordinary; modern.

quake, v. **1.** shake, shudder, tremble, shiver, vibrate, stagger, quaver, quiver. —n. **2.** temblor, earthquake, tremor, seismic activity.

qualify, v. **1.** fit, suit, adapt, prepare, equip, ready, condition, certify, make eligible. **2.** characterize, call, name, designate, label, signify. **3.** modify, limit, mitigate, restrain, narrow, restrict. **4.** moderate, mitigate, meliorate, soften, ameliorate, mollify, soothe, ease, assuage, temper, reduce, diminish.

quality, n. **1.** characteristic, attribute, property, character, feature, mark, distinction, trait. **2.** grade, kind, sort, caliber, status, rank, condition. **3.** excellence, superiority.
—Ant. inferiority, baseness; failure.
—Syn. Study. QUALITY, ATTRIBUTE, PROPERTY refer to a distinguishing feature or characteristic of a person, thing, or group. A QUALITY is an innate or acquired characteristic that, in some particular, determines the nature and behavior of a person or thing: the qualities of patience and perseverance. An ATTRIBUTE is a quality that we assign or ascribe to a person or to something personified;

it may also mean a fundamental or innate characteristic: an attribute of God; attributes of a logical mind. PROPERTY is applied only to a thing; it refers to a principal characteristic that is part of the constitution of a thing and serves to define or describe it: the physical properties of limestone.

qualm, n. uneasiness, second thoughts, doubt, uncertainty, hesitation, reluctance, disinclination, queasiness, apprehensiveness, compunction, scruple, twinge, remorse, misgiving, pang, worry, concern, sinking feeling.
—Ant. self-assurance, confidence, certainty.

quandary, n. dilemma, predicament, strait, uncertainty, doubt, plight, difficulty.
—Syn. Study. See PREDICAMENT.

quarrel, n. **1.** dispute, altercation, disagreement, argument, contention, controversy, dissension, feud, breach, break, rupture, debate, discord, row, squabble, scuffle, fracas, melee, donnybrook, difference, spat, tiff, fight, misunderstanding, wrangle, brawl, tumult. —v. **2.** squabble, fall out, disagree with, differ, disagree, be at odds, feud, battle, scrap, bicker, dispute, argue, wrangle, spar, brawl, clash, jar, fight.
—Syn. Study. QUARREL, DISSENSION refer to disagreement and conflict. QUARREL applies chiefly to a verbal disagreement between individuals or groups and is used with reference to a large variety of situations, from a slight and petty difference of opinion to a violent altercation: It was little more than a domestic quarrel. Their quarrel led to an actual fight. DISSENSION usu. implies a profound disagreement and bitter conflict. It also applies chiefly to conflict within a group or between members of the same group: dissension within the union; dissension among the Democrats.

quarrelsome, adj. argumentative, disputatious, cantankerous, disagreeable, fractious, querulous, choleric, contrary, dyspeptic, hostile, dissident, contentious, testy, petulant, irascible, irritable, peevish, cross, curmudgeonly, cranky, grouchy, combative, belligerent, truculent, pugnacious, antagonistic.
—Ant. peaceable, amicable.

queasy, adj. **1.** squeamish, fastidious, finicky, finical, picky, particular. **2.** nauseated, nauseous, qualmish, sickish, seasick, airsick, carsick, queer, queerish, green around the gills, woozy, bilious. **3.** uncomfortable, uneasy, nervous, apprehensive, worried, troubled, ill at ease, doubtful, hesitant.

queer, adj. strange, unconventional, odd, singular, curious, fantastic, uncommon, weird, peculiar, extraordinary, eccentric, freakish, anomalous, bizarre, uncanny, exotic, fey, outlandish, outré, unorthodox, atypical, offbeat.
—Ant. conventional, ordinary, common.

quell, v. **1.** suppress, stifle, extinguish, put an end to, crush, quash, subdue, overpower, overcome. **2.** vanquish, put down, defeat, conquer. **3.** quiet, allay, calm, pacify, compose, lull, hush.
—Ant. encourage, foster; defend, lose; agitate, disturb, perturb.

querulous, adj. complaining, petulant, peevish, snappish, abrupt, irritable, irascible, fractious, perverse, ill-natured, crotchety, cantankerous, curmudgeonly, choleric, dyspeptic, cross, testy, sour, crabby, quarrelsome, fretful, whining, touchy, waspish; caviling, carping, faultfinding, hypercritical, censorious, fussy,

finicky, overparticular, annoyed, piqued.
—Ant. calm, equable; pleased, contented.

question, n. **1.** inquiry, query, interrogation. **2.** dispute, controversy. —v. **3.** interrogate; ask, inquire, query, examine, quiz, test, interview, sound out, grill, pump. **4.** doubt, mistrust, distrust, suspect. **5.** dispute, challenge.
—Ant. answer, reply; agree, concur.

questionable, adj. doubtful, uncertain, dubitable, dubious, debatable, disputable, controvertible, moot, borderline, suspect, suspicious, shady, problematical, unreliable, unsure, ambiguous.
—Ant. certain, sure, positive.

quibble, n. **1.** evasion, prevarication, equivocation, sophistry, sophism, hair-splitting, nitpicking, subterfuge, cavil. —v. **2.** evade, prevaricate, equivocate, cavil, shuffle, trifle, split hairs, be evasive, pettifog, nitpick.

quick, adj. **1.** prompt, immediate, rapid, fast, swift, speedy, instantaneous, fleet, hasty, hurried, expeditious. **2.** impatient, hasty, abrupt, curt, short, precipitate, sharp, unceremonious; testy, waspish, snappish, irritable. **3.** lively, keen, acute, sensitive, alert, sharp, shrewd, intelligent, discerning. **4.** vigorous, energetic, active, nimble, animated, agile, lively, alert, brisk.
—Ant. slow; patient, deliberate; calm; dull, stupid; lethargic, lazy.
—Syn. Study. QUICK, FAST, SWIFT, RAPID describe a speedy rate of motion or progress. QUICK applies particularly to an action or reaction that is almost instantaneous, or of brief duration: to take a quick look around. FAST refers to a person or thing that acts or moves speedily; when used of communication or transportation, it suggests a definite goal and continuous movement: a fast swimmer; a fast train. SWIFT, a more formal word, suggests great speed as well as graceful movement: The panther is a swift animal. RAPID applies to one or a series of actions or movements; it stresses the rate of speed: to perform rapid calculations. See also SHARP.

quiet, n. **1.** tranquility, rest, repose, calm, stillness, quietude, serenity, peace, calmness, silence. —adj. **2.** peaceable, peaceful, pacific, calm, tranquil, serene, silent. **3.** motionless, still, unmoving, unmoved, fixed, stationary, at rest, inactive, composed, unexcited. **4.** inconspicuous, subdued; repressed, unstrained, unobtrusive. —v. **5.** still, hush, silence. **6.** tranquilize, pacify, calm, compose, lull, soothe.
—Ant. disturbance, perturbation; war; warlike, noisy, clamorous; conspicuous, obvious, blatant.

quip, v. **1.** joke, banter, jest, gibe, wisecrack, josh, crack wise. —n. **2.** witticism, joke, jest, ad lib, barb, aphorism, epigram, pun, double entendre, one-liner, crack, wheeze, chestnut, smart remark, jape, gibe, wisecrack, gag, bon mot, sally.

quit, v. **1.** stop, cease, discontinue, desist. **2.** depart from, leave, go, withdraw or retire from, exit, decamp, desert, flee, forsake, abandon, take off, skip. **3.** give up, let go, relinquish, release, resign, surrender. —adj. **4.** released, free, clear, rid, absolved, acquitted, discharged.
—Ant. start; initiate, originate; continue; arrive, enter; chained, confined.

quiver, v. **1.** shake, tremble, vibrate, quake, shudder, shiver. —n. **2.** tremble, tremor, shudder, shiver, trembling, shake, spasm, quaver.

quixotic, adj. idealistic, impractical, unrealistic, fantastic, chimerical, fanciful, dreamy, starry-eyed, optimistic, Pollyannaish, rash, absurd, mad, foolhardy, preposterous, ridiculous, visionary, impracticable, romantic, imaginary, wild.
—Ant. realistic, practicable, practical.

quizzical, adj. **1.** questioning, curious, puzzled, inquisitive, inquiring, interrogatory. **2.** skeptical, suspicious, dubious, doubting, wary, distrustful, incredulous, unbelieving.

R

rabid, adj. **1.** overwrought, violent, berserk, hysterical, frantic, frenzied, frenetic, furious, raging, wild, mad, maniacal. **2.** extreme, extremist, radical, fanatic, fanatical, fervent, perfervid, overzealous, irrational, wild-eyed, over the top.
—Ant. calm, composed, reasonable.

race, n. **1.** competition, contest. **2.** course, stream. **3.** nation, people, clan, family, tribe; generation, stock, line, lineage, breed, kin, kindred, progeny, descendants, offspring, children. **4.** humankind. —v. **5.** run, speed, hurry, hasten, hie, dash, sprint, fly, rush, scramble, step on it, get a move on.

rack, n. **1.** torment, anguish, torture, pain, agony. —v. **2.** torture, distress, torment, agonize, excruciate. **3.** strain, force, wrest, stretch, wrench, batter, beat, tear at.

racket, n. din, uproar, noise, clamor, fuss, tumult, hubbub, outcry, disturbance, row, rumpus, hullaballoo, ado, commotion, brouhaha, pandemonium, to-do, hue and cry.
—Ant. quiet, tranquility, peace.
—Syn. Study. See NOISE.

racy, adj. **1.** vigorous, lively, animated, spirited. **2.** suggestive, risqué, ribald, bawdy, off-color, smutty, salacious, vulgar, pornographic, obscene, naughty, earthy, lewd, blue, indecent, adult.
—Ant. dispirited, dejected; mild, bland.

radiant, adj. shining, bright, brilliant, beaming, effulgent, resplendent, sparkling, splendid, glittering, luminous, shimmering, scintillating, dazzling, twinkling, incandescent, lustrous, gleaming, glossy, glowing.
—Ant. dull.

radiate, v. **1.** shine, beam, glow, gleam, burn, luminesce, incandesce, twinkle, glimmer, sparkle, flash, blaze, shimmer, glisten, glitter, coruscate, scintillate. **2.** diffuse, disperse, emit, spread, propagate, scatter, emanate, throw off, give off.

radical, adj. **1.** fundamental, basic, original, constitutional, elementary, inherent, cardinal, principal, primary, deep-seated, profound, underlying, organic, natural, rudimentary, essential, innate, ingrained. **2.** thoroughgoing, extreme, complete, entire, total, exhaustive, comprehensive, drastic, severe, revolutionary, unqualified, thorough, fanatical, excessive, immoderate, extravagant, violent. —n. **3.** extremist, revolutionary, rebel, nonconformist, iconoclast, nihilist, pioneer, trail-blazer, progressive, zealot, fanatic, militant, anarchist, Jacobin, terrorist.
—Ant. superfluous; incomplete, moderate.

rage, n. **1.** anger, ire, fury, frenzy, passion, vehemence, wrath, exasperation, madness, raving. **2.** fury, violence, turbulence, tumultuousness, storm. **3.** ardor, fervor, enthusiasm, eagerness, desire, passion, frenzy,

vehemence. **4.** mode, fashion, fad, craze, vogue, mania. **—*v.* 5.** rave, fume, storm, fret, rant, go berserk, explode, boil, seethe, smolder, fulminate, blow up, hit the roof *or* ceiling, go ape, have a fit.
—Ant. calm, equanimity.
—Syn. Study. See ANGER.

ragged, *adj.* **1.** tattered, torn, shredded, rent, ripped, frayed, threadbare, patched. **2.** shabby, poor, mean, seedy, tacky, grungy.
—Ant. neat, whole.

raid, *n.* **1.** onset, attack, seizure, onslaught, blitz, expedition. **2.** invasion, inroad, incursion.
—Ant. defense.

raillery, *n.* banter, kidding, kidding around, teasing, joshing, frivolity, repartee, joking, jesting, ridicule, ribbing, ragging, twitting, fooling around, badinage, persiflage.

raise, *v.* **1.** lift, lift up, elevate, heave, hoist, loft. **2.** rouse, arouse, awake, awaken, call forth, evoke, stir up, excite. **3.** build, erect, construct, rear, set up. **4.** cause, promote, cultivate, grow, propagate. **5.** originate, engender, give rise to, bring up *or* about, produce, effect, cause. **6.** invigorate, animate, inspirit, heighten, intensify. **7.** advance, elevate, promote, exalt. **8.** gather, collect, muster, marshal, assemble, bring together. **9.** increase, intensify, heighten, aggravate, amplify, augment, enhance, enlarge.
—Ant. lower; pacify; destroy, raze; kill; weaken, dispirit; debase, dishonor; scatter, disperse, broadcast.

ramble, *v.* **1.** stroll, amble, walk, wander, saunter, stray, roam, travel, drift, hike, trek, meander, rove, range, straggle. **—*n.* 2.** walk, stroll, amble, excursion, tour, promenade, tramp, hike, trek.

rambling, *adj.* wandering, aimless, irregular, straggling, straying; meandering, maundering, labyrinthine, muddled, discursive, roundabout, circuitous, tortuous, disjointed, illogical, circumlocutory, incoherent, periphrastic.
—Ant. direct, pointed.

rambunctious, *adj.* boisterous, high-spirited, exuberant, roisterous, rollicking, unrestrained, uninhibited, irrepressible, untamed, knockabout, uproarious, wild, rowdy; unruly, disobedient, riotous, obstreperous, disorderly, fractious.
—Ant. docile.

rampage, *n.* **1.** spree, tear, binge, outburst, orgy, riot, furor, tumult, uproar, frenzy, rage, turmoil, fury, convulsion. **—*v.* 2.** rage, storm, rave, rant, tear, tear around, riot, go berserk, run amok.

ramshackle, *adj.* shaky, rickety, flimsy, dilapidated, broken down, tumbledown, crumbling, decrepit, ruined, run-down, neglected, derelict, jerry-built.
—Ant. luxurious, sumptuous, palatial.

rancor, *n.* resentment, antipathy, antagonism, hostility, vindictiveness, vengefulness, spleen, acrimony, animus, bad feeling, bad blood, bitterness, ill will, hatred, malice, spite, venom, malevolence, animosity, enmity.
—Ant. amiability, goodwill, benevolence.

random, *adj.* haphazard, chance, fortuitous, accidental, serendipitous, arbitrary, nonspecific, unplanned, unsystematic, unpremeditated, incidental, hit or miss, casual, aimless.
—Ant. specific, particular.

range, *n.* **1.** extent, limits, scope, sweep, latitude, reach, span, radius, sphere, orbit, area, compass. **2.** rank, class, order, kind, sort. **3.** row, line, series, tier, file. **4.** area, trace, region. **—*v.* 5.** align, rank, classify, class, order, arrange, array, dispose. **6.** vary, fluctuate, spread, run the gamut, course. **7.** extend, stretch out, run, go, lie. **8.** roam, rove, wander, stroll, straggle. **9.** extend, be found, occupy, lie, run, cover.
—Syn. Study. RANGE, COMPASS, LATITUDE, SCOPE refer to extent or breadth. RANGE emphasizes extent and diversity: *the range of one's interests.* COMPASS suggests definite limits: *within the compass of one's mind.* LATITUDE emphasizes the idea of freedom from narrow confines, thus breadth or extent: *granted latitude of action.* SCOPE suggests great freedom but a proper limit: *the scope of one's obligations.*

rank, *n.* **1.** position, standing, station, order, class, level, status, grade, echelon, division. **2.** row, line, tier, series, range. **3.** weight, authority, ascendancy, superiority, influence, power, prestige, distinction, eminence, dignity. **4.** order, arrangement, array, alignment. **—*v.* 5.** arrange, line up, align, array, range. **6.** classify, dispose, sort, class, arrange. **—*adj.* 7.** tall, vigorous, luxuriant, abundant, overabundant, exuberant. **8.** strong, gamy, pungent, offensive, noxious, fetid, rancid, putrid. **9.** utter, absolute, complete, entire, sheer, gross, extravagant, excessive. **10.** offensive, disgusting, repulsive, repellent, miasmatic, mephitic. **11.** coarse, indecent, foul, gross, vulgar, lurid, vile, obscene.

rankle, *v.* irritate, annoy, vex, distress, plague, nettle, fester, gall, inflame, incense, embitter, rile, aggravate, chafe, grate, torment, pain, provoke, anger, exasperate, irk.
—Ant. placate, please.

ransom, *n.* **1.** redemption, rescue, emancipation, deliverance, liberation, release. **—*v.* 2.** redeem, release, restore, deliver, deliver up.

rapid, *adj.* speedy, fast, quick, swift, fleet, high-speed, brisk, prompt, express, lightning-fast, hurried, hasty, precipitate.
—Ant. slow.
—Syn. Study. See QUICK.

rapidity, *n.* swiftness, speed, fleetness, quickness, haste, velocity, alacrity, celerity, promptness, dispatch, briskness, expeditiousness.
—Ant. lethargy, slowness.

rapport, *n.* relationship, interrelationship, affinity, attraction, bond, sympathy, empathy, closeness, understanding, like-mindedness, accord, concord, harmony, compatibility, fellow feeling, fellowship, kinship, oneness, camaraderie.
—Ant. enmity, incompatibility.

rapt, *adj.* **1.** engrossed, preoccupied, occupied, absorbed, abstracted, thoughtful, bemused, faraway, singleminded, concentrated, fixed, fixated. **2.** enraptured, rapturous, transported, ecstatic, transfigured, enthralled, fascinated, enchanted, gripped, held, riveted, spellbound, entranced, bewitched, captivated, mesmerized, hypnotized, delighted, under a spell.
—Ant. distracted.

rapture, *n.* ecstasy, joy, delight, transport, bliss, beatitude, exultation, exaltation, elation, euphoria, thrill, enchantment, pleasure.
—Ant. misery, disgust, revulsion.

rare, *adj.* **1.** scarce, uncommon, exceptional, atypical, unusual, sparse, infrequent, extraordinary, singular, phenomenal, recherché, unique, one of a kind, limited, few and far between. **2.** excellent, admirable, fine, choice, exquisite, incomparable.
—Ant. common, usual, frequent, ordinary; base, inferior.

rarefied, *adj.* **1.** thin, attenuated, tenuous, ethereal, vaporous, insubstantial, airy, gaseous, diffuse, diluted, dilute, adulterated, weak, watered down, porous. **2.** refined, esoteric, special, secret, recondite, inside, privileged.

rascal, *n.* imp, devil, mischief-maker, cad, villain, blackguard, good-for-nothing, wastrel, wretch, knave, rogue, scamp, scoundrel, miscreant, scapegrace.

rash, *adj.* hasty, impetuous, reckless, headlong, precipitate, impulsive, thoughtless, heedless, indiscreet, incautious, unwary, injudicious, imprudent, wild, madcap, harebrained, hotheaded, adventurous, quixotic, bold, brash, daring, devil-may-care, foolhardy, audacious.
—Ant. thoughtful, considered, discreet, cautious.

ratify, *v.* confirm, corroborate, consent to, agree to, approve, sanction, substantiate, validate, establish, endorse, support, uphold, sustain, verify, certify, affirm, clinch, settle.
—Ant. refute, veto, disapprove.

ration, *n.* **1.** allowance, portion, share, quota, allotment, helping, part, provision, percentage, dole, amount. **—*v.* 2.** apportion, distribute, mete, dole, deal, parcel out.

rational, *adj.* **1.** reasonable, sensible, well-balanced, sane, sound, normal, logical, clearheaded, cleareyed, sober, of sound mind. **2.** intelligent, wise; judicious, discreet, sagacious, enlightened. **3.** sane, lucid, sound, sober, common-sense, practical, pragmatic, down-to-earth, acceptable.
—Ant. irrational, unreasonable; unintelligent, stupid, unwise, indiscreet; unsound.

rationalize, *v.* **1.** explain, clarify, elucidate, explicate, illuminate. **2.** justify, excuse, alibi, exculpate, extenuate, explain away, vindicate, whitewash, gloss over.

raucous, *adj.* **1.** noisy, discordant, strident, harsh, dissonant, earsplitting, thunderous, rackety, cacophonous, stridulant, shrill, grating, piercing, jarring, screechy, shrieky, squawky. **2.** obstreperous, riotous, disorderly, boisterous, unruly, rowdy, rambunctious, uproarious, irrepressible, wild, tumultuous, rollicking, turbulent, fractious.
—Ant. melodious, sweet-sounding.

ravage, *n.* **1.** devastation, destruction, ruin, waste, desolation, damage, havoc, despoilment, plunder, pillage. **—*v.* 2.** damage, demolish, raze, wreck, mar, ruin, devastate, destroy, lay waste; despoil, plunder, pillage, sack, ransack, loot.

ravenous, *adj.* ravening, voracious, greedy, swinish, piggish, hoggish, starved, hungry, famished, insatiable, gluttonous, devouring; rapacious, raptorial, predacious, predatory.
—Ant. sated, satisfied.

raw, *adj.* **1.** unprepared, unfinished, unrefined, unmade, crude, rude, rough, makeshift. **2.** uncooked, unprepared, fresh, natural. **3.** ignorant, inexperienced, new, unseasoned, immature, untrained, undisciplined, green, unskilled, untried, unpracticed. **4.** damp, chilly, cold, wet, windy, frigid, freezing, nippy, biting, penetrating.
—Ant. prepared, finished, refined, done, polished; cooked, done; intelligent, disciplined, skilled; dry, warm, arid.
—Syn. Study. RAW, CRUDE, RUDE refer to something not in a finished or highly refined state. RAW applies particularly to material not yet changed by a process, by manufacture, or by preparation for consumption: *raw leather.* CRUDE refers to that which still needs refining: *crude petroleum.* RUDE refers to what is still in a condition of rough simplicity or in a roughly made form: *rude agricultural implements.*

reach, *v.* **1.** get to, attain, arrive at, come to. **2.** touch, seize, outstretch, extend, hold out. **3.** stretch, extend. **—*n.* 4.** extent, distance, range, compass, area, sphere, influence, stretch, scope, grasp.

reactionary, *n.* conservative, ultraconservative, rightist, right-winger, enemy of progress, establishmentarian, nonprogressive, hard-liner, royalist, moderate, orthodox, traditionalist, tory, mossback, fundamentalist, throwback, old fogy, puritan, fuddy-duddy, stuffed shirt, bluenose, stick-in-the-mud, fossil, square.
—Ant. radical.

ready, *adj.* **1.** prepared, set, fitted, fit. **2.** equipped, geared, completed, adjusted, arranged. **3.** willing, agreeable, cheerful, disposed, inclined. **4.** prompt, quick, alert, acute, sharp, keen, adroit, facile, clever, skillful, nimble. **—*v.* 5.** make ready, prepare, equip, fit out, get ready.
—Ant. unprepared, unfit; unwilling, indisposed, disinclined; slow, deliberate, unskillful.

real, *adj.* true, actual, faithful, factual, authentic, legitimate, verifiable, bonafide, official, valid, genuine; sincere, unfeigned, honest, unaffected.
—Ant. false, fake, counterfeit, fraudulent; insincere.

realistic, *adj.* practical, hardheaded, clear-eyed, clear-sighted, clearheaded, down-to-earth, common sense, sensible, reasonable, levelheaded, sane, rational, no-nonsense, hard-nosed, businesslike, sober, blunt, factual, pragmatic, toughminded, undeceived, ungullible, unsentimental, unromantic.
—Ant. impractical, flighty.

realize, *v.* **1.** grasp, understand, comprehend, appreciate, recognize, perceive, see, conceive. **2.** accomplish, effect, effectuate, perform, produce, achieve, fulfill.

realm, *n.* kingdom, empire, sovereignty, sphere, domain, province, department; area, territory, responsibility, jurisdiction, bailiwick.

rear, *n.* **1.** back, background. **—*v.* 2.** bring up, nurture, raise, nurse. **3.** raise, elevate, lift, loft, lift up, hold up; build, put up, erect, construct.
—Ant. front; face.
—Syn. Study. See BACK.

reason, *n.* **1.** ground, cause, motive, purpose, end, design, *raison d'être,* objective, aim, object. **2.** justification, explanation, excuse, rationale, ratiocination, rationalization. **3.** judgment, common sense, understanding, intellect, intelligence, mind. **4.** sanity, rationality, mind. **—*v.* 5.** argue, ratiocinate, justify; rationalize. **6.** conclude, infer. **7.** persuade, convince, influence.
—Syn. Study. REASON, CAUSE, MOTIVE are terms for a circumstance (or circumstances) that brings about or explains certain results. A REASON is an explanation of a situation or circumstance that made certain results seem possible or appropriate: *The reason for the robbery was the victim's careless display of money.* The CAUSE is the way in which the circumstances produce the effect; that is, make a specific action seem necessary or desirable: *The cause was the robber's immediate need of money.* A MOTIVE is the hope, desire, or other force that starts the action (or

an action) in an attempt to produce specific results: *The motive was to use the stolen money to gamble.*

reasonable, *adj.* **1.** rational, logical, sensible, intelligent, wise, judicious, right, fair, equitable. **2.** moderate, tolerable, adequate, satisfactory, acceptable, equitable, fair, conservative. **3.** sane, rational, sober, sound, sensible, judicious, level-headed.
—Ant. unreasonable, illogical, irrational; immoderate, intolerable; unsound, insane.

reassure, *v.* encourage, hearten, embolden, buoy up, cheer, uplift, brace, support, bolster, comfort, inspirit, put (someone's) mind at rest.
—Ant. disconcert, unnerve, dishearten, discourage.

rebel, *n.* **1.** insurgent, insurrectionist, mutineer, revolutionary, resister, freedom fighter; nonconformist, heretic, dissenter, apostate, schismatic. **—*adj.* 2.** insurgent, mutinous, rebellious, insubordinate. **—*v.* 3.** revolt, mutiny, rise up, take up arms; dissent, disobey, defy, challenge, resist, flout.
—Ant. patriot; loyal, obedient.

rebellion, *n.* resistance, defiance, insurrection, mutiny, sedition, revolution, revolt; insubordination, disobedience, contumacy.

rebellious, *adj.* defiant, insubordinate, mutinous, rebel, seditious, insurgent; refractory, disobedient, contumacious, incorrigible, unruly, difficult, unmanageable, obstinate, obstreperous, recalcitrant, fractious, rambunctious.
—Ant. subordinate, obedient, patriotic.

rebuff, *v.* **1.** reject, snub, slight, spurn, cut, dismiss, drop, repulse, repel, brush off. **—*n.* 2.** rejection, snub, dismissal, repulsion, brushoff, kissoff, repudiation, slight, refusal.
—Ant. welcome, embrace.

rebuke, *v.* **1.** reprove, reprimand, censure, upbraid, chide, reproach, reprehend, lecture, berate, castigate, criticize, take to task, revile, chew out, give (someone) a piece of one's mind, bawl out, admonish, scold, remonstrate with. **—*n.* 2.** reproof, reprimand, censure, reproach, reprehension, chiding, scolding, remonstration, tongue-lashing.
—Ant. praise.

recalcitrant, *adj.* stubborn, obstinate, disobedient, uncompliant, refractory, rebellious, contumacious, opposing, willful, defiant, headstrong, perverse, contrary, fractious, unruly, insubordinate, intractable, adamant, inflexible, immovable, uncontrollable, wayward.
—Ant. obedient, compliant.
—Syn. Study. See UNRULY.

recall, *v.* **1.** recollect, think back to, reminisce, call to mind, remember. **2.** call back, revoke, rescind, retract, withdraw, recant, repeal, annul, countermand, nullify. **—*n.* 3.** memory, recollection. **4.** revocation, retraction, repeal, cancellation, annulment, disavowal, denial, withdrawal, recantation, nullification; impeachment.
—Ant. forget; enforce; ratify; sanction.

recent, *adj.* late, modern, up-to-date, fresh, new, novel, just out, brand-new, current, late-model.
—Ant. early, old, ancient.
—Syn. See MODERN.

receptive, *adj.* responsive, open, open-minded, hospitable, welcoming, sympathetic, impressionable, susceptible, amenable, reachable, teachable, educable, swayable, persuadible, suggestible, tractable, flexible, pliant, interested, willing, responsive.
—Ant. resistant.

recherché, *adj.* **1.** unusual, exotic, rare, novel, uncommon, unfamiliar, strange, foreign, unheard of, mysterious. **2.** quaint, choice, exquisite, precious, special, superior, select, peerless, superlative. **3.** affected, overrefined, unnatural, artificial, put-on, stagy, theatrical.
—Ant. down-to-earth, everyday.

recital, *n.* account, narrative, description, recitation, rehearsal, relation, history, story, report, narration, telling, recounting, rendition, version, repetition, recap.

recite, *v.* repeat, relate, narrate, recount, describe, quote, present, report, detail, chronicle, list, share, recapitulate, tell, recap.
—Syn. Study. See RELATE.

reckless, *adj.* careless, rash, heedless, incautious, negligent, foolhardy, injudicious, impulsive, irresponsible, thoughtless, imprudent, improvident, remiss, inattentive, indifferent, regardless, unconcerned, daredevil, breakneck, madcap, harebrained, mad, wild.
—Ant. careful, heedful, cautious, thoughtful, provident.

reckon, *v.* **1.** count, compute, calculate, enumerate. **2.** suppose, assume, presume, venture, imagine, conclude, daresay, esteem, consider, regard, account, deem, estimate, judge, evaluate.

reclaim, *v.* recover, bring *or* get back, regain, restore, rescue, redeem, salvage, retrieve, save.

recognize, *v.* **1.** identify, place, recall, recollect, remember, detect. **2.** acknowledge, perceive, understand, realize, accept, allow, see, admit, concede, appreciate, grant, respect, be aware of. **3.** approve, sanction, accept, endorse, ratify, validate, acknowledge. **4.** honor, reward, pay respect, pay homage, give recognition to, salute, show appreciation, acknowledge, show one's gratitude.
—Ant. forget; deny; reject; ignore.

recoil, *v.* **1.** draw *or* shrink back, falter, flinch, quail. **2.** rebound, spring *or* fly back, react, reverberate.
—Ant. advance.
—Syn. Study. See WINCE.

recommend, *v.* **1.** commend, approve, condone, endorse, praise, push, favor, support, promote, second, vouch for, back, plug. **2.** advise, counsel, guide, urge, exhort, suggest, propose, advocate, propound, persuade.
—Ant. condemn, disapprove.

recompense, *v.* **1.** repay, remunerate, reward, requite, compensate for. **—*n.* 2.** compensation, payment, reward, requital, remuneration, repayment, amends, indemnification, retribution, reparation, atonement, redress, restitution.

reconcile, *v.* **1.** content, win over, convince, persuade. **2.** pacify, conciliate, placate, propitiate, appease. **3.** compose, settle, adjust, make up, harmonize, make compatible *or* consistent.
—Ant. dissuade; anger, arouse, disturb.

record, *v.* **1.** set down, enter, register, enroll, transcribe, document, note, log, chronicle, report, itemize, list, enumerate, catalog. **—*n.* 2.** account, chronicle, history, note, register, memorandum, report, document, log, journal, archive, annal, diary, list, catalog.

recount, *v.* relate, narrate, tell, recite, describe, enumerate, report, communicate, impart, reveal, review, detail, specify.
—Syn. Study. See RELATE.

recourse, *n.* resource, resort, refuge, hope, expedient, means, device, help, strength, last resort, backup, reserve, alternative, remedy, place to turn.

recover, *v.* **1.** regain, get again, reclaim, retrieve, restore, recoup, repossess, recapture, redeem, win *or* take back. **2.** heal, mend, recuperate, rally, convalesce, improve, revive, pull through, get back on one's feet, regain one's strength.

rectify, *v.* **1.** set right, correct, remedy, mend, emend, amend, revise, improve, redress, cure, repair, fix, square, better, ameliorate. **2.** adjust, regulate, put right, straighten.
—Ant. worsen, ruin.

redeem, *v.* **1.** buy *or* pay off, ransom, recover, reclaim, repossess, retrieve, buy back, repurchase. **2.** ransom, free, liberate, rescue, save, deliver, emancipate, release.

redress, *n.* **1.** reparation, restitution, amends, indemnification, compensation, satisfaction, indemnity, restoration, remedy, relief, atonement. **—*v.* 2.** remedy, repair, correct, amend, mend, emend, right, rectify, adjust, relieve, ease.
—Ant. blame, punishment; damage.
—Syn. Study. REDRESS, REPARATION, RESTITUTION suggest making amends or giving compensation for a wrong. REDRESS may refer either to the act of setting right an unjust situation or to satisfaction sought or gained for a wrong suffered: *the redress of grievances.* REPARATION refers to compensation or satisfaction for a wrong or loss inflicted. The word may have the moral idea of amends, but more frequently it refers to financial compensation: *to make reparation for one's neglect; the reparations demanded of the aggressor nations.* RESTITUTION means literally the giving back of what has been taken from the lawful owner, but may refer to restoring the equivalent of what has been taken: *The servant convicted of robbery made restitution to his employer.*

reduce, *v.* **1.** diminish, decrease, shorten, abridge, curtail, retrench, abate, lessen, contract. **2.** subdue, suppress, subject, subjugate, conquer, vanquish, overcome, overpower, overthrow, depose. **3.** debase, depress, lower, degrade.
—Ant. increase; defend; honor, exalt, elevate.

refer, *v.* **1.** direct, commit, deliver, consign. **2.** assign, attribute, ascribe, impute. **3.** relate, apply, obtain, pertain, belong, respect. **4.** advert, allude, hint at, mention, indicate, quote, cite, note.

reference, *n.* **1.** naming, remark, indication, hint, intimation, innuendo, insinuation, specification, notation, quotation, direction, allusion, referral, mention, citation. **2.** witness; testimonial, endorsement, relation, regard, respect, concern, connection, relevance, pertinence.

refined, *adj.* **1.** cultivated, polished, genteel, elegant, polite, courteous, courtly, civilized, well-bred. **2.** purified, clarified, distilled, strained. **3.** subtle, discriminating, fastidious, nice, sophisticated. **4.** minute, precise, exact, exquisite.
—Ant. unrefined, inelegant, impolite, discourteous; polluted, contaminated; obvious, direct; general, inexact.

reflect, *v.* **1.** mirror, cast *or* throw back, rebound. **2.** reproduce, demonstrate, exhibit, illustrate, reveal, expose, suggest, show, manifest, espouse. **3.** meditate, think, ponder, ruminate, cogitate, muse, deliberate, study, contemplate, consider.
—Syn. Study. See STUDY.

reflection, *n.* **1.** image, representation, counterpart. **2.** consideration, thought, deliberation, cogitation, rumination, meditation, study, contemplation, thinking, musing. **3.** imputation, aspersion, reproach, censure.
—Ant. original; thoughtlessness; praise.

reflective, *adj.* pensive, meditative, contemplative, musing, thoughtful, pondering, deliberating, reflecting, reasoning.
—Ant. thoughtless, inconsiderate, unthinking.
—Syn. Study. See PENSIVE.

reform, *n.* **1.** improvement, amendment, correction, reformation, change, modification, rectification, rehabilitation, recovery, renovation, betterment, amelioration. **—*v.* 2.** better, rectify, correct, amend, emend, ameliorate, mend, improve, repair, restore.
—Ant. deterioration; worsen, deteriorate.

reformation, *n.* improvement, betterment, correction, reform, amendment, reorganization, rehabilitation, renovation, rectification, modification, change, transformation, melioration.

refrain, *v.* restrain, cease, abstain, desist, forbear, keep from, eschew, avoid, renounce, leave off, curb oneself, hold oneself back, withhold.
—Ant. continue, persist.

refresh, *v.* **1.** reinvigorate, revive, stimulate, freshen, resuscitate, vitalize, energize, fortify, exhilarate, brace, cheer, enliven, reanimate. **2.** restore, repair, renovate, renew, retouch.
—Ant. dispirit, discourage.

refuge, *n.* shelter, protection, cover, security, safety; asylum, retreat, sanctuary, hiding place, haven, harbor, stronghold, safehouse, citadel, hideaway, hideout.

refurbish, *v.* renovate, refurnish, redecorate, brighten, restore, polish, renew, spruce up, remodel, overhaul, repair, revamp.

refuse, *v.* **1.** decline, reject, spurn, turn down, deny, rebuff, repudiate. **—*n.* 2.** rubbish, trash, waste, litter, dirt, debris, detritus, castoffs, junk, garbage; slag, lees, dregs, scum, sediment, dross.
—Ant. allow, permit, sanction, approve.
—Syn. Study. REFUSE, REJECT, SPURN, DECLINE imply nonacceptance of something. REFUSE is direct and emphatic in expressing a determination not to accept what is offered or proposed: *to refuse an offer of help.* REJECT is even more forceful and definite: *to reject an author's manuscript.* To SPURN is to reject with scorn: *to spurn a bribe.* DECLINE is a milder and more courteous term: *to decline an invitation.*

regain, *v.* recover, recapture, repossess, retrieve, get back.
—Ant. lose, miss.

regal, *adj.* royal, kingly, queenly, magisterial, majestic, noble, sovereign, imperial, exalted, stately, princely, splendid.
—Ant. servile.

regale, *v.* amuse, divert, entertain, beguile, refresh, please, delight, indulge, fascinate, entrance, enchant, charm, gladden, titillate, tickle.

regard, *v.* **1.** look upon, think of, consider, esteem, account, judge, deem, hold, suppose, estimate. **2.** respect, esteem, honor, revere, reverence, value. **3.** look at, observe, notice, note, see, remark, mark. **4.** relate to, concern, refer to, respect. **—*n.* 5.** reference, relevance, association, bearing, connection, relation.

6. point, particular, detail, matter, consideration. **7.** thought, concern, attention. **8.** look, gaze, view. **9.** respect, deference, concern, esteem, estimation, consideration, reverence. **10.** liking, affection, interest, love.
—**Ant.** disregard; disrespect, dishonor; inattention; dislike.

region, *n.* part, area, division, district, section, portion, quarter, district, zone, locality, sector, dominion, precinct, province, territory, locale, site, sphere, vicinity, vicinage, space, tract, domain, field, jurisdiction, bailiwick.

register, *n.* **1.** record, catalog, account book, ledger, archive. **2.** roll, roster, catalog, list, record, chronicle, schedule, annals. **3.** registry, entry, registration, enrollment. —*v.* **4.** enroll, list, record, catalogue, chronicle, enter. **5.** demonstrate, show, evince, display, express, indicate, reveal, betray, divulge, reflect.

regret, *v.* **1.** deplore, lament, feel sorry about, grieve at, bemoan, bewail, rue, mourn for, repent. —*n.* **2.** sorrow, lamentation, woe, mournfulness, grief. **3.** remorse, penitence, contrition, repentance, compunction, guilt, conscience, qualm, self-reproach, self-condemnation, second thoughts.
—**Ant.** rejoice; joy; unregeneracy.
—**Syn. Study.** REGRET, REMORSE imply a sense of sorrow about events in the past, usu. wrongs committed or errors made. REGRET is a feeling of sorrow or disappointment for what has been done or not been done: *I remembered our bitter quarrel with regret.* REMORSE is a deep sense of guilt and mental anguish for having done wrong: *The killer seemed to have no remorse.*

regular, *adj.* **1.** usual, normal, customary, routine, ordinary, common, commonplace, traditional, time-honored, conventional, typical, habitual, familiar, standard, predictable, scheduled, fixed, invariable, methodical. **2.** conforming, symmetrical, uniform, even, systematic, formal, fixed, orderly, invariant, harmonious, classic, well-proportioned, unvarying, methodical, constant. **3.** recurrent, periodic, habitual, established, fixed, steady, systematic, rhythmic, dependable, orderly, uniform, automatic.
—**Ant.** irregular.

regulate, *v.* control, direct, manage, rule, order, adjust, modify, modulate, balance, fix, govern, organize, maintain, monitor, handle, run, operate, administer, oversee, arrange, set, systematize, dispose, conduct, guide.

regulation, *n.* **1.** rule, order, direction, law, precept, ruling, code, bylaw, edict, ordinance, statute, decree, dictate. **2.** direction, control, management, arrangement, ordering, disposition, disposal, adjustment.
—**Ant.** misdirection, mismanagement.

rehearse, *v.* **1.** recite, act, practice, drill, train, exercise, study, repeat. **2.** relate, enumerate, recount, delineate, describe, portray, narrate, recapitulate, repeat, review, report, recap.
—**Ant.** extemporize.

reign, *n.* **1.** rule, sway, dominion, sovereignty, ascendancy, hegemony, command, leadership, jurisdiction, control, domination, governance, government, mastery, power, influence. —*v.* **2.** rule, govern, prevail, predominate, hold sway, influence, command, dominate, control, run the show, manage.
—**Ant.** obey.

reject, *v.* **1.** refuse, repudiate, decline, disallow, spurn, veto, shun, spurn, dismiss, turn thumbs down, brush off, brush aside, turn down, deny, rebuff, repel, renounce. **2.** discard, throw away, exclude, eliminate, jettison, scrap, junk, scratch, disown.
—**Ant.** accept.
—**Syn. Study.** See REFUSE.

relate, *v.* **1.** tell, recite, narrate, recount, rehearse, report, describe, delineate, detail, repeat, communicate, present, divulge, impart, reveal, make known. **2.** associate, connect, ally, couple, link.
—**Ant.** dissociate, disconnect, separate.
—**Syn. Study.** RELATE, RECITE, RECOUNT mean to tell, report, or describe in some detail an occurrence or circumstance. To RELATE is to give an account of happenings, events, circumstances, etc.: *to relate one's adventures.* To RECITE may mean to give details consecutively, but more often applies to the repetition from memory of something learned with verbal exactness: *to recite a poem.* To RECOUNT is usu. to set forth consecutively the details of an occurrence, argument, experience, etc., to give an account in detail: *to recount an unpleasant experience.*

relation, *n.* **1.** connection, relationship, association, alliance, dependence. **2.** reference, regard, respect. **3.** narration, recitation, recital, description, rehearsal, relating, telling; narrative, account, report, story, chronicle, tale, history.
—**Ant.** independence.

relationship, *n.* **1.** relation, connection, association, affiliation, bearing, link, tie, interconnection, reference, pertinence. **2.** kinship, affinity, family tie, consanguinity, blood tie.
—**Ant.** dissociation.

relax, *v.* **1.** loosen, slacken, moderate, release, relieve, reduce, ease up on. **2.** diminish, ebb, wane, mitigate, weaken, lessen, reduce, remit, abate, debilitate, enervate. **3.** ease, unbend, relent, soften.
—**Ant.** tighten; intensify, increase; harden.

release, *v.* **1.** free, dismiss, discharge, liberate, set free, loose, unloose, unfasten, set at liberty, deliver. **2.** disengage, loose, extricate. —*n.* **3.** liberation, deliverance, emancipation, discharge, freedom, rescue, salvation.
—**Ant.** fasten, fetter, imprison; engage, involve; incarceration, imprisonment.
—**Syn. Study.** RELEASE, FREE, DISMISS, DISCHARGE, LIBERATE all mean to let loose or let go. RELEASE and FREE both suggest a helpful action; they may be used of delivering a person from confinement or obligation: *to release prisoners; to free a student from certain course requirements.* DISMISS usually means to force to go unwillingly; however, it may also refer to giving permission to go: *to dismiss an employee; to dismiss a class.* DISCHARGE usually means to relieve of an obligation, office, etc.; it may also mean to permit to go: *The soldier was discharged. The hospital discharged the patient.* LIBERATE suggests particularly the deliverance from unjust punishment, oppression, or the like, and often means to set free through forcible or military action: *to liberate occupied territories.*

relentless, *adj.* unrelenting, inflexible, rigid, stern, severe, unbending, unforgiving, unappeasable, implacable, merciless, ruthless, unmerciful, stubborn, perseverent, dogged, intransigent, determined, steely, tough, stiff-necked, pitiless, hard, obdurate, adamant, unyielding, remorseless, inexorable.
—**Ant.** flexible, soft, pliant, merciful.

relevant, *adj.* pertinent, applicable, germane, apposite, appropriate, suitable, fitting, apt, proper, suited, related, relative, significant, akin, allied, to the point.
—**Ant.** irrelevant.
—**Syn. Study.** See APT.

reliable, *adj.* trustworthy, trusty, dependable, infallible, unfailing, honest, principled, conscientious, punctilious, honorable, safe, sure, certain, secure, sound, responsible, predictable, stable, reputable.
—**Ant.** unreliable, untrustworthy, undependable.

relief, *n.* **1.** deliverance, alleviation, ease, assuagement, mitigation, abatement, release, remission, liberation, amelioration, comfort. **2.** help, assistance, aid, succor, redress, remedy.
—**Ant.** intensity, intensification.

relieve, *v.* **1.** ease, alleviate, assuage, mitigate, allay, lighten, reduce, abate, lift, raise, palliate, soften, comfort, soothe, lessen, diminish. **2.** unburden, disburden, free, rid, liberate, disencumber, rescue, release, save, ease. **3.** aid, help, assist, succor, remedy, support, sustain.
—**Ant.** intensify, increase; burden.

religious, *adj.* **1.** pious, holy, devout, faithful, reverent, godly, churchgoing, God-fearing, spiritual. **2.** conscientious, scrupulous, exacting, punctilious, strict, rigid, rigorous, fastidious, meticulous, sedulous, assiduous, demanding.
—**Ant.** irreligious, impious, unfaithful, irreverent; flexible, lenient.
—**Syn. Study.** RELIGIOUS, DEVOUT, PIOUS indicate a spirit of reverence toward God. RELIGIOUS is a general word, indicating adherence to a particular set of beliefs and practices: *a religious family.* DEVOUT indicates a fervent spirit, usu. genuine and often independent of outward observance: *a deeply devout though unorthodox church member.* PIOUS implies constant attention to, and extreme conformity with, outward observances; it can also suggest sham or hypocrisy: *a pious hypocrite.*

relinquish, *v.* renounce, surrender, give up, resign, yield, cede, waive, forswear, forgo, abdicate, leave, forsake, desert, renounce, quit, abandon, let go, resign, drop, vacate, retire from.
—**Ant.** demand, require.

relish, *n.* **1.** liking, taste, enjoyment, appreciation, gusto, zest, avidity, anticipation, appetite, fondness, pleasure, propensity, proclivity, inclination, bent, partiality, predilection, preference. **2.** taste, flavor, savor. —*v.* **3.** like, enjoy, appreciate, prefer, delight in, take pleasure in, be partial to, fancy, savor, anticipate.
—**Ant.** distaste, aversion.

reluctant, *adj.* unwilling, disinclined, hesitant, loath, averse, indisposed, unenthusiastic, opposed; cautious, chary, leery, circumspect, careful.
—**Ant.** willing, agreeable, amenable, unhesitating, eager, avid.
—**Syn. Study.** RELUCTANT, LOATH, AVERSE describe disinclination toward something. RELUCTANT implies some sort of mental struggle, as between disinclination and sense of duty: *reluctant to expel students.* LOATH describes extreme disinclination: *loath to part from a friend.* AVERSE describes a long-held dislike or unwillingness, though not a particularly strong feeling: *averse to an idea; averse to getting up early.*

remain, *v.* **1.** continue, stay, last, abide, endure. **2.** wait, tarry, linger, loiter, dally, stop over, delay, stay, rest. —*n.* **3.** (*plural*) remnants, scraps, remainder, refuse, leavings, crumbs, orts, residue, relics, detritus, leftovers, rest.
—**Ant.** leave, depart.

remainder, *n.* residuum, remnant, excess, residue, rest, balance, surplus, others, leftovers.

remark, *v.* **1.** say, observe, note, perceive, heed, regard, notice; comment, state. —*n.* **2.** notice, regard, observation, heed, attention, consideration. **3.** comment, utterance, note, observation, declaration, assertion, statement.
—**Ant.** disregard, ignore; inattention.

remarkable, *adj.* notable, conspicuous, unusual, extraordinary, exceptional, impressive, phenomenal, astonishing, astounding, incredible, noteworthy, striking, wonderful, uncommon, strange, rare, distinguished, prominent, singular, signal, special, marvelous, unique, outstanding, memorable, unforgettable.
—**Ant.** common, usual, ordinary.

remedy, *n.* **1.** cure, relief, medicine, treatment, restorative, therapy, prescription, drug, cure-all, nostrum, medicament, medication, ointment, balm. **2.** antidote, corrective, antitoxin, counteraction, countermeasure, relief, redress, answer, solution. —*v.* **3.** cure, heal, put *or* set right, restore, recondition, repair, redress. **4.** counteract, remove, correct, right, improve, rectify, ameliorate, straighten out, repair.
—**Ant.** sicken, worsen.

remember, *v.* **1.** recall, recollect, reminisce, think *or* look back; call to mind, turn one's mind *or* thoughts back, hark back, return. **2.** retain, memorize, keep *or* bear in mind.
—**Ant.** forget.

remembrance, *n.* reminder, keepsake, memento, souvenir, trophy, token, memorial, memento mori.

remiss, *adj.* **1.** negligent, careless, thoughtless, lax, slack, forgetful, unmindful, neglectful, inattentive, heedless. **2.** languid, sluggish, dilatory, slothful, slow, tardy, lax, delinquent.
—**Ant.** careful, thoughtful, attentive; energetic, quick.

remission, *n.* **1.** pardon, forgiveness, absolution, indulgence, exoneration, discharge, deliverance, amnesty, reprieve, release, exemption, acquittal. **2.** abatement, diminution, lessening, relaxation, moderation, mitigation. **3.** release, relinquishment. **4.** decrease, subsidence, respite, stoppage, pause, interruption, relief, hiatus, suspense, suspension, abatement.
—**Ant.** blame, censure, conviction; increase, intensification; increase.

remnant, *n.* remainder, remains, residue, residuum, rest; trace, vestige, leftover, relic, fragment, scrap, shred, end, bit.

remorse, *n.* regret, compunction, penitence, contrition, repentance, ruefulness, sorrow, woe, guilt, bad conscience, humiliation, self-reproach, mortification, shame, bitterness.
—**Ant.** conviction.
—**Syn. Study.** See REGRET.

remorseful, *adj.* regretful, penitent, contrite, repentant, rueful, sorry, apologetic, conscience-stricken, guilt-ridden, humiliated, mortified, shamefaced, ashamed, humbled, bitter.
—**Ant.** impenitent.

remorseless, *adj.* relentless, pitiless,

uncompassionate, unrelenting, merciless, unmerciful, ruthless, cruel, savage, implacable, inexorable, callous, heartless, hardhearted, inhumane, barbarous.
—Ant. merciful, compassionate.

remote, *adj.* **1.** distant, far apart, far-off, outlying, inaccessible, removed; alien, foreign; outside, irrelevant, unrelated, unconnected. **2.** slight, faint, inconsiderable. **3.** abstracted, aloof, detached, withdrawn, reserved, standoffish.
—Ant. close, near; connected, related; considerable, substantial.

remove, *v.* **1.** replace, displace, dislodge, transfer, transport, carry. **2.** take, withdraw, separate, extract, eliminate. **3.** kill, assassinate, do away with, destroy, murder, dispose of, purge.

rend, *v.* tear apart, wrench, mangle, shred, split, divide, rip, rive, sunder, sever, cleave, chop, fracture, tear, dissever, crack, snap, lacerate, rupture.

render, *v.* **1.** make, cause to be, cause to become. **2.** do, perform, play. **3.** deliver, hand in, present, offer, provide, tender, furnish, supply, give, contribute, afford. **4.** exhibit, show, demonstrate; depict, represent, portray, execute, achieve. **5.** present, give, assign. **6.** deliver, return. **7.** translate, interpret, decode, decipher, convert, explain, restate, rephrase. **8.** give back, restore, return, give up, surrender, cede, yield, relinquish, resign, provide.

renew, *v.* **1.** restore, replenish, restock. **2.** re-create, rejuvenate, regenerate, restore, reinstate, renovate, repair, mend. **3.** revive, reestablish, resurrect, resume, reopen, recommence.
—Syn. Study. RENEW, RENOVATE, REPAIR, RESTORE suggest making something the way it formerly was. RENEW means to bring back to an original condition of freshness and vigor: *to renew one's faith.* RENOVATE means to bring back to a good condition, or to make as good as new: *to renovate an old house.* To REPAIR is to put into good or sound condition after damage, wear and tear, etc.: *to repair the roof of a house.* To RESTORE is to bring back to a former, original, or normal condition or position: *to restore a painting.*

renounce, *v.* **1.** give up, put aside, forsake, forgo, relinquish, abandon, forswear, leave, quit, resign, abdicate. **2.** repudiate, disown, disclaim, reject, disavow, deny, recant.
—Ant. claim, accept, desire.

renovate, *v.* redecorate, remodel, modernize, refurbish, refurnish, refit, restore, revamp, repair, overhaul, fix up.

renown, *n.* repute, fame, celebrity, glory, prominence, mark, luster, stardom, distinction, note, eminence, reputation, name, honor, esteem, acclaim, prestige, éclat.
—Ant. disrepute, infamy; oblivion.

rent, *n.* **1.** rental, return, payment, hire, lease, fee. **2.** tear, split, fissure, slit, crack, crevice, cleft, rift, gap, opening, rip, rupture, breach, break, fracture, laceration. **3.** schism, separation, disunion, breach. *—v.* **4.** lease, let, hire, charter, farm out.
—Syn. Study. See HIRE.

repair, *v.* **1.** restore, mend, remodel, renew, renovate, patch, revamp, adjust, amend, fix. **2.** make good, make up for, remedy, retrieve. **3.** make amends for, atone for, redress.
—Ant. break, destroy, ruin.
—Syn. Study. See RENEW.

repay, *v.* pay back, return, reimburse, indemnify, refund; recompense, compensate, requite, reciprocate, reward, return the favor, settle up, square with.

repeat, *v.* **1.** reiterate, recapitulate, iterate, recite, rehearse, relate, restate, retell, quote, recount, recap. **2.** reproduce, echo, reecho, redo. *—n.* **3.** repetition, iteration; duplicate, copy, reproduction, replica, encore, reprise.
—Syn. Study. REPEAT, RECAPITULATE, REITERATE refer to saying or doing a thing more than once. To REPEAT is to say or do something over again: *to repeat an order.* To RECAPITULATE is to restate in brief form often by repeating the principal points in a discourse: *to recapitulate a news broadcast.* To REITERATE is to say (or, sometimes, to do) something over and over again, often for emphasis: *to reiterate a refusal.*

repel, *v.* **1.** repulse, parry, ward off. **2.** resist, withstand, rebuff, oppose, confront. **3.** reject, decline, refuse, discourage. **4.** offend, disgust, sicken, nauseate, revolt, turn one's stomach, make one's skin crawl, give one the creeps, turn one off.
—Ant. attract; approve, accept.

repent, *v.* regret, atone, be contrite, be sorry, rue, feel remorse, be penitent, lament, bemoan, apologize, be ashamed.

repentance, *n.* compunction, contrition, contriteness, penitence, remorse, sorrow, regret, shame, atonement, embarrassment, humiliation, mortification.
—Ant. impenitence.

replace, *v.* **1.** supersede, supplant, substitute, succeed. **2.** restore, return, make good, refund, repay; replenish.
—Syn. Study. Study. REPLACE, SUPERSEDE, SUPPLANT refer to putting one thing or person in place of another. To REPLACE is to take the place of, to succeed: *Ms. Jones will replace Mr. Smith as president.* SUPERSEDE implies that that which is replacing another is an improvement: *The computer has superseded the typewriter.* SUPPLANT implies that that which takes the other's place has ousted the former holder and usurped the position or function, esp. by art or fraud: *to supplant a former favorite.*

reply, *v.* **1.** answer, respond, echo, rejoin. *—n.* **2.** answer, rejoinder, retort, comeback, reaction, rise, riposte, replication, response, feedback.
—Syn. Study. See ANSWER.

represent, *v.* **1.** designate, stand for, denote, symbolize, exemplify, typify, embody, epitomize, illustrate, image, depict, express, portray, personate, delineate, figure, present. **2.** set forth, describe, state, delineate, characterize, report, assert, define, outline, sketch, depict, picture, portray, paint; pretend.

repress, *v.* **1.** check, suppress, subdue, put down, quell, quash, reduce, crush. **2.** check, restrain, curb, bridle, control, stifle, squelch, contain, constrain, inhibit, hamper, hinder, frustrate, discourage.
—Ant. foster, support, help, aid.

reprisal, *n.* retaliation, revenge, vengeance, redress, vendetta, retribution, requital, vindication, repayment, recompense, getting even.
—Syn. Study. See REVENGE.

reproach, *v.* **1.** chide, abuse, reprimand, condemn, criticize, rebuke, scold, reprove, call to account, censure, blame, remonstrate with, castigate, find fault with, shame, abash, discredit, reprehend, upbraid. *—n.* **2.** blame, censure, upbraiding, reproof, abuse, vilification, discredit, reprehension, rebuke, criticism, remonstrance, condemnation, expostulation, disapproval, disapprobation. **3.** disgrace, dishonor, shame, disrepute, odium, scandal, obloquy, opprobrium, ignominy, indignity, infamy, insult, scorn, offense.
—Ant. praise, honor.

reproduce, *v.* **1.** copy, duplicate, repeat, imitate, represent, replicate, recreate, simulate, match. **2.** generate, propagate, beget, give birth, breed, multiply, procreate, spawn, foal.
—Ant. initiate, originate.

repudiate, *v.* **1.** reject, disclaim, disavow, disown, scorn, retract, rescind, reverse, abandon, abrogate, forswear, forgo, deny, discard, renounce. **2.** condemn, disapprove.
—Ant. accept; approve, commend.

repugnance, *n.* distaste, aversion, dislike, repulsion, abhorrence, disgust, abomination, execration, nausea, hatred, hostility, antipathy.
—Ant. attraction, liking, sympathy.

repugnant, *adj.* **1.** repulsive, off-putting, repellant, revolting, vile, abominable, loathsome, foul, unpalatable, unsavory, intolerable, noisome, obnoxious, nauseating, sickmaking, unpleasant, horrid, distasteful, objectionable, offensive. **2.** opposing, objecting, protesting, averse, unfavorable, antagonistic, inimical, adverse, contrary, hostile, opposed.
—Ant. attractive, tasteful; favorable, amiable.

reputation, *n.* **1.** estimation, regard, repute, standing, stature, status, position, name, character. **2.** credit, esteem, honor, fame, celebrity, distinction, renown, name, notoriety, acclaim, repute.
—Ant. dishonor, infamy.
—Syn. Study. REPUTATION and CHARACTER are often confused. REPUTATION, however, is the word which refers to the position one occupies or the standing that one has in the opinion of others, in respect to attainments, integrity, and the like: *a fine reputation; a reputation for honesty.* CHARACTER is the combination of moral and other traits which make one the kind of person one actually is (as contrasted with what others think of one): *Honesty is an outstanding trait of her character.*

repute, *n.* **1.** estimation, reputation. **2.** name, reputation, distinction, credit, honor. *—v.* **3.** consider, esteem, account, regard, hold, deem, reckon.

request, *n.* **1.** solicitation, petition, suit, entreaty, plea, application, supplication, prayer, demand. *—v.* **2.** ask for, sue, petition, entreat, beg, supplicate, solicit, beseech, require, plead for, importune, seek.

require, *v.* **1.** need, demand, command, press for, instruct, coerce, force, insist, call for, request, order, enjoin, direct, ask. **2.** obligate, necessitate, want, need, call for, lack, desire.
—Ant. forgo.
—Syn. Study. See LACK.

requirement, *n.* **1.** requisite, need, claim, requisition, prerequisite, demand, precondition, condition, stipulation, criterion, sine qua non, provision, proviso, necessity, essential, desideratum, must. **2.** mandate, order, command, directive, injunction, ukase, charge, claim, precept.
—Syn. Study. REQUIREMENT, REQUISITE refer to that which is necessary. A REQUIREMENT is some quality or performance demanded of a person in accordance with certain fixed regulations: *requirements for admission to college.* A REQUISITE is not imposed from outside; it is a factor that is judged necessary according to the nature of things, or to the circumstances of the case: *Efficiency is a requisite for success in business.* REQUISITE may also refer to a concrete object judged necessary: *the requisites for perfect grooming.*

requisite, *adj.* **1.** required, necessary, essential, indispensable, needed, needful. *—n.* **2.** necessity, requirement, criterion, sine qua non.
—Ant. dispensable, unnecessary; luxury, superfluity.
—Syn. Study. See NECESSARY. See also REQUIREMENT.

requite, *v.* **1.** repay, remunerate, reimburse, recompense, pay, satisfy, compensate. **2.** retaliate, avenge, revenge, punish.
—Ant. dissatisfy; forgive.

rescue, *v.* **1.** save, deliver, liberate, set free, emancipate, manumit, release, redeem, ransom, extricate; recover, preserve. *—n.* **2.** liberation, release, redemption, ransom, recovery, deliverance, salvation, emancipation.
—Ant. incarceration, imprisonment.

research, *n.* **1.** inquiry, investigation, examination, scrutiny, study, exploration, delving, digging, fact-finding, inspection, probe, analysis, experimentation, checking. *—v.* **2.** investigate, study, inquire, examine, scrutinize.

resemblance, *n.* **1.** similarity, likeness, analogy, semblance, similitude, correspondence, congruity, equivalence, comparability, agreement. **2.** appearance, representation, semblance, image.
—Ant. dissimilarity; misrepresentation.

resentful, *adj.* bitter, embittered, envious, spiteful, jealous, begrudging, vindictive, indignant, disgruntled, acrimonious, peeved, irritated, riled, piqued, irate, annoyed, provoked, furious, incensed, agitated, upset, worked up, antagonistic, hostile, hateful, rancorous, malevolent.
—Ant. grateful, benevolent, friendly.

reserve, *v.* **1.** keep back, save, retain, husband, withhold, conserve, preserve, keep, hold, store up. **2.** set apart, set aside, bank. *—n.* **3.** reservation, qualification, exception. **4.** store, stock, supply. **5.** self-restraint, restraint, reticence, silence, taciturnity, constraint, coldness, coolness, aplomb, detachment, formality, aloofness, cool.
—Ant. splurge, squander, waste; prodigality; warmth, enthusiasm.
—Syn. Study. See KEEP.

reside, *v.* **1.** dwell, abide, live, sojourn, stay, lodge, inhabit, remain. **2.** abide, lie, be present, inhere, exist.

residence, *n.* **1.** dwelling, house, home, habitation, domicile, abode, place, living quarters. **2.** tenancy, visit, residency, stay, sojourn.
—Syn. Study. See HOUSE.

resign, *v.* give up, submit, yield, cede, surrender, abdicate, relinquish, forgo, abandon, forsake, quit, leave, renounce, withdraw, vacate, retire, release.

resignation, *n.* **1.** abdication, abandonment, surrender, relinquishment. **2.** submission, meekness, patience, acquiescence, endurance, compliance, forbearance, sufferance, acceptance, capitulation, passivity, reconciliation.
—Ant. application; boldness, rebelliousness.

resilient, *adj.* ductile, elastic, flexible, springy, supple, recoiling; buoyant, cheerful, bouncy.
—**Ant.** rigid, inflexible, inelastic.

resist, *v.* **1.** withstand, strive against, oppose, confront, thwart, impede, block, obstruct, combat, battle, oppugn, countervail, defy, weather, stand up to, hold at bay, hold the line against, fight, assail, attack, counteract, rebuff. **2.** refrain *or* abstain from, refuse, forgo, turn down, deny.
—**Ant.** defend; accept.
—**Syn. Study.** See OPPOSE.

resolute, *adj.* resolved, firm, steadfast, determined, set, adamant, staunch, dogged, single-minded, indefatigable, tireless, unflagging, unswerving, perseverant, persistent, tenacious, deliberate, immutable, opinionated, purposeful, earnest, sincere, fixed, unflinching, unwavering, inflexible, hardy, unshaken, bold, undaunted, pertinacious.
—**Ant.** weak, feeble, frail, flexible, lenient.
—**Syn. Study.** See EARNEST.

resolve, *v.* **1.** fix *or* settle on, determine, decide, confirm, establish, agree, undertake, fix. **2.** work out, figure out, clear up, answer, explain, explicate, solve. —*n.* **3.** resolution, determination, decision, purpose, intention, obstinacy, dedication, devotion, perseverance, doggedness, tenacity, constancy, indefatigability.
—**Ant.** indecision.
—**Syn. Study.** See DECIDE.

respect, *n.* **1.** particular, detail, point, regard, feature, matter, aspect, quality, trait, characteristic, attribute, element, property. **2.** relation, reference, connection, regard. **3.** esteem, deference, regard, estimation, veneration, reverence, homage, honor, admiration, approbation, approval, affection, feeling. —*v.* **4.** honor, revere, reverence, esteem, venerate, regard, consider, defer to, admire, adulate, adore, love. **5.** regard, heed, attend to, pay attention to, obey, notice, consider.
—**Ant.** disregard.
—**Syn. Study.** RESPECT, ESTEEM, VENERATION imply recognition of a person's worth, or of a personal quality, trait, or ability. RESPECT is commonly the result of admiration and approbation, together with deference: *to feel respect for a great scholar.* ESTEEM is deference combined with admiration and often with affection: *to hold a friend in great esteem.* VENERATION is an almost religious attitude of reverence and love, such as one feels for persons or things of outstanding superiority, endeared by long association: *veneration for noble traditions.*

respectable, *adj.* **1.** estimable, worthy, honorable, upright, honest, respected, reputable, unimpeachable, aboveboard. **2.** proper, decent, presentable, moral, modest, chaste, innocent, pure, clean. **3.** fair, fairly good, moderate, middling, passable, tolerable, considerable, large, appreciable, sizable, substantial, significant, satisfactory, tidy.
—**Ant.** unworthy, dishonorable; improper; poor, small, insignificant.

respectful, *adj.* courteous, polite, well-mannered, cordial, gracious, obliging, considerate, thoughtful, well-bred, decorous, civil, deferential.
—**Ant.** disrespectful, discourteous, impolite.

respite, *n.* **1.** relief, delay, hiatus, cessation, postponement, intermission, break, interruption, breather, holiday, interval, rest, recess. **2.** stay, reprieve, suspension, postponement, pause.
—**Ant.** continuation.

response, *n.* answer, reply, rejoinder, riposte, retort, reaction, return, comeback, feedback.
—**Syn. Study.** See ANSWER.

responsible, *adj.* **1.** accountable, answerable, liable. **2.** chargeable, guilty, at fault, culpable, to blame, accountable, blamable, censurable. **3.** capable, able, reliable, solvent, trustworthy, trusty, dutiful, honest, dependable, stable, creditable, ethical.
—**Ant.** innocent; incapable, unreliable.

rest, *n.* **1.** sleep, nap, doze, slumber, repose, siesta, snooze, shuteye. **2.** relaxation, intermission, break, interval, recess, breather, holiday, respite, interlude, time off, cessation, vacation. **3.** leisure, ease, indolence, relaxation, idleness, loafing, inactivity. **4.** remainder, balance, remains, remnants, leftovers, others, excess, surplus, overage. —*v.* **5.** lie down, recline, relax, repose, unwind, loll about, loaf, laze about, take one's ease, put up one's feet, take it easy, nap, lounge, snooze, sleep, doze, catch forty winks, sack out, hit the hay. **6.** lie, be placed *or* situated, reside, be found, remain, stay. **7.** place, position, put, lay, set, lean, prop.

restful, *adj.* calm, tranquil, peaceful, undisturbed, serene, pacific; relaxing, soothing, sedative, comforting, soporific, hypnotic.
—**Ant.** perturbed, disturbed, agitated; upsetting.

restitution, *n.* reparation, redress, indemnification, restoration, recompense, amends, compensation, remuneration, requital, satisfaction, repayment.
—**Syn. Study.** See REDRESS.

restive, *adj.* **1.** uneasy, restless, nervous, impatient, ill at ease, edgy, fidgety, jumpy, skittish, high-strung, fretful, apprehensive, anxious, agitated, jittery, uptight, hyper, excitable, unquiet. **2.** refractory, disobedient, obstinate, mulish, stubborn, pigheaded, intractable, fractious.
—**Ant.** restful, patient, quiet, serene; obedient.

restore, *v.* **1.** reestablish, replace, reinstate, renew. **2.** renew, refurbish, rehabilitate, fix, touch up, revive, rejuvenate, renovate, repair, mend. **3.** return, give back, make restitution; replace, reimburse, return, repay. **4.** reproduce, reconstruct, rebuild.
—**Ant.** disestablish, destroy; break, ruin; accept, receive; raze.
—**Syn. Study.** See RENEW.

restrain, *v.* **1.** check, keep down, repress, curb, bridle, suppress, hold, keep, constrain. **2.** restrict, circumscribe, confine, hinder, abridge, hamper, limit, inhibit, curtail, stifle, interfere with, handicap.
—**Ant.** unbridle; broaden, widen.
—**Syn. Study.** See CHECK.

restrict, *v.* confine, limit, restrain, abridge, curb, circumscribe, bound, impede, regulate, demarcate.
—**Ant.** free, broaden, disencumber.

result, *n.* **1.** outcome, consequence, effect, conclusion, issue, event, end, termination, product, fruit, upshot, development, sequel, followup, denouement. —*v.* **2.** spring, arise, proceed, follow, flow, come, issue, ensue, rise, originate. **3.** terminate, end, resolve, eventuate, end, conclude, culminate.
—**Ant.** cause.
—**Syn. Study.** See FOLLOW. See also EFFECT.

retain, *v.* **1.** keep, hold, withhold, preserve, detain, reserve. **2.** recollect, memorize, remember, recall. **3.** hire, engage, employ, commission, take on.
—**Ant.** loose, lose; forget; disengage, fire.
—**Syn. Study.** See KEEP.

retaliate, *v.* avenge, requite, return, repay, revenge, counter, reciprocate, settle a score, give as good as one gets, give (someone) a taste of his *or* her own medicine, wreak vengeance, strike back, get even.
—**Ant.** forgive, pardon.

retard, *v.* slow, delay, hinder, hamper, impede, decelerate, clog, obstruct, check, stall, thwart, balk, restrict, frustrate, interfere with.
—**Ant.** speed, expedite, accelerate.

reticent, *adj.* taciturn, silent, reserved, quiet, uncommunicative, quiet, shy, timid, retiring, unresponsive, laconic, tightlipped.
—**Ant.** voluble, communicative.

retire, *v.* withdraw, leave, depart, go away, retreat, seclude oneself, fall back, recede; retract.
—**Ant.** advance, attack.

retired, *adj.* withdrawn, secluded, sequestered, cloistered, isolated, removed, apart, solitary, abstracted.
—**Ant.** advanced.

retort, *v.* **1.** counter, fling back, rebut, come back with, reply, respond, return, answer, retaliate, rejoin. —*n.* **2.** reply, response, answer, riposte, rejoinder, rebuttal, comeback.
—**Syn. Study.** See ANSWER.

retreat, *n.* **1.** departure, withdrawal, retirement, seclusion, privacy, solitude. **2.** sanctuary, den, haven, hideaway, hideout, sanctum sanctorum, shelter, refuge, asylum. —*v.* **3.** retire, withdraw, leave, depart, draw back, turn tail, decamp, evacuate, flee, take flight.
—**Ant.** advance.

retribution, *n.* requital, revenge, vengeance, retaliation, reprisal, redress, quid pro quo, satisfaction, punishment, justice, just deserts, repayment, reward, recompense, compensation.
—**Ant.** forgiveness, pardon.
—**Syn. Study.** See REVENGE.

retrieve, *v.* recover, regain, restore, save, rescue, recoup, reclaim.

reveal, *v.* make known, communicate, disclose, divulge, unveil, uncover, discover, publish, impart, tell, announce, proclaim, expose, display, give vent to, air, ventilate, leak.
—**Ant.** conceal, hide, veil, cover.

revenge, *n.* **1.** vengeance, retaliation, requital, reprisal, retribution. **2.** vindictiveness, revengefulness, vengefulness, spitefulness. —*v.* **3.** avenge, retaliate, requite, vindicate, exact retribution.
—**Ant.** forgiveness, pardon.
—**Syn. Study.** REVENGE, REPRISAL, RETRIBUTION, VENGEANCE suggest a punishment or injury inflicted in return for one received. REVENGE is the carrying out of a bitter desire to injure another for a wrong done to oneself or to those who are close to oneself: *to plot revenge for a friend's betrayal.* REPRISAL is used specifically in the context of warfare; it means retaliation against an enemy: *The guerrillas expected reprisals for the raid.* RETRIBUTION usu. suggests deserved punishment for some evil done: *a just retribution for wickedness.* VENGEANCE is usu. vindictive, furious revenge: *He swore vengeance against his enemies.*

revengeful, *adj.* vindictive, spiteful, malevolent, resentful, malicious, malignant, implacable, grudging, bitter, invidious.
—**Ant.** forgiving, benevolent.

reverence, *n.* **1.** worship, honor, esteem, admiration, glorification, beatification, sanctification, idolization, adulation, adoration, fealty, deference, obeidhsance, veneration, respect, homage, awe. —*v.* **2.** venerate, revere, honor, adore, adulate, worship, idolize, respect, enshrine, sanctify, beatify, glorify, esteem, admire.
—**Ant.** disrespect; despise.

reverse, *n.* **1.** opposite, antithesis, contrary, converse, counterpart. **2.** check, misfortune, defeat, mishap, misadventure, affliction. —*v.* **3.** overturn, upend, turn topsy-turvy, transpose, invert. **4.** alter, change, modify; renounce, recant, take back. **5.** revoke, annul, repeal, veto, rescind, overthrow, countermand, quash, override, nullify, invalidate, undo, negate, upset.
—**Ant.** same.

review, *n.* **1.** critique, criticism, evaluation, commentary, notice, opinion, judgment, survey. **2.** rereading, rehash, postmortem, reassessment, study, reconsideration, reexamination. **3.** inspection, examination, investigation. —*v.* **4.** survey, inspect, criticize, examine, study, weigh, scrutinize, consider.

revive, *v.* **1.** reactivate, revitalize, reanimate, resuscitate, revivify, reinvigorate, reinspirit, jump-start. **2.** bring back, quicken, renew, refresh, rouse. **3.** recover, reawake, come around, regain consciousness.
—**Ant.** kill; languish, die.

revoke, *v.* take back, withdraw, annul, cancel, reverse, rescind, repudiate, renounce, recant, repeal, retract, deny, invalidate, void, nullify, negate, quash, veto, abrogate, abolish.

revolt, *v.* **1.** rebel, mutiny, rise. **2.** disgust, repel, shock, nauseate, offend, horrify, repulse, sicken. —*n.* **3.** insurrection, rebellion, mutiny, revolution, uprising, overthrow, sedition, coup d'état, putsch, takeover.
—**Ant.** attract, delight.

revolution, *n.* **1.** overthrow, sea change, revolt, rebellion, mutiny, coup, uprising, insurgency, insurrection, upheaval. **2.** cycle, rotation, circuit, turn, round, orbit, spin, lap, circle, gyration.

revolve, *v.* **1.** rotate, spin, circulate, turn, roll, orbit, circle. **2.** consider, think about, ruminate on, ponder, reflect on, brood over, study, weigh, contemplate, meditate on, chew over.
—**Syn. Study.** See TURN.

reward, *n.* **1.** recompense, prize, desert, compensation, pay, award, favor, return, tribute, honor, remuneration, requital, merit. **2.** bounty, premium, bonus. —*v.* **3.** recompense, requite, compensate, pay, remunerate, redress.

ribald, *adj.* scurrilous, offensive, coarse, wanton, irreverent, loose, indecent, low, obscene, pornographic, blue, indelicate, naughty, shameless, lusty, gross, filthy, dirty, vulgar, bawdy, earthy, lubricious, lewd, licentious, racy, lascivious, smutty, rude.
—**Ant.** pure, inoffensive, refined, polished, elegant.

rich, *adj.* **1.** well-to-do, wealthy, moneyed, opulent, affluent, prosperous, well-off, flush, well-heeled, well-fixed, loaded. **2.** abounding, abundant, bounteous, bountiful, fertile, plenteous, plentiful, copious, ample, luxuriant, productive, fruitful, prolific. **3.** valuable, valued, precious, costly, estimable, sumptuous, elegant. **4.** deep, strong, vivid, intense, vibrant, lustrous, lively, bright, gay.

—**Ant.** poor, impoverished; scarce, barren, sterile; weak; dull.

riddle, *n.* conundrum, puzzle, enigma, poser, question, problem, mystery, brainteaser.

ridicule, *n.* **1.** derision, mockery, gibes, jeers, taunts, raillery, satire, sendup, burlesque, sarcasm, sneer, banter, wit, irony. —*v.* **2.** deride, tease, chaff, twit, mock, taunt, make fun of, sneer at, burlesque, satirize, rail at, lampoon, jeer *or* scoff at, rib, roast, send up.

—**Ant.** praise, honor; respect.

—**Syn. Study.** RIDICULE, DERIDE, MOCK, TAUNT mean to make fun of a person. To RIDICULE is to make fun of, either playfully or with the intention of humiliating: *to ridicule a pretentious person.* To DERIDE is to laugh at scornfully: *a student derided for acting silly.* To MOCK is to make fun of by imitating the appearance or actions of another: *She mocked the seriousness of his expression.* To TAUNT is to call attention to something annoying or humiliating, usu. maliciously and in the presence of others: *The bully taunted the smaller boy.*

ridiculous, *adj.* absurd, preposterous, laughable, nonsensical, inane, asinine, funny, ludicrous, droll, comical, farcical, hilarious, sidesplitting, risible, outlandish, bizarre, grotesque, zany, wild, far-out.

—**Ant.** sensible.

—**Syn. Study.** See ABSURD.

rife, *adj.* **1.** common, prevalent, widespread, prevailing. **2.** abundant, plentiful, numerous, plenteous, abounding, copious, ubiquitous, multitudinous.

—**Ant.** rare, unusual; scarce, scanty.

right, *adj.* **1.** just, good, equitable, fair, upright, honest, lawful, licit, legal, moral, proper, correct, righteous, virtuous, ethical, fair, true, honorable, principled, aboveboard, legitimate. **2.** correct, proper, suitable, fit, appropriate, becoming, *de rigueur,* befitting, seemly, *comme il faut.* **3.** correct, true, exact, precise, perfect, factual, sound, valid, accurate. —*n.* **4.** claim, title, due, ownership. **5.** virtue, justice, fairness, integrity, equity, equitableness, uprightness, rectitude, goodness, lawfulness.

—**Ant.** wrong.

righteous, *adj.* moral, upright, holy, God-fearing, virtuous, good, honest, fair, right, equitable, law-abiding, just, upstanding, ethical, honorable, reputable, trustworthy.

—**Ant.** immoral, bad, dishonest, unfair.

rigid, *adj.* **1.** stiff, unyielding, unbending, firm, hard, inelastic, inflexible. **2.** unmoving, immovable, static, stationary. **3.** inflexible, strict, severe, stern, rigorous, austere, unbending, harsh, stringent, puritanical, hard and fast, hard-nosed, hardline, adamant, straitlaced, obdurate, resolute, relentless, inexorable.

—**Ant.** flexible, soft; compliant, elastic, lenient.

—**Syn. Study.** See STRICT.

rigorous, *adj.* **1.** rigid, severe, harsh, stern, austere, strict, hard, inflexible, stiff, unyielding, stringent. **2.** exact, demanding, finical, punctilious, precise, literal, meticulous.

—**Ant.** flexible, soft; inaccurate.

—**Syn. Study.** See STRICT.

rim, *n.* **1.** edge, border, lip, margin, brim, boundary, verge, skirt. —*v.* **2.** edge, border, bound, margin, confine.

—**Ant.** center, inside.

—**Syn. Study.** RIM, BRIM refer to the boundary of a circular or curved area. A RIM is a line or surface bounding such an area; an edge or border: *the rim of a glass.* BRIM usu. means the inside of the rim, at the top of a hollow object (except of a hat), and is used particularly when the object contains something: *The cup was filled to the brim.*

ring, *n.* **1.** circlet, loop, hoop; annulus. **2.** arena, enclosure, rink, circle. **3.** circle, organization, band, pack, team, crew, confederation, cartel, bloc, clan, society, cabal, faction, group, alliance, federation, coalition, union, affiliation, clique, coterie, set, combination, confederacy, league; gang, mob, syndicate. —*v.* **4.** surround, encircle, circle. **5.** peal, resonate, vibrate, reverberate, resound, reecho, tinkle, jingle, jangle, chime, toll, knell, ding-dong, clang, gong.

riot, *n.* **1.** outbreak, disorder, brawl, uproar, tumult, disturbance, commotion, fray, melee, altercation, rumpus, turbulence, fracas, pandemonium, donnybrook, unrest, row, strife, imbroglio, anarchy, disruption, violence, rampage, storm, ruckus, confusion. **2.** revelry, festivity. —*v.* **3.** revolt, rebel, take to the streets, mount the barricades, protest, go on a rampage, run riot, storm, create a disorder, disturb the peace, create a disturbance, brawl, fight. **4.** carouse, revel.

rip, *v.* **1.** cut, tear, tear apart, slash, slit, rend. —*n.* **2.** rent, tear, laceration, cut, split, gash, slash, rift, rupture, cleft.

ripe, *adj.* **1.** mature, mellow, grown, aged. **2.** full, complete, consummate, perfect, finished. **3.** developed, ready, prepared, set, enthusiastic, eager, fit.

—**Ant.** immature; imperfect, unfinished; undeveloped, unprepared.

ripen, *v.* mature, age, grow, develop, mellow, grow up, maturate, evolve, blossom, flower, come into season.

rise, *v.* **1.** get up, arise, stand, stand up. **2.** revolt, rebel, mutiny, oppose, resist. **3.** spring up, grow. **4.** come into existence, appear, come forth. **5.** occur, happen. **6.** originate, issue, arise, come up, be derived, proceed. **7.** move upward, ascend, mount, arise. **8.** succeed, be promoted, advance. **9.** swell, puff up, enlarge, increase. —*n.* **10.** rising, ascent, mounting. **11.** advance, elevation, promotion. **12.** increase, augmentation, enlargement, swelling. **13.** source, origin, beginning, commencement, birth, fountainhead, wellspring.

—**Ant.** sink; support; die; fail; decrease, deflate; open.

risible, *adj.* funny, amusing, comic, comical, laugh-provoking, laughable, droll, humorous, hilarious, rich, ludicrous, absurd, ridiculous, farcical, priceless, hysterical, sidesplitting.

—**Ant.** sober, solemn.

risk, *n.* **1.** hazard, chance, danger, dangerous chance, venture, chance, gamble, peril, jeopardy, exposure. —*v.* **2.** hazard, take a chance, endanger, imperil, jeopardize. **3.** venture upon, dare.

rite, *n.* ceremony, procedure, practice, observance, form, usage, ritual, formality, custom, routine, solemnity, sacrament, solemnization.

ritual, *n.* **1.** ceremony, rite, formality, routine, practice, convention, custom, protocol. —*adj.* **2.** ceremonial, formal, sacramental, ceremonious.

—**Ant.** unceremonious, informal.

rival, *n.* **1.** competitor, contestant, challenger, adversary, contender, antagonist, opponent. —*adj.* **2.** competing, competitive, opposed, emulating, opposing. —*v.* **3.** compete *or* contend with, oppose, challenge, contest, combat, vie with, struggle against. **4.** match, equal, emulate, measure up to, compare with.

—**Ant.** ally, friend.

roam, *v.* walk, go, travel, ramble, wander, peregrinate, rove, stray, meander, amble, perambulate, drift, saunter, dawdle, dally, stroll, range, prowl, traipse, cruise, gallivant, jaunt, mosey, loiter.

roar, *v.* **1.** cry, bellow, bawl, shout, yell, vociferate. **2.** laugh, guffaw, howl, hoot. **3.** resound, boom, thunder, peal.

rob, *v.* **1.** rifle, sack, steal, deprive, plunder, pillage, pilfer, pinch, burgle, loot, ransack, hijack, burglarize, mug, hold up, roll, shoplift. **2.** defraud, cheat, deprive, rook, rip off, prey upon, swindle, fleece, bilk, victimize.

robber, *n.* thief, second-story man, kleptomaniac, shoplifter, pilferer, brigand, bandit, marauder, freebooter, pirate, pickpocket, burglar, cat burglar, sneak thief, mugger, holdup man, ripoff artist, hijacker, carjacker.

—**Syn. Study.** See THIEF.

robust, *adj.* sturdy, healthy, strong, hardy, vigorous, stalwart, hale, powerful, firm, sound, athletic, brawny, muscular, sinewy, fit, hearty, stout, tough, able-bodied, strapping, rugged, lusty, well-knit, husky, buff, pumped up.

—**Ant.** weak, feeble, unhealthy.

rogue, *n.* rascal, scamp, mischief-maker, wastrel, good-for-nothing, miscreant, outlaw, desperado, villain, scoundrel, trickster, swindler, cheat, mountebank, quack, sharper, charlatan, louse, rat, creep, stinker, bum, SOB.

roil, *v.* **1.** muddy, foul, dirty, pollute, befoul, contaminate. **2.** disturb, agitate, perturbate, stir, stir up, churn, whip, whip up. **3.** rile, anger, irritate, irk, vex, peeve, provoke, gripe.

—**Ant.** clarify, calm.

roll, *v.* **1.** turn, revolve, rotate, wheel, gyrate, spin, cycle, tumble, somersault, whirl, bowl. **2.** billow, rise and fall, wave, undulate. **3.** sway, rock, swing, list, tilt. —*n.* **4.** register, list, record, directory, slate, docket, index, schedule, annals, inventory, catalogue, roster. **5.** cylinder, roller, spindle.

—**Syn. Study.** See LIST.

romance, *n.* **1.** novel, tale, story, fiction; (*slang*) bodice ripper. **2.** fancy, fabrication, extravagance, exaggeration; falsehood, fable, fiction, lie. **3.** love affair, amour, liaison, relationship, dalliance, intrigue. **4.** sentiment, mystery, nostalgia, adventure, glamour, fascination, exoticism, intrigue, fantasy, imaginativeness, colorfulness, color.

romantic, *adj.* **1.** fanciful, unpractical, quixotic, extravagant, exaggerated, wild, imaginative, unrealistic, fantastic. **2.** improbable, imaginary, fantastic, chimerical, fictitious, fabulous, unreal. **3.** picturesque, exotic, glamorous, sentimental, emotional, nostalgic, sweet. **4.** amorous, aroused, ardent, affectionate, lustful, passionate, impassioned, overfriendly, loving, lovey-dovey, fresh, on the make.

—**Ant.** practical, realistic; probable.

romp, *v.* **1.** play, frolic, gambol, frisk, cavort, caper, rollick, revel, roister, lark about, kick up one's heels. —*n.* **2.** gambol, frolic, caper, revel, escapade. **3.** triumph, easy victory, runaway, pushover.

rosy, *adj.* **1.** cherry, cerise, rose-red, ruby, pink, reddish, roseate. **2.** red, rubicund, flushed, glowing, blushing, florid, apple-cheeked, blooming, ruddy, healthy. **3.** bright, promising, cheerful, optimistic, favorable, auspicious, sunny, hopeful, encouraging, sanguine.

—**Ant.** dark, dim, cheerless, pessimistic.

rot, *v.* **1.** decompose, decay, mold, molder, putrefy, spoil, corrupt. **2.** waste *or* wither away, languish, die, decline, atrophy, deteriorate, degenerate. —*n.* **3.** decay, putrefaction, decomposition, corruption, mold, blight, disintegration, deterioration.

—**Ant.** purify.

—**Syn. Study.** See DECAY.

rotate, *v.* turn, spin, revolve, gyrate, pirouette, go round, wheel, whirl, twirl, pivot, reel.

—**Syn. Study.** See TURN.

rotten, *adj.* **1.** decomposed, decayed, putrefied, putrescent, putrid, tainted, foul, miasmatic, noxious, ill-smelling, fetid, rank. **2.** corrupt, offensive, amoral, immoral, venal, degenerate, villainous, iniquitous, evil, wicked, vile, base, perverted, depraved, unscrupulous, unprincipled, warped. **3.** contemptible, disgusting, unwholesome, treacherous, dishonest, deceitful, corrupt, heinous, despicable, miserable, wretched, nasty, filthy, low, mean, lousy, stinking, lowdown, terrible, awful, horrible.

—**Ant.** pure; moral; wholesome, honest.

rough, *adj.* **1.** uneven, bumpy, irregular, rugged, jagged, coarse, craggy. **2.** violent, disorderly, wild, boisterous, turbulent, riotous; sharp, severe, harsh. **3.** turbulent, choppy, roiled, storm-tossed, disturbed, stormy, agitated, tempestuous, inclement. **4.** harsh, grating, jarring, noisy, cacophonous, inharmonious, discordant, flat, raucous. **5.** uncultured, indelicate, unrefined, impolite, uncivil, unpolished, rude, inconvenient, uncomfortable, crude, coarse. **6.** rudimentary, crude, raw, rough-hewn, formless, unshaped, plain, imperfect, unpolished, uncorrected, unfinished, unwrought, undressed, unprepared, unset, uncut. **7.** general, approximate, cursory, quick, hasty, sketchy, ballpark, vague, inexact, incomplete.

—**Ant.** even, regular; orderly; fair; harmonious; cultured, refined; finished, polished; precise, exact.

round, *adj.* **1.** circular, disklike; ring-shaped, hooplike, annular; curved, arched; cylindrical; spherical, globular, rotund, orbed. **2.** full, complete, entire, whole, unbroken. —*n.* **3.** circle, ring, curve; cylinder. **4.** course, cycle, revolution, period, series, succession.

—**Ant.** angular, square, rectangular, polygonal.

rouse, *v.* **1.** stir, excite, animate, kindle, fire, inflame, stimulate, awaken, provoke, electrify, galvanize, prompt, goad, prod, move, spur. **2.** anger, provoke, incite, ire, fire up.

—**Ant.** calm; pacify.

—**Syn. Study.** See INCITE.

row, *n.* **1.** argument, disagreement, quarrel, dispute, altercation, tiff, squabble, fight, set-to, donnybrook, scrap, knock-down-drag-out. —*v.* **2.** argue, quarrel, squabble, fight, dispute, disagree, wrangle, cross swords, have words, bicker, have a tiff, scrap, fall out.

rowdy, *adj.* **1.** boisterous, noisy, raucous, rackety, rambunctious, disorderly, unruly, brawling, roistering, obstreperous, rip-roaring, riotous, ruffian, rough and tumble. —*n.* **2.** mischief-maker, ruffian, hooligan, brawler, streetfighter, tough, street tough, hood, hoodlum, hooligan, thug, bullyboy, bully, yahoo, lout, skinhead.

royal, *adj.* regal, majestic, kingly, queenly, sovereign, stately, august,

impressive, imposing, imperial, princely.
—**Ant.** servile.

ruckus, *n.* commotion, disturbance, fuss, row, to-do, hubbub, rumpus, uproar, racket, turmoil, brouhaha.

rude, *adj.* **1.** discourteous, unmannerly, ill-mannered, impolite, ungallant, ungracious, ill-bred, oafish, loutish, unrefined, uncivil, coarse; curt, brusque, saucy, pert, impertinent, impudent, insolent, offensive, disrespectful, flippant, gruff, tactless, undiplomatic, fresh. **2.** unlearned, untutored, uneducated, untaught, ignorant, uncultured, unrefined, untrained, uncivilized, philistine, oafish, loutish, coarse, uncouth, vulgar, boorish. **3.** rough, harsh, ungentle, coarse, rugged, crude. **4.** unwrought, raw, crude, rough, shapeless, amorphous. **5.** inartistic, inelegant, primitive, rustic, artless, clumsy, bumbling, makeshift, homespun, basic, bare, simple, unadorned, unpolished, undecorated.
—**Ant.** courteous, mannerly; learned; gentle; artistic, elegant.
—**Syn. Study.** See RAW.

rudimentary, *adj.* **1.** basic, essential, introductory, abecedarian, formative, first, primal, seminal, elementary, fundamental, primary, initial. **2.** undeveloped, embryonic, elementary, imperfect, crude, coarse, primitive, immature, vestigial, primordial.
—**Ant.** advanced; mature, perfect.

ruffle, *v.* **1.** disarrange, rearrange, disorder, rumple, wrinkle, dishevel, mix up, tousle, tangle, muss up, damage, derange. **2.** disturb, discompose, irritate, vex, annoy, upset, agitate, trouble, torment, plague, harry, harass, worry, molest, disconcert, confuse, perturb, disorient, unnerve, fluster, affect, bother, intimidate, rattle, throw, shake up. —*n.* **3.** disturbance, perturbation, annoyance, vexation, confusion, commotion, flurry, tumult, bustle, agitation, ripple, stir, wrinkle.
—**Ant.** arrange, order; compose; composure, peace.

rugged, *adj.* **1.** broken, uneven, rocky, hilly, craggy, irregular. **2.** rough, harsh, stern, severe, hard, austere. **3.** severe, hard, trying, difficult, arduous, Spartan, rigorous, onerous, demanding, burdensome. **4.** harsh, grating, inharmonious, cacophonous, scabrous. **5.** rude, uncultivated, unrefined, unpolished, crude. **6.** hardy, durable, strong, sturdy, robust, tough, stalwart; independent, self-reliant, individualistic, bold, self-sufficient.
—**Ant.** even, smooth, regular; easy, flexible; fair; harmonious; cultivated, refined; weak wimpy.

ruin, *n.* **1.** decay, dilapidation, ruination, perdition, destruction, dissolution, degradation, corruption, failure, collapse, debacle, havoc, damage, disintegration, devastation, spoliation. **2.** downfall, destruction, fall, overthrow, defeat, undoing, subversion, wreck. —*v.* **3.** spoil, demolish, destroy, damage, devastate, annihilate, dissolve, wipe out, overthrow, raze, shatter, wreck, crush, flatten, pulverize, smash, wreak havoc on, reduce to ruin; corrupt, dishonor, defile, debase.
—**Ant.** construction; creation; create, build.

rule, *n.* **1.** principle, regulation, standard, law, canon, ruling, ordnance, decree, statute, direction, guideline, guide, precept, order. **2.** control, government, dominion, command, domination, mastery, sway, authority, direction. —*v.* **3.** administer, command, govern, manage, control, handle, lead, direct, guide, conduct. **4.** decree, decide, deem, judge, settle, establish, order, demand.

rumor, *n.* story, talk, gossip, hearsay, information, scoop, tidings, chat, chitchat, leak, disclosure, revelation, inside story, bruit, news, report, tittle-tattle, scandal, item, whisper, *on dit,* calumny, obloquy, buzz, dish, talk of the town, scuttlebutt, grapevine, jungle telegraph, lowdown, info, poop, dirt.

run, *v.* **1.** race, hasten, hurry, sprint, scurry, dart, bolt, dash, tear, scoot, scuttle, zip, gallop, jog, trot, lope, rush, scramble, hustle, step on it, step lively, hotfoot it, get the lead out, get cracking, scud, speed, scamper. **2.** flow, diffuse, flood, gush, spill, dribble, spurt, trickle, spout, cascade, seep, pour, stream; go, move, proceed. **3.** flee, escape, take flight, abscond, take to one's heels, bolt, decamp, clear out, retreat, retire, make a getaway, scram, skedaddle, skip out, fly the coop, head for the hills, vamoose. **4.** leak, overflow, flood, spread. **5.** operate, function, perform, work, go, continue. **6.** extend, stretch, reach, spread. **7.** contend, compete, challenge. **8.** pursue, hunt, chase. **9.** convey, transport, ferry, drive, carry. **10.** operate, carry on, conduct, manage, direct, control, oversee, supervise, head, lead, administer, coordinate. —*n.* **11.** period, spell, interval. **12.** series, set, course, passage, motion, extent, progress.

rupture, *n.* **1.** breaking, bursting; breach, fracture, break, split, burst, disruption, breakup, schism, disunity, severance, division, separation. —*v.* **2.** break, fracture, split, burst, disrupt, separate, cleave, divide, breach, part, sunder.
—**Ant.** seam, union; unite, organize.

rural, *adj.* **1.** country, pastoral, sylvan, bucolic, rustic, Arcadian, exurban, agrarian, agricultural. **2.** peasant, plain, simple, homespun, down-home, countrified, hillbilly, backwoods, awkward, cloddish, gawky, uncultured, unrefined, guileless, artless, ingenuous, oafish, bumptious, hayseed, hick, backwater, naive, unsophisticated, rugged, rough; crude, boorish, loutish.
—**Ant.** urban.
—**Syn. Study.** RURAL and RUSTIC are terms that refer to the country. RURAL is the neutral term: *rural education.* It is also used subjectively, usu. in a favorable sense: *the charm of rural life.* RUSTIC, however, may have either favorable or unfavorable connotations. In a derogatory sense, it means provincial, boorish, or crude; in a favorable sense, it may suggest a homelike simplicity and lack of sophistication: *rustic manners.*

rush, *v.* **1.** hurry, hasten, run, race, make haste, speed, dash, sprint, hustle, bustle, scurry, scamper, scramble, scoot, scuttle, move it, hotfoot it, skedaddle, make it snappy, step on it, hightail it, shake a leg, dart, bolt, tear, zip, step lively, get the lead out, get cracking, fly, get a wiggle on. —*n.* **2.** hurry, haste, speed, quickness, immediacy, hustle, bustle, dash, busyness, turmoil, flurry, commotion, ferment, fluster, ado, to-do, excitement, harum-scarum, activity, urgency, exigency. —*adj.* **3.** urgent, top-priority, emergency, exigent, hurry-up.
—**Ant.** delay, retard; sloth, lethargy, sluggishness; low-priority.

ruthless, *adj.* pitiless, merciless, unpitying, unmerciful, cruel, hard, harsh, severe, hardhearted, uncompassionate, unrelenting, adamant, relentless, inexorable, fell, truculent, inhuman, ferocious, savage, barbarous, unsympathetic, fierce, remorseless, vicious, callous, unfeeling, tough, heartless, brutal, brutish, mean.
—**Ant.** merciful, compassionate, humane.

S

sabotage, *n.* **1.** subversion, subversiveness, damage, destruction, impairment, injury, undermining, weakening; treachery, betrayal, traitorousness. —*v.* **2.** undermine, subvert, damage, hurt, disable, weaken, incapacitate, wreck, disrupt, spoil, ruin, cripple, disable, monkey with.

saccharine, *adj.* **1.** oversweet, sickly sweet, cloying, treacly, sugary. **2.** mawkish, oversentimental, maudlin, bathetic, sticky, treacly, cloying, mushy, soppy, sappy, icky. **3.** ingratiating, fawning, obsequious, insinuating, silken, silky, suave, sycophantic.
—**Ant.** astringent, bracing.

sack, *n.* **1.** bag, pouch. **2.** pillaging, looting, plundering, pillage, destruction, devastation, desolation, spoliation, ruin, ruination, waste, ravage, rapine. —*v.* **3.** pillage, loot, rob, spoil, despoil, ruin, lay waste, plunder, devastate, demolish, destroy, ravage, rape.

sacred, *adj.* **1.** consecrated, holy, blessed, sanctified, awe-inspiring, sainted, venerable, hallowed, divine, worshipful. **2.** dedicated, consecrated, revered. **3.** secure, protected, sacrosanct, immune, inviolate, inviolable, untouchable. **4.** religious, spiritual, ceremonial, churchly, priestly, ecclesiastical, ritual, solemn, sacramental, liturgical, hieratic.
—**Ant.** blasphemous.
—**Syn. Study.** See HOLY.

sacrifice, *v.* **1.** give up, forgo, forfeit, forsake, relinquish, surrender, lose, yield, renounce, forswear; forbear, desist, cease, stop, refrain from, deny oneself, waive, swear off, eschew. —*n.* **2.** forfeiture, loss, relinquishment, renunciation, surrender, forswearing, deprivation, privation, denial, self-denial, abdication, abrogation, yielding, forbearance, waiver, abjuration, abstention, eschewal.
—**Ant.** indulge in; continue, persist; reward, indulgence.

sacrilege, *n.* blasphemy, impiety, irreverence, profanity, desecration, profanation, heresy, sin, offense, abomination, violation, crime, infamy, disgrace, scandal, debasement, defilement, contamination, perversion, outrage, secularization.

sad, *adj.* **1.** sorrowful, mournful, unhappy, despondent, disconsolate, depressed, dejected, melancholy, discouraged, gloomy, morose, low, glum, lugubrious, heartsick, crestfallen, disheartened, blue, heartbroken, woebegone, wretched, miserable, down in the dumps, singing the blues, tearful, downcast, downhearted. **2.** somber, dark, dull, dismal, dreary, bleak, funereal, dispiriting, depressing. **3.** grievous, deplorable, disastrous, dire, calamitous, unfortunate, lamentable, sorry, pathetic, lousy, rotten, awful, terrible.
—**Ant.** happy.

safe, *adj.* **1.** secure, protected, sheltered, shielded, guarded. **2.** dependable, sound, risk-free, solid, bona fide, tried and true, conservative, trustworthy, sure, reliable. **3.** cautious, wary, careful.
—**Ant.** unsafe.

safeguard, *n.* **1.** defense, guard, protection, precaution, bulwark, shield, aegis, armor, armament, cushion, security, insurance. —*v.* **2.** defend, guard, protect, shield, secure, bulwark, preserve, shelter, conserve, save, keep, care for, look after.

saga, *n.* edda, epic, tale, tradition, legend, history, story, adventure, narrative, chronicle, romance.

sagacious, *adj.* wise, sage, shrewd, discerning, clever, intelligent, judicious, rational, acute, sharp, keen, perspicacious, sharp-witted.
—**Ant.** unwise, irrational.

sage, *n.* **1.** wise man, philosopher, savant, expert, elder, guru, pundit, oracle, authority. —*adj.* **2.** prudent, sagacious, sensible, profound, discerning, reasonable, logical, common-sense, thoughtful, circumspect, wary, careful, insightful, sapient, astute, knowledgeable, learned, enlightened, erudite, knowing.
—**Ant.** dolt; imprudent.

sailor, *n.* mariner, salt, tar, seaman, seafarer, seafaring man *or* woman, seadog, skipper, swabbie, gob, yachtsman, yachtswoman, deckhand.
—**Ant.** landlubber.
—**Syn. Study.** SAILOR, SEAMAN, MARINER, SALT are terms for a person who leads a seafaring life. A SAILOR or SEAMAN is one whose occupation is on board a ship at sea, esp. a member of a ship's crew below the rank of petty officer: *a sailor before the mast; an able-bodied seaman.* MARINER is a term found in certain technical expressions: *mariner's compass* (ordinary compass as used on ships); the word now seems elevated or quaint: *The Rime of the Ancient Mariner.* SALT is an informal term for an experienced sailor: *an old salt.*

sake, *n.* **1.** cause, account, interest, score, regard, consideration, benefit, welfare, advantage, behalf, respect, reason. **2.** purpose, end, reason, objective.

salacious, *adj.* lusty, lecherous, rakish, lewd, carnal, wanton, lascivious, libidinous, concupiscent; obscene, pornographic, prurient.
—**Ant.** modest, prudish.

salient, *adj.* prominent, conspicuous, important, remarkable, outstanding, pronounced, noticeable, significant, important, marked, striking, impressive, distinctive, unique, principal, chief, primary, noteworthy, notable, eminent.
—**Ant.** inconspicuous; unimportant.

sallow, *adj.* pallid, washed out, wan, waxen, sickly, bloodless, anemic, pasty, pasty-faced, whey-faced, greenish, green around the gills, yellowish, jaundiced.

salvage, *v.* rescue, redeem, deliver, save, recover, regain, retrieve, recoup, ransom, recycle, reclaim.
—**Ant.** discard.

same, *adj.* **1.** identical; similar, like, corresponding, interchangeable, equal. **2.** agreeing; unchanging, constant, uniform, unvarying, verbatim, monotonous.
—**Ant.** different; disagreeing.

sample, *n.* specimen, example, illustration, pattern, model, representation, cross section, exemplar; taste, nibble, bite.

sanctify, *v.* bless, consecrate, dedicate, hallow, purify, beatify, enshrine, glorify, exalt, canonize.
—**Ant.** desecrate.

sanctimonious, *adj.* hypocritical,

unctuous, pious, canting, mealy-mouthed, smarmy, two-faced, pretentious, dissembling, feigning, insincere, self-satisfied, complacent, pietistic, pharisaical, holier than thou, smug, Tartuffian, Pecksniffian, simon-pure, self-righteous, goody-goody, goody-two-shoes.
—**Ant.** sincere.

sanction, *n.* **1.** authority, permission, countenance, approval, confirmation, legalization, legitimation, validation, license, certification, imprimatur, seal of approval, support, ratification, solemnification, authorization. —*v.* **2.** authorize, countenance, approve, confirm, ratify, support, allow, bind.
—**Ant.** disapproval; disallow, disapprove.

sanctuary, *n.* church, temple, shrine, altar, sanctum, chapel, synagogue, mosque, house of worship *or* God; asylum, refuge, retreat, shelter, safety, protection.

sane, *adj.* rational, reasoning, reasonable, lucid, clearheaded, clear-thinking, sound, normal, all there, *compos mentis*, wise, judicious, sapient, sagacious, sage, prudent, sensible.
—**Ant.** insane, foolish.

sanitary, *adj.* hygienic, unpolluted, clean, aseptic, disinfected, sterile, antiseptic, germ-free; healthy, salutary, wholesome, salubrious, healthful.
—**Ant.** polluted; unhealthy, unwholesome.

sarcasm, *n.* scorn, contumely, acrimony, acerbity, harshness, asperity, venom, poison, virulence, spite, spitefulness, malice, malevolence, satire, cynicism, disdain, irony, derision, bitterness, ridicule; taunt, gibe, jeer.

sarcastic, *adj.* cynical, biting, cutting, mordant, bitter, derisive, ironical, sardonic, satirical, scornful, contumelious, nasty, trenchant, incisive, acrimonious, acerbic, acid, acidic, acidulous, acrid, harsh, aspersive, venomous, virulent, poisonous, spiteful, disdainful, mocking, contemptuous, critical, censorious, captious, caviling, scathing, caustic, sneering, malignant, malicious, malefic, malevolent.

satanic, *adj.* evil, wicked, diabolical, devilish, infernal, hellish, malicious, fiendish, immoral, amoral, dark, black, demonic, ghoulish, sinister, iniquitous, depraved, perverted, perverse, godless, ungodly, impious, unholy.
—**Ant.** godly, angelic, benevolent.

satiate, *v.* cloy, glut, stuff, gorge, sate, surfeit; gall, disgust, bore, tire, weary.

satire, *n.* irony, sarcasm, ridicule, lampoon, pasquinade, burlesque, exposure, denunciation, mockery, spoof, sendup, takeoff.

satirical, *adj.* mocking, spoofing, irreverent, derisive, disparaging, abusive, scornful, flippant, ridiculing, chaffing, trenchant, cynical, sarcastic, sardonic, ironical, taunting, biting, keen, sharp, cutting, severe, mordant, mordacious, bitter, acid.

satisfaction, *n.* **1.** gratification, enjoyment, pleasure, contentment, ease, comfort. **2.** reparation, restitution, amends, expiation, atonement, damages, compensation, indemnification, remuneration, recompense, requital. **3.** payment, discharge, repayment.
—**Ant.** dissatisfaction, displeasure, discomfort.

satisfy, *v.* **1.** gratify, meet, appease, pacify, content, please. **2.** fulfill, fill, satiate, sate, suffice, surfeit. **3.** assure, convince, persuade, reassure, content.
—**Ant.** dissatisfy, displease.

saturate, *v.* soak, impregnate, imbue, wet, drench, waterlog, steep.
—**Ant.** dry.

saucy, *adj.* impudent, disrespectful, audacious, brassy, bold, pert, cheeky, flippant, irrepressible, forward, impertinent, cocky, sassy, fresh, flip, insolent, brazen.

savage, *adj.* **1.** wild, rugged, uncultivated, sylvan, rough. **2.** barbarous, uncivilized, rude, unpolished, wild. **3.** fierce, ferocious, wild, untamed, feral, ravenous. **4.** enraged, furious, angry, irate, infuriated. **5.** cruel, brutal, beastly; inhuman, fell, merciless, unmerciful, pitiless, ruthless, bloodthirsty, truculent, sanguinary.
—**Ant.** cultivated, cultured; tame; calm; merciful.

savant, *n.* scholar, sage, intellectual, polymath, expert, authority, pundit, egghead, wonk, brain, rocket scientist, maven, Einstein, wizard, whiz, genius, guru, connoisseur.

save, *v.* **1.** rescue, salvage, preserve, deliver, retrieve, free, redeem, liberate. **2.** safeguard, keep, protect, secure, shelter, shield, guard, preserve. **3.** set apart, reserve, lay by, economize, hoard, store up, husband, put away *or* aside, retain, preserve, conserve, scrimp, scrape.

savior, *n.* rescuer, deliverer, saver, lifesaver, safekeeper, preserver, liberator, redeemer, emancipator, salvation, champion, friend in need, Good Samaritan, knight in shining armor, paladin.

savor, *n.* **1.** taste, flavor, relish; odor, scent, fragrance. —*v.* **2.** taste, sample, perceive, detect, sense; enjoy, relish, indulge in, appreciate, delight in, value, cherish.

say, *v.* **1.** utter, pronounce, speak, remark, affirm, allege. **2.** express, state, word, declare, tell, argue. **3.** recite, repeat, iterate, reiterate, rehearse. **4.** report, allege, maintain, hold, assert, mention, rumor, suggest, hint, whisper.

scamp, *n.* rascal, imp, mischief-maker, cutup, rogue, little devil, scalawag, urchin, brat, slyboots, sly dog, smooth operator.
—**Ant.** goody-two-shoes.

scandal, *n.* **1.** disgrace, damage, discredit, dishonor, offense, embarrassment, sin, outrage, infamy, degradation, shame, disrepute, opprobrium, odium, ignominy. **2.** defamation, rumor, hearsay, whisper, talk, bruit, *on dit*, scuttlebutt, gossip, slander, character assassination, aspersion, detraction, calumny, obloquy, libel, innuendo, insinuation, abuse, dirt, slur, smear, stigma, smirch, spot, taint, blemish, black mark, dish, talk of the town.
—**Ant.** honor, repute; praise, kudos.

scanty, *adj.* meager, sparse, insufficient, inadequate, deficient, scarce, minimal, measly, skimpy, thin, spare, small, paltry, poor, stinted, lean.
—**Ant.** abundant, adequate.
—**Syn. Study.** SCANTY, MEAGER, SPARSE refer to insufficiency or deficiency in quantity, number, etc. SCANTY denotes smallness or insufficiency of quantity, number, supply, etc.: *a scanty supply of food.* MEAGER indicates that something is poor, stinted, or inadequate: *meager fare; a meager income.* SPARSE applies particularly to that which grows thinly or is thinly distributed: *sparse vegetation; a sparse population.*

scapegoat, *n.* patsy, goat, fall guy, whipping boy, sacrifice, offering, victim, target, stooge, front, dupe, gull, cat's-paw, straw man, sucker.

scarce, *adj.* rare, insufficient, deficient, scanty, scant, inadequate, wanting, lacking, meager, rare, unusual, in short supply, hard to come by, at a premium, uncommon, infrequent.
—**Ant.** abundant, sufficient.

scare, *v.* **1.** terrify, alarm, startle, frighten, shock, intimidate, dismay, daunt, appall, terrorize, threaten, menace, cow, intimidate, horrify, spook, make one's hair stand on end, make one's flesh crawl *or* creep, give one goosebumps. —*n.* **2.** fright, terror, alarm, panic, shock, surprise, start.

scatter, *v.* **1.** sprinkle, broadcast, strew, spread, diffuse, shower, litter, distribute, sow, disseminate. **2.** dispel, disperse, dissipate, separate, drive away, break up, disband.
—**Ant.** gather.
—**Syn. Study.** SCATTER, DISPEL, DISPERSE, DISSIPATE imply separating and driving something away so that its original form disappears. To SCATTER is to separate something tangible into parts at random and drive these in different directions: *The wind scattered leaves all over the lawn.* To DISPEL is to drive away or scatter usu. intangible things so that they vanish: *Your explanation has dispelled my doubts.* To DISPERSE is usu. to cause a compact or organized tangible body to separate or scatter in different directions, to be reassembled if desired: *Tear gas dispersed the mob.* To DISSIPATE is usu. to scatter by dissolving or reducing to small atoms or parts that cannot be reunited: *He dissipated his money and his energy in useless activities.*

scene, *n.* **1.** location, site, place, area, locale, spot, locality, sphere, milieu, whereabouts, backdrop, background. **2.** view, scenery, sight, panorama, vista, picture, prospect, landscape. **3.** incident, episode, situation; commotion, upset, row, disturbance, brouhaha, furor, tantrum. **4.** exhibition, demonstration, spectacle, show, display.
—**Syn.** See VIEW.

scent, *n.* **1.** odor, aroma, fragrance, bouquet, whiff, trace, smell, savor, redolence, perfume. **2.** track, trail, spoor. —*v.* **3.** detect, perceive, smell, determine, discern, sense, sniff out, get wind of, recognize.
—**Syn. Study.** See ODOR.

schedule, *n.* **1.** roll, catalogue, table, list, inventory, register; timetable. —*v.* **2.** enter, register, list, enroll, tabulate, classify, program, organize, plan, outline, arrange, book, assign, earmark.

scheme, *n.* **1.** plan, design, program, project, system, plot, course of action, outline, method, technique, approach, game plan, scenario. **2.** plot, intrigue, stratagem, cabal, conspiracy, contrivance, machination, ploy, subterfuge, ruse, maneuver, tactic, trick, dodge, racket. **3.** system, pattern, diagram, schema, arrangement. —*v.* **4.** plan, plot, contrive, project, devise, design, intrigue, hatch, conspire, machinate, connive, concoct, maneuver, formulate, organize.

scholar, *n.* **1.** academic, professor, researcher, teacher, pedagogue, authority, expert, pundit, man *or* woman of letters, bookman, bluestocking, intellectual, highbrow, bookworm, brain, egghead, longhair, wonk, connoisseur, savant, wise man, sage. **2.** student, pupil, disciple, learner, undergraduate, schoolchild.
—**Ant.** ignoramus, dropout.

scholarship, *n.* learning, knowledge, erudition, information, science, wisdom, lore, expertise, know-how; study, research, investigation, academic inquiry.
—**Ant.** ignorance.
—**Syn. Study.** See LEARNING.

schooling, *n.* education, training, teaching, guidance, instruction, tuition, tutelage, learning, preparation, indoctrination, edification, enlightenment.

scientific, *adj.* orderly, methodical, systematic, meticulous, thorough, precise, detailed, painstaking, well-organized, rational.

scoff, *n., v.* mock, scorn, jeer, gibe, sneer, disdain, despise, flout, taunt, ridicule, deride, belittle, disparage, dismiss, make light *or* fun of, spoof, lampoon, tease, rib, kid, rag.
—**Ant.** envy, praise, exalt.
—**Syn. Study.** SCOFF, JEER, SNEER imply behaving with scornful disapproval toward someone or about something. To SCOFF is to express insolent doubt or derision, openly and emphatically: *to scoff at a new invention.* To JEER suggests expressing disapproval and scorn more loudly, coarsely, and unintelligently than in scoffing: *The crowd jeered at the pitcher.* To SNEER is to show by facial expression or tone of voice ill-natured contempt or disparagement: *He sneered unpleasantly in referring to his opponent's misfortunes.*

scold, *v.* **1.** chide, reprove, reproach, berate, censure, rail at, reprimand, blame, rebuke, admonish, criticize, tonguelash, rate, revile, vituperate, upbraid, find fault with, lecture, castigate, bawl out, dress down, give (someone) a piece of one's mind, chew out, give (someone) a tongue-lashing *or* talking-to, rake (someone) over the coals, haul (someone) on the carpet. —*n.* **2.** nag, shrew, fishwife, hellcat, fury, tigress, old battle-ax, Xanthippe, virago, termagant, maenad, bacchante.
—**Ant.** praise, honor.

scope, *n.* range, extent, space, reach, area, compass, expanse, breadth, sphere, orbit, span, sweep, gamut, radius, ken, purview, horizon; leeway, space, spread, elbowroom, freedom, capacity, stretch, opportunity, margin, room, latitude, liberty; tract, area, length.
—**Syn. Study.** See RANGE.

scorch, *v.* sear, blacken, roast, broil, sizzle, burn, singe, char, blister, parch, shrivel, wither.

score, *n.* **1.** record, account, reckoning, register, tally, number, count, amount, sum, total. **2.** notch, scratch, stroke, line, nick, groove, cut, mark. **3.** account, reason, rationale, basis, cause, provocation, ground, consideration, motive, purpose. —*v.* **4.** record, reckon, tabulate, count. **5.** notch, mark, scratch, incise, groove, nick, cut. **6.** gain, win, succeed, triumph, have an impact, make an impression *or* hit.

scorn, *n.* **1.** contempt, contemptuousness, deprecation, abuse, dismissal, rejection, disdain, contumely, superciliousness, insolence. **2.** mockery, derision, derisiveness, ridicule, sneering, scoffing, taunting. —*v.* **3.** disdain, reject, rebuff, disown, disavow, disregard, ignore, shun, snub, flout, hold in contempt, spurn, put down, look down one's nose at, disparage, high-hat, despise, detest.
—**Ant.** affection, pleasure.
—**Syn. Study.** See CONTEMPT.

scoundrel, *n.* villain, knave, rogue, evildoer, mischief-maker, devil, demon, brute, fiend, beast, monster, blackguard, bounder, wretch, scamp, cad, rascal, fox, cur, hound, dog, miscreant, trickster, sharper, cheat, fake, charlatan, mountebank, wretch, good-for-nothing, heel, louse, con artist, smooth operator,

sly dog, stinker.
—Ant. hero.

scourge, *n.* **1.** curse, misfortune, evil, bane, adversity, torment, torture, misery, woe, affliction, calamity, plague, pest, nuisance. —*v.* **2.** flog, beat, horsewhip, whale, belt, flagellate, lash, whip. **3.** punish, chastise, chasten, correct, discipline, castigate, afflict, torment.

scramble, *v.* **1.** hasten, rush, scurry, hurry, run, race, scoot, dash, skedaddle, hightail it, hotfoot it, scamper, scuttle, bustle, hustle. **2.** clamber, creep, scrabble, claw, climb, struggle, crawl, go on all fours. **3.** vie, compete, contend, jostle, struggle, strive. **4.** mix, intermix, blend, mix up, mingle, jumble. **5.** confuse, mix up, muddle, garble. —*n.* **6.** bustle, rush, hurry, flurry, flutter, commotion. **7.** clutter, jumble, mix, mishmash. **8.** struggle, tussle, competition, contest, disorder, riot, pandemonium, free-for-all, hassle.

scrap, *n.* **1.** fragment, piece, portion, particle, mite, sliver, snippet, whit, iota, speck, molecule, atom, dab, trace, hint, scintilla, suggestion; morsel, crumb, bit, bite. —*adj.* **2.** fragmentary, piecemeal; waste. —*v.* **3.** break up, demolish, dismantle, destroy, pull to pieces, wreck, smash, ruin. **4.** throw away, discard, reject, abandon, forsake, forget, get rid of, discard, dispose of, consign to the scrapheap, trash, junk, dispense with, shed, slough.
—Ant. whole.

scream, *v.* **1.** shriek, screech, cry, squeal, yowl, wail, caterwaul, howl. —*n.* **2.** outcry, cry, shriek, screech, squeal, yowl, wail, caterwaul, howl, yell, bellow, roar, shout.

screen, *n.* **1.** partition, divider, wall; shelter, cover, protection, guard, shield, defense. —*v.* **2.** shelter, protect, veil, defend, shield, conceal, guard, camouflage, hide, cover, cloak, mask, shroud.

scruple, *n.* **1.** hesitation, hesitancy, reluctance, misgiving, second thoughts, doubt, uncertainty, apprehension, uneasiness, discomfort, squeamishness, pang of conscience, restraint, compunction, demurral, suspicion, mistrust, qualm. —*v.* **2.** hesitate, waver, pause, falter, vacillate, demur, be loath to, balk at, shrink from, have doubts *or* compunctions about, have misgivings *or* qualms, think twice, be reluctant.

scrupulous, *adj.* **1.** conscientious, reluctant, hesitant, cautious, wary, careful, circumspect. **2.** punctilious, meticulous, overnice, strict, fastidious, particular, fussy, finicky, painstaking, religious, minute, careful, exacting, exact, accurate, precise, demanding, rigorous. **3.** honorable, righteous, upstanding, principled, high-minded, ethical, moral, just, honest.
—Ant. remiss, careless, sloppy; unprincipled, dishonest, shifty.
—Syn. Study. SCRUPULOUS, PUNCTILIOUS imply being very careful to do the right or proper thing. SCRUPULOUS implies conscientious care in attending to details: *The scientist described his observations with scrupulous accuracy.* PUNCTILIOUS suggests strictness and rigidity, esp. in observance of social conventions: *punctilious adherence to the rules of etiquette.*

scrutinize, *v.* examine, investigate, analyze, probe, inspect, check, survey, observe, assess, evaluate, critique, criticize, review, eyeball, peruse, scan, audit, ponder, consider, view, contemplate, weigh, research, anatomize, dissect, study, sift.
—Ant. neglect, overlook.

scrutiny, *n.* examination, investigation, dissection, study, analysis, probe, exploration, sifting, check, observation, evaluation, critique, once-over, perusal, research, inquiry, inspection, inquisition, search.
—Syn. Study. See EXAMINATION.

scurrilous, *adj.* **1.** foulmouthed, profane, scabrous, nasty, derogatory, defamatory, disparaging, calumnious, malign, aspersive, vile, low, derisive, abusive, opprobrious, vituperative, reproachful, insolent, insulting, offensive, contumelious. **2.** coarse, ribald, licentious, gross, indecent, dirty, smutty, off-color, prurient, salacious, lewd, lascivious, pornographic, foul, filthy, vulgar, obscene.
—Ant. decent, polite; proper.

seamless, *adj.* smooth, continuous, unvarying, integrated, indivisible, unbroken, uninterrupted, connected, uniform, homogeneous.
—Ant. disjointed, fragmented.

seamy, *adj.* sordid, nasty, dark, disreputable, shameful, unwholesome, unsavory, distasteful, squalid, depraved, degenerate, debased, low, degraded, foul, vile, odious, abhorrent, ugly, repulsive, repellent, contemptible, despicable, shabby, base, miserable, rotten, ignoble, mean.

search, *v.* **1.** look for, seek, explore, investigate, examine, scrutinize, inspect, check, comb through, scour, scout out, hunt *or* rummage through, probe; pierce, penetrate. —*n.* **2.** exploration, examination, investigation, inspection, scrutiny, research, analysis, probe, study, perusal, searching, inquiry, inquisition; pursuit, quest, hunt.

seasonable, *adj.* suitable, timely, apt, fitting, providential, propitious, well-timed, proper, welcome, fortunate, auspicious, lucky, favorable, advantageous, happy, felicitous, gratifying, opportune, fit, convenient, appropriate.
—Ant. unseasonable, unsuitable, untimely, inopportune.

seasoned, *adj.* experienced, knowledgeable, proficient, accomplished, adept, practiced, well-versed, skilled, prepared, established, veteran, long-standing, proven, professional, habituated, acclimated, accustomed, familiar, tempered, hardened, strengthened, toughened, grizzled, aged, well-developed, mature.
—Ant. inexperienced, immature, green, new, unproven, unaccustomed.

seasoning, *n.* **1.** flavoring, flavor, tang, piquancy, zest, relish, sauce, essence, extract, condiment, spice, herb. **2.** experience, practice, exercise, training, discipline, maturation, development, mellowing, tempering, aging, hardening, strengthening, toughening, acclimatization, habituation, familiarization.

seat, *n.* **1.** place, chair, bench, banquette, sofa, couch, settee, easy chair, throne, stool. **2.** bottom, base, fundament. **3.** site, situation, location, locality, locale; residence, home, domicile, abode, estate, realm, sphere.

secede, *v.* abdicate, withdraw, retire, abandon, forsake, apostasize, break away from, quit, drop out, separate, resign, turn one's back on, wash one's hands of, defect, split off.
—Ant. join.

secluded, *adj.* withdrawn, isolated, separate, lonely, alone, solitary, detached, desolate, deserted, retired, sequestered, cloistered, monastic, hermitic, eremitic, reclusive, private.
—Ant. public, open, sociable.

secrecy, *n.* mystery, privacy, stealth,

surreptitiousness, concealment, furtiveness, covertness, sneakiness, confidentiality, secretiveness, clandestineness, inscrutability, slyness.

secret, *adj.* **1.** clandestine, hidden, shrouded, undisclosed, stealthy, surreptitious, furtive, underhand, concealed, secreted, screened, buried, masked, disguised, covert, private, confidential, quiet, undercover, hush-hush, off the record, backstair, dissembling, cloak-and-dagger, unrevealed, mysterious, unknown. **2.** reticent, close-mouthed, secretive. **3.** retired, withdrawn, reclusive, monastic, solitary, secluded, private. **4.** occult, obscure, cryptic, arcane, incomprehensible, esoteric, cabalistic, inscrutable, mysterious, latent, abstruse, recondite, puzzling, perplexing, mystifying.
—Ant. open, manifest, obvious, apparent.

secrete, *v.* hide, conceal, cover, cache, bury, camouflage, cloak, mask, stash, screen, ensconce, shroud, disguise.
—Ant. reveal, expose, uncover.
—Syn. Study. See HIDE.

secular, *adj.* worldly, temporal, terrestrial, mundane, earthly, earthy, lay, nonclerical, nonecclesiastical, nonreligious, civil, state, material, unspiritual, profane.
—Ant. religious, spiritual, ecclesiastical.

secure, *adj.* **1.** safe, protected, sheltered, shielded, guarded, defended, invincible, invulnerable, impregnable, unassailable, unthreatened, immune, unimperiled, snug, cozy. **2.** steady, firm, moored, anchored, sound, solid, sturdy, fixed, stable, fast, locked, fastened, riveted, attached, affixed. **3.** sure, definite, established, inevitable, probable, evident, easy, positive, certain, confident, assured, guaranteed. —*v.* **4.** obtain, procure, get, acquire, gain, win, earn. **5.** protect, guard, safeguard, shelter, shield, defend. **6.** make certain, ensure, assure, guarantee. **7.** make firm, fasten, affix, attach, anchor, rivet, moor.
—Ant. insecure; unstable; unsure; lose; unloose, loosen.
—Syn. Study. See GET.

sedate, *adj.* **1.** calm, quiet, composed, peaceful, even-tempered, sober, undisturbed, unexcited, staid, cool, collected, serene, placid, tranquil, unruffled, unperturbed, imperturbable, detached, unflappable, controlled, solemn, earnest, serious, settled, demure, grave, thoughtful, contemplative. **2.** proper, formal, decorous, dignified, refined, old-fashioned, conventional, staid, strait-laced, fussy, prim, prudish.
—Ant. agitated, perturbed, excited, nervous; wanton, improper, undignified, abandoned, unrestrained, indecorous.

sedative, *n.* **1.** sleeping pill, depressant, soporific, tranquilizer, opiate, drug, narcotic, calmative, barbiturate, antispasmodic, hypnotic, quieter, quietener, soother, pacifier, anodyne, downer, knockout drops, Mickey Finn. —*adj.* **2.** soothing, relaxing, calming, depressing, hypnotic, sleep-inducing, tranquilizing, narcotic, calmative, somniferous, soporific, palliative.
—Ant. stimulant.

sediment, *n.* lees, dregs, grounds, precipitate, deposit, remains, residue, detritus.

sedition, *n.* agitation, rabble-rousing, fomentation, instigation, incitement to riot, whipping *or* stirring *or* firing up; insurgency, insurgence, treachery, treason, subversion, dissidence, Putsch, disaffection, insubordination, mutiny, rebellion, revolt, revolution,

riot, insurrection, uprising.
—Ant. pacification; fidelity, loyalty, fealty, allegiance, patriotism.
—Syn. Study. See TREASON.

seduce, *v.* tempt, lead astray, debauch, deprave, pervert, corrupt, entice, beguile, inveigle, decoy, attract, tantalize, enchant, entrance, bewitch, allure, lure, delude, deceive, mislead, charm, captivate, fascinate, entrap, ensnare, sweet-talk.
—Ant. repel; reform.
—Syn. Study. See TEMPT.

seductive, *adj.* tempting, captivating, alluring, enticing, appealing, tantalizing, inviting, enchanting, entrancing, bewitching, fascinating, flirtatious, coquettish, on the make, provocative, irresistible, winning, prepossessing, unctuous, attractive, beguiling; deceptive.
—Ant. unattractive, repellent, abhorrent, dull, insipid, prudish.

see, *v.* **1.** perceive, look at, spy, espy, mark, spot, witness, recognize, catch sight of, glimpse, note, notice, discern, descry, remark, observe, distinguish, behold, regard, gaze, gape, stare, glare. **2.** view, visit, watch, attend, take in, survey. **3.** perceive, discern, penetrate, understand, comprehend, remark, apprehend, appreciate, fathom, grasp, realize, know, take in, be conscious *or* aware of, get the drift of. **4.** learn, ascertain, find out, determine, investigate, discover, learn. **5.** experience, endure, survive, live through, know, feel, meet with, suffer, undergo. **6.** receive, entertain, visit with. **7.** go out with, date, socialize with, consort *or* associate with; attend, escort, accompany, show, lead, usher, conduct, take, bring. **8.** consider, think, deliberate, make up one's mind, mull over, contemplate, decide, ruminate, reflect, brood over.

seedy, *adj.* shabby, run-down, dilapidated, worn, decayed, deteriorated, mangy, grubby, squalid, sleazy, ramshackle, ragged, shoddy, shopworn, scruffy, tatty, ratty, down-at-heel, flyblown, motheaten.
—Ant. spruce, trim, smart.

seek, *v.* **1.** search for, look for, hunt for, quest after, pursue, follow, solicit, go after. **2.** ask for, request, inquire after, beg, solicit, demand, invite. **3.** aspire, aim, undertake, try, endeavor, essay.

seem, *v.* appear, look; pretend, assume, makebelieve, play, play-act.
—Syn. Study. SEEM, APPEAR, LOOK refer to an outward aspect that may or may not be contrary to reality. SEEM is applied to something that has an aspect of truth and probability: *It seems warmer today.* APPEAR suggests the giving of an impression that may be superficial or illusory: *The house appears to be deserted.* LOOK more vividly suggests the use of the eye (literally or figuratively) or the aspect as perceived by the eye: *She looked frightened.*

seemly, *adj.* fitting, becoming, suited, well-suited, suitable, appropriate, proper, apt, *comme il faut*, apposite, apropos, characteristic, reasonable, congruous, compatible, consonant, congenial, befitting, meet; decent, decorous, right, demure, sedate, dignified, genteel, prudent, discreet, diplomatic, politic.
—Ant. unsuitable, inappropriate; indecorous, improper.

seethe, *v.* **1.** fume, smolder, burn, rage, rant, rave, be angry *or* incensed, get red in the face *or* hot under the collar, blow up. **2.** boil, stew, simmer, bubble, surge, foam, froth.
—Syn. Study. See BOIL.

segregate, *v.* isolate, separate, set apart, dissociate, segment, partition, seclude, sequester, exclude, ostracize, discriminate against, practice apartheid *or* Jim Crow.
—**Ant.** unite, associate, blend; desegregate.

seize, *v.* **1.** grasp, grab, clutch, grip, snatch, take hold of. **2.** capture, take into custody, arrest, apprehend, entrap, trap, catch, take, pick up, nab, collar, cop, snare, pinch. **3.** confiscate, appropriate, commandeer, liberate, capture, impound, annex, usurp, take possession of, arrogate.
—**Ant.** loose.

select, *v.* **1.** choose, prefer, pick, hand pick, pick out, opt for, single out, settle on, elect, decide on, cull. —*adj.* **2.** selected, chosen, preferred, choice, special, preferable, favorite, exceptional, first-rate, world-class, superior, prime, valuable, excellent. **3.** exclusive, selective, limited, restrictive, eclectic, privileged, elite, closed, private, rarefied, hoity-toity, discriminatory.
—**Ant.** reject.

selective, *adj.* discriminating, choosy, scrupulous, particular, demanding, exacting, discerning, eclectic, fastidious, picky, fussy, finicky.
—**Ant.** undiscriminating.

self-conscious, *adj.* shy, modest, retiring, unsure, embarrassed, sheepish, shamefaced, coy, diffident, self-effacing, shrinking, apprehensive, insecure, reserved, timid, backward, awkward, gauche, uncomfortable, uneasy, hesitant, nervous, halting, stammering, faltering, ill at ease, bashful, reticent, reluctant, chary, meek, abashed, confused, unassuming, demure.
—**Ant.** self-confident, self-assured, poised.

self-evident, *adj.* evident, obvious, patent, incontrovertible, definite, express, distinct, clear-cut, apparent, undeniable, unmistakable, palpable, tangible, true, axiomatic, self-explanatory, clear.
—**Ant.** mysterious.

selfish, *adj.* greedy, covetous, grasping, avaricious, acquisitive, materialistic, self-indulgent, self-aggrandizing, self-centered, self-absorbed, self-serving, monomaniacal, self-interested, self-seeking, egoistic, egotistical; mercenary, tightfisted, miserly, niggardly, pennypinching, cheeseparing, grudging, uncharitable, possessive, thoughtless, inconsiderate, illiberal, parsimonious, stingy, mean.
—**Ant.** unselfish, generous, liberal, charitable, noble, self-sacrificing.

self-satisfied, *adj.* content, complacent, smug, satisfied, sanctimonious, holier-than-thou, priggish, overconfident, conceited, self-important, vain, pompous, swellheaded, arrogant, overweening, overbearing.
—**Ant.** modest, unassuming.

sell, *v.* trade, barter, vend, exchange, transfer, convey, dispose of; market, merchandise, offer, peddle, hawk, handle, traffic in, retail, stock, furnish, supply, push, promote, auction, consign, deal in.
—**Ant.** buy.

semblance, *n.* **1.** appearance, aspect, form, show, exterior, image, figure, look, mask, facade, front, face, veneer, form, shape, mien, bearing, air, likeness, similarity, similitude, analogy, congruousness, affinity, resemblance. **2.** guise, pretense, simulation, impression, affectation, pose, air.
—**Ant.** dissimilarity, difference.

seminal, *adj.* original, progenitive, creative, primary, primal, basic, fundamental, basal, founding, formative, innovative, imaginative, unprecedented, precedent-setting, landmark, influential; germinal, germinative, generative, embryonic, incipient, potential, latent, undeveloped, in utero.
—**Ant.** derivative, imitative.

send, *v.* **1.** transmit, dispatch, forward, convey, deliver, assign, remit, ship, mail. **2.** impel, throw, cast, hurl, toss, propel, fling, project, release, discharge, shoot, fire, let fly.
—**Ant.** receive.

senile, *adj.* senescent, decrepit, weak, infirm, feeble, geriatric, doddering, doddery, declining, failing, in one's dotage, superannuated, old, aged, elderly, rickety, fogyish, old-fogyish, forgetful, absentminded, oblivious, simple-minded, childish, in one's second childhood, over the hill, out of it.
—**Ant.** youthful, alert.

sensation, *n.* **1.** sense, percept, image, sensibility, feeling, perception, impression; foreboding, awareness, consciousness, sneaking suspicion, presentiment, prescience. **2.** excitement, stimulation, animation; agitation, commotion, perturbation, stir, thrill, furor, tumult, uproar, disturbance, to-do, brouhaha, fuss.

sensational, *adj.* startling, thrilling, exciting, stimulating, electrifying, galvanizing, shocking, stirring, staggering, spine-tingling, hair-raising, show-stopping, breathtaking, astounding, astonishing, amazing, mind-boggling, mind-blowing, incredible, unbelievable, spectacular, out of this world, fantastic, extravagant, marvelous, wonderful, matchless, superb, peerless, phenomenal, extraordinary, fabulous, stupendous.
—**Ant.** prosaic, dull.

sense, *n.* **1.** feeling, perception, impression, sensation. **2.** awareness, recognition, realization, apprehension, appreciation, understanding, cognizance, consciousness. **3.** perception, estimation, appreciation, discernment, discrimination, penetration, insight, acumen. **4.** meaning, signification, signficance, import, interpretation, denotation, connotation, intelligibility, coherence, drift, gist, nuance, message, substance. **5.** opinion, judgment, feeling, idea, notion, sentiment. —*v.* **6.** perceive, feel, detect, intuit, divine, suspect, have a hunch *or* feeling, realize, pick up on, apprehend, become aware *or* conscious of, discern, appreciate, recognize.
—**Syn. Study.** See MEANING.

senseless, *adj.* **1.** insensate, unconscious, insensible, inert, stunned, comatose, dead to the world, anesthetized, numb, knocked out cold. **2.** unperceiving, undiscerning, unappreciative, unfeeling, apathetic, uninterested. **3.** stupid, foolish, silly, idiotic, dizzy, moronic, fatuous, imbecilic, brainless, mindless, half-witted, birdbrained, harebrained, empty-headed, simple, weak-minded, witless; nonsensical, pointless, illogical, irrational, absurd, ridiculous, ludicrous, inane, meaningless, asinine; crazy, demented, insane, wild, mad, wacky, screwball, screwy, nutty, batty.
—**Ant.** sensitive; intelligent; rational; sane.

sensibility, *n.* **1.** responsiveness, sensitiveness, perceptiveness, alertness, awareness, susceptibility. **2.** quickness, intelligence, judgment, judiciousness, keen-wittedness, penetration, discernment, insight, perception, keenness, acumen, acuity, acuteness, sensitivity, sensitiveness. **3.** consciousness, appreciation, awareness, perception, intuition, feeling, sentience, understanding. **4.** delicacy, tenderness, concern, sympathy, warmth, sentiment, sentimentalism, sentimentality.
—**Ant.** insensibility; dullness; callousness.

sensible, *adj.* **1.** commonsensical, common-sense, rational, reasonable, logical, realistic, practical, pragmatic, expedient, sound, sane, wise, sage, sagacious, judicious, discreet, politic, intelligent, down-to-earth, sober, clearheaded, cleareyed, efficient, hardheaded, tactful, tactical, well-thought-out, well-considered, appropriate, advisable, circumspect, cautious, careful. **2.** cognizant, aware, conscious, acquainted with, sensitive to, mindful of, in touch with, alert, awake, wise to, perceptive, alive, understanding, observant. **3.** appreciable, considerable, significant, substantial, substantive, noticeable, perceptible. **4.** perceptible, discernible, detectable, evident, recognizable, manifest, palpable, tangible, material, physical, substantive, corporeal, visible, observable, phenomenal, objective, identifiable.
—**Ant.** insensible, irrational, unsound; unaware; trifling.
—**Syn. Study.** See PRACTICAL.

sensitive, *adj.* **1.** impressionable, susceptible, easily affected, touchy, emotional, vulnerable, thin-skinned, high-strung, hypersensitive, volatile, excitable, temperamental; irritable, testy, irascible, petulant, quick-tempered. **2.** tender, sore, feeling, susceptible, sensate. **3.** delicate, responsive, subtle, acute, reactive, finely tuned.
—**Ant.** insensitive; phlegmatic, thick-skinned, unemotional; numb, insenate; nonresponsive.

sensual, *adj.* **1.** voluptuous, sensuous, luxurious; sumptuous, rich, sybaritic, hedonistic, epicurean, physical, carnal, bodily, fleshly, animal, animalistic. **2.** libidinous, lustful, lusty, sexual, erotic, lecherous, goatish, abandoned, wanton, profligate, debauched, dissipated, lubricious, salacious, prurient, loose, dirty, lewd, unchaste, gross, licentious, lascivious, dissolute.
—**Ant.** modest, prudish.
—**Syn. Study.** SENSUAL, SENSUOUS both refer to experience through the senses. SENSUAL refers to the enjoyments derived from the senses, esp. to the gratification or indulgence of physical appetites: *sensual pleasures.* SENSUOUS refers to that which is aesthetically pleasing to the senses: *sensuous poetry.* See also CARNAL.

sensuous, *adj.* sentient, feeling, sensible, perceptible, sensory; sybaritic, hedonistic, epicurean, sumptuous, rich, luxurious, voluptuous, luscious, delectable, delightful, aesthetic; physical, carnal, fleshly, animal.
—**Ant.** Spartan, austere.
—**Syn. Study.** See SENSUAL.

sentient, *adj.* aware, alive, conscious, awake, cognizant, sensitive, sensible, witting, susceptible, susceptive, feeling, perceptive, responsive, receptive, impressionable, sensate, reactive, discriminative, discriminatory.
—**Ant.** dulled, numb, insensate.

sentiment, *n.* **1.** attitude, disposition, opinion, feeling, notion, idea, judgment, view, outlook, position, belief, conviction, persuasion, thought. **2.** emotion, sentimentality, feeling, susceptibility, nostalgia, sentimentalism, mawkishness, bathos; sensitiveness, sensibility, tenderness, tenderheartedness, affection, passion.
—**Ant.** coolness, apathy, pragmatism, rationality.
—**Syn. Study.** See FEELING. See also OPINION.

sentimental, *adj.* **1.** emotional, compassionate, tenderhearted, tender, sympathetic, warmhearted, heart-felt, poignant, affecting, touching, moving, stirring. **2.** romantic, maudlin, mawkish, emotional, nostalgic, tearful, teary-eyed, tear-jerking, weepy, simpering, sweet, oversweet, saccharine, mushy, soppy, corny, schmaltzy, icky-sweet, yucky.

sentimentality, *n.* emotionalism, romanticism, nostalgia, pathos, bathos, mawkishness, tenderness, teariness, tearfulness, mush, soppiness, schmaltz, corn, kitschiness.
—**Ant.** reason.

separate, *v.* **1.** keep apart, divide, partition, divorce, detach, unhook, rend, part, put apart, disjoin, disconnect, dissever, sever, disunite, sunder, disengage, dissociate, split, break up, disassemble, disentangle, unravel. **2.** withdraw, cleave, part company *or* ways, disband, divorce, secede, diverge. —*adj.* **3.** separated, disjoined, disunited, disconnected, disassociated, unattached, apart, divided, severed, detached, distinct, discrete, apart, withdrawn, solitary, removed, cloistered, secluded, shut away, locked up, segregated, free, independent, sequestered, alone, isolated. **4.** independent, individual, particular, different, unrelated, other, unique, sole, lone, single, solitary.
—**Ant.** unite, connect; together, whole; social, sociable; integral, same, identical, general.

separation *n.* **1.** splitup, split, breakup, break, rift, estrangement, divorce, disunion. **2.** division, split, schism, partition, disassociation, independence, dissociation, severance, detachment, removal. **3.** fracture, fragmentation, disintegration, shattering, rupture, disjunction, split, breakup, dismemberment, segregation, division, sundering.

sequence, *n.* **1.** succession, order, arrangement, series, progression, set, run, concatenation, system, chain, string, train, course, cycle, organization, suit, suite. **2.** outcome, sequel, consequence, result, followup, upshot, issue, development.
—**Syn. Study.** See SERIES.

serendipity, *n.* luck, chance, happenstance, accident, break, fortuity, fortuitousness, adventitiousness, randomness, fortune, fluke, flukiness, dumb luck.
—**Ant.** premeditation, fate, predestination, logic.

serene, *adj.* **1.** calm, peaceful, tranquil, quiet, still, noiseless, silent, pacific, peaceable, halcyon, restful, idyllic, pastoral, bucolic; unruffled, undisturbed, imperturbable, unperturbed, untroubled; poised, self-possessed, even-tempered, temperate, nonchalant, easygoing, laidback, placid, composed, sedate, staid, collected, cool. **2.** fair, clear, unclouded, bright.
—**Ant.** agitated, disturbed, excitable, mercurial, irritable, self-conscious, nervous; cloudy, inclement.
—**Syn. Study.** See PEACEFUL.

serenity, *n.* calmness, composure, self-possession, poise, aplomb, nonchalance, unflappability; tranquility, peacefulness, calm, sereneness, peace, quiet, restfulness, stillness.
—**Ant.** perturbation, disturbance, agitation, pandemonium, uproar, hurly-burly.

series, *n.* sequence, succession, set, progression, run, cycle, string, train, concatenation, suit, suite, line; order, arrangement, organization, system.

—**Syn. Study.** SERIES, SEQUENCE, SUCCESSION are terms for an orderly following of things one after another. SERIES is applied to a number of things of the same kind, usu. related to each other, arranged or happening in order: *a series of base-ball games.* SEQUENCE stresses the continuity in time, thought, cause and effect, etc.: *The scenes came in a definite sequence.* SUCCESSION implies that one thing is followed by another or others in turn, usu. though not necessarily with a relation or connection between them: *a succession of calamities.*

serious, *adj.* **1.** thoughtful, reflective, contemplative, meditative, deep, profound, grave, unsmiling, poker-faced, pensive, humorless, somber, grim, dour, severe, austere, stern, ascetic, solemn, sober, sedate, staid, earnest. **2.** weighty, important, momentous, vital, significant, consequential, grave, urgent, pressing, crucial, dangerous, life-or-death, deep, profound, grave, critical.

—**Ant.** lighthearted, jocular; trivial.

—**Syn. Study.** See EARNEST.

sermonize, *v.* preach, evangelize, homilize, preachify, prelect, lecture, hold forth, discourse, dilate, expatiate, dogmatize, moralize.

servant, *n.* domestic, help, helper, employee, menial, factotum, lackey, dogsbody; housekeeper, maid, handyman, valet, butler, cleaning woman *or* man, nanny, au pair, cook, chef.

—**Ant.** employer.

serve, *v.* **1.** wait on, attend, minister to, look after, be at (someone's) beck and call. **2.** assist, help, aid, succor, accommodate, oblige, gratify, be of assistance. **3.** function, answer, do, suffice, be useful, fill the bill, suit, be adequate *or* suitable. **4.** promote, contribute, forward, advance, assist. **5.** provide, cater, satisfy, purvey, distribute, supply, offer, make available, dish *or* dole *or* deal out, pass around *or* out, handle.

serviceable, *adj.* **1.** working, workable, functional, operating, operative; helpful, useful, handy, utile, aidful, employable, utilitarian, advantageous, profitable, convenient, available, effective, valuable; durable, tough, long-lasting, wear-resistant. **2.** adequate, tolerable, passable, fair, fairish, unexceptional, middling, so-so, decent, respectable, acceptable, satisfactory.

servile, *adj.* submissive, obsequious, slavish, compliant, sheepish, docile, obedient, passive, subservient, craven, acquiescent, deferential, ingratiating, toadying, truckling, wheedling, flattering, unctuous, timeserving, apple-polishing, bootlicking, smarmy, brown-nosing, menial, cringing, cowering, low, fawning, abject, ignoble, inferior, mean, base, sycophantic, groveling.

—**Ant.** proud, noble, masterful, independent, dignified, disobedient, mutinous, insolent, disrespectful.

—**Syn. Study.** SERVILE, OBSEQUIOUS, SLAVISH describe the submissive or compliant behavior of a slave or an inferior. SERVILE suggests cringing, fawning, and abject submission: *servile responses to questions.* OBSEQUIOUS implies the ostentatious subordination of oneself to the wishes of another, either from fear or from hope of gain: *an obsequious waiter.* SLAVISH stresses the dependence and laborious toil of one who follows or obeys without question: *slavish attentiveness to orders.*

set, *v.* **1.** put, place, position, pose, locate, situate, post, appoint, station, site, lay, install, lodge, mount, deposit, drop, park, plant. **2.** fix, appoint, ordain, settle, establish, determine, fasten on, prescribe, assign, define, predetermine. **3.** adjust, arrange, order, dispose, place. **4.** turn, synchronize, fix, calibrate, coordinate, regulate. **5.** decline, sink, subside, fall, wane, go down. **6.** solidify, congeal, jell, freeze, stiffen, coagulate, clot, thicken, harden. —*n.* **7.** assortment, outfit, group, combination, number, selection, arrangement, grouping, collection, series. **8.** group, clique, coterie, company, circle, class, ring, crowd, gang, faction, sect. **9.** direction, bent, inclination, disposition, attitude. **10.** bearing, carriage, mien, posture, appearance, aspect. **11.** stage, scene, set, mounting, *mise en scène,* scenery, decor, backdrop, setting. —*adj.* **12.** fixed, established, prearranged, decided, determined, settled, prefixed, predetermined. **13.** prescribed, foreordained. **14.** customary, normal, regular, habitual, traditional, conventional, scheduled, routine, standard, unvarying, unchanging, wonted, usual. **15.** fixed, rigid, immovable. **16.** resolved, determined, stubborn, fixed, obstinate, stiff, unyielding.

—**Ant.** displace, abolish; rise; soften, melt.

settle, *v.* **1.** fix, agree upon, decide, appoint, confirm, affirm, conclude, make sure of, determine, choose, select, set, establish. **2.** pay, discharge, repay, satisfy, clear, quit, defray, liquidate. **3.** locate in, emigrate, put down roots, relocate, take up residence, stay, dwell, reside, make one's home, abide, inhabit, live, set up housekeeping; populate, pioneer, people, colonize. **4.** quiet, tranquilize, calm, compose, still, pacify. **5.** stabilize, establish, decide, arrange, agree, order, dispose, organize, straighten out, compose, put to rights, reconcile, resolve, conclude, put an end to, adjust, calm down, subside, quiet down, become tranquil, rest, sink down, decline, sink, fall, gravitate.

—**Ant.** unsettle.

sever, *v.* separate, divide, cut apart, part, cut, cleave, lop, chop, hack, hew, slice, shear, dock, rend, split, sunder, break off, disunite, disjoin, detach, disengage, disconnect; dissolve, terminate, suspend, abandon, discontinue.

—**Ant.** unite.

severe, *adj.* **1.** harsh, extreme, fierce, trenchant, biting, acerb, bitter, caustic, satirical, keen, stinging, mordant, mordacious, sharp, cutting. **2.** serious, grave, stern, forbidding, glowering, dour, grim, stiff, sober, unsmiling, cold, frigid, aloof, austere, rigid, rigorous, strict, straitlaced, sedate; unfeeling, unsympathetic, cruel, harsh, brutal, stonyhearted, flinty, ironhanded, oppressive, obdurate, pitiless, merciless, punitive, ruthless, despotic, dictatorial, authoritative, autocratic, relentless, hard, unrelenting, inexorable, abrupt, peremptory, curt, short. **3.** restrained, modest, spare, plain, simple, unadorned, stark, bare, austere, ascetic, monastic, Spartan, crude, undecorated, unembellished, unembroidered, unornamented, chaste. **4.** uncomfortable, distressing, unpleasant, acute, afflictive, violent, intense, dangerous, critical, dreadful, awful, life-threatening, dire; mortal, fatal, terminal. **5.** rigid, strict, painstaking, fastidious, exigent, taxing, exact, critical, demanding, accurate, methodical, systematic, exacting.

—**Ant.** mild; gradual; flexible; comfortable; inaccurate.

—**Syn. Study.** See STERN.

sexy *adj.* **1.** erotic, exciting, seductive, suggestive, arousing, sensual, sensuous, carnal, fleshly, voluptuous, earthy, lustful, animal, provocative, inviting, alluring, flirtatious, coquettish, appealing, attractive, fascinating, captivating, stunning, bedroom, come-hither. **2.** pornographic, explicit, X-rated, obscene, smutty, lewd, gross, libidinous, lascivious, lubricious, licentious, indecent, dirty, filthy, vulgar, coarse, off-color, ribald, risqué, bawdy, titillating, indelicate, suggestive, shameless, raunchy.

shabby, *adj.* **1.** threadbare, worn, ragged, bedraggled, shopworn, moth-eaten, tattered, scruffy, tatty, out at the elbows. **2.** shoddy, ramshackle, run-down, neglected, decrepit, seedy, squalid, sordid, slummy, wretched. **3.** mean, mean-spirited, base, contemptible, deplorable, egregious, scurvy. **4.** disreputable, discreditable, dishonorable, shameful, ignominious, shady. **5.** unfair, inequitable, unjust, unsporting, unsportsmanlike, discriminatory.

shack, *n.* shanty, hut, shed, hutch, hovel, cabin, crib, outbuilding, outhouse, lean-to, dump.

shackle, *n.* **1.** fetter, chain, anklet, iron, ball and chain, restraint, cuff, bracelet, handcuff, manacle, hobble. **2.** restriction, restraint, deterrent, check, barrier, hindrance, bar, impediment, obstacle, obstruction, encumbrance. —*v.* **3.** confine, bind, tie, secure, truss, tether, trammel, restrain, restrict, fetter, chain, manacle, handcuff, hobble, hog-tie. **4.** restrict, trammel, impede, encumber, obstruct, block, restrain, hold back, deter, hinder, discourage, handicap, curb, control, inhibit, limit, rein, bridle, check, circumscribe, confine, slow, stultify, dull.

—**Ant.** disencumber, extricate, release, liberate, free.

shade, *n.* **1.** darkness, dimness, shadiness, murkiness, shadow, obscurity, gloom, gloominess, dusk, umbrage, penumbra. **2.** specter, ghost, apparition, spirit, phantom, phantasm, wraith, vision, banshee, spook, revenant, haunting. **3.** variation, amount, degree, hair, trace, hint, intimation, tinge, modicum, soupçon, suspicion, touch, scintilla, nuance, undertone, overtone, speck, dash, vestige, suggestion. —*v.* **4.** obscure, dim, darken, cloud, shadow, veil, blot out, shroud, mask, camouflage, blur, obfuscate. **5.** screen, hide, shield, protect, conceal, cover, shelter.

—**Ant.** light.

shake, *v.* **1.** sway, vibrate, fluctuate, oscillate, pulsate, gyrate, swing, wiggle, wriggle, squirm, shimmy, twitch, jiggle, waggle, roll, bump, grind; quake, wobble, dither, teeter, quiver, waver, tremble, agitate, rock, convulse, shudder, shiver, totter. **2.** brandish, wave, display, show off, exhibit, flap, flutter, parade, flourish. **3.** agitate, disturb, move, intimidate, frighten, daunt, upset, disconcert, discombobulate, unnerve, discomfort, worry, fluster, disquiet, confound, confuse, perplex, rattle, throw for a loop. **4.** unsettle, undermine, impair, harm, damage, discourage, weaken, enfeeble. —*n.* **5.** tremor, blow, disturbance, shock.

shaky, *adj.* **1.** unsteady, unstable, rickety, dilapidated, ramshackle, decrepit, on its last legs, feeble, unbalanced, teetery, teetering, tottery, tottering, wobbly, doddering, fragile, spindly. **2.** tremulous, aflutter, faint, shuddering, unsteady, dizzy,

vertiginous, shivering, quivering, apprehensive, fidgety, flustered, edgy, fretful, agitated, upset, uneasy, anxious, nervous, jittery, jumpy, skittish. **3.** unstable, unsound, flimsy, tenuous, questionable, unsubstantiated, untrustworthy, undependable, unreliable, uncertain, unsure, doubtful, dubious, precarious, problematic, risky, ticklish, dicey, iffy.

—**Ant.** steady, solid, stable; confident; certain, reliable, proven, safe.

shallow *adj.* superficial, skin-deep, surface, outward, external, slight, trivial, insignificant, unimportant, frivolous, trifling, thin, slim, slender, flimsy, foolish, idle, cursory, uncritical, insubstantial, meaningless, cosmetic, nominal, passing, nonessential, petty, paltry, empty, hollow, idle, vain.

sham, *n.* **1.** imitation, pretense, fake, fraud, hoax, humbug, forgery, counterfeit, phony, copy, imposture, cheat, deception, simulacrum. —*adj.* **2.** pretended, counterfeit, false, fake, fraudulent, paste, simulated, make-believe, fictitious, ersatz, bogus, artificial, synthetic, phony, pseudo, spurious, mock. —*v.* **3.** pretend, simulate, counterfeit, assume, affect, imitate, deceive, feign, defraud, impose, make believe, hoax, con.

—**Ant.** genuine, authentic, bona fide, real.

—**Syn. Study.** See FALSE.

shame, *n.* **1.** embarrassment, humiliation, chagrin, mortification, remorsefulness, loss of face, abashment. **2.** disgrace, derision, ignominy, dishonor, disrepute, degradation, vilification, calumny, abasement, reproach, obloquy, opprobrium, odium, infamy, contempt. **3.** scandal, stigma, denigration, defamation, descredit, derogation, disparagement. **4.** modesty, humility, decorum, decency, propriety, respectability, shyness, coyness, diffidence, timidity, prudishness, bashfulness, meekness. —*v.* **5.** abash, humiliate, mortify, embarrass, chagrin, put down, chasten, take (someone) down a peg, humble, confuse, disconcert. **6.** disgrace, reproach, dishonor, calumniate, degrade, defame, discredit, stigmatize, scandalize, debase, tarnish, stain, taint, smear, blacken, besmirch, sully, soil. **7.** force, bully, coerce, drive, push, impel, compel, intimidate, pressure.

—**Ant.** honor.

—**Syn. Study.** SHAME, EMBARRASSMENT, HUMILIATION, CHAGRIN designate different kinds or degrees of painful feeling caused by injury to one's pride or self-respect. SHAME is a painful feeling caused by the consciousness or exposure of unworthy or indecent conduct or circumstances: *One feels shame at being caught in a lie.* It is similar to guilt in the nature and origin of the feeling. EMBARRASSMENT usu. refers to a less painful feeling, one associated with less serious situations, often of a social nature: *embarrassment over breaking a vase at a party.* HUMILIATION is a feeling of embarrassment at being humbled in the estimation of others: *Being ignored gave him a sense of humiliation.* CHAGRIN is humiliation mingled with vexation or anger: *She felt chagrin at her failure to do well on the test.*

shameful, *adj.* disgraceful, blameworthy, scandalous, mortifying, humiliating, dishonorable, ignominious, disreputable, degrading, indecent, inglorious, deplorable, corrupt, unprincipled, unethical, immoral, outrageous, infamous, vicious, villainous, iniquitous, vile, base, mean, evil, wicked, horrid, shocking, indecorous, unseemly, low. —**Ant.** honorable.

shameless, *adj.* **1.** immodest, wild, flagrant, unrestrained, wanton, uncontrolled, barefaced, audacious, unblushing, brazen, indecent, indecorous, brash, rude, improper, forward, impudent, bold, insolent, indelicate, unabashed, unashamed, shocking, outrageous. **2.** corrupt, impure, indecent, dishonorable, sinful, unprincipled, depraved, profligate, abandoned, wanton, dissolute, reprobate, vicious, hard, hardened, callous, incorrigible, lost. —**Ant.** shy, diffident, bashful, modest; proper, pure, chaste, decent, principled, honorable, righteous, upstanding, incorruptible.

shape, *n.* **1.** outline, lines, contours, profile, silhouette; build, body, physique, form, figure; appearance, aspect. **2.** guise, disguise, likeness, image, form, appearance. **3.** arrangement, order, configuration, pattern. **4.** condition, situation, state, status, trim, order. **5.** mold, cast, pattern, form, structure. —*v.* **6.** make, fabricate, manufacture, forge, form, fashion, mold, model, cast, sculpt; carve, trim, hew, hack. **7.** word, express, term, formulate, put, pose, embody in words. **8.** adjust, adapt, frame, fit, accommodate, change, modify, remodel.

shapeless, *adj.* **1.** formless, unformed, amorphous, unstructured, indefinite, undefined, vague, nebulous, uncertain, hazy, fuzzy, rough, rude, crude, chaotic, inchoate. **2.** deformed, misshapen, lumpy, distorted, twisted, battered, bent, malformed, contorted, warped, gnarled, grotesque, abnormal, monstrous, illformed, badly proportioned, ungraceful.

share, *n.* **1.** portion, part, allotment, division, allocation, allowance, due, ration, apportionment, contribution, quota, lot, proportion, cut, piece, stake, slice. —*v.* **2.** divide, distribute, dispense, apportion, allot, portion, parcel out, allocate, ration, split, partition, deal out, dole, mete out. **3.** partake, participate, join in, engage in, take part, receive, enter into.

sharp, *adj.* **1.** keen, acute, edged, pointed, knifelike, peaked. **2.** abrupt, precipitous, sheer, marked, vertical, sudden. **3.** distinct, marked, clear. **4.** pungent, biting, acrid, spicy, burning, hot, mordacious, bitter, piquant, tangy, harsh, acid, tart, sour. **5.** shrill, piercing, loud, high, high-pitched, penetrating, piercing, strident, loud, earsplitting. **6.** cold, piercing, freezing, nipping, cutting, severe, fierce, biting. **7.** painful, distressing, intense, severe, extreme, acute, piercing, fierce, excruciating, agonizing. **8.** harsh, merciless, unmerciful, severe, acute, cutting, incisive, caustic, trenchant, scathing, malicious, nasty, malevolent, malignant, acid, sarcastic, sardonic, acrimonious, mordant, mordacious, piercing, probing, penetrating, pointed, biting, unkind, spiteful, virulent, venomous, poisonous. **9.** fierce, violent, intense. **10.** vigilant, alert, awake, on the qui vive, attentive. **11.** acute, shrewd, keen-witted, smart, agile, astute, clever, penetrating, discerning, perspicacious, ingenious, discriminating, ready, smart, cunning, intelligent, bright, quick, sensitive, alert, observant, incisive, vigorous, understanding, active, reasoning. **12.** dishonest, shady, unlawful, deceitful, artful, crafty, foxy, sly, cunning, calculating, unscrupulous, corrupt, treacherous, deceptive, sneaky, cheating.

—**Ant.** dull, blunt; unclear; mild; soft; warm; merciful; stupid, dim; honest, aboveboard.

—**Syn. Study.** SHARP, KEEN, INTELLIGENT, QUICK may all be applied to mental qualities and abilities. SHARP means mentally alert or acute; it implies a clever and astute quality: *a sharp mind.* KEEN suggests an incisive, observant, or penetrating nature: *a keen observer.* INTELLIGENT means not only acute, alert, and active, but also able to reason and understand: *an intelligent reader.* QUICK suggests lively and rapid comprehension, prompt response to instruction, and the like: *quick at figures.*

shatter, *v.* break, crush, shiver, disintegrate, burst, pulverize, smash, splinter, fragment, fracture, rupture, crash, split, crack; explode, implode, destroy, ruin, wreck, demolish, devastate, blast, undermine, blow to bits *or* smithereens, reduce to rubble; overcome, overwhelm, paralyze, confound, confuse, stupefy, stun, knock for a loop.

sheer, *adj.* **1.** transparent, diaphanous, thin, clear, revealing, see-through, filmy, gauzy, gossamer, translucent, light, peekaboo. **2.** absolute, unmitigated, out-and-out, unalloyed, plain, total, rank, complete, arrant, thoroughgoing, outright, unmixed, mere, simple, pure, downright, unadulterated, unqualified, utter. **3.** steep, precipitous, abrupt, perpendicular, bluff, vertical. —**Ant.** opaque; gradual.

shelter, *n.* **1.** protection, safeguard, refuge, retreat, asylum, cover, screen, safety, security, defense, concealment, bastion, safe house, bulwark, sanctuary, shield, haven, port, ark, harbor. —*v.* **2.** protect, guard, cover, safeguard, screen, keep, secure, defend, shield, hide, shroud, house, harbor, receive, accept, admit, lodge, board, entertain. —**Ant.** exposure; betray, expose, abandon, evict.

shiftless, *adj.* **1.** lazy, indolent, slothful, unambitious, slack, dilatory, uninspired, unmotivated, unenterprising, idle, lackadaisical, irresponsible, aimless, time-wasting, clock-watching, goldbricking, good-for-nothing. **2.** improvident, inefficient, unresourceful. —**Ant.** ambitious, energetic, enterprising, sedulous, hard-working.

shimmer, *v., n.* glisten, shine, flash, glance, sparkle, glitter, scintillate, coruscate, twinkle, glister, spark, gleam, glimmer, glow, flicker, glint.

shine, *v.* **1.** beam, glare, gleam, glisten, glimmer, shimmer, sparkle, flare, glitter, coruscate, twinkle, scintillate, glint, flicker, flash, glow, radiate. —*n.* **2.** radiance, light, brightness, gleam, glow, shimmer. **3.** polish, luster, gloss, brilliance, twinkle, scintillation, glow, sheen, patina, brightness, sparkle, shimmer, glitter, gleam, radiance.

shining, *adj.* **1.** radiant, gleaming, glowing, shimmering, glossy, glassy, beaming, glittering, twinkling, dazzling, coruscating, sparkling, scintillating, flickering, lambent, fulgent, bright, brilliant, resplendent, glistening, effulgent, lustrous. **2.** conspicuous, fine, outstanding, distinguished, eminent, prime, splendid, choice, excellent, select.

shirk, *v.* evade, avoid, dodge, shun, get out of, shrink from, duck, elude, escape, sidestep, malinger, goldbrick, slack off, goof off, waste time, lollygag.

shiver, *v.* **1.** tremble, quake, quaver, totter, wobble, shimmy, teeter,

shudder, shake, quiver, vibrate, rattle. **2.** shake, quake, tremble, shudder, quiver, thrill, frisson, tremor, flutter; goosebumps, chill.

shock, *n.* **1.** blow, impact, collision, encounter, concussion, clash, tingle, jolt, jar. **2.** surprise, thunderbolt, bombshell, revelation, eye-opener, jolt; disturbance, commotion, agitation; trauma, stupor, paralysis, collapse, breakdown, prostration. —*v.* **3.** startle, stagger, surprise, stun, jar, jolt, shake up, numb, daze, appall, astonish, flabbergast, astound, paralyze, stupefy, bewilder, dumbfound. **4.** frighten, petrify, traumatize, repel, upset, horrify, disgust, outrage, nauseate, offend, sicken, revolt.

shoddy *adj.* shabby, second-rate, imperfect, poor, inferior, bad, cheap, cheapjack, meretricious, tacky, chintzy, Drummagem, pinchbeck, tawdry, tinselly, artificial, plastic, trashy, junky, ratty, mangy, low-quality, mediocre, substandard, low-grade, gimcrack, crummy, lousy, tasteless, tinny, rundown, seedy, insubstantial, flimsy. —**Ant.** first-rate, superior, well-made, quality, perfect.

short, *adj.* **1.** little, small, tiny, diminutive, wee, slight, petite, dwarfish, squat, runty, stunted, stubby, pint-sized, sawn-off, knee-high to a grasshopper. **2.** concise, pithy, epigrammatic, brief, terse, succinct, laconic, condensed, compendious, compressed, abbreviated, abridged, curt, sententious. **3.** abrupt, curt, sharp, blunt, bluff, brusque, gruff, drabby, waspish, snappish, discourteous, impolite, curmudgeonly, petulant, short-tempered, testy, uncivil, rude. **4.** scanty, poor, insufficient, deficient, inadequate, wanting, lacking, needful, shy of, low on. **5.** substandard, inferior, unacceptable, below par. —*adv.* **6.** suddenly, abruptly, peremptorily, instantly, unexpectedly, hurriedly, hastily, out of the blue, without notice *or* warning. —**Ant.** tall, long.

—**Syn. Study.** SHORT, BRIEF are opposed to LONG, and indicate slight extent or duration. SHORT may imply duration but is also applied to physical distance and certain purely spatial relations: *a short journey.* BRIEF refers esp. to duration of time: *brief intervals.*

shortage *n.* lack, scarcity, scarceness, want, shortfall, need, deficiency, deficit, dearth, paucity, insufficiency, inadequacy, scantiness, meagerness.

shortcoming *n.* imperfection, blemish, flaw, weak spot, handicap, liability, drawback, weakness, frailty, defect, failure, failing, deficiency, inadequacy, foible, fault, Achilles' heel, lack, blind spot, vice.

shorten, *v.* **1.** curtail, abbreviate, cut, trim, prune, compress, truncate, summarize, contract, shrink, abstract, digest, epitomize, abridge, condense, lessen, limit, restrict, reduce, retrench. **2.** take in, reduce, decrease, diminish, lessen, contract. —**Ant.** lengthen, elongate, extend.

—**Syn. Study.** SHORTEN, ABBREVIATE, ABRIDGE, CURTAIL mean to make shorter or briefer. SHORTEN is a general word meaning to make less in extent or duration: *to shorten a dress; to shorten a prison sentence.* The other three terms suggest methods of shortening. ABBREVIATE usu. means to shorten a word or group of words, as by omission of letters: *to abbreviate a name.* To ABRIDGE is to reduce in length or size by condensing, summarizing, and the like: *to abridge a document.* CURTAIL suggests a lack of completeness due to

the omission of some part: *to curtail an explanation.*

short-lived, *adj.* temporary, fleeting, passing, brief, transitory, transient, ephemeral, evanescent, impermanent, momentary, fugitive, fly-by-night, quick, hasty, not long for this world. —**Ant.** permanent, enduring, lasting, everlasting, stable, perpetual, eternal, constant, abiding.

shortsighted, *adj.* **1.** myopic, dim-sighted, near-sighted. **2.** unthinking, unimaginative, unprogressive; improvident, injudicious, careless, heedless, reckless, thoughtless, imprudent, impulsive, brash, rash, unwary, blind, foolhardy, irresponsible; wasteful, profligate, prodigal, spendthrift, happy-go-lucky. —**Ant.** presbyopic, far-sighted; visionary, thoughtful, prudent.

shout, *v.* cry out, hoot, exclaim, vociferate, yell, scream, bawl, bellow, howl, roar, hoot, clamor, call out, yelp. —**Ant.** whisper.

shove, *v.* **1.** push, propel, impel, thrust, drive, force, move, press on, set in motion, jar, jolt, launch, start; constrain, compel, oblige, coerce. **2.** jostle, elbow, shoulder, nudge, bump, knock, jab, push aside, jar, strike, hit, butt into.

show, *v.* **1.** exhibit, display, present, expose, manifest, evidence, evince, offer, tender, parade, flaunt, demonstrate. **2.** point out, indicate. **3.** guide, accompany, lead, usher, escort, direct, lead, conduct. **4.** interpret, make clear *or* known, clarify, elucidate, explain, express, discover, reveal, disclose, divulge, publish, proclaim. **5.** prove, confirm, argue, prove, substantiate, corroborate, verify, certify, authenticate, demonstrate, evidence. **6.** accord, grant, bestow, confer. **7.** look, appear, seem, be visible. —*n.* **8.** display, ostentation, pomp, pretension, pretentiousness, affectation, exhibition, flourish, dash, pageantry, ceremony. **9.** showing, spectacle, exhibition, production, presentation, exhibit, exposition, fair, appearance. **10.** deception, pretense, pretext, simulation, illusion. —**Ant.** hide, conceal.

showy, *adj.* ostentatious, pompous, flamboyant, conspicuous, pretentious, florid, bravura, opulent, resplendent, sumptuous, gorgeous, luxurious; flashy, tawdry, gaudy, meretricious, garish, loud; fancy, elaborate, fussy, ornate, overdone, excessive, intricate, baroque, rococo, Byzantine. —**Ant.** subtle, discreet, austere, plain, simple, modest, unassuming.

shrewd, *adj.* astute, sharp, acute, clever, smart, cunning, canny, foxy, sly, crafty, artful, wily, manipulative, calculating, knowing, diplomatic, politic, smooth, suave, quick, discerning, discriminating, perceptive, perspicuous, perspicacious, keen, intelligent, penetrating, ingenious, sagacious, wise, sage, ingenious, inventful, resourceful, prudent, sensible, judicious. —**Ant.** dull, unworldly, naive, guileless, stupid, imperceptive.

shriek, *n., v.* cry, scream, screech, yell, squeal, squawk, squall, yelp.

shrink, *v.* **1.** retreat, recede, withdraw, draw back, back away, cower, cringe, wince, shy away, balk at, quail, boggle, scruple, demur, avoid, recoil, flinch, retire. **2.** contract, constrict, compress, condense, deflate, reduce, wither, shrivel, lessen, diminish, decrease, dwindle, wane, peter out; shorten, condense, abbreviate, cut, curtail, abridge.

—**Ant.** advance, attack; swell, expand, amplify, distend, inflate, dilate, increase.

—**Syn. Study.** See DECREASE. See also WINCE.

shrivel, *v.* wither, wrinkle, wizen, dry up, desiccate, dehydrate, parch, scorch, sear; decrease, pucker up, curl up, contract, shrink.

—**Ant.** blossom, expand.

shroud, *v.* cover, veil, cloak, shield, screen, mask, disguise, camouflage, blanket, shade, protect, swathe, envelop, wrap, surround, curtain, hide, conceal, obscure, cloud, becloud.

—**Ant.** reveal, expose.

shudder, *n.* shiver, quaver, quake, quiver, shake, twitch, tremble, convulsion, paroxysm, spasm, fit; rattle, vibration.

shun, *v.* elude, avoid, evade, eschew, sidestep, skirt, circumvent, dodge, steer clear of, shrink from, flee *or* escape from; rebuff, refuse, spurn, disdain, reject, cold-shoulder, repudiate, scorn, brush off.

—**Ant.** confront, pursue, seek.

shut, *v.* **1.** close, fasten, secure, shut, lock, bolt, seal, slam. **2.** confine, enclose, jail, imprison. **3.** bar, exclude, prohibit, preclude. —*adj.* **4.** closed, fastened, sealed, locked, bolted.

—**Ant.** open.

shy, *adj.* **1.** bashful, diffident, retiring, timid, coy, withdrawn, reserved, private, meek, mild, modest, sheepish, self-conscious, introverted, apprehensive, nervous. **2.** suspicious, distrustful, wary, heedful, cautious, careful, chary, reluctant, leery, guarded, afraid, fearful, anxious, worried, distrustful, cowardly, craven, timid. **3.** short, missing, lacking, deficient. —*v.* **4.** recoil, draw back, shrink, flinch, balk.

—**Ant.** self-confident, aggressive, obtrusive, forward; trusting; incautious, careless; advance, attack.

sick, *adj.* **1.** ill, unwell, ailing, infirm, unhealthy, diseased, afflicted, under the weather, out of sorts, laid up, not up to snuff, indisposed. **2.** nauseous, vomiting, nauseated, queasy, squeamish, green around the gills. **3.** pale, wan, ashen, pasty, wheyfaced, haggard, woebegone, weak, drawn, peaked, pallid, white, sickly. **4.** affected, troubled, stricken, wretched, miserable, woeful.

—**Ant.** well, hale, healthy.

—**Syn. Study.** See ILL.

sickly, *adj.* **1.** unhealthy, ailing, sick, unwell, puny, weak, frail, feeble, delicate, wan, anemic, infirm. **2.** weak, mawkish, mushy, maudlin, cloying, insipid, schmaltzy, sentimental, faint.

—**Ant.** strong, healthy.

sidekick, *n.* partner, associate, colleague, partner in crime, ally, comrade, comrade in arms, companion, confederate, cohort, henchman, subordinate, stooge, assistant, right hand, man Friday, girl Friday, factotum.

—**Ant.** enemy, foe, adversary, opponent.

sign, *n.* **1.** token, signal, notice, indication, trace, evidence, clue, symptom, manifestation, betokening, vestige, hint, suggestion. **2.** mark, device, representation, emblem, brand, stamp, insigne, badge, character, note, symbol. **3.** omen, presage, portent, augury, foreboding, warning, forewarning, indication, prophecy, prognostication, foreshadowing, handwriting on the wall. —*v.* **4.** signify, betoken, indicate, mean, signal. **5.** affix a signature to, autograph, inscribe, witness, mark, sign on the dotted line.

—**Syn. Study.** SIGN, OMEN, PORTENT refer to something that gives evidence of a future event. SIGN is a general word for a visible trace or indication of an event, either past, present, or future: *Dark clouds are a sign of rain.* An OMEN is a happening or phenomenon that serves as a warning of things to come; it may foreshadow good or evil: *She believed it was a bad omen if a black cat crossed her path.* PORTENT also refers to an indication of future events, usu. ones that are momentous or of ominous significance: *the portents of war.*

significance, *n.* **1.** import, importance, consequence, moment, weight, weightiness, relevance, value, worth, excellence, merit, prestige, authority, influence. **2.** import, meaning, sense, purport, message, idea, point, implication, pith, essence, gist, implication, drift, vein, impression, connotation, signification.

—**Ant.** triviality.

—**Syn. Study.** See IMPORTANCE. See also MEANING.

significant, *adj.* **1.** important, consequential, momentous, weighty, substantial, substantive, noteworthy, notable, valued, valuable, meretorious, relevant, signal, outstanding, impressive, critical, crucial, vital. **2.** meaningful, expressive, eloquent, pithy, pregnant, informative, sententious, cogent, telling, convincing, signifying, indicative *or* suggestive of.

—**Ant.** insignificant.

signify, *v.* **1.** signal, make known, express, indicate, communicate. **2.** convey, symbolize, betoken, represent, mean, connote, suggest, portend, denote, indicate, purport, imply. **3.** matter, count, carry weight, be consequential *or* important, impress, stand out, merit consideration.

silent, *adj.* **1.** quiet, still, noiseless, hushed, tranquil, peaceful, calm, soundless. **2.** speechless, dumb, mute; closemouthed, taciturn, uncommunicative, tightlipped, mum, reticent, reserved, secretive, private, discreet, restrained, inhibited, prudent. **3.** inactive, dormant, quiescent, hidden. **4.** unspoken, tacit, implicit, understood, implied, unexpressed.

—**Ant.** noisy, clamorous; voluble, talkative; spoken, stated.

silly, *adj.* **1.** foolish, stupid, idiotic, foolhardy, irresponsible, simple, dopey, vacuous, simpering, birdbrained, dullwitted, dimwitted, witless, childish, puerile, jejune, juvenile, sophomoric, fatuous, unwise, imbecilic, moronic. **2.** absurd, ridiculous, inane, asinine, senseless, ludicrous, laughable, risible, macaronic, frivolous, trivial, nonsensical, preposterous, mad, crazy, insane, irrational, illogical, pointless, idiotic, wishy-washy, insipid.

—**Ant.** sensible, mature, sane, rational, serious.

similar, *adj.* like, alike, identical, akin, analagous, comparable, parallel, homogeneous, equivalent, equal, correspondent, complementary, resembling.

—**Ant.** dissimilar, different, opposite, contradictory, contrary, antithetical.

similarity, *n.* likeness, resemblance, congruity, equivalence, comparability, sameness, analogy, affinity, agreement, correspondence, accordance, harmony, similitude, correspondence, parallelism.

—**Ant.** difference, dissimilarity.

simple, *adj.* **1.** clear, intelligible, uncomplicated, plain, comprehensible, clear, straightforward, easy, elementary, basic, facile, light, effortless, understandable, unmistakable, lucid. **2.** plain, modest, clean, undecorated, unostentatious, unpretentious, uncluttered, stark, classic, severe, austere, homey, Spartan, unadorned, natural, unaffected, unembellished, neat. **3.** unaffected, unassuming, homely, unpretentious. **4.** mere, bare, pure, sheer, absolute, elementary, simplex, uncomplicated. **5.** sincere, frank, candid, open, unaffected, uncomplicated, unpretentious, aboveboard, straightforward, direct, forthright, upright, righteous, honest; undesigning, green, childlike, innocent, natural, artless, naive, guileless, ingenuous, unsophisticated. **6.** humble, inferior, mean, base, common, subservient, subordinate, lowly. **7.** unimportant, insignificant, trifling, trivial, nonessential, unnecessary, immaterial, inconsequential. **8.** common, ordinary, usual, customary. **9.** unlearned, ignorant, uneducated, untutored, dull-wittted, half-witted, slow-witted, simple-minded, feebleminded, thick, bovine, obtuse, dumb, dull, backward, witless, brainless, stupid, dense, silly, naive, foolish, credulous, shallow.

—**Ant.** complicated, complex; fancy, ornate, ostentatious; pretentious; compound; pompous; grand, magisterial; important; unusual; erudite, learned, profound.

simulate, *v.* imitate, mimic, pretend, feign, parrot, ape, copy, assume, affect, counterfeit, act, fake, sham, play-act, put on, dissemble, disguise, cloak, mask.

sin, *n.* **1.** transgression, trespass, violation, crime, infraction, dereliction, misdemeanor, infringement, breach, misdeed, impiety, fault, profanation, desecration, iniquity, evil, sacrilege, peccadillo, foible, failing, frailty, offense, wrong; wickedness, vice, corruption, ungodliness, evil, immorality, depravity, irreverence, guilt. —*v.* **2.** transgress, trespass, do wrong, offend, fall from grace, stray, lapse, go astray, err.

—**Ant.** virtue.

—**Syn. Study.** See CRIME.

sincere, *adj.* candid, honest, open, truthful, aboveboard, straightforward, direct, frank, upfront, on the level, honorable, conscientious, scrupulous, upright, forthright, earnest, guileless, artless, plain, simple; veracious, heartfelt, unequivocal, serious, deep, fervent, hearty, wholehearted, genuine, true, unaffected, real, unfeigned.

—**Ant.** insincere.

—**Syn. Study.** See EARNEST.

sincerity, *n.* honesty, candor, frankness, truthfulness, openness, straightforwardness, forthrightness, seriousness, earnestness, artlessness, veracity, uprightness, trustworthiness, integrity, probity, genuineness, artlessness, ingenuousness, guilelessness.

—**Ant.** insincerity.

—**Syn. Study.** See HONOR.

sinful, *adj.* wicked, iniquitous, depraved, evil, immoral, amoral, corrupt, wrongful, vile, base, profligate, criminal, ungodly, unholy, sacrilegious, irreligious, impious, irreverent, demonic, profane, diabolical, satanic, fiendish, shameful, dissolute, heinous, debased, degenerate, perverted, unrepentant, unregenerate, bad, mischievous, piacular.

sing, *v.* trill, croon, vocalize, carol, lilt, give voice, descant, chant, intone, pipe, belt, warble.

single, *adj.* **1.** separate, only, individual, sole, distinct, particular, singular, solitary, one, lone, unique. **2.** alone, solitary, isolated. **3.** unmarried, unwed, unattached, free. **4.** simple, unmixed, pure, uncompounded, unadulterated. —*n.* **5.** one, individual, monad, singleton.

—**Ant.** accompanied; multiple, together; married, wed, conjugal; adulterated, mixed.

singleminded, *adj.* resolute, firm, resolved, determined, dedicated, devoted, uncompromising, unswerving, unfaltering, persistent, relentless, purposeful, persevering, unwavering, tireless, committed, obstinate, dogged, tenacious.

—**Ant.** undecided, distracted, dilatory.

singular, *adj.* **1.** extraordinary, remarkable, unusual, uncommon, rare, different, abnormal, aberrant, atypical, special, outlandish, offbeat, outré, far-out, strange, peculiar, odd, bizarre, fantastic, peculiar, unusual, eccentric, queer, curious, unaccountable. **2.** outstanding, noteworthy, significant, important, conspicuous, notable, signal, superior, prominent, preeminent, eminent, exceptional, unparalleled, unprecedented. **3.** unique, separate, individual, single, lone, isolated, rare, distinct, unique, one of a kind.

—**Ant.** common, ordinary; mediocre, second-rate; imitative, duplicate.

sinister, *adj.* **1.** threatening, menacing, fateful, foreboding, dark, gloomy, portentous, ominous, inauspicious, unlucky, unfavorable, unpropitious, baleful, malign, malefic, unfortunate, disastrous. **2.** bad, evil, base, wicked, malevolent, malignant, malign, harmful, pernicious, treacherous, nefarious, diabolical, demonic, satanic, sinful, piacular, depraved, corrupt, perverse, spiteful, dishonest, crooked, baleful, villainous, insidious, sneaky, furtive, underhanded.

—**Ant.** benign, favorable, fortunate; good, honest.

sip, *v.* **1.** drink; sample, savor, taste. —*n.* **2.** drink, taste, sample, soupçon, drop, bit, swallow, nip, dram, swig, spoonful, thimbleful, mouthful, shot.

sit, *v.* **1.** be seated, roost, perch, settle down, take a seat, take a load off; rest, relax. **2.** be situated, dwell, settle, lie, rest, remain, abide, repose, stay. **3.** meet, assemble, gather, get together, be in session, convene.

—**Ant.** stand, lie.

situation, *n.* **1.** location, position, setting, site, place, locality, locale, spot. **2.** condition, case, instance, quandary, dilemma, plight, state, status, status quo, state of affairs, lay of the land, juncture, pass, circumstances, predicament. **3.** position, post, job, employment, place, office, berth, appointment, capacity.

size, *n.* **1.** dimensions, proportions, measurements, expanse, range, scope, area, square footage, spread, stretch, amplitude, magnitude, extent; volume, bulk, weight, mass. **2.** immensity, vastness, enormousness, hugeness, greatness.

skeptic, *n.* doubter, questioner, scoffer, cynic, doubting Thomas, disbeliever, agnostic, atheist, infidel, heathen, nullifidian.

—**Ant.** believer, theist.

skeptical, *adj.* skeptic, doubtful, dubious, doubting, questioning, disbelieving, unbelieving, incredulous, mistrustful, distrustful, scoffing, cynical, agnostic.

—**Ant.** trusting, gullible, credulous.

—**Syn. Study.** See DOUBTFUL.

sketch, *n.* **1.** drawing, outline, draft, diagram, tracing, blueprint, plan, schematic, design, delineation. **2.** skit, play, act, routine, stint. —*v.* **3.** depict, draw, diagram, trace, plan, outline, design, rough out, delineate, portray, represent.

sketchy, *adj.* hasty, hurried, imperfect, slight, cursory, incomplete, unfinished, patchy, skimpy, rough, vague, crude, fuzzy, indistinct, ill-defined, unrefined, unpolished, rough-hewn, perfunctory, once-over, slipshod, superficial.
—**Ant.** finished, well-defined, polished.

skill, *n.* **1.** ability, aptitude, talent, expertise, expertness, facility, artistry, art, mastery, handiness, knack, technique, cleverness, adeptness, adroitness, dexterity, ingenuity, proficiency, deftness, quickness, cunning, craft, artifice, efficiency, effectiveness, readiness, facility, ease. **2.** capability, strength, gift, faculty, know-how, accomplishment, forte.
—**Ant.** clumsiness, inability; weakness, failure.

skillful, *adj.* skilled, expert, ready, able, talented, capable, adroit, deft, adept, proficient, efficient, effective, dexterous, competent, qualified, practiced, masterly, masterful, gifted, accomplished, apt, clever, ingenious, resourceful, creative, knowledgeable, professional, trained, experienced, conversant, versed.
—**Ant.** unskillful, inexpert, maladroit, awkward, inept, unqualified.
—**Syn. Study.** SKILLFUL, SKILLED, EXPERT refer to ability or competence in an occupation, craft, or art. SKILLFUL suggests adroitness and dexterity: *a skillful watchmaker.* SKILLED implies having had long experience and thus having acquired a high degree of proficiency: *not an amateur but a skilled worker.* EXPERT means having the highest degree of proficiency; it may mean much the same as SKILLFUL or SKILLED, or both: *expert workmanship.*

skin, *n.* **1.** hide, pelt, fur, fleece, epidermis, derma, integument. **2.** covering, peel, rind, hull, bark, shell, husk, crust, coat, coating, outside, incrustation, pellicle, veneer, lamina, overlay, outer layer, film, membrane. —*v.* **3.** flay, peel, hull, shell, pare, strip, husk, excoriate, decorticate.

skinny, *adj.* thin, bony, underweight, slim, slender, lean, slight, narrow, lanky, lank, gaunt, gangling, gangly, rawboned, scraggy, spare, anemic, emaciated, starved, half-starved, anorexic, anorectic, undernourished, pinched, hollow-cheeked, haggard, wasted, shrunken, angular, skeletal, scrawny, wiry; cadaverous, all skin and bones.
—**Ant.** fleshy, fat, obese, corpulent, zaftig.

skip, *v.* **1.** spring, jump, gambol, cavort, frisk, prance, romp, dance, leap, bound, caper, hop. **2.** omit, overlook, avoid, ignore, cut, steer clear of, disregard, skip over, skim over, leave out, pass by. —*n.* **3.** leap, cavort, gambol, frisk, prance, romp, jump, spring, bound, caper, hop, dance.

skirmish, *n.* encounter, brush, action, battle, fight, engagement, confrontation, showdown, struggle, set-to, contest, conflict, combat, brush, fray, clash, fracas, melee, scrap, tussle, dust-up.

skittish, *adj.* **1.** uneasy, restless, restive, impatient, unquiet, hectic, feverish, sensitive, nervous, tense, agitated, flustered, ruffled, jittery, fretful, uptight, shaky, on pins and needles, in a dither *or* tizzy, anxious, jumpy, quivery, flighty, fidgety, edgy, fluttery, excitable, high-strung. **2.** unconfident, self-conscious, cowardly, craven, shy, timid, bashful, timorous, coy. **3.** frisky, lively, giddy, frivolous, whimsical, capricious. **4.** unpredictable, uncertain, variable, fickle, erratic, fitful, volatile, mercurial, unreliable, fluctuating, unstable. **5.** cautious, guarded, suspicious, apprehensive, leery, wary, chary, hesitant.
—**Ant.** down-to-earth, stable, calm, confident, resolute, determined.

skulk, *v.* lurk, slink, sneak, hide, prowl, steal, lie low, creep, slip, tiptoe, pussyfoot, lie in wait.
—**Ant.** emerge, appear.
—**Syn. Study.** See LURK.

slack, *adj.* **1.** loose, relaxed, limp, droopy, sagging, flaccid, floppy, soft, baggy. **2.** indolent, slothful, negligent, lazy, remiss, careless, lax, neglectful, delinquent, inattentive. **3.** slow, sluggish, dilatory, tardy, late, lingering, laggard, easygoing, slothful, sluggish, lethargic, shiftless. **4.** dull, inactive, blunted, idle, quiet. —*n.* **5.** decrease, decline, lull, pause, cutback, lessening, reduction, abatement, downturn, dwindling, lag, slowing, loosening; relaxation, indolence, negligence, laziness, remissness, laxness, inattentiveness, delinquency, lethargy, sloth. —*v.* **6.** shirk, neglect, goldbrick, malinger, loaf, idle, goof off, lollygag. **7.** relax, ease up, let up on, decline, decrease, diminish, weaken, abate, reduce, slacken, moderate, mitigate.
—**Ant.** tight, tense, taut; diligent, industrious, busy, expeditious, quick.

slacken, *v.* **1.** loosen, relax, relieve, abate, mitigate, moderate, temper, qualify, remit, lessen, diminish. **2.** restrain, inhibit, delay, retard, slow, detain, check, curb, bridle, repress, subdue, control.
—**Ant.** quicken.

slant, *v.* **1.** slope, lean, incline, tilt, angle, pitch, cant, bend, list, tip. —*n.* **2.** tilt, ramp, gradient, deflection, leaning, lean, angle, cant, incline, inclination, pitch, slope, obliquity, obliqueness. **3.** bent, leaning, prejudice, bias, inclination, partiality, turn, one-sidedness. **4.** viewpoint, angle, spin, attitude, approach, standpoint, aspect, idea, twist.

slapdash, *adj.* careless, slipshod, sketchy, perfunctory, rough, crude, patchy, skimpy, sloppy, haphazard, any which way, hit or miss, hurried, hasty, superficial, cursory, lick and a promise, quick and dirty, once over lightly.
—**Ant.** careful, meticulous.

slash, *v.* **1.** cut, slit, slice, gash, hack, score, knife, lacerate, scar, wound, pierce, enter, penetrate. **2.** cut, reduce, decrease, drop, lower, trim, alter, abridge, abbreviate. —*n.* **3.** stroke, cut, wound, gash, slit, incision, slice, gouge, tear, rip, laceration, piercing, penetration, opening, slit, hole.

slaughter, *n.* **1.** killing, butchering, butchery, massacre, carnage, homicide, murder, manslaughter, slaying, execution, sacrifice, bloodshed, genocide, bloodletting, blood bath, extermination, liquidation, pogrom. —*v.* **2.** butcher, execute, exterminate, liquidate, destroy, put to death, persecute, massacre, murder, slay, kill, wipe out, devastate, decimate.
—**Syn. Study.** SLAUGHTER, BUTCHER, MASSACRE all imply violent and bloody methods of killing when applied to human beings. SLAUGHTER and BUTCHER emphasize brutal or indiscriminate killing: *to slaughter enemy soldiers in battle; to butcher tribal peoples.* MASSACRE indicates a wholesale destruction of helpless or unresisting victims: *to massacre an entire village.*

slave, *n.* lackey, peon, drudge, workhorse, laborer, toiler, grind, hack, dogsbody, gofer; scullion, odalisque, helot, bondswoman, bondsman, bondservant, esne, thrall, villein, serf, vassal.
—**Ant.** master.

slavery, *n.* **1.** enslavement, bondage, servitude, serfdom, vassalage, thralldom, subjection, captivity, yoke, enthrallment. **2.** toil, drudgery, exertion, pains, chores, travail, grind, strain, sweat, hard labor, laboriousness, labor, donkey work, hack work, scut work.
—**Syn. Study.** SLAVERY, BONDAGE, SERVITUDE refer to involuntary subjection to another or others. SLAVERY emphasizes the idea of complete ownership and control by a master: *to be sold into slavery.* BONDAGE indicates a state of subjugation or captivity often involving burdensome and degrading labor: *in bondage to a cruel master.* SERVITUDE is compulsory service, often such as is required by a legal penalty: *penal servitude.*

slavish, *adj.* **1.** submissive, abject, passive, sheepish, docile, obedient, subservient, craven, deferential, toadying, servile, groveling, menial, drudging, obsequious, fawning, sycophantic, cringing. **2.** base, mean, ignoble, sordid, low, inferior, slimy, unctuous, smarmy.
—**Ant.** independent; elevated, exalted.
—**Syn. Study.** See SERVILE.

sleek, *adj.* smooth, slick, glossy, polished, lustrous, shiny, silky, silken, velvety, velvet, satiny, satin, glabrous; bright, lustrous, brilliant, even; suave, urbane, well-groomed, elegant, trim, graceful, streamlined, svelte.

sleep, *v.* **1.** rest, repose, slumber, catnap, nap, drowse, doze, drop off, snore, snooze, catch forty winks, catch some Z's. —*n.* **2.** dormancy, inactivity; slumber, rest, repose, nap, catnap, doze, siesta, forty winks, beauty sleep.

slender, *adj.* **1.** slight, slim, thin, lean, willowy, sylphlike, svelte, lissome, lithe, graceful, lanky, spare, narrow. **2.** slim, slight, little, scanty, small, trivial, meager, trifling, insignificant, inadequate, insufficient. **3.** thin, weak, slim, narrow, slight, poor, unlikely, remote, small, meager, puny, feeble, flimsy.
—**Ant.** large, fat, obese, corpulent; substantial; likely, certain.
—**Syn. Study.** SLENDER, SLIGHT, SLIM imply a tendency toward thinness. As applied to the human body, SLENDER implies a generally attractive and pleasing thinness: *slender hands.* SLIGHT often adds the idea of frailness to that of thinness: *a slight, almost fragile, figure.* SLIM implies a lithe or delicate thinness: *a slim and athletic figure.*

slide, *v.* slip, slither, glide, coast, skim, skate, glissade, skid, sled, toboggan, creep, slink; drop, fall, decline, decrease.

slight, *adj.* **1.** small, insignificant, superficial, shallow, trivial, nugatory, negligible, minor, unlikely, inconsequential, tenuous, paltry, unimportant. **2.** slender, slim, petite, delicate, diminutive, tiny, short, miniature, wee, bantam, pint-sized. **3.** unstable, insubstantial, insecure, inadequate, rickety, precarious, dainty, frail, flimsy, weak, feeble, delicate, fragile. **4.** unsubstantial, inconsiderable, infinitesimal, trifling, minute, tiny, slender. —*v.* **5.** ignore, disregard, omit, forget, reject, disrespect, neglect, disdain, overlook, shun, snub, rebuff, cut, cold-shoulder, despise, flout, scoff at, scorn, (*slang*) dis. —*n.* **6.** neglect, disregard, disdain, indifference, snub, coldness, rebuff, rejection, scorn, contumely, contempt, inattention. **7.** affront, insult, disrespect, slur, offense, indignity, outrage.
—**Ant.** considerable; compliment, welcome, honor.
—**Syn. Study.** SLIGHT, DISREGARD, NEGLECT, OVERLOOK mean to pay no attention or too little attention to someone or something. To SLIGHT is to ignore or treat as unimportant: *to slight one's neighbors.* To DISREGARD is to ignore or treat without due respect: *to disregard the rules.* To NEGLECT is to fail in one's duty toward a person or thing: *to neglect one's correspondence.* To OVERLOOK is to fail to notice or consider someone or something, possibly because of carelessness: *to overlook a bill that is due.* See INSULT. See also SLENDER.

slim, *adj.* **1.** slender, thin, slight, lean, spare, scrawny, bony, skinny, svelte, lithe, lanky, lissome, graceful, willowy, sylphlike. **2.** small, poor, slight, insignificant, trifling, trivial, nugatory, unimportant, paltry, meager, inadequate, remote, negligible, minor, feeble, flimsy, tenuous, inconsiderable, scanty, weak, thin, unsubstantial.
—**Ant.** fat; considerable, substantial.
—**Syn. Study.** See SLENDER.

slip, *v.* **1.** slide, skid, slither, glide. **2.** be mistaken, err, blunder, make a mistake, miscalculate, go astray *or* wrong, transgress, sin, mess up. —*n.* **3.** mistake, error, blunder, fault, inadvertance, blooper, lapse, boner, carelessness, negligence, oversight; faux pas, indiscretion, gaffe, impropriety, transgression, sin, peccadillo, backsliding.
—**Syn. Study.** See MISTAKE.

slippery, *adj.* **1.** slick, smooth, lubricious, slithery, oily, lubricated, glassy, sleek, icy, slimy, greased. **2.** risky, precarious, dangerous, hazardous, unsafe, ticklish. **3.** changeable, volatile, mutable, unstable, shifting, uncertain. **4.** untrustworthy, shifty, tricky, unreliable, undependable, treacherous, perfidious, disloyal, dishonest, deceitful, devious, evasive, wily, slick, crafty, sly, foxy, cunning, sneaky, shady, slimy, smarmy, cagey.

slope, *v., n.* slant, incline, decline, rise, fall, dip, sink, drop, angle, pitch, tip, tilt.

sloppy, *adj.* slovenly, slatternly, frowzy, blowzy, untidy, messy, dirty, grungy, disorderly, careless, loose, bedraggled, disheveled, unkempt, dowdy, frumpy, shabby, scruffy, unwashed, unclean, disorganized, cluttered, haphazard, topsy-turvy, in disarray, unorganized, lax, hit or miss, slipshod, slapdash, negligent, slack, remiss, indifferent, unconcerned.
—**Ant.** careful, fastidious, tidy, neat, well-groomed, organized, methodical, meticulous.

slothful, *adj.* idle, sluggardly, indolent, lazy, sluggish, inactive, inert, dilatory, shirking, dronish, goldbricking, lethargic, apathetic, phlegmatic, indifferent, lax, shiftless, donothing, slow, laggard, languorous, languid, lackadaisical, layabout, torpid, slack, supine.
—**Ant.** industrious, busy, diligent, active, energetic.
—**Syn. Study.** See IDLE.

slow, *adj.* **1.** deliberate, gradual, leisurely, progressive, measurable, perceptible, by degrees, moderate. **2.** lazy, sluggish, sluggardly, dilatory, indolent, lazy, slothful, laggard, torpid, dawdling, leaden, ponderous, plodding, snail-like, tortoiselike, creeping, crawling; unhurried, leisurely, easy, relaxed, restful, lackadaisical. **3.** dull, dense, stupid, unintelligent, thick, dumb, simple, simpleminded, obtuse, backward, dimwitted, bovine, unresponsive, cloddish, doltish, unimaginative, stolid, slow on the uptake, not too swift. **4.** slack, inactive, quiet, unproductive, sluggish. **5.** dragging, late, unpunctual, delayed, dilatory, lagging, tardy, behindhand. **6.** tiresome, wearisome, monotonous, tame, uneventful, dead, dry, ennuyant, soporific, sleepy, somnolent, uninteresting, tedious, humdrum, dull, boring. —*v.* **7.** retard, hinder, impede, obstruct; slack off, hold back, take it easy, ease up, relax.

—Ant. fast; energetic, industrious; hurried, rapid, swift; quick, quick-witted; busy; punctual; lively, eventful, exciting, invigorating; advance, promote; hurry, race.

—Syn. Study. SLOW, DELIBERATE, GRADUAL, LEISURELY mean unhurried or not happening rapidly. SLOW means acting or moving without haste: *a slow procession of cars.* DELIBERATE implies the slowness that marks careful consideration: *a deliberate and calculating manner.* GRADUAL suggests the slowness of something that advances one step at a time: *a gradual improvement.* LEISURELY means moving with the slowness allowed by ample time or the absence of pressure: *a leisurely stroll.*

sluggish, *adj.* inactive, slow, lazy, lethargic, languid, languorous, laggard, lax, sluggardly, dilatory, shiftless, slack, do-nothing, lackadaisical, slothful, indolent, dull, inert, torpid, dronish, stuperous, comatose, phlegmatic, indifferent, apathetic, soporific, sleepy, somnolent, lifeless, limp, tired, drowsy.

—Ant. quick, active, energetic.

slur, *v.* **1.** slight, disregard, pass over, gloss over, give short shrift, ignore, overlook. **2.** affront, smear, insult, offend, brand, stigmatize, slight, calumniate, disparage, slander, depreciate, asperse. —*n.* **3.** smear, calumny, aspersion, discredit, insinuation, imputation, putdown, slander, libel, disparagement, slight, innuendo, insult, affront, blot, stain, stigma, brand, black mark, disgrace.

—Ant. compliment, praise.

sly, *adj.* **1.** cunning, wily, artful, foxy, crafty, clever, guileful, astute, scheming, designing, conniving, tricky, shrewd, deceitful, disingenuous. **2.** stealthy, surreptitious, furtive, insidious, secret, underhanded, crooked, devious, covert, sneaky, shady, shifty, subtle, clandestine. **3.** naughty, impish, devilish, arch, waggish, puckish, mischievous, roguish.

—Ant. direct, straightforward, guileless, ingenuous.

small, *adj.* **1.** little, tiny, diminutive, short, petite, mignonne, miniature, minute, minuscule, midget, mini, elfin, Lilliputian, baby, bantam, undersized, pint-sized, peewee. **2.** slender, slim, petite, skinny, thin, slight, narrow. **3.** unimportant, trivial, minor, slight, secondary, lesser, trifling, trivial, nugatory, inconsequential, petty, paltry, insignificant, puny, negligible; limited, diminished, reduced. **4.** uninspired, shallow, unoriginal, unimaginative, flat, commonplace, mundane, everyday. **5.** mean-spirited, mean, stingy, ungenerous, parsimonious, niggardly, selfish, tight, illiberal, narrow, skimpy, uncharitable, scanty, meager, cheap, petty, stinting, grudging, miserly, tightfisted, tight, close. **6.** foolish, humiliated, embarrassed, chagrined, disconcerted, uncomfortable, ashamed, mortified, abashed.

—Ant. large.

small-minded, *adj.* **1.** narrow-minded, narrow, small, illiberal, selfish, stingy, grudging, ungenerous, uncharitable, mean, petty, closeminded, bigoted, hidebound, rigid, puritanical, shortsighted, myopic, unimaginative, intolerant. **2.** provincial, parochial, insular, limited, confined.

—Ant. liberal, broadminded, tolerant, flexible, free-thinking, imaginative, urbane.

smarmy, *adj.* **1.** insincere, false, sly, deceitful, guileful, disingenuous, hypocritical, mealymouthed, sanctimonious **2.** suave, sleek, smug, insinuating, unctuous, slimy, fulsome, oily. **3.** obsequious, servile, toadying, brown-nosing, bootlicking, craven, wheedling, flattering, sycophantic, ingratiating.

smart, *v.* **1.** pain, hurt, sting, pinch, ache, throb, burn, prickle, tingle, stab, pierce. **2.** hurt, wound, insult, affront. —*adj.* **3.** quick, swift, sharp, keen, stinging, poignant, penetrating, painful, severe. **4.** brisk, vigorous, active, energetic, effective, animated, spirited, perky, breezy, lively. **5.** quick, prompt, nimble, agile, alert, active. **6.** intelligent, astute, brilliant, adept, quick-witted, acute, ingenious, capable, apt, bright, sharp, clever, expert, adroit. **7.** canny, perceptive, discerning, witty, trenchant, knowledgeable, erudite, aware, shrewd, cunning, streetwise, savvy, hip, with it. **8.** neat, trim, dashing, spruce, jaunty. **9.** elegant, chic, fashionable, voguish, à la mode, modish, stylish, soignée, well-groomed, dapper.

—Ant. mild, gentle; sluggish, slow; dull, stupid, slow-witted; witless, imperceptive; unfashionable, dowdy, frumpy.

smell, *n.* odor, scent, aroma, fragrance, perfume, bouquet, whiff; stink, stench, reek, fetor, fetidness, effluvium, noxiousness.

smitten, *adj.* enamored, captivated, enthralled, enchanted, enraptured, charmed, infatuated, bewitched, beguiled, lovestruck, moonstruck, besotted, doting, gaga, swept off one's feet, bowled over, on cloud nine.

—Ant. repelled, antipathetic.

smooth, *adj.* **1.** level, even, plain, regular, flush, plane, flat. **2.** bald, hairless, naked, bare, cleanshaven, depilated. **3.** flat, unruffled, calm, undisturbed, calm, peaceful, tranquil, pacific, peaceable. **4.** elegant, polished, fluent, facile, honey-tongued, syrupy, eloquent, diplomatic, glib, voluble, soft-spoken, slippery, slick, slimy, suave, unctuous, persuasive, charming, urbane, winning, plausible, nonchalant. **5.** pleasant, agreeable, polite, courtly, courteous. —*v.* **6.** sand, plane, stroke, polish, buff, refine, burnish, scrape; level, press, flatten, iron, roll, even out. **7.** tranquilize, ameliorate, allay, minimize, mitigate, lessen, reduce, temper, calm, soothe, assuage, mollify, better, gloss over, palliate, soften, appease.

—Ant. rough, uneven, irregular; hairy; wrinkled, rumpled, disturbed; bluff, brusque.

smug, *adj.* complacent, self-satisfied, hypocritical, pharisaical, holier than thou, sanctimonious, arrogant, haughty, conceited, self-centered, egotistical, self-important, overconfident, condescending, self-righteous, overweening, opinionated, superior, cavalier, pompous, highhanded.

—Ant. humble, modest.

snare, *n.* **1.** trap, noose, net, seine, springe, pitfall, boobytrap, ambush, lure, bait, decoy; trick, ruse, wile, stratagem, subterfuge, deception, chicanery. —*v.* **2.** trap, entrap, entangle, catch, seize, capture, net, bag; lure, entice, decoy, inveigle, seduce, tempt, captivate.

sneak, *v.* **1.** slink, lurk, skulk, steal, creep, cower, prowl, sidle, pussyfoot. —*n.* **2.** sneaker, prowler, lurker; informer, rat, tattletale, nark, stoolpigeon, stoolie, snitch, fink.

—Syn. Study. See LURK.

sneaky, *adj.* underhanded, devious, sly, cunning, wily, secretive, unscrupulous, shifty, slippery, slimy, furtive, disingenuousness, deceitful, dishonest, clandestine, covert, undercover, insidious, artful, untrustworthy, misleading, insincere, guileful, crafty, scheming, duplicitous, lying, cheating, double-dealing.

—Ant. forthright, aboveboard, trustworthy, sincere.

sneer, *v.* **1.** smirk, curl one's lip, sniff; scorn, jeer, gibe, scoff, despise, mock, flout, disdain, deride, ridicule, criticize, underrate. —*n.* **2.** scorn, contempt, mockery, ridicule, scoff, gibe, jeer, derision, disdain.

—Syn. Study. See SCOFF.

snide, *adj.* derogatory, nasty, mean, deprecatory, denigrating, disparaging, belittling, demeaning, offensive, insulting, hurtful, spiteful, abusive, churlish, surly, cruel, insinuating, vicious, slanderous, libelous.

—Ant. complimentary, favorable.

snobbish, *adj.* pretentious, affected, pompous, self-important, self-satisfied, haughty, supercilious, lordly, conceited, vain, arrogant, self-centered, egotistical, smug, superior, lofty, condescending, patronizing, disdainful, scornful, contemptuous, presumptuous, snooty, snotty, uppity, highfalutin, high and mighty, hoity-toity, stuck-up, high-hat, social-climbing, overweening, putting on airs.

—Ant. egalitarian, humble, unaffected, modest.

snub, *v.* **1.** disdain, humiliate, humble, slight, scorn, shun, ignore, avoid, cold-shoulder, high-hat, rebuff, cut, disregard, overlook, deny, spurn, refuse, dismiss, repudiate, brushoff, reject, put down, freeze (someone) out. —*n.* **2.** rebuke, rebuff, rejection, denial, refusal, dismissal, repudiation, putdown, brushoff, cut, cold shoulder, slight, affront, insult.

—Ant. accept, welcome.

soak, *v.* **1.** steep, drench, wet, sop, immerse, douse, bathe, inundate, waterlog, saturate. **2.** permeate, osmose, penetrate, impregnate.

—Ant. dry.

soar, *v.* **1.** fly, glide, rise, hover, float, hang. **2.** tower, rise, rocket, surge, levitate, dart, shoot, ascend, mount; increase, climb, escalate, spiral upward, skyrocket, shoot up.

sober, *adj.* **1.** unintoxicated; temperate, continent, abstinent, abstemious, dry, on the wagon, teetotaling, nonindulgent. **2.** serious, grave, solemn, quiet, sedate, somber, plain, simple, repressed, dreary, gloomy, subdued, staid. **3.** calm, serene, tranquil, peaceful, cool, moderate, dignified, cool, composed, unexcited, unimpassioned, unruffled, collected, dispassionate, unconcerned, reasonable, rational, earnest, steady, levelheaded, balanced, practical, realistic, controlled, sane, sound. **4.** somber, drab, colorless, dreary, dull, neutral, dark.

—Ant. drunk; frivolous, flippant, wild; immoderate.

—Syn. Study. See GRAVE.

sociable, *adj.* social, friendly, affable, approachable, gregarious, outgoing, extroverted, amiable, amicable, congenial, convivial, cordial, neighborly, chummy.

—Ant. unsociable, unfriendly.

social, *adj.* sociable, friendly, amiable, companionable, genial, affable, accessible, cooperative, convivial, hospitable, familiar.

—Ant. antisocial, unfriendly.

society, *n.* **1.** organization, association, circle, fellowship, club, league, institute, alliance, academy, guild, union, group, order, fraternity, brotherhood, sorority, sisterhood, sodality, company, partnership, corporation. **2.** community, culture, civilization, world; organization, system; humankind, people, the public. **3.** companionship, company, fellowship, sodality, camaraderie, friendship.

soft, *adj.* **1.** yielding, cushiony, spongy, squeezable, plushy, compressible, flexible, pliant, supple, pliable, plastic, moldable, malleable, impressible. **2.** smooth, agreeable, delicate. **3.** muted, quiet, mellow, faint, soothing, smooth, gentle, low, subdued, melodious, mellifluous, dulcet, sweet, pleasing, pleasant, flowing. **4.** gentle, mild, balmy, moderate, halcyon, summery, springlike, restful, relaxing, lazy, genial. **5.** gentle, mild, lenient, easy-going, tolerant, kind, merciful, indulgent, permissive, liberal, lax, easy, benign, compassionate, tender, sympathetic. **6.** smooth, soothing, ingratiating, mollifying. **7.** impressionable, yielding, compliant, flexible, irresolute, submissive, deferential, tame, undecided, weak, delicate, sensitive. **8.** weak, feeble, frail, effete, delicate, puny, flabby, poor, wishy-washy.

—Ant. hard, inflexible, unyielding, harsh, rough.

soften, *v.* **1.** melt, affect, mollify, mellow, soothe, relax, appease, palliate, tenderize. **2.** appease, assuage, mollify, moderate, mitigate, modify, soothe, alleviate, diminish, reduce, cushion, lessen, relieve, calm, quell, still, quiet, ease, allay, lighten, abate, qualify, temper, blunt, dull.

—Ant. harden.

solace, *n.* **1.** comfort, alleviation, condolence, succor, support, help, reassurance, cheer, consolation, relief. —*v.* **2.** comfort, console, cheer, soothe, condole, support, succor, reassure, hearten; gladden, delight, please, gratify. **3.** relieve, alleviate, soothe, mitigate, ameliorate, alleviate, lighten, assuage, allay, soften.

—Ant. aggrieve, aggravate.

sole, *adj.* only, single, solitary, alone, lone, singular, personal, exclusive, select, individual, unattended, unique, separate, particular.

solemn, *adj.* **1.** grave, sober, reserved, earnest, sedate, staid, taciturn, mirthless, unsmiling, morose, morbid, gloomy, grim, somber, glum, serious. **2.** impressive, awe-inspiring, awesome, momentous, moving, sublime, superb, august, imposing, venerable, grand, majestic, pompous, stately. **3.** formal, stately, conventional, plenary, dignified, serious, ceremonious, ritual, ceremonial. **4.** religious, holy, divine, sacramental, liturgical, ecclesiastical, hallowed, reverential, devotional, sacred, ritualistic.

—Ant. jovial; unimpressive; informal; profane.

—Syn. Study. See GRAVE.

solicit, *v.* seek, entreat, ask for, request, apply for, beseech, pray, beg, importune, urge, implore, crave, supplicate, sue, petition, appeal to.

solid, *adj.* **1.** three-dimensional, cubic. **2.** dense, compact, firm, hard, stable, concrete, concentrated, consolidated, compacted. **3.** unbroken, continuous, undivided, unrelieved, complete, whole, entire, uniform. **4.** firm, cohesive, compact. **5.** dense, thick, tough, sturdy, firm, durable, rugged, heavy, substantial, sound, stable, dependable, well-made, stout. **6.** real, genuine, complete, sound, good. **7.** sober-minded, sober, cogent, weighty, valid, reasonable, authoritative, incontrovertible, irrefutable, powerful, forceful, convincing, persuasive, sensible. **8.** thorough, vigorous, dynamic, telling, powerful, effective, forceful, mighty, intensive, downright, firm, strong, great, stout. **9.** united, consolidated, unanimous. **10.** successful, solvent, wealthy, rich; reliable, honorable, law-abiding, steady, stable, stalwart, steadfast, upstanding, upright, estimable, worthy, dependable, sober, well-established, sound, trustworthy, honest, sure, safe.

—Ant. flat, two-dimensional; fluid, liquid; loose; divided; sparse; counterfeit; weak; separate; unsuccessful.

solitary, *adj.* **1.** unaccompanied, solo, unattended, alone, friendless, single, sole, individual, unsocial, lonesome, forlorn, lone, lonely. **2.** isolated, retired, reclusive, hermetic, withdrawn, distant, desolate, out-of-the-way, forsaken, abandoned, lonely, deserted, unfrequented, remote, secluded.

solitude, *n.* **1.** seclusion, isolation, solitariness, aloneness, withdrawal, retreat, remoteness, loneliness, retirement, privacy, refuge, asylum. **2.** desert, waste, wilderness, emptiness.

somber, *adj.* **1.** gloomy, dark, foreboding, bleak, leaden, dreary, overcast, shadowy, dim, unlighted, dusky, murky, cloudy, dull, sunless, dismal. **2.** depressing, depressed, morose, sad, cheerless, joyless, unsmiling, grave, gloomy, grim-faced, long-faced, saturnine, dismal, lugubrious, mournful, dolorous, doleful, funereal, melancholy.

—Ant. cheerful.

soothe, *v.* **1.** tranquilize, pacify, solace, calm, relieve, comfort, refresh. **2.** allay, mitigate, assuage, alleviate, appease, mollify, soften, lull, quell, quiet, ease, lighten, palliate.

—Ant. upset, disturb.

—Syn. Study. See COMFORT.

sophisticated, *adj.* **1.** cosmopolitan, urbane, suave, polished, elegant, refined, cultured, cultivated, experienced, knowledgeable, knowing, soigné, blasé, worldly-wise, savvy, knowing, worldly. **2.** advanced, complex, multifaceted, highly developed, complicated, intricate, elaborate, fancy, subtle, high-tech, modern, contemporary, sleek, streamlined, improved, cutting-edge, fashionable, trendy, voguish, modish, in style, hot, deluxe, posh, elegant, high-class, superior, chic, smart, up-to-date, up-to-the-minute, exclusive.

—Ant. unsophisticated.

sorcery, *n.* magic, wizardry, witchery, enchantment, witchcraft, spell, necromancy, divination, charm, alchemy, shamanism, black art, satanism.

sordid, *adj.* **1.** dirty, filthy, soiled, unclean, foul, squalid, unsanitary, polluted, fetid, maggoty, flyblown, putrid, slimy, slummy, seamy, seedy, mean, wretched, sleazy. **2.** mean, abject, ignoble, amoral, degraded, depraved, corrupt, vile, debased, ignominious, shameful, dishonorable, despicable, disreputable, shabby, scurvy, rotten, scurvy, low, base. **3.** selfish, self-seeking, mercenary, avaricious, stingy, tight, close, close-fisted, greedy, grasping, swinish, rapacious, money-grubbing, materialistic, venal, cheap, miserly, niggardly.

—Ant. clean; honorable; generous.

sore, *adj.* **1.** painful, sensitive, tender, raw, inflamed, smarting, chafed, burning, hurting, throbbing, irritated. **2.** grieved, distressed, upset, irritated, irked, agitated, disturbed, perturbed, ruffled, aggrieved, sorrowful, hurt, pained, depressed, vexed. **3.** grievous, distressing, painful, depressing, severe, sharp, troublesome, harrowing, agonizing, bitter, onerous, heavy, burdensome, fierce, oppressive. **—*n.* 4.** injury, damage, swelling, rawness, inflammation, bruise, abrasion, cut, laceration, scrape, burn, infection, abscess, wound, ulcer, pustule, boil, cancer, canker.

—Ant. tough.

sorrow, *n.* **1.** heartache, heartbreak, torment, agony, dolor, unhappiness, desolation, mourning, grieving, sadness, depression, dejection, melancholy, distress, anxiety, anguish, grief, sadness, woe, suffering, misery, wretchedness, regret. **2.** affliction, adversity, trouble, trial, tribulation, hardship, hard luck, cares, strain, misfortune. **—*v.* 3.** grieve, mourn, bemoan, regret, agonize, moan, suffer, cry, weep, wail, sob, groan, bewail, lament.

—Ant. joy, gladness, delight.

sorrowful, *adj.* **1.** grief-stricken, grieved, sad, unhappy, melancholy, gloomy, downcast, blue, dispirited, heartsick, broken-hearted, heavy-hearted, disconsolate, inconsolable, depressed, dejected, aggrieved, afflicted, mournful, regretful, sorry, crestfallen, wretched, rueful, woeful, tearful, plaintive. **2.** distressing, grievous, lamentable, dismal, dreary, doleful, unfortunate, bitter, unlucky, hapless, sorry.

—Ant. happy; lucky.

sorry, *adj.* **1.** regretful, penitent, repentant, apologetic, remorseful, contrite, guilt-ridden, conscience-stricken. **2.** pitiable, miserable, deplorable, abject, depressing, wretched, pathetic, dismal, sordid, grim, star-crossed, unfortunate, sad, grievous, painful. **3.** sorrowful, grieved, sad, unhappy, melancholy, depressed. **4.** wretched, poor, mean, pitiful, base, ignoble, sordid, low, vile, abject; contemptible, bad, scurvy, despicable; paltry, worthless, shabby, petty, trifling, trivial.

—Ant. happy.

—Syn. Study. See MISERABLE.

sort, *n.* **1.** kind, species, classification, category, brand, make, mark, stamp, mold, stripe, ilk, variety, class, group, family, description, order, race, rank, character, description, nature, type. **2.** character, quality, nature. **3.** example, pattern, sample, exemplar. **4.** manner, fashion, way, method, means, style. **—*v.* 5.** arrange, assort, organize, systematize, catalogue, group, pigeonhole, order, classify, class, file, rank, grade, categorize, combine, merge, alphabetize, separate, divide, distribute.

soul, *n.* spirit, anima, breath, vital force, being, inner *or* true self, essence, psyche, heart, mind, intellect, reason, brain, brains, intelligence, wit, wits, powers, faculties, emotions, vitality, animation, life, consciousness.

—Ant. body.

sound, *n.* **1.** noise, tone, din, cacophony, ring. **—*v.* 2.** resound, echo, reverberate, resonate. **3.** utter, articulate, voice, vocalize, enunciate, pronounce, express. **4.** plumb, test, check, question, probe, examine, inspect, survey, investigate, fathom, ascertain, determine. **—*adj.* 5.** undamaged, intact, in good shape, unscathed, uninjured, unharmed, unbroken, whole, entire, complete, intact, perfect, unimpaired. **6.** healthy, fit, blooming, rosy-cheeked, wholesome, strong, hale, hearty, robust, hardy, vigorous. **7.** solvent, secure, well-established, safe, conservative, nonspeculative, riskless. **8.** reliable, dependable, trustworthy, responsible, right-minded, upstanding, solid, loyal, virtuous, honest, honorable. **9.** true, truthful, just, fair, judicious, reasonable, rational, sane, sensible, balanced, lucid, logical, practical, prudent, wise, common-sense. **10.** enduring, substantial, firm, solid, strong, sturdy, tough, rugged, durable, reliable, dependable, well-constructed. **11.** correct, orthodox, right, proper. **12.** unbroken, deep, profound, uninterrupted, untroubled, peaceful, fast, undisturbed.

—Ant. silence; damaged; unhealthy; unreliable; risky; irrational; unstable, flimsy, jerry-built; improper; fitful, troubled, disturbed.

sour, *adj.* **1.** acid, acidic, vinegary, lemony, acerbic, bitter, astringent, tart. **2.** fermented, turned, spoiled, curdled, rancid, bad, gone off. **3.** distasteful, disagreeable, unpleasant, nasty, bad, terrible, regrettable, unhappy, bitter. **4.** harsh, embittered, bitter, churlish, curmudgeonly, grouchy, curt, caustic, brusque, gloomy, edgy, sullen, glum, dour, saturnine, vexatious, spiteful, ill-tempered, bad-tempered, austere, severe, morose, peevish, testy, short-tempered, hot-tempered, touchy, acrimonious, cross, petulant, crabbed, snappish, waspish, uncivil, rude, crude, rough.

—Ant. sweet, pleasant, delightful; good-natured, cheerful.

sovereign, *n.* **1.** monarch, king, queen, emperor, empress, prince, princess; chief, head, master, mistress, lady, lord, ruler, potentate. **—*adj.* 2.** regal, royal, majestic, princely, imperial, noble, lordly, aristocrat, monarchical, queenly, kingly. **3.** supreme, chief, highest, foremost, ranking, leading, commanding, directing, superior, ruling, preponderant, preeminent, reigning, governing, absolute, omnipotent, all-powerful, transcendent, surpassing, ultimate, paramount, principal, dominant, predominant. **4.** utmost, extreme, greatest. **5.** potent, effective, efficacious, effectual.

—Ant. dependent.

spacious, *adj.* **1.** ample, large, enormous, commodious, sizable, voluminous, outsize, oversize, capacious, roomy, wide. **2.** extensive, vast, huge, extended, tremendous, broad, great, immense, enormous, broad, wide, deep.

—Ant. small, cramped, restricted, claustrophobic.

span, *n.* **1.** distance, amount, piece, length, extent. **2.** extension, reach, extent, stretch, period, course, interval, time, term, spell. **—*v.* 3.** bridge, extend over, reach, pass over, stretch across, cross, compass.

spare, *v.* **1.** forgo, sacrifice, avoid, dispense with, manage, without, surrender. **2.** save, rescue, redeem, deliver; pardon, release, liberate, free, let go, have mercy on, let off, forgive, acquit, excuse, grant amnesty. **—*adj.* 3.** extra, reserve, superfluous, surplus, additional, auxilliary, supplementary; leftover, unused, idle, free, leisure, unspoken for, available, unoccupied. **4.** economical, temperate, moderate, careful, restricted, meager, frugal, skimpy, modest, thrifty, stingy, sparse, scant, sparing, scanty, parsimonious. **5.** lean, thin, slender, slight, gaunt, scrawny, cadaverous, gangling, wiry, slim, underweight, sinewy, lank, skinny, rawboned, emaciated, anorexic, skin and bones, bony, angular, skeletal.

—Ant. splurge; condemn; inadequate; corpulent, fat, plump; profuse, profligate.

sparkle, *v.* **1.** glisten, glitter, shine, shimmer, glint, flicker, blink, twinkle, glimmer, flash, spark, twinkle, gleam, coruscate, scintillate. **2.** effervesce, fizz, bubble. **—*n.* 3.** luster, dazzle, spark, gleam, brilliance, radiance, brightness, éclat, scintillation, glister, glitter, twinkle, twinkling, coruscation. **4.** vivacity, fire, wittiness, effervescence, ebullience, animation, brilliance, liveliness, spirit, vigor, energy, élan, gaiety, joy, cheerfulness, gusto, glow, piquancy, pizzazz, oomph.

sparse, *adj.* **1.** thin, scattered, dispersed, spotty, scarce, few and far between, sporadic, occasional, infrequent, uncommon, here and there. **2.** little, scanty, meager, spare, insignificant, inappreciable, limited, restricted.

—Ant. abundant.

—Syn. Study. See SCANTY.

speak, *v.* utter, talk, voice, converse, discourse, remark, observe, declare, assert, aver, mention, discuss, give voice to, orate, air, communicate, disclose, reveal, enunciate, pronounce, say, articulate, express, address, state, tell, comment, lecture, expatiate, descant.

special, *adj.* distinct, distinctive, distinguished, different, particular, rare, unorthodox, unconventional, unique, specialized, remarkable, inimitable, idiosyncratic, curious, odd, strange, bizarre, weird, notable, noteworthy, especial, peculiar, characteristic, singular, specific, certain, individual, single, unusual, uncommon, extraordinary, exceptional.

—Ant. common, ordinary, familiar, usual, customary, conventional.

specific, *adj.* particular, definite, precise, exact, express, explicit, definitive, distinct, set, fixed, determined, predetermined, indicated, spelled out, established, unambiguous, specified, restricted, limited, clear-cut, unequivocal, individual, peculiar, certain.

—Ant. generic, vague.

specimen, *n.* type, example, sample, model, pattern, instance, exemplar, representive, illustration, case in point.

specter, *n.* ghost, phantom, spirit, wraith, vision, revenant, doppelgänger, chimera, illusion, apparition, shade, shadow, hallucination, image, spook, bogeyman, undead, zombie.

—Ant. reality.

speculation, *n.* **1.** thinking, meditation, reflection, deliberation, evaluation, rumination, cogitation, cerebration, pondering, wondering, ratiocination, analysis, pensiveness, study, musing, contemplation, consideration. **2.** conclusion, supposition, conjecture, surmise, view, hypothesis, theory, guesswork, guess, postulation, opinion, analysis, idea, notion.

speech, *n.* **1.** statement, utterance, remark, observation, declaration, assertion, asseveration, averral, comment, mention, talk. **2.** talk, oration, address, lecture, disquisition, sermon, homily, discourse; tirade, phillipic, filibuster, harangue. **3.** language, words, lingo, tongue, dialect, patois, idiom, jargon, tongue, parlance, slang. **4.** conversation, parley, discussion, discourse, communication.

—Syn. Study. SPEECH, ADDRESS, ORATION, HARANGUE are terms for a communication to an audience. SPEECH is the general word, with no implication of kind or length, or whether planned or not. An ADDRESS is a rather formal, planned speech, appropriate to a particular subject or occasion. An ORATION is a polished, rhetorical address, given usu. on a notable occasion, that employs eloquence and studied methods of delivery. A HARANGUE is an impassioned, vehement speech intended to arouse strong feeling and sometimes to lead to mob action.

speechless, *adj.* **1.** dumbfounded, shocked, dazed, paralyzed, nonplussed, stunned, flummoxed, dumbstruck, wordless, tonguetied, thunderstruck, inarticulate. **2.** silent, inarticulate, voiceless, dumb, mute.

—Ant. loquacious, voluble, talkative.

speed, *n.* **1.** rapidity, alacrity, celerity, quickness, fleetness, velocity, speediness, briskness, promptness, timeliness, swiftness, dispatch, expedition, haste, hurry, momentum, pace, headway, impetus, drive. *—v.* **2.** promote, facilitate, boost, accelerate, help, assist, aid, drive, impel, advance, further, forward, expedite, favor; accelerate, quicken, hasten, hurry, precipitate. **3.** rush, hurry, hasten, run, race, dart, bolt, sprint, hustle, tear, fly, scurry, zip, zoom, skedaddle, make tracks, burn rubber, hightail it, step on the gas, go like greased lightning, put the pedal to the metal, go like a bat out of hell, fly like the wind.

—Ant. sloth.

—Syn. Study. SPEED, VELOCITY, CELERITY refer to swift or energetic movement or operation. SPEED may apply to human or nonhuman activity; it emphasizes the rate in time at which something travels or operates: *the speed of an automobile; the speed of thought.* VELOCITY, a more technical term, is commonly used to refer to high rates of speed: *the velocity of a projectile.* CELERITY, a somewhat literary term, usu. refers to human movement or operation, and emphasizes dispatch or economy in an activity: *the celerity of his response.*

spend, *v.* **1.** disburse, expend, pay *or* lay out, dispose of; squander, throw away, fritter away, go through, splurge, be prodigal, waste, lavish, dissipate. **2.** exhaust, use up, consume. **3.** employ, use, allot, assign, invest, put in, pass, apply, devote.

—Ant. earn, save.

sphere, *n.* **1.** ball, orb; globe, earth; planet, star. **2.** field, environment, orbit, area, place, province, territory, bailiwick, jurisdiction, reach, scope, circle, compass, coterie, set, realm, domain, quarter. **3.** stratum, walk of life, rank, class, caste, level, station, position.

spin, *v.* **1.** draw out, twist, wind. **2.** circle, wheel, swirl, eddy, revolve, twist, pivot, reel, pirouette, twirl, whirl, turn, rotate, gyrate. **3.** invent, concoct, make up, devise, produce, fabricate, evolve, develop. **4.** tell, narrate, relate, weave, retail, recount, unfold. **5.** draw out, extend, protract, prolong, lengthen, perpetuate, continue, keep going.

—Syn. Study. See TURN.

spineless, *adj.* limp, weak, feeble, flabby, weak-willed, indecisive, irresolute, ineffectual, ineffective, powerless, impotent; cowardly, fearful, timid, lily-livered, craven, chicken, yellow, wimpy, nebbishy.

—Ant. strong, decisive, brave.

spirit, *n.* **1.** animation, vitality, soul, psyche, self, heart, breath, anima, being, power, essence, life, mind, consciousness. **2.** goblin, sprite, elf, fairy, hobgoblin; angel, genius, demon, *prāna.* **3.** ghost, specter, apparition, phantom, phantasm, revenant, wraith, spook, reincarnation, shade, shadow. **4.** courage, fortitude, resolution, tenacity, pluck, grit, backbone, strength, might, power, forcefulness, spunk, mettle, zest, panache, élan, gusto, passion, eagerness, avidity, vigor, liveliness, enthusiasm, energy, zeal, zealousness, ardor, fervor, fire, vivacity, enterprise, ambition, resourcefulness. **5.** character, temperament, temper, disposition, attitude, mood, bent, inclination, humor, sort, frame of mind. **6.** character, nature, drift, tenor, gist, sense, complexion, quintessence, essence. **7.** meaning, intent, intention, significance, purport, implication, message, core, heart, meat, pith, marrow, substance.

spirited, *adj.* excited, animated, sprightly, sparkling, dynamic, bouyant, ebullient, effervescent, vivacious, ardent, active, energetic, enthusiastic, eager, avid, keen, passionate, ardent, fervent, lively, vigorous, courageous, intrepid, audacious, valiant, brave, impetuous, bold.

—Ant. dispirited, inactive, indolent.

spite, *n.* **1.** spitefulness, vindictiveness, vengefulness, vengeance, ill will, malevolence, maliciousness, malice, rancor, gall, malignity, poison, venom, spleen, animosity, resentment, hostility, bitterness, antagonism, animus, antipathy, grudge, hate, pique, hatred. *—v.* **2.** annoy, irritate, vex, upset, disconcert, offend, provoke, pique, thwart, injure, hurt, harm, wound, needle.

—Ant. forgiveness, benevolence.

spiteful, *adj.* malicious, venomous, malevolent, revengeful, vengeful, vindictive, bitter, acrimonious, invidious, hostile, antagonistic, mean, cruel, hateful, rancorous, splenetic, unforgiving, retaliatory, retributive, punitive.

—Ant. benevolent, friendly.

splendid, *adj.* **1.** splendorous, gorgeous, magnificent, sumptuous, luxurious, superb, resplendent, showy, marvelous, spectacular, lavish, ornate, majestic, brilliant, extraordinary, awe-inspiring, awesome, lush, plush, rich, supreme, sublime, transcendent, dazzling, imposing, grand, beautiful, impressive. **2.** glorious, renowned, famed, famous, illustrious, eminent, conspicuous, distinguished, prominent, superior, noteworthy, exemplary, admirable, sublime, outstanding, successful, remarkable, celebrated, brilliant, noble. **3.** marveleous, exceptional, extraordinary, superior, excellent, fabulous, fantastic, incredible, first-class, peerless, unrivaled, matchless, nonpareil, capital, superlative, laudable, praiseworthy, fine, striking, admirable.

—Ant. sordid, squalid; ignoble.

splendor, *n.* **1.** magnificence, radiance, resplendence, sumptuousness, stateliness, majesty, panoply, spectacle, glory, luxury, lavishness, brilliance, grandeur, pomp, show, display, dash, élan, éclat. **2.** distinction, glory, brillance, fame, eminence, renown, celebrity. **3.** brightness, brilliance, light, luster, dazzle, refulgence.

—Ant. squalor, anonymity.

spoil, *v.* **1.** damage, impair, ruin, wreck, disfigure, destroy, demolish, upset, undermine, injure, hurt, corrupt, vitiate, mar, harm. **2.** baby, pamper, coddle, mollycoddle, indulge, pet, dote on, suffocate, cater to, overindulge, favor, gratify, treat, cosset. **3.** decay, molder, decompose, turn, go off, ferment, sour, rot, putrefy, disintegrate, crumble. *—n.* **4.** (*often plural*) booty, plunder, loot, pillage, prizes, pickings, swag, take, boodle.

—Ant. preserve, conserve, save; abuse, discipline, punish; sweeten.

—Syn. Study. SPOIL, HUMOR, INDULGE imply attempting to satisfy the wishes or whims of oneself or others. SPOIL implies being so lenient or permissive as to cause harm to a person's character: *to spoil a grandchild.* To HUMOR is to comply with a mood, fancy, or caprice, as in order to satisfy, soothe, or manage: *to humor an invalid.* INDULGE suggests a yielding, though temporary or infrequent, to wishes that perhaps should not be satisfied: *to indulge an irresponsible son.*

spontaneous, *adj.* impulsive, instinctive, automatic, unpremeditated, unannounced, unplanned, impromptu, extemporaneous, extempore, impromptu, improvised, off the cuff, ad hoc, ad-libbed, offhand, spur-of-the-moment, natural, unexpected, unrehearsed, unprepared, unconstrained, voluntary, gratuitous, free, unselfish.

—Ant. premeditated, rehearsed, stilted, unnatural, stiff.

sport, *n.* **1.** pastime, game, athletics, distraction, relaxation, pleasure, enjoyment, merriment, jollity, mirth, glee, hilarity, amusement, diversion, fun, entertainment, frolic, gambol, rollicking, romp, jest, recreation, play. **2.** derision, jesting, ridicule, mockery, taunting, teasing, ribbing, kidding, twitting, bullying, raillery. *—v.* **3.** play, frolic, gambol, romp, caper, cavort, lark, roister, rollick, fool around, be frisky. **4.** ridicule, make fun, make a monkey of, chaff, mock, deride, bully, laugh at, roast, taunt, jibe, twit, rib, kid, jeer, rail, razz, josh, make a laughingstock of, send up, caricature, lampoon, needle.

spot, *n.* **1.** mark, stain, blot, speck, blotch, patch, fleck, particle, mote. **2.** blemish, flaw, stain, taint, stigma, smudge, discoloration, splotch. **3.** place, location, locality, locale, scene, setting, section, neighborhood, area, site, situation. *—v.* **4.** stain, mark, blot, speckle, fleck, spray, splash, spatter, soil, sully, dirty, taint, smudge, besmirch, blemish, stigmatize, tarnish.

spread, *v.* **1.** unroll, unfold, open, display, extend, lay out, fan out, unfurl, expand, stretch out, draw out. **2.** extend, protract, prolong, drag out, disperse, distribute, stretch, expand, dilate. **3.** dispose, distribute, diffuse, disseminate, broadcast, strew, sow, dissipate, shed, scatter, disperse. **4.** overlay, smear, apply, smooth, rub, layer, plaster, overspread, cloak, blanket, cover, coat. **5.** emit, scatter, diffuse, radiate. **6.** publicize, make known, air, announce, make public, herald, disseminate, broadcast, publish, circulate, divulge, promulgate, propagate, disperse. *—n.* **7.** expansion, development, increase, proliferation, growth, mushrooming, extension, enlargement, broadening, dispersion, dissemination, distribution, dispensing, diffusion. **8.** extent, reach, area, span, sweep, vastness, range, limits, bounds, size, dimensions, breadth, depth, compass; stretch, scope, span, amplitude, magnitude, expanse.

spring, *v.* **1.** leap, jump, bound, hop, dart, fly, bounce, vault. **2.** arise, appear, grow, emerge, loom, sprout, shoot up, burst forth; start, originate, commence, begin, evolve, rise, issue, emanate, flow, proceed from, stem from, derive from, develop from. **3.** grow, develop, increase, wax, thrive. *—n.* **4.** leap, jump, hop, bounce, skip, bound, vault. **5.** elasticity, bounciness, bounce, flexibility, sprightliness, airiness, springiness, suppleness, resilience, resiliency, buoyancy, vigor. **6.** source, origin, mouth, fountainhead, fount, wellspring, beginning, root, inception, cause, head.

spry, *adj.* active, nimble, agile, brisk, flexible, light, vigorous, strenuous, robust, sound, hale, hearty, lively, energetic, animated, quick, smart, alert, ready, prompt.

—Ant. doddering.

spur, *n.* **1.** goad, prick, prod, urging, prompting, pressure, encouragement, whip, goad, incitement, stimulus, stimulation, motive, motivation, impetus, incentive, inducement, cause, provocation, impulse, instigation. *—v.* **2.** urge, prod, egg on, impel, prompt, press, push, drive, pressure, goad, prick, whip, incite, provoke, encourage, animate, excite, motivate, stimulate, induce, instigate.

—Ant. discourage.

spurn, *v.* reject, disdain, scorn, despise, refuse, decline, repudiate, rebuff, snub, sneer at, scoff at, brush off, cold-shoulder, turn down, turn one's nose up, sneeze at.

—Ant. accept.

—Syn. Study. See REFUSE.

spurt, *v.* **1.** gush, spout, flow, issue, spew, squirt, shoot, erupt, burst, surge, stream, jet, well, spring. *—n.* **2.** spate, outbreak, effort, rise, increase, jet, spout.

—Ant. drip, ooze.

squalid, *adj.* **1.** sordid, slummy, seamy, seedy, shabby, sleazy, mean, vile, fetid, neglected, slovenly, unkempt, sloppy, slipshod, frowzy, foul, repulsive, unclean, dirty, filthy, nasty. **2.** sordid, wretched, miserable, degraded, debased, ignoble, scurvy, rotten, deplorable, sorry, pathetic, pitiful, abject, awful, shameful.

—Ant. splendid, palatial.

squeamish, *adj.* **1.** moral, proper, puritanical, prim, staid, rigid, modest, prudish; blue. **2.** particular, scrupulous, fastidious, finical, finicky, punctilious, demanding, critical, exacting, difficult, fussy, fastidious, meticulous, painstaking, persnickety, dainty, delicate, hypercritical, faultfinding, caviling, carping, captious, nice.

—Ant. liberal, loose, lackadaisical.

stab, *v.* **1.** pierce, wound, gore, stick, puncture, prick, jab, impale, knife, skewer, spit, slash, spear, penetrate, pin, transfix; poke, plunge, thrust, insert. **2.** attempt, try, essay; guess, conjecture, estimate, guesstimate. *—n.* **3.** thrust, blow; wound, puncture, jab, laceration, incision, slash.

stability, *n.* permanence, constancy, steadiness, balance, poise, security, safety, evenness, regularity, firmness, continuance, solidity, soundness, sturdiness, durability, staunchness, steadfastness, dependability, reliability, tenacity, perseverance, persistence, perdurability, endurance, faithfulness, fixedness, strength, immovability, fixedness.

—Ant. instability.

stable, *adj.* **1.** firm, steady, fixed, strong, sturdy, established, set, regular, safe, secure, durable, immovable, permanent, invariable, unvarying, steadfast, staunch, resolute, unchangeable, unchanging. **2.** enduring, permanent, constant, persisting, persistent, perdurable, last-

ing, abiding, secure, fast, perpetual, eternal, everlasting. **3.** unwavering, steadfast, staunch, constant, reliable, steady, solid.
—**Ant.** unstable, changeable, rocky, shaky, inconstant, fluctuating, volatile; short-lived, temporary; dilatory.

stagger, *v.* **1.** sway, reel, totter, lurch, teeter, wobble, rock, pitch. **2.** waver, falter, vacillate, hesitate, doubt. **3.** shock, astound, astonish, stun, perplex, overwhelm, overcome, stupefy, bewilder, flabbergast, flummox, floor, startle, jolt, tax, burden, bowl over, confound, amaze, nonplus, dumbfound, surprise. **4.** alternate, zigzag, rearrange, reorder, overlap, vary, space out.

staid, *adj.* sedate, settled, sober, serious, proper, decent, demure, seemly, smug, priggish, complacent, decorous, correct, rigid, stiff, prim, dignified, restrained, cool, collected, quiet, composed, serene, calm, solemn, grave.
—**Ant.** wild, indecorous.

stain, *n.* **1.** discoloration, spot, blemish, defect, flaw, mark, imperfection, smirch, blot. **2.** stigma, disgrace, dishonor, taint, black eye, brand, blot, tarnish. **3.** dye, reagent, tint, coloring, tinge, pigment, tincture. —*v.* **4.** discolor, taint, spot, streak, soil, dirty, blemish, blot. **5.** blemish, sully, spot, taint, soil, tarnish, disgrace, dishonor, stigmatize, corrupt, spoil, ruin, besmirch, shame, disgrace, debase, defile, contaminate, pollute. **6.** tint, dye, tinge, color.

stake, *n.* **1.** wager, bet, ante, pot; risk, jeopardy, chance, peril, hazard. —*v.* **2.** risk, hazard, put money on, gamble, take a chance, chance, jeopardize, wager, venture, bet, imperil, put at risk, run a risk.

stale, *adj.* **1.** vapid, flat, dry, hardened, hard, tasteless, sour, insipid, spoiled, rotten, turned, gone off. **2.** old, banal, overused, antiquated, old-fashioned, clichéd, threadbare, uninteresting, hackneyed, trite, unoriginal, tired, boring, tiresome, warmed over, shopworn, familiar, stock, stereotyped, old-hat, common, commonplace.
—**Ant.** fresh, modern.

stalemate, *n.* impasse, deadlock, standstill, standoff, tie, Mexican standoff.

stalwart, *adj.* **1.** strong, stout, well-developed, robust, sturdy, brawny, mighty, powerful, rugged, lusty, solid, able-bodied, fit, hearty, hale, husky, beefy, sinewy, muscular, athletic, strapping, vigorous, pumped up, buff. **2.** strong, brave, valiant, redoubtable, undaunted, courageous, heroic, stouthearted, audacious, plucky, lion-hearted, spirited, red-blooded, bold, valorous, intrepid, daring, fearless, firm, resolute, indomitable, gallant. **3.** firm, steadfast, resolute, determined, tenacious, unyielding, unwavering, unfaltering, unflinching, unflagging, indefatigable, tireless, relentless, uncompromising, redoubtable, formidable.
—**Ant.** weak, feeble; fearful; infirm, unsteady.

stamina, *n.* strength, vigor, energy, endurance, ruggedness, resistance, staying power, mettle, might, staunchness, steadfastness, health, robustness, hardiness, fortitude, indefatigability, stick-to-itiveness, grit, guts.
—**Ant.** weakness.

stammer, *v.* stutter, pause, hesitate, stumble, hem and haw, falter.

stamp, *v.* **1.** strike, beat, trample, tramp, tread, step, stomp, crush, pound. **2.** eliminate, abolish, annihilate, kill, exterminate, terminate,

destroy, extinguish, extirpate, quell, subdue, suppress, repress, squelch, squash, quash, eradicate. **3.** tag, term, name, style, characterize, designate, identify, classify, categorize, denominate, mark, label, brand. **4.** impress, imprint, print, mark, record, register, inscribe, engrave, emboss. —*n.* **5.** impression, design, pattern, brand, mark, print, seal. **6.** character, kind, type, sort, description, cut, style, cast, mold, fashion, grade, genre, class, level, classification, description, variety, form, make.

stand, *v.* **1.** halt, stop, pause. **2.** remain, continue, persist, stay, abide, prevail, obtain, apply, exist, be firm *or* resolute *or* steadfast *or* steady. **3.** set, erect, place, put, fix. **4.** face, meet, encounter, resist, oppose. **5.** endure, undergo, submit to, survive, tolerate, brook, countenance, face, confront, withstand, experience, cope with, brave, stand for, handle, bear, sustain, weather, outlast, abide, stomach, suffer, admit, allow. —*n.* **6.** halt, stop, stopover, rest, stay. **7.** position, stance, posture, policy, standpoint, viewpoint, opinion, belief, philosophy, sentiment, feeling, line, attitude. **8.** resistance, defense, effort, opposition, defiance, fight.
—**Syn. Study.** See BEAR.

standard, *n.* **1.** criterion, measure, benchmark, archetype, touchstone, yardstick, paradigm, paragon, type, ideal, requirement, precept, principle, law, canon, axiom, fundamental, gauge, test, model, example, exemplar, sample, basis, pattern, guide, rule. **2.** average, norm, par, mean, rating, level. —*adj.* **3.** recognized, usual, accepted, customary, habitual, orthodox, set, approved, definitive, established, traditional, classic, conventional, prevalent, regular, familiar, ordinary, stock, typical, normal, staple, universal, prescribed, defined, authoritative, official, required, textbook, basic, exemplary, guiding, sample.
—**Syn. Study.** STANDARD, CRITERION refer to the basis for making a judgment. A STANDARD is an authoritative principle or rule that usu. implies a model or pattern for guidance, by comparison with which the quantity, excellence, correctness, etc., of other things may be determined: *She could serve as the standard of good breeding.* A CRITERION is a rule or principle used to judge the value, suitability, probability, etc., of something, without necessarily implying any comparison: *Wealth is no criterion of a person's worth.*

standing, *n.* **1.** position, status, station, place, grade, order, level, stratum, rank, condition; reputation, repute, eminence, prominence. **2.** existence, continuation, duration, residence, membership, experience. —*adj.* **3.** still, static, stationary, stagnant, unmoving, motionless. **4.** continuing, continuous, fixed, ongoing, perpetual, unceasing, constant, permanent, unchanging, steady, lasting, durable. **5.** operative, in force, effective, in effect, established, settled.

stare, *v.* gaze, gape, goggle, watch, gawk, rubberneck, glare, peer, watch, glower, scowl.

stark, *adj.* **1.** sheer, utter, downright, complete, perfect, thoroughgoing, unmitigated, unconditional, unqualified, flagrant, patent, gross, rank; arrant, simple, mere, pure, absolute, entire, unmistakable. **2.** severe, austere, spartan, bare, plain, simple, cold, harsh, grim, bald, blunt, unadorned. **3.** harsh, grim,

desolate, dreary, severe, bleak, austere, barren, depressing, empty, vacant. —*adv.* **4.** utterly, absolutely, wholly, entirely, totally, fully, completely, quite, irrevocable, certifiably, plainly, obviously, clearly.

start, *v.* **1.** begin, be on one's way, set out *or* forth, go, leave, hit the road, move, get going, get under way, commence, depart. **2.** issue, emerge, crop up, develop, get under way, begin, originate, spring up, come up, come, arise. **3.** jump, jerk, flinch, quail, shy, recoil, wince, shrink, draw back, twitch, spring back. **4.** set up, begin, commence, originate, open, activate, get off the ground, embark on, set in motion, kick off, create, inaugurate, conceive, invent, start up, organize, establish, found, institute, initiate. —*n.* **5.** beginning, opening, outset, initiation, commencement, creation, origin, birth, genesis, inception, startup, emergence, rise, onset, inauguration, kickoff, founding, foundation, establishment. **6.** jerk, recoil, wince, flinch, balk, shy, cringe, spasm, fit, twitch, jump.
—**Ant.** end, terminate.
—**Syn. Study.** See BEGIN.

startle, *v.* disturb, shock, agitate, surprise, unsettle, upset, disconcert, jolt, jar, dismay, perturb, stun, discombobulate, shake up, nonplus, terrify, electrify, thrill, alarm, amaze, astound, astonish, scare, frighten.
—**Ant.** calm, pacify.

state, *n.* **1.** condition, case, circumstances, juncture, predicament, state of affairs, shape, position, posture, mode, pass, plight, emergency, crisis, exigency, quandary, dilemma, situation, status, estate, surroundings, environment, rank, position, standing, stage. **2.** constitution, structure, form, phase, shape, stage. **3.** estate, station, rank, position, standing. **4.** dignity, pomp, display, grandeur, style, splendor, brilliance, glory, magnificence. **5.** nation, country, land, sovereign state, government, federation, commonwealth, community, territory. —*adj.* **6.** public, national, government, federal. **7.** formal, solemn, official, ceremonial, ceremonious, pompous, stately, imposing, sumptuous, dignified. —*v.* **8.** declare, aver, assert, report, articulate, voice, delineate, claim, maintain, allege, submit, confirm, testify, say, relate, recount, narrate, describe, expound, explain, elucidate, interpret, set forth, express, affirm, specify.

stately, *adj.* imposing, grand, august, solemn, distinguished, impressive, striking, awesome, lofty, elevated, noble, imperial, grandiose, dignified, majestic, elegant, magnificent, regal, royal, splendid, glorious, sublime, superb, luxurious, opulent, sumptuous.
—**Ant.** humble, mundane.

statement, *n.* declaration, communication, report, announcement, proclamation, description, explanation, excuse, position, assertion, allegation, expression, account, claim, affirmation, averral, utterance, disclosure, communiqué, manifesto, testimony, affidavit, press release.

station, *n.* **1.** position, post, place, spot, site, situation, location. **2.** depot, train station, bus station, terminal, way station, whistle stop. **3.** position, place, status, caste, level, class, office, standing, rank. —*v.* **4.** assign, spot, site, appoint, install, garrison, billet, place, post, position, locate, establish, set, fix.

status, *n.* **1.** condition, state, circumstance, situation, state of affairs, shape, position. **2.** condition, position, standing, rank, station, place,

grade, level, order, stratum. **3.** importance, stature, eminence, preeminence, prominence, significance, reputation, repute.

staunch, *adj.* **1.** firm, steadfast, stable, unflinching, unshrinking, unswerving, unfaltering, undeviating, unwavering, steady, constant, resolute, true, faithful, principled, loyal, dependable, reliable, devoted, true-blue, trusty, trusted. **2.** solid, sturdy, well-built, substantial, tough, rugged, long-lasting, strong, sound, stout.
—**Ant.** unsteady, disloyal.
—**Syn. Study.** See STEADFAST.

stay, *v.* **1.** remain, dwell, reside, live, visit, wait, linger, put up, abide, sojourn, tarry, stop, rest, lodge. **2.** continue, remain, stop, halt, wait, stand, freeze. **3.** pause, wait, loiter, tarry, stop, delay, linger, procrastinate, lag. **4.** arrest, stop, thwart, prevent, halt, interrupt, block, hold back, detain, restrain, obstruct, arrest, check, hinder, delay, postpone, discontinue, put off, defer, suspend, adjourn, hold, curb, retard, slow, impede, foil, hamper, discourage, deter, suppress, quell, prevent. **5.** sustain, bolster, strengthen, uphold. —*n.* **6.** stop, stoppage, arrest, setback, check, prevention, discontinuation, halt, pause, delay, standstill; interruption, blockage, postponement, delay, deferral, deferment, reprieve, suspension, adjournment, break, hiatus, lacuna. **7.** stop, stopover, visit, layover, sojourn, rest, repose. **8.** prop, buttress, brace, support; crutch.
—**Ant.** leave.

steadfast, *adj.* **1.** fixed, immovable, enduring, constant, deep-rooted, regular, set, fast, firm, established, perdurable, lasting, abiding, stable. **2.** staunch, steady, determined, resolved, single-minded, dedicated, sure, dependable, trustworthy, trusty, reliable, resolute, constant, strong, firm, loyal, regular, purposeful, persevering, indefatigable, persistent, tireless, true, faithful, unwavering, unflinching, unfaltering.
—**Ant.** unsteady; weak; sporadic, unfaithful.
—**Syn. Study.** STEADFAST, STAUNCH, STEADY imply a sureness and continuousness that may be depended upon. STEADFAST literally means fixed in place, but is chiefly used figuratively to indicate undeviating constancy or resolution: *steadfast in one's faith.* STAUNCH literally means watertight, as of a vessel, and therefore strong and firm; figuratively, it is used of loyal support that will endure strain: *a staunch advocate of free trade.* Literally, STEADY is applied to that which is relatively firm in position or continuous in movement or duration: *a steady flow;* figuratively, it implies sober regularity or persistence: *a steady worker.*

steady, *adj.* **1.** firm, fixed, steadfast, stable, even, equable, poised, balanced, regular, uniform, habitual, direct. **2.** undeviating, invariable, unvarying, unwavering, changeless, regular, constant, unchanging, uninterrupted, uniform, unremitting, continuous, perpetual, nonstop, persistent, unbroken, uninterrupted, endless, relentless. **3.** solid, substantial, strong, sound, stout, firm, stable. **4.** firm, devoted, staunch, faithful, loyal, inveterate, confirmed, longstanding, consistent, persistent, unwavering, steadfast. **5.** settled, dignified, poised, sensible, serious, levelheaded, practical, down-to-earth, reliable, dependable, trustworthy, staid, sedate, sober. —*v.* **6.** stabilize, hold fast, support, brace, secure, strengthen.

—**Ant.** unsteady.
—**Syn. Study.** See STEADFAST.

steal, *v.* **1.** take, pilfer, rifle, thieve, burglarize, purloin, filch, appropriate, shoplift, walk *or* make off with, liberate, misappropriate, usurp, rob, cheat, overcharge, fleece, defraud, pocket, pirate, abscond with, loot, plunder, strip, despoil, pillage, defalcate, embezzle, swindle, lift, pinch, boost, borrow, hijack, nick, swipe, rip off, snitch, cop. **2.** win, gain, draw, lure, allure.
—**Ant.** provide, donate.

stealthy, *adj.* furtive, surreptitious, secretive, sneaking, slinking, skulking, secret, clandestine, cunning, crafty, tricky, artful, wily, sly, sneaky, covert, sub rosa, undercover, underhanded, backstairs, closet, hidden, private, confidential.
—**Ant.** obvious, open, manifest.

stem, *v.* **1.** rise, arise, originate, develop, derive, issue, generate, flow, spring, sprout, emanate, descend, proceed, result. **2.** stop, check, dam up, stanch, halt, arrest, curb, control, quell, suppress, obstruct, hinder, stay, retard, diminish, reduce, lessen, tamp, plug, tighten.

stereotyped, *adj.* stock, routine, clichéd, set, standard, customary, familiar, fixed, settled, conventional, hackneyed, overused, run-of-the-mill, overdone, overworked, commonplace, trite, banal, dull, ordinary, lifeless, uninteresting, stale, jejune, tiresome, tired, old, tedious, platitudinous, bromidic, dreary, boring, worn, pointless, insipid, dead, deadly, unimaginative, old-hat, moldy, mediocre, unoriginal, humdrum, moth-eaten.
—**Ant.** original, unique, one-of-a-kind, imaginative, rare, uncommon, unusual, interesting, fresh.

sterile, *adj.* **1.** pure, aseptic, sanitary, germ-free, sterilized, uninfected, uncontaminated, unpolluted, uncorrupted, antiseptic. **2.** infertile, impotent, childless, gelded, fixed, spayed, barren, unproductive, fruitless, unfruitful, bare, dry, unprofitable, poor, infecund.
—**Ant.** septic, contaminated; fertile, prolific.

stern, *adj.* **1.** severe, harsh, firm, strict, adamant, austere, stringent, demanding, critical, rigid, rigorous, flinty, steely, authoritarian, tough, uncompromising, Spartan, ascetic, disciplined, hard, inflexible, unremitting, obdurate, hardhearted, unsparing, unforgiving, merciless, unyielding, unrelenting, steadfast, implacable, forbidding, unsympathetic, rough, cruel, unfeeling. **2.** unsmiling, frowning, serious, somber, saturnine, sour, grim, grave, gloomy, funereal, lugubrious, dour, gruff, crabby, churlish.
—**Ant.** soft, lenient, flexible.
—**Syn. Study.** STERN, SEVERE, HARSH mean strict or firm and can be applied to methods, aspects, manners, or facial expressions. STERN implies uncompromising, inflexible firmness, and sometimes a forbidding aspect or nature: *a stern parent.* SEVERE implies strictness, lack of sympathy, and a tendency to discipline others: *a severe judge.* HARSH suggests a great severity and roughness, and cruel, unfeeling treatment of others: *a harsh critic.*

stew, *v.* **1.** simmer, boil, seethe, bubble, scald, cook, parboil; agonize, fret, brood, chafe, smolder, worry, get upset, get hot under the collar. —*n.* **2.** ragout, goulash, salmagundi, mixture, mishmash, hash, olla podrida, gallimaufry, potage, hotpot, pot au feu, chowder, bouillabaisse.
—**Syn. Study.** See BOIL.

stick, *n.* **1.** stake, twig, branch, shoot, switch, rod, staff, pole, cane, wand, baton, club, cudgel, bat. —*v.* **2.** poke, thrust, impale, spike, skewer, spit, run through, jab, prick, perforate, drill, bore, riddle, pierce, puncture, stab, penetrate, spear, transfix, pin, gore. **3.** fasten, infix, implant, attach, glue, affix, nail, pin, weld, solder, bond, tie, unite, join, cement, paste. **4.** adhere, cohere, cling, cleave, hold. **5.** hold, last, endure, dwell, continue, persevere, remain, stay, persist, abide. **6.** balk, shy, scruple, demur, boggle, object, kick, protest, vacillate, falter, hesitate, waver, doubt.
—**Ant.** sever, separate; detach, disengage.
—**Syn. Study.** STICK, ADHERE, COHERE mean to be fastened or attached to something. STICK is the general term; it means to be fastened with glue, pins, nails, etc.: *A gummed label will stick to a package.* Used figuratively, STICK means to hold faithfully or keep steadily to something: *to stick to a promise.* ADHERE is a more formal term meaning to cling or to stay firmly attached: *Wallpaper will not adhere to a rough surface.* Used figuratively, ADHERE means to be attached as a follower: *to adhere to religious beliefs.* COHERE means to hold fast to something similar to itself: *The particles of sealing wax cohered into a ball.* Used figuratively, COHERE means to be logically connected or attached: *The pieces of evidence did not cohere.*

stiff, *adj.* **1.** rigid, firm, solid, unflexible, unbendable, unbending, unyielding, inelastic, brittle, starchy, starched, hard, tough, solidified, congealed, thick, dense, compact. **2.** violent, strong, steady, powerful, brisk, forceful, gusty, howling, unremitting, fresh. **3.** firm, purposive, energetic, staunch, dogged, tenacious, indomitable, relentless, strong, stout, unrelenting, unyielding, resolved, resolute, obstinate, stubborn, pertinacious. **4.** graceless, awkward, maladroit, gauche, clumsy, inelegant, crude, abrupt. **5.** formal, ceremonious, punctilious, constrained, starched, frigid, cool, haughty, wooden, stuffy, aloof, tense, unrelaxed, pompous, stilted, mannered, snobbish, reserved, standoffish, chilly, unfriendly, uptight, forced, artificial, labored, pedantic, turgid, prim, priggish. **6.** laborious, difficult, excruciating, rough, intense, arduous, tiring, exhausting, harrowing, challenging, tough. **7.** harsh, punitive, hurtful, punishing, abusive, drastic, distressing, severe, rigorous, straitlaced, austere, strict, dogmatic, uncompromising, positive, absolute, inexorable, overwhelming, unbearable, merciless, cruel. **8.** excessive, steep, exorbitant, dear, expensive, great, high. **9.** taut, tight, tense. —*n.* **10.** prude, prig, stuffed shirt, puritan, blue nose, reactionary, conservative, stick-in-the-mud, old fogy, wallflower, bore, fuddy-duddy, square, fossil, anachronism; skinflint, miser, cheapskate, tightwad, piker.
—**Ant.** flexible.

stifle, *v.* **1.** smother, suffocate, strangle, garrote, choke, throttle, asphyxiate. **2.** keep *or* choke back, repress, check, stop, suppress, withhold, restrain, control, prevent, cover up, hold in. **3.** crush, stop, halt, obviate, prevent, preclude, put down, destroy, suppress, demolish, extinguish, kill, eliminate, stamp out, quash, silence, check, curb, decimate.
—**Ant.** encourage, further, foster.

stigma, *n.* mark, stain, reproach, smirch, demerit, blemish, scar, taint, blot, spot, brand, defilement, sullying, tarnish, disgrace, infamy, defamation, deprecation, calumny, condemnation, disparagement, disrepute, ignominy, scandal, pillory, dishonor, opprobrium, odium, shame, blot on the escutcheon.
—**Ant.** laurels, honor.

still, *adj.* **1.** in place, at rest, motionless, stationary, unmoving, inert, even, flat, smooth, undisturbed, unruffled, quiescent. **2.** soundless, quiet, hushed, restful, comfortable, noiseless, silent, mute. **3.** tranquil, calm, peaceful, peaceable, pacific, placid, serene. —*v.* **4.** silence, lull, hush, quiet, mute, stifle, muffle, smother. **5.** calm, appease, allay, assuage, alleviate, relieve, mollify, subdue, suppress, repress, soothe, compose, pacify, smooth, tranquilize. —*n.* **6.** stillness, quiet, silence, tranquility, serenity, peace, noiselessness, hush, calm.
—**Ant.** stirring, mobile, moving; noisy, clamorous, agitated, disturbed; noise.

stimulate, *v.* **1.** rouse, arouse, stir, rally, waken, awaken, activate, incite, incentivize, animate, excite, quicken, pique, galvanize, energize, vitalize, enliven, vivify, invigorate, urge, provoke, instigate, goad, spur, prod, prick, inflame, fire, inspire, encourage, fuel, nourish, jolt, whip up. **2.** invigorate.
—**Ant.** discourage, unnerve, deaden.

stimulus, *n.* incentive, incitement, spur, goad, prompt, urge, fillip, impetus, drive, impulse, push, enticement, stimulation, motive, motivation, inspiration, encouragement, provocation; stimulant.
—**Ant.** discouragement; wet blanket; soporific.

stingy, *adj.* parsimonious, miserly, niggardly, penurious, pennypinching, cheeseparing, economical, skimpy, sparing, frugal, tightfisted, mercenary, greedy, covetous, money-grubbing, cheap, uncharitable, selfish, closefisted, stinting, petty, mean-spirited, measly, unaccommodating, small-minded, petty, grudging, grasping, illiberal, venal, skinflinty, extortionate, usurous, shabby, near, churlish, sordid, mean, close, tight, avaricious.
—**Ant.** generous.
—**Syn. Study.** STINGY, PARSIMONIOUS, MISERLY mean reluctant to part with money, possessions, or other things. STINGY means unwilling to give, share, or spend anything of value: *a stingy employer; an expert stingy with advice.* PARSIMONIOUS describes a stinginess arising from excessive frugality or unwillingness to spend money: *a parsimonious family.* MISERLY implies a pathological pleasure in acquiring and hoarding money: *a miserly recluse.*

stint, *v.* **1.** limit, restrict, control, curb, confine, restrain; pinch, straiten, starve, famish, skimp, scrimp, begrudge, economize, cut corners, withhold. —*n.* **2.** limit, limitation, restriction, restraint, constraint, control, curb, check, condition, reservation, qualification. **3.** share, rate, allotment, portion, quota, bit, assignment, stretch, term, shift, time, turn, duty, responsibility, charge, obligation, job, task, chore.
—**Ant.** liberate, free.

stir, *v.* **1.** move, trouble, perturb, affect, upset, activate, agitate, disturb, mix, merge, blend, scramble, amalgamate, beat, whip up, shake. **2.** incite, instigate, prompt, motivate, encourage, hearten, inspire, inspirit, excite, move, drive, impel, rouse, foment, arouse, provoke, stimulate, animate, urge, goad, spur, prod, induce, persuade, convince, awaken, waken, rally, quicken, galvanize, energize. **3.** affect, touch, impress, strike, hit hard, have a profound effect on, alter one's feelings, excite, move. —*n.* **4.** movement, bustle, ado, to-do, agitation, commotion, disorder, uproar, tumult, activity, action, flurry, confusion, fuss, disturbance, excitement, hubbub, din, uproar, pandemonium, babel.

stock, *n.* **1.** store, goods, inventory, stockpile, armamentarium, cache, selection, goods, wares, supplies, supply, provision, reserve, reservoir, assortment, selection, variety, range, hoard. **2.** race, bloodline, dynasty, genealogy, extraction, roots, breeding, heritage, family tree, lineage, family, descent, pedigree, ancestry, line, parentage, house, tribe. —*adj.* **3.** staple, standard, standing, customary, ordinary, regular, routine, permanent. **4.** common, commonplace, ordinary, usual, routine, banal, clichéd, stereotypical, stale, hackneyed, everyday, standard, traditional, orthododox, conventional, trite, worn-out, old, tired, tiresome, run-of-the-mill, boring, corny. —*v.* **5.** supply, store, fill, handle, market, inventory, furnish, provide, offer, keep.

stocky, *adj.* thickset, squat, chunky, stubby, stumpy, dumpy, chunky, solid, burly, beefy, heavyset, portly, memomorphic, short, thick, solid.

stoop, *v.* **1.** bend, lean, bow, crouch, duck, hunch, hunker, slouch. **2.** descend, condescend, sink, deign, lower *or* abase *or* degrade *or* humble *or* humiliate oneself. **3.** stoop down, descend.

stop, *v.* **1.** cease, leave off, break off, bring to a close, give up, quit, halt, terminate, end, finish, conclude, abandon, discontinue, desist *or* refrain from. **2.** arrest, check, halt, interrupt, suspend, stay, postpone, defer, restrain, intermit, terminate, end. **3.** cut off, intercept, withhold, thwart, interrupt, obstruct, impede, hinder, prevent, thwart, frustrate, foil, balk, preclude, delay, restrain, repress, suppress. **4.** block, obstruct, close, jam, plug, clog, choke off, seal off, blockade. **5.** cease, pause, break, interrupt, take a breather, rest, quit. —*n.* **6.** halt, cessation, arrest, ban, prohibition, close, standstill, conclusion, finish, end, termination, check. **7.** stay, visit, break, rest, layover, sojourn, stopover. **8.** station, depot, terminal. **9.** block, blockage, obstruction, obstacle, hindrance, impediment.
—**Ant.** start, commence, initiate.
—**Syn. Study.** STOP, ARREST, CHECK, HALT imply causing a cessation of movement or progress (literal or figurative). STOP is the general term for the idea: *to stop a clock.* ARREST usu. refers to stopping by imposing a sudden and complete restraint: *to arrest development.* CHECK implies bringing about an abrupt, partial, or temporary stop: *to check a trotting horse.* To HALT means to make a temporary stop, esp. one resulting from a command: *to halt a company of soldiers.*

storm, *n.* **1.** turbulence, roaring, inclement, weather, tempest; gale, hurricane, tornado, cyclone, typhoon, shower, cloudburst, downpour, deluge, flood, monsoon, duststorm, squall, noreaster, rainstorm, whirlwind, hailstorm, snowstorm, ice storm, blizzard, thunderstorm. **2.** upheaval, agitation, stir, rumpus, furor, turmoil, disorder, disruption, ferment, tumult, perturbation, hurly burly, chaos, riot, uproar, brouhaha, melee, violence, commotion, disturbance, strife. **3.** outburst, outcry, eruption, furor, explosion, uproar, outbreak. —*v.* **4.** blow; rain, snow, sleet, squall, howl, hail, thunder and lightning. **5.** rage, rave, bluster, thunder, explode, blow one's top *or* stack, have a temper tantrum, act up, roar, rant, fume, complain. **6.** rush, attack, assault, besiege, assail, raid, blitz, bombard, shell, bomb.

story, *n.* **1.** narrative, tale, legend, recounting, yarn, account, recital, fairy tale, story, myth, epic, saga, fable, romance, anecdote, allegory, parable, record, history, chronicle. **2.** lie, fib, confabulation, falsehood, untruth, alibi, excuse, tall tale. **3.** article, item, report, news, feature, information, scoop, lowdown, copy, dispatch, release, file. **4.** contention, testimony, assertion, version, representation, report, account, description, statement, allegation.

stout, *adj.* **1.** rotund, obese, tubby, overweight, heavyset, big, burly, heavy, plump, bulky, thickset, fat, corpulent, plump, portly, fleshy. **2.** bold, hardy, undaunted, dauntless, brave, gutsy, gritty, plucky, valorous, valiant, gallant, intrepid, fearless, staunch, resolute, doughty, invincible, indomitable, courageous. **3.** firm, stubborn, obstinate, determined, intent, contumacious, resolute. **4.** strong, stalwart, sturdy, brawny, healthy, robust, strapping, lusty, hulking, beefy, husky, sinewy, athletic, brawny, muscular, hefty, vigorous, energetic, dynamic, able-bodied. **5.** strong, substantial, sturdy, durable, tough, solid, heavy-duty, reinforced. —**Ant.** slim, slender, thin; fearful; weak; light.

straight, *adj.* **1.** candid, frank, open, honest, direct, straightforward, explicit, blunt, unequivocal, unambiguous. **2.** honorable, honest, virtuous, upright, erect, just, fair, equitable, impartial, aboveboard, respectable, decent, trustworthy, dependable, reliable, upfront, straight-shooting, principled, moral, ethical, on the up-and-up, truthful, straightforward. —**Ant.** devious, crooked, dishonest.

straightforward, *adj.* **1.** direct, straight, undeviating, unwavering, unswerving, to the point. **2.** honest, truthful, above-board, upright, plainspoken, on the level, on the up and up, honorable, just, fair. —**Ant.** devious; dishonest.

strain, *v.* **1.** stretch, tighten, tauten; force, overtax, burden, overwork, push; surpass, exceed. **2.** try hard, make an effort, struggle, strive, push, labor, toil, exert oneself. **3.** sprain, impair, injure, hurt, harm, damage, tax, pull, weaken, wrench, twist, tear, overexert. **4.** filter, sift, sieve, drain, filtrate, purify, percolate, ooze, seep through. —*n.* **5.** force, stress, tension, burden, anxiety, worry, obligation, demand, pressure, effort, exertion. **6.** sprain, damage, harm, impairment, weakness, injury, wrench. **7.** family, stock, descent, race, pedigree, lineage, ancestry, extraction. **8.** tenor, tone, drift, quality, spirit, complexion, vein, theme, mood, humor, cast, thread, impression, character, tendency, trait. **9.** streak, trace, vein, suspicion, touch, soupçon, dash, tinge, smack, dash, hint, suggestion, scintilla, iota, jot, bit.

strait, *n.* difficulty, distress, need, vicissitude, rigor, fix, quandary, emergency, exigency, crisis, pinch, dilemma, predicament, plight, trouble, mess, bind, pickle, jam, scrape, tight spot, hot water. —**Ant.** ease.

straitlaced, *adj.* prim, stuffy, hidebound, prudish, moralistic, rigid, proper, staid, strict, narrowminded, overscrupulous, conservative, old-fashioned, stiff, goody-goody, goody

two-shoes, priggish, puritanical, bluenosed, finicky, finial, fuddy-duddy, fussy, prissy, Victorian. —**Ant.** liberal, free-thinking, bohemian, loose, free and easy, relaxed.

strange, *adj.* **1.** unusual, atypical, aberrant, extraordinary, curious, bizarre, odd, queer, eerie, wierd, uncommon, funny, quaint, fantastic, singular, peculiar, unfamiliar, inexplicable, unaccountable, uncanny, offbeat, far-out, unexplained, irregular, unconventional, rare, mysterious, mystifying, eccentric, abnormal, out of the ordinary, grotesque, remarkable, surprising, amazing, astounding, astonishing, flabbergasting, anomalous, exceptional. **2.** alien, foreign, exotic, outlandish, unfamiliar, unheard of, unknown. **3.** unacquainted, unaccustomed, unfamiliar, unknown, unexperienced. **4.** distant, reserved, aloof, detached, indifferent, standoffish, haughty, snobbish, formal, remote, withdrawn, reticent, unfriendly, unsociable, frigid, chilly, cold, supercilious, superior. —**Ant.** usual, commonplace.

stranger, *n.* alien, foreigner, outlander, *Auslander,* immigrant, emigré, outsider, visitor, newcomer, unknown quantity. —**Ant.** friend, relative, ally. —**Syn. Study.** STRANGER, ALIEN, FOREIGNER all refer to someone regarded as outside of or distinct from a particular group. STRANGER may apply to one who does not belong to some group—social, professional, national, etc.—or may apply to a person with whom one is not acquainted. ALIEN emphasizes a difference in political allegiance and citizenship from that of the country in which one is living. FOREIGNER emphasizes a difference in language, customs, and background.

strangle, *v.* garrote; choke, stifle, suffocate, smother, throttle, asphyxiate, wring (someone's) neck.

stratagem, *n.* plan, scheme, trick, ruse, deception, artifice, wile, feint, expedient, intrigue, device, maneuver, contrivance, machination, dodge, subterfuge, lure, plan, plot, ploy, tactic, conspiracy. —**Syn. Study.** See TRICK.

strategy, *n.* tactics, plan, design, scheme, policy, procedure, blueprint, scenario, game plan, master plan; skillful management.

stream, *n.* **1.** current, rivulet, rill, brook, tributary, freshet, run, waterway, channel, kill, branch, creek, streamlet, run, river. **2.** flow, current, outpouring, effusion, rush, spurt, spout, fountain, flood, deluge, cataract, cascade, course, tide. **3.** flow, succession, torrent, rush, series, barrage, line, chain, string. —*v.* **4.** pour, flow, run, issue, emit, course, rush, surge, pour, gush, flood, spurt, shoot.

street, *n.* way, road, roadway, avenue, boulevard, concourse, lane, thoroughfare, drive, passage, byway, thruway, highway; path, footpath, alley, alleyway.

strength, *n.* **1.** power, force, vigor, muscle, sinew, intensity, focus, toughness, health, might, potency, energy, resources, assets, means, ability, capacity. **2.** firmness, courage, backbone, stamina, tenacity, willpower, perseverance, persistence, nerve, determination, gameness, grit, pluck, fortitude, resolution. **3.** effectiveness, efficacy, potency, cogency, soundness, weight, incisiveness, persuasiveness, validity. **4.** intensity, brightness, loudness, vividness, pungency. —**Ant.** weakness.

strenuous, *adj.* **1.** difficult, hard,

tough, arduous, laborious, toilsome, tiring, exhausting, taxing, demanding, uphill. **2.** vigorous, energetic, active, enthusiastic, dynamic, intense, indefatigable, tireless, persistent, dogged, tenacious, animated, spirited, eager, zealous, ardent, resolute, determined, forceful, earnest. —**Ant.** easy.

stress, *n.* **1.** anxiety, worry, distress, pain, suffering, grief, anguish, pressure, tension, tenseness, overwork, exhaustion, troubles, misery, woes, overexertion, burden, upset, pressure, strain. **2.** importance, significance, emphasis, weight, insistence, urgency, accent, force. —*v.* **3.** underscore, underline, highlight, mark, note, bring home, make a point of, spotlight, feature, emphasize, press, focus on, accent. —**Ant.** ease; insignificance; overlook.

stretch, *v.* **1.** draw out, extend, distend, dilate, expand, widen, enlarge, broaden, lengthen, elongate. **2.** hold out, reach forth, reach, extend, stretch forth, spread. **3.** tighten, tauten, strain, exaggerate. —*n.* **4.** length, span, spread, sweep, area, tract, distance, expanse, extent, extension, range, reach, compass. **5.** elasticity, give, resilience, stretchiness. —**Ant.** curtail, abbreviate.

strict, *adj.* **1.** rigid, rigorous, narrow, constrictive, restrictive, stringent, inflexible, stiff, severe, firm, hard, tough, unbending, unyielding, exacting, demanding, stern, narrow, illiberal, uncompromising, harsh, austere, authoritarian, tyrannical, repressive, autocratic, ironfisted, coldblooded, ruthless, merciless, pitiless, unsympathetic, straitlaced. **2.** exact, precise, accurate, scrupulous, meticulous, compulsive, punctilious, finicky, attentive, conscientious, particular. **3.** close, careful, minute, precise, exact, faithful, critical. **4.** absolute, perfect, thorough, complete. —**Ant.** flexible. —**Syn. Study.** STRICT, RIGID, RIGOROUS, STRINGENT imply inflexibility, severity, and an exacting quality. STRICT suggests close conformity to rules, requirements, obligations, or principles: *to maintain strict discipline.* RIGID suggests an inflexible, uncompromising, or unyielding nature or character: *a rigid parent.* RIGOROUS suggests that which is harsh or severe, esp. in action or application: *rigorous self-denial.* STRINGENT refers to something that is vigorously exacting, or absolutely binding: *stringent measures to suppress disorder.*

strife, *n.* **1.** conflict, discord, disharmony, rivalry, competition, dispute, dissension, bickering, quarreling, squabbling, arguing, variance, difference, disagreement, contrariety, opposition. **2.** quarrel, struggle, clash, fight, conflict; animosity, antagonism, friction, hostility, hatred, enmity, ill will, bad blood. —**Ant.** peace.

strike, *v.* **1.** thrust, hit, smite, knock, smack, batter, pummel, thrash, punch, hammer, batter, belabor, pelt, bludgeon, horsewhip, flog, slap, slug, whack, wallop, sock, belt, bash, lambaste, bop, beat, pound, cuff, buffet. **2.** catch, arrest, impress. **3.** come across, meet with, meet, encounter, discover, find, stumble upon, chance upon, hit upon. **4.** affect, overwhelm, impress, influence, afflict, hit. —**Syn. Study.** See BEAT.

strip, *v.* **1.** uncover, peel, decorticate,

skin, bare, denude. **2.** remove, confiscate, seize, expropriate. **3.** withhold, deprive, divest, dispossess, dismantle. **4.** rob, plunder, despoil, pillage, ransack, loot, spoliate, ravage, rifle, sack, devastate, spoil, desolate, lay waste. —**Ant.** cover; furnish; invest.

strive, *v.* **1.** endeavor, try, attempt, strain, make every effort, work at, exert oneself, essay, struggle, toil. **2.** contend, battle, wrestle, compete, fight, struggle. —**Syn. Study.** See TRY.

stroke, *n.* **1.** striking, blow, hitting, smack, whack, swipe, slam, wallop, strike, beating, beat, knock, rap, tap, pat, thump. **2.** apoplexy, paralysis, seizure, fit, spasm, embolism, aneurysm, cerebrovascular accident, shock, attack. **3.** feat, achievement, action, act, work, example, accomplishment. —*v.* **4.** caress, rub gently, massage, pet, pat, touch.

stroll, *v.* **1.** ramble, saunter, meander, perambulate, promenade, amble, walk, wander, roam, rove, stray. —*n.* **2.** ramble, saunter, promenade, amble, walk, wander, constitutional.

strong, *adj.* **1.** powerful, vigorous, hale, hearty, healthy, robust, mighty, sturdy, brawny, wiry, athletic, sinewy, strapping, sturdy, burly, stout, beefy, hefty, husky, buff, pumped up, hardy, muscular, stout, stalwart, herculean. **2.** powerful, able, competent, talented, skilled, experienced, qualified, trained, knowledgeable, potent, capable, puissant, efficient. **3.** firm, courageous, valiant, brave, valorous, bold, intrepid, fearless. **4.** influential, resourceful, persuasive, convincing, compelling, trenchant, profound, formidable, telling, cogent, impressive. **5.** clear, firm, loud. **6.** well-supplied, rich, substantial. **7.** cogent, forceful, forcible, effective, efficacious, conclusive, irrefutable, substantial, potent, powerful. **8.** resistive, resistant, solid, firm, secure, compact, impregnable, impenetrable. **9.** firm, determined, staunch, unswerving, committed, devoted, unfaltering, tenacious, unwavering, resolute, solid, tough, stout. **10.** intoxicating, alcoholic, potent, spiritous, hard. **11.** intense, brilliant, glaring, vivid, dazzling. **12.** distinct, marked, sharp, stark. **13.** strenuous, energetic, forceful, active, dynamic, unflagging, tireless, diligent, indefatigable, steadfast, rabid, staunch, fervent, vehement, incompromising, assiduous, sedulous, hardworking, vigorous, zealous, eager, earnest, ardent. **14.** hearty, fervent, fervid, thoroughgoing, vehement, stubborn, dogged, obstinate, pertinacious, perseverant, persistent. **15.** pungent, redolent, intense, concentrated, heady, penetrating, fragrant, aromatic, odoriferous; sharp, acrid, piquant, spicy, hot, biting. **16.** smelly, rank, noisome, stinky, foul, rotten, putrid, putrescent, odoriferous. —**Ant.** weak.

structure, *n.* **1.** construction, organization, anatomy, skeleton, system, arrangement, form, makeup, framework, order, design, nature, character, composition, organism, scheme, complex, configuration, shape. **2.** building, edifice, house, construction, pile.

struggle, *v.* **1.** strain, expend energy, exert oneself, make an effort, cope, endeavor, try, attempt; contend, strive, oppose, contest, fight, vie, rival, wrestle, battle, conflict. —*n.* **2.** contention, competition, contest, rivalry, dust up, brush, clash, tusssle, match, fray, melee, encounter, skirmish, fight, battle, conflict, strife. **3.** effort, strife, strain, endeavor, exertion, labor, toil, work, travail, drudgery, pains.

strut, v. swagger, parade, flaunt, show off, bristle, display oneself, act like a peacock, promenade, prance, vaunt, brag, boast, crow, gasconade.
—**Syn. Study.** STRUT and SWAGGER refer esp. to carriage in walking. STRUT implies swelling pride or pompousness; it means to walk with a stiff, seemingly affected or self-conscious gait: *A turkey struts about the barnyard.* SWAGGER implies a domineering, sometimes jaunty, superiority or challenge and a self-important manner: *to swagger down the street.*

stubborn, adj. obstinate, dogged, persistent, perverse, contrary, tenacious, pertinacious, determined, stiff-necked, intractable, refractory, inflexible, intransigent, unrelenting, uncompromising, recalcitrant, unyielding, unbending, rigid, stiff, contumacious, headstrong, pigheaded, mulish, bullheaded, adamant, wayward, willful, singleminded, obdurate, fixed, set, opinionated, resolute, persevering, hard, tough, stiff, strong, stony.
—**Ant.** tractable, amenable, adaptable, pliable, pliant, flexible; irresolute.
—**Syn. Study.** STUBBORN, OBSTINATE, DOGGED, PERSISTENT imply fixity of purpose or condition and resistance to change. STUBBORN and OBSTINATE both imply resistance to advice, entreaty, protest, or force; but STUBBORN implies an innate characteristic and is the term usu. used when referring to inanimate things: *a stubborn child; a stubborn lock; an obstinate customer.* DOGGED implies willfulness and tenacity, esp. in the face of obstacles: *dogged determination.* PERSISTENT implies having staying or lasting qualities, resoluteness, and perseverance: *persistent questioning.*

student, n. pupil, learner, disciple, undergraduate, schoolchild, trainee, apprentice, beginner, tyro, abecedarian, scholar; observer, commentator, critic, admirer, follower, devotee, fan, maven.
—**Ant.** teacher.

studied, adj. deliberate, premeditated, calculated, planned, intentional, voluntary, conscious, contrived, feigned, labored, forced, wooden, artificial, designed, overwrought, stale, predetermined, willful, considered, elaborate.
—**Ant.** unpremeditated, spontaneous, extempore, ad-libbed, ad hoc, impulsive, instinctive.

study, n. **1.** attention, application, exploration, scrutiny, learning, lessons, bookwork, cramming, concentration, investigation, inquiry, research, reading, reflection, meditation, cogitation, thought, consideration, contemplation. **2.** field, area, subject, topic, sphere, theme, bailiwick, specialty, major. **3.** zealousness, endeavor, effort, assiduity, enterprise, sedulousness, assiduousness. **4.** overview, presentation, article, paper, analysis, review, discussion, survey, results, research, thesis, results, opinion. **5.** library, den, office, haunt, studio, retreat, sanctum sanctorum. —v. **6.** read, investigate, memorize, rehearse, analyze, scrutinize, survey, inspect, scan, review, look into, observe, practice. **7.** think, reflect, consider, muse, deliberate, meditate, ponder, weigh, estimate, examine, contemplate, scrutinize, turn over, ruminate, chew on.
—**Syn. Study.** STUDY, CONSIDER, REFLECT, WEIGH imply fixing the mind upon something, generally doing so with a view to some decision or action. STUDY implies an attempt to obtain a grasp of something by methodical or exhaustive thought: *to study a problem.* CONSIDER implies fixing the mind on something and giving it close attention before making a decision or taking action: *to consider the alternatives.* REFLECT implies looking back quietly over past experience and giving it consideration: *to reflect on similar cases in the past.* WEIGH implies a deliberate and judicial estimate, as by a balance: *to weigh a decision.*

stuff, n. **1.** material, substance, matter, fabric, ingredients, essentials, makings, building blocks, fundamentals, essence, basics, elements, makeup, components, constituents, parts, units, pieces, segments, factors, features, details, items, specifics, particulars, rudiments, principles. **2.** character, qualities, temperament, attitude, spirit, substance, grit, talent, abilities, background, attributes, experience, professionalism, capabilities. **3.** rubbish, trash, waste, nonsense, twaddle, balderdash, humbug, rot, garbage, tripe, poppycock, malarkey, hogwash, bunk, swill, eyewash, baloney, claptrap, piffle, bull, inanity, absurdity. —v. **4.** fill, cram, pack, jam, ram, crowd, compress, squeeze, squash, shove, force, press, stow. **5.** stop up, clog, block up, choke, plug, obstruct.

stun, v. **1.** knock out, shock, dizzy, daze, traumatize, numb, benumb, strike, hit, smack. **2.** startle, astound, stupefy, daze, dazzle, overpower, boggle the mind, disarm, astonish, amaze, overcome, bewilder, paralyze, stagger, jar, jolt, shake up, bowl over, excite, overwhelm, confound, confuse, perplex, nonplus, dumbfound, flabbergast, discombobulate.

stupid, adj. **1.** unintelligent, obtuse, dense, simple, simpleminded, subnormal, feebleminded, fatuous, fatheaded, bovine, dull, dullwitted, lumpish, doltish, moronic, cretinous, idiotic, imbecilic, weakminded, thick, thickheaded, thickwitted, witless, brainless, brain-dead, mindless, emptyheaded, birdbrained, boneheaded, addled, slow, slowwitted, dumb, dopey, sluggish, stolid, impassive, slow on the pickup, dead between the ears, shallow, mentally deficient *or* incompetent, vacant, nobody home, driveling, cloddish, intellectually challenged, unteachable. **2.** foolish, foolhardy, trifling, trivial, silly, frivolous, harebrained, crazy, insane, mad, crackbrained, scatterbrained, screwball, screwy, absurd, ludicrous, idiotic, risible, laughable, ridiculous, nonsensical, bootless, irrational, half-baked, cuckoo, inane, asinine, senseless, simple, half-witted, witless, dumb. **3.** dull, vapid, pointless, prosaic, tedious, uninteresting, stale, monotonous, unimaginative, vacuous, boring, insipid, flat, humdrum, tiresome, heavy.
—**Ant.** bright, intelligent, clever, shrewd.

sturdy, adj. **1.** well-built, strong, energetic, vigorous, healthy, solid, tough, lusty, robust, stalwart, hardy, muscular, rugged, substantial, strapping, burly, athletic, husky, hefty, brawny, sinewy, stout, powerful. **2.** stalwart, formidable, staunch, steadfast, firm, stout, indomitable, unbeatable, unconquerable, persevering, resolute, vigorous, determined, uncompromising, unyielding, enduring, pertinacious, dogged.
—**Ant.** weak, decrepit.

style, n. **1.** kind, sort, type, variety, category, class, make, brand, genre, design, look, fashion, pattern, cut, shape, line, form, appearance, character. **2.** mode, manner, method, approach, system. **3.** sophistication, refinement, polish, savvy, savoirfaire, fashion, elegance, smartness, chic, stylishness, taste, flair, dash, panache, cachet, vogue, class, élan, éclat, pizzazz, swankiness, spiffiness, trendiness. **4.** touch, characteristic, mark. —v. **5.** call, denominate, name, designate, address, entitle, title, christen, dub, label, tag, brand, characterize, term.

suave, adj. smooth, polished, cultivated, cosmopolitan, debonair, gracious, nonchalant, civilized, courteous, charming, diplomatic, disarming, smooth-talking, persuasive, winning, knowing, savvy, fashionable, politic, genteel, fulsome, sleek, slick, unctuous, sociable, cordial, genial, congenial, affable, ingratiating, agreeable, polite, urbane, sophisticated, worldly, mundane.
—**Ant.** bluff, self-conscious, clumsy, gauche, unsophisticated, naive, country.

subdue, v. **1.** conquer, defeat, suppress, overthrow, rout, beat, lick, quell, quash, crush, control, master, dominate, gain the upper hand, get the best of, put down, punish, subjugate, vanquish, overcome, overpower, subject. **2.** repress, surmount, sublimate, stifle, suffocate, reduce, overcome. **3.** tame, break, humble, bridle, chasten, train, correct, discipline, domesticate. **4.** tone down, soften, mollify, moderate, temper, hush, mute, mellow, softpedal, curb, check.
—**Ant.** liberate; awaken; intensify.
—**Syn. Study.** See DEFEAT.

subject, n. **1.** topic, theme, argument, text, leitmotif, conception, point, thesis, issue, angle, gist, substance, business, affair, object, subject matter. **2.** ground, motive, reason, basis, source, excuse, rationale, cause. **3.** minion, underling, vassal, inferior, menial, dependent, subordinate. —adj. **4.** subordinate, subservient, submissive, controlled, inferior, answerable, dependent, secondary, collateral, subjected, inferior. **5.** obedient, tractable, docile, compliant, biddable, amenable, submissive. **6.** open, exposed, prone, vulnerable, susceptible, sensitive, apt, likely, liable. **7.** dependent, relative, conditional, contingent. —v. **8.** dominate, control, influence, conquer, subjugate, subdue, enslave, humble, crush, vanquish, master, put down. **9.** make liable, lay open, expose, submit, put through, impose on, cause to undergo.
—**Ant.** sovereign, dominant; exempt.
—**Syn. Study.** SUBJECT, TOPIC, THEME refer to the central idea or matter considered in speech or writing. SUBJECT refers to the broad or general matter treated in a discussion, literary work, etc.: *The subject of the novel was a poor Southern family.* TOPIC often applies to one specific part of a general subject; it may also apply to a limited and well-defined subject: *We covered many topics at the meeting. The topic of the news story was an escaped prisoner.* THEME usu. refers to the underlying idea of a discourse or composition, perhaps not clearly stated but easily recognizable: *The theme of social reform runs throughout her work.*

subjective, adj. **1.** mental, inner, unreal, visionary, notional, abstract, chimerical, theoretical, imaginary, illusory, fancied, imagined. **2.** personal, individual, idiosyncratic. **3.** introspective, contemplative, introverted, meditative, ruminative, thoughtful, pensive.
—**Ant.** objective.

submerge, v. submerse, dip, sink, inundate, wash, soak, drench, saturate, douse, souse, wet, dunk, plunge, immerse, duck, dive, flood, swamp, engulf, drown, overwhelm.
—**Ant.** surface.

submissive, adj. **1.** unresisting, yielding, acquiescent, deferential, accomodating, flexible, manageable, biddable, humble, obedient, tractable, compliant, pliant, yielding, amenable, agreeable. **2.** menial, mean, lowly, abject, degraded, debased, obsequious, servile, subservient, subject, submissive, slavish, ingratiating, sycophantic, toadying, truckling, bootlicking, brownnosing, passive, resigned, patient, docile, tame, long-suffering, subdued, meek, timid, uncomplaining.
—**Ant.** rebellious, intractable, refractory, fractious, unruly, disobedient, proud.

submit, v. yield, surrender, bow, capitulate, cave in, concede, consent, accede, defer, succumb, bend, knuckle under, resign oneself, accept, acquiesce, put up with, comply, obey, agree.
—**Ant.** resist, disobey, disagree.
—**Syn. Study.** See YIELD.

subordinate, adj. **1.** lower, inferior, below, beneath, under. **2.** secondary, unimportant, ancillary, minor. **3.** subservient, dependent, accessory, secondary, subject, ancillary, tributary, auxiliary, contributory. —n. **4.** inferior, subject, underling, minion, menial, drudge, stooge, aide, assistant, factotum, junior, hireling, lackey, servant, slave. —v. **5.** lower, subject, reduce, make secondary.
—**Ant.** superior; primary, chief, leading, dominant.

subside, v. **1.** sink, lower, decline, drop, recede, precipitate, descend, settle. **2.** quiet, abate, calm, moderate, let up, die down, wear off, decrease, diminish, lessen, wane, ebb.
—**Ant.** rise; increase.

substance, n. **1.** matter, material, fabric, composition, make up, stuff. **2.** essence, subject matter, quintessence, quiddity, gravamen, theme, subject. **3.** meaning, gist, nub, crux, heart, core, kernel, meat, sum total, significance, import, pith, essence, purport, point.

substantial, adj. **1.** real, actual, physical, worldly, mundane, palpable, valid, true, hard, solid, material, corporeal. **2.** ample, generous, abundant, goodly, tidy, healthy, major, large, massive, bulky, monumental, considerable, sizable. **3.** solid, stout, firm, well-built, durable, sturdy, strong, stable, sound. **4.** wealthy, well-heeled, affluent, rich, well-to-do, successful, prosperous, propertied, influential, responsible, reliable, consequential, powerful, significant, worthy, estimable. **5.** worthy, valuable, consummate, worthwhile, profitable, rewarding.
—**Ant.** airy, ethereal, insubstantial, immaterial: trivial; unstable, unsound; poor; unworthy.

substitute, n. **1.** surrogate, makeshift, stopgap, replacement, alternative, relief, standby, stand-in, understudy, proxy, alternate, representative, deputy, agent, temporary, relief, expedient, duplicate, copy, reproduction, contrivance, pinch hitter, double. —v. **2.** replace, displace, relieve, exchange places, make do, stand in, supplant, switch, take the place of, double for, cover for, pinch-hit-for.
—**Ant.** original, starter, regular.

succeed, v. **1.** flourish, prosper, thrive, win, triumph, achieve, make good, progress, advance, get ahead, make it, arrive, get to the top, do well, make a hit, go swimmingly, prevail. **2.** follow, replace, ensue, come after, supervene; displace, supplant, replace, supersede. —**Ant.** fail; precede.

—**Syn. Study.** SUCCEED, FLOURISH, PROSPER, THRIVE mean to do well. To SUCCEED is to turn out well or do well; it may also mean to attain a goal: *The strategy succeeded. She succeeded in school.* To FLOURISH is to grow well or fare well: *The plants flourished in the sun. The business flourished under new management.* To PROSPER is to do well, esp. materially or financially: *They worked hard and prospered.* To THRIVE is to do well, esp. to achieve wealth; it may also mean to grow or develop vigorously: *The shopping center thrived. The dog thrived on the new diet.* See also FOLLOW.

succession, *n.* **1.** order, sequence, progression, set, suit, suite, chain, train, string, concatenation, flow, procession, course, series. **2.** descent, transmission, lineage, race, dynasty, birthright, descendants, bloodline, ancestry.

—**Syn. Study.** See SERIES.

successive, *adj.* consecutive, following, sequential, ordered, sequent, serial; uninterrupted, continuous, unbroken, continual, succeeding.

sudden, *adj.* unexpected, abrupt, unannounced, precipitate, immediate, rapid, accelerated, expeditious, hurried, fast, swift, brisk, unplanned, unlooked for, unforeseen, quick, unanticipated; hasty, headlong, impetuous, rash, impulsive; unwonted, surprising, startling. —**Ant.** deliberate, premeditated, foreseen.

suffer, *v.* **1.** undergo, experience, endure, live through, brook, face, confront, withstand, sustain, submit to, take, abide, accept, receive, bow, bear, tolerate, allow, permit, humor, indulge, stomach, stand, meet with, feel. **2.** agonize, hurt, smart, ache, throb, sweat, grieve, sorrow, anguish, moan, shed tears, mourn, weep, cry, complain.

sufficient, *adj.* enough, adequate, ample, satisfactory, competent, suitable, requisite, fitting, passable, acceptable, middling, so-so, fair, tolerable, not bad. —**Ant.** insufficient.

suggest, *v.* propose, recommend, indicate, hint, insinuate, intimate, advance, urge, advocate, support, offer, present, mention, introduce, prompt, advise, counsel; adumbrate, shadow. —**Ant.** express.

—**Syn. Study.** See HINT.

suggestion, **1.** recommendation, proposition, proposal, advice, counsel, plan, scheme, opinion, idea, notion, view, guidance; warning, admonition, hint, caveat. **2.** touch, suspicion, hint, indication, trace, whisper, insinuation, innuendo, intimation, implication, soupçon, breath, tinge, tincture, shade, dash, vein, streak, strain, smack, iota, jot.

suggestive, *adj.* evocative, indicative, reminiscent, provocative, representative, symbolic.

sullen, *adj.* **1.** silent, reserved, sulky, taciturn, melancholy, depressed, dejected, brooding, pouting, temperamental, glum, dour, lugubrious, somber, sober, saturnine, pessimistic, cynical, despondent, downhearted, desolate, morose, moody. **2.** ill-humored, sour, resentful, aloof, surly, cross, churlish, grumpy, petulant, perverse, crotchety, choleric, crabby, cranky, irritable, glowering, spiteful, malevolent, malign,

acrimonious, vexatious, splenetic, bad-tempered. **3.** gloomy, dismal, cheerless, clouded, overcast, somber, mournful, depressing, funereal, dispiriting, dreary, lowering, shadowy, tenebrous, murky, black, sunless, gray, obscure, dusky, subfusc, dark. —**Ant.** cheerful.

summary, *n.* **1.** brief, digest, synopsis, summarization, recapitulation, encapsulation, condensation, shortening, consolidation, review, distillation, extract, abstract, compendium, epitome, epitomization, essence, outline, précis, résumé, quintessence, skeleton, heart, core, kernel, nub, abridgment. —*adj.* **2.** brief, comprehensive, concise, short, condensed, compendious, concentrated, compact, succinct, pithy. **3.** curt, abrupt, quick, short, perfunctory, terse, peremptory, laconic.

—**Syn. Study.** SUMMARY, BRIEF, DIGEST, SYNOPSIS are terms for a short version of a longer work. A SUMMARY is a brief statement or restatement of main points, esp. as a conclusion to a work: *a summary of a chapter.* A BRIEF is a concise statement, usu. of the main points of a legal case: *The attorney filed a brief.* A DIGEST is a condensed and systematically arranged collection of literary, legal, or scientific matter: *a digest of Roman law.* A SYNOPSIS is a condensed statement giving a general overview of a subject or a brief summary of a plot: *a synopsis of a play.*

summit, *n.* top, peak, apex, pinnacle, acme, vertex, culmination, crown, climax, apogee, zenith. —**Ant.** base, bottom.

summon, *v.* **1.** call, invite, command, order, enjoin, ask, send for, bid; convene, assemble, gather together, convoke. **2.** call forth, rouse, mobilize, muster, invoke, gather, evoke, elicit, arouse, activate, incite.

superb, *adj.* wonderful, marvelous, superior, glorious, divine, outstanding, sensational, unequaled, noteworthy, peerless, unrivaled, matchless, first-rate, superlative, perfect, classic, exceptional, extraordinary, striking, dazzling, brilliant, marvelous, fantastic, miraculous, incredible, unbelievable, fabulous, stupendous, staggering, mind-boggling, breathtaking, smashing, terrific, super, (*slang*) def, phat, unreal, stately, majestic, grand, magnificent, admirable, fine, excellent, exquisite, elegant, splendid, sumptuous, rich, luxurious, gorgeous. —**Ant.** inferior.

superficial, *adj.* shallow, external, outward, exterior, slight, skin-deep, surface, outside, cursory, uncritical, cosmetic, perfunctory, slapdash, sloppy, once-over, light, insubstantial, minor, hasty, hurried, summary, passing, rushed, mechanical, careless, spotty, patchy, sketchy, nominal, meaningless. —**Ant.** basic, profound, radical.

superfluous, *adj.* unnecessary, extra, gratuitous, dispensable, uncalled-for, unneedful, needless, *de trop*, redundant, excessive, superabundant, surplus, supernumerary, spare, overabundant, supererogatory. —**Ant.** essential.

superior, *adj.* **1.** first-rate, excellent, outstanding, exceptional, consummate, glorious, sublime, superb, high-ranking, high-level, high-class, upper-class, lofty, noble, better, classy, elevated, distinguished, preferred, choice, select, elite, superlative, matchless, unequaled, peerless, unrivaled, nonpareil, supreme, notable, noteworthy, worthy, estimable, transcendent, surpassing. **2.** supercilious, lordly, lofty, pretentious,

highfalutin, haughty, arrogant, condescending, snobbish, snooty, disdainful, patronizing, overweening, overbearing, scornful, pompous, high and mighty, stuffy, hoity-toity, uppity, stuck-up, la-di-da. —**Ant.** inferior, second-rate, worse, lower-class, undistinguished; humble.

superiority, *n.* **1.** lead, dominance, preeminence, ascendancy, supremacy, dominance, leadership, primacy, predominance, hegemony. **2.** prominence, eminence, importance, distinction, prestige, renown, excellence, greatness, magnificence, inimitability, worthiness; fame, notability, illustriousness, brilliance, éclat, power, influence, consequence, accomplishment, esteem. —**Ant.** inferiority.

supernatural, *adj.* **1.** unnatural, superhuman, miraculous, preternatural, phantasmagorical, occult, ghostly, spectral, metaphysical, unearthly, otherworldly, mystic, paranormal, psychic, uncanny, weird, eerie, mysterious, arcane, unreal, magical, dark. **2.** extraordinary, abnormal, unusual, odd, exceptional, remarkable, out of the ordinary, fabulous, rare, fantastic, inexplicable. —**Syn. Study.** See MIRACULOUS.

supersede, *v.* **1.** replace, displace, oust, substitute for, take the place of, supplant, succeed, remove. **2.** void, overrule, annul, neutralize, revoke, nullify, cancel, suspend, stay, rescind. —**Syn. Study.** See REPLACE.

supplant, *v.* displace, supersede, oust, turn out, eject, expel, dismiss, unseat, substitute, exchange, replace, succeed, remove. —**Syn. Study.** See REPLACE.

supple, *adj.* flexible, bendable, elastic, pliant, pliable; lithe, limber, lissome, willowy, nimble, graceful, athletic, bouncy. —**Ant.** rigid, inflexible.

supplement, *n.* **1.** reinforcement, appendage, adjunct, accessory, codicil, insert, sequel, extension, addition, complement, addendum, appendix, epilogue, postscript. —*v.* **2.** add to, extend, augment, lengthen, expatiate on, expand, amplify, enhance, magnify, develop, flesh out, elaborate on, enlarge on, append, attach, complement. —**Syn. Study.** See COMPLEMENT.

supply, *v.* **1.** furnish, provide, give, endow, purvey, present, deliver, accommodate, provision, replenish, stock, fill. **2.** make up, make up for, satisfy, fulfill, replenish. **3.** fill, substitute for, occupy. —*n.* **4.** stock, store, stockpile, quantity, inventory, hoard, reserve, reservoir, cache, accumulation, fund.

support, *v.* **1.** bear, hold up, sustain, uphold. **2.** undergo, endure, suffer, sustain, withstand, weather, brook, abide, countenance, face, submit to, tolerate, bear, stand, stomach, go through, put up with. **3.** sustain, keep up, maintain, pay for, fund, finance, sponsor, underwrite, bankroll, provide for, nourish, nurture. **4.** back, bolster, strengthen, fortify, boost, champion, promote, advance, stand up for, brace, buttress, sanction, uphold, second, further, advocate, endorse, forward, defend, protect, shield. **5.** aid, reassure, sympathize with, maintain, help, assist, advocate, succor, abet, relieve, patronize. **6.** corroborate, confirm, verify, authenticate, certify, substantiate, affirm, endorse, attest to, vouch for, validate, ratify, bear out. —*n.* **7.** maintenance, sustenance, living, expenses, upkeep, funding, resources, finances, budget, bread, livelihood, subsistence, keep. **8.**

help, aid, succor, assistance, relief, backing, backup, reinforcement, bolstering, encouragement. —**Ant.** fail, abandon, deny, undermine.

suppose, *v.* **1.** assume, presume, surmise, infer, presuppose, take for granted. **2.** believe, think, consider, judge, deem, conclude, fancy, imagine. **3.** hypothesize, theorize, postulate, posit, assume, propose.

supposed, *adj.* **1.** reputed, putative, conjectural, alleged, assumed, presumed, imagined, suppositious, hypothetical, theoretical, postulated, speculative, soi-disant, self-styled. **2.** expected, obliged, required; intended, meant.

sure, *adj.* **1.** undoubted, indubitable, indisputable. **2.** confident, certain, definite, persuaded, cocksure, satisfied, positive, assured, convinced. **3.** reliable, dependable, steadfast, unshakable, undeviating, unfaltering, certain, trusty, trustworthy, honest, infallible, unfailing. **4.** firm, established, stable, solid, safe, secure, steady. **5.** unerring, accurate, precise, certain, foolproof, effective, sure-fire, unfailing, infallible. **6.** inevitable, unavoidable, guaranteed, inexorable, ineluctable, inescapable, foreordained, destined. —**Ant.** unsure, uncertain.

surface, *n.* **1.** outside, exterior, covering, skin, integument, top, façade, face, boundary, interface. —*v.* **2.** materialize, appear, show up, emerge, arise, rise, come up, pop up, crop up. —**Ant.** inside, interior; disappear, vanish.

surpass, *v.* exceed, excel, transcend, best, worst, better, top, cap, leave behind, prevail over, outdo, beat, outstrip, outdistance, outperform, outclass, outshine, overshadow, eclipse.

surplus, *n.* remainder, excess, overage, leftover, oversupply, overdose, glut, extra, spare, surfeit, superfluity, overabundance, redundance, superabundance, residue. —**Ant.** insufficiency, inadequacy.

surprise, *v.* astonish, amaze, shock, take aback, nonplus, dumbfound, dazzle, stun, stagger, strike, hit, awe, floor, flabbergast, bowl over, knock out, dizzy, discombobulate, catch unawares, stupefy, open (someone's) eyes, astound, take unawares, startle, disconcert, bewilder, confuse.

surrender, *v.* **1.** yield, give *or* deliver up, cede, abandon, deliver, hand over, forsake, sacrifice, eschew, relinquish, renounce, resign, waive, forgo. **2.** submit, yield, capitulate, quit, cry uncle, succumb, submit, acquiesce, comply, concede, crumble, give up, throw in the towel, raise the white flag. —*n.* **3.** resignation, submission, renunciation, transferal, concession, conveyance, capitulation, relinquishment. —**Syn. Study.** See YIELD.

surveillance, *n.* watch, vigil, stakeout, oversight, inspection, examination, care, control, management, supervision, superintendence, observation, scrutiny, reconaissance.

survey, *v.* **1.** view, scan, observe, watch, inspect, examine, scrutinize, appraise, evaluate, study, measure, assess, investigate, review, criticize, look into, size up, contemplate, ponder. —*n.* **2.** examination, inspection, critique, appraisal, study, evaluation, measure, scan, scrutiny, inquiry, investigation, review, poll, questionnaire, research.

survive, *v.* continue, persist, live, remain, succeed, outlive, subsist, last, endure, persist, pull through. —**Ant.** languish, die, fail.

—**Syn. Study.** SURVIVE, OUTLIVE refer to remaining alive longer than someone else or after some event. SURVIVE usu. means to succeed in staying alive against odds, to live after some event that has threatened one: *to survive an automobile accident.* It also means to live longer than another person (usu. a relative) but, today, it is used mainly in the passive, as in the fixed expression: *The deceased is survived by his wife and children.* OUTLIVE stresses capacity for endurance, the time element, and sometimes a sense of competition: *She outlived all her enemies.* It is also used, however, of a person or thing that has lived or lasted beyond a certain point: *The machine has outlived its usefulness.*

suspect, *v.* **1.** distrust, mistrust, disbelieve, be suspicious, have suspicions, doubt. **2.** imagine, believe, surmise, feel, think, sense, fancy, imagine, theorize, hypothesize, postulate, have a funny *or* queer feeling, feel in one's bones *or* gut, have a hunch, consider, suppose, guess, conjecture. —*adj.* **3.** suspected, suspicious, questionable, dubious, doubtful, shady, shifty. —**Ant.** trust.

suspend, *v.* **1.** hang, attach, dangle, swing, fasten. **2.** defer, postpone, delay, withhold, shelve, table, keep in abeyance. **3.** stop, cease, desist, hold up, hold off, discontinue, intermit, interrupt, arrest, debar.

suspense, *n.* **1.** uncertainty, doubt, indefiniteness, insecurity, irresolution, expectancy, unsureness, incertitude, indetermination. **2.** indecision, vacillation, hesitation, hesitancy, wavering, second thoughts, scruple, misgiving. **3.** anxiety, tension, apprehension, nervousness, anticipation, agitation, anxiousness, expectancy, expectation, fearfulness, dread, angst, uneasiness, disquiet, foreboding, stress, strain, edginess, jumpiness. —**Ant.** certainty; decision.

suspicion, *n.* **1.** distrust, doubt, mistrust, misgiving, dubiousness, skepticism, qualm, wariness, apprehensiveness, apprehension, cautiousness, hesitation, uncertainty, leeriness, second thoughts, funny feeling. **2.** imagination, hunch, notion, idea, supposition, conjecture, guess. **3.** trace, hint, suggestion, shade, strain, inkling, soupçon, touch, shadow, tinge, taste, scintilla, jot, iota, dash, glimmer, flavor, streak, bit. —**Ant.** trust.

—**Syn. Study.** SUSPICION, DISTRUST are terms for a feeling that appearances are not reliable. SUSPICION is the positive tendency to doubt the trustworthiness of appearances and therefore to believe that one has detected possibilities of something unreliable, unfavorable, menacing, or the like: *to feel suspicion about the honesty of a prominent man.* DISTRUST may be a passive want of trust, faith, or reliance in a person or thing: *to feel distrust of one's own ability.*

suspicious, *adj.* **1.** dubious, doubtful, debatable, questionable, suspect, under suspicion, shady, fishy. **2.** skeptical, leery, apprehensive, wary, uncertain, uneasy, anxious, tense,

disbelieving, unbelieving, distrustful, mistrustful, dubious, in doubt.

sustain, *v.* **1.** hold *or* bear up, bear, maintain, continue, keep up, preserve, prolong, persist in, carry, support, uphold. **2.** undergo, stand, withstand, experience, tolerate, weather, brave, support, suffer, endure, bear. **3.** maintain, support, provide subsistence for, nourish, nurture. **4.** purvey, supply, cater, furnish, support, aid, countenance, help. **5.** uphold, confirm, establish, recognize, allow, approve. **6.** confirm, ratify, approve, sanction, authorize, endorse, validate, corroborate, justify. —**Ant.** fail; disapprove.

swagger, *v.* **1.** strut, parade, prance, sashay, promenade, vaunt, show off, strut like a peacock. **2.** boast, brag, trumpet, crow, gasconade, talk big, lay it on thick, exaggerate, go on about, toot one's own horn, bluster, blow. —*n.* **3.** boasting, bragging, arrogance, display, ostentation, posturing, cockiness, conceit, machismo, boastfulness, virility, pomposity, bluster, insolence, pride, affectation, braggadocio. —**Syn. Study.** See STRUT.

swallow, *v.* **1.** eat, consume, devour, dispatch, ingest, taste, savor, take in, gorge, gulp, engorge, imbibe, drink, gulp, guzzle, swill, put away. **2.** consume, assimilate, absorb, engulf, devour. **3.** accept, receive, believe, credit, take on faith, buy, fall for. —*n.* **4.** mouthful, bite, morsel, nibble, guzzle, swig, gulp, drink, sip, taste.

swarm, *n.* **1.** horde, bevy, crowd, multitude, throng, mass, host, flock, cloud, army, drove, flood, pack, bunch, stream. —*v.* **2.** crowd, throng, mass, congregate, gather, flock, stream, flow, abound, teem. —**Syn. Study.** See CROWD.

sway, *v.* **1.** swing, wave, brandish, flourish, display. **2.** incline, lean, bend, tend. **3.** fluctuate, vacillate, oscillate, rock, undulate, waver, totter. **4.** rule, reign, govern, lead, prevail. **5.** direct, dominate, control, persuade, convince, impress, bring around, incline, influence. —*n.* **6.** rule, dominion, leadership, control, power, sovereignty, government, authority, mastery, predominance, ascendency. **7.** influence, control, command, grip, hegemony, power, authority, bias.

swear, *v.* **1.** declare, affirm, avow, aver, vouchsafe, warrant, depose, state, vow, testify. **2.** promise, vow, take a solemn oath, guarantee, assure, give one's word, pledge, agree. **3.** curse, imprecate, blaspheme, execrate, use profanity, utter profanities, use four-letter words.

sweeping, *adj.* **1.** broad, wide, extensive, comprehensive, wholesale, all-inclusive, general, universal, widespread, blanket, umbrella, catholic, exhaustive, radical, thorough, across the board, vast. **2.** exaggerated, overstated, extravagant, unqualified, hasty. —**Ant.** narrow; qualified.

sweet, *adj.* **1.** sugary, honeyed, syrupy, saccharine; cloying, sentimental, treacly, precious, gushy, sticky, soppy, sloppy, icky, maudlin, schmaltzy, sickening. **2.** fresh, pure, clean, new. **3.** musical, melodious,

euphonious, euphonic, lyrical, golden, silvery, mellifluous, harmonious, tuneful, in tune, dulcet, tuneful, mellow. **4.** fragrant, redolent, aromatic, perfumed, ambrosial, balmy, scented. **5.** pleasing, pleasant, agreeable, pleasurable, enjoyable, delightful, charming, lovable, kind, amiable, genial, warm, unassuming, easygoing, gracious, engaging, winning, winsome, attractive, gentle. **6.** dear, beloved, precious, treasured, prized. **7.** considerate, attentive, thoughtful, kindhearted, generous, solicitous, compassionate, sympathetic, gracious, accommodating. —**Ant.** sour, bitter.

swell, *v.* **1.** inflate, dilate, distend, increase, enlarge, dilate, wax, mushroom, balloon, bloat, grow, expand, blow up. **2.** bulge, protrude. **3.** grow, increase, augment, enlarge. **4.** arise, grow, well up, glow, warm, thrill, heave, expand. —*n.* **5.** bulkiness, distention, inflation, swelling. **6.** bulge, protuberance, augmentation, growth. —*adj.* **7.** stylish, elegant, fashionable, posh, ritzy, classy, luxurious, smart, chic, chichi, swanky, deluxe, grand. **8.** grand, fine, first-rate, marvelous, superb, splendid, spectacular, thrilling, super, terrific, wonderful, dandy, brilliant. —**Ant.** decrease, diminish.

swift, *adj.* **1.** speedy, quick, fleet, hasty, lively, rapid, fast, expeditious; brisk, sudden, abrupt. **2.** quick, prompt, ready, eager, alert, zealous. —**Ant.** slow, slothful. —**Syn. Study.** See QUICK.

swindle, *v.* **1.** cheat, cozen, defraud, dupe, trick, gull, victimize, deceive, inveigle, bilk, hoodwink, fleece, fool, exploit, sucker, gyp, buffalo, sting, screw, bamboozle, diddle, rook, rip off, con. —*n.* **2.** fraud, trickery, confidence game, gyp, three-card monte, shell game, chicanery, hoax, flimflam, cheating, racket, rip off, scam, deception.

swindler, *n.* confidence man, con artist, scoundrel, villain, fraud, fourflusher, cheat, deceiver, charlatan, mountebank, flimflam man, bunco artist, schemer, ripoff artist, scam artist, rogue, rascal, knave, sharper, trickster, impostor, embezzler.

swing, *v.* **1.** sway, oscillate, rock, fluctuate, wave, vibrate. **2.** suspend, hang, dangle, flap, waggle. —*n.* **3.** sway, vibration, oscillation, fluctuation. **4.** freedom, margin, range, scope, trend, play, sweep.

symbolic, *adj.* figurative, allegorical, emblematic, typical, representative, characteristic, symptomatic, metaphorical, allusive, denotative, connotative, suggestive, expressive, betokening, signifying, exemplifying, illustrative, epitomizing.

symmetry, *n.* balance, proportion, harmony, evenness, orderliness, uniformity, congruity, correspondence, agreement, consistency, equality, uniformity, symmetricalness, equilibrium, order, regularity. —**Ant.** disorder, lopsidedness, imbalance, disequilibrium. —**Syn. Study.** SYMMETRY, BALANCE, PROPORTION, HARMONY all denote qualities based on a correspondence or agreement, usu. pleasing, among

the parts of a whole. SYMMETRY implies a regularity in form and arrangement of corresponding parts: *the perfect symmetry of pairs of matched columns.* BALANCE implies equilibrium of dissimilar parts, often as a means of emphasis: *a balance of humor and seriousness.* PROPORTION implies a proper relation among parts: *His long arms were not in proportion to his body.* HARMONY suggests a consistent, pleasing, or orderly combination of parts: *harmony of color.*

sympathetic, *adj.* **1.** sympathizing, comforting, consoling, soothing, solacing, sensitive, compassionate, commiserating, kind, understanding, comprehending, supportive, caring, concerned, thoughtful, solicitous, responsive, well-meaning, considerate, empathetic, empathic, warmhearted, kindhearted, benign, benevolent, tender, affectionate. **2.** compatible, consonant, agreeable, pleasant, likeminded, simpatico, in tune with, on the same wavelength, attractive, congenial, attached, affected *or* touched by. —**Ant.** unsympathetic, apathetic, insensitive, uncaring; incompatible.

sympathy, *n.* **1.** compassion, pity, empathy, commiseration, tenderness, understanding, warmth, warmheartedness, solicitousness, consolation, caring, solace, sensitivity, thoughtfulness, responsiveness, consideration, fellow feeling, concern, support. **2.** compatibility, affinity, rapport, concord, agreement, harmony, camaraderie, fellowship, closeness, congeniality, unity. —**Ant.** antipathy, apathy; enmity. —**Syn. Study.** SYMPATHY, COMPASSION, PITY, EMPATHY denote the tendency or capacity to share the feelings of others. SYMPATHY signifies a general kinship with another's feelings, no matter of what kind: *sympathy with their yearning for freedom; sympathy for the bereaved.* COMPASSION implies a deep sympathy for the sorrows or troubles of another, and a powerful urge to alleviate distress: *compassion for homeless refugees.* PITY suggests a kindly, but sometimes condescending, sorrow aroused by the suffering or misfortune of others: *Mere pity for the flood victims is no help.* EMPATHY refers to a vicarious participation in the emotions of another, or to the ability to imagine oneself in someone else's predicament: *to feel empathy with a character in a play.*

system, *n.* **1.** organization, arrangement, classification, order, network, nexus, pattern, setup, set, group, structure, organism, economy, assemblage, combination, complex, correlation. **2.** plan, method, approach, modus operandi, process, technique, scheme, procedure, practice, routine, way, methodology, fashion, project, arrangement, classification.

systematic, *adj.* orderly, well-ordered, organized, well-organized, methodical, standard, standardized, routine, planned, businesslike, regular. —**Ant.** slapdash, messy, sloppy, disorderly, disorganized.

T

taboo, *adj.* **1.** forbidden, interdicted, out of bounds, sinful, wrong, anathema, off limits, prohibited, banned, sacred, unclean, dirty, trayf, verboten, restricted, unspeakable, untouchable, unacceptable, rude, impolite, indecent, outlawed, illegal, unlawful. **—*n.* 2.** prohibition, interdiction, outlawing, ban, proscription, anathema, restriction, forbidden fruit, exclusion, ostracism.
—Ant. allowed, sanctioned, approved; permission, approval.

tacit, *adj.* silent, unexpressed, undeclared, unstated, unvoiced, unspoken, unsaid, implied, implicit, understood, inferred.
—Ant. expressed, overt.

tacky, *adj.* **1.** inferior, tinny, junky, tinselly, secondhand, shoddy, broken-down, shabby, rundown, ramshackle, decrepit, shopworn, seedy, tatty, threadbare. **2.** unfashionable, unstylish, dowdy, frumpy, frumpish, frowzy, drab, stale, old-fashioned, outmoded, stodgy, colorless. **3.** tasteless, gaudy, vulgar, chintzy, cheap, tawdry, cheesy, brummagem, glitzy, sleazy, loud, garish, low-class, low-rent.
—Ant. elegant, classy.

tactful, *adj.* diplomatic, discreet, prudent, judicious, delicate, dexterous, discerning, knowing, politic, poised, savvy, suave, polite, courteous, urbane, gallant, adroit, skillful, careful, acute, clever, perceptive, sensitive, considerate, thoughtful, understanding.
—Ant. tactless, maladroit.
—Syn. Study. See DIPLOMATIC.

tactic, *n.* strategy, move, ploy, plan, ruse, device, scheme, design, campaign, operation, master plan, blueprint, maneuver, procedure.

take, *v.* **1.** get, acquire, procure, win, lay hold of, lay one's hands on, gain possession of, gain, obtain, secure. **2.** seize, catch, capture, clasp, snatch, clutch, grab, grasp, grip, embrace. **3.** pick, select, choose, opt for, settle on, decide on, fasten on, elect. **4.** subtract, deduct, discard, remove, take away *or* off *or* from. **5.** carry, bear, transport, bring, haul, ferry, deliver, cart, convey, transfer. **6.** conduct, escort, convey, guide, accompany, lead. **7.** obtain, exact, demand. **8.** occupy, use up, consume. **9.** attract, hold, draw. **10.** captivate, enthrall, capture, lure, seduce, charm, delight, attract, interest, engage, bewitch, fascinate, allure, enchant. **11.** assume, adopt, accept, bear, undertake, arrogate, acknowledge. **12.** ascertain, determine, fix. **13.** experience, feel, perceive. **14.** regard, view, accept, assess, believe, think, judge, deem, feel, consider, suppose, assume, presume, hold. **15.** perform, discharge, assume, adopt, appropriate. **16.** grasp, gather, conclude, deduce, infer, apprehend, comprehend, understand. **17.** suffer, brave, abide, undergo, swallow, stomach, brook, countenance, undergo, experience, bear, stand, tolerate, submit to, endure. **18.** employ, establish, put in place, effect, apply, adopt, resort to, use, make use of. **19.** require, need, necessitate, call for, demand. **20.** deceive, cheat, trick, fool, impose upon, dupe, hoodwink, swindle, con, bamboozle, bilk, hoax, humbug, gull, lead down the garden path, pull the wool over (someone's) eyes, swindle, defraud. **21.** catch, engage, fix.
—Ant. give.

tale, *n.* **1.** story, narrative, narration, report, record, chronicle, history, anecdote, story, fable, account, fiction, memoir, novel, novella, legend, myth. **2.** lie, fib, falsehood, fabrication, untruth, exaggeration, cock-and-bull story, prevarication, tall tale. **3.** rumor, gossip, scandal, slander, allegation, dish, whispering, scuttlebutt.

talent, *n.* ability, aptitude, capacity, power, flair, facility, knack, ingenuity, endowment, strength, proclivity, capability, gift, genius, faculty, forte.
—Ant. inability, incapability, weakness.
—Syn. Study. See ABILITY.

talk, *v.* **1.** speak, converse, discourse, communicate, express oneself. **2.** consult, confer, discuss, parley, chat, confabulate, rap, gossip. **3.** chatter, prattle, jabber, blather, babble, gibber, cackle, rattle on, run off at the mouth, jaw, beat one's gums, prate. **4.** orate, lecture, speak, sermonize, give an address *or* speech, speechify, harangue, discourse. **5.** utter, speak, mention. **—*n.* 6.** speech, talking, conversation, discussion, meeting, consultation, palaver, chat, tête-à-tête, colloquy, discourse, dialogue, chat, communication, parley, conference, confabulation, one-on-one, pow wow, rap session. **7.** report, rumor, gossip, tittle-tattle, tattle, gab, blabbing, hearsay, information, news, dope, dish, lowdown, inside story, bruit. **8.** prattle, empty words, claptrap, verbiage, hot air, nonsense, chatter, rubbish, poppycock, malarky, applesauce, hooey, baloney, horse hockey, hogwash, bull, horsefeathers. **9.** language, dialect, lingo, idiom, speech, jargon, parlance, argot, cant, patois.

talkative, *adj.* garrulous, loquacious, wordy, verbose, prolix, longwinded, voluble, chatty, effusive, loggorheic, big-mouthed, chatty, gabby, longdrawn.
—Ant. taciturn, silent, laconic, terse.
—Syn. TALKATIVE, GARRULOUS, LOQUACIOUS characterize a person who talks a great deal. TALKATIVE is a neutral or mildly unfavorable word for a person who is much inclined to talk, sometimes without significance: *a talkative child.* The GARRULOUS person talks with wearisome persistence, usu. about trivial things: *a garrulous cab driver.* A LOQUACIOUS person, intending to be sociable, talks continuously and at length: *a loquacious host.*

tall, *adj.* high, elevated, towering, big, soaring, giant, gigantic, monumental, colossal, sky-scraping, lofty, long-legged, leggy, lanky, gangling, rangy, huge, gigantic, large.
—Ant. short.

tame, *adj.* **1.** domesticated, housebroken, broken, trained, obedient, disciplined, subdued, submissive, defanged, docile, gentle. **2.** mild, gentle, fearless, unafraid. **3.** tractable, pliant, compliant, amenable, biddable, obedient, docile, submissive, meek, subdued, crushed, suppressed, under (someone's) thumb, passive, unassertive, ineffective. **4.** dull, insipid, unanimated, spiritless, flat, empty, vapid, vacuous, jejune, tiresome, bland, lifeless, prosaic, humdrum, dead, prosaic, boring, uninteresting, uninspired, uninspiring, run-of-the-mill, ordinary, commonplace, toothless, tedious. **5.** spiritless, cowardly, pusillanimous, timid, timorous, fainthearted, lily-livered, yellow, chicken, wimpy. **—*v.* 6.** domesticate, break, subdue, train, house-train, master, discipline, civilize, make tractable. **7.** soften, tone down, temper, moderate, mute, mitigate, subdue, mollify, pacify, defang, calm, tranquilize, control, curb, repress, subjugate, enslave.
—Ant. feral, savage, wild; fearful; refractory, disobedient; exciting, spirited; brave, intrepid, valiant.

tamper, *v.* **1.** meddle, interfere, intrude, tinker, monkey around, intervene; damage, misuse, alter. **2.** bribe, suborn, seduce, lead astray, corrupt.

tangible, *adj.* **1.** physical, tactile, solid, concrete, sensible, appreciable, visible, objective, touchable, discernible, material, substantial, palpable, corporeal. **2.** real, actual, genuine, manifest, ostensive, patent, certain, open, plain, positive, obvious, evident, in evidence, perceptible. **3.** definite, certain, specific, ineluctable, inescapable.
—Ant. intangible; unreal, imperceptible.

tantalize, *v.* torment, tease, torture, taunt, tempt, bait, frustrate, plague, harass, harry, irritate, vex, provoke, annoy, bother, try, afflict, pester.

tardy, *adj.* **1.** late, behindhand, unpunctual, overdue, behind schedule, delayed, detained, retarded, slack, dilatory, slow, backward. **2.** slow, dilatory, belated, slack, retarded, sluggish, reluctant, indolent, lackadaisical, listless, phlegmatic, slothful, lethargic, languid, languorous, lazy, laidback, laggard.
—Ant. early, punctual, prompt.

tart, *adj.* **1.** sour, sourish, acidic, acidulous, dry, lemony, vinegary, tangy, astringent, acerbic, sharp, piquant, acrid, harsh, pungent, bitter. **2.** bitter, acid, corrosive, mordant, astringent, acerbic, incisive, keen, barbed, nasty, sardonic, vicious, cynical, trenchant, caustic, sarcastic, acrimonious, cutting, biting, stinging.
—Ant. sweet, mellow.

task, *n.* **1.** duty, job, assignment, business, charge, stint, mission, undertaking, employment, occupation, métier, profession, function, work, labor, drudgery, toil. **2.** struggle, strain, effort, test, trial, exertion, travail, striving, strife, pains, trouble.
—Syn. Study. TASK, CHORE, ASSIGNMENT, JOB refer to a specific instance or act of work. TASK refers to a clearly defined piece of work, usu. of short or limited duration, assigned to or expected of a person: *the task of collecting dues.* A CHORE is a minor, usu. routine task, often more tedious than difficult: *the chore of taking out the garbage.* ASSIGNMENT usu. refers to a specific task assigned by someone in authority: *a homework assignment.* JOB is the most general of these terms, referring to almost any work or duty, including one's livelihood: *the job of washing the windows; a well-paid job in advertising.*

taste, *v.* **1.** try, sip, savor, nibble; sample, examine, assess, judge, rate. **2.** undergo, experience, feel, sample, know, encounter, come up against, meet with. **3.** smack, savor. **—*n.* 4.** sensation, flavor, savor, scent. **5.** morsel, bit, sip, bite, nip, morsel, swig, swallow, mouthful, sample. **6.** relish, palate, penchant, fancy, appetite, stomach, tolerance, gusto, zest, liking, fondness, predilection, disposition, partiality, preference, predisposition. **7.** discernment, perception, discrimination, cultivation, refinement, polish, elegance, stylishness, sense, judgment, appreciation, understanding, penetration, insight, acumen, connoiseurship. **8.** manner, style, mode, fashion, form, design, motif, character.

tasteful, *adj.* proper, decorous, fitting, fit, approprioate, refined, cultivated, cultured, finished, polite, polished, restrained, correct, tactful, discreet, discriminating, *comme il faut,* harmonious, aesthetic, fastidious, elegant, graceful, charming.

tasteless, *adj.* **1.** flavorless, insipid, bland, dull, savorless, flat, watery, uninteresting, wishy-washy, vapid, unsavory, blah. **2.** inappropriate, unseemly, wrong, unsuitable, inapt, improper, ill-chosen, infelicitous. **3.** distasteful, unsavory, gross, base, low, indelicate, offensive, indecorous, uncouth, uncultured, gauche, boorish, maladroit, objectionable, coarse, crass, crude, garish, gaudy, meretricious, cheap, flashy, unaesthetic, tacky, vulgar.
—Ant. tasteful.

tasty, *adj.* delicious, flavorful, delectable, luscious, ambrosial, scrumptious, savory, palatable, appetizing, toothsome, mouthwatering, yummy.
—Ant. bland.

taunt, *v.* **1.** reproach, insult, censure, deride, blame, twit, deride, chide, reprove, berate, scorn, upbraid, sneer at, flout, revile. **2.** ridicule, tease, torment, annoy, razz, ride, insult, burlesque, lampoon, poke fun at, kid, rib, roast, put down, rag, hassle, bug, get on (someone's) case, mock, jeer, scoff at, make fun of, twit, provoke. **—*n.* 3.** gibe, jeer, derision, sneer, raspberry, Bronx cheer, dig, sarcasm, scorn, contumely, reproach, challenge, scoff, derision, insult, reproach, censure, ridicule.
—Syn. Study. See RIDICULE.

taut, *adj.* tense, stretched, rigid, unrelaxed, inelastic, tight, drawn, stiff, strained.
—Ant. loose, relaxed.

tawdry, *adj.* cheap, gaudy, showy, garish, loud, tatty, tinselly, tacky, tinny, shabby, cheapjack, ostentatious, flashy, meretricious, plastic.
—Ant. tasteful, elegant.

teach, *v.* instruct, tutor, train, educate, inform, guide, coach, edify, mentor, counsel, advise, impart, develop, communicate, enlighten, discipline, drill, practice, exercise, school, indoctrinate, implant, instill, inculcate, demonstrate, show, familiarize, acquaint, give lessons to, drum into (someone's) head.
—Ant. learn.
—Syn. Study. TEACH, INSTRUCT, TUTOR, TRAIN, EDUCATE share the meaning of imparting information, understanding, or skill. TEACH is the most general of these terms, referring to any practice that furnishes a person with skill or knowledge: *to teach children to write.* INSTRUCT usu. implies a systematic, structured method of teaching: *to instruct paramedics in first aid.* TUTOR means to give private instruction, focusing on an individual's difficulties in a specific subject: *to tutor him in geometry every Thursday afternoon.* TRAIN stresses the development of a desired proficiency or behavior through practice, discipline, and instruction: *to train military recruits.* EDUCATE stresses the development of reasoning and judgment; it often involves preparing a person for an occupation or for mature life: *to educate the young.*

teacher, *n.* instructor, tutor, lecturer, professor, don, guide, coach, mentor, guru, educator, lecturer, trainer, counselor, adviser, schoolteacher.
—Ant. student, pupil.

tear, *n.* **1.** (*plural*) grief, sorrow, woe,

lamentation, regret, remorse, sadness, anguish, suffering, weeping, sobbing, weepiness, whimpering, blubbering, regret, affliction, misery. **2.** rip, rent, rupture, hole, split, slash, gore, cut, slit, gash, rift, laceration, fissure. **3.** rage, passion, flurry, outburst. —*v.* **4.** pull apart, rend, rip, rive, rupture, shred, mutilate, mangle, claw, sunder, sever. **5.** distress, shatter, afflict, upset, disturb, disconcert, affect. **6.** rend, split, divide, rip, cleave, slit, slash, cut, separate. **7.** cut, lacerate, wound, injure, mangle, damage, impair.

tease, *adj.* irritate, bother, bait, taunt, torment, beleaguer, bedevil, needle, worry, pester, goad, provoke, badger, twit, tantalize, frustrate, aggravate, rag, pick on, rib, kid, roast, give (someone) a hard time, inflame, importune, fret, gall, trouble, provoke, disturb, annoy, rail at, vex, plague, molest, harry, harass, chafe, chaff, hector.
—**Ant.** calm, assuage, mollify.

technique, *n.* method, system, approach, tack, line, process, apparatus, procedure, practice, mechanism, routine, modus operandi, way, manner, fashion, style, mode.

tedious, *adj.* long, prolonged, overlong, endless, long-winded, wordy, tiresome, irksome, jading, wearying, wearisome, prolix, labored, laborious, repetitive, repetitious, mechanical, wearing, exhausting, tiring, fatiguing, monotonous, dull, boring, dreary, dry, drab, colorless, vapid, insipid, flat, banal, unexciting, prosaic, soporific, sleep-inducing, humdrum, routine, two-dimensional.
—**Ant.** interesting.

tell, *v.* **1.** narrate, relate, give an account of, recount, describe, report, recite. **2.** communicate, make known, apprise, acquaint, inform, teach, impart, explain. **3.** announce, proclaim, make known, air, broadcast, impart, release, break, advertise, trumpet, herald, publish, publicize. **4.** utter, express, word, mouth, mention, speak. **5.** reveal, divulge, disclose, intimate, leak, betray, declare; acknowledge, own, confess, admit, unbosom, get off one's chest, blab, tattle, let the cat out of the bag, spill the beans, spill one's guts, squeal, rat, blow the whistle. **6.** say, make plain. **7.** discern, identify, describe, distinguish, discover, make out. **8.** bid, order, command, urge, require, charge, direct, dictate, instruct. **9.** mention, cite, enumerate, count, reckon, number, compute, calculate. **10.** operate, have force *or* effect, carry weight, be influential.

temper, *n.* **1.** temperament, constitution, character, personality, individuality, complexion, makeup, nature. **2.** state *or* frame of mind, vein, disposition, mood, humor. **3.** passion, tantrum, fit of pique, fury, rage, frenzy, irritation, anger, resentment. **4.** calmness, self-control, self-possession, sang-froid, balance, restraint, aloofness, moderation, coolness, equanimity, tranquility, composure. —*v.* **5.** modify, qualify, adjust, regulate, fix, lighten, palliate, reduce, relax, slacken, appease, moderate, mitigate, assuage, mollify, alleviate, relieve, tone down, mute, mellow, soften, soothe, calm, pacify, tranquilize, restrain. **6.** suit, adapt, fit, accommodate, adjust.

temperament, *n.* disposition, humor, frame of mind, mood, vein, complexion, composition, makeup, temper, constitution, nature, attitude, personality, individuality.

temperamental, *adj.* moody, irascible, petulant, impatient, waspish, peevish, snappish, irritable, sensitive, hypersensitive, volatile, mercurial, excitable, explosive, capricious, erratic, changeable, thin-skinned, difficult, touchy, testy, hot-tempered, bad-tempered, short-tempered, cantankerous, hotheaded, hot-blooded, curmudgeonly; crabby, grumpy, huffy, crotchety, cranky, grouchy, cross, tetchy.
—**Ant.** serene, composed.

temperate, *adj.* moderate, reasonable, disciplined, forbearing, controlled, sensible, sane, rational, abstinent, abstemious, economical, thrifty, judicious, sparing, discreet, cautious, restrained, continent; composed, steady, stable, equable, sober-sided, sober, calm, cool, reserved, detached, dispassionate, imperturbable, self-possessed, quiet, serene, placid.
—**Ant.** intemperate, immoderate.
—**Syn. Study.** See MODERATE.

temporary, *adj.* transient, transitory, impermanent, makeshift, stopgap, standby, provisional, substitute, acting, part-time, occasional, discontinuous, fleeting, passing, momentary, fly-by-night, unstable, brief, changeable, fugitive, evanescent, short-lived, ephemeral.
—**Ant.** permanent, lasting, perdurable, infinite.
—**Syn. Study.** TEMPORARY, TRANSIENT, TRANSITORY agree in referring to that which is not lasting or permanent. TEMPORARY implies an arrangement established with no thought of continuance but with the idea of being changed soon: *a temporary structure.* TRANSIENT describes that which is in the process of passing by, and which will therefore last or stay only a short time: *a transient condition.* TRANSITORY describes an innate characteristic by which a thing, by its very nature, lasts only a short time: *Life is transitory.*

tempt, *v.* **1.** seduce, induce, persuade, entice, allure, attract, lead astray, invite, inveigle, decoy, lure, whet one's appetite, seduce, captivate, coax, cajole. **2.** tantalize, frustrate, dare, provoke, test, try, prove.
—**Syn. Study.** TEMPT, SEDUCE both mean to allure or entice someone into an unwise, wrong, or wicked action. To TEMPT is to attract by holding out the probability of gratification or advantage, often in regard to what is wrong or unwise: *to tempt a high official with a bribe.* To SEDUCE is to lead astray, as from duty or principles, but more often from moral rectitude, chastity, etc.: *to seduce a soldier from loyalty.*

tempting, *adj.* enticing, inviting, persuasive, seductive, attractive, alluring, tantalizing, captivating, appealing, irrestible, titillating, fetching, winsome, appetizing, mouthwatering.
—**Ant.** repulsive, repellent.

tenacious, *adj.* dogged, determined, resolute, diligent, steadfast, stalwart, staunch, strong-willed, single-minded, uncompromising, unyielding, obdurate, mulish, pigheaded, adamant, refractory, immovable, firm, unfaltering, unswerving, unwavering, strong, sturdy, solid, pertinacious, persistent, stubborn, obstinate, opinionated, sure, positive, certain.
—**Ant.** dilatory, irresolute, lackadaisical, uncertain.

tenacity, *n.* perseverance, persistency, pertinacity, obstinacy, grit, purposefulness, stamina, assiduity, strength, diligence, sudulousness, stick-to-itiveness, unshakeability, toughness, resilience, fortitude, determination, backbone.
—**Ant.** weakness, irresolution, dilatoriness.
—**Syn. Study.** See PERSEVERANCE.

tendency, *n.* direction, trend, disposition, predisposition, proneness, propensity, predilection, susceptibility, readiness, partiality, affinity, fondness, liking, turn, tenor, current, penchant, proclivity, inclination, leaning, bias, prejudice, drift, bent, movement.
—**Ant.** stasis, disinclination.

tender, *adj.* **1.** soft, delicate, gentle, light, soothing. **2.** weak, delicate, feeble, frail, infirm, unstable, shaky, unsound, sickly, ailing. **3.** young, immature, youthful, inexperience, callow, raw, tenderfooted, green, impressionable, vulnerable, undeveloped, uninitiated, juvenile. **4.** gentle, delicate, soft, lenient, mild. **5.** softhearted, responsive, sensitive, considerate, caring, solicitous, humane, benevolent, charitable, generous, altruistic, good-natured, feeling, thoughtful, sympathetic, tenderhearted, compassionate, pitiful, kind, merciful, affectionate. **6.** affectionate, loving, sentimental, fond, romantic, adoring, amorous, amatory. **7.** considerate, careful, chary, reluctant. **8.** acute, raw, inflamed, hurting, aching, painful, sore, sensitive. **9.** fragile, breakable, frangible, friable. **10.** touchy, tricky, difficult, troublesome, precarious, ticklish, delicate, sensitive. —*v.* **11.** offer, proffer, propose, extend, submit, advance, put forth, present. —*n.* **12.** offer, bid, presentation, proposition, offering, proposal, proffer.
—**Ant.** coarse, rough; healthy, sound, strong; mature, experienced, adult; merciless, ruthless; apathetic; inconsiderate; tough; accept.
—**Syn. Study.** See OFFER.

tenet, *n.* belief, principle, doctrine, fundamental, axiom, article of faith, ideology, precept, dogma, opinion, notion, position, conviction, idea, axiom, canon, credo, creed, teaching, persuasion, view.

tense, *adj.* **1.** tight, taut, stretched, inelastic, inflexible, unbendable, wooden, stiff, rigid, strained. **2.** nervous, neurotic, jittery, unquiet, uneasy, apprehensive, fearful, expectant, holding one's breath, on edge, edgy, on pins and needles, agitated, perturbed, upset, alarmed, excited, strained.
—**Ant.** loose, limp, flaccid, lax; relaxed, expansive.

tentative, *adj.* experimental, trial, provisional, impermanent, undecided, undetermined, temporary, acting, probationary, indefinite.
—**Ant.** definite, confirmed, definitive.

tenuous, *adj.* **1.** thin, slender, small, slim, slight, attenuated, minute. **2.** rare, thin, airy, rarefied. **3.** unimportant, insignificant, negligible, inconsequential, trivial, trifling, nugatory, unsubstantial.
—**Ant.** thick, dense, substantial, significant.

terminate, *v.* **1.** end, finish, stop, cease, discontinue, abolish, extinguish, conclude, close, complete. **2.** bound, restrict, abate, limit. **3.** issue, result, turn out, eventuate, prove.
—**Ant.** begin, open.

terrible, *adj.* **1.** dreadful, awful, fearful, frightful, appalling, dire, horrific, horrible, horrifying, terrifying, terrific, horrendous, horrid, gruesome, hideous, monstrous. **2.** distressing, shocking, appalling, severe, extreme, excessive.
—**Ant.** delightful, pleasant; moderate.

terrify, *v.* frighten, scare, alarm, terrorize, shock, horrify, paralyze, stun, petrify, startle, panic, dismay, apall, upset, agitate, perturb, daunt, cow, intimidate, browbeat, bully, make one's blood run cold, make one's hair stand on end, fill with dread.
—**Ant.** pacify, soothe, calm.

terror, *n.* horror, fear, panic, fright, apprensiveness, fearfulness, agitation, perturbation, disquiet, upset, discomposure, alarm, dread, trepidation, dismay, consternation.
—**Ant.** security, calm.

terrorize, *v.* dominate, coerce, terrify, frighten, alarm, dismay, scare, taunt, disconcert, make uneasy, cow, bulldoze, browbeat, compel, impel, push around, bully, force, persecute, intimidate, threaten, mau-mau.
—**Ant.** befriend, hearten.

terse, *adj.* brief, concise, pithy, neat, laconic, precise, short, crisp, clear-cut, exact, compact, succinct, curt, sententious, condensed, abbreviated, abstracted, summary, concentrated.
—**Ant.** wordy, diffuse, garrulous.

test, *n.* **1.** trial, proof, assay, evaluation, checkup, investigation, study, analysis. **2.** examination, quiz, exam. —*v.* **3.** try, check, evaluate, assess, probe, investigate, essay, prove, examine; refine, assay.

testimony, *n.* evidence, deposition, avowal, statement, affidavit, claim, assertion, witnessing, attestation, declaration, confirmation, verification, authentication, affirmation, corroboration.

testy, *adj.* temperamental, thin-skinned, querulous, quarrelsome, disagreeable, irritable, impatient, touchy, tetchy, petulant, edgy, on edge, short-tempered, peevish, vexatious, fractious, contentious, choleric, snappish, waspish, splenetic, crusty, grumpy, grouchy, bearish, cross, cranky, irascible, fretful, crotchety, crabby, cantankerous, captious, carping, faultfinding.
—**Ant.** even-tempered, imperturbable, cool, composed, calm.

thankful, *adj.* grateful, appreciative, pleased, glad, satisfied, content, indebted, beholden, obligated, obliged.
—**Ant.** thankless, ungrateful.

theatrical, *adj.* dramatic, histrionic, melodramatic, stagy, operatic, exaggerated, forced, unnatural, showy, pretentious, pompous, ostentatious, sensational, artificial, mannered, affected, overdone, overwrought, hyperbolic, camp, campy, ham, hammy, phony, false, fake, unrealistic.
—**Ant.** modest, low-key.

theft, *n.* robbery, larceny, burglary, stealing, pilfering, thievery, appropriation, filching, purloining, lifting, shoplifting, embezzlement, hijacking, pinching, pocketing, liberation, swiping, ripoff, heist.

theme, *n.* **1.** subject, topic, thesis, idea, notion, concept, keynote, gist, essence, core, substance, argument, point, text. **2.** composition, essay, review, study, article, piece, exercise, dissertation, treatise, tract, disquisition, monograph, paper. **3.** motif, leitmotif, thread, tenor, ideas; pattern, trend.
—**Syn. Study.** See SUBJECT.

theory, *n.* **1.** hypothesis, assumption, presumption, supposition, presupposition, law, rationale, explanation, system, conjecture, guess, speculation, proposition, postulate, inference, plan, scheme, proposal. **2.** view, contemplation, notion, opinion, judgment, conclusion, conception.
—**Syn. Study.** THEORY, HYPOTHESIS are used in non-technical contexts

to mean an untested idea or opinion. A THEORY in technical use is a more or less verified or established explanation accounting for known facts or phenomena: *Einstein's theory of relativity.* A HYPOTHESIS is a conjecture put forth as a possible explanation of phenomena or relations, which serves as a basis of argument or experimentation to reach the truth: *This idea is only a hypothesis.*

therapeutic, *adj.* healing, curative, remedial, corrective, restorative, healthy, salubrious, medicinal, medical, adjuvant, alleviative, palliative, helpful, beneficial, salutary.
—**Ant.** harmful, toxic.

thick, *adj.* **1.** broad, wide, solid, bulky, substantial, ample, massive; thickset, stocky, squat, stout, plump, portly, chunky, dumpy. **2.** dense, close, concentrated, condensed, compact, compressed, impenetrable, opaque, obscure, hazy, choking; full, filled, deep, clotted, chock-full, teeming, swarming, crawling, crammed, brimming, alive, crowded, jam-packed, bursting. **3.** inarticulate, indistinct, distorted, hoarse, gruff, rough, guttural, husky, raspy, gravelly. **4.** pronounced, marked, strong, distinct, obvious, decided, typical. **5.** heavy, dense, viscous, gelatinous, coagulated, clotted, jelled, congealed, stiff, firm, rigid, solid. **6.** friendly, close, intimate, inseperable, devoted, familiar, confidential, chummy, on good terms, palsy-walsy. **7.** stupid, slow, slow-witted, dense, stolid, obtuse, thickheaded, dull, dull-witted, half-witted, dimwitted, dopey, slow on the pickup, doltish, imbecilic, moronic, obtuse, bovine, simple, brainless; insensitive, thick-skinned.
—**Ant.** thin.

thick-skinned, *adj.* insensate, numb, apathetic, unfeeling, hard, hardhearted, unsympathetic, unaffected, affectless, insensitive, dull, obtuse, callous, invulnerable, stoical, steely, hardened, toughened, tough, inured, insusceptible, impervious, hard-boiled.
—**Ant.** sensitive, vulnerable.

thief, *n.* robber; pickpocket, purse-snatcher, mugger, burglar, pirate, swindler, con artist, embezzler, looter, pilferer, bandit, thug, purloiner, shoplifter, hijacker, cheat, charlatan, trickster, flimflam man, crook, ruffian, outlaw, desperado; kleptomaniac.
—**Syn. Study.** THIEF, ROBBER refer to one who steals. A THIEF takes the goods or property of another by stealth without the latter's knowledge: *like a thief in the night.* A ROBBER trespasses upon the house, property, or person of another, and makes away with things of value, even at the cost of violence: *An armed robber held up the store owner.*

thin, *adj.* **1.** slim, slender, lean, spare, slight, lanky, spindly, gangling, underweight, undernourished, underfed, skinny, gaunt, scrawny, skeletal, cadaverous, puny, starved, anorexic, anemic, pinched, wasted, haggard, hollow-cheeked, emaciated. **2.** unplentiful, sparse, scanty, slimpy, paltry, piddling, meager. **3.** unsubstantial, slight, flimsy. **4.** transparent, translucent, see-through, filmy, gauzy, gossamer, sheer, light, silky, delicate, diaphanous. **5.** faint, slight, poor, feeble. —*v.* **6.** rarefy, dilute, reduce, attenuate, decrease, water down, weaken, diminish.
—**Ant.** thick, fat, overweight, obese; abundant; substantial; increase, thicken, strengthen.

think, *v.* **1.** conceive, imagine, fancy, realize, envision, invent, concoct, picture. **2.** consider, regard, suppose, look upon, judge, infer, deduce, conclude, evaluate, reckon, deem, esteem, count, characterize. **3.** bear in mind, call to mind, recollect, recall, remember. **4.** intend, mean, design, propose, entertain the idea *or* notion of, purpose. **5.** believe, suppose, imagine, dream, fantasize. **6.** anticipate, expect. **7.** cogitate, meditate, reason, speculate, deliberate, mull over, consider, reflect, muse, ponder, ruminate, contemplate.

thirst, *n.* desire, wish, craving, eagerness, yen, longing, pining, hankering, yearning, hunger, appetite, rapacity, greed, cupidity, covetousness, avidity, voracity, voraciousness, ravenousness, lust, passion, enthusiasm, fancy, itch.
—**Ant.** distaste, repugnance, abhorrence, apathy.

thorough, *adj.* complete, entire, thoroughgoing, unqualified, perfect, downright, out-and-out, sheer, utter, absolute, unmitigated, unalloyed; painstaking, methodical, exhaustive, careful, scrupulous, conscientious, extensive, detailed, comprehensive, total, encyclopedic, all-out.
—**Ant.** incomplete, partial.

thought, *n.* **1.** concept, conception, opinion, view, sentiment, persuasion, judgment, belief, idea, notion, tenet, conviction, speculation, brainstorm, observation, impression. **2.** consideration, contemplation, meditation, reflection, musing, brooding, pondering, rumination, deliberation, mental activity, cerebration, brown study, cogitation, thinking. **3.** intention, design, plan, scheme, purpose, intent. **4.** anticipation, expectation, hope, prospect, dream, vision, fancy. **5.** consideration, attention, thoughtfullness, kindliness, kindheartedness, concern, compassion, solicitude, sympathy, tenderness, care, regard.
—**Syn. Study.** See IDEA.

thoughtful, *adj.* **1.** contemplative, speculative, musing, pondering, in a brown study, brooding, meditative, reflective, pensive, deliberative, serious, grave, earnest, abstracted, engrossed, preoccupied, rapt, intent, absorbed, introspective, sober, woolgathering, daydreaming. **2.** careful, heedful, mindful, cautious, judicious, discriminating, vigilant, watchful, attentive, discreet, prudent, wary, circumspect. **3.** considerate, attentive, concerned, solicitous, compassionate, sensitive, kind, kind-hearted, tender, sympathetic, charitable, helpful, courteous, polite, gallant, chivalrous, gracious, tactful.
—**Ant.** thoughtless.

thoughtless, *adj.* **1.** unthinking, unreflective, absentminded, forgetful, careless, heedless, inattentive, inadvertent, indifferent, unconcerned, ill-considered, imprudent, negligent, neglectful, lax, remiss, unmindful, unobservant, unwatchful, reckless, rash, foolhardy, foolish, stupid, silly, flighty, scatterbrained. **2.** inconsiderate, rude, impolite, tactless, insensitive, ill-mannered, unthinking, discourteous, unchivalrous, ungracious, unkind, clumsy, awkward, gauche.
—**Ant.** thoughtful.

threaten, *v.* **1.** menace, endanger, jeopardize, imperil, terrorize, bully, browbeat, daunt, cow, **2.** loom, indicate, presage, impend, portend, augur, forebode, foreshadow, prognosticate.
—**Ant.** protect, defend.

threatening, *v.* daunting, fearsome, dire, intimidating, menacing, ominous, looming, sinister, foreboding, portentous, inauspicious, imminent, impending

thrifty, *adj.* frugal, provident, economical, sparing, saving, prudent, foresighted, careful, parsimonious, scrimping, skimping, tightfisted, penurious, penny-pinching, niggardly, stingy, cheap, on a tight budget.
—**Ant.** wasteful, prodigal, improvident.
—**Syn. Study.** See ECONOMICAL.

thrill, *v.* excite, stimulate, arouse, stir, rouse, quicken, rally, animate, galvanize, electrify, enliven, move, titillate, touch, strike, grip, rivet, give (someone) a kick *or* bang *or* charge, inspire, turn on, energize, stir up, inflame, impassion, inspirit, intoxicate, exhilarate.
—**Ant.** disappoint, bore, deaden, depress.

thrive, *v.* prosper, succeed, flourish, grow, boom, bloom, wax, develop, burgeon, ripen, increase, advance, luxuriate.
—**Ant.** languish, die.
—**Syn. Study.** See SUCCEED.

throng, *n.* **1.** multitude, crowd, congregation, gathering, assembly, assemblage, swarm, horde, host, mass, crush, bevy, herd, flock, press, jam, pack. —*v.* **2.** swarm, assemble, crowd, press, fill, pack, cram, crush, jam, flock, mass, congregate, jostle, herd.
—**Syn. Study.** See CROWD.

throw, *v.* project, propel, cast, hurl, pitch, toss, fling, launch, send, sling, clash, let fly.

thrust, *v.* **1.** push, force, shove, impel, ram, propel, prod, press, drive. **2.** stab, pierce, enter, plunge, stick, jab, poke, puncture, penetrate. —*n.* **3.** lunge, stab, push, drive, tilt, shove, poke, prod, puncture, penetration.

thwart, *v.* frustrate, baffle, oppose, prevent, hinder, obstruct, check, curb, arrest, impede, stymie, foil, stop, stump, balk, block, negate, nullify, circumvent, outwit, bar, overcome, surmount, restrain, forestall, anticipate, defeat.
—**Ant.** favor, encourage, support, help.

tidy, *adj.* clean, neat, trim, shipshape, spruce, spick-and-span, well-kept, snug; orderly, systematic, meticulous, fastidious, scrupulous, well-organized, methodical.
—**Ant.** unkempt, messy, sloppy, untidy, slovenly, slipshod.

tie, *v.* **1.** bind, fasten, knot, lash, secure, attach, couple, moor, tether, rivet, anchor, join, unite, connect, link, knit, yoke, lock. **2.** confine, restrict, limit, obligate, constrain, curtail, hamper, hinder, curb, cramp. **3.** equal. —*n.* **4.** lace, throng, line, leash, ribbon, cord, string, rope, band, ligature. **5.** draw, deadlock, stalemate, equality, dead heat. **6.** link, connection, bond, relationship, affiliation, involvement, entanglement, liaison.
—**Ant.** untie, loosen, release.

tight, *adj.* **1.** secure, fixed, firm, fast, sealed, close-fitting, impervious, impenetrable, impermeable, snug, airtight, leakproof, waterproof. **2.** taut, tense, stretched, constricting, shrunken, contracted, compressed, condensed. **3.** strict, stringent, restrictive, tough, severe, rigorous, stern, harsh, austere, uncompromising, inflexible, unyielding, hard and fast, autocratic, despotic, tyrannical.
—**Ant.** loose.

time, *n.* **1.** duration, stretch, patch, period, interval, term, spell, span, space. **2.** epoch, era, period, season, age, date, day, heyday, lifetime. **3.** opportunity, occasion, chance, break; juncture, pass, contingency. —*v.* **4.** regulate, gauge, measure, schedule, set, control, organize, fix, adjust.

timely, *adj.* seasonable, opportune, fortunate, lucky, providential, propitious, favorable, auspicious, appropriate, fit, seemly, proper, convenient, well-timed, prompt, punctual.
—**Ant.** untimely, inappropriate, inopportune.

timid, *adj.* fearful, shy, diffident, sheepish, apprehensive, afraid, nervous, anxious, bashful, retiring, coy, blushing, modest, mousy, wary, chary, circumspect, shrinking, timorous, fainthearted, tremulous, cowardly, yellow, lily-livered, chicken, chicken-hearted, gutless, pusillanimous.
—**Ant.** bold, fearless, intrepid, valiant.

tinny, *adj.* **1.** unresonant, harsh, metallic, twangy, reedy, thin, hollow, weak, feeble. **2.** inferior, cheap, low-grade, insubstantial, shoddy, tacky, tatty, tinselly, shabby, tawdry, flimsy, cheapjack.
—**Ant.** resonant; well-made, superior, substantial.

tint, *n.* **1.** color, hue, tinge, dye, wash, cast, touch, hint, trace, suggestion, shade, stain, tincture, rinse. —*v.* **2.** color, tinge, stain, dye, rinse, touch up.

tiny, *adj.* small, little, minute, microscopic, wee, teeny, miniature, diminutive, minuscule, mini, micro, infinitesimal, midget, petite, slight, delicate, dainty, elfin, pygmy, Lilliputian, bantam, pint-sized, puny, inconsequential, insignificant, negligible, trifling, paltry, itty-bitty, itsy-bitsy.

tirade, *n.* denunciation, outburst, diatribe, phillipic, jeremiad, screed, invective, harangue, declamation.

tire, *v.* **1.** exhaust, weary, fatigue, tucker out, weaken, drain, sap, enervate, debilitate, frazzle, deplete, wear out, jade. **2.** exasperate, bore, weary, irk, annoy, pester, bother, irritate, vex, tax, needle, hassle, get up (someone's) nose.

tired, *adj.* exhausted, fatigued, sleepy, worn out, spent, drained, sapped, weary, wearied, enervated, bushed, pooped, all in, wiped out, beat, ready to drop, bone-tired, dead on one's feet.
—**Ant.** energetic, fiery, tireless.

tireless, *adj.* untiring, indefatigable, vital, vigorous, dynamic, lively, spirited, strenuous, energetic, active, industrious, enterprising, hard-working, unfaltering, unflagging, dogged, persistent, steadfast, determined, resolute, diligent, persevering, perseverant, assiduous, staunch, unwavering, tenacious.
—**Ant.** tired, slothful.

tiresome, *adj.* **1.** wearisome, tedious, boring, monotonous, flat, insipid, bland, soporific, dry, prosaic, dreary, unexciting, uninteresting, drab, vapid, dull, fatiguing, humdrum. **2.** annoying, vexatious, vexing, irritating, irksome, bothersome, burdensome, trying, exasperating, oppressive, disagreeable, troublesome, onerous, arduous.
—**Ant.** interesting, enchanting.

title, *n.* **1.** name, designation, epithet, appellation, denomination, cognomen. **2.** championship, crown. **3.** right, interest, privilege, ownership, deed, prerogative, birthright, claim. —*v.* **4.** designate, entitle, denominate, term, call, style, name, label, christen, baptize.

toil, *n.* **1.** work, labor, effort, drudgery, exertion, travail, pains, sweat of one's brow, grind, trouble. —*v.* **2.** labor, work, strive, sweat, grind, exert oneself, struggle, drudge.

—**Ant.** indolence, sloth.
—**Syn. Study.** See WORK.

tolerance, *n.* **1.** toleration, patience, leniency, indulgence, long-suffering, sufferance, forbearance, endurance, resistance, imperviousness. **2.** liberality, catholicity, impartiality, permissiveness, generosity, evenhandedness, fairness, charity, magnanimity, broadmindedness, openmindedness. **3.** play, clearance, allowance, variation.
—**Ant.** intolerance.

tool, *n.* instrument, implement, utensil, contrivance, device, gadget, apparatus, appliance, aid, mechanism, contraption, gizmo.
—**Syn. Study.** TOOL, IMPLEMENT, INSTRUMENT, UTENSIL refer to contrivances for doing work. A TOOL is a contrivance held in and worked by the hand and used for cutting, digging, etc.: *a carpenter's tools.* An IMPLEMENT is any tool or contrivance designed or used for a particular purpose: *agricultural implements.* An INSTRUMENT is anything used in doing certain work or producing a certain result, esp. such as requires delicacy, accuracy, or precision: *surgical or musical instruments.* A UTENSIL is usu. an article for domestic use: *kitchen utensils.* When used figuratively of human agency, TOOL is generally used in a contemptuous sense; INSTRUMENT, in a neutral ·or good sense: *a tool of unscrupulous men; an instrument of Providence.*

top, *n.* **1.** apex, zenith, acme, peak, crest, head, crown, height, high point, apogee, meridian, summit, pinnacle, vertex, culmination. —*adj.* **2.** highest, topmost, uppermost, upper. **3.** best, greatest, leading, preeminent, first, finest, choicest, foremost, chief, principal. —*v.* **4.** surpass, excel, outdo, better, outstrip, exceed, beat, trancend, overshadow.
—**Ant.** bottom, foot; lowest; worst.

topic, *n.* subject, theme, thesis, argument, text, issue, question, point, area of study *or* inquiry, keynote, gist, substance, thread, angle, subject matter.
—**Syn. Study.** See SUBJECT.

torment, *v.* **1.** afflict, pain, rack, grill, try, torture, abuse, mistreat, maltreat, harrow, harass, harry, hector, bait, badger, bully, vex, annoy, irritate, agonize, distress, excruciate, crucify. **2.** plague, worry, annoy, pester, tease, provoke, needle, nettle, bedevil, nag, persecute, irk, exasperate, aggravate, beleaguer, trouble, tantalize, fret, hassle. —*n.* **3.** agony, wretchedness, suffering, affliction, torture, misery, distress, anguish, woe, travail, affliction, pain, curse, hell, horror.
—**Ant.** please; delight; soothe, mollify; joy, pleasure, amelioration.

torrent, *n.* stream, flow, downpour, flood, deluge, rush, effusion, gush, outpouring, inundation, overflow, tide, cascade, outburst, spate.
—**Ant.** drop, drip, dribble.

torrid, *adj.* **1.** hot, humid, muggy, steamy, tropical, burning, sultry, stifling, sweltering, sizzling, boiling, blistering, arid, scorching, fiery, parching. **2.** ardent, lustful, amorous, erotic, sexy, hot, inflamed, impassioned, passionate, fervent, intense.
—**Ant.** arctic, frigid, cold; dispassionate, cool.

torture, *v.* torment, afflict, try, rack, grill, abuse, mistreat, maltreat, maim, mutilate, mangle, trouble, distress, wrong, oppress, persecute, agonize, worry, annoy, harass, bully, badger, bait.

toss, *v.* throw, cast, fling, hurl, pitch, lob, send, launch, lash,

heave, sling, propel, thrust, catapult, let fly, chuck.

total, *adj.* **1.** whole, entire, complete, gross, overall, comprehensive, finished, final, full; absolute, utter, unalloyed, unmitigated, thorough, perfect, outright, out-and-out, all-out, downright, unconditional, unqualified. —*n.* **2.** sum, whole, amount, total number, quantity, entirety, totality, aggregate, gross.

totality, *n.* total, all, sum total, aggregate, whole, grand total, everything, entirety, all and sundry, kit and caboodle, whole nine yards, whole bit, whole schmear, whole shebang, whole shooting match, whole ball of wax, the works, the lot, beginning and end, be-all and end-all, alpha and omega.

touch, *v.* **1.** handle, feel, palpate, stroke. **2.** tap, pat, brush against, caress, rub, pet, strike, hit. **3.** come up to, attain, reach, arrive at. **4.** approach, rival, match, equal, compare with, hold a candle to, stack up against, be on a par with, be in the same league *or* class with. **5.** affect, impress, sway, quicken, influence, disturb, arouse, excite, impassion, stimulate, move, strike, stir, melt, soften. **6.** pertain *or* relate to, concern, regard, affect. —*n.* **7.** stroke, pat, hit, brush, caress, tap, blow. **8.** hint, trace, suggestion, dash, intimation, soupçon, tinge, suspicion, streak, bit, whiff, speck.

touchy, *adj.* **1.** sensitive, hypersensitive, thin-skinned, temperamental, excitable, explosive, mercurial, changeable, unstable, tense, highstrung, volatile. **2.** irritable, irascible, cranky, crabby, crotchety, grouchy, querulous, quarrelsome, captious, petulant, peevish, choleric, dyspeptic, splenetic, argumentative, disputatious, snappish, bearish, waspish, short-tempered, curmudgeonly, caviling, faultfinding, cross, cantankerous, testy, tetchy. **3.** delicate, ticklish, difficult, tricky, sticky, precarious, slippery, perilous, parlous, dangerous, critical, touch-and-go, sensitive, risky, chancy, hazardous, uncertain, hair-raising, nerve-racking, terrifying.
—**Ant.** imperturbable.

tough, *adj.* **1.** firm, strong, hard, long-lasting, substantial, stout, rugged, sound, well-built, hardy, sturdy, hardy, durable. **2.** difficult, hard, demanding, taxing, troublesome, exacting, strenuous; baffling, perplexing, thorny, knotty, irksome, puzzling, mystifying. **3.** hardened, incorrigible, troublesome, stubborn, obstinate, obdurate, refractory, adamant, callous, hard-boiled, hardnosed, intractable, unsentimental, cold, stony, unbending, inflexible, rigid.
—**Ant.** weak, feeble, sickly; flexible, soft.

tour, *n.* excursion, trip, journey, expedition, visit, travel, voyage, pilgrimage, junket, jaunt, outing, peregrination, safari, drive, cruise, trek.

towering, *adj.* tall, lofty, high, soaring, outstanding, sky-high, imposing, impressive, huge, gigantic, superior, paramount, supreme, unparalleled, unsurpassed, unrivaled, overwhelming, colossal, enormous, great, elevated.
—**Ant.** short, low.

toxic, *adj.* harmful, injurious, hazardous, dangerous, damaging, deleterious, poisonous, venomous, virulent, malignant, deadly, lethal, pestilent, pestilential.
—**Ant.** beneficial, healthful.

trace, *n.* **1.** vestige, mark, sign, remnant, track, spoor, scent, footprint, trail, record. **2.** mark, sign, token, clue, hint, indication, evidence. **3.**

hint, suggestion, touch, taste, intimation, whiff, suspicion, tinge, dash, spot, bit, speck, soupçon. —*v.* **4.** track, follow, trail, dog, pursue, stalk, shadow, tail. **5.** ascertain, find out, discover, investigate, determine, detect, seek, search for, hunt down, unearth. **6.** draw, map, chart, sketch, reproduce, draft, plot, copy, delineate, outline, diagram.
—**Ant.** abundance, plethora.
—**Syn. Study.** TRACE, VESTIGE agree in denoting marks or signs of something, usu. of the past. TRACE, the broader term, denotes any mark or slight indication of something past or present: *a trace of ammonia in water.* VESTIGE is more limited and refers to some slight, though actual, remains of something that no longer exists: *vestiges of one's former wealth.*

tract, *n.* **1.** stretch, extent, district, area, zone, belt, expanse, spread, vicinity, locality, section, sector, patch, quarter, parcel, plot, portion, lot, territory, region. **2.** treatise, pamphlet, booklet, brochure, leaflet, broadside, essay, sermon, thesis, text, monograph, article, paper, critique, homily, dissertation, disquisition, phillipic, jeremiad, diatribe, screed.

trade, *n.* **1.** commerce, traffic, business, dealing, exchange, barter, industry, buying and selling, merchandising, marketing. **2.** purchase, sale, exchange, swap. **3.** occupation, vocation, métier, livelihood, living, employment, pursuit, work, job, career, position, place, situation, business, profession, craft, calling. —*v.* **4.** barter, exchange, swap, return, switch, interchange. **5.** barter, transact *or* do business, merchandise, market, bargain, traffic *or* deal in.

tragic, *adj.* mournful, melancholy, sad, depressing, lamentable, funereal, forlorn, dolorous, grievous, dismal, lugubrious, unhappy, cheerless, miserable, pathetic, distressing, pitiful, piteous, pitiable, appalling, wretched, shocking, upsetting, unfortunate, ill-fated, star-crossed, illstarred, inauspicious, unlucky, calamitous, sorrowful, disastrous, fatal, dire, awful, horrible, terrible, deplorable, catastrophic, crushing, dreadful.
—**Ant.** comic, happy, fortunate, auspicious.

trail, *v.* **1.** drag, draw, tow, haul, pull, tag along, trawl. **2.** track, trace, hunt down, follow, pursue, dog, shadow, stalk, chase, tail. —*n.* **3.** path, track, route, way, course; scent, spoor, smell, trace.

train, *v.* discipline, teach, instruct, drill, coach, prepare, exercise, tutor, guide, indoctrinate, raise, rear, bring up.

trance, *n.* daze, daydream, reverie, spell, transport, exaltation, brown study, stupor, coma, swoon, hypnotic *or* cataleptic state, semiconsciousness, rapture, ecstasy, fugue, stupefaction, absorption, paralysis.

tranquil, *adj.* calm, peaceful, serene, placid, halcyon, quiet, silent, still, unruffled, noiseless, relaxed, sedate, unperturbed, undisturbed, even, cool, self-possessed, composed, collected, mild, gentle, restful.
—**Ant.** troubled, perturbed, raucous.

transact, *v.* carry on, enact, conclude, settle, perform, manage, negotiate, conduct, handle, administer, discharge, perform, complete, finish.

transform, *v.* change, alter, convert, metamorphose, metamorphosize, modify, morph, transmogrify, mutate, vary, evolve, develop, mature,

transfigure, transmute.
—**Ant.** retain.
—**Syn. Study.** TRANSFORM, CONVERT mean to change one thing into another. TRANSFORM means to radically change the outward form or inner character: *a frog transformed into a prince; delinquents transformed into responsible citizens.* CONVERT usually means to modify or adapt so as to serve a new or different use or function: *to convert a barn into a house.*

transient, *adj.* transitory, temporary, fleeting, passing, flitting, flying, ephemeral, short-lived, momentary, evanescent, short-term, impermanent, fly-by-night, brief, fugitive.
—**Ant.** permanent, perpetual, lasting, stable, durable, perdurable.
—**Syn. Study.** See TEMPORARY.

translation, *n.* paraphrase, version, transliteration, conversion, gloss, rewording, interpretation, rendition, rendering, treatment.

translucent, *adj.* semitransparent, see-through, pellucid, sheer, diaphanous, filmy, lucid, limpid, clear, translucid.
—**Ant.** opaque, dense, solid.
—**Syn. Study.** See TRANSPARENT.

transparent, *adj.* **1.** diaphanous, clear, pellucid, lucid, limpid, crystalline, translucent. **2.** direct, unambiguous, unequivocal, straightforward, forthright, aboveboard, plainspoken, artless, guileless, ingenuous, open, frank, candid. **3.** plain, apparent, evident, undisguised, recognizable, patent, unmistakable, crystal clear, manifest, obvious.
—**Ant.** opaque; clandestine, secretive; concealed.
—**Syn. Study.** TRANSPARENT, TRANSLUCENT agree in describing material that light rays can pass through. That which is TRANSPARENT allows objects to be seen clearly through it: *Clear water is transparent.* That which is TRANSLUCENT allows light to pass through, diffusing it, however, so that objects beyond are not distinctly seen: *Ground glass is translucent.*

transport, *v.* **1.** carry, convey, bear, remove, transfer, ship, haul, transmit, forward, shift, send, move, deliver, dispatch. **2.** banish, exile, deport, send away, expatriate, ostracize, expel, oust, eject. —*n.* **3.** conveyance, carrier, shipment, transfer, transportation. **4.** joy, bliss, rapture, ecstasy, happiness, exaltation, exultation, delight, bliss, exhilaration, elation, euphoria, nirvana, seventh heaven, paradise, cloud nine, beatitude, felicity, enthusiasm, passion, fervor, ardor, fury, frenzy.

trap, *n.* **1.** pitfall, snare, springe, lure, bait, decoy. **2.** ambush, pitfall, artifice, maneuver, wile, machination, ruse, plot, conspiracy, subterfuge, device, deception, deceit, con game, hoax, sham, pretense, scam, flimflam, stratagem, trick. —*v.* **3.** snare, ensnare, entrap, bag, catch, capture, nab, cop, net, seize, ambush. **4.** trick, fool, deceive, dupe, con, inveigle, beguile, mislead, cajole, bamboozle, delude, betray, hoax, lead on.

traumatic, *adj.* injurious, harmful, hurtful, damaging, wounding, acute, upsetting, wrenching, painful, disturbing, distressing, dreadful, troubling, shattering, shocking, stunning, devastating, excruciating, agonizing, torturous, racking.

travesty, *n.* burlesque, parody, mockery, farce, lampoon, caricature, takeoff, sendup.

treacherous, *adj.* **1.** traitorous, turncoat, renegade, seditious, unfaithful, faithless, untrustworthy, treasonable, treasonous, perfidious, disloyal.

2. deceptive, unreliable, insidious, recreant, deceitful, false, double-crossing, betraying, deceiving, misleading, two-faced, hypocritical, underhanded, Machiavellian, conspiratorial. 3. dangerous, perilous, hazardous, unsound, parlous, tricky, ticklish, touchy, uncertain, unstable, insecure.
—**Ant.** faithful, trustworthy, loyal; reliable; stable, secure.

treachery, *n.* betrayal, treason, apostasy, recreance, recreancy, defection, abandonment, desertion, disloyalty, faithlessness, double-dealing, duplicity, guile, underhandedness, double-cross, perfidy, sabotage, subversion, deceit, chicanery, knavery, villainy, iniquity.
—**Ant.** loyalty, fealty.

treason, *n.* sedition, disloyalty, sellout, betrayal, perfidy, subversiveness, deception, double-crossing, treachery, disaffection, lese majesty, mutiny, insurrection, incitement to riot, rebellion.
—**Ant.** loyalty, allegiance.
—**Syn. Study.** TREASON, SEDITION mean disloyalty or treachery to one's country or its government. TREASON is any attempt to overthrow the government or impair the well-being of a state to which one owes allegiance. According to the U.S. Constitution, it is the crime of levying war against the U.S. or giving aid and comfort to its enemies. SEDITION is any act, writing, speech, etc., directed unlawfully against state authority, the government, or the constitution, or calculated to bring it into contempt or to incite others to hostility or disaffection; it does not amount to treason and therefore is not a capital offense.

treasure, *n.* 1. wealth, riches, fortune, money, cash, cache, hoard, funds; valuables, jewels. —*v.* 2. prize, cherish, love, hold dear, value, appreciate, esteem, respect, admire, regard highly, adore.

treat, *v.* 1. act *or* behave toward. 2. look upon, consider, regard, deal with. 3. discuss, deal with, handle, manage, study, examine, consider, touch on, investigate, explore, scrutinize, analyze, review, criticize. 4. entertain, take out, wine and dine, pay for, host, regale, feast. 5. negotiate, settle, bargain, come to terms, confer, consult, advise. —*n.* 6. favor, gift, present, bonus, freebie, perk; feast, fête, entertainment, banquet.

tremble, *v.* 1. shake, quiver, quaver, quake, shiver, shudder. 2. vibrate, wobble, teeter, shimmy, oscillate, totter.

tremendous, *adj.* 1. huge, gigantic, stupendous, monumental, prodigious, monstrous, enormous, immense, vast, gargantuan, outsize, oversized, towering, colossal. 2. dreadful, awful, horrid, alarming, startling, frightening, staggering, stunning, dire, horrendous, terrible, terrifying, horrifying, appalling. 3. amazing, astounding, astonishing, dazzling, stunning, staggering, awesome, flabbergasting, wonderful, remarkable, fabulous, extraordinary, marvelous, terrific
—**Ant.** small, tiny, microscopic.
—**Syn. Study.** See HUGE.

tremor, *n.* 1. trembling, shaking, shuddering, vibration, oscillation, shivering, quivering, quaking. 2. quake, earthquake, temblor, seismic activity, tectonic shift.

trend, *n.* 1. course, drift, tendency, tenor, current, disposition, predisposition, leaning, bias, bent, proneness, propensity, direction, inclination. 2. fashion, style, vogue, rage, fad, mode, look, craze. —*v.* 3. tend, veer, extend, stretch, run, incline, lean, bend, drift, swing, shift, head.

trespass, *n.* 1. invasion, encroachment, intrusion, infringement. 2. offense, sin, wrong, transgression, violation, infraction, breach, contravention, vice, crime, misdemeanor, misdeed, error, fault. —*v.* 3. encroach, infringe, intrude, invade, butt in, interfere, intervene. 4. transgress, offend, err, do wrong, sin.
—**Syn. Study.** TRESPASS, ENCROACH, INFRINGE imply overstepping boundaries or violating the rights of others. To TRESPASS is to invade the property or rights of another, esp. to pass unlawfully within the boundaries of private land: *The hunters trespassed on the farmer's fields.* To ENCROACH is to intrude, gradually and often stealthily, on the territory, rights, or privileges of another, so that a footing is imperceptibly established: *The sea slowly encroached on the land.* To INFRINGE is to break in upon or invade another's rights, customs, or the like, by violating or disregarding them: *to infringe on a patent.*

trial, *n.* 1. test, proof, experiment, tryout, trial run, checking, dry run, demonstration, inspection, experience, scrutiny, examination, testing. 2. attempt, effort, endeavor, struggle, try, venture, shot, stab, fling, whirl, essay. 3. test, assay, criterion, proof, touchstone, standard. 4. affliction, suffering, tribulation, difficulty, distress, sorrow, grief, trouble, misery, agony, anguish, adversity, misfortune, vicissitude, cross, rigor, woe, hardship, hard luck, hard times.
—**Ant.** consolation.

trick, *n.* 1. artifice, ruse, stratagem, device, expedient, maneuver, humbug, fraud, imposture, hoax, subterfuge, intrigue, wile, deception, fraud, trickery, cheating, deceit, duplicity, machination, conspiracy, con. 2. prank, joke, practical joke, antic, horseplay, tomfoolery, caper, mischief, gag, shenanigans. 3. jugglery, sleight of hand, legerdemain, prestidigitation, magic, stunt, illusion, hocus-pocus. —*v.* 4. cheat, swindle, beguile, gull, hoax, hoodwink, bamboozle, mislead, outwit, circumvent, outmaneuver, bilk, rook, outfox, dupe, fool, deceive, defraud, delude.
—**Syn. Study.** TRICK, ARTIFICE, RUSE, STRATAGEM are terms for crafty or cunning devices intended to deceive. TRICK, the general term, refers usu. to an underhanded act designed to cheat someone, but it sometimes refers merely to a pleasurable deceiving of the senses: *to win by a trick.* Like TRICK, but to a greater degree, ARTIFICE emphasizes the cleverness or cunning with which the proceeding is devised: *an artifice of diabolical ingenuity.* RUSE and STRATAGEM emphasize the purpose for which the trick is designed; RUSE is the more general term, and STRATAGEM sometimes implies a more elaborate procedure or a military application: *We gained entrance by a ruse. His stratagem gave the army command of the hill.* See also CHEAT.

trickery, *n.* artifice, trick, stratagem, dissimulation, guile, cunning, wiles, wiliness, duplicity, fraud, deception, deceit, chicanery, double-dealing, subterfuge, imposture, cheating, fraud, humbug, knavery, shrewdness, slyness, craftiness, craft, evasiveness, hanky-panky, skulduggery, hocus-pocus.
—**Ant.** honesty, sincerity, trustworthiness, guilelessness.

trifling, *adj.* 1. trivial, insignificant, unimportant, petty, paltry, negligible, puny, measly, picayune, minor, inconsequential, nugatory, slight, worthless, piddling, immaterial. 2. frivolous, shallow, inane, jejune, banal, vapid, insipid, superficial, lightweight, light, empty.
—**Ant.** important, significant, substantial, major; profound, serious.
—**Syn. Study.** See PETTY.

trim, *v.* 1. shorten, abbreviate, crop, snip, dock, reduce, pare, clip, prune, shave, shear, cut, lop, curtail. 2. modify, adjust, prepare, arrange. 3. dress up, array, deck, bedeck, ornament, beautify, decorate, adorn, embellish, garnish, embroider, trick out. —*n.* 4. condition, order, form, health, fitness, repair, shape, situation, state. 5. dress, array, equipment, gear, trappings, trimmings. 6. trimming, edging, embroidery, border, frill, fringe, ornamentation, adornment, embellishment, decoration; cutting, clipping, priming, reduction. —*adj.* 7. neat, smart; well-groomed, well-kempt, crisp, dapper, spick-and-span, shipshape, spruce, tidy, well-ordered, orderly, ordered.
—**Ant.** augment, increase.

trip, *n.* 1. expedition, journey, pilgrimage, voyage, excursion, travel, tour, jaunt, junket, outing, trek, peregrination, cruise, drive, safari. 2. stumble, misstep, fall, faltering. 3. slip, mistake, error, blunder, erratum, faux pas, indiscretion, lapse, oversight, miss. —*v.* 4. stumble, misstep, fall down, tumble, lurch, flounder, topple, sprawl, plunge, falter, stagger. 5. bungle, blunder, err, slip, miss, overlook. 6. tip, tilt.
—**Syn. Study.** TRIP, EXPEDITION, JOURNEY, PILGRIMAGE, VOYAGE are terms for a course of travel made to a particular place, usu. for some specific purpose. TRIP is the general word, indicating going any distance and returning, for either business or pleasure, and in either a hurried or a leisurely manner: *a trip to Europe; a bus trip.* An EXPEDITION, made often by an organized group, is designed for a specific purpose: *an archaeological expedition.* JOURNEY indicates a trip of considerable length, mainly by land, and is usu. applied to travel that is more fatiguing than a trip: *an arduous journey to Tibet.* A PILGRIMAGE is made as to a shrine, from motives of piety or veneration: *a pilgrimage to Lourdes.* A VOYAGE usu. indicates leisurely travel by water to a distant place: *a voyage around the world.*

trite, *adj.* commonplace, ordinary, common, threadbare, shopworn, stereotyped, old-hat, hackneyed, clichéd, bromidic, antiquated, archaic, obsolete, banal, flat, insipid, jejune, vapid, stale.
—**Ant.** original, fresh, uncommon, unusual, extraordinary.

triumph, *n.* 1. victory, conquest, subjugation, routing, overthrow, success, achievement, accomplishment, attainment, coup. 2. joy, exultation, ecstasy, rejoicing, elation, rapture, glory, delight, exhilaration, jubilation, celebration. —*v.* 3. win, succeed, prevail, dominate, defeat, vanquish, conquer, beat, rout, overcome, overwhelm, subdue. 4. rejoice, exult, celebrate, glory, be elated *or* glad, delight, rejoice.
—**Ant.** defeat, loss.
—**Syn. Study.** See VICTORY.

trivial, *adj.* trifling, petty, unimportant, insignificant, nugatory, futile, vain, fruitless, bootless, meaningless, inconsequential, nonessential, minimal, minor, paltry, puny, measly, picayune, lightweight, slight, immaterial, frivolous, small.
—**Ant.** important, significant, weighty, momentous.
—**Syn. Study.** See PETTY.

trophy, *n.* 1. token, remembrance, record, reminder, memento, souvenir, keepsake, commemoration, memorial. 2. prize, award, reward, laurels, garland, loving cup, wreath, medal, citation, palm, booty, spoils.

trouble, *v.* 1. disturb, distress, ail, undermine, try, anguish, alarm, worry, concern, agitate, upset, discompose, disquiet, perturb, grieve, disorder, disarrange, distract, perplex, puzzle, baffle, discombobulate, confuse, derange, embarrass, disconcert, abash. 2. inconvenience, put out, burden, encumber, discommode, incommode. 3. annoy, vex, bother, afflict, provoke, needle, nettle, exasperate, aggravate, gall, beleaguer, irritate, irk, pester, plague, fret, torment, torture, harry, hector, harass, nag, bully, pick at *or* on, badger, molest, get on one's nerves *or* under one's skin, give (someone) a hard time. —*n.* 4. molestation, harassment, annoyance, bother, irritation, nuisance, vexation, difficulty, embarrassment. 5. misery, distress, affliction, concern, worry, grief, agitation, care, agony, anguish, torment, torture, cross, catastrophe, suffering, calamity, dolor, adversity, bad luck, hard times, strife, vicissitude, tribulation, trial, misfortune, woe, pain, sorrow. 6. disturbance, agitation, row, turbulence, unrest, discord, turmoil, tumult, fighting, uprising, skirmish, revolt, rebellion, outbreak, disorder. 7. inconvenience, exertion, fuss, ado, stir, flurry, pains, effort.
—**Ant.** calm, mollify; support, accommodate; happiness, joy, celebration; peace, serenity, tranquility.

troublesome, *adj.* 1. annoying, worrisome, worrying, irksome, irritating, exasperating, bothersome, pestiferous, pesky, vexatious, confusing, baffling, perplexing, galling, nagging, harassing. 2. laborious, difficult, arduous, strenuous, tiring, tiresome, rigorous, excruciating, taxing, hard, burdensome, wearisome.
—**Ant.** simple, easy, trouble-free.

true, *adj.* 1. factual, actual, real, bona fide, authentic, genuine, veracious, truthful, realistic, valid, verified, verifiable, veritable. 2. sincere, earnest, wholehearted, honest, honorable, just, faithful, equitable, fair. 3. loyal, faithful, trusty, trustworthy, devoted, dedicated, fast, firm, stable, dependable, reliable, resolute, true blue, staunch, constant, steady, steadfast, unswerving, unwavering, unfaltering. 4. accurate, exact, faithful, correct, literal, unvarnished, unadulterated, precise; agreeing. 5. right, proper, legitimate, rightful. 6. reliable, sure, unfailing, persisting, certain, persevering.
—**Ant.** untrue, false.

trust, *n.* 1. reliance, confidence, dependence, sureness, positiveness, assurance, security, conviction, certitude, certainty, belief, faith, credence, credit. 2. expectation, hope, faith. 3. credit, reliability, dependability, trustworthiness, credibility. 4. obligation, responsibility, charge. 5. commitment, office, duty, charge. —*v.* 6. rely on, confide in, count on, bank on, reckon on, have confidence in, depend upon. 7. believe, credit. 8. expect, hope, look for, have faith. 9. entrust, commit, consign, delegate, empower, assign, sign *or* hand over.
—**Ant.** mistrust, distrust.

trustworthy, *adj.* reliable, true, dependable, trusty, tried, safe, secure, constant, stable, honest, honorable, faithful, staunch, loyal, steadfast,

steady, straightforward, honest, upright, scrupulous.
—**Ant.** deceitful, dubious

truth, *n.* **1.** fact, reality, verity, veracity. **2.** genuineness, reality, authenticity, actuality. **3.** honesty, uprightness, integrity, sincerity, candor, frankness, openness, ingenuousness, probity, fidelity, virtue. **4.** accuracy, correctness, rightness, precision, exactness, nicety.
—**Ant.** lie, fiction, fabrication, untruth; fraudulence; dishonesty; inaccuracy.

try, *v.* **1.** attempt, essay, endeavor, struggle, undertake, venture, seek, take a shot *or* crack *or* stab at, strive, make an effort. **2.** test, prove, demonstrate, inspect, scrutinize, analyze, evaluate, check out, sample, appraise, assess, judge, examine, investigate.
—**Syn. Study.** TRY, ATTEMPT, ENDEAVOR, STRIVE all mean to put forth an effort toward a specific end. TRY is the most often used and most general term: *to try to decipher a message; to try hard to succeed.* ATTEMPT, often interchangeable with TRY, sometimes suggests the possibility of failure and is often used in reference to more serious or important matters: *to attempt to formulate a new theory of motion.* ENDEAVOR emphasizes serious and continued exertion of effort, sometimes aimed at dutiful or socially appropriate behavior: *to endeavor to fulfill one's obligations.* STRIVE stresses persistent, vigorous, even strenuous effort, often in the face of obstacles: *to strive to overcome a handicap.*

tumult, *n.* **1.** commotion, disturbance, disorder, turbulence, uproar, upset, disquiet, bedlam, chaos, brouhaha, stir, ado, pandemonium, hullabaloo, brawl, donnybrook, furor, row, turmoil, frenzy, rage, rumpus, ruckus, hubbub, fracas, agitation, affray, melee; riot, outbreak, uprising, revolt, insurrection, rampage, revolution, mutiny. **2.** agitation, perturbation, confusion, excitement, ferment.
—**Ant.** peace, order; calm, serenity.

tumultuous, *adj.* **1.** uproarious, chaotic, frenzied, furious, hectic, wild, savage, frantic, hysterical, tempestuous, stormy, fierce, turbulent, riotous, violent. **2.** noisy, disorderly, irregular, boisterous, clamorous, rowdy, unruly, obstreperous. **3.** disturbed, agitated, excited, perturbed, confused, unquiet, restive, restless, nervous, uneasy.
—**Ant.** calm, peaceful, pacific; regular, orderly; quiet, restful.

tuneful, *adj.* musical, melodious, melodic, euphonious, mellifluent, mellow, smooth, harmonic, harmonious, dulcet, sweet, rich, rhythmic.
—**Ant.** discordant, sour, flat.

turmoil, *n.* commotion, disturbance, tumult, agitation, disquiet, upset, chaos, confusion, ferment, frenzy, violence, fury, turbulence, stir, ado, brouhaha, hysteria, disorder, bustle, trouble, uproar.
—**Ant.** quiet, serenity, order, peace.

turn, *v.* **1.** rotate, spin, revolve, roll, reel, pivot, swivel, gyrate, circle, whirl, twirl, wheel, swirl, pirouette, eddy. **2.** change, reverse, divert, deflect, avert, sheer, veer, swerve, deviate, diverge, shift, digress, depart, transfer. **3.** change, alter, metamorphose, transmute, transform, adapt, reorganize, modify, shape, reform, convert. **4.** direct, point, aim. **5.** shape, form, create, concoct, formulate, construct, cast, coin, fashion, mold. **6.** curve, bend, twist, wind, loop, arc, meander, snake, zigzag, coil. **7.** go bad, spoil, curdle, rot, decay, molder, putrefy, become rancid, sour, ferment. —*n.* **8.** rotation, spin, cycle, circuit, round, spin, whirl, twirl, gyration, revolution. **9.** change, reversal, alteration, shift. **10.** direction, drift, trend. **11.** change, deviation, twist, bend, turning, vicissitude, variation. **12.** shape, style, mode, form, mold, cast, fashion, manner. **13.** inclination, bent, tendency, disposition, predisposition, bias, leaning, penchant, prejudice, proneness, predilection, aptitude, talent, proclivity, propensity.
—**Syn. Study.** TURN, REVOLVE, ROTATE, SPIN indicate moving in a more or less rotary, circular fashion. TURN is the general and popular word for motion on an axis or around a center, but it is used also of motion that is less than a complete circle: *A gate turns on its hinges.* REVOLVE refers esp. to movement in an orbit around a center, but is sometimes exchangeable with ROTATE, which refers only to the motion of a body around its own center or axis: *The moon revolves about the earth. The earth rotates on its axis.* To SPIN is to rotate very rapidly: *A top spins.*

tutor *v.* teach, instruct, educate, train, enlighten, advise, guide, prepare, direct, ground, mentor, coach, drill, indoctrinate, school.

twilight, *n.* **1.** evening, dusk, eventide, gloaming, sunset, sundown, half-light, dimness, obscurity, shadows, nightfall, crepuscule. **2.** decline, diminution, waning, ebb, weakening, close, end, ending, finish, conclusion, downturn, slump, decay.
—**Ant.** dawn; waxing.

twist, *v.* **1.** intertwine, braid, plait, weave, entwine, interlace, interweave; combine, associate. **2.** contort, distort, change, alter, pervert, warp, bias, color, falsify, misrepresent, misconstrue, garble. **3.** wind, snake, meander, turn, zigzag, coil, curve, bend, roll. **4.** writhe, squirm, wriggle. **5.** turn, spin, rotate, revolve. —*n.* **6.** curve, bend, turn. **7.** turning, turn, rotation, rotating, spin. **8.** spiral, helix, coil.

twit, *v.* **1.** taunt, gibe, banter, ridicule, mock, pick on, scoff, jeer, tweak, make fun of, razz, ride, rib, roast, kid, rag, tease. **2.** deride, reproach, upbraid, chide, reprove, censure, blame, berate, scorn, revile, sneer at.

tycoon, *n.* magnate, leader, captain of industry, top executive, baron, czar, personage, mogul, CEO, chairman of the board, business leader, financier, millionaire, billionaire, panjandrum, nabob, VIP, worthy, big shot, wheel, wheeler-dealer, big cheese, big wheel, bigwig, brass hat, big-time operator, big enchilada, top dog.
—**Ant.** nobody, nonentity, cipher; underling, subordinate, lackey, flunky.

type, *n.* **1.** kind, sort, class, category, genre, order, variety, species, breed, strain, ilk, classification, group, family, genus, phylum, form, stamp. **2.** sample, specimen, example, representative, prototype, paradigm, epitome, personification, standard, quintessence, pattern, model, exemplar, original, archetype. **3.** form, character, stamp. **4.** image, figure, device, sign, symbol, emblem, mark, token.

typical *adj.* **1.** normal, standard, ordinary, regular, natural, general, generic, common, universal, representative, characteristic, specific. **2.** conventional, usual, commonplace, common, ordinary, run-of-the-mill, orthodox, classic, in keeping, in character, to be expected.
—**Ant.** atypical, distinctive, unusual, unexpected, unorthodox.

tyrannical, *adj.* arbitrary, despotic, authoritarian, fascistic, autocratic, bullying, totalitarian, dictatorial, cruel, harsh, severe, oppressive, unjust, overbearing, highhanded, ironfisted, absolute, magisterial, imperious, domineering, dominating, inhuman.
—**Ant.** judicious, liberal, just, humane, democratic, egalitarian.

tyrant, *n.* despot, autocrat, dictator, authoritarian, overlord, slave driver, bully, Hitler, czar, martinet, fascist, Nazi, supremacist, absolute ruler *or* monarch, totalitarian, oppressor.
—**Ant.** democrat, egalitarian, liberator.

U

ugly, *adj.* **1.** repulsive, offensive, hideous, grotesque, ghastly, gruesome, monstrous, ill-favored, unlovely, unattractive, unsightly, homely. **2.** revolting, terrible, base, sordid, evil, foul, perverted, depraved, degenerate, abominable, execrable, despicable, odious, vile, monstrous, corrupt, heinous, amoral. **3.** disagreeable, unpleasant, offensive, nasty, loathsome, repugnant, repulsive, revolting, obnoxious, objectionable. **4.** troublesome, uncomfortable, awkward, hazardous, perilous, touchy, precarious, threatening. **5.** surly, spiteful, ill-natured, quarrelsome, argumentative, peevish, irritable, cross, crabby, querulous, curmudgeonly, rude, irascible, churlish, disagreeable, hostile, nasty, cantankerous, crotchety, mean, obnoxious, obstreperous, peevish, testy, tetchy, rancorous, malicious, vicious, bad-tempered.
—**Ant.** beautiful.

ulterior, *adj.* unacknowledged, underlying, surreptitious, underhanded, unavowed, unexpressed, hidden, concealed, covert, secret, private, personal, confidential, latent, obscure, ambiguous, cryptic, enigmatic.
—**Ant.** open, explicit.

ultimate, *adj.* final, decisive, last, latest, terminal, conclusive, eventual, supreme, utmost, absolute, extreme, furthest, farthest, remotest.
—**Ant.** prime, primary.

ultimatum, *n.* warning, notice, threat, demand, requirement, condition, stipulation, insistence, final offer.

unable *adj.* **1.** not able, unfit, unqualified, powerless, impotent, incapable, helpless, incompetent, ineffective, ineffectual. **2.** disabled, incapacitated, crippled, paralyzed, debilitated, weak, feeble.
—**Ant.** able.

unaccountable, *adj.* **1.** not answerable, not responsible, independent, autonomous, sovereign. **2.** inexplicable, inscrutable, strange, mysterious, puzzling, baffling, odd, peculiar, weird, uncanny, unfathomable, incomprehensible, unintelligible.
—**Ant.** accountable.

unaccustomed, *adj.* unusual, unfamiliar, uncommon, unexpected, unprecedented, peculiar, curious, rare, new.
—**Ant.** common, typical, familiar.

unaffected, *adj.* **1.** sincere, genuine, honest, real, unfeigned, natural, unpretentious, unassuming, unstudied, down to earth, plain, naive, simple, guileless, straightforward, ingenuous, unsophisticated, artless. **2.** unmoved, untouched, unimpressed, immune, impervious, aloof, unresponsive, cold, remote, unconcerned, unstirred.
—**Ant.** affected.

unanimity, *n.* accord, agreement, unanimousness, harmony, unity, unison, uniformity, concurrence, consensus, concord, concordance, solidarity, likemindedness.
—**Ant.** discord, disagreement, dissension.

unassuming, *adj.* modest, unpretentious, humble, simple, approachable, friendly, warm, accessible, unaffected, down-to-earth, self-effacing, unostentatious.
—**Ant.** immodest, pretentious, pompous, self-important.

unbearable, *adj.* unendurable, intolerable, insufferable, insupportable, unacceptable, outrageous, unreasonable, inhuman, unthinkable, unspeakable.
—**Ant.** bearable, tolerable.

unbecoming, *adj.* **1.** inappropriate, ill-suited, unsuited, unapt, unsuitable, unfitted, unfitting, unfit, out of place *or* character. **2.** unseemly, improper, indecent, indelicate, indecorous, clumsy, awkward, gauche, maladroit, tasteless, rude, impolite, offensive, objectionable.
—**Ant.** becoming, appropriate; seemly, proper.
—**Syn. Study.** See IMPROPER.

unbelievable, *adj.* incredible, beyond belief, doubtful, dubious, unimaginable, inconceivable, implausible, unlikely, improbable, unthinkable, far-fetched, unrealistic, preposterous, absurd, ridiculous, mind-boggling.
—**Ant.** believable, credible, realistic.

unbiased, *adj.* fair, equitable, impartial, tolerant, unprejudiced, openminded, even-handed, just, reasonable, fair-minded, objective, judicious, dispassionate, detached, unbigoted, aloof, uncolored, nonpartisan, undogmatic, liberal, neutral, disinterested.
—**Ant.** biased, prejudiced.

uncalled-for, *adj.* unnecessary, needless, unoprovoked, unsolicited, unwelcome, unjustified, unfounded, unjustifiable, improper, out of line *or* order, impertinent, intrusive, officious, unwarranted, gratuitous, wanton, supererogatory.
—**Ant.** necessary, essential, proper.

uncanny, *adj.* strange, preternatural, supernatural, weird, odd, eerie, singular, erratic, eccentric, queer, mysterious, inexplicable, unfathomable, inscrutable, extraordinary, ghostly, unearthly, spooky, creepy.
—**Ant.** common, usual, natural.
—**Syn. Study.** See WEIRD.

uncertain, *adj.* **1.** insecure, precarious, unsure, doubtful, dubious, unpredictable, problematical, touchy, ticklish, touch-and-go, unstable, unreliable, unsafe, fallible, perilous, dangerous, hazardous, risky. **2.** unsure, undecided, indeterminate, unfixed, unsettled, indefinite, ambiguous, questionable, dubious, up in the air, conjectural, speculative, debatable, touch and go. **3.** doubtful, vague, hazy, indefinite, fuzzy, obscure, ambiguous, indistinct. **4.** undependable, unreliable, changeable, variable, capricious, unsteady, irregular, fitful, desultory, chance, fickle, erratic, wavering, sporadic, occasional.
—**Ant.** certain.

uncivil, *adj.* uncivilized, ill-mannered, unmannerly, rude, impolite, discourteous, ungracious, unchivalrous, ill-bred, vulgar, disrespectful, uncouth, boorish, loutish, churlish, crusty, blunt, tactless, undiplomatic, brusque, curt, impudent.
—**Ant.** civil.

uncivilized, *adj.* ill-mannered, uncultured, unrefined, uneducated, unpolished, unsophisticated, inelegant, uncouth, boorish, loutish, coarse, crude, gross, philistine, provincial, rough, rude, gauche, maladroit, clumsy, awkward, vulgar, tasteless, unenlightened, lowbrow, crass.
—**Ant.** civilized.

unclean, *adj.* **1.** dirty, soiled, filthy, grimy, unwashed, untidy, slovenly, squalid, smudged, bedraggled, slatternly, besmirched, sullied, stained, nasty, foul. **2.** evil, vile, base, impure, unvirtuous, unchaste, sinful, corrupt, polluted.
—**Ant.** clean.

uncomfortable, *adj.* **1.** disquieting, embarassing, disconcerting, upsetting, unnerving, unsettling, disturbing, discomforting. **2.** uneasy, ill at ease, embarrassed, queasy, flustered, agitated, upset, shaken, unsettled, perturbed, rattled, troubled, disturbed, unhappy, miserable.
—**Ant.** comfortable.

uncommon, *adj.* unusual, rare, scarce, infrequent, unexpected, occasional, sporadic, unique, atypical, different, odd, singular, strange, peculiar, remarkable, queer, extraordinary, exceptional.
—**Ant.** common.

uncommunicative, *adj.* reserved, taciturn, tightlipped, closemouthed, reticent, inexpressive, silent, mute, secretive.
—**Ant.** communicative, talkative, voluble, outgoing.

uncompromising, *adj.* unyielding, unwavering, staunch, loyal, committed, devoted, tried and true, dependable, faithful, unfaltering, resolute, determined, single-minded, immovable, inveterate, confirmed, wholehearted, inflexible, rigid, firm, steadfast, obstinate, subborn, adamant.
—**Ant.** irresolute, half-hearted, flexible.

unconditional, *adj.* unrestricted, absolute, complete, total, utter, sheer, unqualified, unconditioned, unreserved, categorical.
—**Ant.** conditional, restricted, qualified.

unconscionable, *adj.* **1.** unscrupulous, unprincipled, unethical, immoral, amoral, conscienceless, evil, wicked, criminal, unjust, unfair, contemptible, despicable, base, ignoble, shady, dishonest, unlawful. **2.** inexcusable, unacceptable, unforgivable, unpardonable, indefensible, unreasonable, excessive, extravagant, outrageous, extortionate, egregious, inordinate, immoderate, exorbitant.
—**Ant.** scrupulous; reasonable.

uncouth, *adj.* awkward, clumsy, gauche, maladroit, boorish, loutish, oafish, uncivilized, lowbrow, base, vulgar, crude, gross, crass, barbaric, coarse, insensitive, ignorant, unmannerly, discourteous, rude, ill-mannered, uncivil, ucivilized.
—**Ant.** courteous, urbane, well-bred.

uncover, *v.* lay bare, disclose, dig up, unveil, show, unearth, excavate, discover, dredge up, turn up, reveal, expose, open, strip.
—**Ant.** conceal, bury.

undeniable, *adj.* irrefutable, indisputable, indubitable, incontrovertible, incontestable, unquestionable; obvious, evident, clear, certain, sure, unimpeachable, unassailable.
—**Ant.** doubtful, dubitable, questionable.

undergo, *v.* experience, suffer, bear, weather, stand, withstand, submit to, survive, countenance, face, tolerate, sustain, endure.
—**Ant.** avoid.

underground, *adj.* **1.** subterranean, subterrestrial, subsurface, belowground, underearth, buried, sunken, covered. **2.** secret, clandestine, hidden, concealed, covert, stealthy, shrouded, furtive, sneaky, subversive, underhanded, backstairs, undercover, cabalistic, surreptitious. **3.** avant-garde, experimental, antiestablishment, revolutionary, radical, subversive, altetrnative, nonconformist, guerrilla.

underhanded, *adj.* secret, stealthy, covert, furtive, backstairs, sneaky, devious, tricky, wily, sly, crafty, dishonorable, deceitful, dishonest, cunning, clandestine, surreptitious.
—**Ant.** straightforward, aboveboard, forthright, open, candid.

understand, *v.* **1.** perceive, grasp, realize, comprehend, interpret, conceive, know, see, apprehend, discern, envision, appreciate, recognize, get the drift of, be conversant with, catch on to. **2.** learn, hear, gather, get wind of, take it, be advised.
—**Ant.** misunderstand.
—**Syn. Study.** See KNOW.

understanding, *n.* **1.** comprehension, awareness, grasp, knowledge, mastery, acquaintance, familiarity, deftness, adroitness, skill, competence, proficiency, expertise, know-how. **2.** interpretation, opinion, apprehension, opinion, reading, view, judgment, perception, estimation, viewpoint. **3.** intelligence, wisdom, intellect, mind, brain, reason, sense; discernment, insight, intuition, sensitivity, discrimination, penetration, sympathy, enlightenment, sagacity, savvy. **4.** agreement, contract, bargain, settlement, pact, covenant, accord, treaty, reconciliation, settlement, arrangement, alliance.

undying, *adj.* immortal, deathless, endless, unceasing, interminable, infinite, perpetual, continuous, imperishable, timeless, constant, indestructible, sempiternal, perdurable, lasting, unending, eternal, everlasting, permanent.
—**Ant.** mortal, temporary, short-lived, evanescent, ephemeral.

unearthly, *adj.* otherworldly, extraterrestrial, extrasensory, supernatural, preternatural, ghostly, spectral, unnatural, inexplicable, weird, unreal, uncanny, spooky, creepy, strange, eerie, bizarre; sublime, celestial, heavenly, empyreal.
—**Ant.** earthly, terrestrial.

uneasy, *adj.* disquieted, upset, ill at ease, unquiet, nervous, restless, restive, impatient, jittery, jumpy, skittish, fidgety, hectic, agitated, disturbed, perturbed, anxious, worried, concerned, apprehensive, on edge, edgy, uncomfortable, flustered, discombobulated, troubled, angst-ridden, fretful, uncertain.
—**Ant.** comfortable, at ease, relaxed, confident.

uneducated, *adj.* untutored, unschooled, unenlightened, benighted, uninstructed, unread, uncultured, uncultivated, untaught, uninformed, unlettered, illiterate, ignorant.
—**Ant.** cultivated, cultured, literate.
—**Syn.** See IGNORANT.

unemployed, *adj.* unoccupied, idle, out of work, inactive, at leisure, at liberty, jobless, between engagements.
—**Ant.** employed, working, on the job, busy.

unequaled, *adj.* unparalleled, nonpariel, transcendant, sublime, surpassing, supreme, superlative, superior, outstanding, extraordinary, superb, unique, original, sui generis, matchless, unmatched, unsurpassed, unrivaled, peerless, inimitable, incomparable, beyond compare.
—**Ant.** ordinary, run-of-the-mill, mediocre.

unexpected, *adj.* unforeseen, unlooked-for, unannounced, undreamt-of, unanticipated, precipitate, sudden, abrupt; surprising, shocking, stunning, startling, fortuitous, chance.
—**Ant.** expected, foreseen, anticipated, gradual.

unfair, *adj.* **1.** biased, partial, prejudiced, jaundiced, unjust, inequitable, unreasonable. **2.** unscrupulous, dishonest, underhanded, dishonerable, crooked, untrustworthy, corrupt, base, heinous, iniquitous, wrongful, cheating, sneaky, shifty, wily.
—**Ant.** fair.

unfaithful, *adj.* **1.** false, disloyal, perfidious, faithless, treacherous, treasonous, seditious, traitorous, deceitful, recreant, untrustworthy, unreliable, undependable. **2.** fickle, untrue, inconstant; philandering, cheating, adulterous.
—**Ant.** faithful, steadfast, loyal, true, constant.

unfavorable, *adj.* disadvantageous, unpropitious, inauspicious, inopportune, unfortunate, ominous, disastrous, adverse, inimical.
—**Ant.** favorable.

unfeeling, *adj.* insensible, insensate, numb; callous, unsympathetic, inured, hardened, tough, stolid, unresponsive, cold, heartless, affectless, unaffected, insensitive, stonyhearted, uncompassionate, thick-skinned, hard-boiled, hard-nosed, apathetic, uncaring, indifferent, hard, hardhearted.
—**Ant.** feeling, sympathetic.

unfortunate, *adj.* **1.** unlucky, unhappy, luckless, unsuccessful, jinxed, cursed, woebegone, pathetic, doomed, ill-fated, pitiable, pitiful, wretched, miserable, sorry, hopeless, hapless, star-crossed, ill-starred. **2.** inauspicious, unpropitious, ominous, sinister, portentous.
—**Ant.** fortunate.

unfriendly, *adj.* inimical, antagonistic, contrary, unsympathetic, inhospitable, cold, remote, aloof, distant, haughty, standoffish, formal, unsociable, unapproachable, rancorous, adversarial, contentious, hateful, malevolent, hostile, unkind.
—**Ant.** friendly.

ungodly, *adj.* irreligious, impious, godless, antireligious, heathen, accursed, blasphemous, heretical, iconoclastic, atheistic, sacrilegious, demonic, diabolical, satanic, feindish, infernal, hellish, damnable, damned, sinful, piacular, profane; wicked, depraved, dissolute, iniquitous, beastly, degenerate, unrepentant, filthy, indecent, polluted, corrupted, base, immoral, heinous, dissolute, blackhearted, perverted, lawless, execrable, vile, evil.
—**Ant.** godly.

unguarded, *adj.* **1.** unprotected, undefended, open, naked, uncovered, exposed, vulnerable, helpless, assailable, in jeopardy, at risk, defenseless. **2.** incautious, inattentive, heedless, unthinking, indiscreet, unwise, hasty, imprudent, thoughtless, careless.
—**Ant.** guarded, protected; cautious, careful.

unhappy, *adj.* **1.** sad, miserable, wretched, sorrowful, depressed, dejected, melancholy, gloomy, glum, dolorous, dispirited, troubled, crestfallen, chapfallen, down in the dumps *or* mouth, despondent, woeful, woebegone, downcast, cheerless, disconsolate, inconsolable, distressed. **2.** unlucky, unfortunate, hapless, hopeless, woebegone, pitiable, pitiful, doomed, cursed, jinxed, ill-starred, star-crossed, unsuccessful. **3.** unfavorable, disastrous, ill-omened, calamitous, inauspicious, unpropitious. **4.** infelicitous, inappropriate, inapt, inexpedient, ill-advised.
—**Ant.** happy.

unhealthy, *adj.* **1.** sick, sickly, delicate, frail, weak, feeble, enfeebled, ill, ailing, under the weather, off one's feed, not up to snuff, unwell, debilitated, unsound, indisposed, bed-ridden, invalid, out of commission, diseased, afflicted. **2.** unwholesome, unhealthful, unsanitary, unhygienic, insalubrious, deleterious, poisonous, harmful, detrimental, injurious, malign, toxic, noxious.
—**Ant.** healthy.

uniform, *adj.* **1.** homogeneous, consistent, unaltered, invariable, unchanging, unwavering, unvarying, unvaried, unchanged, constant, steady, stable, regular. **2.** undiversified, unvariegated, dun, solid, plain. **3.** regular, even, unbroken, smooth. **4.** agreeing, alike, similar, parallel, identical, analagous, comparable, akin.
—**Ant.** heterogeneous; variegated; uneven; dissimilar.

unimportant, *adj.* trivial, trifling, paltry, nugatory, secondary, insignificant, petty, slight, unimposing, puny, insubstantial, nonsubstantive, negligible, minor, irrelevant, obscure, inconsequential, small-time, second-rate, niggling, piddling, picayune, inappreciable, worthless, not worth mentioning, silly, frivolous, of no account *or* concern, immaterial, unimpressive, low-level, bush-league, minor-league, penny-ante, small potatoes, not worth shaking a stick at, not worth one's time.
—**Ant.** important.

union, *n.* **1.** junction, combination, conjunction, amalgamation, fusion, synthesis, mixture, unification, solidarity, integration, concatenation, unity, coalition. **2.** society, association, organization, club, circle, fellowship, syndicate, coalition, federation, fraternity, sorority, brotherhood, sisterhood, team, gang, party, bloc, league, confederacy, alliance. **3.** marriage, matrimony, wedlock. **4.** agreement, harmony, congruity, coherence, compatibility, consonance, accord.
—**Ant.** separation, sundering; divorce; disharmony, incongruity.
—**Syn. Study.** See ALLIANCE.

unique, *adj.* **1.** sole, only, single, lone, solitary, separate, particular. **2.** unequaled, unexcelled, unparalleled, unrivaled, incomparable, beyond compare, second to none, unsurpassed, inimitable, matchless, peerless. **3.** rare, unusual, singular, odd, quaint, curious, peculiar, strange, uncommon, once in a lifetime, exceptional, infrequent.
—**Ant.** common, usual.

unite, *v.* **1.** join, combine, unify, merge, intermix, relate, integrate, bring together, incorporate, connect, couple, link, yoke, associate. **2.** combine, amalgamate, compound, blend, coalesce, bond, alloy, bind, glue, fasten, fuse, weld, consolidate. **3.** marry, wed, join together, link, connect, merge.
—**Ant.** separate, part, sever.
—**Syn. Study.** See JOIN.

unity, *n.* **1.** oneness, union, singleness, singularity, individuality, integrity, congruity, uniformity, homogeneity, identity, similarity, sameness, likeness. **2.** concord, harmony, agreement, unison, concert, unanimity, uniformity, consistency, constancy, consensus, solidarity,

compatibility, concurrence, continuity, rapport, sympathy, likemindedness.
—**Ant.** difference; disagreement.

universal, *adj.* general, generic, prevalent, widespread, ubiquitous, omnipresent, catholic, common, worldwide, wide-ranging, comprehensive, all-encompassing, cosmic.
—**Ant.** particular.
—**Syn. Study.** See GENERAL.

unjust, *adj.* **1.** inequitable, partial, unfair, prejudiced, biased, unreasonable, jaundiced. **2.** undeserved, unjustified, unjustifiable, unmerited, unfounded, illegitimate, wrongful, improper, unlawful, indefensible, unwarranted, inexcusable.
—**Ant.** just, evenhanded, objective, impartial; condign, fitting, well-deserved.

unkind, *adj.* harsh, cruel, unmerciful, unfeeling, unsympathetic, insensitive, uncaring, heartless, thoughtless, unthoughtful, inconsiderate, callous, tough, stern, severe, mean.
—**Ant.** kind.

unlawful, *adj.* illegal, illicit, illegitimate, criminal, felonious, lawless, outlawed, banned, forbidden, taboo, prohibited, proscribed, interdicted, disallowed, unauthorized, unsanctioned.
—**Ant.** lawful, legal.
—**Syn. Study.** See ILLEGAL.

unlike, *adj.* different, dissimilar, diverse, distinct, opposite, contrasting, divergent, separate, incompatible, incongruous, unequal, disparate, variant, heterogeneous.
—**Ant.** like.

unlikely, *adj.* improbable, implausible, doubtful, dubious, unrealistic, far-fetched, remote, hard to imagine, unimaginable, unexpected, unthinkable, inconceivable, unanticipated, unpredictable, questionable, surprising, startling, odd, peculiar, strange, weird, unsuitable, inappropriate.
—**Ant.** likely.

unlimited, *adj.* unrestricted, unconstrained, unrestrained, unqualified, unconditional, full, absolute; endless, immense, immeasurable, innumerable, myriad, boundless, unfettered, limitless, unbounded, vast, extensive, infinite, inexhaustible, interminable, never-ending.
—**Ant.** limited.

unlucky, *adj.* **1.** luckless, unfortunate, hapless, hopeless, doomed, cursed, wretched, miserable, pathetic, unhappy, star-crossed, ill-fated, unsuccessful, ill-omened. **2.** sinister, portentious, ominous, menacing, inauspicious, unpropitious, unpromising, fateful, baneful, malign, adverse.
—**Ant.** lucky.

unmindful, *adj.* heedless, indifferent, lax, remiss, derelict, slack, inadvertent, careless, inattentive, neglectful, negligent, unobservant, forgetful, oblivious.
—**Ant.** mindful, solicitous, careful, concerned, attentive.

unmistakable, *adj.* clear, plain, manifest, unambiguous, unequivocal, explicit, indisputable, unquestionable, definite, evident, obvious, palpable, patent.
—**Ant.** unclear, dim.

unmitigated, *adj.* unqualified, absolute, categorical, sheer, total, perfect, plain, utter, unalloyed, relentless, out-and-out, thoroughgoing, complete, consummate.
—**Ant.** softened, lessened.

unnatural, *adj.* **1.** affected, forced, strained, theatrical, artificial, contrived, labored, stilted, self-conscious, mannered, insincere, feigned, false. **2.** unusual, strange, abnormal, irregular, anomalous, aberrant, odd, peculiar, queer, unexpected, uncharacteristic, out of character, atypical. **3.** bizarre, weird, uncanny, freakish, outlandish, preternatural, supernatural, queer, grotesque, spooky, strange, extraordinary, monstrous, prodigious, fantastic, abnormal.
—**Ant.** natural.

unnecessary, *adj.* needless, superfluous, extra, dispensable, expendable, disposable, surplus, inessential, supererogatory, *de trop*.
—**Ant.** necessary.

unnerve, *v.* weaken, enfeeble, sap, undermine, undo, discourage, enervate, disarm, agitate, perturb, ruffle, rattle, dismay, faze, shake, fluster, disconcert, upset, nonplus, throw for a loop, intimidate, bewilder, distract, confound, stupefy, stun, discombobulate.
—**Ant.** steel, encourage.

unparalleled, *adj.* matchless, unmatched, unequaled, unrivaled, peerless, incomparable, inimitable, superlative, singular, unique, rare, one of a kind, exceptional, consummate.
—**Ant.** typical, ordinary, mediocre.

unpleasant, *adj.* unpleasing, disagreeable, objectionable, uncomfortable, unsavory, unpalatable, unappetizing, offensive, obnoxious, noisome, repulsive, repellent, revolting, nauseating, odious, abominable, noxious.
—**Ant.** pleasant.

unpretentious, *adj.* modest, unassuming, unpresuming, simple, plain, homely, ordinary, unexceptional, self-effacing, humble, demure, diffident, reticent, unostentatious, inconspicuous, understated, moderate, reserved, retiring, unobtrusive, down-to-earth.
—**Ant.** pretentious.

unprincipled, *adj.* unscrupulous, unethical, immoral, amoral, lawless, ungodly, dishonest, dishonorable, corrupt, perverse, perverted, base, calculating, conniving, tricky, shrewd, cagey, crafty, scheming, canny, wily, guileful, sneaky, duplicitous, deceptive, perfidious, treacherous, double-dealing, underhanded, conscienceless, criminal, unjust, untrustworthy, disreputable, louche, crooked, fiendish, diabolical, iniquitous, indecent, depraved, dissolute, wicked, bad, evil, vile, selfish, Machiavellian.
—**Ant.** principled, scrupulous.
—**Syn. Study.** See UNSCRUPULOUS.

unqualified, *adj.* **1.** unfit, incompetent, ineligible, unsuited, untrained, unprepared, ill-suited, unsuitable. **2.** absolute, unmitigated, out-and-out, thorough, complete, direct, unrestricted, unreserved, unconditional, categorical, consummate, perfect, sheer, outright, downright.
—**Ant.** qualified, competent, capable, able.

unquestionable, *adj.* indisputable, indubitable, incontrovertible, undeniable, irrefutable, incontestable, unequivocal, unmistakable, unambiguous, unimpeachable, positive, certain, sure, definite, patent, clear, obvious, conclusive.
—**Ant.** questionable, dubious, uncertain.

unquiet, *adj.* restless, restive, impatient, troubled, anxious, worried, concerned, hectic, feverish, fevered, disordered, unsettled, turbulent, tumultuous, disturbed, agitated, upset, vexed, dismayed, alarmed, apprehensive, ill at ease, uneasy, nervous, perturbed, fidgety, jittery, skittish, jumpy, edgy, on edge, on pins and needles, on tenterhooks, discombobulated.
—**Ant.** quiet.

unreal, *adj.* **1.** imaginary, fantastic, phantasmagorical, fanciful, fancied, fictitious, illusory, supernatural, chimerical, spectral, nonexistent, make-believe, made-up, mythical, pretend. **2.** synthetic, mock, counterfeit, fake, phony, bogus, falsified, false, unnatural, simulated, imitation, artificial, sham, spurious. **3.** unrealistic, visionary, idealistic, unworkable, speculative, hypothetical, conjectural, suppositional, pie in the sky, abstract, academic, theoretical, impractical.
—**Ant.** real.

unreasonable, *adj.* **1.** irrational, illogical, brainless, senseless, foolish, silly, preposterous, ridiculous, ludicrous, laughable, insane, crazy, far-fetched, absurd, stupid, nonsensical, idiotic, fatuous, asinine, myopic, blind. **2.** immoderate, exorbitant, excessive, inordinate, outrageous, unwarranted, unjustifiable, extortionate, unjust, unfair, extravagant.
—**Ant.** reasonable.

unrefined, *adj.* **1.** unpurified, impure, raw, natural, unprocessed, coarse, harsh, crude. **2.** unpolished, uncultivated, unsophisticated, plebeian, ill-bred, inelegant, callow, uncultured, rude, boorish, loutish, uncouth, gauche, bumbling, awkward, provincial, primitive, ignorant, barbaric, brutish, vulgar, gross.
—**Ant.** refined.

unrelenting, *adj.* unabating, relentless, continual, unremitting, implacable, inexorable, merciless, ruthless, remorseless, pitiless, grim, obdurate, adamant, inflexible, rigid, severe, cruel, hard, bitter, harsh, stern, austere.
—**Ant.** forbearing.

unruffled, *adj.* smooth, calm, placid, unperturbed, tranquil, serene, collected, imperturbable, cool, sedate, steady, even, untroubled, self-possessed, relaxed, laid-back, dispassionate, composed, peaceful, self-controlled, undisturbed.
—**Ant.** ruffled, agitated, turbulent.

unruly, *adj.* ungovernable, undisciplined, uncooperative, defiant, wayward, disobedient, insubordinate, unmanageable, uncontrollable, refractory, fractious, adamantine, stubborn, obstreperous, recalcitrant, intractable, willful, headstrong, rebellious, contumacious, perverse, contrary; lawless, turbulent, tumultuous, mutinous, violent, tempestuous, rowdy, boisterous, wild, disorderly, riotous.
—**Ant.** obedient, tractable, docile.
—**Syn. Study.** UNRULY, INTRACTABLE, RECALCITRANT, REFRACTORY describe persons or things that resist management or control. UNRULY suggests constant disorderly behavior or character: *an unruly child; unruly hair.* INTRACTABLE suggests in persons a determined resistance to all attempts to guide or direct them, and in things a resistance to attempts to shape, improve, or modify them: *an intractable social rebel; an intractable problem.* RECALCITRANT implies a stubborn rebellion against authority or direction: *a recalcitrant prisoner.* REFRACTORY also implies a mulish disobedience, but leaves open the possibility of eventual compliance: *The refractory youth needs more understanding.*

unsatisfactory, *adj.* disappointing, deficient, wanting, lacking, failing, losing, incomplete, inadequate, insufficient, imperfect, faulty, defective, flawed, inferior, mediocre, unacceptable, weak, below par, substandard, displeasing, unfulfilling, intolerable.
—**Ant.** satisfactory.

unsavory, *adj.* tasteless, unpleasant, offensive, obnoxious, disagreeable, objectionable, unappetizing, unpalatable, disgusting, repellent, nauseating, revolting, sickening, rotten, distasteful.
—**Ant.** savory, tasteful.

unscrupulous, *adj.* conscienceless, unprincipled, dishonorable, dishonest, unethical, immoral, amoral, wicked, evil, lawless, antisocial, corrupt, untrustworthy, treacherous, iniquitous, insidious, sly, cunning, shifty, slippery, sneaky, crooked, vile, depraved, dissolute, unregenerate, reprobate, nefarious, base, villainous, Machiavellian, double-dealing, deceptive, deceitful.
—**Ant.** scrupulous, principled, moral, ethical.
—**Syn. Study.** UNSCRUPULOUS, UNPRINCIPLED refer to a lack of moral or ethical standards. UNSCRUPULOUS means not controlled by one's conscience and contemptuous of what one knows to be right or honorable: *an unscrupulous landlord.* UNPRINCIPLED means lacking or not aware of moral standards that should restrain one's actions: *an unprincipled rogue.*

unseemly, *adj.* in poor *or* bad taste, out of place, undignified, unfitting, unbecoming, improper, indecorous, indecent, naughty, offensive, objectionable, coarse, rude, indelicate, unbefitting, shameful, disreputable, unsuitable, discreditable, inappropriate.
—**Ant.** seemly, fitting, proper, appropriate.
—**Syn. Study.** See IMPROPER.

unselfish *adj.* generous, giving, magnanimous, kind, kindly, openhanded, good, bighearted, beneficient, benevolent, charitable, lavish, unstinting, ungrudging, unsparing, liberal, altruistic, selfless, high-minded, self-sacrificing, self-abnegating, humane, humanitarian, philanthropic, obliging, considerate, thoughtful, compassionate, solicitous, gracious, caring, loving.
—**Ant.** selfish, grasping, self-indulgent, mean.

unsettled, *adj.* unstable, unsteady, shaky, undependable, unsure, unfixed, undetermined, indeterminate, changeable, variable, inconstant, unpredictable, fluctuating, wavering, vacillating, fickle, faltering, irresolute.
—**Ant.** settled, stable, steady.

unsightly, *adj.* unpleasant, unprepossessing, homely, plain, ill-favored, unattractive, ugly, disagreeable, hideous, frightful, awful, monstrous, grotesque, repulsive.
—**Ant.** beautiful.

unskillful, *adj.* untrained, inexpert, unaccomplished, untalented, inept, incompetent, unqualified, unprofessional, bumbling, all thumbs, awkward, bungling, clumsy, maladroit.
—**Ant.** skillful.

unsophisticated, *adj.* simple, inexperienced, childlike, unworldly, innocent, green, callow, artless, ingenuous, guileless, naive, provincial, down-home, natural, unrefined, unpolished, uncultured, uncultivated, inelegant.
—**Ant.** sophisticated.

unsound, *adj.* **1.** diseased, debilitated, feeble, afflicted, impaired, sickly, sick, ill, unwell, ailing, delicate, injured, wounded, infirm, unhealthy, unwholesome. **2.** fallacious, unfounded, invalid, false, erroneous, untenable, illogical, flawed, specious, meretricious, spurious, faulty. **3.** frail, rickety, shaky, wobbly, defective, decayed, rotten, fragile, breakable, frangible. **4.** insane, mad, crazy, unbalanced, unstable, deranged, demented.
—**Ant.** sound; healthy; valid; sturdy; sane.

unstable, *adj.* **1.** unsteady, shaky, insecure, unfixed, unmoored, unattached, loose, precarious. **2.** changeable, variable, unpredictable, unreliable, erratic, volatile, fluctuating, indefinite, mutable, inconstant, fickle, capricious, mercurial, flighty, wavering, vacillating, unsettled.
—**Ant.** stable, secure, fixed, firm; constant, invariable, predictable.

unsteady, *adj.* **1.** unstable, infirm, wobbly, tottering, off-balance, swaying, rocky, shaky, stumbling, trembling, staggering, teetering, unbalanced, lurching, listing, floundering, foundering, faltering. **2.** fluctuating, wavering, flickering, moving, inconstant, vacillating, fickle, changeable, unstable, irregular, uneven, erratic, variable. **3.** irregular, uneven, stop-and-go, halting, sporadic, fitful, intermittent, periodic, spasmodic.
—**Ant.** steady; upright, stable; constant, even; regular, uniform, consistent.

unsuccessful, *adj.* **1.** ineffective, inefficient, ineffectual, unproductive, unprofitable, worthless, vain, unavailing, useless, fruitless, bootless, abortive, sterile, luckless, pointless, futile, losing, purposeless. **2.** defeated, beaten, foiled, confounded, stumped, hindered, frustrated, balked, checked, stopped, blocked, stymied, overcome, down and out, crushed, finished, whipped, thwarted, disappointed, met one's Waterloo, ruined, checkmated, on the ropes *or* skids, KOed, knocked out, flummoxed, bankrupt, thrown in the towel, down for the count.
—**Ant.** successful.

unsuitable, *adj.* **1.** unseemly, improper, infelicitous, indecent, indecorous, inappropriate, unfitting, unbefitting, unbecoming. **2.** unqualified, inapt, wrong, unfit, ill-equipped, incorrect, incongruous.
—**Ant.** suitable, fitting, appropriate.

unsympathetic, *adj.* uncaring, unfeeling, callous, indifferent, impassive, stolid, apathetic, stony, pitiless, ruthless, aloof, hardened, hardhearted, antipathetic, averse, unmoved, unaffected, untouched, unresponsive, cold.
—**Ant.** sympathetic, compassionate, empathetic, understanding.

unthinkable, *adj.* **1.** inconceivable, incredible, beyond belief, unimaginable, incomprehensible, mind-boggling. **2.** unacceptable, impossible, out of the question, preposterous, absurd, illogical, ludicrous, laughable, unlikely.
—**Ant.** credible; plausible, possible.

untidy, *adj.* slovenly, disordered, sloppy, messy, disheveled, unkempt, dirty, littered, cluttered, chaotic.
—**Ant.** tidy.

untimely, *adj.* unpropitious, unseasonable, inappropriate, inopportune, premature, early, advanced, precocious.
—**Ant.** timely, well-timed.

untruth, *n.* falsehood, fib, lie, fiction, story, tale, tall tale, fabrication, fable, forgery, invention, misrepresentation, prevarication, equivocation, deceit, mendacity, dishonesty, distortion, duplicity.
—**Ant.** truth, veracity.

unusual, *adj.* uncommon, irregular, atypical, different, unconventional, unorthodox, extraordinary, infrequent, exceptional, rare, strange, remarkable, singular, curious, queer, peculiar, bizarre, freakish, unique, weird, odd.
—**Ant.** usual, typical, common, ordinary.

unwary, *adj.* incautious, unguarded, imprudent, unwise, indiscreet, hasty, careless, rash, heedless, precipitous, impetuous, foolhardy, reckless, thoughtless, headlong.
—**Ant.** wary, careful, prudent.

unwholesome, *adj.* unhealthy, unhygienic, unhealthful, deleterious, detrimental, harmful, injurious, noxious, noisome, poisonous, toxic, baneful, pernicious.
—**Ant.** wholesome.

unwieldy, *adj.* bulky, unmanageable, clumsy, awkward, cumbersome, ungainly, oversized, ponderous, heavy.
—**Ant.** manageable, light.

upbraid, *v.* reproach, chide, reprove, reprimand, scold, rebuke, berate, chastise, castigate, blame, censure, take to task, rake (someone) over the coals, call (someone) on the carpet, bawl out, chew out.
—**Ant.** praise.

uphold, *v.* **1.** support, sustain, maintain, approve, sanction, embrace, back, defend, protect, justify, aid, vindicate, promote, preserve, espouse, endorse, advocate, champion. **2.** raise, elevate.
—**Ant.** attack, subvert.

uplifting, *adj.* spiritual, civilizing, elevating, exalting, inspiriting, inspiring, edifying, improving, bettering, educational, instructive, enlightening.
—**Ant.** debasing, degrading.

uppity, *adj.* arrogant, haughty, impertinent, insolent, pompous, pretentious, overweening, high and mighty, affected, disdainful, scornful, presumptuous, cocky, sassy, saucy, supercilious, snobbish, snobby, stuck-up, snooty, hifalutin, hoity-toity, on one's high horse.
—**Ant.** modest, unassuming, down to earth.

upright, *adj.* honest, just, fair, conscientious, scrupulous, principled, moral, ethical, righteous, honorable, straight, straightforward, aboveboard, virtuous, true, good, pure, high-minded, upstanding, decent, trustworthy, unimpeachable, incorruptible.
—**Ant.** dishonest, conniving.

uprising, *n.* insurrection, revolt, revolution, rebellion, mutiny, riot, coup d'état, dissension, conflict, strife, violence.
—**Ant.** pacification.

uproar, *n.* disturbance, tumult, disorder, turbulence, commotion, hubbub, furor, din, clamor, noise; outcry, babel, bedlam, pandemonium, strife, discord, brouhaha, racket, rumpus, brawl, donnybrook, fracas, melee, riot.
—**Ant.** peace, quiet.

upset, *v.* **1.** overturn, capsize, upend, invert, spill, topple, turn topsy-turvy, reverse. **2.** overthrow, defeat, depose, displace, thrash, rout, overcome, vanquish, beat, triumph over. **3.** disturb, distress, trouble, ruffle, dismay, worry, bother, unsettle, frighten, derange, unnerve, disconcert, agitate, perturb, fluster. —*n.* **4.** overturn, overthrow, defeat, conquest, triumph, victory, rout. —*adj.* **5.** disordered, muddled, confused, chaotic, untidy, messy; sloppy. **6.** worried, troubled, unnerved, distracted, dismayed, apprehensive, nervous, anxious, angst-ridden, frightened, fearful, on edge, distressed, deranged, off balance, flustered, queasy, uneasy, sick at heart, disheartened, bewildered, rattled, fazed, discombulated, concerned, disconcerted, agitated, disturbed, perturbed, irritated, vexed, bothered, in a state, freaked out, beside oneself.
—**Ant.** steady, stable.

urbane, *adj.* sophisticated, knowing, diplomatic, tactful, civil, poised, cultured, cultivated, well-bred, courteous, courtly, polite, refined, elegant, polished, smooth, savvy, suave.
—**Ant.** unsophisticated, unrefined, boorish.

urge, *v.* **1.** push, force, impel, drive. **2.** press, push, hasten, accelerate, speed, hurry, rush, hustle. **3.** impel, constrain, move, activate, animate, incite, instigate, goad, stimulate, spur, egg on, prompt, exhort. **4.** induce, persuade, solicit, beg, beseech, importune, entreat, implore. **5.** insist upon, allege, assert, aver, argue, demand, affirm, hold, declare. **6.** recommend, suggest, counsel, persuade, advocate, advise. —*n.* **7.** impulse, pressure, impetus, desire, compulsion, itch, yen, hunger, drive, longing, yearning, thirst, craving, lust, appetite, passion.
—**Ant.** deter, discourage.

urgent, *adj.* **1.** pressing, compelling, vital, life-and-death, exigent, emergency, rush, imperative, immediate, top priority, requisite, necessary. **2.** insistent, earnest, eager, energetic, tenacious, firm, forceful.
—**Ant.** unimportant.

use, *v.* **1.** employ, utilize, make use of, apply, avail oneself of, exercise, resort to, have recourse to. **2.** expend, deplete, run through, consume, use up, waste, exhaust. —*n.* **3.** employment, usage, utilization, application, exercise. **4.** utility, function, account, usefulness, service, advantage, profit, benefit, avail. **5.** help, profit, good, purpose, point, object, reason, end, advantage. **6.** custom, practice, usage, habit, routine. convention, tradition. **7.** treatment, management, operation, manipulation, wielding, handling.
—**Syn. Study.** USE, UTILIZE mean to put something into action or service. USE is a general word referring to the application of something to a given purpose: *to use a telephone.* USE may also imply that the thing is consumed or diminished in the process: *I used all the butter.* When applied to persons, USE implies a selfish or sinister purpose: *He used his friend to advance himself.* UTILIZE, a more formal word, implies practical, profitable, or creative use: *to utilize solar energy to run a machine.*

useful, *adj.* **1.** serviceable, advantageous, profitable, helpful, expedient, valuable, fruitful, productive, worthwhile, effectual, effective, efficacious, beneficial, salutary. **2.** practical, practicable, workable, functional, utilitarian, usable.
—**Ant.** useless.

useless, *adj.* **1.** unavailing, futile, fruitless, vain, ineffectual, ineffective, abortive, impractical, pointless, idle, unsuccessful, profitless, bootless, valueless, worthless, hopeless. **2.** unserviceable, unusable, inept, hopeless, incompetent, inefficient, unproductive.
—**Ant.** useful.
—**Syn. Study.** USELESS, FUTILE, VAIN refer to something that is of no use, value, profit, or advantage. USELESS refers to something of no avail because of the circumstances or because of some inherent defect: *It is useless to reason with him.* FUTILE suggests wasted or ill-advised effort and complete failure to achieve a desired end: *Their attempts to save the business were futile.* VAIN describes something that is fruitless or unsuccessful in spite of all possible effort: *It is vain to keep on hoping.*

usual, *adj.* habitual, accustomed, same, customary; common, ordinary, familiar, prevailing, prevalent, everyday, conventional, stock, workaday, normal, routine, typical, general, frequent, regular, expected, predictable, settled, constant, fixed, well-known, established, traditional, set, stereotypical, unexceptional, unremarkable, unoriginal.
—**Ant.** unusual.
—**Syn. Study.** USUAL, CUSTOMARY, HABITUAL refer to something that is familiar because it is commonly met with or observed. USUAL indicates something that is to be expected by reason of previous experience, which shows it to occur more often than not: *There were the usual crowds at the monument.* CUSTOMARY refers to something that accords with prevailing usage or individual practice: *customary courtesies; a customary afternoon nap.* HABITUAL refers to a practice that has become fixed by regular repetition: *a clerk's habitual sales pitch.*

usually, *adv.* as a rule, for the most part, generally, typically, almost always, predominantly, chiefly, in the main, mainly, by and large, mostly, normally, commonly, regularly, predominantly.

utensil, *n.* instrument, tool, vessel, gadget, household item, implement, appliance, device, contrivance, contraption, invention.

utilitarian, *adj.* useful, practical, serviceable, helpful, functional, pragmatic, workaday, handy, convenient, effective, valuable, advantageous.
—**Ant.** impractical, useless.

utter, *v.* **1.** express, speak, enunciate, articulate, pronounce, say, voice, vent, air, broach. **2.** publish, declare, proclaim, announce, promulgate. —*adj.* **3.** complete, total, sheer, thorough, thoroughgoing, unreserved, out-and-out, downright, categorical, absolute, unconditional, unqualified, entire.
—**Ant.** partial, incomplete, relative.

V

vacant, *adj.* **1.** empty, void, hollow, devoid *or* destitute of, lacking, wanting. **2.** untenanted, unoccupied, empty, uninhabited, deserted, abandoned. **3.** free, unoccupied, unemployed, spare, extra, unfilled, unengaged, unspoken-for, leisure, unencumbered. **4.** unthinking, thoughtless, abstracted, vacuous, blank, expressionless, deadpan, dull, absentminded, uncomprehending, inane, fatuous.
—**Ant.** full; occupied; busy; thoughtful.

vacate, *v.* quit, abandon, leave, depart, abandon, evacuate, desert, forsake, withdraw from, relinquish, clear *or* move out.
—**Ant.** occupy.

vacillate, *v.* fluctuate, waver, hesitate, falter, demur, scruple, vary, seesaw, shift, change.
—**Syn. Study.** See WAVER.

vacuous, *adj.* vacant, empty, hollow, void, blank, insipid, vapid, fatuous, foolish, silly, asinine, inane, spacey, abstracted, absentminded, oblivious, uncomprehending, emptyheaded, airheaded, bubblebrained, out to lunch, nobody home.
—**Ant.** serious, attentive, alert, on the qui vive, intelligent.

vague, *adj.* **1.** indefinite, unspecific, general, ill-defined, hazy, fuzzy, blurred, misty, foggy, shadowy, unclear, inexact, inchoate, shapeless, amorphous, imprecise, obscure, dim, indistinct. **2.** unclear, indeterminate, ambiguous, equivocal, nonspecific, unspecified, inexact, in

doubt, uncertain, unknown, unfixed, lax, loose.
—**Ant.** definite, specific, lucid.

vain, *adj.* **1.** useless, hollow, idle, unsuccessful, empty, abortive, unproductive, worthless, unimportant, nugatory, otiose, empty, puny, paltry, petty, trifling, trivial, ineffective, ineffectual, unavailing, pointless, profitless, bootless, unfruitful, futile. **2.** conceited, haughty, boastful, bragging, cocky, self-centered, self-important, swellheaded, narcissistic, egotistical, complacent, self-satisfied, smug, proud, arrogant, overweening, preening, pompous, inflated, stuck-up, stuck on oneself.
—**Ant.** useful, productive, successful, effective; modest, down to earth, meek, diffident, humble.
—**Syn. Study.** See USELESS.

valiant, *adj.* brave, bold, courageous, stouthearted, intrepid, heroic, gallant, dauntless, undaunted, daring, audacious, fearless, staunch, stalwart, tough, strong, gutsy, plucky, spunky, spirited, determined, resolute, tenacious, indomitable.
—**Ant.** timid, cowardly.
—**Syn. Study.** See BRAVE.

valid, *adj.* just, well-founded, sound, convincing, telling, conclusive, definitive, decisive, substantial, logical, analytical, subtle, cogent, authoritative, forceful, effective, binding, legal, lawful, licit.
—**Ant.** invalid, fallacious, deceptive, misleading.

valor, *n.* courage, boldness, heroism, prowess, gallantry, daring, audacity, mettle, tenacity, resolution, determination, fortitude, strength, invincibility, bravery, intrepidity, spirit, fearlessness, backbone, pluck, spunk, guts.
—**Ant.** timidity, cowardice, faintheartedness.

valuable, *adj.* **1.** costly, expensive, rare, precious, dear, invaluable, priceless. **2.** prized, treasured, valued, appreciated, esteemed, admired, respected, worthy, estimable. **3.** useful, desirable, excellent, important, beneficial, advantageous, profitable, helpful, fruitful, productive, effective, worthwhile, significant, consequential, vital, substantial.
—**Ant.** worthless, meretricious.

value, *n.* **1.** worth, merit, desirability, usefulness, utility, importance, significance, benefit. **2.** expense, charge, cost, price. **3.** valuation, evaluation, assessment, appraisal, estimation. **4.** importance, consequence, weight, significance. —*v.* **5.** estimate, rate, price, evaluate, assay, assess, appraise. **6.** regard, esteem, appreciate, prize, treasure, cherish, admire, respect.
—**Syn. Study.** VALUE, WORTH both imply excellence and merit. VALUE is excellence based on desirability, usefulness, or importance; it may be measured in terms of its equivalent in money, goods, or services: *the value of sunlight; the value of a painting.* WORTH usu. implies inherent excellence based on spiritual and moral qualities that command esteem: *Few knew her true worth.* See also APPRECIATE.

vanish, *v.* **1.** disappear, evanesce, fade, melt away, evaporate, vaporize, dissolve, deliquesce, dwindle, disperse, dissipate, disintegrate, decompose, diminish, become invisible. **2.** end, come to an end, stop, finish, conclude, terminate, die out, perish, become extinct, peter out, expire, cease, fade.
—**Ant.** appear; begin.
—**Syn. Study.** See DISAPPEAR.

vanity, *n.* **1.** pride, conceit, arrogance, cockiness, haughtiness, hauteur, amour-propre, self-esteem, egotism, immodesty, narcissism, smugness, complacency, self-satisfaction, self-aggrandizement, self-importance, swell headedness, high opinion of oneself. **2.** ostentation, pretentiousness, pretension, pomposity, pompousness, pomp, exhibitionism, flamboyance, flashiness, flash, flaunting, showiness, showing off, affectation, airs, posturing, grandiosity, preening.
—**Ant.** humility, modesty, diffidence.
—**Syn. Study.** See PRIDE.

vanquish, *v.* conquer, defeat, eliminate, overthrow, overwhelm, overcome, overpower, destroy, triumph *or* prevail over, be victorious over, get the better of, win out over, subjugate, suppress, subdue, crush, quell, rout, reduce, surmount, foil, outwit, beat, best, lick, trounce, thrash, whip, shatter.
—**Ant.** lose, surrender, capitulate.

variable, *adj.* **1.** changeable, alterable, adjustable, adaptable, mutable, protean, chameleon-like, versatile, flexible. **2.** inconstant, fickle, flighty, mercurial, capricious, volatile, unpredictable, erratic, inconsistent, indecisive, irresolute, indefinite, unstable, uncertain, unreliable, undependable. **3.** changing, irregular, unfixed, vacillating, wavering, fluctuating, unsteady.
—**Ant.** invariable; constant.

variance, *n.* **1.** variation, disparity, disagreement, deviation, divergence, discrepancy, diversity, disparateness, incongruity, inconsistency, unlikeness, difference. **2.** disagreement, contention, conflict, misunderstanding, argument, debate, schism, rift, difference of opinion, dispute, quarrel, controversy, dissension, discord, strife.
—**Ant.** similitude, sameness, agreement.

variation, *n.* **1.** change, mutation, permutation, modulation, transformation, metamorphosis, morphing, conversion, alteration, modification, vicissitude. **2.** variance, deviation, divergence, difference, dissimilarity, unlikeness, incongruity, disparateness, discrepancy; variety, diversity.
—**Ant.** sameness.

variety, *n.* **1.** variation. **2.** diversity, multiplicity, multifariousness, diversification, heterogeneity, miscellaneousness, miscellany. **3.** assortment, mixture, mix, choice, selection, range, choice, collection, group. **4.** kind, sort, type, category, brand, make, breed, order, genre, strain, class, species.
—**Ant.** sameness, monotony.

various, *adj.* **1.** differing, different, distinct, separate, individual. **2.** several, many, multiple, numerous, manifold, multifarious, miscellaneous, diverse, sundry, divers, varied.
—**Ant.** uniform, identical, same, similar.
—**Syn. Study.** VARIOUS, DIVERSE, DIFFERENT, DISTINCT describe things that are not identical. VARIOUS stresses the multiplicity and variety of sorts or instances of a thing or class of things: *various kinds of seaweed.* DIVERSE suggests an even wider variety or disparity: *diverse opinions.* DIFFERENT points to a separate identity, or a dissimilarity in quality or character: *two different versions of the same story.* DISTINCT implies a uniqueness and lack of connection between things that may possibly be alike: *plans similar in objective but distinct in method.*

vary, *v.* **1.** change, alter, diversify, reorganize, modulate, modify. **2.** transform, metamorphose, convert, transmute, change. **3.** differ, deviate, depart, diverge, digress. **4.** alternate, switch, fluctuate, vacillate, shift, seesaw.

vast, *adj.* extensive, voluminous, capacious, massive, immense, huge, enormous, gigantic, colossal, tremendous, great, prodigious, stupendous, colossal, titantic, monstrous, monumental, mammouth, elephantine, Brobdingnagian, behemoth; measureless, immeasurable, unbounded, boundless, unlimited, limitless, infinite, interminable, endless, never-ending, incalcuable, indeterminate, inexhaustible.
—**Ant.** limited, small.

vehement, *adj.* **1.** impassioned, passionate, ardent, zealous, fervent, fervid, burning, fiery, afire, ablaze. **2.** angry, rancorous, truculent, ferocious, furious, wrathful, incensed, infuriated, fuming, all steamed up, hot under the collar, on the warpath. **3.** intense, fierce, powerful, potent, energetic, vigorous, violent, forceful.
—**Ant.** mild, subdued, cool, dispassionate.

veneration, *n.* respect, reverence, worship, adoration, deference, homage, esteem, honoring, obeisance, regard, devotion, admiration, idolization, piety, adulation, deification, awe.
—**Ant.** disrespect, irreverence.
—**Syn. Study.** See RESPECT.

vengeance, *n.* avenging, revenge, retribution, requital, retaliation, reprisal, recompense, punishment, castigation, chastisement, punitive measure.
—**Ant.** forgiveness, pardon, forbearance.
—**Syn. Study.** See REVENGE.

venial, *adj.* excusable, forgivable, pardonable, tolerable, trifling, trivial, petty, minor, insignificant, unimportant, inconsequential.
—**Ant.** inexcusable, unforgivable, mortal, heinous.

venom, *n.* **1.** poison, toxin, bane, snakebite. **2.** malice, malignity, maliciousness, animosity, hostility, enmity, antagonism, rancor, spite, spitefulness, acrimony, bitterness, acerbity, malevolence, gall, spleen, poisonousness, virulence, viciousness, meaness, jealousy, hatred, hate, contempt.
—**Syn. Study.** See POISON.

venture, *n.* **1.** hazard, danger, chance, jeopardy, risk, peril. **2.** speculation, bet, gamble, experiment, plunge, fling, wager, undertaking, enterprise. —*v.* **3.** endanger, imperil, risk, jeopardize, hazard; chance, gamble, bet, wager. **4.** dare, presume, make bold, volunteer, hazard, broach, offer, put forward.

verbal, *adj.* worded, linguistic, oral, vocal, enunciated, articulated, expressed, viva voce, aloud, spoken, word-of-mouth, conversational, colloquial; unwritten.
—**Ant.** unarticulated, unspoken, silent, tacit; written.

verbose, *adj.* wordy, prolix, diffuse, redundant, loquacious, talkative, voluble, garrulous, grandiloquent, bombastic, flowery.
—**Ant.** laconic, terse, succinct.

verge, *n.* **1.** edge, rim, margin, brim, lip, border, brink, limit, bound, end, confine, perimeter, circumference, compass, belt, strip. —*v.* **2.** border, approach, come close to. **3.** tend, lean, incline, slope, sink, extend, stretch.

vernacular, *adj.* **1.** colloquial, informal, conversational, spoken, nonliterary, nonacademic, vulgate, vulgar, demotic, general, popular, everyday, familiar, ordinary, commonplace. **2.** local, native, regional, indigenous, autochthonous. —*n.* **3.** vocabulary, terminology, phraseology, language, nomenclature, lexicon; tongue, speech, talk, idiom, argot, patois, patter, slang, cant, jargon, dialect, lingo.
—**Syn. Study.** See LANGUAGE.

versatile, *adj.* adaptable, flexible, adjustable, changeable, multipurpose, multifaceted, many-sided, all-round, all-purpose, general, diversified, encyclopedic, protean, resourceful, handy, inventive, creative, imaginative, ingenious, gifted, talented, multitalented, Renaissance, polymathic, polyhistoric.
—**Ant.** one-sided, one-note, limited, rigid, specialized.

versed, *adj.* conversant, acquainted, informed, familiar, intimate, grounded, competent, accomplished, proficient, knowledgeable, expert, experienced, practiced, skilled, well-read, learned, lettered, cultured, cultivated.
—**Ant.** uninformed, ignorant, inexpert, incompetent.

version, *n.* **1.** account, story, rendition, rendering, view, side, report, chronicle, telling, description, interpretation. **2.** variant, form, rendition, model, style, adaptation, variation, variety, type, portrayal, idea, notion, concept, conception.

verve, *n.* spirit, buoyance, dash, style, stylishness, animation, life, liveliness, sparkle, energy, vigor, exuberance, effervescence, joie de vivre, brio, élan, gusto, panache, flair, enthusiasm, ardor, zeal, passion, fire, esprit, vivacity, vivaciousness, vitality, zest, oomph, zing, pizazz, flash.

vestige, *n.* **1.** remnant, residue, relic, remains, reminder, memorial, fragment, shard, shred, scrap. **2.** trace, hint, suggestion, mark, evidence, token, glimmer, inkling, taste, sign, suspicion, soupçon.
—**Syn. Study.** See TRACE.

vet, *v.* examine, inspect, check out, look over, scan, scrutinize, review, investigate, size up; appraise, verify, check, authenticate, validate, certify, corroborate, substantiate, vouch for, guarantee, warrant, back up.

vex, *v.* **1.** irritate, annoy, pester, bother, exasperate, chafe, gall, peeve, badger, plague, harass, provoke, anger, irk, fret, nettle, hassle, get on (someone's) nerves, get up (someone's) nose, get in (someone's) face. **2.** torment, trouble, distress, dismay, perturb, upset, worry, agonize.
—**Ant.** delight.

viable, *adj.* tenable, sustainable, supportable, operable; workable, doable, achievable, feasible, reasonable, sensible, possible, practical, practicable.
—**Ant.** tenuous, precarious; dubious, doubtful, impractical, unworkable.

vibrate, *v.* **1.** oscillate; swing, sway, waver, fluctuate, undulate; shake, tremble, wobble, jiggle, shudder, rock, quake, quaver, quiver, shiver; pulsate, pulse, beat, throb, palpitate. **2.** resound, echo, reverberate, resonate, ring.

vice, *n.* **1.** sin, offense, crime, scandal, transgression, trespass, infraction, breach, immorality, depravity, iniquity, sinfulness, degeneracy, evil, venality, profligacy, wickedness, corruption. **2.** shortcoming,

foible, fault, failing, frailty, weakness, infirmity; flaw, blemish, blot, imperfection, defect, deficiency.
—**Ant.** virtue.
—**Syn. Study.** See FAULT.

vicinity, *n.* area, neighborhood, locale, locality, territory, environs, precincts, district, surroundings, environment, milieu.

vicious, *adj.* **1.** immoral, depraved, evil, villainous, nefarious, degenerate, debauched, perverted, debased, dissolute, reprobate, iniquitous, vile, profligate, sinful, corrupt, abandoned, wanton, lecherous, libidinous, lewd. **2.** spiteful, malign, malignant, malicious, malevolent, mean, nasty, venomous, rancorous, vindictive, hateful, bitter, acrimonious, defamatory, slanderous. **3.** savage, ferocious, fierce, violent, wild, untamed, brutal, bestial, ravening, feral, fiendish, unruly, ill-tempered, bad-tempered, refractory.
—**Ant.** moral; virtuous; benign, benevolent, kindly; tame, gentle, docile, sweet.

victim, *n.* prey, quarry; martyr, sufferer, casualty, injured party, sacrificial lamb, scapegoat; dupe, fool, butt, chump, fall guy, patsy, sap, sucker, schlemiel, schnook.

victimize, *v.* **1.** persecute, prey on, bully, harass, pursue, pick on, vex, exploit, take advantage of, use, maltreat, abuse, molest, afflict, torment, torture, oppress, tyrannize. **2.** dupe, swindle, cheat, bilk, take in, take for a ride, get the better of, set up, beguile, deceive, trick, defraud, fool, con, gull, outwit, outsmart, outfox, bamboozle, snooker, rook, flimflam, hoodwink, sucker, shaft, screw.
—**Syn. Study.** See CHEAT.

victory, *n.* conquest, triumph, win, ascendancy, supremacy, superiority, mastery, championship, vanquishment, upper hand, domination, defeat, subjugation, rout, success, coup.
—**Ant.** defeat.
—**Syn. Study.** VICTORY, CONQUEST, TRIUMPH refer to a successful outcome of a struggle. VICTORY suggests the decisive defeat of an opponent in a contest of any kind: *victory in battle; a football victory.* CONQUEST implies the taking over of control by the victor, and the obedience of the conquered: *a war of conquest; the conquest of Peru.* TRIUMPH implies a particularly outstanding victory: *the triumph of a righteous cause; the triumph of justice.*

vie, *v.* compete, rival, oppose, contend, struggle, strive, endeavor, fight, challenge, confront, battle, combat, joust.

view, *n.* **1.** sight, look, glimpse, glance, peek, peep. **2.** prospect, outlook, aspect, perspective, panorama, spectacle, landscape, picture, scene, vista. **3.** aspect, perspective, angle, position, slant, appearance. **4.** scrutiny, observation, vision, sight, study, scanning, contemplation, examination, survey, inspection. **5.** aim, intention, expectation, hope, dream, vision, prospect, purpose, reason, end, design, intent, objective, object. **6.** version, story, side, interpretation, rendition, rendering, telling, report, account, description. **7.** point of view, approach, position, conviction, standpoint, conception, idea, notion, opinion, theory, belief, judgment, estimation, assessment, understanding, feeling, sentiment, impression. —*v.* **8.** see, behold, witness, contemplate, regard, watch, observe, scrutinize, take in, look at, survey, inspect, examine, consider, assess, gauge.
—**Syn. Study.** VIEW, PROSPECT, SCENE, VISTA refer to whatever lies open to sight. VIEW is the general word: *a fine view of the surrounding countryside.* PROSPECT suggests a sweeping and often distant view, as from a vantage point: *The prospect from the mountaintop was breathtaking.* SCENE suggests an organic unity in the details, as is found in a picture: *a woodland scene.* VISTA suggests a long, narrow view, as along an avenue between rows of trees: *a pleasant vista.* See also OPINION.

vigilant, *adj.* watchful, attentive, wary, alert, observant, wide-awake, sharp, eagle-eyed, on the lookout, on the qui vive, on one's toes, on one's guard, guarded, circumspect, cautious, careful, chary.
—**Ant.** inattentive, unmindful, negligent, lax, slack.

vigorous, *adj.* energetic, strenuous, dynamic, active, powerful, forceful, spirited, vital, lively, lusty, virile, hardy, hearty, stalwart, fit, athletic, tough, strong, robust, sturdy, sound, healthy, spry, peppy, full of beans.
—**Ant.** weak, inactive, lethargic, languorous.

vile, *adj.* **1.** immoral, wicked, sinful, base, low, vicious, evil, depraved, corrupted, perverted, debauched, debased, dissolute, reprobate, despicable, execrable, shameless, fiendish, iniquitous. **2.** offensive, noxious, obnoxious, unpleasant, loathsome, distasteful, unsavory, objectionable, repulsive, disgusting, revolting, repellent, nauseating, repugnant, sickening, foul, filthy, nasty, dirty. **3.** vulgar, obscene, coarse, gross, lewd, licentious, salacious, scabrous, crass, smutty, rude. **4.** mean, menial, degrading, lowly, low, ignominious, ignoble, servile, demeaning, slavish, abject, sordid, shameful, beneath contempt, contemptible. **5.** valueless, paltry, miserable, wretched, petty, mean, inferior, second-rate, sorry, puny, pitiful, pathetic, worthless, cheap, tawdry, trashy, shabby, shoddy, sleazy, seedy, tacky, two-bit, chintzy, lousy, cheapjack, cheesy, crappy.
—**Ant.** virtuous, moral; pleasant, delightful, tasteful; refined, genteel, elevated; noble, dignified, prestigious; valuable, first-rate.

villain, *n.* antagonist, scoundrel, criminal, traitor, turncoat, quisling, Judas, Benedict Arnold, blackguard, knave, rascal, rogue, wretch, malefactor, miscreant, reprobate, evildoer, fiend, demon, devil, archfiend, ogre, monster, brute, beast, dog, cur, hound, rat, viper, reptile, snake in the grass, heel, degenerate, pervert, bad guy, worm, swine, good-for-nothing, stinker, louse, creep, bum, bastard, black hat, SOB, fink.
—**Ant.** hero, protagonist.

vindicate, *v.* **1.** clear, exonerate, exculpate, absolve, acquit, excuse, dispel, suspicion. **2.** uphold, justify, maintain, defend, assert, support, argue for, advocate, make a case for, show evidence for.
—**Ant.** convict, indict.

vindictive, *adj.* revengeful, vengeful, spiteful, acrimonious, bitter, grim, unforgiving, rancorous, malign, malicious, vicious, venomous, mean, nasty, unrelenting, relentless, merciless, implacable.
—**Ant.** forgiving, merciful.

violation, *n.* **1.** breach, disturbance, infringement, infraction, trespass, offense, sin, crime, vice, transgression. **2.** desecration, profanation, sacrilege, blasphemy, disrespect, irreverence, defilement. **3.** rape, defloration, deflowering, outrage, attack, defilement, assault, molestation, harassment, abuse, victimization.
—**Ant.** respect, reverence, honoring.
—**Syn. Study.** See BREACH.

violence, *n.* **1.** injury, wrong, harm, damage, wounding, outrage, injustice. **2.** force, compulsion, coercion, duress, constraint. **3.** vehemence, force, ferocity, fierceness, virulence, immoderation, roughness, fury, intensity, severity, might, power, strength, energy, vigor, acuteness. **4.** brutality, savagery, bestiality, bloodthirstiness, murderousness, wildness, frenzy, passion, cruelty, barbarousness.

virgin, *adj.* **1.** pure, stainless, unsullied, undefiled, unblemished, wholesome, clean, chaste, decent, modest, virtuous, moral, good, continent, abstinent, intact. **2.** untouched, untried, unused, inexperienced, untested, unfledged, untrained, unripe, immature, budding, fresh, new, raw, green; first, initial, inaugural, maiden.
—**Ant.** impure, unchaste; experienced, mature, seasoned.

virile, *adj.* masculine, manly, male, manful; dynamic, forceful, spirited, vital, lively, lusty, vigorous, potent, powerful, strong, robust, fit, hardy, stalwart, tough, athletic.
—**Ant.** effeminate; impotent.
—**Syn. Study.** See MALE.

virtue, *n.* **1.** goodness, uprightness, righteousness, fairness, nobility, good conduct, morality, probity, rectitude, integrity, honor, honesty, decency, high-mindedness, character, respectability. **2.** chastity, virginity, purity, honor, innocence, abstinence, continence, self-restraint, incorruptibility. **3.** justice, prudence, temperance, fortitude; faith, hope, charity. **4.** excellence, worth, value, credit, strength, good point, merit, quality, asset. **5.** effectiveness, efficacy, force, power, potency, strength, might.
—**Ant.** vice.
—**Syn. Study.** See GOODNESS.

virtuous, *adj.* **1.** right, upright, moral, ethical, noble, just, honorable, honest, high-principled, upstanding, respectable, righteous, just, fair, high-minded, scrupulous, trustworthy, reliable, uncorrupted, uncorruptible, good. **2.** chaste, pure, innocent, decent, proper, unsullied, virginal.
—**Ant.** immoral, evil.

virulent, *adj.* **1.** venomous, poisonous, toxic, pernicious, septic, miasmic, lethal, life-threatening, fatal, noxious, baneful, deleteriuos, harmful, pestilential, unhealthy, unwholesome, destructive, malignant, deadly. **2.** hostile, antagonistic, hateful, malicious, splenetic, bitter, acrimonious, spiteful, vicious, acerbic, acid, mordant, trenchant, caustic, nasty, trenchant, sarcastic.
—**Ant.** harmless.

visible, *adj.* **1.** perceptible, discernible, detectable, noticeable, obvious, unmistakable, plain, clear, open. **2.** apparent, manifest, obvious, evident, open, clear, patent, palpable, conspicuous, observable, prominent, distinct, identifiable, unmistakable.
—**Ant.** invisible.

vision, *n.* **1.** sight, eyesight, perception, acuity. **2.** perception, discernment, farsightedness, foresight, insight, imagination, understanding. **3.** view, perspective, image, conception, idea, notion, dream, plan, scheme, expectation. **4.** apparition, specter, shade, wraith, revenant, ghost, phantom, phantasm, illusion, chimera, fantasy, fancy, delusion, mirage, hallucination, daydream, dream, nightmare; revelation, prophecy.

visionary, *adj.* fanciful, fantastic, chimerical, quixotic, dreamy, wishful, unrealizable, unpractical, impractical, impracticable, fancied, unreal, unrealistic, idealistic, ideal, transcendent, abstract, imaginary, speculative, illusory, chimerical, romantic, sentimental, utopian, ambitious, pretentious.
—**Ant.** practical, practicable.

vital, *adj.* indispensable, imperative, fundamental, cardinal, requisite, required, mandatory, compulsive, crucial, basic, central, pivotal, essential, necessary, needful, significant, consequential, momentous, weighty, important, critical.
—**Ant.** unnecessary, optional, dispensable, secondary, unimportant.

vivacious, *adj.* lively, animated, effervescent, bubbly, gay, buoyant, merry, blithe, playful, jaunty, sprightly, spirited, brisk, energetic, ebullient, cheerful, sunny.
—**Ant.** dull, inactive, languid, lethargic.

vivid, *adj.* **1.** bright, brilliant, intense, clear, lucid, strong, fresh, dazzling, rich, colorful, glowing, lively. **2.** picturesque, graphic, pictorial, true to life, lifelike, realistic, detailed. **3.** clear, sharp, keen, acute, lucid, powerful. **4.** strong, distinct, striking, dramatic, memorable.
—**Ant.** dull, obscure, vague.

vocation, *n.* business, occupation, career, profession, calling, trade, métier, employment, pursuit, job, line of work.

vogue, *n.* **1.** fashion, style, trend, craze, look, taste, fad, latest thing, last word, *dernier cri.* **2.** popularity, preference, prevalence, fashionableness, currency, acceptance, favor, usage, custom, practice.

void, *adj.* **1.** invalid, not binding, unenforceable, inoperative, unavailing, futile, idle, pointless, useless, ineffectual, vain, ineffective, nugatory. **2.** empty, deserted, vacant, unoccupied, vacated, unfilled, unused, blank, clear. —*n.* **3.** emptiness, nothingness, vacantness, blankness, barrenness, desolation, vacuity, black hole, outer space, vacuum. **4.** gap, opening, space, vacancy, place, slot, niche, emptiness. —*v.* **5.** invalidate, nullify, annul, cancel, delete, vacate, quash, reverse, rescind, abrogate. **6.** empty, drain, purge, clear, discharge, evacuate, vacate, emit.
—**Ant.** valid, full, occupied; validate; fill.

voluble, *adj.* fluent, glib, eloquent, articulate, vocal, facile; talkative, garrulous, chatty, windy, long-winded, wordy, bombastic, loquacious.
—**Ant.** stammering, hesitant; curt, terse, taciturn.
—**Syn. Study.** See FLUENT.

volume, *n.* **1.** size, extent, dimensions, area, capacity, measure, amount, magnitude. **2.** bulk, mass, quantity, amount, supply, aggregate, abundance.

voluntary, *adj.* **1.** deliberate, considered, purposeful, premeditated, volitional, willful, intentional, intended, designed, planned. **2.** spontaneous, free, elective, willing, unsolicited, gratuitous, unforced, natural, unconstrained.
—**Ant.** involuntary.
—**Syn. Study.** See DELIBERATE.

voluptuous, *adj.* **1.** sensual, sensuous, carnal, sybaritic, opulent, sumptuous, indulgent, libidinous, hedonistic, pleasure-loving, gratifying, luxurious, epicurean. **2.** seductive, alluring, ravishing, enticing, luscious, shapely, buxom, full-figured, well-endowed, zaftig, sexy, curvaceous, stacked, dishy.
—**Ant.** ascetic; skinny.

voracious, *adj.* ravenous, gorging, gluttonous, insatiable, avaricious, prodigious, grasping, acquisitive, covetous, predacious, greedy, rapacious.
—**Ant.** temperate, forbearing, abstemious.

vow, *v.* pledge, promise, swear, give one's word, take an oath, assure, declare, guarantee.

voyage, *n.* trip, pilgrimage, journey, expedition, excursion, tour, trek, flight, cruise, sailing.
—**Syn. Study.** See TRIP.

vulgar, *adj.* **1.** coarse, gross, obscene, indelicate, indecent, indecorous, tasteless, improper, dirty, off-color, lewd, smutty, filthy, pornographic, raunchy, ribald, crude, rude, low, base, vile. **2.** low-class, unrefined, boorish, uncouth, oafish, uncultivated, uncultered, gauche, baseborn, ill-bred, inelegant, tasteless, common, mean, ignoble, plebeian. **3.** commonplace, common, ordinary, undistinctive, unaesthetic, banal, pedestrian.
—**Ant.** decent, proper, refined; distinctive.
—**Syn. Study.** See COMMON.

vulnerable, *adj.* **1.** defenseless, exposed, naked, open, unfortified, unprotected, unguarded, helpless, at risk, in jeopardy, assailable, at (someone's) mercy. **2.** open, susceptible, sensitive, ingenuous, naive, unwary, easily led, credulous, weak-minded, childlike, unworldly, unsuspecting, gullible, guileless, trusting, receptive, persuadable, pliant, impressionable, suggestible, liable, predisposed.
—**Ant.** invulnerable, impregnable, invincible, impervious; wary, hardened, insusceptible.

W

wacky, *adj.* eccentric, irrational, whimsical, knockabout, clownish, slapstick, comical, hilarious, nonsensical, absurd, ludicrous, inane, lunatic, preposterous, wild, zany, madcap, foolish, silly, crazy, screwball, goofy, oddball, nuts, nutty, loony, crackpot, cracked, cuckoo, screwy, bonkers, meshuga, flaky.
—**Ant.** serious, sobersided.

waffle, *v.* vacillate, dither, equivocate, double-talk, sidestep, skirt, evade, dodge, mislead, deceive, hedge, quibble, be undecided, waver, seesaw, fluctuate, hem and haw, shilly-shally, beat around the bush, yo-yo.

wage, *n.* **1.** (*usually plural*) money, fee, payment, pay, salary, stipend, earnings, emolument, compensation, remuneration, income, allowance; recompense, return, reward, comeuppance. —*v.* **2.** carry on, undertake, pursue, conduct, practice, proceed with, engage in.

wait, *v.* **1.** stay, rest, remain, be inactive, repose, linger, abide, tarry, pause, delay, postpone, loiter, bide one's time, mark *or* waste time, sit tight, shilly-shally, hang fire. —*n.* **2.** delay, stay, holdup, postponement, lull, interruption, discontinuation, halt, pause, stop, break, rest, interval, gap, hiatus, intermission, recess, breather, abeyance, lapse, rest period.
—**Ant.** go, depart, leave, proceed.

waive, *v.* **1.** relinquish, forgo, resign, abdicate, forsake, cede, abandon, yield, forbear, sacrifice, surrender, renounce, give up, remit. **2.** defer, put off *or* aside, postpone, overlook, disregard, ignore.
—**Ant.** require, demand, claim.

wake, *v.* **1.** awake, stir, come to, regain consciousness, rise, arise, get up. **2.** rouse, waken, arouse, stir, rally, awaken. **3.** stimulate, activate, animate, inspire, bring to life, vitalize, kindle, provoke, motivate, excite, quicken, galvanize, inflame, fire, impel, drive. —*n.*
—**Ant.** sleep; lull; subdue, pacify.

walk, *v.* **1.** step, stride, stroll, pace, trot, amble, stride, ramble, shamble, pad, shuffle, saunter, sashay, flounce, mince, trip, sidle, tiptoe, waddle, perambulate, promenade, parade, swagger, strut, prance, stamp, march, tramp, hike, trudge, slog, trek, plod, traipse, trek, trundle, tread, go by shanks' mare. —*n.* **2.** stroll, promenade, trek, slog, amble, saunter, ramble, march, tramp, hike, constitutional.

wan, *adj.* washed out, pale, pallid, sickly, ashen, white, livid, pasty, bloodless, sallow, colorless, ghastly, drawn, haggard, worn, cadaverous, fatigued, tired, anemic, weak, feeble.
—**Ant.** ruddy, robust.
—**Syn. Study.** See PALE.

wander, *v.* **1.** ramble, rove, roam, stray, range, stroll, meander, saunter, prowl, gad about, traipse, gallivant, drift, cruise. **2.** ramble, curve, wind, meander, zigzag, bend, twist, snake. **3.** deviate, err, go astray, digress, drift, lapse. **4.** rave, be delirious *or* incoherent, babble, ramble, gibber, maunder.

wane, *v.* decrease, decline, dwindle, lessen, abate, subside, ebb, fade, diminish, fail, sink.
—**Ant.** wax.

wangle, *v.* manipulate, maneuver, engineer, manage, fix, fiddle, finagle, connive, machinate, scheme, plot, intrigue, connive, con, talk into, pull off, angle, swing.

want, *v.* **1.** desire, wish, long for, pine for, hope for, crave, covet, lust after, hunger *or* thirst for, have an itch *or* yen for, yearn for, aspire to, aim for, pant after; need, miss, demand, necessitate, require, lack. —*n.* **2.** necessity, need, exigency, requirement, desideratum. **3.** lack, absence, privation, shortage, dearth, scarcity, scarceness, inadequacy, insufficiency, scantiness, paucity, meagerness, deficiency, defect, defectiveness. **4.** destitution, poverty, need, homelessness, pinch, bankruptcy, insolvency, privation, penury, indigence, straits.
—**Ant.** reject; plenty, abundance, plethora, superfluity; wealth, affluence.
—**Syn. Study.** See LACK.

wanton, *adj.* **1.** immoral, evil, wicked, vicious, cruel, violent, malicious, malevolent, merciless, inhumane, spiteful, perverse, contrary. **2.** deliberate, calculated, willful, unprovoked, groundless, arbitrary, gratuitous, unjustifiable, supererogatory, unwarranted, uncalled for. **3.** unruly, wayward, ungovernable, intractable, daring, heedless, foolhardy, uninhibited, unrestrained, unbridled, wild, reckless. **4.** unchaste, abandoned, dissipated, debauched, degenerate, depraved, hedonistic, loose, lascivious, lewd, licentious, dissolute, lustful, prurient, libertine, lecherous, salacious, incontinent, concupiscent, libidinous. **5.** extravagant, excessive, profligate, lavish, wasteful, extreme, outrageous, profuse, immoderate, intemperate, improvident, undue, unwarranted, unconscionable, incontinent.
—**Ant.** moral, virtuous; justifiable, restrained, sober, inhibited; chaste, pure; moderate, temperate.

war, *n.* **1.** fighting, warfare, military action, military operations, military expedition, military campaign, clash of arms, armed conflict, combat, struggle, conflict, hostilities, aggression, strife, battle, pitched battle, encounter, engagement, clash, fray, confrontation, attack, counterattack, assault, skirmish, encroachment, invasion, offensive, offense, onslaught, slaughter, bloodshed, blood feud, blitzkrieg, Armageddon, holocaust. **2.** belligerence, bellicosity, discord, competition, conflict, disagreement, dissension, dispute, antagonism, rivalry, contest, contention, fracas, match, debate, wrangle, altercation, controversy, feud, quarrel, squabble, row, tiff, breach of the peace, scrap, bickering, standoff, showdown. —*v.* **3.** fight, battle, contend, combat, oppose, struggle, strive, resist, withstand, attack, assault, campaign against, stand up to, take up arms, cross swords, joust, fence.
—**Ant.** peace.

warlike, *adj.* martial, military, militaristic, hawkish, war-mongering, jingoistic; bellicose, belligerent, hostile, inimical, pugnacious, contentious, combative, aggressive, unfriendly, bloodthirsty.
—**Ant.** peaceful, peaceable.

warm, *adj.* **1.** heated, lukewarm, tepid, moderate, comfortable. **2.** hearty, enthusiastic, earnest, sincere, passionate, heartfelt, wholehearted, fervent, ardent, eager. **3.** amiable, genial, hospitable, welcoming, friendly, neighborly, kind, warmhearted, responsive, cordial, hearty. **4.** attached, friendly, amiable, amicable, affectionate, tender, sympathetic, compassionate, loving, amorous, close, inimate. **5.** heated, irritated, annoyed, testy, touchy, irascible, vexed, angry, irate, furious. **6.** animated, spirited, lively, brisk, vigorous, vehement. —*v.* **7.** cheer, please, delight, move, animate, stir, rouse, arouse.
—**Ant.** cool.

warn, *v.* caution, admonish, forewarn, advise, counsel, exhort, urge, notify, apprise, inform, alert, tip off, signal, sound an alarm.
—**Syn. Study.** WARN, CAUTION, ADMONISH imply attempting to prevent someone from running into danger or unpleasant circumstances. To WARN is to inform plainly and strongly of possible or imminent trouble, or to advise that doing or not doing something will have dangerous consequences: *The scout warned the fort of the attack. I warned them not to travel to that country.* To CAUTION is to advise to be careful and to take necessary precautions: *Tourists were cautioned to watch their belongings.* To ADMONISH is to advise of negligence or a fault in an earnest, authoritative, but friendly way, so that corrective action can be taken: *to admonish a student for constant lateness.*

warning, *n.* **1.** caution, admonition, threat, caveat, tip, notification, heads-up, signal, counsel, advice. **2.** omen, sign, signal, indication, forewarning, foreshadowing, prophecy, augury, portent.

warrant, *n.* **1.** authorization, sanction, justification, approval, certification. **2.** pledge, guarantee, assurance, security, surety, warranty. **3.** certificate, affidavit, document, credential, license, permit, voucher, writ, order, mandate, decree. —*v.* **4.** authorize, sanction, approve, justify, vindicate, endorse, guarantee, vouch for. **5.** assure, certify, uphold, back up, stand behind, promise, guarantee, secure, affirm, vouch for, attest.

wary, *adj.* alert, cautious, vigilant, chary, fearful, apprehensive, suspicious, on edge, on guard, careful, circumspect, watchful, discreet, prudent, observant, foresighted.
—**Ant.** foolhardy, careless.
—**Syn. Study.** See CAREFUL.

wash, *v.* **1.** cleanse, clean, launder, scrub, mop, swab, rub, scour, soak, rinse, flush. **2.** bathe, shower, shampoo, soap up, lather, sponge off.

washout, *n.* **1.** failure, total loss, disaster, disappointment, debacle, rout, calamity, catastrophe, farce, setback, misfire, shellacking, flop, fiasco, botch, fizzle, clinker, lead balloon, lemon, bomb, bummer. **2.** failure, flop, nonstarter, loser, misfit, nebbish, schlemiel, schnook, sad sack, dud, bust, dead duck, turkey, also-ran.
—**Ant.** success.

waste, *v.* **1.** consume, misuse, burn up, fritter away, spend, throw away, expend, squander, misspend, splurge, dissipate. **2.** destroy, consume, wear away, erode, eat away, reduce, wear down, exhaust, disable, debilitate, emaciate, enfeeble. **3.** destroy, demolish, wreck, decimate, lay waste, devastate, desolate, ruin, ravage, pillage, plunder, sack, loot, despoil. **4.** diminish, dwindle, deteriorate, decline, wither, shrink, ebb, wane, decay. —*n.* **5.** consumption, misuse, dissipation, diminution, decline, loss, destruction, decay, impairment. **6.** extravagance, prodigality, improvidence, squandering, overindulgence, lavishness. **7.** desert, tundra, wilderness, wild, badlands, wasteland, emptiness. **8.** refuse, rubbish, trash, garbage, detritus, scrap, litter, junk, debris. —*adj.* **9.** unused, useless, superfluous, worthless, leftover, surplus, extra, *de trop.* **10.** rejected, unproductive, unsalvageable, unrecyclable, useless, worthless, purposeless, unusable.
—**Ant.** preserve.

watch, *v.* **1.** look, see, observe, note, notice, pay attention to, follow, scrutinize, examine, inspect. **2.** contemplate, regard, mark, view, gaze at, stare at, take in, behold, eye, survey, observe, look at *or* upon. **3.** wait for, await, expect, anticipate, be watchful *or* vigilant, be prepared *or* ready. **4.** guard, protect, tend, mind, supervise, look after, keep an eye on, keep safe, take care of, chaperone, baby-sit. —*n.* **5.** observation, inspection, attention, vigil, watchfulness, alertness, surveillance, lookout.

watchful, *adj.* vigilant, alert, observant, attentive, heedful, careful, circumspect, cautious, wary, wakeful, wide-awake, awake.
—**Ant.** careless, heedless, inattentive.

wave, *n.* **1.** ridge, swell, undulation, whitecap, billow, heave, comber, ripple, breaker, surf, sea; surge, upsurge, tide, current, flood. —*v.* **2.** undulate, billow, ripple, fluctuate, oscillate. **3.** flutter, swing, flap, quiver, wag, shake, wiggle, float, sway, rock.
—**Ant.** hollow.

waver, *v.* **1.** wave, sway, flutter, flicker, hover, flit, flitter, float. **2.** shake, rock, tremble, quiver, quaver, shudder, shiver. **3.** vacillate, fluctuate, waffle, dither, equivocate, seesaw, yo-yo, falter, balk, boggle, demur, shy, hedge, shilly-shally, vary, alternate, hesitate.
—**Syn. Study.** WAVER, VACILLATE refer to an inability to decide or to stick to a decision. WAVER usu. implies a state of doubt, uncertainty, or fear that prevents one from pursuing a chosen course: *He made plans to move, but wavered at the last minute.* VACILLATE means to go back and forth between choices without reaching a decision, or to make up one's mind and change

it again suddenly: *Stop vacillating and set a day.*

wax, *v.* increase, intensify, extend, grow, expand, magnify, amplify, swell, spread, distend, lengthen, elongate, widen, broaden, stretch, enlarge, dilate, augment, snowball, develop, burgeon, flourish, proliferate.
—**Ant.** wane.

way, *n.* **1.** manner, mode, fashion, means, technique, procedure, system, approach, method, modus operandi. **2.** manner, character, nature, behavior, style, pattern, conduct, habit, custom, usage, practice, approach, spirit, feeling, sense, disposition, temperament, personality. **3.** means, course, plan, method, scheme, device. **4.** respect, aspect, sense, feature, point, particular detail, part. **5.** direction; passage, progression, advance, headway. **6.** distance, space, interval. **7.** path, street, trail, course, road, route, track, avenue.
—**Syn. Study.** See METHOD.

wayward, *adj.* **1.** contrary, headstrong, stubborn, balky, insubordinate, contumacious, rebellious, recalcitrant, obstinate, disobedient, unruly, refractory, intractable, willful, perverse. **2.** capricious, unstable, unpredictable, volatile, flighty, whimsical, fickle, mercurial, erratic, variable, inconstant, changeable.
—**Ant.** agreeable, amenable, obedient, tractable; constant, stable.
—**Syn. Study.** See WILLFUL.

weak, *adj.* **1.** fragile, frail, breakable, delicate, frangible, flimsy, shaky, rickety, unsound, unsteady, unstable. **2.** feeble, senile, anile, doddering, doting, infirm, decrepit, weakly, sickly, unhealthy, unwell, debilitated, enervated, anemic, exhausted, wan, haggard, vitiated, effete, invalid. **3.** impotent, ineffectual, ineffective, inefficient, inadequate, inefficacious, useless, worthless. **4.** unconvincing, inconclusive, lame, unpersuasive, empty, hollow, pathetic, pitiful, half-baked, puny, unbelievable, illogical, unsatisfactory, vague. **5.** unintelligent, simple, foolish, stupid, senseless, silly. **6.** unassertive, retiring, spineless, feckless, irresolute, weak-kneed, namby-pamby, wishy-washy, meek, timid, cowardly. **7.** faint, slight, feeble, dim, inconsiderable, flimsy, poor, meager, paltry, puny. **8.** deficient, inadequate, unsatisfactory, faulty, imperfect, inferior, flawed, defective, insufficient.
—**Ant.** strong.

weaken, *v.* worsen, enfeeble, debilitate, enervate, emasculate, unnerve, undermine, sap, cripple, disable, injure, damage, impair, handicap, exhaust, deplete, diminish, lessen, lower, impoverish, vitiate, degrade, reduce, mitigate, moderate, minimize, dilute, thin, attenuate, extenuate, adulterate, contaminate.
—**Ant.** strengthen.

weakling, *n.* coward, born victim, born loser, pushover, lightweight, second-rater, washout, mouse, milksop, namby-pamby, creampuff, softie, baby, doormat, yes-man, milquetoast, jellyfish, weak sister, empty suit, invertebrate, wuss, wimp, schnook, schlemiel, nerd, twerp, turkey, drip, dweeb, crybaby, mama's boy, pantywaist, sissy, nebbish, gutless wonder, chicken, quitter, nervous Nellie, yellow-belly, pansy, patsy, sucker, lame.

weakness, *n.* **1.** feebleness, fragility, frailty, delicacy, vulnerability, infirmity. **2.** flaw, defect, fault, shortcoming, foible, failing, imperfection, liability, blemish, deficiency. **3.** fondness, preference, affection,

appreciation, tenderness, liking, inclination, bent, leaning, proclivity, propensity, partiality, appetite, taste, soft spot.
—**Ant.** strength.
—**Syn. Study.** See FAULT.

wealth, *n.* **1.** property, riches, assets, holdings, capital, funds, cash, valuables, bankroll. **2.** abundance, profusion, fullness, plethora, bounty, store, plenitude, plenty, copiousness, richness, amplitude. **3.** assets, possessions, goods, property. **4.** prosperity, affluence, opulence, fortune, treasure, wherewithal, resources, means.
—**Ant.** poverty, indigence.

wealthy, *adj.* rich, affluent, opulent, prosperous, well-to-do, well-off, comfortable, flush, well-heeled, loaded, fat, moneyed, upper-class, privileged, to the manor born, noveau riche, rolling in dough, rich as Croesus *or* Rockefeller, well-fixed, well-provided-for.
—**Ant.** poor, poverty-stricken, indigent.

wearisome, *adj.* **1.** fatiguing, tiring, exhausting, debilitating, vitiating, wearing, taxing. **2.** tiresome, boring, tedious, soporific, monotonous, humdrum, dull, bland, insipid, vapid, jejune, prosaic, vexatious, trying, irritating, irksome, exasperating, bothersome, annoying.
—**Ant.** vitalizing, energizing, interesting, exciting.

weary, *adj.* **1.** exhausted, tired, wearied, enervated, debilitated, fatigued, spent, drained, sapped, knocked out, bone-tired, finished, all in, frazzled, tuckered out, dead on one's feet, pooped, zonked, shot. **2.** impatient, bored, indignant, sick and tired, fed up, dissatisfied. —*v.* **3.** fatigue, tire, exhaust, tire *or* wear out, jade, drain, tax, enervate, debilitate, sap, weaken. **4.** annoy, bother, irritate, burden, vex, exasperate, irk.
—**Ant.** energetic; forbearing, patient; invigorating; enliven, energize; delight.

weep, *v.* shed tears, cry, sob, wail, whimper, blubber, moan, sigh, groan, bawl, whine, snivel, mewl, pule, murmur, mope, lament, sorrow, suffer, grieve, complain, deplore, bewail, bemoan, turn on the waterworks.
—**Ant.** laugh, rejoice, celebrate.

weigh, *v.* consider, balance, ponder, contemplate, study, revolve, meditate, muse, reflect, think over, mull over, ruminate, chew over, brood, examine, review, pore over, judge, assess, evaluate.
—**Syn. Study.** See STUDY.

weight, *n.* influence, authority, prestige, credit, importance, substance, force, impact, value, worth, seriousness, gravity, moment, import, consequence, significance, efficacy, effectiveness, power.

weighty, *adj.* **1.** heavy, ponderous, massive, bulky, cumbersome, hefty. **2.** burdensome, irksome, troublesome, wearisome, oppressive, distressing, onerous. **3.** important, momentous, significant, serious, crucial, grave, consequential. **4.** influential, powerful, important, forceful, authoritative, prestigious, prominent.
—**Ant.** light; unimportant, insignificant.

weird, *adj.* eerie, strange, uncanny, mysterious, unnatural, unearthly, supernatural, preternatural, fearsome, dreadful, awful, odd, peculiar, queer, curious, fantastic, bizarre, grotesque, outlandish, freakish, freaky, spooky, creepy.
—**Ant.** natural.
—**Syn. Study.** WEIRD, EERIE, UNCANNY refer to that which is myste-

rious and apparently outside natural law. WEIRD suggests the intervention of supernatural influences in human affairs: *weird doings in the haunted house; a weird coincidence.* EERIE refers to something ghostly that makes one's flesh creep: *eerie moans from a deserted house.* UNCANNY refers to an extraordinary or remarkable thing that seems to defy the laws established by experience: *an uncanny ability to recall numbers.*

welfare, *n.* well-being, commonweal, prosperity, good fortune, good health, success, happiness, benefit, good, profit, advantage, interest.

well, *adv.* **1.** satisfactorily, favorably, adequately, agreeably, nicely, advantageously, fortunately, happily. **2.** commendably, meritoriously, excellently, successfully, superbly, splendidly, admirably. **3.** properly, correctly, skillfully, efficiently, accurately. **4.** justly, reasonably, easily, in fairness, with propriety, properly. **5.** adequately, sufficiently, satisfactorily. **6.** thoroughly, soundly, carefully, abundantly, amply, fully. **7.** considerably, rather, quite, fairly. **8.** personally, intimately, closely, thoroughly, profoundly, deeply, entirely. —*adj.* **9.** sound, healthy, hale, hearty, robust, fit, vigorous, wholesome, strong, in good shape, in fine fettle. **10.** satisfactory, good, fine, pleasing, agreeable, all right. **11.** proper, fitting, gratifying, suitable, befitting, appropriate. **12.** fortunate, successful, well-off, happy.
—**Ant.** poorly, badly; unwell, infirm, weak, ill, sick.

well-built, *adj.* **1.** well-endowed, well-knit, well-proportioned, sinewy, hunky, luscious, alluring, appealing, desirable, stunning, gorgeous, muscular, powerful, strapping, rugged, robust, sturdy, broad-shouldered, athletic, brawny, burly, stacked, curvaceous, shapely, comely, graceful, lissome, svelte, slender, slim, voluptuous, zaftig, buxom, sexy, dishy, eye-popping, an eyeful, eye candy, built. **2.** sturdy, strong, durable, solid, rugged, sound, stout, substantial, enduring, heavy-duty, long-wearing, dependable, well-constructed.
—**Ant.** scrawny, frail; unsound, rickety.

wet, *adj.* **1.** soaked, drenched, sopping, soppy, saturated, dripping, sodden, damp, dampened, waterlogged, flooded, moist, moistened. **2.** damp, moist, dank, humid, dewy, foggy, misty, drizzling, rainy.
—**Ant.** dry.

wherewithal, *n.* means, resources, wealth, riches, supplies, means, fortune, money, cash, funds, capital, bankroll, finances, holdings, assets, property, credit.

whim, *n.* fancy, fantasy, vision, dream, idea, notion, caprice, whimsy, humor, vagary, quirk, inclination, playfulness, impulse, impetuosity, crotchet.
—**Ant.** plan.

whimsical, *adj.* **1.** capricious, mercurial, volatile, erratic, flighty, fickle, unpredictable, inconsistent, impetuous, changeable. **2.** crotchety, freakish, fanciful, odd, peculiar, curious, singular, queer, quaint, eccentric, fey, playful.
—**Ant.** deliberate, serious, sober.

whine, *v.* complain, grouse, mutter, wail, carp, gripe, squawk, grouch, beef, kick, cavil, fret, grumble; moan, lament, groan, wail, whimper, howl, sob, snivel, pule, mewl, cry.
—**Syn. Study.** See COMPLAIN.

whip, *v.* lash, beat, flog, thrash, horsewhip, cane, spank, strap, scourge, beat, switch, flagellate;

chastise, castigate, punish, discipline.

whirl, *v.* gyrate, pirouette, spin, swirl, turn, circle, eddy, rotate, revolve, twirl, wheel.

whitewash, *v.* **1.** gloss over, cover up, hide, conceal, disguise, camouflage, paper over, mask, mislead, cloak, dissemble, sugarcoat, prevaricate, stonewall. **2.** justify, condone, equivocate, excuse, exculpate, extenuate, qualify, minimize, downplay, rationalize, explain away, vindicate.
—**Ant.** confess, reveal.

whole, *adj.* **1.** entire, full, total, all, gross; together, undiminished, undivided, integral, complete, uncut, unbroken, unimpaired, perfect, uninjured, faultless, undamaged, unharmed, unscathed, in one piece, solid, inviolate, sound, intact. —*n.* **2.** totality, total, sum, entirety, aggregate, sum total, everything, *(slang)* the full monty.
—**Ant.** partial; part.

wholesome, *adj.* salutary, beneficial, helpful, healthful, salubrious, nourishing, nutritious, healthy, invigorating, tonic, bracing, lifegiving, restorative.
—**Ant.** unwholesome.
—**Syn. Study.** See HEALTHY.

wicked, *adj.* evil, bad, immoral, amoral, lawless, unrepentant, unprincipled, sinful, piacular, unrighteous, ungodly, godless, sacrilegious, satanic, demonic, fiendish, ghoulish, hellish, impious, profane, blasphemous; profligate, corrupt, depraved, dissolute, blackhearted, beastly, base, low, debased, degenerate, perverse, perverted, foul, offensive, abominable, shameful, disgraceful, shameless, unregenerate, criminal, heinous, vicious, vile, iniquitous, abandoned, flagitious, nefarious, treacherous, villainous, atrocious.
—**Ant.** good, virtuous.

wide, *adj.* broad, extensive, roomy, vast, spacious, ample; comprehensive, large, expanded, distended, encyclopedic, inclusive, wide-ranging, far-reaching, widespread.
—**Ant.** narrow.

wild, *adj.* **1.** untamed, undomesticated, feral, savage, vicious, unbroken, ferocious. **2.** uncultivated, uninhabited, desolate, empty, barren, deserted, waste, virgin, unpopulated. **3.** uncivilized, barbarous, savage, primitive, backward, fierce, barbarian. **4.** violent, furious, boisterous, tempestuous, stormy, disorderly, frenzied, turbulent, impetuous. **5.** frantic, mad, distracted, distraught, hysterical, frenzied, unhinged, berserk, manic, rabid, crazy, insane. **6.** enthusiastic, eager, anxious, agog, fervent, impatient, excited. **7.** ardent, passionate, exciting, romantic, tempestuous, intense, chaotic, crazy, madcap. **8.** undisciplined, willful, unruly, obstreperous, fractious, disobedient, refractory, intractable, boisterous, rowdy, lively, uproarious, freewheeling, unconventional, lawless, turbulent, headstrong, self-willed, ungoverned, unrestrained, riotous, wayward. **9.** unrestrained, unrestricted, unchecked, unbridled, uncontrolled, untrammeled. **10.** absurd, irrational, imprudent, foolhardy, reckless, rash, extravagant, unworkable, impractical, impracticable. **11.** queer, grotesque, bizarre, strange, fantastic, far-out, freakish, imaginary, fanciful, visionary. **12.** disorderly, disheveled, unkempt, messy, sloppy, tousled, windblown. —*n.* **13.** waste, wilderness, tundra, desert, heath, wasteland, emptiness.
—**Ant.** tame, domesticated.

wild-eyed, *adj.* **1.** wild, manic, maniacal, rabid, frantic, frenzied, raving, mad, crazy, berserk. **2.** visionary, quixotic, unrealistic, extreme, fanatical, fanatic, far-out, off the wall, harebrained.
—**Ant.** calm, composed; sensible, practical.

wile, *n.* **1.** trick, artifice, stratagem, feint, subterfuge, ploy, conspiracy, dodge, trap, snare, ruse, deception, move, gambit, maneuver. **2.** deceit, cunning, duplicity, guile, slyness, foxiness, craftiness, artfulness, trickery, chicanery, fraud, cheat, defrauding, imposture, imposition.

will, *n.* **1.** determination, commitment, resolve, resolution, resoluteness, decision, forcefulness. **2.** volition, choice, election, preference. **3.** wish, desire, longing, liking, pleasure, disposition, inclination. **4.** intention, intent, purpose, determination. **5.** order, direction, command, behest, bidding. —*v.* **6.** decide, decree, determine, direct, command, bid, order, ordain, require.

willful, *adj.* **1.** willed, willing, deliberate, conscious, premeditated, purposeful, voluntary, intentional, volitional. **2.** self-willed, headstrong, perverse, obstinate, recalcitrant, immovable, dogged, determined, uncompromising, pertinacious, intractable, wayward, stubborn, intransigent, contrary, contumacious, perverse, refractory, disagreeable, pigheaded, cantankerous, unruly, inflexible, obdurate, adamant.
—**Ant.** unintentional, involuntary; tractable, docile, obedient.
—**Syn. Study.** WILLFUL, HEADSTRONG, PERVERSE, WAYWARD refer to a person who stubbornly persists in doing as he or she pleases. WILLFUL implies opposition to those whose wishes, suggestions, or commands ought to be respected or obeyed: *a willful son who ignored his parents' advice.* HEADSTRONG is used in a similar way, but implies foolish and sometimes reckless behavior: *headstrong teens who could not be restrained.* PERVERSE implies stubborn persistence in opposing what is right or acceptable, often with the express intention of being contrary or disagreeable: *taking a perverse delight in arguing with others.* WAYWARD suggests stubborn disobedience that gets one into trouble: *a reform school for wayward youths.*

wily, *adj.* crafty, cunning, artful, sly, shrewd, astute, sneaky, shifty, disingenuous, sharp, smooth, slick, oily, unctuous, slippery, cagey, foxy, tricky, intriguing, arch, designing, calculating, perfidious, deceitful, treacherous, crooked, Machiavellian, duplicitous, double-dealing, underhanded.
—**Ant.** guileless, ingenuous.

win, *v.* **1.** succeed, advance, win out, triumph, progress, overcome, conquer, prevail, be victorious, take first prize, carry the day. **2.** obtain, gain, procure, secure, earn, acquire, achieve, attain, reach, collect, receive, realize, net, bag. **3.** win over, persuade, convince, induce, prevail upon, influence, sway, charm, bring around.
—**Ant.** lose.
—**Syn. Study.** See GAIN.

wince, *v.* recoil, shrink, quail, shy, falter, stagger, blanch, cower, balk, demur, cringe, flinch, draw back, squirm, writhe.
—**Syn. Study.** WINCE, RECOIL, SHRINK, QUAIL all mean to draw back from what is dangerous, fearsome, difficult, or unpleasant. WINCE suggests an involuntary contraction of the facial features triggered by pain, embarrassment, or revulsion: *to wince as a needle pierces*

the skin; to wince at coarse language. RECOIL denotes a physical movement away from something disgusting or shocking, or a similar psychological shutting out or avoidance: *to recoil at the sight of a dead body; to recoil from the idea of retiring.* SHRINK may imply a fastidious and scrupulous avoidance of the distasteful, or a cowardly withdrawal from what is feared: *to shrink from mentioning a shameful act; to shrink from asking for a raise.* QUAIL often suggests trembling or other physical manifestations of fear: *to quail before an angry mob.*

wind, *n.* **1.** air, whiff, puff, breath, current, blast, draft, zephyr, breeze, gust, blow, gale, hurricane, whirlwind, cyclone, tornado, twister, typhoon, waterspout. **2.** noise, bombast, bluster, boasting, braggadocio, blather, maundering, yammering, windiness, flatulence, emptiness, idle talk, nonsense, humbug, hot air, claptrap, hooey, rot, hogwash, baloney, bull. —*v.* **3.** change direction, bend, turn, meander, curve, twist, snake, zigzag, ramble, veer, coil, sheer, swerve, deviate, spiral, angle, dogleg, skew, be tortuous *or* sinuous *or* circuitous *or* indirect. **4.** coil, twine, twist, encircle, spiral, curl, wrap, wreathe.
—**Syn. Study.** WIND, BREEZE, ZEPHYR, GUST, BLAST refer to a current of air set in motion naturally. WIND applies to air in motion, blowing with any degree of gentleness or violence: *a strong wind; a westerly wind.* A BREEZE is usu. a cool, light wind; technically, it is a wind of 4–31 mph: *a refreshing breeze.* ZEPHYR, a literary word, refers to a soft, mild breeze: *a zephyr whispering through palm trees.* A GUST is a sudden, brief rush of air: *A gust of wind scattered the leaves.* A BLAST is a brief but more violent rush of air, usu. a cold one: *a wintry blast.*

winning, *adj.* engaging, endearing, prepossessing, fetching, enchanting, bewitching, charming, captivating, attractive, alluring, charismatic, magnetic, magical, entrancing, seductive, winsome, persuasive, convincing, dynamic, compelling.
—**Ant.** repellent, obnoxious.

wisdom, *n.* **1.** discretion, judgment, judiciousness, perspicacity, perception, foresight, discernment, sense, common sense, reason, penetration, acumen, acuity, intelligence, sagacity, insight, understanding, prudence, savvy. **2.** knowledge, information, lore, scholarship, learning, erudition, enlightenment.
—**Ant.** foolishness; ignorance.

wise, *adj.* **1.** discerning, judicious, discreet, sage, sensible, penetrating, sagacious, intelligent, perspicacious, perceptive, insightful, intelligent, acute, astute, brilliant, clever, bright, quick-witted, profound, rational, prudent, reasonable. **2.** learned, erudite, schooled, scholarly, enlightened, knowing, well-read, cultivated, cultured, versed, knowledgeable, informed. **3.** advisable, sensible, judicious, discreet, expedient, tactful, strategic, diplomatic, prudent, politic, proper, appropriate, fitting.
—**Ant.** unwise.

wish, *v.* **1.** want, crave, desire, have an appetite for, thirst for, yearn, hope, long for; need, lack. **2.** bid, require, request, demand, direct, command, order. —*n.* **3.** desire, passion, whim, keenness, longing, craving, yearning, thirst, appetite, hunger, urge, fondness, want, preference, predisposition, inclination.

wit, *n.* **1.** drollery, facetiousness, repartee, waggishness, raillery, levity, joking, jocularity, pungency, piquancy, sarcasm, irony, wisecrack, humor. **2.** understanding, judgment, discernment, insight, intelligence, sagacity, wisdom, intellect, mind, brains, cleverness, brilliance, acuity, sense.
—**Syn. Study.** See HUMOR.

withdraw, *v.* **1.** draw back *or* away, recoil, shrink, shy, wince, quail, demur, flinch; take back, subtract, remove, retract, cancel, void, annul, recall, disavow, recant, revoke, rescind. **2.** depart, retire, retreat, repair, absent oneself, quit, clear out, abscond, decamp, escape, fly, flee, scramble, scram.
—**Ant.** advance, arrive.

wither, *v.* shrivel, fade, decay, wrinkle, wizen, contract, constrict, shrink, dry, parch, desiccate, wilt, languish, droop, waste away.
—**Ant.** flourish, thrive.

withhold, *v.* hold back, restrain, retain, reserve, control, curb, bridle, inhibit, check, keep back, suppress, repress, hide, conceal.
—**Ant.** grant, concede, unleash, reveal.
—**Syn. Study.** See KEEP.

withstand, *v.* resist, oppose, combat, defy, stand up to, confront, face, face up to, hold out against, bear, endure, countenance, brook, undergo, experience, weather, tolerate, suffer.
—**Ant.** submit, yield, surrender.
—**Syn. Study.** See OPPOSE.

witness, *v.* **1.** see, perceive, observe, view, behold, spot, watch, look at, mark, notice, note. **2.** testify, affirm, swear, certify, vouch for, verify, confirm, prove, show, bear witness. —*n.* **3.** observer, onlooker, bystander, beholder, spectator, eyewitness. **4.** testimony, evidence, deposition, corroboration, statement.

witty, *adj.* facetious, droll, humorous, funny, amusing, entertaining, diverting, clever, original, ingenious, subtle, piquant, pungent, penetrating, astute, insightful, trenchant, mordant, waggish, wisecracking, sparkling, scintillating, brilliant, jocose, jocular.
—**Ant.** silly, stupid.

wizard, *n.* **1.** enchanter, magician, sorcerer, alchemist, shaman, magus, Merlin, mystic, necromancer, conjurer, charmer, diviner, seer, soothsayer. **2.** expert, adept, virtuoso, artist, marvel, miracle worker, genius, master, past master, whiz.

woe, *n.* distress, affliction, trouble, sorrow, grief, misery, anguish, hardship, adversity, calamity, misfortune, tribulation, trial, agony, wretchedness, heartache, regret, suffering, lamentation, gloom, depression, melancholy.
—**Ant.** joy, happiness, bliss, exultation.

woman, *n.* female, lady.
—**Ant.** man.
—**Syn. Study.** WOMAN, FEMALE, LADY are nouns referring to adult human beings who are biologically female, that is, capable of bearing offspring. WOMAN is the general, neutral term: *a wealthy woman.* In scientific, statistical, and other objective use FEMALE is the neutral contrastive term to MALE: *104 females to every 100 males.* FEMALE is sometimes used disparagingly: *a gossipy female.* LADY in the sense "polite, refined woman" is a term of approval: *We know you will always behave like a lady.*

womanly, *adj.* womanlike, womanish; feminine, female; attractive, mature, motherly, fully developed, ripe, nurturing.

—**Syn. Study.** WOMANLY, WOMANLIKE, WOMANISH mean having traits or qualities considered typical of or appropriate to adult human females. WOMANLY, a term of approval, suggests such admirable traits as self-possession, modesty, and motherliness: *a womanly consideration for others.* WOMANLIKE may be a neutral synonym for WOMANLY, or it may convey mild disapproval: *womanlike tears and reproaches.* WOMANISH is usually disparaging. Applied to women, it suggests traits not socially approved: *a womanish petulance;* applied to men, it suggests traits not culturally acceptable for men but (in what is regarded as a sexist notion) typical of women: *a womanish shrillness in his speech.* See also FEMALE.

wonder, *v.* **1.** think, speculate, muse, theorize, puzzle, be curious, mull over, conjecture, meditate, ponder, question, inquire. **2.** marvel, be astonished *or* thunderstruck *or* awed *or* dumbstruck *or* dumbfounded *or* astounded; gape, stare. —*n.* **3.** surprise, stupefaction, fascination, astonishment, amazement, awe, bewilderment, perplexity, mystification, puzzlement; admiration.

wonderful, *adj.* marvelous, extraordinary, remarkable, awesome, startling, wondrous, miraculous, spectacular, stunning, fascinating, surprising, prodigious, astonishing, amazing, astounding, phenomenal, unique, curious, strange, odd, peculiar, rare.
—**Ant.** usual, ordinary, common.

word, *n.* **1.** expression, utterance; assertion, affirmation, declaration, statement. **2.** guarantee, vow, oath, assurance, promise, pledge. **3.** intelligence, tidings, news, report, facts, data, bulletin, message, communiqué, account, advice, information, inside story, lowdown, scuttlebutt, gossip, dish, dope. **4.** signal, order, instruction, high sign, command. —*v.* **5.** express, style, phrase, say, put into words, couch, utter, term, state, set forth.

wordy, *adj.* prolix, redundant, repetitious, diffuse, inflated, turgid, windy, flatulent, bombastic, rambling, longwinded, talky, loquacious, garrulous, verbose, superfluous, long-drawn, grandiloquent, magniloquent, endless, interminable, overlong.
—**Ant.** terse, concise, succinct.
—**Syn. Study.** WORDY, PROLIX, REDUNDANT, VERBOSE all mean using more words than necessary to convey the desired meaning. WORDY, the broadest of these terms, may merely refer to the use of many words but usu. implies that the speech or writing is wearisome or ineffectual: *a wordy review that obscured the main point.* PROLIX refers to speech or writing extended to tedious length by the inclusion of inconsequential details: *a prolix style that robs the story of all its excitement.* REDUNDANT refers to unnecessary repetition by using different words or expressions to convey the same idea: *The editor cut four redundant paragraphs from the article.* VERBOSE adds the idea of pompous or bombastic speech or writing that has little substance: *a verbose speech that put everyone to sleep.*

work, *n.* **1.** exertion, labor, toil, trouble, pains, travail, industriousness, sweat of one's brow, drudgery, effort. **2.** undertaking, task, duty, assignment, chore, enterprise, project, responsibility. **3.** employment, industry, occupation, job, position, situation, business, profession, trade, craft, calling, career, line, livelihood, pursuit, vocation, métier. **4.** deed, performance, fruit, fruition, feat, creation, accomplishment, opus, output, artifact, production, handiwork, piece, composition, masterpiece, achievement. *—v.* **5.** labor, toil, drudge, sweat, slave, exert oneself, take pains. **6.** act, operate, function, go. **7.** operate, ply, apply, wield, control, use, manipulate, manage, handle. **8.** bring about, perform, produce, cause, do, execute, finish, effect, originate, accomplish, achieve. **9.** mold, create, shape, construct, make, fashion, execute, finish.

—Ant. leisure, indolence, idleness, sloth.

—Syn. Study. WORK, DRUDGERY, LABOR, TOIL refer to exertion of body or mind in performing or accomplishing something. WORK is a general word that refers to exertion that is either easy or hard: *pleasurable work; backbreaking work.* DRUDGERY suggests continuous, dreary, and dispiriting work, esp. of a menial or servile kind: *Cleaning these blinds is sheer drudgery.* LABOR denotes hard manual work, esp. for wages: *Repairing the bridge will require months of labor.* TOIL suggests wearying or exhausting labor: *The farmer's health was failing from constant toil.*

worldly, *adj.* **1.** nonspiritual, secular, earthly, mundane, temporal, terrestrial, material, physical, corporeal, fleshly, human, mortal, profane. **2.** worldly-wise, sophisticated, experienced, savvy, knowledgeable, refined, polished, cultured, cultivated, soigné, blasé, poised, stylish, in the know, knowing, urbane, cosmopolitan, suave.

—Ant. celestial, heavenly, sacred, spiritual; naive.

—Syn. Study. See EARTHLY.

world-weary, *adj.* apathetic, anomic, jaded, indifferent, bored, dull, suffering from ennui, dégagé, blasé, impassive, detached, melancholic, listless, burned out, pessimistic, cynical.

—Ant. optimistic, enthusiastic, cheerful, hopeful.

worry, *v.* **1.** fret, torment oneself, agonize, be anxious *or* fearful *or* concerned *or* nervous, be upset *or* distressed, chafe, be troubled *or* vexed, fidget, stew, brood, sweat bullets, despair, mope, pine, eat one's heart out, imagine the worst, dread, feel edgy *or* jumpy, lose sleep, tear one's hair out. **2.** upset, agitate, perturb, trouble, try, torture, torment, annoy, plague, pester, bother, vex, tease, harry, hector, harass, tantalize, molest, persecute, badger, irritate, disquiet, disturb, distress, irritate, rankle. *—n.* **3.** uneasiness, anxiety, agita, misgiving, nervousness, distress, agitation, perturbation, apprehension, foreboding, solicitude, concern, disquiet, misgiving, anguish, woe, heartache, uncertainty, doubt.

—Ant. comfort, solace; sang-froid, equanimity.

—Syn. Study. See CONCERN.

worsen, *v.* **1.** increase, intensify, heighten, deepen, magnify, exacerbate, aggravate, inflame. **2.** weaken, decline, dwindle, fade, give way, degrade, disintegrate, deteriorate, degenerate, slip, slide, backslide, fall apart, crumble, erode, fail, decay, go from bad to worse, go downhill, got to pot, go to the dogs.

—Ant. abate; improve.

worship, *n.* **1.** reverence, homage, veneration, devotion, respect, esteem, exaltation, adoration, honor, praise, admiration, adulation, glorification, magnification, regard, idolizing, idolatry, deification. *—v.* **2.** revere, respect, venerate, reverence, honor, glorify, adore, extol, exalt, praise, admire, glorify, regard highly, adulate, idolize, deify, love, dote on, put on a pedestal, bow down before.

—Ant. detest, execrate, scorn.

worth, *—n.* usefulness, value, benefit, advantage, significance, importance, merit, worthiness, profit, credit, virtue, perfection, indispensability, excellence, quality.

—Ant. worthlessness.

—Syn. Study. See VALUE.

worthy, *adj.* commendable, meritorious, worthwhile, deserving, qualified, creditable, estimable, praiseworthy, excellent, exemplary, distinguished, first-rate, righteous, upright, honest.

—Ant. unworthy.

wound, *n.* **1.** injury, hurt, damage, handicap, trauma; cut, gash, puncture, bruise, slit, burn, contusion, laceration, lesion. **2.** harm, slight, blow, distress, torment, torture, offense, wrong, insult, pain, grief, anguish. *—v.* **3.** injure, hurt, harm, damage, maim, disable, handicap, traumatize; cut, stab, lacerate, shoot, burn.

wrath, *n.* anger, ire, rage, resentment, indignation, irritation, fury, spleen, vexation, annoyance, outrage, temper, displeasure, exasperation.

—Ant. forbearance, mercy, toleration.

wrathful, *adj.* angry, irate, vexed, outraged, mad, acrimonious, infuriated, furious, choleric, livid, splenetic, fuming, enraged, raging, incensed, provoked, exasperated, indignant, on a rampage, hot under the collar, on the warpath, at the end of one's patience, in high dudgeon, ticked off, POed, having a fit.

—Ant. lenient, understanding, indulgent.

wreck, *n.* **1.** ruin, destruction, demolition, decimation, annihilation, spoilation, obliteration, leveling, devastation, desolation. *—v.* **2.** spoil, destroy, demolish, raze, decimate, smash, crush, annihilate, wipe out, devastate, ruin, shatter, lay waste to, flatten, pulverize, ravage, eradicate, trash.

—Ant. create.

wretched, *adj.* **1.** miserable, pitiable, dejected, dismal, despondent, distressed, woeful, afflicted, woebegone, forlorn, unhappy, despairing, hopeless, melancholy, heartbroken, heartsick, inconsolable, crestfallen, desolate, depressed. **2.** sorry, miserable, despicable, mean, base, vile, bad, contemptible, poor, pitiful, worthless, sordid, squalid, abject, shameful, inferior.

—Ant. happy.

—Syn. Study. See MISERABLE.

wrong, *adj.* **1.** bad, evil, wicked, sinful, immoral, corrupt, iniquitous, reprehensible, unjust, unfair, unethical, illegal, illicit, illegitimate, unlawful, criminal, crooked, dishonest, disgraceful, dishonorable, blameworthy, opprobrious, shameful. **2.** erroneous, inaccurate, incorrect, false, untrue, fallacious, misleading, deceptive, in error, mistaken. **3.** improper, inappropriate, unfit, infelicitous, out of place, wrongheaded, imprudent, misguided, ill-considered, unsuitable. **4.** awry, amiss, askew, astray, flawed, defective, unsound, not working, out of order. *—n.* **5.** evil, wickedness, misdoing, evil deed, misdeed, sin, vice, immorality, iniquity; trespass, transgression, offense, infraction, violation, crime, felony, misdemeanor, breach of the law, peccadillo, mistake, lapse in judgment, personal failing. *—v.* **6.** injure, harm, maltreat, mistreat, misuse, abuse, oppress, cheat, defraud, dishonor, discredit, malign, calumniate, take advantage of, violate, offend, insult, wound, victimize.

—Ant. right.

wrongheaded, *adj.* perverse, misguided, injudicious, unwise, erroneous, deluded, opinionated, contrary, ornery, mulish, balky, bullheaded, wayward, obstinate, unreasonable, difficult, barking up the wrong tree.

—Ant. reasonable, compliant.

wry, *adj.* witty, waggish, wisecracking, droll, humorous, biting, trenchant, mordant, pungent, piquant, pointed, ironic, sardonic, sarcastic.

X

xenophobic, *adj.* chauvinistic, insular, separatist, segregationist, discriminatory, intolerant, biased, bigoted, racist, ethnocentric, restrictive, exclusive, exclusionary, closed-door, selective, restricted, restrictive.

—Ant. inclusive, welcoming.

X-rated, *adj.* erotic, sexually explicit, sexy, sexual, adult, salacious, lewd, racy, coarse, licentious, lubricious, lascivious, scabrous, risqué, foulmouthed, prurient, offensive, taboo, obscene, pornographic, smutty, blue, off-color, dirty, filthy, indecent, vulgar, crude, raw, foul, gross, raunchy.

—Ant. clean, wholesome, innocuous.

Y

yahoo, *adj.* **1.** boor, vulgarian, oaf, philistine, lowbrow, lout, barbarian, know-nothing, ignoramus, illiterate, redneck, ruffian, hooligan, Neanderthal, subhuman, slob. **2.** country bumpkin, provincial, peasant, backwoodsman, hillbilly, clodhopper, rube, yokel, hayseed, hick. **3.** nincompoop, ass, jackass, pinhead, clod, clot, idiot, nit, nitwit, moron, bird brain, jerk, sap, imbecile, dope, dunce, halfwit, fool, lummox, galoot, dolt, dimwit, bozo, boob, retard, butthead.

yearn, *v.* long, hanker, pine, yen, ache, itch, thirst, lust, crave, hunger, covet, pant, desire, want, wish, fancy, prefer, aspire, aim.

—Syn. Study. YEARN, LONG, HANKER, PINE all mean to feel a strong desire for something. YEARN stresses the depth and power of the desire: *to yearn to begin a new life.* LONG implies a wholehearted desire for something that is or seems unattainable: *to long to relive one's childhood.* HANKER suggests a restless or incessant craving: *to hanker after fame and fortune.* PINE adds the notion of physical or emotional suffering due to the real or apparent hopelessness of one's desire: *to pine for a lost love.*

yearning, *n.* longing, craving, desire, hankering, pining, itch, thirst, hunger, appetite, yen, wish, urge, passion, lust, aspiration, aim.

—Syn. Study. See DESIRE.

yell, *v.* cry out, shout, scream, bellow, howl, roar, yap, bark, bawl, vociferate, yelp, caterwaul, squall, shriek, wail, whoop, cheer, screech, squeal, hoot, thunder, bay, clamor, boom, rumble, snarl, growl.

—Ant. whisper.

yes-man, *n.* flatterer, sycophant, hanger-on, doormat, jackal, lickspittle, toady, apple-polisher, stooge, boot-licker, flunky, lackey, rubber stamp; menial, underling, hireling, inferior, minion, slave, dogsbody, gofer.

yield, *v.* **1.** give forth, produce, furnish, supply, render, bear, impart, afford, bestow, turn out, generate, engender, breed, propagate. **2.** give up, cede, surrender, submit, give way, concede, knuckle under, capitulate, succumb, throw in the towel, collapse; relinquish, abandon, abdicate, resign, waive, forgo. *—n.* **3.** produce, harvest, fruit, crop, output, production; reward, profit, gain, earnings, proceeds, take.

—Syn. Study. YIELD, SUBMIT, SURRENDER mean to give way or give up to a person or thing. To YIELD is to relinquish or concede under some degree of pressure, either from a position of weakness or from one of advantage: *to yield ground to an enemy; to yield the right of way.* To SUBMIT is to give up more completely to authority or superior force and to cease opposition, usu. with reluctance: *The mutineers finally submitted to the captain's orders.* To SURRENDER is to give up complete possession of and claim to, usu. after resistance: *to surrender a fortress; to surrender one's rights.*

young, *adj.* **1.** youthful, juvenile, teenage, adolescent, pubescent, prepubescent, underage, minor, junior, underaged, in one's prime, at a tender age, blooming, in the flower of one's life, immature, jejune, puerile, boyish, girlish, childish, childlike, babyish, virgin, inexperienced, undeveloped, unfledged, unsophisticated, innocent, naive, callow, green, wet behind the ears. **2.** fresh, vigorous, robust, fit, strong, healthy, strapping, spry, lively, energetic. *—n.* **3.** offspring, children, spawn, issue, babies, progeny, brood, litter, rug rats, kids.

—Ant. aged, old, ancient; mature, grown-up, full-fledged, experienced, progenitors, parents.

youth, *n.* **1.** youngness, youthfulness, prime, bloom, childhood, salad days, schooldays, younger generation, springtime of life, heyday, minority, adolescence, teens, puberty, pubescence, early years, boyhood, girlhood, infancy, babyhood, immaturity, puerility, callowness, naiveté, innocence, virginity. **2.** young man *or* woman, youngster, teenager, adolescent stripling, lad, boy, girl, juvenile, minor, virgin, innocent, naif.

—Ant. maturity; man, woman, adult.

yo-yo, *v.* vacillate, fluctuate, vary, be undecided, hedge, quibble, shift, dither, equivocate, waffle, hesitate, waver, seesaw, fluctuate, hem and haw, shilly-shally.

—Ant. decide.

yucky, *adj.* unappetizing, unpalatable, unsavory, disgusting, sickening, nauseating, repugnant, repellent, repulsive, revolting, sick-making, distasteful, off-putting, noisome, fulsome, stomach-turning, foul, gross, vile, rotten, objectionable, execrable, horrid, horrible, abhorrent, offensive, loathsome, intolerable.

—Ant. appealing, agreeable, yummy.

yummy, *adj.* delicious, savory, luscious, delectable, delightful, appetizing, tasty, appealing, juicy, tempting, succulent, toothsome,

enjoyable, gratifying, pleasing, satisfying, rich, mouthwatering, sensuous, luxurious, voluptuous, sumptuous, splendid, opulent, lavish, lush, velvety, creamy, ambrosial, piquant, redolent.
—**Ant.** sickening, unappetizing, yucky.

Z

zaftig, *adj.* rounded, Rubenesque, chubby, well-fed, full-figured, plump, pleasingly plump, curvaceous, curvy, buxom, busty, voluptuous, pneumatic, built for comfort, well-built, well-upholstered, broad in the beam.
—**Ant.** skinny, emaciated.

zany, *adj.* **1.** comic, comical, farcical, clownish, amusing, wise-cracking, witty, merry, funny, droll, whimsical, waggish, playful, gay, madcap, eccentric, antic, prankish, lunatic, ludicrous, absurd, nonsensical, inane, silly, foolish, hilarious, crazy, kooky, off-the-wall, loopy, nutty, goofy, wacky, loony, crackpot. —*n.* **2.** comic, clown, comedian, joker, jokester, jester, fool, wag, wit, eccentric, stooge, cutup, merry prankster, merry-andrew, madcap, buffoon, kook, nut, weirdo, laughingstock, screwball.

zap, *v.* attack, hit, strike, defeat, destroy, kill, slaughter, murder, liquidate, eliminate, annihilate, terminate, take out, waste, jolt, bombard, nuke, cancel, stop, undo, do in, finish off, rub out, polish off, snuff out, ice, knock out, abort, scrub, censor, skip over, edit out, delete, erase.

zeal, *n.* ardor, enthusiasm, diligence, industriousness, indefatigability, eagerness, fervor, desire, endeavor, fervency, warmth, earnestness, seriousness, vehemence, energy, forcefulness, intensity, passion, spirit.
—**Ant.** apathy, stolidness, impassivity.

zealot, *n.* enthusiast, partisan, adherent, disciple, follower, devotee; fanatic, maniac, extremist, radical, militant, terrorist, bigot, skinhead.

zealous, *adj.* ardent, enthusiastic, devoted, diligent, industrious, eager, earnest, fervid, fervent, intense, vehement, forceful, energetic, lively, passionate, spirited, take-no-prisoners.
—**Ant.** apathetic, uninterested, dispassionate, cool.

zero, *n.* cipher, nothing, nil, naught, aught, zip, nada, nix, goose egg, diddly, diddly-squat, squat, zilch.

zest, *n.* taste, flavor, relish, gusto, pungency, piquancy, edge, bite, zip, zing, pizazz, spiciness, spice, tang; enjoyment, delight, pleasure; zeal, ardor, enthusiasm, passion, spiritedness.
—**Ant.** dullness.

zone, *n.* belt, tract, area, region, quarter, sector, sphere, territory, province, department, district, section, part, segment, precinct, locale, locality, domain, realm, bailiwick.

PUNCTUATION RULES

There is a considerable amount of variation in punctuation practices. At one extreme are writers who use as little punctuation as possible. At the other extreme are writers who use too much punctuation in an effort to make their meaning clear. The principles presented here represent a middle road. As in all writing, consistency of style is essential.

The punctuation system is presented in six charts. Since punctuation marks are frequently used in more than one way, some marks appear on more than one chart. Readers who are interested in the various uses of a particular mark can scan the left column of each chart to locate relevant sections.

1. Sentence-Level Punctuation

	Guidelines	Examples
.	Ordinarily an independent clause is made into a sentence by beginning it with a capital letter and ending it with a period.	Some of us still support the mayor. Others think he should retire. There's only one solution. We must reduce next year's budget.
,	Independent clauses may be combined into one sentence by using the words *and, but, yet, or, not, for,* and *so.* The first clause is usually, but not always, followed by a comma.	The forecast promised beautiful weather, but it rained every day. Take six cooking apples and put them into a flameproof dish.
;	The writer can indicate that independent clauses are closely connected by joining them with a semicolon.	Some of us still support the mayor; others think he should retire. There was silence in the room; even the children were still.
:	When one independent clause is followed by another that explains or exemplifies it, they can be separated by a colon. The second clause may or may not begin with a capital letter.	There's only one solution: we must reduce next year's budget. The conference addresses a basic question: How can we take the steps needed to protect the environment?
?	Sentences that ask a question should be followed by a question mark.	Are they still planning to move to Houston? What is the population of Norway?
!	Sentences that express strong feeling may be followed by an exclamation mark.	Watch out! That's a stupid thing to say!
. ? !	End-of-sentence punctuation is sometimes used after groups of words that are not independent clauses. This is especially common in advertising and other writing that seeks to reflect the rhythms of speech.	Somerset Estates has all the features you've been looking for. Like state-of-the-art facilities. A friendly atmosphere. And a very reasonable price. Sound interesting? Phone today!

2. Separating Elements in Clauses

When one of the elements in a clause is compounded—that is, when there are two or more subjects, predicates, objects, and so forth—punctuation is necessary.

	Guidelines	Examples
	When two elements are compounded, they are usually joined together with a word such as *and* or *or* without any punctuation. Occasionally more than two elements are joined in this way.	Haiti and the Dominican Republic share the island of Hispaniola. Tuition may be paid by check or charged to a major credit card. I'm taking history and English and biology this semester.
,	Compounds that contain more than two elements are called series. Commas are used to separate items in a series, with a word such as *and* or *or* usually occurring between the last two items.	England, Scotland, and Wales share the island of Great Britain. Environmentally conscious businesses use recycled paper, photocopy on both sides of a sheet, and use ceramic cups. We frequently hear references to government of the people, by the people, for the people.
; ,	When the items in a series are very long or have internal punctuation, separation by commas can be confusing, and semicolons may be used instead.	Next year, they plan to open stores in Pittsburgh, Pennsylvania; Cincinnati, Ohio; and Baltimore, Maryland. Students were selected on the basis of grades; tests of vocabulary, memory, and reading; and teacher recommendations.

Note: Some writers omit the final comma when punctuating a series, and newspapers and magazines often follow this practice. Book publishers and educators, however, usually follow the practice recommended above.

3. Quotations

Quotations are used for making clear to a reader which words are the writer's and which have been borrowed from someone else.

Guidelines	Examples
" " When writers use the exact words of someone else, they must use quotation marks to set them off from the rest of the text.	In 1841, Ralph Waldo Emerson wrote, "I hate quotations. Tell me what you know."
Indirect quotations—in which writers report what someone else said without using the exact words—should not be set off by quotation marks.	Emerson said that he hated quotations and that writers should instead tell the reader what they themselves know.
When quotations are longer than two or three lines, they are often placed on separate lines. Sometimes shorter line length and/or smaller type is also used. When this is done, quotation marks are not used.	In his essay "Notes on Punctuation," Lewis Thomas* gives the following advice to writers using quotations: If something is to be quoted, the exact words must be used. If part of it must be left out because of space limitations, it is good manners to insert three dots to indicate the omission, but it is unethical to do this if it means connecting two thoughts that the original author did not intend to have tied together.
• • • If part of a quotation is omitted, the omission must be marked with points of ellipsis. When the omission comes in the middle of a sentence, three points are used. When the omission includes the end of one or more sentences, four points are used. **• • • •**	Lewis Thomas offers this advice: If something is to be quoted, the exact words must be used. If part of it must be left out…insert three dots to indicate the omission, but it is unethical to do this if it means connecting two thoughts which the original author did not intend to have tied together.
When writers insert something within a quoted passage, the insertion should be set off with brackets. Insertions are sometimes used to supply words that make a quotation easier to understand.	Lewis Thomas warns that "it is unethical to [omit words in a quotation]…if it means connecting two thoughts which the original author did not intend to have tied together."
[ ] Writers can make clear that a mistake in the quotation has been carried over from the original by using the word *sic,* meaning "thus."	As Senator Claghorne wrote to his constituents, "My fundamental political principals [*sic*] make it impossible for me to support the bill in its present form."
, Text that reports the source of quoted material is usually separated from it by a comma.	Mark said, "I've decided not to apply to law school until next year." "I think we should encourage people to vote," said the mayor.
When quoted words are woven into a text so that they perform a basic grammatical function in the sentence, no introductory punctuation is used.	According to Thoreau, most of us "lead lives of quiet desperation."
' ' Quotations that are included within other quotations are set off by single quotation marks.	The witness made the same damaging statement under cross-examination: "As I entered the room, I heard him say, 'I'm determined to get even.'"
Final quotation marks follow other punctuation marks, except for semicolons and colons.	Ed began reading Williams's "The Glass Menagerie"; then he turned to "A Streetcar Named Desire."
" " Question marks and exclamation marks precede final quotation marks when they refer to the quoted words. They follow when they refer to the sentence as a whole.	Once more she asked, "What do you think we should do about this?" What did Carol mean when she said, "I'm going to do something about this"? "Get out of here!" he yelled.

* *New England Journal of Medicine*, Vol. 296, pp. 1103–05 (May 12, 1977). Quoted by permission.

4. Word-Level Punctuation

The punctuation covered so far is used to clarify the structure of sentences. There are also punctuation marks that are used with words.

Guidelines	Examples
' The apostrophe is used with nouns to show possession:	The company's management resisted the union's demands. She found it impossible to decipher the students' handwriting.
(1) An apostrophe plus *s* is added to all words—singular or plural—that do not end in *-s*.	the boy's hat children's literature a week's vacation
(2) Just an apostrophe is added at the end of plural words that end in *-s*.	the boys' hats two weeks' vacation
(3) An apostrophe plus *s* is usually added at the end of singular words that end in *-s*. Just an apostrophe is added to names of classical or biblical derivation that end in *-s*.	the countess's daughter Dickens's novels Achilles' heel Moses' brother
An apostrophe is used in contractions to show where letters or numerals have been omitted.	he's didn't let's ma'am four o'clock readin', writin', and 'rithmetic the class of '55
An apostrophe is sometimes used when making letters or numbers plural.	45's ABC's
• A period is used to mark shortened forms like abbreviations and initials.	Prof. M. L. Smith 14 ft. 4:00 p.m. U.S.A. or USA etc.
– A hyphen is used to end a line of text when part of a word must be carried over to the next line.	... insta- bility
Hyphens are sometimes used to form compound words.	twenty-five self-confidence
In certain situations, hyphens are used between prefixes or suffixes and root words.	catlike *but* bull-like preschool *but* pre-Christian recover *vs.* re-cover
Hyphens are often used to indicate that a group of words is to be understood as a unit.	a scholar-athlete hand-to-hand combat
When two modifiers containing hyphens are joined together, common elements are often not repeated.	The study included fourth- and twelfth-grade students.

Note: It is important not to confuse the hyphen (-) with the dash (—), which is more than twice as long. The hyphen is used to group words and parts of words together, while the dash is used to clarify sentence structure. With a typewriter, a dash is formed by typing two successive hyphens(--). Many word-processing programs will create a dash automatically.

HOW TO WRITE A GOOD COLLEGE ESSAY

By The Princeton Review

Grammar and Form

You should strive to make your college essay clear, concise, candid, structurally sound, and 100 percent grammatically accurate. Clarity and conciseness are achieved through a lot of reading, rereading, and rewriting. Without question, repeated critical revision by yourself and by others is the surest way to trim, tune, and improve your prose.

As candor cannot be superimposed after the fact, your writing should be sincere from the outset. Let's be frank: You're probably pretty smart. You can probably fake candor if absolutely necessary, but don't. For one thing, it involves a lot more work. Moreover, no matter how good your insincere essay may be, we're confident that the honest and authentic one you write will be even better.

Structural soundness is the product of a well-crafted outline. Sketch out the general themes of your essay first; worry about filling in the particulars later. Many people like to start by putting ideas onto paper in the form of "bubble outlines"—they'll write down the names of things that they're passionate or know a lot about, circle the ones that they really think describe who they are, then connect with lines ideas that complement one another. Others start writing lists of things that they like or have done, lists and lists and lists, until an overall theme starts to take shape. If you go about it this way, you have the details of your essay written down even before you decide what your theme will be.

The idea is to get thinking, get your thoughts onto paper, then settle down to attack the task of building a formal outline. Pay close attention to the structure of your essay and to the fundamental message it communicates. Make sure you have a thesis statement and a well-conceived narrative. Your essay should flow from beginning to end. Use paragraphs properly and make sure they are in logical order. The sentences within each paragraph should be complete and also flow in logical order.

Grammatical accuracy is key. A thoughtful essay that offers true insight will undoubtedly stand out, but if it is riddled with poor grammar and misspelled words, it will not receive serious consideration. *It is critical that you avoid grammatical errors.* We can't stress this enough. Misspellings, awkward constructions, run-on sentences, and misplaced modifiers cast doubt on your efforts. Admissions officers will question the amount of care you put into the essay's composition.

Things to Remember

Good writing is writing that is easily understood. You want to get your point across, not bury it in words. Don't talk in circles. Your prose should be clear and direct. If an admissions officer has to struggle to figure out what you are trying to say, you're in trouble.

Get to the point in three pages. Don't be long-winded and boring. Admissions officers don't like long essays. Would you, if you were in their shoes? Be brief. Be focused. If there is a word limit, abide by it.

Proofread your essay from beginning to end, proofread it again, then proofread it some more. Read it aloud. Keep in mind, the more time you spend with a piece of your own writing, the less likely you are to spot errors. Ask friends, teachers, siblings—somebody other than yourself—to read your essay and comment on it. Ask them if it reflects your personality and tells a coherent story. If it doesn't, work on it more. Do not get content ideas from them. Then have an English teacher or another stickler for grammar make sure your essay is clear, concise, candid, structurally sound, and 100 percent grammatically accurate.

What Colleges Want to See in Your Essay: Writing Ability and Insight into Who You Are

The admissions officers reading your essay want it to show that you can write at the college level. This means you have command of the English language and can use it to craft a cogent written statement. They are not interested in your vocabulary skills, so give the thesaurus to mom and have her hide it. You should write your essay without fancy words whose meanings you don't understand. It is painfully obvious to admissions officers when you do this; they're almost embarrassed *for* you.

Part 1: Essay Fundamentals

Admissions officers are interested in seeing that you understand sentence and paragraph structure and can pace a narrative—and that you know what a narrative is in the first place. If you're a little unsure, a narrative is simply a story. Unless you're William Faulkner, the story your essay tells to admissions officers needs to be brief, flow logically from one event to the next, and have a convincing conclusion.

You'd have to be a really clever wordsmith, for example, to convince a reader that a chain smoker could enter the New York City Marathon and win it just because he "had a lot of heart." Your essay should not read like a work of fiction and require admissions officers to suspend disbelief. Keep it brief and coherent.

This does not mean that you or someone else should edit your essay down to nothing. It also shouldn't sound like a marketing piece. It should sound the way you talk (when you speak with correct grammar, of course).

An additional point we hope you will pick up on is that no matter how impressive your grades, test scores, and extracurriculars are, admissions decisions by these top-flight schools involve subjective elements you can't control. You shouldn't try to be someone else whom you think admissions officers want to see. That's the job of a con artist, and it almost never works. Besides, admissions officers are paid to find students who are good matches for their institution. A dishonest essay may lead you to the wrong school. Who wants to fill out transfer applications?

Time and again admissions officers tell us that they want students to write their college essays about the things they, the students, actually care about. You should write your essay about something you do, not something you would do if you were president of the United States (unless specifically asked to do so). Admissions officers want to know how and why you spent every Wednesday afternoon last year teaching an underprivileged boy how to use a computer, even when you didn't want to or didn't think you had time. They even want to know why you're passionate about Spider-Man comics.

But notice the "why." The essay isn't just an opportunity for you to show you're a character who would bring some much-needed uniqueness to campus. It's an opportunity for you to give admissions officers real insight into who you are. This means your essay absolutely must include a "why." There are no exceptions. Why do you love Spider-Man?

Is it something he is or isn't? Is Spidey's story somehow an allegory for selfless service to others? If you're an artist, is it the care with which every frame is crafted? The detail? If you're a cultural anthropologist, is it Spidey's continued ability to resonate with readers, both old and young? Your essay should show that you have thought about why you love what you love, believe what you believe, or are who you are.

The "why" in your essay will show that you know how to reflect and analyze in college.

Topics that Work, Topics that Don't

Opinion differs from college to college regarding what's a good essay topic and what isn't. There are a few topics, however, that almost invariably send shudders down admissions officers' spines.

These include sex (especially *your* sex life), drugs (especially *your* drug use), and violent events in which you participated. Admissions officers also tire of reading travelogues and stories of how you recovered from a sports injury. Want to make them groan? Rehash the extracurricular activities that you already listed on your application, or editorialize on the top news item of the day.

Swearing isn't effective, either. They appreciate humor, but if you're not funny in person, you shouldn't try to be so on paper. If your essay relies on humor, you should have a teacher read it; if your humor doesn't elicit the right response from them, it most likely won't get the reaction you're looking for in the admissions office.

Admissions officers also don't want to read an essay you wrote for another school. If you use the same essay for all the schools to which you apply, make sure the correct school's name appears in each version (if applicable). It's common courtesy.

Excerpted from *College Essays That Made A Difference, 2nd Edition*, ISBN 978-0-375-76568-1, Random House, September 2006

COMMONLY CONFUSED WORDS

Words are often confused if they have similar or identical forms or sounds. You may have the correct meaning in mind, but choosing the wrong word will change your intended meaning. An *ingenuous* person is not the same as an *ingenious* person. Similarly, you may be using a word that is correct in a different context but does not express your intended meaning. To *infer* something is not the same as to *imply* it.

Use of the wrong word is often the result of confusing words that are identical or very similar in pronunciation but different in spelling. An example of a pair of words with the same pronunciation is "compliment, complement." The confusion may arise from a small difference in spelling, as the pair "canvas, canvass"; or the soundalikes may be spelled quite differently, as the pairs "manor, manner" and "brake, break." An example of a pair of words with similar but not identical pronunciation is "accept, except"; they are very different in usage and grammatical function.

Words may also be confused if they are spelled the same way but differ in meaning or in meaning and pronunciation, as the soundalikes *bear* "animal" and *bear* "carry, support" or the lookalikes *row* (rō) "line" and *row* (rou) "fight."

Errors in word choice may also result if word groups overlap in meaning or usage. In informal contexts, *aggravate* may be used to mean "annoy" and *mad* may be used to mean "angry." *Leave* and *let* are interchangeable when followed by the word "alone" in the sense "to stop annoying or interfering with someone."

The following glossary lists words that are commonly confused and discusses their meanings and proper usage.

accept/except *Accept* is a verb meaning "to receive": *Please accept a gift. Except* is usually a preposition or a conjunction meaning "other than" or "but for": *He was willing to accept an apology from everyone except me.* When *except* is used as a verb, it means "to leave out": *He was excepted from the new regulations.*

accidentally/accidently The correct adverb is *accidentally,* from the root word *accidental,* not *accident* (*Russell accidentally slipped on the icy sidewalk*). *Accidently* is a misspelling.

adoptive/adopted *Adoptive* refers to the parent: *He resembles his adoptive father. Adopted* refers to the child: *Their adopted daughter wants to adopt a child herself.*

adverse/averse Both words are adjectives, and both mean "opposed" or "hostile." *Averse,* however, is used to describe a subject's opposition to something (*The minister was averse to the new trends developing in the country*), whereas *adverse* describes something opposed to the subject (*The adverse comments affected his self-esteem*).

advice/advise *Advice,* a noun, means "suggestion or suggestions": *Here's some good advice. Advise,* a verb, means "to offer ideas or suggestions": *Act as we advise you.*

affect/effect Most often, *affect* is a verb, meaning "to influence," and *effect* is a noun meaning "the result of an action": *His speech affected my mother very deeply, but had no effect on my sister at all. Affect* is also used as a noun in psychology and psychiatry to mean "emotion": *We can learn much about affect from performance.* In this usage, it is pronounced with the stress on the first syllable. *Effect* is also used as a verb meaning "to bring about": *His letter effected a change in their relationship.*

aggravate/annoy In informal speech and writing, *aggravate* can be used as a synonym for *annoy.* However, in formal discourse the words mean different things and should be used in this way: *Her back condition was aggravated by lifting the child, but the child's crying annoyed her more than the pain.*

agree to/agree with *Agree to* means "to consent to, to accept" (usually a plan or idea). *Agree with* means "to be in accord with" (usually a person or group): *I can't believe they will agree to start*

a business together when they don't agree with each other on anything.

aisle/isle *Aisle* means "a passageway between sections of seats": *It was impossible to pass through the airplane aisle during the meal service. Isle* means "island": *I would like to be on a desert isle on such a dreary morning.*

all ready/already *All ready,* a pronoun and an adjective, means "entirely prepared"; *already,* an adverb, means "so soon" or "previously": *I was all ready to leave when I noticed that it was already dinnertime.*

allusion/illusion An *allusion* is a reference or hint: *He made an allusion to the past.* An *illusion* is a deceptive appearance: *The canals on Mars are an illusion.*

a lot/alot/allot *A lot* is always written as two words. It is used informally to mean "many": *The unrelenting heat frustrated a lot of people. Allot* is a verb meaning "to divide" or "to set aside": *We alloted a portion of the yard for a garden. Alot* is not a word.

altogether/all together *Altogether* means "completely" or "totally"; *all together* means "all at one time" or "gathered together": *It is altogether proper that we recite the Pledge all together.*

allude/elude Both words are verbs. *Allude* means "to mention briefly or accidentally": *During our conversation, he alluded to his vacation plans. Elude* means "to avoid or escape": *The thief has successfully eluded capture for six months.*

altar/alter *Altar* is a noun meaning "a sacred place or platform": *The couple approached the altar for the wedding ceremony. Alter* is a verb meaning "to make different; to change": *He altered his appearance by losing fifty pounds, growing a beard, and getting a new wardrobe.*

amount/number *Amount* refers to quantity that cannot be counted: *The amount of work accomplished before a major holiday is always negligible. Number,* in contrast, refers to things that can be counted: *He has held a number of jobs in the past five months.* But some concepts, like time, can use either *amount* or *number,* depending how the elements are identified in the specific sentence: *We were surprised by the amount of time it took us to settle into our new surroundings. The number of hours it took to repair the sink pleased us.*

ante-/anti- The prefix *ante-* means "before" (*antecedent, antechamber, antediluvian*); the prefix *anti-* means against (*antigravity, antifreeze*). *Anti-* takes a hyphen before an *i* or a capital letter: *anti-Marxist, anti-inflationary.*

anxious/eager Traditionally, *anxious* means "nervous" or "worried" and consequently describes negative feelings. In addition, it is usually followed by the word "about": *I'm anxious about my exam. Eager* means "looking forward" or "anticipating enthusiastically" and consequently describes positive feelings. It is usually followed by "to": *I'm eager to get it over with.* Today, however, it is standard usage for *anxious* to mean "eager": *They are anxious to see their new home.*

anybody, any body/anyone, any one *Anybody* and *anyone* are pronouns; *any body* is a noun modified by "any" and *any one* is a pronoun or adjective modified by "any." They are used as follows: *Was anybody able to find any body in the debris? Will anyone help me? I have more cleaning than any one person can ever do.*

any more/anymore *Any more* means "no more"; *anymore,* an adverb, means "nowadays" or "any longer": *We don't want any more trouble. We won't go there anymore.*

apt/likely *Apt* is standard in all speech and writing as a synonym for "likely" in suggesting chance without inclination: *They are apt to call any moment now. Likely,* meaning "probably," is frequently preceded by a qualifying word: *The new school budget* *will very likely raise taxes.* However, *likely* without the qualifying word is standard in all varieties of English: *The new school budget will likely raise taxes.*

ascent/assent *Ascent* is a noun that means "a move upward or a climb": *Their ascent up Mount Rainier was especially dangerous because of the recent rock slides. Assent* can be a noun or a verb. As a verb, *assent* means "to concur, to express agreement": *The union representative assented to the agreement.* As a noun, *assent* means "an agreement": *The assent was not reached peacefully.*

assistance/assistants *Assistance* is a noun that means "help, support": *Please give us your assistance here for a moment. Assistants* is a plural noun that means "helpers": *Since the assistants were late, we found ourselves running behind schedule.*

assure, ensure, insure *Assure* is a verb that means "to promise": *The plumber assured us that the sink would not clog again. Ensure* and *insure* are both verbs that mean "to make certain," although some writers use *insure* solely for legal and financial writing and *ensure* for more widespread usage: *Since it is hard to insure yourself against mudslide, we did not buy the house on the hill. We left late to ensure that we would not get caught in traffic.*

bare/bear *Bare* is an adjective or a verb. As an adjective, *bare* means "naked, unadorned": *The wall looked bare without the picture.* As a verb, *bare* means "to reveal": *He bared his soul. Bear* is a noun or a verb. As a noun, *bear* refers to the animal: *The teddy bear was named after Theodore Roosevelt.* As a verb, *bear* means to carry: *He bears a heavy burden.*

before/prior to *Prior to* is used most often in a legal sense: *Prior to settling the claim, the Smiths spent a week calling the attorney general's office.* Use *before* in almost all other cases: *Before we go grocery shopping, we sort the coupons we have clipped from the newspaper.*

beside/besides Although both words can function as prepositions, they have different shades of meaning: *beside* means "next to"; *besides* means "in addition to" or "except": *Besides, Richard would prefer not to sit beside the dog. There is no one here besides John and me. Besides* is also an adverb meaning "in addition": *Other people besides you feel the same way about the dog.*

bias/prejudice Generally, a distinction is made between *bias* and *prejudice.* Although both words imply "a preconceived opinion" or a "subjective point of view" in favor of something or against it, *prejudice* is generally used to express unfavorable feelings.

blonde/blond A *blonde* indicates a woman or girl with fair hair and skin. *Blond*, as an adjective, refers to either sex (*I have three blond children. He is a cute blond boy*), but *blonde*, as an adjective, still applies to women: *The blonde actress and her companion made the front page of the tabloid.*

borrow/lend *Borrow* means "to take with the intention of returning": *The book you borrow from the library today is due back in seven days. Lend* means "to give with the intention of getting back": *I will lend you the rake, but I need it back by Saturday.* The two terms are not interchangeable.

brake/break The most common meaning of *brake* as a noun is a device for slowing a vehicle: *The car's new brakes held on the steep incline. Brake* can also mean "a thicket" or "a species of fern." *Break*, a verb, means "to crack or make useless": *Please be especially careful that you don't break that vase.*

breath/breathe *Breath*, a noun, is the air taken in during respiration: *Her breath looked like fog in the frosty morning air. Breathe*, a verb, refers to the process of inhaling and exhaling air: *"Please breathe deeply," the doctor said to the patient.*

bring/take *Bring* is to carry toward the speaker: *She brings it to me. Take* is to carry away from the speaker: *She takes it away.*

buy/by *Buy*, a verb, means "to acquire goods at a price": *We have to buy a new dresser. By* can be a preposition, an adverb, or an adjective. As a preposition, *by* means "next to": *I pass by the office building every day.* As an adverb, *by* means "near, at hand": *The office is close by.* As an adjective, *by* means "situated to one side": *They came down on a by passage.*

canvas/canvass *Canvas*, a noun, refers to a heavy cloth: *The boat's sails are made of canvas. Canvass*, a verb, means "to solicit votes": *The candidate's representatives canvass the neighborhood seeking support.*

capital/Capitol *Capital* is the city or town that is the seat of government: *Paris is the capital of France. Capitol* refers to the building in Washington, D.C., in which the U.S. Congress meets: *When I was a child, we went for a visit to the Capitol.* When used with a lowercase letter, *capitol* is the building of a state legislature. *Capital* also means "a sum of money": *After the sale of their home, they had a great deal of capital.* As an adjective, *capital* means "foremost" or "first-rate": *He was a capital fellow.*

censor/censure Although both words are verbs, they have different meanings. To *censor* is to remove something from public view on moral or other grounds, and to *censure* is to give a formal reprimand: *The committee censored the offending passages from the book and censured the librarian for placing it on the shelves.*

cite/sight/site To *cite* means to "quote a passage": *The scholar often cited passages from noted authorities to back up his opinions. Sight* is a noun that means "vision": *With her new glasses, her sight was once again perfect. Site* is a noun that means "place or location": *They picked out a beautiful site overlooking a lake for their new home.*

climatic/climactic The word *climatic* comes from the word "climate" and refers to weather: *This summer's brutal heat may indicate a climatic change. Climactic*, in contrast, comes from the word "climax" and refers to a point of high drama: *In the climactic last scene the hideous creature takes over the world.*

clothes/cloths *Clothes* are garments: *For his birthday, John got some handsome new clothes. Cloths* are pieces of fabric: *Use these cloths to clean the car.*

coarse/course *Coarse*, an adjective, means "rough or common": *The horsehair fabric was too coarse to be made into a pillow. Although he's a little coarse around the edges, he has a heart of gold. Course*, a noun, means "a path" or "a prescribed number of classes": *They followed the bicycle course through the woods. My courses include English, math, and science.*

complement/compliment Both words can function as either a noun or a verb. The noun *complement* means "that which completes or makes perfect": *The rich chocolate mousse was a perfect complement to the light meal.* The verb *complement* means "to complete": *The oak door complemented the new siding and windows.* The noun *compliment* means "an expression of praise or admiration": *The mayor paid the visiting officials the compliment of escorting them around town personally.* The verb *compliment* means "to pay a compliment to": *Everyone complimented her after the presentation.*

complementary/complimentary *Complementary* is an adjective that means "forming a complement, completing": *The complementary colors suited the mood of the room. Complimentary* is an adjective that means "expressing a compliment": *The complimentary reviews ensured the play a long run. Complimentary* also means "free": *We thanked them for the complimentary tickets.*

continual/continuous Use *continual* to mean "intermittent, repeated often" and *continuous* to mean "uninterrupted, without stopping": *We suffered continual losses of electricity during the hurricane. They had continuous phone service during the hurricane. Continuous* and *continual* are never interchangeable with regard to spatial relationships, *a continuous series of passages.*

corps/corpse Both words are nouns. A *corps* is a group of people acting together; the word is often used in a military context: *The officers' corps assembled before dawn for the drill.* A *corpse* is a dead body: *The corpse was in the morgue.*

counsel/council *Counsel* is a verb meaning "to give advice": *They counsel recovering gamblers. Council* is a noun meaning "a group of advisers": *The trade union council meets in Ward Hall every Thursday.*

credible/creditable/credulous These three adjectives are often confused. *Credible* means "believable": *The tale is unusual, but seems credible to us. Creditable* means "worthy": *Sandra sang a creditable version of the song. Credulous* means "gullible": *The credulous Marsha believed that the movie was true.*

descent/dissent *Descent*, a noun, means "downward movement": *Much to their surprise, their descent down the mountain was harder than their ascent had been. Dissent*, a verb, means "to disagree": *The town council strongly dissented with the proposed measure. Dissent* as a noun means "difference in sentiment or opinion": *Dissent over the new proposal caused a rift between colleagues.*

desert/dessert *Desert* as a verb means to abandon; as a noun, an arid region: *People deserted in the desert rarely survive. Dessert*, a noun, refers to the sweet served as the final course of a meal: *My sister's favorite dessert is strawberry shortcake.*

device/devise *Device* is a noun meaning "invention or contrivance": *Do you think that device will really save us time? Devise* is a verb meaning "to contrive or plan": *Did he devise some device for repairing the ancient pump assembly?*

die/dye *Die*, as a verb, means "to cease to live": *The frog will die if released from the aquarium into the pond. Dye* as a verb means "to color or stain something": *I dye the drapes to cover the stains.*

discreet/discrete *Discreet* means "tactful;" *discrete*, "separate." For example: *Do you have a discreet way of refusing the invitation? The mosaic is made of hundreds of discrete pieces of tile.*

disinterested/uninterested *Disinterested* is used to mean "without prejudice, impartial" *(He is a disinterested judge)* and *uninterested* to mean "bored" or "lacking interest." *(They are completely uninterested in sports).*

dominant/dominate *Dominant*, an adjective, means "ruling, controlling": *Social scientists have long argued over the dominant motives for human behavior. Dominate*, a verb, means "to control": *Advice columnists often preach that no one can dominate you unless you allow them to.*

elicit/illicit *Elicit*, a verb, means "call forth;" *illicit*, an adjective, means "against the law": *The assault elicited a protest against illicit handguns.*

emigrate/immigrate *Emigrate* means "to leave one's own country to settle in another": *She emigrated from France. Immigrate* means "to enter a different country and settle there": *My father immigrated to America when he was nine years old.*

eminent/imminent *Eminent* means "distinguished": *Marie Curie was an eminent scientist in the final years of her life. Imminent* means "about to happen": *The thundershower seemed imminent.*

envelop/envelope *Envelop* is a verb that means "to surround": *The music envelops him in a soothing atmosphere. Envelope*, a noun, is a flat paper container, usually for a letter: *Be sure to put a stamp on the envelope before you mail that letter.*

especially/specially The two words are not interchangeable: *especially* means "particularly," *specially* means "for a specific reason." For example: *I especially value my wedding ring; it was made specially for me.*

ever so often/every so often *Ever so often* means happening very often and *every so often* means happening occasionally.

everyday/every day *Everyday* is an adjective that means "used daily, typical, ordinary"; *every day* is made up of a noun modified by the adjective "every" and means "each day": *Every day they had to deal with the everyday business of life.*

exam/examination *Exam* should be reserved for everyday speech and *examination* for formal writing: *The College Board examinations are scheduled for this Saturday morning at 9:00.*

explicit/implicit *Explicit* means "stated plainly;" *implicit* means "understood," "implied": *You know we have an implicit understanding that you are not allowed to watch any television shows that contain explicit sex.*

fair/fare *Fair* as an adjective means "free from bias," "ample," "unblemished," "of light hue," or "attractive." As an adverb, it means "favorably." It is used informally to mean "honest." *Fare* as a noun means "the price charged for transporting a person" or "food."

farther/further Traditionally, *farther* is used to indicate physical distance *(Is it much farther to the hotel?)* and *further* is used to refer to additional time, amount, or abstract ideas *(Your mother does not want to talk about this any further).*

flaunt/flout *Flaunt* means "to show off"; *flout*, "to ignore or treat with disdain." For example: *They flouted convention when they flaunted their wealth.*

flounder/founder *Flounder* means "to struggle with clumsy movements": *We floundered in the mud. Founder* means "to sink": *The ship foundered.*

formally/formerly Both words are adverbs. *Formally* means "in a formal manner": *The minister addressed the king and queen formally. Formerly* means "previously": *Formerly, he worked as a chauffeur; now, he is employed as a guard.*

forth/fourth *Forth* is an adverb meaning "going forward or away": *From that day forth, they lived happily ever after. Fourth* is most often used as an adjective that means "next after the third": *Mitchell was the fourth in line.*

gibe/jibe/jive The word *gibe* means "to taunt; deride; jeer." The word *jibe* means "to be in agreement with; accord; correspond": *The facts of the case didn't jibe.* The word *jive* is slang, and means "to tease; fool; kid."

healthy/healthful *Healthy* means "possessing health;" *healthful* means "bringing about health": *They believed that they were healthy people because they ate healthful food.*

historic/historical The word *historic* means "important in history": *a historic speech; a historic battlefield.* The word *historical* means "being a part of, or inspired by, history": *historical records; a historical novel.*

home in/hone in The expression *home in* means "to approach or focus on (an objective)." It comes from the language of guided missiles, where *homing in* refers to locking onto a target. The expression *hone in* is an error.

human/humane Both words are adjectives. *Human* means "pertaining to humanity": *The subject of the documentary is the human race. Humane* means "tender, compassionate, or sympathetic": *Many of her patients believed that her humane care speeded their recovery.*

idea/ideal *Idea* means "thought," while *ideal* means "a model of perfection" or "goal." The two words are not interchangeable. They should be used as follows: *The idea behind the blood drive is that our ideals often move us to help others.*

imply/infer *Imply* means "to suggest without stating": *The message on Karen's postcard implies that her vacation has not turned out as she wished. Infer* means "to reach a conclusion based on understood evidence": *From her message I infer that she wishes she* had stayed home. When used in this manner, the two words describe two sides of the same process.

incredible/incredulous *Incredible* means "cannot be believed;" *incredulous* means "unbelieving": *The teacher was incredulous when she heard the pupil's incredible story about the fate of his term project.*

individual/person/party *Individual* should be used to stress uniqueness or to refer to a single human being as contrasted to a group of people: *The rights of the individual should not supersede the rights of a group. Person* is the preferred word in other contexts. *What person wouldn't want to have a chance to sail around the world? Party* is used to refer to a group: *Send the party of five this way, please. Party* is also used to refer to an individual mentioned in a legal document.

ingenious/ingenuous *Ingenious* means "resourceful, clever": *My sister is ingenious when it comes to turning leftovers into something delicious. Ingenuous* means "frank, artless": *The child's ingenuous manner is surprising considering her fame.*

later/latter *Later* is used to refer to time; *latter,* the second of two items named: *It is later than you think. Of the two shirts I just purchased, I prefer the latter.*

lay/lie *Lay* is a transitive verb that means "to put down" or "to place." It takes a direct object: *Please lay the soup spoon next to the teaspoon. Lie* is an intransitive verb that means "to be in a horizontal position" or "be situated." It does not take a direct object: *The puppy lies down where the old dog had always lain. The hotel lies on the outskirts of town.* The confusion arises over *lay,* which is the present tense of the verb *lay* and the past tense of the verb *lie.*

- To lie (recline)
- Present: *Spot lies (is lying) down.*
- Future: *Spot will lie down.*
- Past: *Spot lay down.*
- Perfect: *Spot has (had, will have) lain down.*
- To lay (put down)
- Present: *He lays (is laying) his dice down.*
- Future: *He will lay his dice down.*
- Past: *He laid his dice down.*
- Perfect: *He has (had, will have) laid his dice down.*

Although *lie* and *lay* tend to be used interchangeably in all but the most careful, formal speech, the following phrases are generally considered nonstandard and are avoided in written English: *Lay down, dears. The dog laid in the sun. Abandoned cars were laying in the junkyard. The reports have laid in the mailbox for a week.*

lead/led *Lead* as a verb means "to take or conduct on the way": *I plan to lead a quiet afternoon. Led* is the past tense: *He led his followers through the dangerous underbrush. Lead,* as a noun, means "a type of metal": *Pipes are made of lead.*

learn/teach *Learn* is to acquire knowledge: *He learned fast. Teach* is to impart knowledge: *She taught well.*

leave/let *Leave* and *let* are interchangeable only when followed by the word "alone": *Leave him alone. Let him alone.* In other instances, *leave* means "to depart" or "permit to remain in the same place": *If you leave, please turn off the copier. Leave the extra paper on the shelf. Let* means "to allow": *Let him work with the assistant, if he wants.*

lessen/lesson *Lessen* is a verb meaning "to decrease": *To lessen the pain of a burn, apply ice to the injured area. Lesson* is most often used as a noun meaning "material assigned for study": *Today, the lesson will be on electricity.*

lightening/lightning *Lightening* is a form of the verb that means "to brighten": *The cheerful new drapes and bunches of flowers went a long way in lightening the room's somber mood. Lightning* is most often used as a noun to mean "flashes of light generated during a storm": *The thunder and lightning frightened the child.*

loose/lose *Loose* as an adjective meaning "free and unattached": *The dog was loose again. Loose* can also be a verb meaning "let loose": *The hunters loose the dogs as soon as the ducks fall. Lose* is a verb meaning "to part with unintentionally": *He will lose his keys if he leaves them on the countertop.*

mad/angry Traditionally, *mad* has been used to mean "insane"; *angry* has been used to mean "full of ire." While *mad* can be used to mean "enraged, angry," in informal usage, you should replace *mad* with *angry* in formal discourse: *The president is angry at Congress for overriding his veto.*

maybe/may be *Maybe,* an adverb, means "perhaps": *Maybe the newspapers can be recycled with the plastic and glass. May be,* a verb, means "could be": *It may be too difficult, however.*

moral/morale As a noun, *moral* means "ethical lesson": *Each of Aesop's fables has a clear moral. Morale* means "state of mind" or "spirit": *Her morale was lifted by her colleague's good wishes.*

orient/orientate The two words both mean "to adjust to or familiarize with new surroundings; place in a particular position." There is no reason to prefer or reject either word, although sometimes people object to *orientate.*

passed/past *Passed* is a form of the verb meaning "to go by": *Bernie passed the same buildings on his way to work each day. Past* can function as a noun, adjective, adverb, or preposition. As a noun, *past* means "the history of a nation, person, etc.": *The lessons of the past should not be forgotten.* As an adjective, *past* means "gone by or elapsed in time": *John is worried about his past deeds.* As an adverb, *past* means "so as to pass by": *The fire engine raced past the parked cars.* As a preposition, *past* means "beyond in time": *It's past noon already.*

patience/patients *Patience,* a noun, means "endurance": *Chrissy's patience makes her an ideal baby-sitter. Patients* are people under medical treatment: *The patients must remain in the hospital for another week.*

peace/piece *Peace* is "freedom from discord": *The negotiators hoped that the new treaty would bring about lasting peace. Piece* is "a portion of a whole" or "a short musical arrangement": *I would like just a small piece of cake, please. The piece in E flat is especially beautiful.*

percent/percentage *Percent* is used with a number, *percentage* with a modifier. *Percentage* is used most often after an adjective: *A high percentage of your earnings this year is tax deductible.*

personal/personnel *Personal* means "private": *The lock on her journal showed that it was clearly personal. Personnel* refers to employees: *Attention all personnel!* The use of *personnel* as a plural has become standard in business and government: *The personnel were dispatched to the Chicago office.*

plain/plane *Plain* as an adjective means "easily understood," "undistinguished," or "unadorned": *His meaning was plain to all. The plain dress suited the gravity of the occasion.* As an adverb, *plain* means "clearly and simply": *She's just plain foolish.* As a noun, *plain* is a flat area of land: *The vast plain seemed to go on forever.* As a noun, *plane* has a number of different meanings. It most commonly refers to an airplane, but is also used in mathematics and fine arts and as a tool used to shave wood.

practicable/practical *Practicable* means "capable of being done": *My decorating plans were too difficult to be practicable. Practical* means "pertaining to practice or action": *It was just and practical to paint the floor white.*

precede/proceed Although both words are verbs, they have different meanings. *Precede* means "to go before": *Morning precedes afternoon. Proceed* means "to move forward": *Proceed to the exit in an orderly fashion.*

presence/presents *Presence* is used chiefly to mean "attendance, close proximity": *Your presence at the ceremony will be greatly appreciated. Presents* are gifts. *Thank you for giving us such generous presents.*

principal/principle *Principal* can be a noun or an adjective. As a noun, *principal* means "chief or head official" (*The principal decided to close school early on Tuesday*) or "sum of capital" (*Invest only the interest, never the principal*). As an adjective, *principal* means "first or highest": *The principal ingredient is sugar. Principle* is a noun only, meaning "rule" or "general truth": *Regardless of what others said, she stood by her principles.*

quiet/quite *Quiet*, as an adjective, means "free from noise": *When the master of ceremonies spoke, the room became quiet. Quite*, an adverb, means "completely, wholly": *By the late afternoon, the children were quite exhausted.*

quotation/quote *Quotation*, a noun, means "a passage quoted from a speech or book": *The speaker read a quotation of twenty-five lines to the audience. Quote*, a verb, means "to repeat a passage from a speech, etc.": *Marci often quotes from popular novels. Quote* and *quotation* are often used interchangeably in speech; in formal writing, however, a distinction is still observed between the two words.

rain/reign/rein As a noun, *rain* means "water that falls from the atmosphere to earth." As a verb, *rain* means "to send down, to give abundantly": *The crushed piñata rained candy on the eager children.* As a noun, *reign* means "royal rule," as a verb, "to have supreme control": *The monarch's reign was marked by social unrest.* As a noun, *rein* means "a leather strap used to guide an animal," as a verb, "to control or guide": *He used the rein to control the frisky colt.*

raise/rise/raze *Raise*, a transitive verb, means "to elevate": *How can I raise the cost of my house? Rise*, an intransitive verb, means "to go up, to get up": *Will housing costs rise this year? Raze* is a transitive verb meaning "to tear down, demolish": *The wrecking crew was ready to raze the condemned building.*

respectful/respective *Respectful* means "showing (or full of) respect": *If you are respectful toward others, they will treat you with consideration as well. Respective* means "in the order given": *The respective remarks were made by executive board members Joshua Whittles, Kevin McCarthy, and Warren Richmond.*

reverend/reverent As an adjective (usually capitalized). *Reverend* is an epithet of respect given to a member of the clergy: *The Reverend Mr. Jones gave the sermon.* As a noun, a *reverend* is "a member of the clergy": *In our church, the reverend opens the service with a prayer. Reverent* is an adjective meaning "showing deep respect": *The speaker began his remarks with a reverent greeting.*

right/rite/write *Right* as an adjective means "proper, correct" and "as opposed to left," as a noun it means "claims or titles," as an adverb it means "in a straight line, directly," as a verb it means "to restore to an upright position." *Rite* is a noun meaning "a solemn ritual": *The religious leader performed the necessary rites. Write* is a verb meaning "to form characters on a surface": *The child liked to write her name over and over.*

sensual/sensuous *Sensual* carries sexual overtones: *The massage was a sensual experience. Sensuous* means "pertaining to the senses": *The sensuous aroma of freshly baked bread wafted through the house.*

set/sit *Set*, a transitive verb, describes something a person does to an object: *She set the book down on the table. Sit*, an intransitive verb, describes a person resting: *Marvin sits on the straight-backed chair.*

somebody/some body *Somebody* is an indefinite pronoun: *Somebody recommended this restaurant. Some body* is a noun modified by an adjective: *I have a new spray that will give my limp hair some body.*

someone/some one *Someone* is an indefinite pronoun: *Someone who ate here said the pasta was delicious. Some one* is a pronoun adjective modified by "some": *Please pick some one magazine that you would like to read.*

sometime/sometimes/some time Traditionally, these three words have carried different meanings. *Sometime* means "at an unspecified time in the future": *Why not plan to visit Niagara Falls sometime? Sometimes* means "occasionally": *I visit my former college roommate sometimes. Some time* means "a span of time": *I need some time to make up my mind about what you have said.*

stationary/stationery Although these two words sound alike, they have very different meanings. *Stationary* means "staying in one place": *From this distance, the satellite appeared to be stationary. Stationery* means "writing paper": *A hotel often provides stationery with its name preprinted.*

straight/strait *Straight* is most often used as an adjective meaning "unbending": *The path cut straight through the woods. Strait*, a noun, is "a narrow passage of water connecting two large bodies of water" or "distress, dilemma": *He was in dire financial straits.*

subsequently/consequently *Subsequently* means "occurring later, afterward": *We went to a new French restaurant for dinner; subsequently, we heard that everyone who had eaten the Caesar salad became ill. Consequently* means "therefore, as a result": *The temperature was above 90 degrees for a week; consequently all the tomatoes burst on the vine.*

taught/taut *Taught* is the past tense of "to teach": *My English teachers taught especially well. Taut* is "tightly drawn": *Pull the knot taut or it will not hold.*

than/then *Than*, a conjunction, is used in comparisons: *Robert is taller than Michael. Then*, an adverb, is used to indicate time: *We knew then that there was little to be gained by further discussion.*

their/there/they're Although these three words sound alike, they have very different meanings. *Their*, the possessive form of "they," means "belonging to them": *Their house is new. There* can point out place (*There is the picture I was telling you about*) or call attention to someone or something (*There is a mouse behind you!*). *They're* is a contraction for "they are": *They're not at home right now.*

threw/thru/through *Threw*, the past tense of the verb "throw," means "to hurl an object": *He threw the ball at the batter. Through* means "from one end to the other" or "by way of": *They walked through the museum all afternoon. Through* should be used in formal writing in place of *thru*, an informal spelling.

to/too/two Although the words sound alike, they are different parts of speech and have different meanings. *To* is a preposition indicating direction or part of an infinitive; *too* is an adverb meaning "also" or "in extreme"; and *two* is a number: *I have to go to the store to buy two items. Do you want to come too?*

track/tract *Track*, as a noun, is a path or course: *The railroad track in the Omaha station has recently been electrified. Track*, as a verb, is "to follow": *Sophisticated guidance control systems are used to track the space shuttles. Tract* is "an expanse of land" or "a brief treatise": *Jonathan Swift wrote many tracts on the political problems of his day.*

unexceptional/unexceptionable Although both *unexceptional* and *unexceptionable* are adjectives, they have different meanings and are not interchangeable. *Unexceptional* means "commonplace, ordinary": *Despite the glowing reviews the new restaurant had received, we found it offered unexceptional meals and services.* *Unexceptionable* means "not offering any basis for exception or objection, beyond criticism": *We could not dispute his argument because it was unexceptionable.*

usage/use *Usage* is a noun that refers to the generally accepted way of doing something. The word refers especially to the conventions of language: *"Most unique"* is considered incorrect usage. *Use* can be either a noun or a verb. As a noun, use means "the act of employing or putting into service": *In the adult education course, I learned the correct use of tools.* *Usage* is often misused in place of the noun *use*: *Effective use (not "usage") of your time results in greater personal satisfaction.*

use/utilize/utilization *Utilize* means "to make use of": *They should utilize the new profit-sharing plan to decrease taxable income.* *Utilization* is the noun form of utilize. In most instances, however, *use* is preferred to either *utilize* or *utilization* as less overly formal and stilted: *They should use the new profit-sharing plan to decrease taxable income.*

which/witch *Which* is a pronoun meaning "what one": *Which desk is yours?* *Witch* is a noun meaning "a person who practices magic": *The superstitious villagers accused her of being a witch.*

who's/whose *Who's* is the contraction for "who is" or "who has": *Who's the person in charge here? Who's got the money?* *Whose* is the possessive form of "who": *Whose book is this?*

your/you're *Your* is the possessive form of "you": *Your book is overdue at the library.* *You're* is the contraction of "you are": *You're just the person we need for this job.*

Excerpted from *Random House Webster's Build Your Power Vocabulary*, Random House, 1998.

ALL RIGHT Not "alright."

AMONG/BETWEEN *Among* is used with three or more; *between* is used with two.
- The tin-can telephone line ran *between* the two houses.
- *Among* the twelve members of the committee were only three women.
- Mr. Nuñez distributed the candy *among* the four of us. *Between you and I* is incorrect; *between you and me* is correct.

ANXIOUS This word properly means "filled with anxiety," not "eager." Don't say you're *anxious* for school to end unless the ending of school makes you feel fearful.

AS FAR AS...IS CONCERNED Not a stylish expression, but if you use it, don't leave out the *is concerned*. It is not correct to say, "*As far as* money, I'd like to be rich." Instead, you should say, "*As far as* money *is concerned*, I'd like to be rich."

AS/LIKE You can run like a fox, but you can't run like a fox runs.

   Like is used only with nouns, pronouns, and grammatical constructions that act like nouns.
- Joe runs *like* a fox.
- Joe runs *as* a fox runs.
- Joe runs the way a fox runs.

BIWEEKLY, ETC. *Biweekly* means either twice a week or once every two weeks, depending on who is using it. Likewise with *bimonthly*. If you need to be precise, avoid it (saying "twice a week" or "every other week," instead). *Fortnightly* means once every two weeks.

CAN/MAY *Can* denotes ability; *may* denotes permission. If you *can* do something, you are *able* to do it. If you *may* do something, you are permitted to do it.

CAPITAL/CAPITOL Washington, D.C., is the *capital* of the United States. The building where Congress meets is the *Capitol*.

COMMON/MUTUAL *Common* means "shared"; *mutual* means "reciprocal." If Tim and Tom have a *common* dislike, they both dislike the same thing (anchovies). If Tim and Tom have a *mutual* dislike, they dislike each other.

COMMONPLACE In careful usage, this word is an adjective meaning "ordinary" or "uninteresting." It can also be used as a noun meaning a "trite or obvious observation" or a "cliché." It should not be used sloppily as a substitute for the word "common."
- To say that French food is the best in the world is a *commonplace*.
- It is *commonplace* but neither interesting nor perceptive to say that French food is the best in the world.

COMPARE TO/COMPARE WITH *To compare* an apple *to* an orange is to say that an apple is like an orange. *To compare* an apple *with* an orange is to discuss the similarities and differences between the two fruits.
- Daisuke *compared* his girlfriend's voice *to* the sound of a cat howling in the night; that is, he said his girlfriend sounded like a cat howling in the night.
- I *compared* my grades *with* Bud's and discovered that he had done better in every subject except math.

DIFFERENT FROM *Different from* is correct; "different than" is not.
- My dog is *different from* your dog.

EACH OTHER/ONE ANOTHER *Each other* is used with two; *one another* is used with three or more.
- A husband and wife should love *each other*.
- The fifteen members of the group had to learn to get along with *one another*.

EQUALLY AS Nothing is ever "*equally as*" anything as anything else.
- Your car and Dave's car might be *equally* fast.

   You should never say that the two cars are *equally as* fast. Nor should you say that your car is *equally as* fast as Dave's. You should simply say that it is *as* fast.

FACT THAT/THAT You almost never need to use "*the fact that*"; *that* alone will suffice.

   Instead of saying, "I was appalled by the *fact that* he was going to the movies," say, "I was appalled *that* he was going to the movies."

FARTHER/FURTHER *Farther* refers to actual, literal distance—the kind measured in inches and miles. *Further* refers to figurative distance. Use *farther* if the distance can be measured; use *further* if it cannot.
- Paris is *farther* from New York than London is.
- Paris is *further* from my thoughts than London is.
- We hiked seven miles but then were incapable of hiking *farther*.
- I made a nice outline for my thesis but never went any *further*.

FEWER, LESS *Fewer* is used with things that can be counted, *less* with things that cannot. That is, *fewer* refers to number; *less* refers to quantity.
- I have *fewer* sugar lumps than Henry does.
- I have *less* sugar.

   Despite what you hear on television, it is *not* correct to say that one soft drink contains "*less calories*" than another. It contains *fewer* calories (calories can be counted); it is *less* fattening.

FORMER, LATTER *Former* means the first of two; *latter* means the second of two. If you are referring to three or more things, you shouldn't use *former* and *latter*.

   It is incorrect to say, "The restaurant had hamburgers, hot dogs, and pizzas; we ordered the *former*." Instead, say, "We ordered the first," or, "We ordered hamburgers."

IF/WHETHER Almost everyone uses *if* in situations that call for *whether*. *If* should be used when something may or may not happen, and is usually followed by *then*. *Whether* should be used when more than one alternative is being discussed. For example: "We need to decide *whether* we should go to the show or stay home." The use of *if* in this situation is widely accepted, but the use of *if* in some situations might cause confusion. Consider this sentence: "Let me know *if* you're coming tonight." Someone might interpret this to mean "*If* you're coming tonight, then let me know. *If* you're not coming tonight, then you don't have to reply." To make it clear that you expect a response, use *whether*: "Let me know *whether* you're coming tonight." This should be interpreted as "No matter what you decide, please let me know your plans."

IRREGARDLESS This is not a word. Say *regardless* or *irrespective*.

LAY/LIE The only way to "*lay* down on the beach" is to take small feathers and place them in the sand.

   To *lay* is to place or set.
- Will the widow *lay* flowers by the grave? She already *laid* them, or she has already *laid* them. Who *lies* in the grave? Her former husband *lies* there. He *lay* there yesterday, too. In fact, he has *lain* there for several days.

PRESENTLY *Presently* means "soon," not "now" or "currently."

- The mailman should be here *presently*; in fact, he should be here in about five minutes.
  The mailman is here now.

STATIONARY/STATIONERY *Stationary* means not moving; *stationery* is notepaper.

THAT/WHICH Most people confuse these two words. Many people who know the difference have trouble remembering it. Here's a simple rule that will almost always work: *that* can never have a comma in front of it; *which* always will.

- There is the car *that* ran over my foot.
- Ed's car, *which* ran over my foot, is over there.
- I like sandwiches *that* are dripping with mustard.
- My sandwich, *which* was dripping with mustard, was the kind I like.
  Which is used in place of *that* if it follows another *that*: "We were fond of *that* feeling of contentment *which* follows victory."

Excerpted from *Word Smart, 4th Edition*, ISBN 978-0-375-76575-9, Random House, August 2006.

WORDS OFTEN MISPRONOUNCED

abdomen (ab′də mən)
aborigine (ab′ə rij′ə nē)
agile (aj′əl)
albino (al bī′nō)
apropos (ap′rə pō′)
avoirdupois (av′ər də poiz′)

balk (bôk)
baroque (bə rōk′)
bayou (bī′ōō)
brooch (brōch)
buoy (bōō′ē, boi)

cello (chel′ō)
cerebral (sə rē′brəl, ser′ə-)
chaise longue (shāz′ lông′)
chamois (sham′ē)
chantey (shan′tē)
chauffeur (shō′fər, shō fûr′)
chic (shēk)
cholera (kol′ər ə)
cinchona (sing kō′nə)
clandestine (klan des′tin)
clapboard (klab′ərd)
clique (klēk)
colonel (kûr′nl)
compote (kom′pōt)
conduit (kon′dwit)
consommé (kon′sə mā′)
corps (kôr, kōr)
corpuscle (kôr′pə səl)
cortege (kôr tezh′)
cotillion (kə til′yən)
coup (kōō)
coxswain (kok′sən)
crosier (krō′zhər)
crouton (krōō′ton)
cuisine (kwi zēn′)

dachshund (dāks′hōont′, -hōond′, dash′-)
debris (də brē′, dā′brē)
debut (dā byōō′)
devotee (dev′ə tē′)
dinghy (ding′gē)
diphtheria (dif thēr′ē ə)
diphthong (dif′thəng)
discern (di sûrn′)
draught (draft)
drought (drout)
duodenum (dōō′ə dē′nəm)
dyspepsia (dis pep′shə, -sē ə)

edifice (ed′ə fis)
egregious (i grē′jəs)
emu (ē′myōō)
entree (än′trā)

façade (fə säd′)
facile (fas′il)
fiancé (fē′än sā′, fē än′sā)

frigate (frig′it)
fuchsia (fyōō′shə)
fuselage (fyōō′sə läzh′)
fusillade (fyōō′sə läd′, -lād′)

gendarme (zhän′därm)
gentian (jen′shən)
gestation (jes tā′shən)
gibber (jib′ər)
gladiolus (glad′ē ō′ləs)
glazier (glā′zhər)
glower (glou′ər)
gnu (nōō)
gourmet (gōōr mā′, gōōr′mā)
granary (gran′ə rē)
guerrilla (gə ril′ə)
guillotine (gil′ə tēn′)
gunwale (gun′l)

habitué (hə bich′ōō ā′)
harbinger (här′bin jər)
heifer (hef′ər)
heinous (hā′nəs)
hirsute (hûr′sōot)
holocaust (hol′ə kôst′)
hosiery (hō′zhə rē)

iguana (i gwä′nə)
imbroglio (im brōl′yō)
inchoate (in kō′it)
incognito (in′kog nē′tō, in kog′ni tō′)
indigenous (in dij′ə nəs)
interstice (in tûr′stis)
inure (in yōōr′)
irascible (i ras′ə bəl)
isosceles (ī sos′ə lēz′)
isthmus (is′məs)

jodhpurs (jod′pərz)
joust (joust)

khaki (kak′ē)
kohlrabi (kōl rä′bē)

labyrinth (lab′ə rinth)
lascivious (lə siv′ē əs)
legerdemain (lej′ər də mān′)
leisure (lē′zhər)
lemur (lē′mər)
liaison (lē ā′zən, lē′ə zon′)
lien (lēn)
lieu (lōō)
lineage (lin′ē ij)
lingerie (län′zhə rā′)
liturgy (lit′ər jē)
llama (lä′mə)
locale (lō kal′)
logy (lō′gē)
lorgnette (lôrn yet′)
louver (lōō′vər)
lucid (lōō′sid)
lucre (lōō′kər)

machete (mə shet′ē)
machination (mak′ə nā′shən)
mademoiselle (mad′əm ə zel′, mad′mwə-)
maestro (mīs′trō)
mannequin (man′i kin)
marijuana (mar′ə wä′nə)
marquis (mär′kwis, mär kē′)
matinee (mat′n ā′)
mauve (mōv, môv)
meliorate (mēl′yə rāt′)
mesa (mā′sə)
mien (mēn)
modiste (mō dēst′)
motif (mō tēf′)
murrain (mûr′in)
myrrh (mûr)

naïve (nä ēv′)
naphtha (nap′thə, naf′-)
niche (nich)
nihilism (nī′ə liz′əm)
nirvana (nir vä′nə)
nom de plume (nom′ də plōōm′)
nonpareil (non′pə rel′)
nougat (nōō′gət)
nuance (nōō′äns, nyōō′-)

oblique (ə blēk′)
ocher (ō′kər)
omniscient (om nish′ənt)
onerous (on′ər əs)
onus (ō′nəs)
opiate (ō′pē it)

pachyderm (pak′i dûrm′)
palsy (pôl′zē)
paprika (pa prē′kə)
parfait (pär fā′)
parquet (pär kā′)
paschal (pas′kəl)
pecan (pi kän′, kan′)
pellagra (pə lag′rə)
petit (pet′ē)
philistine (fil′ə stēn′)
pimiento (pi myen′tō)
plebeian (plə bē′ən)
pneumatic (nōō mat′ik, nyōō-)
poignant (poin′yənt)
posthumous (pos′chə məs)
precipice (pres′ə pis)
premier (pri mēr′)
pristine (pri stēn′)
protégé (prō′tə zhā′)
pueblo (pweb′lō)
purulent (pyōōr′ə lənt)

quaff (kwof)
qualm (kwäm)
quay (kē)

ragout (ra gōō′)
regime (rā zhēm′)

120

renege	(ri nig′, -neg′)	specious	(spē′shəs)	usury	(yo͞o′zhə rē)
reveille	(rev′ə lē)	suave	(swäv)		
ricochet	(rik′ə shā′)	subpoena	(sə pē′nə)	valance	(vā′ləns)
rudiment	(ro͞o′də mənt)				
		tarpaulin	(tär pô′lin, tär′pə lin)	worsted	(wo͝os′tid, wûr′stid)
savoir-faire	(sav′wär fär′)				
short-lived	(shôrt′līvd′)	thyme	(tīm)		
sleazy	(slē′zē)	travail	(trə vāl′)		
soufflé	(so͞o flā′)				

Pronunciation Key

a	act, bat	k	kept, make	sh	shoe, push
ā	able, cape	l	low, all	t	ten, bit
âr	air, dare	m	my, him	th	thin, path
ä	art, calm	n	now, on	tħ	that, other
b	back, rub	ng	sing, England	u	up, love
ch	chief, beach	o	box, hot	ûr	urge, burn
d	do, bed	ō	over, no	v	voice, live
e	ebb, set	ô	order, ball	w	west, away
ē	equal, bee	oi	oil, joy	y	yes, young
f	fit, puff	o͝o	book, put	z	zeal, lazy, those
g	give, beg	o͞o	ooze, rule	zh	vision, measure
h	hit, hear	ou	out, loud	ə	occurs only in unaccented
i	if, big	p	page, stop		syllables and indicates the
ī	ice, bite	r	read, cry		sound of a *in* alone e *in* system i
j	just, edge	s	see, miss		*in* easily o *in* gallop u *in* circus

NOTES

NOTES